THE FRONTIER OF PATRIOTISM

BEYOND BOUNDARIES: CANADIAN DEFENCE AND STRATEGIC STUDIES SERIES

Rob Huebert, Series Editor

ISSN 1716-2645 (Print) ISSN 1925-2919 (Online)

Canada's role in international military and strategic studies ranges from peacebuilding and Arctic sovereignty to unconventional warfare and domestic security. This series provides narratives and analyses of the Canadian military from both an historical and a contemporary perspective.

No. 1 · *The Generals: The Canadian Army's Senior Commanders in the Second World War*
J.L. Granatstein

No. 2 · *Art and Memorial: The Forgotten History of Canada's War Art*
Laura Brandon

No. 3 · *In the National Interest: Canadian Foreign Policy and the Department of Foreign Affairs and International Trade, 1909–2009*
Greg Donaghy and Michael K. Carroll

No. 4 · *Long Night of the Tankers: Hitler's War Against Caribbean Oil*
David J. Bercuson and Holger H. Herwig

No. 5 · *Fishing for a Solution: Canada's Fisheries Relations with the European Union, 1977–2013*
Donald Barry, Bob Applebaum, and Earl Wiseman

No. 6 · *From Kinshasa to Kandahar: Canada and Fragile States in Historical Perspective*
Michael K. Carroll and Greg Donaghy

A book in the Campus Alberta Collection, a collaboration of Athabasca University Press, the University of Alberta Press, and the University of Calgary Press.

press.ucalgary.ca | aupress.ca | uap.ualberta.ca

2015

Alberta Oil and the Decline of Democracy in Canada
Meenal Shrivastava and Lorna Stefanick
978-1-77199-029-5 (paperback) | Athabasca University Press

So Far and Yet So Close: Frontier Cattle Ranching in Western Prairie Canada and the Northern Territory of Australia
Warren M. Elofson
978-1-55238-794-8 (paperback) | University of Calgary Press

Upgrading Oilsands Bitumen and Heavy Oil
Murray R. Gray
978-1-77212-035-6 (hardcover) | University of Alberta Press

2016

The Frontier of Patriotism: Alberta and the First World War
Adriana A. Davies and Jeff Keshen
978-1-55238-834-1 (paperback) | University of Calgary Press

Seeking Order in Anarchy: Multilateralism as State Strategy
Robert W. Murray
978-1-77212-139-1 (paperback) | University of Alberta Press

Visiting with the Ancestors: Blackfoot Shirts in Museum Spaces
Laura Peers and Alison K. Brown
978-1-77199-037-0 (paperback) | Athabasca University Press

The Frontier of Patriotism

ALBERTA AND THE FIRST WORLD WAR

Edited by Adriana A. Davies and Jeff Keshen

Beyond Boundaries: Canadian Defence and Strategic Studies Series
ISSN 1716-2645 (Print) ISSN 1925-2919 (Online)

UNIVERSITY OF CALGARY
Press

University of Calgary Press
2500 University Drive NW
Calgary, Alberta
Canada T2N 1N4
press.ucalgary.ca

Library and Archives Canada Cataloguing in Publication

The frontier of patriotism : Alberta and the First World War / edited by Adriana A. Davies and Jeff Keshen.

(Beyond boundaries : Canadian defence and strategic studies series ; 7)
Includes bibliographical references and index.
Issued in print and electronic formats.
ISBN 978-1-55238-834-1 (paperback).—ISBN 978-1-55238-835-8 (open access pdf).—
ISBN 978-1-55238-836-5 (pdf).—ISBN 978-1-55238-837-2 (epub).—
ISBN 978-1-55238-838-9 (mobi)

1. Alberta—History—1905–1945.   2. Alberta—History, Military—20th century.   3. World War, 1914–1918—Canada.   4. Alberta—Social conditions—1905–1945.   5. Canada—History—1914–1918.   I. Keshen, Jeff, 1962–, editor   II. Davies, Adriana A., editor   III. Series: Beyond boundaries series ; no. 7

FC3672.F76 2016   971.23'02   C2016-905366-0
                                         C2016-905367-9

This project was funded in part by the Alberta Historical Resources Foundation. Financial support was also provided by the Ukrainian Canadian Civil Liberties Foundation.

The University of Calgary Press acknowledges the support of the Government of Alberta through the Alberta Media Fund for our publications. We acknowledge the financial support of the Government of Canada through the Canada Book Fund for our publishing activities. We acknowledge the financial support of the Canada Council for the Arts for our publishing program.

Printed and bound in Canada by Friesens
♻ This book is printed on 100% PCW paper

Cover image: McDermid Studio, Glenbow Archives, NC-6-1210
Cover design, page design, and typesetting by Garet Markvoort, zijn digital
Copy editing by Gretchen Albers, Kerri Rubman, and Peter Enman

CONTENTS

ACKNOWLEDGMENTS

The 100th anniversary of the First World War is one of those benchmark events in our history needing to be commemorated by new scholarship. We would like to thank Peter Enman, John King, and John Wright as well as the Board of the University of Calgary Press for being receptive to an anthology that would focus on Alberta and the First World War.

The co-editors are grateful that they found each other and were able to combine expertise in military and twentieth century Canadian history, with Alberta's historical, natural, scientific and technological heritage. This made the commissioning of articles a satisfying and stimulating adventure. While we scoped out thematic areas, new authors came onboard, and they enriched and expanded these themes. All the contributors brought considerable knowledge of primary sources – from local to national – that has made this critical period in Alberta's development come to life. Without Library and Archives Canada, the Provincial Archives of Alberta, Glenbow Archives and local archives, the authors could not have provided the insight into the mobilization of Alberta, and the impact of the war both in the short- and long-term. Resources must be found to enable archives to preserve their collections and to continue to make more and more of them accessible in a digital format.

The authors come from a range of backgrounds including academic historians and their masters and doctoral students as well as local historians undertaking cultural memory and living tradition research that focuses on individual and community experience and transference from one generation to the next. Enormous thanks go to them for their commitment, in particular in meeting the tight timelines that the project required. A project of such scope – the total number of essays grew to a hefty 40 – normally takes years to plan and execute. The commissioning, research, and writing phases spanned 18 months, a challenge everyone met with grace and understanding.

We would like to thank Mount Royal University for its institutional support. Matthew Wangler, Executive Director of the Alberta Historical Resources Foundation, was extremely supportive of the project, while Carina Naranjilla, its Grant Program Coordinator, provided sage advice with respect to grant applications. We gratefully acknowledge the financial support of the Government of Alberta's Lotteries Fund, the Alberta Historical Resources Foundation and the Ukrainian Canadian Civil Liberties Foundation.

Finally, each of us would like to thank our families, Alex, Catherine, Ciaran, and Oliver Davies, and William, Sabrina, and Dawson Davies, and Deborah, Madelaine, and Jacob Keshen. Their moral support and keen interest in our work is a source of inspiration.

INTRODUCTION

Alberta was only nine years old when the First World War started. Its population had reached 375,000 by 1911 and 496,000 five years later.[1] In 1914, the populations of Edmonton and Calgary both exceeded 70,000, though by 1918, they had dropped to just over 50,000. Given the province's youth and small population, it would appear unlikely that it could make a major difference to the war effort. However, this was not the case at all. Alberta made major contributions to Canada's fighting forces. Precise numbers are elusive because many Albertans enlisted outside the province. One comprehensive analysis puts the total at 48,885, or 35.1 percent of the male population aged 18 to 45, placing the province third behind Manitoba at 47.6 and Ontario at 36.8 percent. The figure becomes more impressive given that in 1911, 43.5 percent of Alberta's population was born outside Canada or Britain, more than twice the national average, and 62.1 percent lived in rural settings compared to 54.5 percent nationwide, a segment of the population that tended to provide fewer recruits due to the critical need for farm labour. High recruitment meant significant losses: 6,140 Albertans were killed in action, and some 20,000 were wounded, 5 percent of the population eligible for military service.[2]

There is relatively little scholarship on Alberta's First World War experience. The earliest treatment is John Blue's "Alberta in the Great War," a chapter in his *Alberta Past and Present: Historical and Biographical*, published in 1924.[3] In 1978, John Herd Thompson wrote a brief regional analysis, *The Harvests of War*, examining the Manitoba, Saskatchewan, and Alberta home fronts.[4] The first contemporary, comprehensive examination of Alberta's First World War experience was volume 4 in Ted Byfield's *Alberta in the 20th Century: A Journalistic History of the Province in Twelve Volumes*. Titled *The Great War and Its Consequences*, it was published in 1994. Byfield, a journalist, publisher, and editor, produced a heavily pictorial popular history that also devoted a surprising amount of space to national issues and trends.[5] There is also information to be found in profiles of Alberta military leaders, those who trained in the province, regimental and municipal histories, and accounts of institutions such as the University of Alberta and Mount Royal College (as it was then).[6]

Regional analysis of Canada's First World War effort remains an area in need of further scholarship. Most work is considerably dated. That on Quebec still focuses on debates over conscription; the most comprehensive work on Ontario is largely comprised of reprinted documents; there is no general work on the Maritimes; and a recently published book on wartime British Columbia is a popular, rather episodic account by two CBC journalists.[7]

Historiography on Canada in the First World War

While regional wartime history remains sparse, the general historiography on Canada in the First World War has grown increasingly comprehensive and complex. For many years, studies of Canadian forces overseas have centred on how their performance in battle generated pride and a national spirit, accelerating Canada's trajectory from colony to nation.[8] Unlike Britain or Australia during the interwar years, Canada did not produce a multivolume scholarly "Official History" of its military involvement and performance. Colonel A. Fortescue Duguid, an engineer by training, was put in charge of a small historical section in the Canadian Army.[9] Determined to get every detail correct, and, as a result, to consult every document, Duguid produced only a single volume by the outset of the Second World War. He also hoarded First World War military records, which as a result were not open to researchers until the 1960s. This gap in scholarship did not begin to be addressed until the appearance of G.W.L. Nicholson's 1964 single-volume *Official History of the Canadian Army in the First World War*. Although thorough and balanced, it is more descriptive than analytical. Thus, more popular or even propagandistic books, including those generated during the war, remained widely consulted. Not until 1980 did the first volume of the *Official History of the Royal Canadian Air Force* appear, and not until 2010 that of the Royal Canadian Navy.[10]

The immediate period after the Second World War did not see much scholarly attention devoted to the First World War. The 1960s and 1970s brought little academic military history, reflecting an anti-military and anti-authoritarian ethos prevalent on university campuses during the unpopular Vietnam War. Countering this, however, uplifting popular accounts were published, namely about the battle at Vimy Ridge, that promulgated Canada's growing nationalism, autonomy, and international recognition, especially as the 50th anniversary of the clash coincided with Canada's 100th birthday. This carried into the 1980s with the appearance of popular histories that detailed the harsh, gruesome, and deadly nature of other key battles involving Canadians, but also highlighted the grit, fortitude, and accomplishments of Canadian soldiers.[11]

Recent historiographic trends, namely toward specialization and social history, have resulted in a more complete picture of Canada's overseas military experience. Still, the nationalistic theme persists, notably in discussions of Canada's increasingly improved performance over the course of the conflict, and the emergence of the Canadian Corps as an elite, expertly, Canadian-led formation, arguably the best among the Allies.[12] Demonstrating the influence of social history, Desmond Morton's *When Your Number's Up* and Sandra Gwyn's *Tapestry of War* reconstruct the war experience through the writings of those in the thick of things overseas.[13] Recent scholarship has also examined the complex and not always copacetic relationship between Canadian soldiers and the British.[14] Analyses have challenged the portrayal of

Canada's 1st Division as less prepared and effective, namely at the Second Battle of Ypres.[15] While commending Canadians for their performance at Vimy, other works argue that the battle's importance and impact have been exaggerated and that Canadian tactics, while effective, were not hugely innovative.[16] Tim Cook's monumental two-volume work, *At the Sharp End* and *Shock Troops*, provides an examination of the Canadian Army's experiences from the perspectives of both ordinary soldiers and their leaders.[17] He details the unique world of soldiers, from the banality of trench routines to the men's various coping techniques, such as seeking the protection of supernatural forces or turning to black humour, drinking, swearing, singing, and womanizing.[18] Other works examine the war through presenting letters between soldiers and those on the home front, or through focusing on the experiences of POWs; the application of military discipline; diet and health; and recreation and sports.[19]

Earlier works on the Canadian home front during the First World War typically focused on the national level—principally on how mobilization was managed, with munitions production, recruitment, and conscription being central themes.[20] Perpetual regionalism, or what historian J.M.S. Careless called in 1970 Canada's "limited identities," no doubt prompted several regional-based studies on the First World War. The trend toward more intensive analysis also manifested in recent works on specific communities in wartime, namely Winnipeg, Regina, Toronto, Trois Rivières, Guelph, Lethbridge, and Halifax.[21]

Works on mobilization have explored the ways in which Canadians were influenced to back total war, such as through censorship and propaganda and other forms of state surveillance and repression.[22]

Scholarship has also detailed how classrooms and popular literature were geared toward cultivating patriotism. Works on universities show the beginnings of officer training programs and coordination between government, industry, and academe that advanced military-related scientific research.[23] That on Canadian churches shows that a wide swath of denominations, particularly Protestant branches, promoted the war as a righteous cause against evil, raised money and other means of support, and provided clerics who ministered to men's spiritual and emotional needs overseas.[24]

Social friction in wartime Canada has also become a prominent theme. Much of the work draws inspiration from social history, which seeks to tell the story of groups long under-represented or written out of mainstream, often whiggish historical accounts. Such scholarship has explored increasing discord and radicalism among large segments of Canada's working class over wartime hyperinflation, lack of representation, absence of collective bargaining rights, and the conscription of men but not wealth.[25] Other work shows that jingoism and nativism, buttressed by wartime hysteria, resulted in extreme prejudice against Canadians of German and Ukrainian background. The latter, typically not naturalized as British subjects, were classified as enemy aliens and, in over 8,500 cases, interned.[26] Scholarship also details the wartime experiences of visible minorities, who were initially excluded from volunteering in what was termed a "White Man's War" and, in the case of African-Canadians, eventually restricted to labour battalions to support white troops.[27] Recent academic debate has revolved around the extent to which First Peoples responded to the call and whether their patriotism resulted in meaningful improvements.[28] Further work has enriched understanding of the contributions and war-related changes experienced by women, and probed whether they enhanced longer-term trends toward equality.[29]

Important new work has also focused on the aftermath of the war. Many soldiers carried home the Spanish flu, which took the lives of 50,000 Canadians. As Mark Humphries writes, the pandemic exposed major gaps in Canada's fledgling health-care system and played a key role in generating the creation of a federal Department of Health.[30] Recent scholarship shows that programs to support Canada's First World War veterans had profound shortcomings, but still constituted pioneering social welfare initiatives.[31] Finally, newer cultural history research, exploring memory and commemoration, explains how Canada's First World War has been represented, constructed, and distorted—through, for example, memorials, art, and literature—often to serve particular agendas.[32]

Alberta at War

In the war's early stages, Alberta's young men overwhelmed enlistment centres. Most were motivated by a sense of loyalty and duty to Britain and the conviction that it was essential to halt German aggression and militarism. Many craved travel and adventure and wanted to partake in events that were cast as shaping the destiny of civilization. Some joined for a job, as the West, like the rest of Canada, was mired in a deep recession that lasted until mid-1915. At the outset of the war, Edmonton had an estimated 4,000 unemployed, and rural areas suffered with droughts in 1912 and 1913. Many thought time was of the essence if they wanted to participate

since experts predicted a short conflict, reasoning that the Great Powers could sustain a massive war for only months.

Those who successfully enlisted into what must have initially seemed like an exclusive club found themselves without enough weapons or uniforms. In Edmonton, early recruits paraded through city streets in civilian clothes. In January 1915, the 49th Battalion, known as the Loyal Edmonton Regiment, raised a full complement of 35 officers and 975 other ranks in a matter of days. At Calgary's Sarcee training camp, which became the second largest in Canada, 40,000 men over the course of the war were prepared to go overseas.

Albertans participated in every major battle involving Canadians. Some sent home chilling accounts. In June 1916, from Hooge in Belgium—where the Germans used flamethrowers, machine guns, mortars, and grenades to recapture lost ground—Bruce Davies, a Lethbridge corporal, wrote that the "dead were lying all around. I got out and crawled back into the trench. I found out that I had been hit in the right leg pretty hard, also in the left knee. Previously none of these wounds had been dressed, the reason being that the stretcher bearers kept being blown to pieces . . . My God, it was awful agony."[33] Most, however, in order to appear manly and to avoid upsetting loved ones or running afoul of military censors, emphasized triumphs and heroism, or maintained a lighthearted attitude. An example of the last is Calgary's Harry Jennings, who said of a serious head wound sustained at the Second Battle of Ypres: "I shall have to part my hair in the middle."[34]

Alberta newspapers highlighted heroism by local lads such as Private Cecil Kinross, a 22-year-old from Lougheed, in central Alberta, who won the Victoria Cross at Passchendaele for singlehandedly moving across open ground to capture a German machine gun, killing six. Also venerated were Canada's military leaders such as Brigadier General Archibald MacDonnell, commander of the Loyal Edmonton Regiment and three other battalions as part of the 7th Brigade, who, following the triumph at Vimy Ridge, was given command of Canada's 1st Division. Albertans also figured prominently in Canada's contributions to aerial combat. Major Donald MacLaren, the province's top ace with 54 kills, rose to the rank of squadron commander and was honoured with the DSO, Military Cross and Bar, Distinguished Flying Cross, Croix de Guerre, and Legion d'Honneur ribbon.

Albertans at home rallied to support all major war charities and drives. Women's groups organized bazaars and teas, sponsored entertainment, and ran second-hand shops to raise money for the war effort. Children collected scrap, and, when not learning patriotic lessons in school, put on plays and other events as fundraisers. Redcliff and Monitor, Alberta, received captured German artillery pieces for topping other communities in Canada when it came to purchasing Victory Bonds on a per capita basis.

For other Albertans, it was a much different war. The province was home to some 37,000 people of German and enemy alien background. Germans were fired from government jobs and positions such as teaching. Many Germans tried to pass themselves off as Scandinavians or Dutch. The Alberta *Herold*, the province's only German newspaper, did not survive the war, as the federal government compelled all newspapers written in enemy languages to print in English.

The war also dramatically affected Alberta's First Peoples. Estimates place the First Nations' enlistment rate as high as 35 percent. Some First Peoples felt loyalty to the British Crown who they believed had respected treaty rights. Young Aboriginal people sought to escape the boredom of reserve life and emulate the warrior tradition of their forebears. Some Alberta Natives became renowned for their battlefield performance. Corporal Henry Norwest, a Cree from Fort Saskatchewan, had 115 observed hits as a sniper. Yet, for Aboriginal people, applications for veterans' benefits had to proceed through Indian agents who, typically, recommended against extending credit, even when it was state subsidized, because it was assumed First Peoples were like children and could not cope with debt.

As casualties mounted and Canada's war economy heated up, it became more difficult to obtain adequate numbers of volunteers. Albertans were attracted to well-paid jobs in munitions factories in Central Canada. The province's ranchers faced record demand for beef; its lumber mills operated at peak capacity; and its coal mines struggled to provide adequate supplies to cities and war industries. Fuelled by overseas demand, wheat prices reached $2.21 a bushel in 1917, three times the prewar level. Alberta wheat farms expanded from a total cultivation of 1.8 million hectares in 1911 to 3.03 million hectares in 1916. However, much of this was on lower-quality farmland. Moreover, to obtain quick and maximum output and profits, proper fallowing was ignored, eventually resulting in declining yields.[35] Still, with the war accelerating rural depopulation, farm labour was desperately needed, and wages increased by 25 percent to reach a record average of $50 per month.[36] Shortages in farm labour reached the point where many in rural Alberta opposed conscription. In the riding of Edmonton West, Frank Oliver, federal minister of the Interior from 1905 to 1911 and founder of the Edmonton *Bulletin*, ran for the Liberals, opposing conscription after his eldest son, Allen, was killed in action the previous November. Oliver led against the pro-conscription Union candidate, Brigadier General William Griesbach, a former, popular mayor and first commander of the 49th Battalion, until the overseas soldier vote tipped the balance to Griesbach.

News of the Armistice on 11 November 1918 prompted massive celebrations and outpourings of national pride. But the war also left deep divisions and daunting problems. Prices had increased an estimated 75 percent during the conflict, and the war-charged economy did not easily transition back to peace. Rapid deflation and a deep recession followed, lasting until the mid-1920s. Plunging postwar wheat prices, ultimately to less than one dollar a bushel, produced a collapse in rural Alberta. Coal mines were beset by labour problems, and the oil industry, which seemed promising in 1914 with discoveries in Turner Valley, was in free fall, as the expense of drilling and production proved prohibitive. The federal government's refusal to establish a wheat board to prop up prices (as the Board of Grain Supervisors had controlled rising wheat prices in wartime), and postwar federal budgets that maintained high tariffs in order to protect central Canadian industry despite promises to move to freer trade, sparked a wave of prairie populism. In July 1921, the United Farmers of Alberta, running candidates in just 45 of 61 ridings and with no leader or official platform, won office with 39 seats.

The end of the conflict saw Canada's federal government saddled with massive debt and facing the challenge of funding veteran programs. Although veterans griped about stingy state support, the assistance provided to Canadian veterans was unprecedented for governments that had never before established significant social welfare programs. Indeed, Ottawa launched a fifth national Victory Bond drive for November 1919 that raised $660 million (worth $8.4 billion in 2015)[37] to help pay for veteran programs.

Many who came out for victory celebrations on 11 November 1918 wore a mask because Canada was then in the midst of the Spanish flu pandemic that, by late 1919, had claimed the lives of 3,259 Albertans. Numerous communities were forced into makeshift responses; Claresholm used its School of Agriculture as a hospital. Isolated communities and First Nations reserves, where there was little or no medical assistance, suffered disproportionately. Calgary's Dr. O.D. Weeks, who volunteered to treat those on reserves along the Alberta & Great Western Railway line, found as many as half the population dead in some places. The entire community of Lethbridge was quarantined for two days, as were the people of Taber, Pincher Creek, Legal, and Drumheller.

The Frontier of Patriotism

The Frontier of Patriotism presents, at the provincial level, the complexity of the war experience as reflected in recent historiography. To do this, the editors turned to 40 contributors, both academic and local historians, whose work, collectively, showcases a rich tapestry of activities and experiences in Alberta during the First World War.

Because of the wide range of topics included, most entries were kept brief so that the volume remained at a manageable length, though latitude was provided in cases where the editors agreed greater coverage was warranted. The essays are grouped thematically to cover Albertans in uniform, in battle, on the home front, and to show the aftermath and legacy of the First World War.

Readers will encounter both academic and popular, and broad and highly focused papers. They will learn about military leaders and ordinary soldiers; the wartime experiences of Alberta chaplains, churches, labour, women, First Peoples, conscientious objectors, and those labelled as enemy aliens; what Albertans read about the war; the construction of war-related infrastructure; the varied and profound impact of the struggle on communities; what one can learn from material evidence; the impact of the Spanish flu pandemic; the postwar Soldier Settlement program; and provincial commemoration of the conflict.

For many Albertans, these four tumultuous years represented a time of individual valour and of communities pulling together and sacrificing for what was viewed as a noble cause. For others, such as Albertans of German and enemy alien background, conscientious objectors, First Peoples, labourers, farmers, and significant numbers of veterans, the war left disillusionment and anger. Many, but not all, of these trends were evident elsewhere in Canada, something that speaks to the importance of exploring the regional and local story as well as the national narrative to understand the commonalities and distinctiveness of what it means to be Canadian.

Notes

1   Howard Palmer and Tamara Palmer, eds., *Peoples of Alberta: Portraits of Cultural Diversity* (Saskatoon, SK: Western Producer Prairie Book, 1985), 6–7, 217.

2   C.A. Sharpe, "Enlistment in the Canadian Expeditionary Force 1914–1918: A Regional Analysis," *Journal of Canadian Studies* 18, no. 4 (1983–84): 15–26.

3   John Blue, "Alberta in the Great War," in *Alberta Past and Present: Historical and Biographical*, vol. 3 (Chicago: Pioneer Historical Publishing, 1924).

4   John Herd Thompson, *The Harvests of War: The Prairie West, 1914–1918* (Toronto: McClelland and Stewart, 1978).

5   Ted Byfield, ed., *Alberta in the 20th Century: A Journalistic History of the Province in Twelve Volumes*, vol. 4, *The Great War and Its Consequences* (Edmonton: United Western Communications, 1994).

6   See Robert Rutherdale, *Hometown Horizons: Local Responses to the Great War* (Vancouver: UBC Press, 2004); Whitney Lackenbauer, "The Politics of Contested Space: Controversy and the Construction of Currie Barracks," *Prairie Forum* 28, no. 1 (2003): 45–66; Whitney Lackenbauer, "Under Siege: The CEF Attack on the RNWMP Barracks in Calgary, October 1916," *Alberta History* 49, no. 3 (2001): 2–12; Max Foran, "W.A. 'Billy' Griesbach and World War One," *Alberta History* 32, no. 3 (1984): 1–8; R. Stevens, *A City Goes to War: History of the Loyal Edmonton Regiment (3 PPCLI)* (Edmonton: Charters, 1965); Major Roy Farran, *The History of the Calgary Highlanders 1921–1954* (Calgary: Bryant Press, 1954); Daniel Dancocks, *Gallant Canadians: The Story of the Tenth Canadian Infantry Battalion, 1914–1919* (Calgary: Calgary Highlanders Regimental Funds Foundation, 1990); David Bercuson, *The Patricia's: A Proud History of a Fighting Regiment* (Toronto: Stoddart, 2001); Donald Baker, *Catch the Gleam: Mount Royal, from College to University* (Calgary: University of Calgary Press, 2011); and Rod Macleod, *All True Things: A History of the University of Alberta, 1908–2008* (Edmonton: University of Alberta Press, 2008).

7   Mark Forsythe and Greg Dickson, *From the West Coast to the Western Front: British Columbians and the Great War* (Madiera Park, BC: Harbour Publishing, 2014); Barbara Wilson, *Ontario and the First World War*

(Toronto: University of Toronto Press, 1977); Elizabeth Armstrong, *The Crisis of Quebec, 1914–18* (New York: Columbia University Press, 1937); M.S. Hunt, *Nova Scotia's Part in the Great War* (Halifax: Nova Scotia Veteran, 1920).

8 See Mark Osborne Humphries, "Between Commemoration and History: The Historiography of the Canadian Corps and Military Overseas," *Canadian Historical Review* 95, no. 3 (2014): 384–97.

9 Duguid served in France from 1915 to 1918, and was director of the historical section of the Canadian Army from 1921 to 1945. The Fortescue fonds are located at the National Defence Headquarters Directorate of History and Heritage.

10 Tim Cook, *Clio's Warriors: Canadian Historians and the Writing of the Two World Wars* (Vancouver: UBC Press, 2007); G.W.L Nicholson, *Official History of the Canadian Army in the First World War: Canadian Expeditionary Force, 1914–1919* (Ottawa: Queen's Printer, 1964); S.F. Wise, *Canadian Airmen and the First World War: The Official History of the Royal Canadian Air Force* (Toronto: University of Toronto Press, 1980); William Johnson, William G.P. Rawling, Richard H. Gimblett, and John MacFarlane, *The Seabound Coast: The Official History of the Royal Canadian Navy, 1867–1939*, vol. 1 (Toronto: University of Toronto Press, 2010).

11 Daniel Dancocks, *Legacy of Valour: The Canadians at Passchendaele* (Edmonton: Hurtig, 1988), and Dancocks, *Welcome to Flanders Field* (Toronto: McClelland and Stewart, 1988). This theme is also evident in the co-authored, and more scholarly, account by J.L. Granatstein and Desmond Morton, *Marching to Armageddon: Canadians and the Great War, 1914–1919* (Toronto: Lester & Orpen Dennys, 1989).

12 See, for example, Bill Rawling, *Surviving Trench Warfare: Technology and the Canadian Corps, 1914–1918* (Toronto: University of Toronto Press, 1992); Shane Schreiber, *Shock Army of the British Empire: The Canadian Corps in the Last 100 Days of the Great War* (St. Catharines, ON: Vanwell, 2004); J.L. Granatstein, *Canada's Army: Waging War and Keeping the Peace*

(Toronto: University of Toronto Press, 2002); and Tim Cook, *The Madman and the Butcher: The Sensational Wars of Sam Hughes and General Arthur Currie* (Toronto: Penguin, 2010).

13 Desmond Morton, *When Your Number's Up: The Canadian Soldier in the First World War* (Toronto: Random House, 1993); Sandra Gwyn, *Tapestry of War: A Private View of Canadians in the Great War* (Toronto: HarperCollins, 1994).

14 See Jonathan Vance, *Maple Leaf Empire: Canada, Britain and the Two World Wars* (Toronto: Oxford, 2012); Douglas Delaney, "Mentoring the Canadian Corps: Imperial Officers and the Canadian Expeditionary Force, 1914–1918," *Journal of Military History* 77, no. 3 (2013): 931–53; Luke Flanagan, "Canadians in Bexhill-on-Sea during the First World War: A Reflection of Canadian Nationhood?" *British Journal of Canadian Studies* 27, no. 2 (2014): 131–48.

15 Nathan Greenfield, *Baptism of Fire: The Second Battle of Ypres and the Forging of Canada, April 1915* (Toronto: HarperCollins, 2007); Andrew Iarocci, *Shoestring Soldiers: 1st Canadian Division at War, 1914–1915* (Toronto: University of Toronto Press, 2008).

16 Geoffrey Hayes, Andrew Iarocci, and Michael Bechtold, eds., *Vimy Ridge: A Reassessment* (Waterloo, ON: Wilfrid Laurier University Press, 2007); J.L. Granatstein, *The Greatest Victory: Canada's One Hundred Days, 1918* (Toronto: Oxford, 2014).

17 Tim Cook, *At the Sharp End: Canadians Fighting the Great War, 1914–1916* (Toronto: Penguin, 2007); Tim Cook, *Shock Troops: Canadians Fighting the Great War, 1917–1918* (Toronto: Penguin, 2008). Also see Tim Cook, *No Place to Run: The Canadian Corps and Gas Warfare in the First World War* (Vancouver: UBC Press, 1999).

18 See, for example, Tim Cook, "Fighting Words: Canadian Soldiers' Slang and Swearing in the Great War," *War in History* 20, no. 3 (2013): 323–44; Tim Cook, "'Tokens of Fritz': Canadian Soldiers and the Art of Souveneering in the Great War," *War and Society* 31, no. 3 (2012): 211–26; Tim Cook, "The Singing War:

Canadian Soldiers' Songs of the Great War," *American Review of Canadian Studies* 39, no. 3 (2009): 224–41; Tim Cook, "Politics of Surrender," *Journal of Military History* 70, no. 3 (2006): 637–65; Tim Cook, "Wet Canteens and Worrying Mothers: Alcohol, Soldiers, and Temperance Groups in the Great War," *Histoire sociale/Social History* 35, no. 70 (2003): 311–30; and Tim Cook and Andrew Iarocci, "Animal Soldiers," *Canada's History* 93, no. 5 (2013): 20–27.

19　See, for example, Mark Humphries, "War's Long Shadow: Masculinity, Medicine, and the Gendered Politics of Trauma, 1914–1939," *Canadian Historical Review* 91, no. 3 (2010): 503–31; Kim Pelis, "Taking Credit: The Canadian Army Medical Corps and the British Conversion to Blood Transfusion in WWI," *Journal of the History of Medicine and Allied Sciences* 56, no. 3 (2001): 238–77; Dan Black and John Boileau, *Old Enough to Fight: Canada's Boy Soldiers in the First World War* (Toronto: James Lorimer & Co., 2013); Jonathan Vance, *Objects of Concern: Canadian Prisoners through the Twentieth Century* (Vancouver: UBC Press, 1997); Desmond Morton, *Silent Battle: Canadian Prisoners of War in Germany, 1914–1919* (Toronto: Key Porter, 1992); Teresa Iacobella, *Death or Deliverance: Canadian Court Martials in the Great War* (Vancouver: UBC Press, 2014); Y.A. Bennett, ed., *Kiss the Kids for Dad, Don't Forget to Write: The Wartime Letters of George Timmins, 1916–18* (Vancouver: UBC Press, 2009); Jay Cassell, *The Secret Plague: Venereal Disease in Canada, 1838–1939* (Toronto: University of Toronto Press, 1992); Craig Greenham, "Canadian Soldiers, an Imperial War, and America's National Pastime," *American Review of Canadian Studies* 42, no. 1 (2012): 34–50; J.J. Wilson, "Skating to Armageddon: Canada, Hockey, and the First World War," *International Journal of the History of Sport* 22, no. 3 (2005): 315–42; Andrew Horrall, "Keep-a-Fighting! Play the Game! Baseball and the Canadian Forces during the First World War," *Canadian Military History* 10, no. 2 (2001): 27–40. The strong relationship between sport and war was also evident in recruiting material that advertised chums' and sportsmen's battalions. See Paul Maroney, "The Great Adventure: The Context and Ideology of Recruiting in Ontario, 1914–1917," *Canadian Historical Review* 77, no. 1 (1996): 62–98. Nic Clarke explores the relationship between sport and war through the military career of the Ottawa hockey star, Frank McGee, who was held up as an example of how Canada's soldiers were the cream of the country's manhood. See "'The Greater and Grimmer Game': Sport as an Arbiter of Military Fitness in the British Empire—The Case of 'One-Eyed' Frank Mcgee," *International Journal of the History of Sport* 28, no. 3/4 (2011): 604–22. On recreational services for soldiers, see Sarah Cozzi, "When You're A Long, Long Way From Home," *Canadian Military History* 20, no. 1 (2011): 45–60, and Jason Wilson, *Soldiers of Song: The Dumbells and Other Canadian Concert Parties of the First World War* (Waterloo, ON: Wilfrid Laurier University Press, 2012).

20　See, for example, Robert Craig Brown, *Robert Laird Borden: A Biography*, 2 vols. (Toronto: Macmillan, 1975, 1980); Michael Bliss, *A Canadian Millionaire: The Life and Business Times of Sir Joseph Flavelle, Bart., 1858–1939* (Toronto: University of Toronto Press, 1992); J.L. Granatstein and J.M. Hitsman, *Broken Promises: A History of Conscription in Canada* (Toronto: Oxford, 1977); John English, *The Decline of Politics: The Conservatives and the Party System* (Toronto: University of Toronto Press, 1977). Newer work on the nationally directed war effort and the controversies over conscription include Tim Cook, *War Lords: Borden, Mackenzie King, and Canada's Two World Wars* (Toronto: Penguin, 2012); Martin Auger, "The Canadian Government and the Suppression of the 1918 Quebec Easter Riots," *Canadian Historical Review* 89, no. 4 (2008): 503–40; Andrew Theobald, "Une Loi Extraordinaire: New Brunswick Acadians and the Conscription Crisis of the First World War," *Acadiensis* 34, no. 1 (2004): 80–95; and David Tough, "'The rich . . . should give to such an extent that it will hurt': 'Conscription of Wealth' and Political Modernism in the Parliamentary Debate on the 1917 Income War Tax," *Canadian Historical Review* 93, no. 3 (2012): 382–407.

21 J.M.S. Careless, "Limited Identities in Canada," *Canadian Historical Review* 50, no. 1 (1969): 1–10; Ian Millar, *Our Glory and Our Grief: Torontonians and the Great War* (Toronto: University of Toronto Press, 2002); Rutherdale, *Hometown Horizons*; Jim Blanchard, *Winnipeg's Great War* (Winnipeg: University of Manitoba Press, 2010); J.M. Pitsula, *For All We Have and Are: Regina and the Experience of the Great War* (Winnipeg: University of Manitoba Press, 2008); John Griffith Armstrong, *The Halifax Explosion and the Royal Canadian Navy: Inquiry and Intrigue* (Vancouver: UBC Press, 2002).

22 Jeffrey Keshen, *Propaganda and Censorship during Canada's Great War* (Edmonton: University of Alberta Press, 1996); Gregory Kealey, "State Repression of Labour and the Left in Canada, 1914–20: The Impact of the First World War," *Canadian Historical Review* 73, no. 3 (1992): 281–315; Gregory Kealey, "The Surveillance State: The Origins of Domestic Intelligence and Counter-Subversion in Canada, 1914–1921," *Intelligence and National Security* 7, no. 3 (1992): 179–210.

23 Nancy Sheehan, "The IODE, the Schools, and World War I," *History of Education Review* 13, no. 1 (1984): 29–44; Peter Webb, "'A Righteous Cause': War Propaganda and Canadian Fiction, 1915–1921," *British Journal of Canadian Studies* 24, no. 1 (2011): 31–48; Susan Fisher, *Boys and Girls in No Man's Land: English Canadian Children and the First World War* (Toronto: University of Toronto Press, 2011); and Paul Stortz and E. Lisa Panayotidis, eds., *Cultures, Communities, and Conflict: Histories of Canadian Universities and War* (Toronto: University of Toronto Press, 2012).

24 See J.M. Bliss, "The Methodist Church and World War I," *Canadian Historical Review* 49, no. 3 (1968): 213–33; David Marshall, "Methodism Embattled: A Reconsideration of the Methodist Church in World War I," *Canadian Historical Review* 66, no. 1 (1986): 48–64; Trevor Powell, "The Church on the Home Front: The Church of England in the Diocese of Qu'Appelle and the Great War," *Saskatchewan History* 64, no. 2 (2012): 8–51; Duff Crerar, "The Church in the Furnace: Canadian Anglican Chaplains Respond to the Great War," *Journal of the Canadian Church Historical Society* 35, no. 2 (1993): 75–103; Duff Crerar, *Padres in No Man's Land: Canadian Chaplains and the Great War* (Montreal and Kingston: McGill-Queen's University Press, 1995); and Michelle Fowler, "'Death is not the Worst Thing': The Presbyterian Press in Canada, 1913–1919," *War and Society* 25, no. 2 (2006): 23–38.

25 See Martin Robin, "Registration, Conscription, and Independent Labour Politics, 1916–1917," *Canadian Historical Review* 64, no. 2 (1966): 147–67; Myer Siemiatycki, "Munitions and Labour Militancy: The 1916 Hamilton Machinists' Strike," *Labour/Le Travail* 3 (1978): 131–51; Mike O'Brien, "Producers versus Profiteers: The Politics of Class in Newfoundland during the First World War," *Acadiensis* 40, no. 1 (2011): 45–69.

26 David Edward Smith, "Emergency Government in Canada," *Canadian Historical Review* 50, no. 4 (1969): 429–48; Kealey, "State Repression," and "Surveillance State"; Keshen, *Propaganda and Censorship*; Barbara Roberts, *Whence They Came: Deportation from Canada, 1900–1935* (Ottawa: University of Ottawa Press, 1988); Martin Kitchen, "The German Invasion of Canada in the First World War," *International History Review* 7, no. 2 (1985): 245–60; Peter Moogk, "Uncovering the Enemy Within: British Columbians and the German Menace," *BC Studies* 182 (2014): 45–72; William Campbell, "'We Germans . . . are British Subjects': The First World War and the Curious Case of Berlin, Ontario, Canada," *Canadian Military History* 21, no. 2 (2012): 45–57; Robert Taylor, "The Mark of the Hun: The Image of Germans in Popular Verse Published in Victoria, B.C., during the Great War," *British Columbia History* 42, no. 3 (2009): 2–7; Bill Waiser, *Park Prisoners: The Untold Story of Western Canada's National Parks, 1915–1946* (Saskatoon, SK: Fifth House, 1995); George Buri, "Enemies within Our Gates: Brandon's Alien Detention Centre during the Great War," *Manitoba History* 56 (2011): 3–11; James Farney and Bhadan Kordan, "The Predicament of Belonging: The Status of Enemy

Aliens in Canada, 1914," *Journal of Canadian Studies* 39, no. 1 (2005): 74–89; Frances Sywripa and John Herd Thompson, eds., *Loyalties in Conflict: Ukrainians in Canada during the Great War* (Edmonton: Canadian Institute of Ukrainian Studies, 1983); Lubomyr Luciuk, "Ukrainians and Internment Operations in Ontario during the First World War," *Polyphony* 10 (1988): 27–31.

27 See James W.St.G. Walker, "Race and Recruitment in World War I: Enlistment of Visible Minorities in the Canadian Expeditionary Force," *Canadian Historical Review* 70, no. 1 (1989): 1–26, and Calvin Ruck, *The Black Battalion, 1916–1920: Canada's Best Kept Military Secret* (Halifax: Nova Scotia Historical Review, 1988).

28 While James Dempsey writes of factors like First Peoples' support for the British monarchy, with whom they had treaties, and the warrior ethic as producing a strong, positive response to the war effort, Timothy Winegard and Robert Talbot present the opposite view based on long-standing First Nations' grievances. See James Dempsey, *Warriors of the King: Prairie Indians in World War I* (Regina: Canadian Plains Research Centre, 1999); Timothy Winegard, *For King and Kanata: Canadian Indians and the First World War* (Winnipeg: University of Manitoba Press, 2012), and Robert Talbot, "'It Would Be Best to Leave Us Alone': First Nations Responses to the Canadian War Effort, 1914–18," *Journal of Canadian Studies* 45, no. 1 (2011): 90–120. Also see Katherine McGowan, "'In the Interests of the Indians': The Department of Indian Affairs, Charles Cooke, and the Recruitment of Native Men in Southern Ontario for the Canadian Expeditionary Force, 1916," *Ontario History* 102, no. 1 (2010): 109–24. On the confiscation of First Nations' reserve land for military training, see Whitney Lackenbauer, "'Pay No Attention to Sero': The Mohawks of the Bay of Quinte and Imperial Flying Training during the Great War," *Ontario History* 96, no. 2 (2004): 143–69.

29 The most comprehensive source is Amy Shaw and Sarah Glassford, eds., *A Sisterhood of Suffering and Service: Women and Girls of Canada and Newfoundland during the First World* (Vancouver: UBC Press, 2012), which covers topics that include university women, voluntary nurses, paid workers, indigenous women, and social policy. Also see Tarah Brookfield, "Divided by the Ballot Box: The Montreal Council of Women and the 1917 Election," *Canadian Historical Review* 89, no. 4 (2008): 473–501; Debbie Marshall, *Give Your Other Vote to the Sister: A Woman's Journey into the Great War* (Calgary: University of Calgary Press, 2007); Desmond Morton, *Fight or Pay: Soldiers' Families in the Great War* (Vancouver: UBC Press, 2004); and Linda Quiney, "Borrowed Halos: Canadian Teachers as Voluntary Aid Detachment Nurses during the Great War," *Historical Studies in Education* 15, no. 1 (2003): 78–99.

30 Mark Humphries, *The Last Plague: Spanish Influenza and the Politics of Public Health in Canada* (Toronto: University of Toronto Press, 2012).

31 See Desmond Morton and Glenn Wright, *Winning the Second Battle: Canadian Veterans and the Return to Civilian Life* (Toronto: University of Toronto Press, 1987); Kent Fedorowich, "Ex-Servicemen and the Politics of Soldier Settlement in Canada and Australia, 1915–1925," *War & Society* 20, no. 1 (2002): 47–80; Tim Cook, "From Destruction to Construction: The Khaki University of Canada, 1917–1919," *Journal of Canadian Studies* 37, no. 1 (2002): 109–44; Lara Campbell, "'We Who Have Wallowed in the Mud of Flanders': First World War Veterans, Unemployment, and the Development of Social Welfare in Canada, 1929–1939," *Journal of the Canadian Historical Association* 11 (2000): 125–49; and Andrew Spaull, "Federal Government Policies and the Vocational Training of World War One Veterans: A Comparative Study," *History of Education Review* 26, no. 2 (1997): 33–48.

32 Jonathan Vance, *Death So Noble: Meaning, Memory, and the First World War* (Vancouver: UBC Press, 1997). Also see Alan Young, "'We Throw the Torch': Canadian Memorials of the Great War and the Mythology of Heroic Sacrifice," *Journal of Canadian Studies* 24, no. 4 (1989): 5–28; Michael Haydon, "'Why Are All Those Names on the Walls?': The University of Saskatchewan

and World War I," *Saskatchewan History* 58, no. 2
(2006): 4–15; Mourad Djebabla-Brun, *Se Souvenir de
la Grande Guerre: la mémoire plurielle de 14–18 au Québec*
(Montreal: VLB éditeur, 2004.); Mark Reid, ed., *Canada's Great War Album: Our Memories of the First World War*
(Toronto: HarperCollins, 2014); Christopher Moore,
"1914 in 2014: What We Commemorate When We
Commemorate the First World War," *Canadian Historical Review* 95, no. 3 (2014): 427–32; Yves Frenette,
"Conscripting Canada's Past: The Harper Government
and the Politics of Memory," *Canadian Journal of History* 49, no. 1 (2014): 49–65.

33 Byfield, *Alberta in the 20th Century*, 65.

34 Ibid., 27.

35 *Historical Statistics on Canada* obtained from the
Statistics Canada website, www.statcan.gc.ca/pub/
11-516-x/index-eng.htm, Series E198-208, M34-44.

36 Joan Champ, "The Impact of the First World War on
Saskatchewan Families," prepared for Saskatchewan Western Development Museum's "Winning
the Prairie Gamble" 2005 Exhibit, 16 December
2002, www.wdm.ca/skteacherguide/WDM Research/
ImpactofWWI.pdf.

37 Bank of Canada Inflation Calculator,
www.bankofcanada.ca/rates/related/inflation-
calculator/.

TIMELINE

4 August 1914 | First World War begins

6 August 1914 | 19th Alberta Dragoons authorized by Department of Militia and Defence and recruited in Edmonton; absorbed as "A" Squadron Canadian Corps Cavalry Regiment

7 August 1914 | 9th Battalion authorized and recruited in Edmonton; reorganized to reinforce the 1st, 2nd, 3rd, and 4th battalions.

10 August 1914 | Canadian government announces an expeditionary force of 25,000

22 August 1914 | Passage of the War Measures Act

24 August 1914 | First troops arrive at the Valcartier training camp

30 September 1914 | Internment centre opens at the Lethbridge exhibition grounds

5 November 1914 | 3rd Regiment Canadian Mounted Rifles (CMR) authorized and recruited in Medicine Hat; absorbed by 1st and 2nd Battalion CMR

11 November 1914 | 31st Battalion authorized and recruited throughout Alberta

1 December 1914 | 12th Regiment CMR authorized and recruited in Calgary and Red Deer; absorbed into Canadian Cavalry Depot

1 December 1914 | 13th Regiment CMR authorized and recruited at Pincher Creek, Cardston, and Macleod; absorbed into various units

5 December 1914 | 50th Battalion authorized and recruited in Calgary

4 January 1915 | 49th Battalion authorized and recruited in Edmonton

24 January 1915 | 56th Battalion authorized and recruited in Calgary; absorbed into 9th Reserve Battalion

February 1915 | First Canadian troops arrive in France

12–15 March 1915 | Battle of Neuve Chappelle (Canada's baptism of fire)

21 April–25 May 1915 | Second Battle of Ypres

21 June 1915 | 66th Battalion authorized and recruited in Edmonton; absorbed into the 9th Reserve Battalion

28 June 1915 | 63rd Battalion authorized and recruited in Edmonton, Calgary, and Medicine Hat; absorbed into the 9th Reserve Battalion

4 July 1915 | Internment camps open in Banff National Park

1 September 1915 | 82nd Battalion authorized and recruited in Calgary; absorbed into the 9th Reserve Battalion

1 November 1915 | 89th Battalion authorized and recruited in Calgary; absorbed into the 9th Reserve Battalion and 97th Battalion

11 November 1915 | 137th Battalion authorized and recruited in Calgary; absorbed into the 21st Reserve Battalion

17 November 1915 | 113th Battalion authorized and recruited in Lethbridge

22 November 1915 | 138th Battalion authorized and recruited in Edmonton; absorbed into the 128th Battalion

26 November 1915 | 151st Battalion authorized and recruited in the federal ridings of Battle River, Victoria, Strathcona, and Red Deer; absorbed into the 7th and 9th Reserve Battalions

1 January 1916 | Prime Minister Borden commits Canada to a 500,000-man military

20 January 1916 | 187th Battalion authorized and recruited in the Red Deer district; absorbed into the 9th Reserve Battalion

21 January 1916 | 191st Battalion authorized and recruited in Macleod and district; re-organized in Canada as a draft giving depot battalion

25 January 1916 | 192nd Battalion authorized and recruited in Blairmore and district; absorbed into the 9th Reserve Battalion

28 January 1916 | 194th Battalion authorized and recruited in Edmonton; absorbed into the 9th Reserve Battalion

4 February 1916 | 202nd Battalion authorized and recruited in Edmonton; absorbed into the 9th Reserve Battalion

8 February 1916 | Internment centre opens at the Dominion Park Building in Jasper

23 February 1916 | 218th Battalion authorized and recruited in Edmonton; amalgamated with 211th Battalion and organized as the 8th Battalion, Canadian Railway Troops

27 March–16 April 1916 | Battle of St. Eloi

28 April 1916 | Following Manitoba (28 January 1916) and Saskatchewan (14 March 1916), Alberta women gain the right to vote provincially with passage of the Equal Suffrage Statutory Law Amendment Act

2–13 June 1916 | Battle of Mount Sorrel

1 July 1916 | Beginning of the Somme campaign

12 July 1916 | Prohibition imposed in Alberta

1 October–11 November 1916 | Battle of Ancre Heights

9–14 April 1917 | Battle of Vimy Ridge

7 July 1917 | Liberal Arthur Sifton re-elected Alberta premier; resigns in August to join the Union government led by Robert Borden; Charles Stewart succeeds Sifton as premier

15–25 August 1917 | Battle for Hill 70

29 August 1917 | Passage of the Military Service Act

20 September 1917 | Passage of the Wartime Elections Act

27 October–10 November 1917 | Battle of Passchendaele

17 December 1917 | Unionists led by Robert Borden win the federal election; win 11 of 12 seats and 61 percent of the popular vote in Alberta

1 April 1918 | Federal prohibition order

8–11 August 1918 | Battle of Amiens

27 September–1 October 1918 | Battle for Canal du Nord

8–9 October 1918 | Battle of Cambrai

1–2 November 1918 | Battle of Valenciennes

11 November 1918 | Armistice ends the war

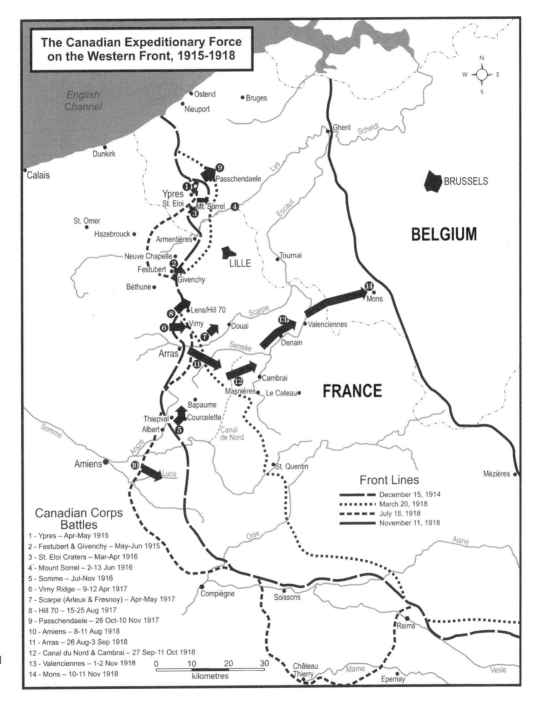

The Canadian Expeditionary Force on the Western Front, 1915-1918

BRUSSELS

BELGIUM

FRANCE

LILLE

English Channel

Ostend
Nieuport
Bruges
Ghent
Dunkirk
Calais
Passchendaele ⑨
St. Omer
Ypres ①
St. Eloi
Mt. Sorrel ④ ③
Hazebrouck
Armentières
Tournai
Neuve Chapelle
Festubert ②
Givenchy
Béthune
Mons ⑭
Lens/Hill 70
⑧
Vimy ⑥ ⑦
Douai
Valenciennes ⑬
Denain
Arras
Sensée
⑪
Cambrai
⑫ Masnières
Le Cateau
Bapaume
Courcelette
Thiepval
Albert ⑤
Canal de Nord
St. Quentin
Somme
Ancre
Amiens
⑩ Luce
Mèzières

Scheldt
Lys
Escaut
Scarpe

Oise
Aisne
Compiègne
Soissons
Reims
Vesle
Château Thierry
Marne
Epernay

Front Lines
— · — December 15, 1914
· · · · · March 20, 1918
– – – July 18, 1918
——— November 11, 1918

Canadian Corps Battles
1 - Ypres – Apr-May 1915
2 - Festubert & Givenchy – May-Jun 1915
3 - St. Eloi Craters – Mar-Apr 1916
4 - Mount Sorrel – 2-13 Jun 1916
5 - Somme – Jul-Nov 1916
6 - Vimy Ridge – 9-12 Apr 1917
7 - Scarpe (Arleux & Fresnoy) – Apr-May 1917
8 - Hill 70 – 15-25 Aug 1917
9 - Passchendaele – 26 Oct-10 Nov 1917
10 - Amiens – 8-11 Aug 1918
11 - Arras – 26 Aug-3 Sep 1918
12 - Canal du Nord & Cambrai – 27 Sep-11 Oct 1918
13 - Valenciennes – 1-2 Nov 1918
14 - Mons – 10-11 Nov 1918

0   10   20   30
kilometres

Map drawn by
Mike Bechthold

SECTION ONE

Albertans at War: The Military

The first formal and comprehensive history of Alberta was John Blue's multi-volume *Alberta Past and Present, Historical and Biographical*, published in 1924. In the chapter titled "Alberta and the Great War," he noted: "The total enlistments in Alberta for the Canadian Expeditionary Force during the period of the Great War (1914–1918) were 45,136 men, comprising twenty battalions of infantry, four mounted regiments, three batteries of artillery and a field ambulance unit."[1] The Alberta-raised infantry battalions were the 9th, 31st, 49th, 50th, 51st, 56th, 63rd, 66th, 82nd, 89th, 113th, 137th, 138th, 151st, 187th, 191st, 192nd, 194th, 202nd and 218th; the mounted regiments: the 3rd Canadian Mounted Rifles, the 12th Canadian Mounted Rifles, the 13th Canadian Mounted Rifles, and the 19th Alberta Dragoons; and the batteries of artillery – the 20th, 39th, and 61st of the Canadian Field Artillery. The No. 2 Tunnelling Company and No. 8 Field Ambulance completed the Alberta contingent. First off the mark were Lieutenant Colonel F.C. Jamieson and Major W.A. Griesbach, who raised the 19th Alberta Dragoons and left for Valcartier, Quebec, on 23 August 1914.

There were also hundreds of reservists from other countries, including Britain, France, Belgium, Serbia, and Italy, resident in Alberta who went overseas to fight. Determining an actual number of enlistees is complicated because some men who resided in Alberta enlisted in other provinces or in Great Britain. In addition, until 1915, when the enlistment forms were revised, they did not list the crucial category "place of residence."[2] As Jonathan Vance notes, the accepted enlistment figures were those established in A.F. Duguid's official history of the war.[3] According to Duguid, 36,165

Albertans served overseas and 12,720 served in Canada, for a total of 48,885. The enlistment number quoted by Blue – 45,136 men – was based on Department of National Defence figures. The 1916 Canadian census puts the male population of Alberta at 277,256; thus the enlistment figures are significant.[4]

Many of the battalions and regiments were established by well-known figures, and this added to the sense of pride of the men in their community and province. Once they arrived in Britain, they were attached to fighting units, and only the 31st, 49th, and 50th battalions retained their identity in France. Letters reveal the disappointment experienced by the men in not being able to fight as part of their original formation. The officers experienced the greatest disappointment, as many were found "surplus" to requirements and, as a result, were given the option of accepting a demotion in rank and being sent to France, or returning to Canada. While no figures are available for the number affected, it would appear that most chose demotion in order to fight.

The casualty rate for Alberta was high: 6,140 killed in action and some 20,000 wounded. The honours received were many; for example, for those who served with the Infantry: Order of St. Michael and St. George, 1; Distinguished Service Order, 6; Order of the British Empire, 3; Military Cross, 46; Distinguished Conduct Medal, 28; and Military Medal, 223. Members of the 49th Battalion were awarded: Victoria Cross, 2; Companion of the Order of Bath, 1 (Brigadier General W.A. Griesbach); Order of St. Michael and St. George, 1 (Brigadier General W.A. Griesbach); Distinguished Service Order, 7; Order of the British Empire, 3; Military Cross, 35; Distinguished Conduct Medal, 27; Military Medal, 184; French Croix de Guerre, 4; and Belgian Croix de Guerre, 3. The 50th Battalion received: Victoria Cross, 1; Distinguished Service Order, 6; Military Cross, 34; Distinguished Conduct Medal, 23; Military Medal, 227; Meritorious Service Medal, 10; Belgian Croix de Guerre, 3; and Russian Cross of St. George, 6.[5]

Section One – Albertans at War: The Military focuses on the contributions of battalions, regiments, and serving men. Rod Macleod covers the involvement of the legendary Western Canadian police officer and soldier, Sam Steele. During the war, Steele was given a leadership role, but solely as a political ploy, and soon felt marginalized. Macleod presents Steele's contributions as a sad ending to a long and distinguished military career. Major John Matthews and Juliette Champagne detail the career of Raymond Brutinel. Following military service in France, Brutinel immigrated to Edmonton, made a fortune and, as part of Canada's army, created the Canadian Automobile Machine Gun Brigade. Patricia Myers traces the early evolution of aviation in Alberta, which produced many barnstormers and combat fighters, in part because the province's vast expanses of flat land provided superior training conditions. Kathryn Ivany examines the construction of Alberta armouries, airfields, and other military infrastructure, including the political factors that sometimes affected their location.

Shifting back to people, James Dempsey writes a detailed account of cautions and contributions of Alberta's First Peoples with respect to the war effort. Duff Crerar traces the considerable enlistment, significant sacrifices, and important legacies from Alberta chaplains in the First World War. Brett Clifton details the strong response from, and local pride expressed in, young men who volunteered for military service from Lethbridge. Michale Lang provides a biographical account largely based on the wartime diary of adventurer, trapper, and mountain guide Sid Unwin, who was mortally wounded in the June 1917 capture of Hill 70. Ryan Flavelle traces the experiences of Alberta's "remittance men": those from moneyed British families who had fallen from grace and were essentially banished to the colonies to start anew, several of whom tried to redeem themselves through military service. Juliette Champagne tells the story of French and Belgian pioneers who homesteaded in northern Alberta but returned to militaries in their former homelands to fight. She does this through a close examination of a collection of postcards sent from France to family and friends in northern Alberta that provides insight into both their passion for their homesteads and age-old French distrust of the Germans as aggressors. David Borys details the tremendous military response at the University of Alberta, both among students and faculty such as Professor H. Moshier, who helped found the 11th Field Ambulance, and President Dr. H.M. Tory, who was instrumental in establishing the 191st Western Universities Battalion and the Khaki University.

Letters are a particularly powerful medium for communicating strong feelings. Adriana Davies covers the overseas wartime experiences of young men from the Strathcona-based Methodist Theological College, as documented in some 300 letters they wrote to Lady Principal Miss Nettie Burkholder, who helped these men keep their faith in a just God while witnessing so much suffering. Antonella Fanella also uses personal correspondence to recreate the love story of Albertans Harold McGill, who was serving in the Canadian Army Medical Corps in France, and Emma Griffis, an army nurse in Bramshott, England.

Caring for the health of enlisted men, whether wounded in action or suffering from everyday ailments, was an enormous challenge. J. Robert Lampard presents an overview of contributions by Alberta medical personnel, many of whom excelled in providing critical care under extreme conditions, and who made breakthroughs in the treatment of wounds and diseases. And finally, Allan Kerr and Doug Styles present a very different expression of a personal war experience: two trench art belts created by Private Stephen Smith of Calgary from souvenirs connected to various phases of his military service.

The essays in this section allow the reader to hear the voices of Albertan serving men on the Front. None emerged unchanged from their experience overseas. There were many whose beliefs were tested and who were left with deep scars. Some even grew callous and cynical in order to survive the horror, which is vividly expressed in letters and memoirs. Re-integration into peacetime society was a hurdle that some never overcame.

Notes

1   John Blue, Provincial Librarian, in the three-volume history of Alberta, *Alberta Past and Present, Historical and Biographical* (Chicago: Pioneer Publishing, 1924) provides a comprehensive history of the new province. Chapter XXIII: "Alberta in the Great War" in volume 1 details the battalions and regiments raised, including the date of their formation and where they served, 399–418.

2   In "Provincial Patterns of Enlistment in the Canadian Expeditionary Force," *Canadian Military History* 17, no. 2 (2008), 75–78, Jonathan Vance outlines a project that he heads in which research assistants are collecting data on all volunteers and conscripts to arrive at more accurate provincial enlistment figures.

3   Enlistment figures are contained in the following: A.F. Duguid, *Official History of the Canadian Forces in the Great War, 1914–1919*, vol. 1: *From the Outbreak of War to the Formation of the Canadian Corps, August 1914–September 1915* (Ottawa: King's Printer, 1938).

4   Howard Palmer and Tamara Palmer, eds., *Peoples of Alberta: Portraits of Cultural Diversity* (Saskatoon, SK: Western Producer Prairie Books, 1985), 217.

5   Blue, *Alberta Past and Present*, 409, 415, and 418.

Stained glass window at St. George's-in-the-Pines Anglican Church, Banff, 2010, Whyte Museum of the Canadian Rockies, v500-166c-na.

(left) An Italian soldier bearing the national flag; (right) Two young women in the regional dress of Alsace and Lorraine appear to be embraced by the French flag, and the slogan "Vive la France" appears below. The rising sun behind the church spire suggests hope that France will regain the territories she lost in the Franco-Prussian War. Germaine Mahé Champagne postcard collection.

(left) Postcards depicting soldiers were extremely popular. *Poilu* was the French popular term for the ordinary soldier. The ruined church and houses in the background suggest what he is fighting for; (right) Allied soldiers depicted with their national flags and the slogan "Towards Victory." The sun is shown breaking through the clouds to herald a new day. Traditional age-old rivalries are forgotten as they fight together to defeat Germany. Germaine Mahé Champagne postcard collection.

Alsace was a deeply contested area and this postcard's slogan, "In Alsace—long live France," is provocative. The young woman on the left is depicted pouring a glass of wine for the French victors. Germaine Mahé Champagne postcard collection.

(left) General Joffre is depicted with the slogan that France's destiny is entrusted to him. The flowers surrounding his image are of the poppy, the marguerite, and cornflower, representing the colours of the French flag; (right) A charming young girl depicts a martial goddess of victory. The Arc de Triomphe is in the background and the slogan "Glory and Immortality!" below. The monument is incredibly important to the French and was designed by Jean Chalgrin in 1806. It depicts classically nude French youths pitted against Germanic warriors in chain mail. It was one of a series of monuments stretching from the Louvre to the Grande Arche de la Défense. In subtext appears another slogan: "We salute the flag!" Germaine Mahé Champagne postcard collection.

POUR LA FRANCE
POUR LA PATRIE
POUR DIEU

REX
4240

Au cher drapeau il on fière place
Sur toutes les maisons d'Alsace.

La Vision

(above left) This postcard juxtaposes a praying nun with young soldiers on the front. Since most combatants were Christians, it was commonly believed that the deity was on their side; thus, the slogan, "For France, for the homeland, for God"; (above right) An Alsatian girl in regional dress holds a flower posy with colours of the French flag. A French aviator appears to be about to drop a floral bouquet for her. French aviation pioneers Henri Farman and Louis Blériot suggested that the airplane could be used for reconnaissance. As early as 1909, the French War Department promoted pilot training for army officers; on 22 October 1910 the *Aéronautique Militaire* was created as a branch of the army, later becoming the French Air Force; (below) A soldier looking at a vision of his sweetheart. Germaine Mahé Champagne postcard collection.

(right) Jeanne d'Arc had been beatified, one of the steps toward sainthood, on 18 April 1909 at Notre-Dame Cathedral in Paris by Pope Pius X. In this scene, women and children are praying for the protection of soldiers on the front, and the slogan reads "Blessed Jeanne d'Arc, protect us"; (below) The horrors of the battlefield are suggested in this picture, and the dog wears a Red Cross emblem as a collar. Germaine Mahé Champagne postcard collection.

Bienheureuse Jeanne d'Arc, protégez-les

The card depicts the flags of the Allies with the slogan "In homage to the Allies!" Germaine Mahé Champagne postcard collection.

Private Stephen Smith framed his two souvenir belts together with his picture, cap badge, and collars. Kerr Collection, Canadian Militaria Preservation Society, Edmonton, Alberta.

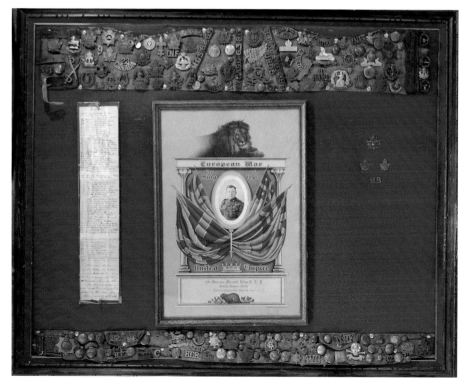

(far left) The small belt (6.5 cm wide, 96 cm long) contains 68 items. The original list was found in the pocket near the belt buckle and is shown left of the picture in the photograph on the previous page; (left) The large belt (14 cm wide, 93 cm long) contains 95 items; (above) The commercially produced memorial picture frame and backing illustrates another type of trench art. Families were contacted, whenever a son or father's name appeared in a newspaper, and offered such products. The backing to Smith's picture frame is marked "COPYRIGHTED BY CHAS E NEVILLE." All images from the Kerr Collection, Canadian Militaria Preservation Society, Edmonton, Alberta.

Lieutenant P.E. Smith.
(Age 18)

~His~
~Spouse~

—THE—
—ARMY—LIFE—OF—
—P.E. SMITH—

General P.E. Smith.
(Age 58)

Colonel P.E. Smith.
(Age 38)

~~The End.~~

(left) An original drawing by soldier Jack Taylor sent by Sam Laycock to Miss Nettie Burkholder in a letter dated 17 January 1918 from France. University of Alberta Archives, 88-66-5; (facing page) Knox Presbyterian Church in Calgary, Alberta, unveiled on Sunday, 2 January 1921, a stained glass memorial window to its war dead. It was designed by A.J. Larshchild of the Pittsburgh Glass Company in Minneapolis.

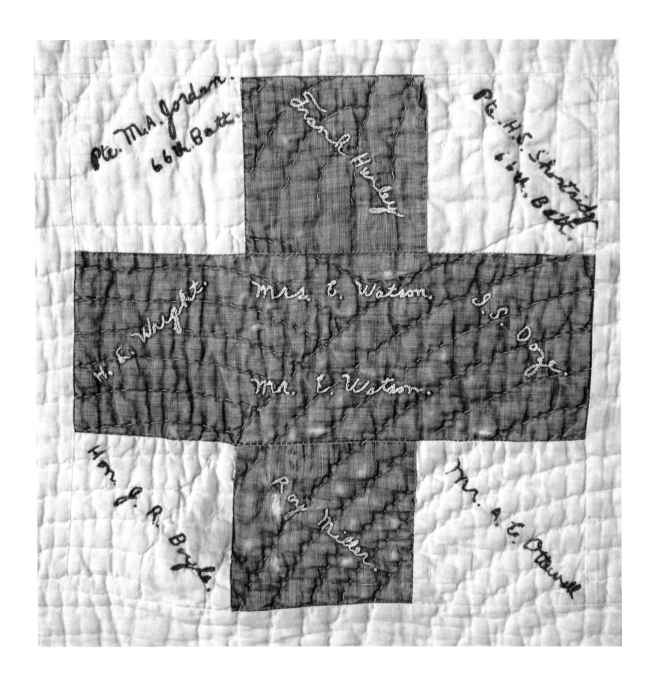

(facing page) 1917 Waskatenau Red Cross signature quilt, post cleaning and stabilization, bearing the names of 300 area residents;
(above) A section of the quilt shows the seven-patch block pattern and varying types of stitches used to embroider the signatures. Photos courtesy of the Royal Alberta Museum.

(this page) Steel helmet, 31st Battalion Canadian Expeditionary Force. This helmet was painted as a commemorative souvenir with the battle honours for all the battles that the 31st Battalion out of Calgary fought in. Collection of the Army Museum of Alberta. Photo: Julie Vincent Photography; (facing page) *War Deed—Story Robe* created by Mike Mountain Horse, from the Kainai (Blood) First Nation in southwest Alberta, with the assistance of Ambrose Two Chiefs, to commemorate his overseas service with Alberta's 50th Battalion. Collection of the Esplanade Arts and Heritage Centre.

Pigeon message canister. This particular canister was used by a signaller from the 187th Battalion from Alberta to send messages across the battlefield when the wires on field telephones were cut. Collection of the Army Museum of Alberta. Photo: Julie Vincent Photography.

An Old Soldier Fades Away: Major General Sir Sam Steele in the First World War

ROD MACLEOD

When the Germans invaded France in August 1914, Sam Steele, age 66, was the best-known Albertan military man, probably the best-known Canadian soldier.[1] He was just finishing his memoirs, and sliding gently toward retirement after nearly half a century of serving his country as a soldier and mounted policeman.[2] He had missed very few opportunities for action during those years. After serving as a private in the Ontario Rifles during the Red River Expedition of 1870 and in "B" Battery, Canadian Artillery, he moved on to the North-West Mounted Police in 1873. He formed and led Steele's Scouts during the 1885 Rebellion. After commanding the Mounted Police in the Yukon during the gold rush, he raised and led Lord Strathcona's Horse in the Boer War. At the end of that conflict, he was one of Lord Baden-Powell's senior officers in the paramilitary South African Constabulary until he returned to Canada and the Canadian Army in 1907, first as commanding officer of Military District No. 13 at Calgary, then of Military District No. 10 at Winnipeg.

The years at Winnipeg from 1907 to 1914 were, on the whole, good ones for Steele. He was with his wife and children, to whom he was devoted, after painful separations while he was in the Yukon and South Africa. Winnipeg was the prosperous metropolis of the booming Canadian West, a city whose business and political elite included many people Steele had befriended at the time of the Red River Expedition. His position as the senior military officer between Thunder Bay and the Rockies made him part of that elite. The job was challenging without being overwhelming. Sir Wilfrid Laurier's Liberal government was in office until 1911 and Steele, who had strong Conservative connections, was in a somewhat uncomfortable situation in what was a highly politicized appointment, but Steele liked and respected the Liberal minister of militia, Sir Frederick Borden.[3]

Canada's military system in the first decade of the twentieth century was based upon a tiny permanent force whose principal duty was to train the large and growing number of part-time militia members.

CAMP SEWELL. 1913.

When Steele returned from South Africa in 1907, the permanent force for all of Canada numbered 2,716 officers and men. It crept up to 3,118 in 1911, and actually dropped to 2,900 the year before the start of the Great War.[4] Canada was by no stretch of the imagination a country of pacifists in this period; it was a militaristic age worldwide, and Canadians fully shared the enthusiasm. In 1911 alone, 33 new militia units were formed across the country, 6 of them in Steele's Military District No. 10. The problem for Steele and his fellow military professionals was that quantity was far outstripping quality. War was becoming rapidly more complex and dangerous, but militia soldiers were still getting the same training—a few days a month of drill and two weeks at a summer camp—that Steele had received at the time of the Fenian raids in the 1860s.

Then it got worse. In 1911 the Conservatives won the election, which should have been a good thing for Steele, but Sam Hughes was appointed minister of militia and defence. Steele had met Hughes in South Africa and was not impressed. He wrote to his wife of one encounter: "He is a blowhard and a nuisance. Does not have enough sense to keep his tongue quiet and makes a show of Canada among the modest but brave soldiers of all parts here. I avoid his company, the fool."[5] Now, he could not avoid Hughes's company and, although he tried his best to be the loyal

(above) Sam Steele, 1913, with (left to right) Sir Ian Hamilton, Sam Hughes, and General G.E. Ellison. Image courtesy of the Bruce Peel Special Collections Library, University of Alberta, 2008.1.3.3.6.3.31; (below) Sam Steele at Camp Sewell, Manitoba, 1913, with his two adjutants, Major Louis Lipsett (left) and Major H.D.B. Ketchen, both of whom became generals during the war. Bruce Peel Special Collections Library, University of Alberta, 2008.1.3.3.6.2.31.

subordinate, it did not take long for the relationship with his new political superior to deteriorate.
In April 1912 he recorded in his diary: "Got a most
scandalously vile and tyrannical telegram from
Sam Hughes."[6] By 1914 he was referring to him in
his diary as "that lunatic and egotist Sam Hughes."[7]
Apart from the obvious personality clash, there were
important differences between the two men over
how Canada's army was to be managed.

Sam Steele was fully aware of the realities of
patronage in the Canadian politics of his time. He
knew that land for new armouries, rifle ranges, and
other military installations would be purchased from
friends of the government in power. He also knew
that the contractors hired to build these facilities
would be members in good standing of the ruling
party. Supplies of all kinds would, as a matter of
course, be purchased only from those firms on the
government's patronage list. But Sam Hughes took
patronage to a new level, demanding that only Conservatives be given commissions or promotions in
the militia. In 1913 Steele confided in his diary:

> Major Corelli called to say that when he was
> down in Ottawa a few days ago he spoke to the
> Minister about a great many things and the
> officers were summoned before Col Hughes
> who made the remark that was in this way,
> why does "Sam Steele recommend those
> damned Grits." I cannot understand him and
> I will continue as I have done viz recommend
> the officers on their merits and fitness.[8]

Sam Hughes had for many years been Canada's
leading exponent of the virtues of amateurism in
military matters. The bravery and enthusiasm of
the "citizen" soldier would vanquish all obstacles.

Portrait of Sam Steele in military uniform in 1914. Image courtesy
of the Bruce Peel Special Collections Library, University of Alberta,
2008.1.3.3.6.1.35.

Basic equipment and a little training was all that was necessary. Hughes regarded all professional soldiers with deep suspicion; they were, he said, "bar-room loafers," who were only in the military because they could not hold down a job in civilian life.[9] The British officers who commanded the Canadian Army in the period before 1914 and who tried, mostly in vain, to raise the standards of training in the permanent force, were, in Hughes's mind, even worse. They were arrogant snobs who refused to recognize the obvious virtues of dedicated amateurs, like Hughes himself. Frederick Borden, who was also a believer in a citizen army but who did not share Hughes's contempt for professionalism, had brought Sam Steele back from South Africa in an effort to help resolve the conflict between amateurs and professionals. Steele had led a group of volunteers, Lord Strathcona's Horse, with great success during the Boer War, but his professionalism had attracted the attention of General Robert Baden-Powell, who recruited him as a senior officer in his South African Constabulary. Steele would, Borden hoped, be able to raise standards of training while remaining acceptable to the amateurs.

When the war came in August 1914, chaos descended on the Canadian militia as Hughes immediately scrapped the existing mobilization plans and built a vast new camp at Valcartier.[10] Three weeks into the war, Steele was ordered there to help sort out the mess. By mid-September a degree of order had been imposed, and the First Canadian Contingent was getting on trains to Halifax for their departure to England. At this point Hughes suggested that Steele might like to command Military District No. 11 in Victoria. Conversations at Valcartier with Minister of Public Works Robert Rogers had given Steele hope that, in spite of his age, his experience and

demonstrated competence might get him an active command. He turned down the offer, something he would come to regret.[11] In December 1914 Steele was promoted to major general and told he would be appointed inspector general for western Canada. Although he got a telegram from Prime Minister Borden congratulating him, the appointment seems not to have happened. Instead, in March 1915 Hughes offered Steele command of the 2nd Canadian Division, which was leaving soon for England.

Steele was elated at the appointment but quickly discovered that it was a poisoned chalice. Hughes had tried to have a Canadian named to command the 1st Division, but Lord Kitchener, the British secretary of state for war, vetoed that idea, pointing out quite correctly that no Canadian officer had commanded anything larger than a battalion in time of war. Hughes knew that the same thing would happen with the 2nd Division but went ahead anyway. If he was going to lose the battle, he would do so in a way that would create the maximum difficulty and embarrassment for Kitchener. Steele had served under Kitchener in South Africa, and the two men liked and respected each other. Steele's high public profile at home would make firing him more awkward. Hughes's knowledge that he would lose this round was less important than his desire to keep the pressure on to promote Canadians to senior commands as they accumulated experience at the front.[12] Sam Steele was collateral damage in this struggle.

Steele found out that he would not be allowed to retain command of the 2nd Division before it left Canada, and offered to resign the position if his appointment would embarrass the government—but Hughes refused to accept the offer.[13] The division sailed in May with Steele in command, recovering from a broken collar bone and other injuries suffered when he was thrown by his horse while reviewing the troops at Toronto. He would remain in command while the division trained in the camp at Shorncliffe in Kent before turning it over to the general who would command it in France. Before he left Canada, Steele was informed by Militia Chief of Staff General Gwatkin that he would be in command of all Canadian troops at Shorncliffe. This logical arrangement was defeated by Sam Hughes's genius for creating administrative confusion.[14]

By the time the 2nd Division arrived in England, Hughes had appointed two officers with competing

Sam Steele with Lord Jellicoe, Lord Kitchener, and King George V reviewing the 2nd Canadian Division, Shorncliffe, 1915. Bruce Peel Special Collections Library, University of Alberta, 2008.1.3.3.6.2.5.

claims to control the Canadians there: Colonel John Carson, who had a rather vague assignment to assist the Canadian high commissioner with administrative arrangements for the troops, and Brigadier General J.C. MacDougall, who had been appointed as temporary commander of all Canadian troops in England when he was rejected for a staff job with the 1st Division in February. Steele, as a major general, was senior to both so, unless another position could be found for him, somebody would have to go. Ironically, it was Kitchener who helped solve the political problem for Hughes. The Shorncliffe area came under the British Army's Eastern Command. The general in charge was due to retire and Steele was appointed to replace him.

Steele was now a Canadian general in command of a British army area whose military camps were almost entirely occupied by Canadians. The purpose of the camps was to train soldiers coming from Canada, the actual training being the responsibility of the British. The principal task of Steele, Carson, and MacDougall was to attempt to maintain a smooth flow of competent officers and men as reinforcements to the 1st and 2nd Divisions in France, and to the 3rd and 4th Divisions assembling in England. Hughes provided no clear division of responsibilities among the three, and disputes inevitably followed. As Desmond Morton noted, "By deliberately creating confusion among the Canadian commanders in England, the minister guaranteed that his own will would remain paramount."[15]

The situation was made worse by the complete lack of any rational system of recruitment in Canada. Instead of recruiting men to sustain existing units in the field, Hughes kept on creating new regiments and sending them across the Atlantic. Once there, the groups had to be broken up to provide the necessary reinforcements. Few had any training to speak of when they arrived and, while privates, NCOs, and lieutenants could be brought up to speed relatively quickly, inexperienced captains, majors, and colonels were a danger to themselves and their troops. Unemployed and disgruntled senior officers piled up at Shorncliffe. Most of them had been chosen for their standing in their communities, and they did not hesitate to make their unhappiness known to the government. Nothing could eliminate this problem as long as surplus officers continued to be fed into the pipeline, but Steele managed to reduce it to manageable proportions. Captains and majors were given the option of taking a reduction in rank to lieutenant to get into the fighting, and many did so. The others were allowed to save face by being sent across for a couple of weeks so that they could go home and, truthfully, state that they had seen fighting.

Steele struggled on as best he could for the year and a half after his appointment. As he had done throughout his life, he worked diligently to keep up with his profession. He studied the fighting in France and incorporated its lessons into the training program, insisting that all newly arrived officers up to the rank of brigadier take the same courses that their soldiers did on grenade throwing, machine guns, and signalling before they were allowed to go to the front.[16] He began taking French lessons because he believed, correctly, that the French army's tactics were more advanced than those of the British. He never stopped campaigning for a more active command, pulling all the strings he could manage.

At the end of 1916, Prime Minister Borden finally lost patience with Sam Hughes and fired him. At last, the Canadian government could set about restoring some semblance of order to its command structure in England, which it did by creating a Ministry of Overseas Military Forces, separate from the Department of Militia and Defence. The Canadian high commissioner, Sir George Perley, was put in charge. He immediately retired General MacDougall and sent him back to Canada. Carson, now a major general, was given a knighthood early in 1917 and also retired. Perley had a higher opinion of Steele's potential usefulness and suggested putting him in charge of recruiting in western Canada.[17] Nothing came of this idea, and Steele was left in his anomalous position for another year, grumbling in his diary that he did not have enough work to do.[18] To make matters worse, the Canadian authorities belatedly decided that, as he held a British command, he should be paid at British rates, lower than the Canadian ones. He was ordered to repay $2,500.[19]

In November 1917, Perley informed Steele that he would be retired soon.[20] He was offered and accepted a KCMG (Knight Commander in the Most Distinguished Order of Saint Michael and Saint George). Becoming Sir Sam Steele softened the blow of retirement somewhat, but his diary makes clear that he would have been happy to trade it for a real job. Negotiations about the terms of his leaving took several months and, on 1 March 1918, Sam Steele's long military career came to an end.[21] He did not return to Canada because he had recently met a very wealthy Ontario businessman named William Perkins Bull who was living in England supervising the hospitals he had established for Canadian soldiers. Bull made Steele a director of one of his western Canadian land companies at a salary well above what he earned as a general.[22] Steele was grateful for the job since it meant he could stay in England. His son, Harwood, was a captain serving with the British army in France and his daughter Flora was a Volunteer Aid

Portrait of Sam Steele in military uniform in 1917. It is clear that the wartime stress has aged him. Image courtesy of the Bruce Peel Special Collections Library, University of Alberta, 2008.1.3.3.6.1.18.

Detachment nurse working in a hospital near Shorn-cliffe. He was reluctant to leave them and, in any case, the prospect of moving his wife and younger daughter back across the Atlantic in wartime was not appealing. He worked diligently in his first civilian job for almost half a century, but his heart was clearly not in it.

By summer 1918 Steele's health was in serious decline. His weight started to drop steadily early in 1917 and by mid-1918 he had lost more than 40 pounds. Steele for the last 20 years of his life feared that he was becoming diabetic, had himself tested regularly, and kept up a rigorous program of diet and exercise. It seems likely that his diagnosis was correct. Starting in early 1918, he was afflicted by severe eczema (another symptom of diabetes), which made sleep difficult. In September Steele spent most of his time in bed, managing to summon enough energy to get out of the house only twice. In October he did not get out of his bed at all, although he continued to follow the final days of the war. His diary entries for most every day of that month, and for November as well, consist of "Still sick in bed." On November 11 he wrote, "The terms of the Armistice with the Central Powers proclaimed at 10:30 AM. All wild with joy."[23] On November 30 the diary he had kept faithfully since 1885 ends. He died two months later on 30 January 1919.

Sam Steele outlived his fame. At the time of his promotion to major general at the beginning of the war, the number of Canadian generals could be counted on the fingers of one hand. Four years later there were dozens, many of them his former subordinates, and all better known to the public than he was because of their roles as brigade or divisional commanders. When he died, some of his friends had a death mask made with the intention of erecting a statue in his honour, but after four years of slaughter in the trenches, there was little appetite for commemorating an old soldier from a very different Canada. The mask lies in the vaults of the Glenbow Museum in Calgary and the monument remains unbuilt.

Notes

1   Sam Steele was born in Ontario, lived in all four western provinces and the Yukon, spent six years in South Africa, and is buried in Winnipeg. Calling Sam Steele an Albertan is based on the fact that he lived more of his adult life in the province (or the part of the North-West Territories that became Alberta) than anywhere else. In all, he lived about 17 years in Alberta, depending on whether or not one counts the time spent in supervising construction on the Canadian Pacific Railway and as part of the Alberta Field Force during the 1885 Rebellion. Fourteen of those years were spent in Fort Macleod and a year each in Fort Saskatchewan and Calgary. The longest he lived in any other place was seven years in Manitoba. He met his wife in Alberta and all three of his children were born at Fort Macleod.

2   S.B. Steele, *Forty Years in Canada: Reminiscences of the Great North-West with Some Account of His Service in South Africa* (Toronto: McClelland, Goodchild, and Stewart, 1915).

3   Borden's son was killed in South Africa, which gave him a bond with the Canadians who served there. He corresponded extensively with Steele about Canadians serving in the South African Constabulary and it was Borden who offered him the opportunity to return to the Canadian army in 1907.

4   Canada, *Sessional Papers*, 1908, 1912, 1914, Annual Reports of the Militia Council.

5   University of Alberta Archives (UAA), Edmonton, Steele Fonds, 2008.2.1.1.1.341, Sam to Marie, 11 May 1900.

6   UAA, Steele Fonds, 2008.1.1.2.60, Diary, 30 April 1912.

7   Ibid., 23 August 1914.

8   Ibid., 10 November 1913.

9   J.L. Granatstein, *Canada's Army: Waging War and Keeping the Peace* (Toronto: University of Toronto Press, 2002), 48.

10 This is the unanimous verdict of historians. Even Hughes's sympathetic biographer, Ronald Haycock, admits it. Ronald G. Haycock, *Sam Hughes: The Public Career of a Controversial Canadian, 1885–1916* (Waterloo, ON: Wilfrid Laurier University Press, 1986), chapter 11.

11 UAA, Steele Fonds, Diary, 15 September 1914.

12 The strategy worked. In September 1915 two Canadian brigade commanders who had done well in the early fighting, Arthur Currie and Richard Turner, were appointed to command the 1st and 2nd Divisions.

13 UAA, Steele Fonds, Diary, 7 April 1915.

14 The extraordinary tangle Hughes created is fully explored in Desmond Morton, *A Peculiar Kind of Politics: Canada's Overseas Ministry in the First World War* (Toronto: University of Toronto Press, 1982).

15 Morton, *A Peculiar Kind of Politics*, 48.

16 UAA, Steele Fonds, Diary, 2 December 1915.

17 Morton, *A Peculiar Kind of Politics*, 123.

18 UAA, Steele Fonds, Diary, 16 March 1917.

19 Ibid., 11 June 1916.

20 Ibid., 13 November 1917.

21 Ibid., 1 March 1918.

22 Ibid., 20 February 1918. William Perkins Bull made an enormous fortune investing in land and early oil developments in Alberta. He was very interested in Canadian history and, among other things, wrote the first history of Canadian sport with the odd title *From Rattlesnake Hunt to Hockey* (Toronto: G.J. McLeod Ltd., 1934).

23 UAA, Steele Fonds, Diary, 11 November 1918.

Works Cited

PRIMARY SOURCES

University of Alberta Archives, Edmonton. Steele Fonds, 2008.2.1.1.1.341.

SECONDARY SOURCES

Cook, Tim. *At the Sharp End: Canadians Fighting the Great War, 1914–1916*. Toronto: Penguin, 2007.

——. *Shock Troops: Canadians Fighting the Great War, 1917–1918*. Toronto: Penguin, 2008.

Granatstein, J.L. *Canada's Army: Waging War and Keeping the Peace*. Toronto: University of Toronto Press, 2002.

Haycock, Ronald G. *Sam Hughes: The Public Career of a Controversial Canadian, 1885–1916*. Waterloo, ON: Wilfrid Laurier University Press, 1986.

Morton, Desmond. *A Peculiar Kind of Politics: Canada's Overseas Ministry in the First World War*. Toronto: University of Toronto Press, 1982.

Nicholson, G.W.L. *Canadian Expeditionary Force 1914–1919: Official History of the Canadian Army*. Ottawa: Queen's Printer, 1962.

Steele, S.B. *Forty Years in Canada: Reminiscences of the Great North-West with Some Account of His Service in South Africa*. Toronto: McClelland, Goodchild and Stewart, 1915.

Raymond Brutinel and the Genesis of Modern Mechanized Warfare

JULIETTE CHAMPAGNE AND MAJOR (RETD.) JOHN MATTHEWS

Raymond Brutinel, a French citizen, made his fortune in Alberta and, in 1914, had machine guns and armoured vehicles made for the Canadian Corps. He rose to the rank of brigadier general, general officer commanding Canadian Machine Gun Corps and, during the Hundred Days (from August 8 through November 1918), commanded a formation called "The Independent Force," sometimes known as "Brutinel's Brigade." In 1919 Prime Minister Robert Borden had British citizenship conferred on him.[1] General F.F. Worthington, considered the founder of the Royal Canadian Armoured Corps (RCAC), wrote: "Brutinel could never have done what he did in any conventional way. It was only possible with the Canadians, without red tape or rigid ideas, and who were commanded by Sir Arthur Currie, a militiaman, who was one of the outstanding Generals of the Western Front."[2]

Today Brutinel remains an unknown figure in the country he served in peace and war. Although there is a short biography in the *Canadian Encyclopedia*, and Brutinel has been the subject of a few articles, little is remembered of him today in Alberta, or for that matter in Canada. Yet he was recognized by three governments. The British awarded him the Distinguished Service Order, the Companion of the Order of the Bath, and the Companion of the Order of St. Michael and St. George; the French named him an Officier de la Légion d'Honneur and Commandeur de la Légion d'Honneur, as well as giving him the Croix de Guerre avec étoile et palme; and Italy gave him the medal of the Chevalier de l'Ordre de St. Maurice et St. Lazare. Other honours included seven British Mentions-in-Despatches and three from the French, a diploma of gratefulness from the City of Westmount (Quebec), and, in 1952, a medal from France for his work in the Resistance.[3] In the months after the November 11 armistice, he prepared two lengthy reports concerning the Canadian Corps and the Canadian Machine Gun Corps for the Canadian government and was asked to take charge of the Historical Service of the Canadian Armies, a position he turned down. Much later, in 1962, he was interviewed at length by a CBC journalist about his activities in the Great War.[4] Dominique and Jacques Baylaucq, two brothers who were close friends of Brutinel and his family, prepared a biography that has been drawn on extensively for this article.

Raymond Pierre Marc Brutinel was born in 1882 at Alet-les-Bains (Aude) in southwest France, Pyrénées region.[5] Educated by the Jesuits in Carcassonne, at 16 he signed on as an apprentice on a fully-rigged sailing ship, which sailed mostly in the Caribbean and along the coast of South America. He rounded Cape Horn three times. Brutinel returned to France for compulsory military service in 1901 with the 53rd Infantry Regiment in Tarbes (Hautes-Pyrénées) where he quickly rose through the ranks, becoming sergeant instructor, then master-at-arms and, eventually, joining a platoon of officers-in-training. In 1903 he married Marie Calumun, daughter of the mayor and regional councillor of the small town of Arreau in the Pyrénées and great-niece to Maréchal Ferdinand Foch, whom he later briefed about Canadian machine gun tactics during the war.

At the turn of the century, France was still in the throes of the anti-Semitic turmoil of the Dreyfus Affair, and in the process of establishing state-provided public schools. With this came the closure of Catholic private schools. The members of religious orders who operated schools found themselves out of work and, in many cases, their residences or convents were seized by the State. In this climate of repression, the scandal known as the "Affaire des fiches" broke. An extensive list had been drawn up identifying more than 25,000 Catholic officers, members of Catholic military organizations, or simply members of charitable church organizations as potentially breaking the 1903 laws of political neutrality, which they had sworn to respect and which effectively eliminated their chances of promotion in the ranks.[6] In light of this, in 1904 the Brutinels immigrated to western Canada along with a group of French soldiers, some of whom were

officers who left in protest.[7] The French ranching community of Trochu, Alberta, attracted some; others established themselves in Calgary. The Brutinels were in Edmonton by September, as can be gathered from a newspaper ad in which Marie was seeking to learn English, and by November they had set up a boarding house on Jasper Avenue and 6th Street.[8] Brutinel was also giving fencing lessons and demonstrations of the sport at a studio he opened with a former member of the Mounted Police. He was also socializing with local businessmen of the French community and the city of Edmonton.[9]

In January 1906 Brutinel began writing a world affairs column for *Le Courrier de l'Ouest*, a weekly newspaper based in Edmonton, which had just been established the previous fall and was then the only French paper in the Canadian West. It was owned by several local entrepreneurs of the French community as well as Liberal politician Frank Oliver.[10] Brutinel's articles provide a sense of his perspective on life. As editor of the front-page column, he covered current events gleaned from newspapers far and wide, including those of France where the ongoing separation of Church and State and the exoneration of Dreyfus in 1906 were sore points for many French Catholics, particularly those who harboured anti-Semitic feelings.[11] After publishing on the first event, a member of the local clergy wrote to the paper protesting that Brutinel was using anti-Catholic sources and, a few months later when the Dreyfus exoneration came through, another cleric wrote a number of letters to that effect. Publishing their letters, Brutinel identified himself as the editor of the world affairs column, which he had been signing with the initials "R.B." and, putting down his editor's pen, replied as a reader. He justified his sources as being moderate and fair, and went on to deplore the anti-Semitic riots that had ensued during the Dreyfus Affair in France and its colonies, stating that the way to settle these matters was not through violence but peaceably, at the ballot box.[12] Finally, the second irate critic, who had written under the pen name "J.B. Surveillant," identified himself as Bishop Émile Legal of the Archdiocese of Edmonton.[13]

By 1907 Brutinel had become one of the directors of a French colonization society in Alberta and was a founding member of a society to welcome and assist French newcomers to the area. By May he had resigned as editor and was on a promotional trip in France for the settlement society.[14] Keeping a hand in journalism, while in Paris he interviewed Sir Wilfrid Laurier and the article was published in the *Courrier de l'Ouest*.[15] By the time he returned to Edmonton, he was employed by a financial syndicate from Montreal affiliated with the Grand Trunk and Pacific Railway, and charged with leading a prospecting crew to explore the region along the future rail line, from the Pembina River to the mouth of the Skeena River, to seek out potential resources—be they timber, water power, coal, or other minerals—and claim them for the syndicate.[16] Working with him was a crew known as "the Frenchmen" that included his friend Armand de Bernis, who had a horse ranch at Trochu, and half a dozen others. Successful in their search, they staked the region now known as the Coal Branch, establishing Pacific Pass Coal Fields Ltd. for the syndicate of which E.B. Greenshields of Montreal was president.

On some land in St. Albert, Brutinel kept a string of saddle and pack horses for the many exploration trips to the mountains. By 1909 he was building a brick home there with all the modern conveniences for his growing family, as he was becoming wealthy through his investments in coal and real estate. In 1911 his office was in Edmonton's Molson's Bank Building, where he was listed as director of Pacific Pass Coal Fields Ltd. and as a financial agent.[17] Locally he invested in and initiated other projects: a coal mine in the St. Albert region, the Edmonton Interurban Railway to St. Albert, a power plant for the town of St. Albert at a time when its residents were still using coal oil lamps (which was never built, as the price was judged to be exorbitant), and the Edmonton-based Great Northern Tannery. By 1913 he had moved to Montreal, where he was in a better position to manage his financial interests.

With the declaration of war on 4 August 1914, Brutinel, like many other French reservists, planned to rejoin his regiment in France. He contacted the French ambassador in Washington, DC, about bringing machine guns with him to France. When Brutinel had done his French military service at the Tarbes Arsenal, it was common knowledge there that the founder of the arsenal was Auguste de Verchère de Reffye, inventor of an early model of the machine gun, who had also developed tactics to use with this weaponry.[18] Keenly interested in this, Brutinel planned to have the guns made by Colt Patent Firearms in Hartford, Connecticut, but, due to the German blockades of the Atlantic, was unable to get French military ammunition from the islands of St. Pierre and Miquelon to calibrate them. Clifford Sifton, formerly minister of the interior in the Laurier government, then chair of the Canadian Commission of Conservation, on hearing of Brutinel's efforts, met with him in Montreal and suggested that he provide the weapons to the Canadian forces. Contacted by telephone, the French ambassador readily agreed, saying that whatever Brutinel did for Canada, he would be doing it for France.[19] Overnight,

Vehicles of the Canadian Automobile Machine Gun Brigade No. 1 moving to the Rockcliffe Ranges, Ottawa, for inspection by the Governor General on 23 September 1914. All variants of the 20 trucks purchased from the Auto Car Company of Ardmore, Pennsylvania, can be seen. Right to left: officers' liaison vehicle, "Auto Car" armoured car, general transport vehicle, shop van and ambulance. Photo courtesy of the Musée Héritage Museum, St. Albert.

Sifton and Brutinel drew up two papers, a general one on the firepower and employment of machine guns, and an innovative one proposing the combination of the firepower of machine guns and the mobility of the automobile: machine guns were to be mounted on a truck chassis with a specially designed armoured body. Presenting this to Sam Hughes, minister of militia and defence, they received verbal approval for the formation of the unit and were able to raise additional funds from some wealthy Montrealers.[20] Hughes had extracts from Brutinel's general paper published in various newspapers, increased the allocation of machine guns from two to four per infantry battalion, and promptly secured

an option on practically the entire production of the Colt Company.[21]

Brutinel immediately made the arrangements in the United States for production of the machine guns and vehicles.[22] Impressed by some rugged delivery trucks he had seen in New York, he ordered twenty vehicles from the Auto Car Company of Ardmore, Pennsylvania. The armoured plate used to construct the bodies for eight weapons carriers came from the Valleyfield Armour Steel Company of Valleyfield, Quebec.[23] These vehicles each carried two machine guns on pedestal mounts. In addition, there were five trucks for ammunition and supplies, a workshop truck, a petrol truck, four command and liaison vehicles (equivalent of the Second World War Jeep), seventeen motorcycles, and sixteen bicycles. An ambulance was donated by the daughter of the president of the Auto Car Company, and Brutinel donated his own automobile.

The vehicles in the unit were all built on the same type of chassis and power train—a mechanic's dream—and indeed all, except for two destroyed in combat, were still in good operating condition at the end of the war. On 2 September 1914, the first entirely motorized unit in the British Empire, the Automobile Machine Gun Brigade No. 1, was officially born. Patterned after the artillery, the brigade comprised two batteries, "A" and "B," each with four auto cars and eight machine guns. The new unit, assigned to the 1st Canadian Division, arrived in England on 20 October 1914, and Brutinel quickly set about moulding it. He sought, first, to build a spirit of "all arms" combat with full cooperation between infantry, artillery, cavalry, and his own motorized machine gunners. Second, he developed the credo of the Automobile Machine Gun Brigade No. 1: that all arms served to support the infantry, which is the only arm capable of occupying and holding ground, and that the machine gun brigade must be prepared to make the supreme sacrifice in so doing. Eliminating as many as 20 percent of the officers and soldiers who proved to be drunkards or troublemakers, he developed intensive training for his machine gunners. While still in Canada, he had written a short manual on the Colt machine gun, an essential tool for instructors, and, by December, was conducting courses for the infantry battalion machine gunners of the entire 1st Division. This gunnery training was one of his major contributions to the success of the Canadian Expeditionary Force (CEF) in the Great War.[24] Even after the Imperial School of Machine

Gunnery was established, Brutinel and "the Motors," as they became known, continued to conduct courses for the battalion machine gunners of the entire 1st Division and, eventually, the entire Canadian Corps. Indeed, Brutinel's ideas on machine gunnery were held in such respect that he was able to influence the content of courses at the Imperial School.

The machine gun is central to the Brutinel story. An early type, the Gatling gun, had been used by Dominion forces to suppress the 1885 Northwest Rebellion, and machine guns were used effectively by the Japanese during the 1904 Sino-Russian war. As this had been closely studied by Brutinel's regiment at Tarbes, he was convinced of their value. However, the British army did not think much of them, and in 1914 their infantry battalions were issued a paltry two Vickers heavy machine guns each.[25] The French army was not much better, but the Germans had invested heavily in them.[26] By 1915, when the 49th Battalion was raised in Edmonton, the British and Canadian allocations had been increased to four guns, but the commanding officer, Lieutenant Colonel William Griesbach, convinced the Edmonton Board of Trade to purchase four additional guns by pointing out that the German army standard was eight guns.[27] As with Edmonton's 49th, many units went overseas with more than the authorized number of machine guns, the money to purchase them raised through local subscription.

The Imperial General Staff and, above all, Field Marshall Lord Kitchener, secretary of state for war, had a disdain for the potential of the machine gun. Brutinel recounted a poignant example of this when King George V inspected the Motor Machine Gun Brigade on 4 February 1915 on Salisbury Plain. The King was impressed by the armoured vehicles with their two mounted machine guns, and said to Lord Kitchener that such a unit should be very useful. Much to Brutinel's dismay, Lord Kitchener replied: "I don't think so, Sir, it would unbalance the fire power of a Division."[28]

The best heavy machine gun available to the British was the Vickers, but the Vickers production line, operating at low capacity, was still preparing guns ordered by the Italians before the war.[29] It was only when David Lloyd George became minister of munitions in May 1915 that he executed a virtual palace revolution by going over the heads of the military establishment and directing the company to go to full capacity. The only Canadian unit equipped with Vickers machine guns was Princess Patricia's Canadian Light Infantry, a force raised at private expense by Sir Hamilton Gault in August 1914 and shipped overseas immediately to join an infantry division of the British army.[30] Canadian battalions of the CEF could not obtain the Vickers and had to use the Colt machine gun, which was more complex and less reliable. As Brutinel put it: "It was the only machine gun available and it was felt that an imperfect gun was better than none at all."[31] After July 1916, the Colts were finally replaced by the Vickers.[32]

When the 1st Canadian Division proceeded to France in February 1915, the British military hierarchy saw no place for the Motors. Thanks to Brutinel's regimen, the unit had the best-trained body of machine gunners in the division, but they remained in England pursuing training activities and filling the role of a mobile reserve against a vaguely defined German invasion threat. After Brutinel wrote to Sifton and informed him that they were languishing in England, Sam Hughes curtly insisted that they be sent to France. Finally, on 17 June 1915, the newly renamed 1st Canadian Motor Machine Gun Brigade

(1st CMMGB) joined the 1st Canadian Division in Rouen. Brutinel, now a lieutenant colonel, set about converting Lieutenant General Edwin Alderson, the British division commander, to his ideas. Once exposed to the reality of combat in France, Alderson became an enthusiastic supporter, as every source of firepower that could be mustered was needed.

With the dispatch of the 2nd Canadian Division to France in September, the Canadian Corps was created. Alderson became its first commander, and Brutinel assumed the informal function of primary advisor to the commander on the employment and training of machine gun units. The 1st Motors now came under the control of the Corps. By October 1915 Brutinel handed over command of the 1st CMMGB and assumed an appointment to the now-regularized position of corps machine gun officer, equivalent to chief engineer and general officer commanding Royal Artillery. He was responsible for all machine gun units throughout the Canadian Corps except for the machine gun sections in the infantry battalions. In the British army, a separate machine gun corps had been authorized, again largely due to the influence of Lloyd George, and these measures, taken with Brutinel's advice, were pushing the CEF in the same direction. As early as late 1915, he had withdrawn the Colts from the infantry battalions to create a Machine Gun Company for each brigade. To replace the Colts, the infantry were receiving the Lewis light machine guns that could accompany assaulting troops. By 1918 these companies in turn were combined into Machine Gun Battalions in each division.

Back in Canada, as part of the progressive expansion of the CEF, the money for three more motorized machine gun units had been raised by private subscription: the Eaton, the Yukon, and the Borden Motor Machine Gun Batteries. Their armoured cars were of a different design from Brutinel's 1914 model. They proceeded overseas and the Eaton Battery arrived in England at the same time as 40 of the new armoured cars but, thanks to the Machiavellian intrigues of the War Office and the Imperial General Staff who considered them to be useless, the cars were never issued to the three batteries.[33] As a result, only Brutinel's original batteries had armoured vehicles. Instead, the three new batteries, designated "c," "d," and "e," were equipped with tricycle motorcycles.

Of the tactical concepts developed by the Canadian machine gunners, the most important was indirect fire. Machine guns, just like artillery, were used to engage targets they could not see. Calculations were made using ammunition firing tables to determine the proper elevation and direction of fire required to hit the target with intensive barrages, just as with artillery. The concept was not original—Brutinel's strength was the ability to take an idea and vigorously pursue it to new perfection and applications. Indirect fire was probably used the first time by the Japanese in the Sino-Russian war of 1904.[34] The British had developed similar ideas, no doubt inspired by Japanese tactics, but the Canadians were particularly aggressive in the use of these techniques and were recognized as being the leaders in this field.

The Motors saw continuous action but, generally, in the dismounted role. In early June 1916, at the end of the battle of Sanctuary Wood, the Germans launched a massive artillery bombardment that left a 600-yard gap in the line of the 3rd Canadian Division through which the Germans could advance on to strategically important Ypres. On his own initiative, Brutinel deployed A and B Batteries of the CMMGB to fill the gap. Eventually, infantry arrived and took positions around the machine gun emplacements. This was a first instance in which the mobility of the Motors was put to use, and presaged the major role they were to play in stopping the German offensive two years later in 1918.

The involvement of the Motors in this action was almost accidental. Brutinel was about to head on leave when the massive bombardment started. At the closest headquarters, that of Brigadier General Louis Lipsett's 2nd Brigade, he was briefed on the situation and, on consulting with Lipsett, concluded that he should ignore a previous order to withdraw one of the batteries from the line, and ordered the other to come forward. Subsequent orders came in to withdraw his batteries, but he ignored them because he knew the batteries were instrumental in holding the line. Eventually, he was vindicated when he explained the entire situation to the new commander of the Canadian Corps, Sir Julian Byng, who confessed he would have fired him if he had *not* disobeyed the order.[35] Brutinel's actions here are a reminder that, for sound military leadership, physical courage alone is insufficient; it must be combined with moral courage.

Vimy Ridge was the coming-of-age of the Canadian Corps, and many would say the Canadian nation itself. The Motors played a unique role in the preparations for the assault. The fire plan included more than 30 days of intensive artillery bombardments. To avoid compromising the positions of the artillery batteries, these fired in the daytime only, since night firing would allow the Germans to locate the gun positions through flash spotting. To prevent the Germans from repairing the damage done in the daytime, the batteries of the 1st CMMGB fired indirect barrage targets at night.

The Canadian operational innovations had started to draw the attention of other Allied armies even before Vimy. The recipe for Canadian success was derived in large part from lessons learned by other armies. Still, the success at Vimy provided proof that the CEF had developed innovations in tactics and training from which others could benefit. Before the attack, French army staff had visited Corps Commander Sir Julian Byng, who had shown them the plans for the upcoming assault. On seeing the machine gun plans, the French commented on their originality; Byng provided copies for their employment before, during, and after the attack. He then told Brutinel to prepare a report for the benefit of the French on lessons learned as soon as the assault was over. Brutinel suggested, instead, that German prisoners be interrogated to get their perspective on the effectiveness of the machine gun fire. As it turned out, the prisoners testified unanimously on the following points:

- By night, machine gun fire made it difficult to repair the trenches knocked down by day by the artillery fire.
- The bringing in of supplies was hampered greatly and was practically impossible during the last few days because of the density of indirect machine gun fire.
- The evacuation of wounded was increasingly difficult and almost impossible during the last three nights before the attack.
- The intense machine gun fire made it impossible to man the parapets when the attack started.[36]

During and after the war, Brutinel was at loggerheads with senior artillery officer Brigadier General Andrew McNaughton over the use of machine gun barrages. The latter viewed them as being wasteful of ammunition and transport, and as trying to do what was better accomplished by the artillery. In this case, the two types of barrages were complementary rather than competitive, and highly effective. Without them, the Germans would have been better prepared to stop the assault that started on Easter Monday, 9 April 1917; moreover, the barrages by the machine gunners that were critical to weakening the German defenses were accomplished with few casualties.[37]

The attack used fire and movement tactics, having machine guns in position and providing fire support to the advancing infantry from the start line to the final objectives.[38] Because of the ground conditions, there was no question of using the vehicles—the Vickers had to be packed to a series of firing positions over successive bounds of several thousand yards. The Vickers alone weighed 15 kg, the tripod another 23 kg, and the water can required for keeping the barrels cool weighed 12 kg, to which was added several thousand rounds of ammunition per gun. The casualties suffered by the Motors in operations to seize Vimy were huge, some 200 out of a unit strength of 350, or 57 percent.[39] In comparison, total Canadian casualties at Vimy were 10,602, including 3,598 fatalities out of a total Canadian strength of 97,184, or 11 percent.[40]

The true vindication of the concept of the 1st CMMGB came during *Operation Michael*, the German spring offensive in 1918. Just weeks before this, the three batteries previously mounted on motorcycles had been given Napier light trucks designated "Auto Car Lorries."[41] The 1st CMMGB now consisted of five batteries each with four weapons carriers armed with two Vickers machine guns per vehicle—a considerable boost. Brutinel's original concept for the Motors was that they be self-sufficient, which was why he had purchased logistics vehicles in 1914. Now the 1st Motors gained its own Transport Company provided from the 2nd Canadian Ammunition Sub-Park, which gave it the resources to keep all five batteries supplied with ammunition, fuel, rations, and mechanics to maintain vehicles.[42] The allotment of motorcyclists was increased to 65. Widely used as scouts, they were also the only reliable means of communication in mobile operations; vehicle mounted radios did not exist and telephones, the main means of communication in static trench situations, were useless for troops on the move.[43]

The 1st Motors and the Canadian Cavalry Brigade were heavily engaged in this battle.[44] The 1st Motors were deployed to reinforce General Hubert Gough's

Canadian Auto Car armoured cars being refurbished after the battles blunting the German Spring Offensive of 1918. This photo shows a clear view of the layout of the Auto Car with its two Vickers HMGs in a near-combat environment. Library and Archives Canada, PA-002614.

5th British Army. They were intended to impede one of the major German objectives: the separation of the French and British armies. General Frank Worthington, then a newly commissioned officer and just posted to one of the truck-mounted batteries of the Motors, later described the very modern-sounding tactics used to engage and blunt the advance of the German army:

> The situation was confused and very fluid. The Germans had overcome the British defenses and were now coming forward in their proper battle formations. The method used by the Motor Machine Guns was very simple. We would take four or eight guns and open fire as the enemy was advancing, and bring him to a halt. Then the enemy would get ready to shell us out. We would move half our guns back to a rear position—maybe five hundred or a thousand yards back—and as the enemy would come on with their artillery support and advance closer we would pull out the forward guns. The battle line would be cleared and the enemy would sort of collect themselves and start moving forward. Then you'd give it to them again. Day after day it was the same thing.[45]

Such tactics were only possible because of the fully motorized nature of the unit. To reach the area of operations, the unit members had made a road move of 103 km, and for the next three weeks they were constantly on the move.[46] The 1st CMMGB achieved its objective of preventing the Germans from separating the 5th British Army from the French Army on its flanks, but at a very heavy price. The unit lost almost half its strength, again proving that its members had learned Brutinel's ethos of giving their all to protect the infantry they existed to support.

As the Motors took their place among the disintegrating 5th Army, Brutinel was at its headquarters conferring with Brigadier General Dill, the chief of operations. They determined that they had sufficient replacements of machine guns, but their manpower was totally committed. The reinforcement pool, Canadian or British, seemed to be totally exhausted, but Brutinel remembered the Horse Guards, the King's personal guard in London. Convinced they could be quickly trained, and that the King would readily agree, Brutinel overcame the staff reluctance to approach the King for help. When contacted, his reply was: "The Horse Guards will be ready to leave tomorrow." Brutinel met them at Boulogne and escorted them to the Machine Gun School to be trained, after which they would take their place in the machine gun detachments—shining another light on his determination to leave no stone unturned to achieve success.[47]

In spite of the success at Vimy, Canadian sources were slow to acknowledge this fine feat of arms, but it did not go unnoticed by British observers. Hamilton Fyfe, editor and war correspondent for the *Daily Mirror*, reported on 1 April 1918:

> When the full story is told of this encounter of giant forces and of the successful withdrawal of the British army in the face of immensely superior German strength a very glowing page of it will have to be devoted to the splendidly gallant and useful part played by the Canadian Motor Machine Guns. The other day, it was the day before Albert fell, I was on the other side of the town and saw some of their grey armoured cars come tearing down

the road in clouds of dust evidently going into action hotfoot. A little later I heard a tremendous tap, tap, tapping and knew they were engaged. They held up the German advance there as they did in a number of other places ... Everywhere they went they steadied the line. They gave the Infantry fresh hope and courage.[48]

Similarly, on April 4, *The Daily Mirror* included this newspaper account:

PARIS, Wednesday. The War correspondent of the *Petit Journal* accords great praise to the Canadian troops. He mentions several episodes evidencing the valour and intrepidity of the soldiers, particularly that on the morning of March 21 regarding the defence of Amiens. Strong Patrols of Uhlans pushed forward an advance guard into Amiens in order to terrorise the inhabitants. Canadians were on guard with armoured motor-cars, which have acquired a great reputation in the British Army, and opposed a resistance so determined and violent that the Germans fled in disorder.[49]

From Field Marshall Haig of the British High Command came firm recognition of the Motors' achievements in his recommendation that their numbers be increased.[50] The six surviving auto cars were withdrawn from the 1st Motors and became a separate unit; all five batteries of the 1st Motors became truck-mounted. A new unit, the 2nd CMMGB, was created with the same structure as the 1st. A new Canadian Motor Machine Gun Mechanical Transport Company, Canadian Army Service Corps, was created, providing additional supply and transport resources for the coming offensive. The mechanics who cared for all vehicles including the armoured cars made modifications such as pedestal machine gun mounts for the Napier light trucks, turning them into "Battle Line Lorries."[51]

Other supporting arms, such as artillery and engineers, were similarly expanded: the Canadian Corps was restructuring and training for a lead role in the last campaign that would bring final victory over the German army. In the campaign that opened with the Battle of Amiens on 8 August 1918, Brutinel, now brigadier general, commanded the Canadian Independent Force (Brutinel's Brigade) including the 1st and 2nd CMMGB, cavalry such as the Canadian Light Horse, cyclists and truck-mounted trench mortars made especially for the operation, and artillery.[52] He even used radio communications in his headquarters to maintain contact with the Canadian Corps HQ. The lack of radios portable enough to be mounted in vehicles was probably the most serious limitation on warfare as they entered the Hundred Days Campaign that ended on 11 November 1918.

Brutinel made a huge contribution to Canada's war effort. When the 1st Division was shipped to England on 3 October 1914 it had as few as 48 machine guns (4 per battalion) plus the 20 of the 1st Motors, with a total of 68 for the entire division. By 11 November 1918, there were 4 Machine Gun Battalions with 96 Vickers each and 92 in the two Motor Machine Gun Brigades, for a total of 476. In 1914 Major Brutinel commanded 135 in all ranks; in 1918 as brigadier general he commanded 8,771.[53] There were now 36 Lewis light machine guns in each of the 48 infantry battalions, for a total of 1,728. In all, the figure soared from 68 in 1914 to 2,152 in 1918![54] He

A Canadian Motor Machine Gun Brigade waiting alongside Arras–Cambrai Road. Advance east of Arras, September 1918. By June 1918 onwards, 6 of the 8 original "Auto Car" armoured cars remained. Each of the CMMGB was equipped with 20 of these "Auto Car Lorries." Clearly visible on the back of the right-hand vehicle is the Vickers HMG on the pedestal mount manufactured by the Canadian Motor Machine Gun Mechanical Transport Company. Library and Archives Canada, PA-003399.

did not do this alone; commanders and staff at all levels took part in the decision-making process, but to him goes much of the credit. However, throughout the war and after, the British and the Canadian hierarchy tended not to acknowledge his contribution, something which hurt him grievously.[55]

Brutinel had the foresight to understand the potential of the machine gun and the importance of armoured vehicles for mobility, and skillfully used his powers of persuasion and political know-how to proselytize for the massive buildup that did so much to lead to victory. His enduring legacy though was in

his first creation, the Motor Machine Gun Brigades, the progenitors of today's armoured units. It is surely no coincidence that Frank Worthington—the true father of the Royal Canadian Armoured Corps, who in the late 1930s almost single-handedly dragged Canada's cavalry into the age of mechanized warfare—had commanded one of Brutinel's batteries during the intense battles of the German Spring Offensive and Canada's Hundred Days Campaign.

Although Brutinel had planned to return to Canada to stay with his family after the conflict, in 1919 when he came back to Montreal he learned that his fortune had been lost by the friends in the law firm to whom he had entrusted his financial affairs. He already knew his house in Westmount had been sold for nonpayment, but things deteriorated further. One of the two lawyers involved committed suicide on the eve of his agreed-upon meeting with Brutinel. The other lawyer had arranged to remove Brutinel from the director positions he held with various coal mining concerns in Canada and abroad. The financial scandal was covered up, but

Staff of the Canadian Motor Machine Gun Corps, 11 November 1919. Seated: Brigadier General Raymond Brutinel; Standing (left to right): Captain J.K. Lawson, Major J.D. Foster, Captain M.R. Levey (Marshall), Lieutenant P.M. Hume. Photo courtesy of the Musée Héritage Museum, St. Albert.

Brutinel was penniless. It was only with the help of a few of his loyal Canadian friends that he was able to re-establish himself in the world of finance. He returned to live in France in 1920, where he became involved in various business dealings: negotiating for the French manufacturing company Schneider-Creusot in the purchase of steel from Germany, selling locomotives to Romania, banking, and many other enterprises.

Brutinel always maintained contacts with his Canadian friends and business associates, even returning to St. Albert in 1928 to purchase additional land in the area at a price that was considered to be extravagant in those days.[56] His house and property there were eventually sold, becoming known locally as the Ball Estate. In France, over time, he owned several palatial homes and three vineyards in the Médoc region. He was a good friend of Sir Winston Churchill, and, at the outbreak of the Second World War, he helped evacuate Georges Vanier and his family and staff of 30 from the Canadian Embassy in Paris to London. During the war, while the Germans commandeered half of his residence, the Château De Bordaberry near Biarritz, he worked with the Resistance, coolly helping to evacuate fallen aviators and Resistance fighters to Spain. He remained active to the end of his life and died in 1964.

Notes

1   R. Brutinel to Mrs. Larry Worthington, 28 April 1964, Powley Fonds, Library and Archives Canada, MG30 E33, vol. 3, Brutinel Gen. R. File, correspondence and notes, 1964.

2   Cited in Dominique Baylaucq and Jacques Baylaucq, *Brutinel, le remarquable destin d'un Français brigadier-général de l'Armée canadienne* (*Brutinel, The*

Extraordinary Story of a French Citizen Brigadier-General in the Canadian Army) (Dominique and Jacques Baylaucq, 2014), 82.

3 Baylaucq and Baylaucq, *Brutinel, le remarquable destin*, 139.

4 Reproduced in Baylaucq and Baylaucq, *Brutinel, le remarquable destin*, 36–79. The tapes were recorded in French and translated into English.

5 Ibid., 12–19.

6 Ruth Harris, *Dreyfus, Politics, Emotion and the Scandal of the Century* (New York: Metropolitan Books, Henry Holt and Company, 2010), 363–66.

7 R. Brutinel to Mrs. Larry Worthington, 28 April 1964, Powley Fonds.

8 *The Edmonton Bulletin*, 9 and 10 September 1905, URL: http://peel.library.ualberta.ca/www.newspapers/EDB; *Le Courrier de l'Ouest* (CDO), 30 November 1905, URL: http://peel.library.ualberta.ca/www.newspapers/CDW.

9 *CDO*, 28 December 1905.

10 Éloi De Grâce, "Le Courrier de l'Ouest (1905–1916)," *Aspects du passé franco-albertain*, edited by A. Trottier, K.J. Munro, and G. Allaire (Histoire franco-albertaine: 1, 1975), 104.

11 *CDO*, 16 April 1906, "Tribune Libre," G. Simonin, Saint-Paul-des-Métis and Brutinel.

12 *CDO*, 2 August 1906, "Tribune Libre," J.B. Surveillant; 9 September 1906, Brutinel; 16 August 1906, J.B. Surveillant; 6 September 1906, Brutinel.

13 In English: Jean-Baptiste Supervisor, *CDO*, 18 October 1906, Mgr. E. Legal.

14 *CDO*, 23 May 1907.

15 Ibid., 25 July 1907, "Sir Wilfrid à Paris."

16 Daniel Kyba and Jane Ross, *Exploring the Historic Coal Branch: A Guide to Jasper's Front Ranges* (Banff, AB: Rocky Mountain Books, ca. 2001), 140.

17 *Henderson's Edmonton City Directory*, 1911.

18 Baylaucq and Baylaucq, *Brutinel, le remarquable destin*, 19.

19 Ibid., 39–40.

20 Sir Clifford Sifton, *Dictionary of Canadian Biography*, URL: http://www.biographi.ca/en/bio/sifton_clifford_15E.html.

21 Baylaucq and Baylaucq, *Brutinel, le remarquable destin*, 40–41.

22 John F. Wallace, *Dragons of Steel: Canadian Armour in Two World Wars* (Burnstown, ON: General Store Publishing House, 1995), 15–16.

23 Cameron Pulsifer, "Canada's First Armoured Unit: Raymond Brutinel and the Canadian Motor Machine Gun Brigades of the First World War," *Canadian Military History* 10, no. 1 (Winter 2001): 46; Baylaucq and Baylaucq, *Brutinel, le remarquable destin*, 25.

24 Yves Tremblay, "Brutinel: A Unique Kind of Leadership," *Warrior Chiefs: Perspectives on Senior Canadian Military Leaders* (Toronto: Dundurn Press, 2001).

25 The Vickers was closely patterned on the Maxim machine gun, as was the German army's *Maschinengewehr 08* (or MG08) and, like the Colts, was classified as a heavy machine gun. Such guns provided a more solid and accurate firing platform and were highly effective in providing fire support as the infantry moved forward, but could not be used to help the assaulting troops fight through the objective. That changed with the Lewis machine gun, which was lighter and could be carried and fired by a single soldier, although others were normally needed to carry spare ammunition magazines.

26 Lt. Col. C.S. Grafton, *The Canadian "Emma Gees": A History of the Canadian Machine Gun Corps* (London, ON: The Canadian Machine Gun Corps Association, 1938), 18–21.

27 G.R. Stevens, *A City Goes to War* (Brampton, ON: Charters Publishing Company, 1964), 21.

28 Baylaucq and Baylaucq, *Brutinel, le remarquable destin*, 46.

29 Ibid., 47.

30 The PPCLI returned to the fold and became part of the 7th Brigade of the 3rd Canadian Division in December 1915.

31 Baylaucq and Baylaucq, *Brutinel, le remarquable destin*, 45.

32 Canadian War Museum Fact Sheet, URL: http://collections.civilization.ca/public/pages/cmccpublic/emupublic/Display.php?irn=1040493.

33 These armoured cars, purchased by Canada, ended up in Ireland and India. Wallace, *Dragons of Steel*, 25.

34 Tremblay, "Brutinel: A Unique Kind of Leadership," 61; also Tape 17, Baylaucq and Baylaucq, *Brutinel, le remarquable destin*, 58–59.

35 Baylaucq and Baylaucq, *Brutinel, le remarquable destin*, 55–58.

36 Ibid., 61.

37 In fact machine gun emplacements that included overhead cover were relatively safe compared to the situation of the infantry in their more open trenches or artillery, whose guns and crews were vulnerable to enemy artillery fire. Machine gun fire was difficult to detect; artillery was vulnerable to being located through flash spotting or sound ranging.

38 For more on the Motors during the battles to seize Vimy Ridge and the operations of 1st CMMGB in the Great War, see Wallace, *Dragons of Steel*.

39 Ibid., 46.

40 There were another 60,000 non-Canadian soldiers attached for the assault on Vimy but these are not included in the calculations. Colonel G.W.L. Nicholson, C.D., *Canadian Expeditionary Force 1914–1919: Official History of the Canadian Army* (Ottawa: Queen's Printer, 1962), 252, 265.

41 *War Diary, Machine Gun Officer, Canadian Corps*, [Brutinel], January 1918.

42 Thanks to these resources, at no time during the very fluid and intense combat did the batteries lack ammunition. *War Diary 1st Canadian Motor Machine Gun Brigade,* March and April 1918.

43 Wallace, *Dragons of Steel*, 52.

44 The cavalry achieved fame and glory at the Battle of Moreuil Wood where Lieutenant Gordon Flowerdew of the Lord Strathcona's Horse won the Victoria Cross.

45 John Marteinson and Michael R. McNorgan, *The Royal Canadian Armoured Corps: An Illustrated History* (Toronto: Robin Brass Studio Inc., 2000), 46–47.

46 A considerable move since the speed of trucks of the era was 24 km per hour at best.

47 Baylaucq and Baylaucq, *Brutinel, le remarquable destin*, 77.

48 Cameron Pulsifer, "Death at Licourt; An Historical and Visual Record of Five Fatalities in the 1st Canadian Motor Machine Gun Brigade, 25 March 1918," *Canadian Military History* 11, no. 3 (Summer 2002): 62. Also cited in Alex Lynch, *The Glory of Their Times; 1st Canadian Motor Machine Gun Brigade March 1918* (Kingston, ON: Lawrence Publications, 2001), 113–14, where the article source is cited as the April 2 edition of the *Continental Daily Mail*.

49 *Daily Mirror* [London], 4 April 1918, 1.

50 Early in 1918 Brutinel and Currie were preparing proposals for the expansion of the Motors to a total of eight Motor Machine gun batteries, but the Canadian staff in London was raising eyebrows at the expense of running these units. As a result, the Motors went into action against the German offensive with their five original batteries. With the extra push from Haig and the testimony of the results of the recent combat, the reorganization went ahead in June 1918 with ten batteries. See *War Diaries Canadian Corps Machine Gun Officer* for January, May, and June 1918.

51 The *War Diaries* continued to refer to them as Auto Car Lorries.

52 The Canadian Light Horse was created by amalgamating the divisional cavalry squadrons into a single unit.

53 Nicholson, *Canadian Expeditionary Force*, 384.

54 Lt. Col. Ian M. McCulloch, "A War of Machines—A Re-assessment of the Canadian Machine Gun Corps: Innovation or Tactical Expedient?" *Canadian Army Journal* 11, no. 2 (Summer 2008): 89.

55 Baylaucq and Baylaucq, *Brutinel, le remarquable destin*, 27.

56 *Edmonton Journal*, 11 May 1928.

Works Cited

PRIMARY SOURCES

Le Courrier de l'Ouest
Edmonton Bulletin
Edmonton Journal
Henderson's Edmonton City Directory, 1911.

Library and Archives Canada. Powley Fonds, MG30 E33, vol. 3, Brutinel Gen. R. File, correspondence and notes, 1964.
——. War Diaries of the First World War. URL: http://www.bac-lac.gc.ca/eng/discover/military-heritage/first-world-war/Pages/war-diaries.aspx, retrieved 14 May 2014.

SECONDARY SOURCES

Baylaucq, Dominique, and Jacques Baylaucq. *Brutinel: The Extraordinary Story of a French Citizen Brigadier-General in the Canadian Army*. Privately printed: Dominique and Jacques Baylaucq, 2014.
——. *Brutinel, le remarquable destin d'un Français brigadier-général de l'Armée canadienne*. Privately printed: Dominique and Jacques Baylaucq, 2014.
Canadian War Museum Fact Sheet. URL: http://collections. civilization.ca/public/pages/cmccpublic/emupublic/ Display.php?irn=1040493, retrieved 14 May 2014.
De Grâce, Éloi. "Le Courrier de l'Ouest (1905–1916)." In *Aspects du passé franco-albertain*, edited by A. Trottier, K.J. Munro, G. Allaire, 100–11. Histoire franco-albertaine: 1. 1975.
Dictionary of Canadian Biography. URL: http://www.biographi.ca.
Grafton, Lt. Col. C.S. *The Canadian "Emma Gees": A History of the Canadian Machine Gun Corps*. London, ON: The Canadian Machine Gun Corps Association, 1938.
Harris, Ruth. *Dreyfus, Politics, Emotion, and the Scandal of the Century*. New York: Metropolitan Books, Henry Holt and Company, 2010.
Kyba, Daniel, and Jane Ross. *Exploring the Historic Coal Branch: A Guide to Jasper's Front Ranges*. Banff, AB: Rocky Mountain Books, ca. 2001.

Lynch, Alex. *Dad, The Motors and the Fifth Army Show*. 2nd ed. Kingston, ON: Lawrence Publications, 2003.
——. *The Glory of Their Times: 1st Canadian Motor Machine Gun Brigade March 1918*. Kingston, ON: Lawrence Publications, 2001.
Marteinson, John, and Michael R. McNorgan. *The Royal Canadian Armoured Corps: An Illustrated History*. Toronto: Robin Brass Studio Inc., 2000.
McCulloch, Lt. Col. Ian M. "A War of Machines— A Re-assessment of the Canadian Machine Gun Corps: Innovation or Tactical Expedient?" *Canadian Army Journal* 11, no. 2 (Summer 2008): 82–92.
Nicholson, Colonel G.W.L. *Canadian Expeditionary Force 1914–1919: Official History of the Canadian Army*. Ottawa: Queen's Printer, 1962.
Pulsifer, Cameron. "Canada's First Armoured Unit: Raymond Brutinel and the Canadian Motor Machine Gun Brigades of the First World War." *Canadian Military History* 10, no. 1 (Winter 2001): 44–57.
——. "Death at Licourt: An Historical and Visual Record of Five Fatalities in the 1st Canadian Motor Machine Gun Brigade, 25 March 1918." *Canadian Military History* 11, no. 3 (Summer 2002): 49–64.
Stevens, G.R. *A City Goes to War: History of the Loyal Edmonton Regiment*. Brampton, ON: Charters Publishing Company, 1964.
Tremblay, Yves. "Brutinel: A Unique Kind of Leadership." In *Warrior Chiefs: Perspectives on Senior Canadian Military Leaders*, edited by Bernd Horn and Stephen Harris. Toronto: Dundurn Press, 2001.
Wallace, John F. *Dragons of Steel: Canadian Armour in Two World Wars*. Burnstown, ON: General Store Publishing House, 1995.
Worthington, Larry. *Amid the Guns Below, the Story of the Canadian Corps (1914–1919)*. Toronto and Montreal: McClelland and Stewart, ca. 1965.
Worthington, Larry, and Clara Ellen Dignum Worthington. *"Worthy": A Biography of Major-General F.F. Worthington C.B. M.C. M.M.* Toronto: The Macmillan Company of Canada Limited, 1961.

While You Were Away: Alberta's First World War Aviation History

PATRICIA MYERS

"Miss Stinson Makes Daring Aerial Flight in Gale," the *Edmonton Journal* announced on 13 July 1916. The "Famous Woman Aerial Artist" was performing every day at the Edmonton Exhibition, flying at the grandstand in the late afternoon and, again, at 9 at night. The evening before, despite a threatening storm and high wind, Stinson performed loop-the-loops and spirals that showed she was not "only a fair weather flyer, but an aviator in every sense of the word." She had already enthralled Calgary fairgoers, and, after seeing her, members of the Edmonton Exhibition Board reported that she "exceeds any press notice ever written concerning her sensational flights."[1]

The state of aviation in Alberta at the beginning of the First World War in 1914 can be seen in Katherine Stinson's flights: it was rare; it was exciting; and it was largely for entertainment. With the continuation of the war, this attitude gradually changed. In 1916, and when she flew again in Alberta in 1917, Stinson and her Curtiss Jenny aircraft represented a tangible, material link between Albertans and the war in the air. Her loop-the-loops and dazzling spins were the same manoeuvres used in aerial combat. When she returned to the province in July 1918, she

again flew at fairs but she did something different. She climbed into her airplane in Calgary with a bag of letters and took off to fly to Edmonton. In that one act, she represented what the future of flying would look like and made visible the significant role aviation had played in Alberta during the conflict.[2]

In 1914 Albertans were not strangers to aviation. The province had been home to pioneers such as William Gibson, Frank Ellis, and Tom Blakely. Fairs and exhibitions had been booking balloonists (such as the daredevil Louise Belmont) and flight demonstrations for years. Aviators such as Frenchman Didier Masson and American Eugene Ely had put on special flying demonstrations that had thrilled audiences around the province. Newspapers kept up with aviation developments, so Albertans could follow the great air meets in Europe, understand the challenges of setting long-distance flight records, and marvel at the experiments of Dr. Alexander Graham Bell and his associates at the Aerial Experiment Association in Baddeck, Nova Scotia, and of the Wright brothers in North Carolina. While, by the outbreak of the War, the airplane and the idea of flight were no longer so new as to be startling, aviation was certainly not common, or terribly practical or dependable. Aircraft were flimsy things made of wood and canvas, and their small and often unreliable motors kept their lifting capacity low. But the attraction of flight, and the aura of excitement that surrounded it, had convinced many young Alberta men that that was how they wanted to serve their country.[3]

Albertans wanting to fly in the war faced a more rigorous route to enlistment than those who joined the infantry. At least one Albertan had hoped for an easier path for Alberta boys. Early in the War, R.B. Bennett, Member of Parliament for Calgary East, was looking for Department of Militia and Defence support for the formation of an Alberta flying corps. Like most other plans to form some sort of Canadian aviation contingent, it was not welcomed. Overwhelmed by the demands of waging the ground war and raising army contingents, the federal government did not deem aviation to be a critical activity for official involvement. Canada entered the war without a Canadian flying corps. Albertans could join either Britain's Royal Flying Corps or Royal Naval Air Service. Each man had to earn a pilot's certificate on his own before he could be commissioned and posted overseas. Reports of the Stinsons' aviation school in San Antonio, Texas, made Alberta newspapers. An Edmonton and a Calgary man had trained at the school Katherine ran with her sister Marjorie, and these Albertans were now in Europe in aerial combat.[4]

Flying schools such as the Curtiss School outside Toronto welcomed Canadians and Americans who wanted to enlist in the British flying services. Four hundred dollars in 1914 (the equivalent of $8,200 today) bought instruction and approximately 400 minutes in the air.[5] Although he applied early, Frank Ellis, who along with partner Tom Blakely had built and flown a plane they called the "West Wind" in 1914 and 1915 outside Calgary, had to wait until the summer of 1918 to be accepted for flying training at a camp near Toronto.

The Royal Naval Services began recruiting in Canada in early 1915, preferring men between 19 and 23 years of age. The Royal Flying Corps began recruiting shortly after.[6] By the middle of 1918, advertisements in Alberta newspapers carried announcements of the creation of air reserves for men between 17 and 20, preparatory to becoming airplane mechanics. Although the process for enlisting in one of the flying services changed during the war, Albertans' enthusiasm for joining did not. "Seventeen Local Men Enlist in Flying Service," the *Edmonton Journal* reported on 7 May 1918. The young men came from Vermilion, Camrose, Ponoka, Donalda, Forestburg, Tofield, Lamoureaux, and Edmonton.

Nick Carter and "Punch" Dickins are two examples of Albertans who wanted to fly in the war and took different routes to get there. Carter, born on a ranch at Fish Creek in 1894, was attending Queen's University when he enlisted, apparently directly into the Royal Naval Air Service, at Kingston on 23 December 1915. He and a friend travelled to St. Augustine, Florida, to begin training at a newly established flying school. They discovered just how new it was when they arrived: the school's only training plane was still unassembled and boxed up in its packing crates. The students assembled the plane and finally got in the air with their instructor, who did not know how to fly. The school folded quickly and Carter returned to Canada, where he so relentlessly pressured Canadian and British officials that they finally accepted him without flying credentials.[7]

Clennell Haggerston "Punch" Dickins first served with the Canadian army before transferring

Thomas Blakely at the controls of the "West Wind" at Shouldice Park, Calgary, 4 July 1914; just one example of flying going on in Alberta at the time of the First World War. Glenbow Archives, NA-1186-1.

into the flying services. Punch was a mechanical engineering student at the University of Alberta in 1917 when he enlisted in the 196th Western Universities Battalion. As he tells it: "I was discharged from the Canadian Army in London in . . . January 1918 . . . I went down the corridor two doors and was sworn into the British Army and they gave me a temporary commission as an airman in training." He was sent for air training courses in Oxford, then to flight training in Norfolk where he learned on a number of

planes. On 1 April 1918, he became a member of the Royal Air Force.[8]

Accounts of the intensity of the ground war and the great numbers of soldiers involved in it filled newspapers. Reports of battles, casualties, troop movements, and the conditions at the front made thick, black headlines almost daily.[9] Although with less frequency, the air war and aviators' deaths received notice too. George Rogers from Lethbridge completed his aviation course in Canada before he enlisted with the Canadian Expeditionary Force. He fought in France and Belgium for 18 months before being taken on by the Royal Flying Corps. Wounded while flying over enemy lines, he managed to return to his airfield and make a safe landing in his damaged plane. Three days later, on 30 October 1917, he died from his wounds.[10] Sandy Talbot from Lacombe had attended the University of Alberta and was a student in a law firm when he enlisted. His parents received "the sad intelligence" of his death in an "aero" accident. "He was a brave boy," the *Edmonton Journal* reported, "just budding into manhood, of sterling character, and had a host of friends."[11]

Pilots were often called "birdmen," a term given to them very early in the history of flight, and an indication of the relative newness of this technology. "Birdmen Have Busy Time in Old Country," the *Edmonton Journal* noted before reprinting some of Willard Sinclair's letters sent from England to his mother in Calgary. The correspondence provided an interesting view of "an embryo birdman," the article said, before reproducing his daily schedule, which included everything from "early morning flying—if all's well," to practising Morse code, photography, and machine gunning.[12] The death of an Edmonton "birdman" in July 1918 was reported to have resulted when "in evolutions preparatory to attack [on the enemy] one of the British airmen lost the formation and crashed into Capt. Manuel's [John Gerald Manuel, DFC, DSC] machine, sending it down to earth out of control. The commanding officer said that nothing had since been heard of Capt. Manuel. He belonged to the Alberta Dragoons and enlisted in November 1914 initially serving in the Canadian Field Artillery."[13]

Flyers themselves were awash with the thrill of flight. "I just think this flying is the greatest game yet," Edmontonian Paul Calder wrote to a friend while he was just completing his flight training in England. "Dad was down to see me the other day and I took him up for a flight. I looped him about 20 times, rolled him, half rolled, spun, and did every stunt there was, but he said he liked it fine and was tickled to death with his trip." Blasé about the dangers (Calder also wrote, "The other day both my lower wings broke and crumpled at about 1,500 feet when I was stunting but I got down O.K."), flyers expressed an intense desire to get a chance at the enemy. "Believe me I am not afraid of Mr. Fritz if they only give me a machine I can depend on," Calder declared.[14]

"Rufus" Rendall provides another example of the fearless aviator. He had been gassed, then injured by shrapnel as an infantryman. On recovery, he joined the Royal Flying Corps. While Rendall was testing a new plane it plunged to earth, injuring his eyes, breaking his nose, and smashing his leg so badly it had to be amputated. He wanted his friends to know that "when he is fitted with a new limb he hopes to have another 'go' at the Huns."[15]

While some of this is certainly youthful bravado, it is also an indication of the necessity fighting men felt to adopt a brave and heroic stance in letters to loved ones, confirming their membership within accepted norms of masculine identity.[16] Flyers were well aware that, while their lot was not the muddy, shell-blasted quagmire of the infantry, they were no less willing or brave. Nor were they safer, as mortality rates of pilots—often measured in weeks—were higher than those in the infantry. Yet flying over the trenches seemed to be both an adventure and a bit of a relief from the on-the-ground hardship. "This is the greatest life on earth; no more toiling through the mud with infantry for me. Every expedition is a great adventure," wrote a pilot whose letter was reprinted in the *Edmonton Journal* of 22 May 1918. The emergence of the concept of the air ace underscores the image of the individual, daring nature of aerial combat, again positioned firmly within cultural definitions of masculinity that included courage, determination, and decisiveness. While death was always his co-pilot, the fighting pilot's position far above the gas and snipers and barbed wire gave him a seeming independence and clarity of action that soldiers below could only watch.

Katherine Stinson helped communicate the freedom and independence that seemed available to flyers with her solo stunting across the province. Rejected as an active war flyer twice, she had turned to flying and stunting to raise money for the American Red Cross. Flying with a red cross painted on the tail of her plane, she created a level of awareness of the capabilities and possibilities of flight that would not have been achieved without her demonstrations. In 1917 she dropped a fake bomb on exhibition trenches dug out at the Edmonton Exhibition. The spins, dives, and loop-the-loops she performed were the same as those used in combat. "To see her," the *Edmonton Journal* wrote in July 1916, "is to realize a measure [of] the maneuvers of our air navy on the firing line."[17]

There certainly was a difference, though, and Albertans were not fooled. Maimed, injured, and ruined men had been returning from the front since 1915. Newspaper descriptions of battle conditions were unlikely to be misinterpreted: "No Man['s] Land Cobbled with Skulls" could only have one meaning; so could "His Machine Badly Shot up—Crashed Badly on Landing."[18] A woman in a plane trailing coloured smoke through the night sky was no less real to the fairgoers than newspaper reports,

letters, and telegrams concerning their sons and husbands photographing, bombing, and dodging enemy aircraft overseas. The realities diverged over Stinson's gender, and over the huge distance separating Alberta and the war front.

But how did the two realities converge? They met after the war in the likes of Freddie McCall, "Wop" May, and George Gorman, and in the renewed

Wilfrid "Wop" May in England in 1917. He returned to Alberta a war hero and had a great influence on aviation in the province. Glenbow Archives, NA-1258-2.

excitement of the possibilities of flight. When Stinson returned to Alberta in 1918, she stunted at fairs in Edmonton, Lethbridge, Camrose, Red Deer, and Calgary. She did something else too: namely, carry the first airmail in western Canada and just the second in Canada, flying between Calgary and Edmonton with a map, a compass, and a sack of letters in her open cockpit plane. Long-distance flights, greater carrying capacities, and larger and more nimble and durable craft all seemed possible because of the growing numbers of pilots and the advances in airplane design that were being planned well before the end of hostilities.[19]

Aviation in the province was also helped along by the British program to send war surplus planes and aviation equipment to Canada. Aero clubs in Calgary and Edmonton, including at the University of Alberta and the Southern Alberta Institute of Technology,

Katherine Stinson's flight between Calgary and Edmonton, in July 1918, exhibited not only the excitement of flight, but the possibilities of long-distance travel the airplane offered. Glenbow Archives, NA-4350-1.

First World War pilots brought their experience back to Alberta and began flying careers. This photograph shows an Imperial Oil camp in 1921 (probably on Bear Island), with pilots George Gorman (holding broom) and Elmer Fullerton (white suspenders). Glenbow Archives, NA-2309-18.

benefited from this plan. The University of Alberta was planning to establish an aeronautical engineering program. In addition, aspiring aeronautical entrepreneurs could purchase surplus Curtiss JN-4s. In Lethbridge, for example, residents could go up in the air with the Lethbridge Aircraft Company's newly acquired Curtiss Jenny.[20]

Several Alberta flyers—such as Calgary's Captain Freddie McCall and Edmonton's Wilfrid "Wop" May—capitalized on their reputations as daring war heroes to attract audiences to exhibition flying after the war. "Visitors will be afforded a vision of the thrilling work done by these intrepid birdmen, miles above the battlefield in Flanders," the *Calgary Herald* promised in a lead-up to the 1919 Calgary fair. When one of McCall's flights went wrong at the fair, he was forced to land his plane on top of the merry-go-round, something for which he was still praised. "It was a wonderful exhibition of daring aviation, quick thinking, and pluck," the *Calgary Herald* enthused, concluding that it was no wonder he had been so successful in France.[21]

With their goggles and helmets and flowing white scarves, the aviators created a glamorous image of freedom, technical mastery, and aerial wizardry. Everywhere they went in Alberta, people came out to see them. At fairs and in farmers' fields across Alberta, former wartime aviators stunted and took people up for flights. This was not enough for these men, though. They had seen the possibilities of the airplane and they went on to turn their flying and mechanical skills into postwar businesses. Although still stunt flying, by 1920 they had moved on to passenger, mail, and freight carrying and had started building an aviation network throughout the province. They were convinced of the possibilities of the airplane and hoped to win over cities, businesses, and citizens to that vision. They came back from the war full of the same enthusiasm for flight that they had left with, only with bigger and more capable machines that made use of the technological developments spurred on by aerial combat. And they had proponents like Katherine Stinson to thank for making the airplane a more common sight in Alberta, and for keeping the enthusiasm for flight in the public eye while they had been away.

Notes

1   For reports on Stinson's exhibition flying, see *Edmonton Journal*, 1, 8, 10, and 12 July 1916, and *Edmonton Bulletin*, 4, 5, 12, and 13 July 1916. Also see Christine A. Keffeler, "Stinson, Katherine," *Handbook of Texas Online* (www.tshaonline.org/handbook/online/articles/fst97), by the Texas State Historical Association, for a full description of her aviation life.

2   There is a great deal of scholarship and information about the war in the air. See, for example, John H. Morrow, *The Great War in the Air: Military Aviation from 1909 to 1921* (Tuscaloosa: University of Alabama Press, 1993); Ian Mackersey, *No Empty Chairs: The Short and Heroic Lives of the Young Aviators Who Fought and Died in the First World War* (London, UK: Orion Publishing Group, 2012); Michael Molkentin, *Fire in the Sky: The Australian Flying Corps in the First World War* (Crowsnest, AU: Allen and Unwin, 2010); and the multivolume *The War in the Air: Being the Story of the Part played in the Great War by the Royal Air Force*, begun by Sir Walter Raleigh, with the first volume being published in London in 1922. For Canadian participation, the classic works are S.F. Wise, *Canadian Airmen and the First World War: The Official History of The Royal Canadian Air Force*, vol. 1 (Toronto: University of Toronto Press, 1980), and Lieutenant Colonel George A. Drew, *Canada's Fighting Airmen* (Toronto: Maclean Publishing Company, Limited, 1931). Also see David Bashow's *Knights of the Air: Canadian Fighter Pilots in the First World War* (Toronto: McArthur & Co., 2000) for stories and details of Canadian pilots, as well as for the other roles available to aviators, such as observers and machine gunners.

3   For more information on prewar aviation activities in Alberta, see Patricia Myers, *Sky Riders: An Illustrated History of Aviation in Alberta, 1906–1945* (Saskatoon: Fifth House, 1995), chapter 1. For a romantic overview of prewar attitudes to and representations of flight, see Robert Wohl, *A Passion for Wings: Aviation and the Western Imagination, 1908–1918* (New Haven, CT: Yale University Press, 1994).

4   This would finally change in the fall of 1918 with the formation of the Royal Canadian Naval Air Service in Canada and the Canadian Air Force in England. However, both were disbanded after the Armistice. See Wise, *Canadian Airmen,* part 1.

5   Bank of Canada Inflation Calculator, accessed 25 March 2014, URL: http://www.bankofcanada.ca/rates/related/inflation-calculator/.

6   Enlistment requirements and procedures changed at various times during the war, including the dropping of the requirement for a pilot's certificate in mid-1916. Wise suggests this was a consequence of large

losses for the Royal Flying Corps during the Somme offensive and the need for reinforcements. See Wise, *Canadian Airmen*, chapter 2.

7 Nick Carter's training trials can be followed in Jack Harris and Bob Pearson, *Aircraft of World War I, 1914–1918* (London, UK: Amber Books, 2010), 30–32. His war record and attestation papers can be accessed at www.theaerodrome.com/aces/canada/carter2.php.

8 Dickins' attestation papers can be accessed at www.collectionscanada.gc.ca/databases/cef/001042-119.02-e.php/image, and a clip of Dickins describing how he enlisted in the Royal Air Force called "The first plane I ever flew" can be accessed at www.veterans.gc.ca/eng/video-gallery/video/5741. The quotation is taken from the transcript. See Denis Winter, *The First of the Few: Fighter Pilots of the First World War* (London, UK: Allen Lane, 1982) for information on training and flying.

9 For two examples of newspaper reports of the air war, see "Latest British Flying Machines are Giants—Will Carry Big Load of Bombs," *Calgary Daily Herald*, 24 June 1918, and "British Bagged Eleven Planes During Thursday," *Edmonton Journal*, 3 August 1918.

10 See University of Lethbridge Digitized Collections for information on George Rogers, accessed 25 March 2014, URL: http://digitallibrary.uleth.ca/cdm/singleitem/collection/cenotaph/id/230/rec/20.

11 See *Edmonton Journal*, 22 June 1918, for an account of Talbot's death

12 Ibid.

13 Ibid., 20 July 1918.

14 Ibid., 17 August 1918.

15 Ibid., 26 October 1918.

16 See Jessica Meyer, *Men of War: Masculinity and the First World War in Britain* (Basingstoke, UK: Palgrave Macmillan, 2009), for a full discussion of the creation and meanings of various kinds of war writing by fighting men. Most of this literature explores the concept of masculinity by studying infantrymen. See, for example, Joanna Burke, *Dismembering the Male: Men's Bodies, Britain and the Great War* (Chicago: University of Chicago Press, 1996), and Charles Nathan Hatton, "Headlocks on the Homefront: Wrestling in Manitoba during the First World War," *Prairie Forum* 37 (Fall 2012): 173–209. For the brevity of airmen's lives, see Cecil Lewis, *Sagittarius Rising* (New York: Harcourt, Brace, 1936), and Mackersey, *No Empty Chairs*.

17 *Edmonton Journal*, 12 July 1917.

18 Ibid., 8 July 1916.

19 *Red Deer Advocate*, 2 August 1918; *Calgary Herald*, 9 and 10 July 1918. For just one treatment of developments in aviation and airplane design during the war, see Harris and Pearson, *Aircraft of World War I*. For two examples of interest in the possibilities of postwar aviation, see "British Aerial Mail After War is Newest Plan," *Edmonton Journal*, 3 August 1918, and "Air Route Over Atlantic is Now Definite Project," *Edmonton Journal*, 22 June 1918.

20 See Myers, *Sky Riders*, chapter 2. I thank Rod Macleod for bringing the University of Alberta's plans for an aeronautical engineering program to my attention. The program funding was cancelled by the United Farmers of Alberta government.

21 See Myers, *Sky Riders*, chapter 2; *Edmonton Journal*, 18 July 1919; *Calgary Herald*, 5 July 1919; *High River Times*, 2 October 1919; and *Red Deer Advocate*, 27 June and 4, 11, and 18 July 1919. For information on "Wop" May's postwar business ventures, see Canadian Aviation Hall of Fame, Membership Files, W.R. May, Glenbow Archives, Calgary, Wilfrid Reid "Wop" May Papers, M829; and City of Edmonton Archives, MS 322, Class 2, Subclass 10, file 1, Edmonton Exhibition Association Limited Collection.

Works Cited

PRIMARY SOURCES

Calgary Herald
Edmonton Journal
High River Times
Red Deer Advocate

SECONDARY SOURCES

Bashow, David. *Knights of the Air: Canadian Fighter Pilots in the First World War*. Toronto: McArthur & Company, 2000.

Drew, Lieut. Colonel George A. *Canada's Fighting Airmen*. Toronto: The Maclean Publishing Company, Limited, 1931.

Harris, Jack, and Bob Pearson. *Aircraft of World War I, 1914–1918*. London, UK: Amber Books, 2010.

Hunt, C.W. *Dancing in the Sky: The Royal Flying Corps in Canada*. Toronto: Dundurn Press, 2009.

Lewis, Cecil. *Sagittarius Rising*. New York: Harcourt, Brace and Company, 1936.

Mackersey, Ian. *No Empty Chairs: The Short and Heroic Lives of the Young Aviators Who Fought and Died in the First World War*. London, UK: Orion Publishing Group, 2012.

Meyer, Jessica. *Men of War: Masculinity and the First World War in Britain*. Basingstoke, UK: Palgrave Macmillan, 2009.

Molkentin, Michael. *Fire in the Sky: The Australian Flying Corps in the First World War*. Crowsnest, AU: Allen and Unwin, 2010.

Morrow, John H. *The Great War in the Air: Military Aviation from 1909 to 1921*. Tuscaloosa: University of Alabama Press, 1993.

Myers, Patricia. *Sky Riders: An Illustrated History of Aviation in Alberta, 1906–1945*. Saskatoon: Fifth House, 1995.

Raleigh, Walter. *The War in the Air: Being the Story of the Part Played in the Great War by the Royal Air Force*. Oxford, UK: The Clarendon Press, 1922.

Winter, Denis. *The First of the Few: Fighter Pilots of the First World War*. London, UK: Allen Lane, 1982.

Wise, S.F. *Canadian Airmen and the First World War: The Official History of the Royal Canadian Air Force*. Vol. 1. Toronto: University of Toronto Press, 1980.

Wohl, Robert. *A Passion for Wings: Aviation and the Western Imagination, 1908–1918*. New Haven, CT: Yale University Press, 1994.

Building on the Home Front: Armouries and Other Infrastructure

KATHRYN IVANY

Preparations for war, especially those that require bricks and mortar, take time and planning, and significant financial resources. Pundits and prophets had been debating the likelihood of a major European conflict for at least a decade before the Great War began in 1914. Citizens of Canada, far removed from the conflict, were often able to ignore and discount the signs. It should not be surprising, therefore, that in the Canadian West the infrastructure around wartime preparations was lacking in many cities prior to 1914.

Even before ominous signs of war were seen in Europe, the militia in Canada began to grow, and assume an important role. Returned officers from the Boer War (1899–1902) maintained their military connections within their home communities and across the country. They developed clubs for social activities but, more importantly, they established clubs for the purpose of keeping their martial skills honed, and for training others. Those with notable reputations or in positions of influence could move local authorities to take note of militia interests and provide services and infrastructure to assist them.

As early as 1905 in Strathcona (at that time a town separate from Edmonton), the militia was active and looking for a home base. The Militia Department secured the Niblock Street School for an armoury for the Lord Strathcona's Horse and sent out equipment to facilitate its operations.[1] By 1906 other local militias organized. William Antrobus Griesbach, veteran of the Boer War with the Canadian Mounted Rifles and a local legal practitioner, began recruiting for the Alberta Mounted Rifles (AMR). It took as its temporary headquarters the Thistle Curling Rink in downtown Edmonton.[2] Visits of military personnel and government officials provided the AMR with opportunities to publicly show off their martial prowess.[3] In September 1906 the vice regal visit of the governor general, Earl Grey, warranted an escort by the militia.[4] By 1909 the "A" squadron in Edmonton was joined by "B" squadron in Strathcona.

Colonel Elihu Burritt Edwards led another group known as the 101st Fusiliers.[5] Originally from Ontario, Edwards was a solicitor in partnership with Louis Madore, and served on the board of the

The Niblock Street School, south Edmonton's first public school, opened in 1892 and was located at 105th Street and 84th Avenue. In 1905, the Militia Department secured it for an armoury for the Lord Strathcona's Horse and sent out equipment to facilitate its operations. Unknown photographer, n.d. City of Edmonton Archives, EA-10-912.

hospital and the Canadian Club. His interest in the military arose from his duties as brigadier with the 7th Infantry Brigade headquartered in Kingston, Ontario.

Edwards and Griesbach tried to ensure decent training facilities were available in Edmonton. The civilian rifle range at Riverside Park became an important component of the training regimen.

Whether the militia officers were already members or joined it for training purposes, the Rifle Club membership grew steadily under the militia's influence. The militia organizations also started their own (or took over) local athletic clubs to promote the fitness of their members.[6] Competitions in running, riding, and hurling various objects were reported in local newspapers, with the rank of the participants and their regiments being duly noted.

In 1907 Griesbach and Edwards were joined by Major Joseph DeBlois Thibaudeau, who was given the go-ahead from Ottawa to organize another squadron of the Mounted Rifles. It was the general trend for the militia to consist predominantly of men of British stock; this new squadron countered that tradition by recruiting primarily from the district of St. Albert and Morinville, where there was a high proportion of French-Canadians.[7]

Overall, the militia's primary concerns were the lack of storage facilities, drill halls for winter, barracks, and armouries. Colonel F.C. Jamieson, another lawyer in Strathcona (and partner of Premier A.C. Rutherford), approached the Strathcona Board of Trade, late in 1906, hoping it would take advantage of the Dominion government's financial support for the militia. The *Edmonton Bulletin* noted:

> Mr. Jamieson introduced the matter of the location of a permanent force barracks in this town. This question had been discussed as long ago as in 1901 and lately he had seen it stated by the Minister of Militia that a permanent barracks was to be located, and for this a grant had been made recently at Ottawa.[8]

Arrangements had been made for the Edmonton men to parade at the Exhibition grounds, so that

Shooting Range in Riverside Park in Edmonton. Unknown creator, 1924. City of Edmonton Archives, EA-29-103.

drills could be carried out on the racetrack and some of the equipment stored in its buildings. During the summer months, training was also carried out at a two-week camp held outside Calgary. Officers and as many men as could be mustered gathered in camp for intensive drills, long marches for the infantry, and rides for the mounted units; practice in rifle maintenance, shooting, and the use of bayonets in combat; as well as courses for the officers in orienteering and command. One camp was held in Edmonton in 1904 and, in 1909, three squadrons gathered on Groat's Flats for a week long training camp.[9]

The "A" squadron of the Alberta Mounted Rifles used a building (possibly the Condell Block) on the corner of 8th Street and Jasper as its temporary armoury, while it was allowed to drill in the Church of England's Sunday School room on 103rd Street. Archdeacon Gray of All Saints Church served as the squadron's chaplain.

Despite the growth of the militia, and the creation of a new western command division, the 13th (formed out of the 10th, which was headquartered in Winnipeg), support for infrastructure in Alberta was lacking. Equipment was sent out to dress and arm the men, but local units were on their own to find facilities to store equipment, meet, plan, and drill. That began to change in mid-1907. In June a building was finally erected to serve the militia: a wood-frame structure on the market square in Edmonton. The building was nothing remarkable, but it did serve to hold the equipment entrusted to the units.[10]

In the interim, tenders began appearing in local newspapers for the construction of armouries in other locations. The Department of Public Works issued calls for tenders in Brandon, Manitoba, in June, and in Medicine Hat, Alberta, in September. The Strathcona division heard the news via its Member of Parliament, Dr. W. McIntyre, the following July: a grant of $10,000 was promised from the Department of Militia and Defense to build an armoury for the division.[11] The news was not greeted with unanimous approval, for some thought an amount five times that would be necessary to build an adequate facility. When Colonel Sam Steele, the new commander of the western divisions, came to Alberta on an inspection tour, he announced a new armoury for Lethbridge but could not confirm the same for Calgary.[12]

A further promise of support for an armoury on the north side of the river was made in September when the Exhibition Grounds was identified as the proposed location. The *Edmonton Bulletin*'s coverage of the September 1st City Council Meeting detailed a letter from G.P. McKie, DSO, acting for the district officer commanding Military District No. 13, requesting that "the city of Edmonton make a grant of a free site for an armory which it is proposed to erect in the city. The size of the site required is 140 × 250 feet."[13]

City Council expressed itself willing to consider making the donation of a site for an armoury slightly bigger than suggested. The Department of Militia and Defence wrote back asking for an even larger site, and that request was granted.[14] Despite such promises and concessions, no action was taken and,

early in 1909, the militiamen again approached the aldermen. The *Edmonton Bulletin* noted:

> Lt. Col. Edwards, officer commanding the 101st Canadian Fusiliers of Edmonton . . . suggested that if this were done the militia department might act more quickly in this regard. With reference to the site of the proposed armoury which the city had promised to give, Col. Edwards suggested that a site adjoining the proposed high school site on the Hudson Bay property on First Street, might be found most suitable. The council passed a resolution asking the government to hurry along the matter of erecting an armoury in Edmonton . . . The matter was referred to the city commissioners to deal with.[15]

The commissioners corresponded over the next year with the Hudson's Bay Company (HBC), owners of the proposed lands west of 101st Street. Then the Department of Militia and Defence requested an even bigger site—double the size of the one first offered by the City. Once the HBC established the price of the larger property, the restrictions on future use demanded by the company entailed months of back-and-forth correspondence between it and the commissioners. At issue was the clause that the land would be used for an armoury in perpetuity. Eventually the aldermen were able to convince the HBC to accept that the land would be used "in perpetuity for government or public purposes."[16]

The next issue became the City having to donate the site. This nearly became a major sticking point for some councillors, bureaucrats, and citizens, especially since eastern Canadian cities had not been asked to do the same when their armouries were built. City Auditor Charles Leo Richardson recommended against the donation and suggested that the question be vetted by the city solicitor. The *Edmonton Bulletin* noted:

> The city of Edmonton as a corporation has no obligation to perform in connection with the defences of the county. This is entirely a responsibility assumed by the Dominion Government . . . the city will be doing so to the benefit of other cities such as Halifax, Toronto, Winnipeg, Vancouver, where the Dominion government were required to purchase sites for armouries.[17]

Despite Mr. Richardson's interference, the city solicitor found that the council was quite able to make such a donation, and the next move was to issue debentures to purchase the HBC's lands. The motion to pass Bylaw 327 "to provide for the raising by the issue of debentures the sum of $22,000 for the purposes of a Drill Hall and Armoury site" was read three times and provisionally passed at the end of March 1911.[18]

Raising the funds took some time, and as the Dominion government did not take action until the land was transferred, this delayed matters for two years. The commanding officers of the militia in Edmonton and Strathcona, in the meantime, had taken matters into their own hands. Colonel Edwards started lobbying for the use of the curling rink again, while the Strathcona "B" squadron of the Alberta Mounted Rifles requested from the Council of Strathcona the use of the upper floor of the old fire hall until its own armoury could be completed.[19]

Major G.W. Marriott was allowed the use of the fire hall, and Colonel Edwards and the Fusiliers were granted use of a smaller building than the curling rink located beside the Thistle Rink.[20]

In May 1911 tenders were called for the construction of the Strathcona Armoury.[21] It was planned as a two-storey building with a basement, built of brick and sandstone in a style typical of Canada's turn-of-the-century military establishments. Designed by Chief Dominion Architect David Ewart in the Baronial style, it was completed in 1911. Rectangular in shape with symmetrical windows flanking the prominent central entrance, and with an entry parapet and battlemented crenellations on the roofline, it looked the part of an armoury. It was named in honour of the Duke of Connaught, who visited Edmonton in September 1912.

What it would take for the Dominion government to commit to building the Edmonton Drill Hall, however, was a disaster. In late October 1913, the Thistle Rink burned down and took two neighbouring buildings with it. The armoury of the 19th Dragoons (formerly the "A" squadron of the Alberta Mounted Rifles under the command of Major Griesbach) was consumed in flames in under three-quarters of an hour. Unfortunately, all its uniforms, rifles, and equipment, which had been gathered into the armoury for an inspection the previous week, were also lost, with explosions of the ammunition putting on quite a show for the many who had come to watch.[22]

Within two weeks, Ottawa announced the intention of building a significant drill hall and armoury building in Edmonton.[23] Work commenced on the Edmonton Drill Hall in the spring of 1914, halted briefly during the winter until a new appropriation could be confirmed in the House of Commons, for

Royal visit on Market Square in Edmonton in 1919. The wooden building on the east side of the square (upper left) was probably the one used by the militia. City of Edmonton Archives, EA-29-37.

scheduled completion in October 1915.[24] By the time it was ready, the militia units it was intended to house had been enlisted and shipped overseas to France. Instead, the 66th and 51st battalions and the 233rd French-Canadian Battalion were quartered here.

The 19th Dragoons, therefore, commandeered the old land titles office on Victoria Avenue (now 100th Avenue) and renamed it the Victoria Armoury. It served their needs adequately until they mustered in and left for training from Calgary's Sarcee Camp.[25]

The Edmonton Drill Hall was designed by Donald MacVicar, a Montreal architect, possibly as early as 1907, and supervised during construction by E.C. Hopkins, a prominent local architect. The building tender was won by P. Lyall and Sons, also from Montreal. The Gothic Revival style (also described as "Tudorbethan") reminds the viewer today of a medieval castle, with its two-storey brick and sandstone walls with four corner towers and crenellated battlements with narrow slit windows. The central drill hall has steel trusses supporting the

Interior of the Edmonton drill hall. It is typical of the style favoured for military buildings in Canada in the early part of the twentieth century. Unknown photographer, 1924. City of Edmonton Archives, EA-29-146

roof, allowing a large open space for inside drills. Two floors of barrack rooms and offices, as well recreational facilities such as firing ranges, bowling alleys in the basement, and mess halls and lounges on the second floor, provided superior accommodations for the military members stationed there.

Although not available for the military preparations prior to the declaration of war in 1914, the armouries and the drill hall in Edmonton did provide a home base for recruitment and initial training, and for returning soldiers prior to their being mustered out. Several veterans' organizations were formed after the war and, before legion halls could be built to accommodate them, they often maintained headquarters in the armouries that had served their regiments.

After the war, veterans required other facilities besides legion halls. Devastating injuries and illnesses were incurred by the soldiers, and on their return home they required medical care. The first military recovery and treatment hospital was established in Ottawa in 1915 as the Sir Sandford Fleming Convalescent Home.[26] In the West, the first was established in Deer Lodge near Winnipeg in 1916. In Calgary, a former hotel was converted in 1919 into the Ogden Military Convalescent Hospital to house returning soldiers in need of care.[27]

Although it took some time, specialized medical units were created in hospitals to deal with the needs of the First World War veterans. In Edmonton severely injured veterans benefited from the experiences of Frank Hamilton Mewburn, who went overseas as an army surgeon in 1914, and his son, Hank, who enlisted in 1915 and returned to pursue medical training and to assist his father at the Canadian Army Medical Corps facility at Taplow,

Buckinghamshire, England.[28] When they returned to Edmonton, their orthopaedic surgery practice was focused on the needs of returned soldiers and disabled children. Dr. Hank Mewburn accepted a position at the University of Alberta as a professor of surgery, and was able to establish a department of orthopaedic surgery, which was named after him in 1923. The Mewburn Centre continued to care for veterans for many years.

Another aspect of infrastructure that appeared in many communities after the First World War was the Military Field of Honour. The Commonwealth War Graves Commission was formed in 1917 to deal with the creation and maintenance of military graveyards in Europe. The Canadian Agency of the Commission, established in 1921, was responsible for the care of those graves in the Americas, including the Caribbean. In the interim, however, numerous military graves were placed in private and municipal cemeteries by the Imperial War Graves Commission, which offered to support the cemetery companies or municipalities to create fields of honour.[29] The Edmonton Cemetery company was approached in 1919, and soon this led to the erection of a memorial to those who served in the First World War—a 22-foot-high replica of the Cross of Sacrifice found in European fields. The Union Cemetery in Calgary also created a field of honour, as did other municipalities in Alberta. Along with the placing of cenotaphs in prominent parks in Alberta's cities and towns, other commemoration of Alberta's soldiers and veterans has continued even one hundred years after the onset of the First World War.

The remaining infrastructure of the First World War—the armouries, drill halls, hospitals, legion halls, and cemeteries—continues to mark the sacrifice of a generation of Albertans. Despite the political machinations that delayed, or precipitated, their construction, arguments over who would pay for them or how the buildings could be used after their military utility ended, the buildings from the prewar/interwar period that remain provide tangible reminders of the efforts and will of the nation to equip, train, house, and otherwise accommodate the Canadian military during the epic war of 1914–18, and to commemorate that service and sacrifice in the years that followed.

Notes

1   *Edmonton Bulletin*, 12 April 1905, 2.
2   Ibid., 29 May 1906, 2.
3   Ibid., 24 January 1907, 1. Members of "B" and "C" squadrons of the CMR, the 45th Regiment, and the 7th Brigade attended the opening of the Legislative Assembly.
4   Ibid., 11 July 1906, 7.
5   Ibid., 24 April 1909.
6   Ibid.
7   Ibid., 12 March 1907, 1.
8   Ibid., 12 December 1906, 2.
9   "Military Matters," *Edmonton Bulletin*, 12 June 1909.
10 *Edmonton Bulletin*, 16 May 1907, 1.
11 Ibid., 11 July 1908, 4.
12 Ibid., 23 October 1908, 10.
13 Ibid., 16 September 1908, 8.
14 City of Edmonton Archives, City of Edmonton Council minutes, 15 September and 1 December 1908, RG 8, 1908, 359 and 387.
15 Ibid., 10 February 1909, 5.
16 City of Edmonton Archives, City of Edmonton Council minutes, relating to correspondence with H.B. Co between 16 August 1910 and 31 January 1911, RG 8, 1910, 712, 724, and 1911, 5, 9, 20, 24, 29.
17 Ibid., 3 February 1911, 2.
18 City of Edmonton Archives, City Council minutes, March 28, 1911, RG 8, 1911, p. 57.
19 *Edmonton Capital*, 14 September 1910.
20 Ibid., 7 January 1911.
21 *Edmonton Bulletin*, 10 May 1911, 7.
22 Ibid., 31 October 1913, 1.
23 Ibid., 10 November 1913, 2.
24 Ibid., 24 September 1915, 1.
25 "Edmonton Militia is on War Footing Today," *Edmonton Bulletin*, 14 August 1914.
26 Frank Rockland, *Fire on the Hill: A Canadian WWI Historical Suspense Novel* website, http://www.sambiasebooks.ca/fire-on-the-hill/canada-ww1/causalities.html, retrieved 26 March 2014.
27 Deer Lodge Centre website, http://www.deerlodge.mb.ca/aboutHistory.html, retrieved 5 May 2014.
28 History of Orthopaedic Surgery in Edmonton, http://www.orthopaedicsurgery.ualberta.ca/en/AboutUs/History.aspx.
29 John Prociuk, *A Walk Through Time—Edmonton's Municipal Cemeteries*, City of Edmonton Archives reference library, 971.233 PRO.

Works Cited

PRIMARY SOURCES

Edmonton Bulletin

Alberta Heritage Resources, Edmonton. Statement of Significance for the Edmonton Drill Hall, 1982.
City of Edmonton Archives. City of Edmonton Council Minutes, RG 8, 1908, 1910, 1911.
——. Holland Roth Architects. Prince of Wales Armouries Heritage Centre Planning Study for the City of Edmonton: Final Report. 31 March 2008, GP2363-2008-mar.

SECONDARY SOURCES

Deer Lodge Centre website. URL:
    http://www.deerlodge.mb.ca/aboutHistory.html,
    retrieved 26 March 2014.

Prociuk, John. *A Walk Through Time – Edmonton's Municipal
    Cemeteries*. City of Edmonton Archives reference
    library, 971.233 PRO.

Rockland, Frank. *Fire on the Hill: A Canadian WWI Historical
    Suspense Novel* website. URL:
    http://www.sambiase books.ca/fire-on-the-hill/
    canada-ww1/causalities.html, retrieved 26 March
    2014.

Stevens, G. R. *A City Goes to War: History of the Loyal
    Edmonton Regiment*. Brampton, ON: Charters
    Publishing Company, 1964.

University of Alberta website, Faculty of Medicine and
    Dentistry, Division of Orthopaedic Surgery. URL:
    http://www.orthopaedicsurgery.ualberta.ca/en/
    AboutUs/History.aspx, retrieved 26 March 2014.

Aboriginal Alberta and the First World War

L. JAMES DEMPSEY

On the eve of the outbreak of the First World War, western Canadian Indians had preserved many of their old traditions, in spite of government efforts to suppress them. The warrior ethic had survived four decades of attempts to replace it with agricultural values. To young men, the achievement of military distinction remained an ideal. Among the Blackfoot, for example, during the Second World War the age-old tribal saying "It is better for a man to be killed in battle than to die of old age or sickness" remained in common usage.[1]

The Indians of Alberta belonged to two major cultural/geographic areas, the Plains and the Woodlands. Most prominent among the Plains groups were the Blackfoot, Blood, Peigan, Sarcee, Plains Cree, Stoney (Assiniboine), Sioux (Dakota), and Plains Ojibwa (Saulteaux or Chippewa). Among the Woodlands tribes were the Woodlands and Swampy Cree, Ojibwa, Woodlands Stoney, Beaver, Slavey, and Chipewyan.[2] In the mid-nineteenth century, the warrior ethic existed in both cultural areas, but particularly on the Plains. To understand the concept, one that would later lead a number of young western Canadian Indians to enlist in the First World War, one must first review the cultures of both Woodlands

and Plains a century and a half ago. In the nineteenth century, the Plains Indians had a warrior personality. Blackfoot children were brought up to view war as an opportunity to acquire fame and riches. The seasoned Plains Indian raider was a courageous, alert, resourceful fighting man, one who attributed his success in war to the power of his war medicine.[3] Although the Woodlands Indians practised warfare, and shared with the Plains people the wish that their male children be excellent hunters and warriors, the Woodland tribes were less concerned with war. The fur trade actually led them away from warfare.

The cornerstone of Canada's Indian policy was the Royal Proclamation of 1763 that recognized a form of Native title to the land.[4] Before settlement could proceed, the majority of the respective groups of Indians had to consent, at a public meeting, to surrender their lands to the Crown, which alone could purchase them. This policy evolved into a system of treaties, known in western Canada as the "Numbered Treaties," with nine (Treaties 1 through 8 and 10) being signed in the present-day Prairie provinces from 1871 to 1908. The three Great Plains treaties were Treaty 4 (covering present-day southern Saskatchewan), Treaty 6 (present-day central Alberta and Saskatchewan), and Treaty 7 (present-day southern Alberta).[5] The signing of the treaties ultimately affected the Indians during the First World War in two ways. First, it created a strong tie with Queen Victoria and her heirs. Since it was in her name that the treaties were signed, and since the commissioners were considered royal representatives, the Indians saw the treaties as pacts with the Crown, rather than with the government of Canada. Second, the addition of a clause in Treaty 3 greatly affected the Indians forty years later since it allowed the exclusion of Natives from fighting in Canada's wars. During the negotiations, a chief from Fort Francis asked: "If you should get into trouble with the nations, I do not wish to walk out and expose my young men to aid you in any of your wars."[6] Commissioner Alexander Morris replied, "The English never call the Indians out of their country to fight their battles."[7]

A gulf of monumental proportions existed between the Native Indians' outlook and that of the European settler on the eve of war. Even with the government's policy of regulation and integration, the old lifestyle of the warrior continued through the late nineteenth and into the twentieth century. In February 1887, young men on the Blood reserve waited for the snow to melt to permit them to raid the Gros Ventres in Montana. The Bloods, in 1889, raided the Crows in Montana. In 1905, seven Bloods were caught stealing horses from the Mormons and running them over into the Kootenay River area in British Columbia, where they sold them to a local rancher. The temporary success of these young men, instead of creating a fear of reprisal on the reserve, induced others to try and to improve on the undertaking. However, since the opportunity for warfare had been abolished through the treaties, religion

became the main avenue left for males to retain their dignity and find relief from the dull and oppressive reserve life. In the case of the Blackfoot, many religious ceremonies continued to be performed into the reserve period during the Sun Dance. Many of these rituals were originally used as a means of arousing "courage and enthusiasm for war."[8]

By 1913, the Canadian government had controlled the lives of western Canadian Indians for almost two generations, and had implemented a paternalistic policy of assimilation. In the Prairie provinces, the goal of this policy was to transform males of various nomadic tribes into farmers, while their children were to be enrolled in church-run schools. The expected results of these programs would be productive Native farmers and "British educated" Native children, who would embody the ideals, values, and morals of the dominant culture. In reality, despite the efforts of the missionary teachers and Indian agents, the culture and, in particular, the warrior ethic persisted. The old enthusiasm for war openly surfaced during the First World War when, in a complete about-face, the government encouraged the enlistment of Native soldiers. During the war, more than 3,500 Indians enlisted for active service with the Canadian Expeditionary Force (CEF), or approximately one-third of the Indian male population of military age. As Deputy Superintendent General of Indian Affairs Duncan Campbell Scott proudly wrote after the war, the percentage of Indian enlistments was fully equal to that among white communities and, in a number of instances, far higher than the average.[9]

In summer 1914, cadet training was carried out on a few of the reserves. On the Blood reserve, this continued into the war years under the direction of Reverend S.H. Middleton, who had some thirty boys

Officers of St. Paul's cadets, Blood reserve, southern Alberta, ca. 1917. Mountain Horse, at left, was killed in France. The Reverend S.H. Middleton stands at right. Boys with drum, bugle, and rifles kneel at front. Glenbow Archives, NA-4611-41.

in his company at St. Paul's Anglican School. Such training became a first step into the military for students anxious to gain traditional war honours. Two examples can be cited from the Blood reserve alone. Albert Mountain Horse, a St. Paul's graduate said to be "one of the brightest and most enlightened boys on the reserve," had served as a cadet at the Indian boarding school.[10] His interest in army life began in boyhood and, when he was old enough, he was sent to military school where he passed the examination entitling him to hold a commission of lieutenant. When war broke out, Mountain Horse belonged to

a militia group, the 23rd Alberta Rangers, and was taking a course in musketry in Calgary. He applied for, and was granted permission to enlist, though it was as a private rather than a lieutenant, in order to be accepted sooner. He enlisted in the Army Service Corps in Calgary, trained at Valcartier in 1914, and then went overseas.[11] Another Blood Indian, Laurie Plume, was a sergeant in the same corps and later enlisted with a number of friends.[12]

Indians across Canada actively supported the war. The Blackfoot presented a donation to the government in September 1914 stating that the "money

Joe Mountain Horse, Cardston, Alberta, ca. 1900–09, Glenbow Archives, NC-7-69.

and old, schooled and unschooled, eagerly inquire for war news and any news told them of the success of the allied army . . . I am proud of our Indians, proud of the fact that they of their own free will and accord spontaneously suggested the calling of the Council [to donate money to the Patriotic Fund]."[15] Since the agents wrote the majority of these letters and proclamations to Ottawa, one must be skeptical of whose opinion they actually represented. Certainly, the war did cause considerable confusion on reserves. A generation earlier, the western Canadian Indians had been instructed at the signing of treaties to throw away their guns as henceforth the Great White Queen would protect them from all enemies. Now, one of their own, Albert Mountain Horse, had enlisted in part due to the Reverend Middleton's encouragement. Some saw the missionary as a betrayer who had broken the peace treaty and had committed the unpardonable sin of sending a Blood to fight in a foreign country.

Further anxiety arose when a proposal was made by Reverend John McDougall, one of the first Protestant missionaries to work among the Alberta Indians, to the effect that a regiment of Indians be raised to fight for the Empire. McDougall thought it would be an excellent plan, believing that "all these Indians at one time fought in battles amongst themselves, and some of them are the best scouts in the world. If I was suggesting sending a contingent of Indians to fight, I would suggest the taking of a certain number from each tribe and from each reserve, and making up a regiment of about 500. They have all fought at one time, and now are united in loyalty in the empire."[16]

At the outset of the war, however, neither the federal government nor the deputy superintendent of Indian affairs sought the assistance or

was to be used by them in whatever way may be deemed most advantageous to assist in bringing this war to a successful conclusion for our Country and her Allies."[13] A month later, the Sarcees presented $500 to the Canadian Patriotic Fund.[14] In a letter sent to J.D. McLean, the assistant deputy and secretary of Indian affairs, the government's agent to the Blood Indians stated: "Daily our Indians, both young involvement of the Indians. They were not felt to be needed in what Canadians believed would be a short war. In any case, the Indians were wards of the government and, as such, were not obligated to defend the British Empire.[17] During the first few months of the war, Deputy Superintendent General of Indian Affairs Scott and the Indian department opposed the outright recruitment of Indians for the army and declared that "no unit composed solely of Indians will go to the front with the Canadian contingent."[18] At this time, Native enlistments went relatively unnoticed by the Canadian military, and by the Department of Indian Affairs, which did not attempt to keep records of such volunteers.

Due to the relatively large number of Indians desiring to enlist at the beginning of the war, various Indian agents requested Ottawa to inform them of the proper procedure. In December 1914, the Department of Indian Affairs sent a memorandum to the agents instructing that "if the young men of the Indian band in their particular district desire to enlist for active service during the present war . . . take them to the local recruiting office and offer their services."[19] In January 1915, the military authorities themselves wanted the regulations clarified since they did not believe they had official authority to raise a company of Natives for the CEF. The department officer commanding was asked for a definite ruling. It would be the end of the year before a final decision was made. Most Indian agents remained neutral on Native recruiting and simply reported enlistments. Several of the military authorities initially opposed recruiting Indians for military service, and advised that the decision on all-Indian companies be delayed. Some feared that, if they were captured, their "savage" background would lead the enemy to treat them harshly. This argument was put forth by

Eugène Fiset, surgeon general of the Department of Militia and Defence, with the apparent endorsement of Minister Sam Hughes. Fiset graduated in medicine from the University of Laval and had served in the Boer War.

Recruiting efforts of department officials and others failed to enlist enough Natives to form an individual fighting force, and they were scattered throughout the Canadian Army. As the war progressed from an anticipated short conflict in 1914 to extended trench warfare that brought high casualties and declining voluntary enlistment, the government began to perceive Natives as members of the British Empire and, therefore, liable for its defence. As a result, the government reversed its stand late in 1915 and began to call for Indian participation. On 9 December 1915, the military reversed its former position against overseas duty for Natives. Confirmation to allow Indian recruiting came from Eugène Fiset, the department officer commanding, and, subsequently, from Deputy Superintendent General Scott and the Department of Indian Affairs. Instructions were sent to all officers commanding military divisions and districts to accept Natives, if they were up to the standard of the Enlistment Regulations.[20] The 114th Overseas Battalion, based in Ontario, became the first unit officially to accept the enlistment of Indians, who formed two companies staffed by a number of Native officers.[21]

In Alberta, Lieutenant Colonel James K. ("Peace River Jim") Cornwall formed a regiment known as the Irish Guards, a unit that had members who spoke almost every language known to the European continent. The unit, according to one source, included 16 interpreters, with Cornwall himself as the Native interpreter for the 50 Indians who formed part of his 8th Battalion. Reportedly, all of the Indians in the unit could speak some English by the time they reached France.[22]

Due to the drastic need for men, in spring 1916 Deputy Superintendent General Scott introduced a major policy change. He personally endorsed agents' attempts to recruit Indians. In late 1916, officials from the military and Department of Indian Affairs proposed new recruiting campaigns. The plans called for military personnel working in conjunction with a member of the Department of Indian Affairs to raise Native units. Lieutenant Maxwell Graham of the 253rd Battalion pointed out that the enlistment total of 155 Indians from the West (which included, by late 1916, 89 from Manitoba, 57 from Saskatchewan, and just 9 from Alberta) was far below what could be obtained.[23] Across Canada, he estimated there were 22,500 able-bodied adult Indian males, most of whom could understand English, and the three western provinces alone had over 6,000 able-bodied candidates. To aid in the recruitment campaign, Graham recommended that "selected Indians now overseas be brought back for recruiting purposes."[24]

Even before these proposals were made, with Scott's approval, the Canadian Army had used Indians to encourage both Natives and non-Natives to enlist. On the Blood reserve, Joe Healey, an Indian scout and member of the Lethbridge mounted police, proved to be an enthusiastic recruiter. He attempted to enlist members of his tribe during the Sun Dance held on the reserve on behalf of the 191st Battalion of Macleod. However, Healey noted that the young men were too busy with the dance to pay much attention to his recruiting speeches, in which he told them that he would be willing to go to the front with any of them, after obtaining a leave from the mounted police.[25]

As the war dragged on, and Canada's military stepped up its efforts to increase the number of recruits, a real fear existed on the part of some bands that their members might be forced to join the Canadian Army overseas. In southern Alberta, these fears had arisen early in the conflict. In December 1914, the tribes of that area "had been much disturbed by the notion of an Official of this Department asking the different Agents how many Indians would be prepared to go to Europe as scouts in the present war."[26] The letter came from the Chief Inspector of Indian Agencies Glen Campbell (and later the organizer of the 107th Battalion), who stated that it was his intention to organize a company of scouts, drawn from Indian reserves, for service in the present war.[27] These bands remembered the Riel Rebellion 29 years earlier in which they were asked to send men to act as scouts, and they probably assumed that the same request would be made during the current conflict.[28] When he learned of the letter, Assistant Deputy and Superintendent-General of Indian Affairs John D. McLean contacted the agents of the reserves and pointed out:

I may say that the Department has not authorized any such letter to be written by any of its officials and should be glad if you would assure the Indians that the Department has no intention of asking them to volunteer as scouts in the present war or any other capacity, that it is perfectly satisfied from the evidence already shown of their loyalty and is desirous that they should continue in their peaceful vocations.[29]

Most bands had few objections to their members volunteering (this was the accepted method by which

Blood recruits, 191st Battalion, Canadian Expeditionary Force, Fort Macleod, Alberta, 1916, Back row (left to right): George Coming Singer, died overseas, 1919; Joe Crow Chief; Dave Mills; George Strangling Wolf; Mike Foxhead, Blackfoot, died overseas, 1919; front row (left to right): Nick King; Harold Chief Moon; Sergeant Major Bryan; Joe Mountain Horse; Mike Mountain Horse. Glenbow Archives, NA-2164-1. Copy of PA-124-80.

young men joined a raiding party), but they opposed the European means of active recruiting. In the cases where there was strong opposition to recruiting, it was often noted by department and military officials that the source was the older members of the band or as they were referred to by the officials, "the Pagan Indians."[30] After the war, Edward Ahenakew summarized why many elders opposed military service overseas:

> Our old men, who remembered the days of warfare, were opposed to our people taking

part and did what they could to discourage it—not from disloyalty, but because it seemed against nature to them that an Indian should go to fight in a distant land and perhaps lay his body to mingle with earth that was not ours. It did not seem even England's quarrel, and much less Canada's. As they understood, England was helping other nations, and not fighting for her own life. If our land were attacked, they said, then it would be up to every man to fight, but not in this way. Their talk went unheeded. Youth is youth the world over.[31]

At the same time, Scott refused to permit excessive pressure to be applied on possible Indian enlistees. Whenever local Indian agents objected to recruiting practices, the deputy superintendent general supported the agents. On the Blackfoot reserve, for example, Agent J.H. Gooderham experienced a problem with recruiters, and asked for Scott's support.[32] Captain Rankin and Douglas Hardwick, a local rancher, attended an Indian dance and addressed the Indians. They succeeded in enlisting some fifteen men who left for Calgary to join the 191st Battalion. Of that number, the army accepted six.[33] The chiefs were not present at the dance, and when they heard what had happened, they met with Lieutenant Colonel Bryan, commander of the 191st Battalion. They requested that the boys be immediately released, as the agent had promised them that none of their young men would be required to fight for Canada. The meeting was successful, and all the Blackfoot were released before any of them saw action.

The Blackfoot elders also sought the discharge of Mike Foxhead (or Many Bears) and Cyril Foxhead (or Old Woman), who had enlisted earlier. Cyril

Mike Foxhead, Blackfoot soldier in the First World War, with friends, ca. 1918. Left to right: Sorrell Horse's son; Foxhead; Riding Grey Horses. Foxhead served with the 191st Overseas Battalion, Canadian Expeditionary Force and was killed overseas. Glenbow Archives, NA-5-16.

Foxhead had enlisted at Calgary in 1917 with the 191st Battalion at the age of 25, but he now complied with the elders' wishes. The young man petitioned to obtain his release on the grounds that his people opposed any band members going to war. A petition of the chiefs was sent to the deputy superintendent general of Indian affairs citing that many of the men who left the reserve fell victim to disease and died, and they feared this would happen to their boys. As a result of the petition, instructions were sent to the commanding officer of Military District No. 13 to discharge Cyril. Mike Foxhead, however, refused to be released and went overseas with his unit. He died in action.[34]

The fact that some of the elders spoke against overseas service did not mean that they opposed the war effort; as has been noted, the western Canadian Indians contributed a substantial amount of money to the war effort, and participated in Red Cross work and patriotic war activities. A total of $44,545.46 (worth over $850,000 in 2015) was donated to various patriotic funds by the Indians of Canada.[35] As organizations such as the central board of the Canadian Patriotic Fund became aware of the extent of Native financial support, they saw the opportunity to use it for propaganda purposes to shame non-Indians into giving more. On many reserves the Indian women formed Red Cross societies and patriotic leagues. They knitted socks, sweaters, and mufflers, made bandages, and provided various other comforts for the soldiers. Social entertainments were held at which the sale of Native crafts helped to raise money for patriotic purposes.[36] Such support came from Native people, in part, to show their loyalty and support, and at the same time to "buy out their young men."[37]

Prime Minister Robert Borden, in his 1916 New Year's speech, announced that Canada's authorized overseas force would be raised from 250,000 to 500,000 men. Borden informed Parliament that Canada's commitment to recruit 500,000 men did not mean the government would introduce conscription. However, late in 1916, the groundwork for conscription was being laid through the formation of the National Service Board. The national registration of all men and women over sixteen years of age was to take place on 22 June 1917. The object of the registration was to "gather information in the cause of increased production from an agricultural point of view; to ascertain where labour for essential industries may be found; and to prepare for a system of rationing food should it become necessary."[38] A special section was added for the benefit of Indian agents that addressed the question of Indian registration. It argued that registration had absolutely nothing to do with conscription and repeated that Indians had never been forced to serve in the army.[39] However, the section did require every Native to register. Band chiefs were asked not to fail in their duty at this critical hour and were warned, "if by your neglect . . . many do not register, on you will rest most of the responsibility. The result of failure to register will be so serious that very much hardship and suffering may occur on your Reserve."[40] Missionaries and schoolteachers were instructed to make known the requirements and the purposes of the registration in order that no false ideas jeopardize its success.

Confusion, however, ensued as many Indians believed that registration was, in fact, conscription. In answer to inquiries, it was pointed out that "the Indians are under obligation to fill out and sign the National Service cards . . . [but] that these cards do not mean enlistment in the overseas battalions, but a census of the industrial strength of the Dominion."[41] On the Blood reserve, Peter Black Rabbit, George Long Time Squirrel, and John Pace refused to register, and there is no record of any consequences.[42]

The passing of the Military Service Act (MSA) on 18 May 1917 was deemed necessary by Prime Minister Borden in order to meet the country's 500,000 quota, and to compensate for rising casualties. Many Indians protested, saying they should be exempt on the basis that they were not citizens but, rather, wards of the state without the right to vote. Also, in the case of the western Canadian Indians, their treaties contained a clause stipulating that they would not be required to fight in any of Canada's wars. As the protests mounted, Indians on various reserves encouraged their members not to report if conscripted.

The success of registration varied depending on how close the contact was between the agent and his wards. On the Sarcee reserve, for example, the agent registered the entire band. Even though he knew those medically fit were required to enlist, he asked for exemptions for everyone, citing tuberculosis as a reason for their exemption.[43] The agent was aware that the Sarcees were not interested in having their men participate and, by asking for total exemption without the band's knowledge, ensured that the government would show no further interest in the Sarcees. Before the new deadline arrived, however, regulations came into effect exempting the Indians from the Military Service Act. The order in council included provisions that any Indians who had enlisted or been conscripted since the passing of the act could make application for discharge. However, this exemption only included those Indians who had enlisted after the act was passed, and who made an application for exemption on their own behalf, not through a concerned second party.[44] They were also still bound to the national registration, though the practical problems of contacting those in the remote regions resulted in their exclusion.[45] The military police in Alberta did charge Clefus De Coine, an Indian from Lake Wabiscaw, located 160 kilometres north of Athabasca, with breach of the act. De Coine

needed a Cree interpreter for the trial, and it appeared from the evidence that the accused had not the faintest idea of what was expected of him regarding registration for military service. In dismissing the case, Magistrate Harrison regarded the action as showing excessive zeal. The military authorities were ordered to return De Coine safely to his home.

With the advantage of hindsight, Scott later supported the exclusion of Natives from the act, changing his initial view. In his chapter on Indian participation in *Canada in the Great War*, published in 1919, Scott wrote:

> When the Military Service Act was put into force in 1917, it was decided to exclude the Indians ... This action was taken in view of the fact that the Indians, although natural-born British subjects, were wards of the Government, and, as such, minors in the eyes of the law, and that, as they had not the right to exercise the franchise of other privileges of citizenship, they should not be expected to assume responsibilities equal to those of enfranchised persons. It was also taken into consideration that certain old treaties between the Indians and the Crown stipulated that they should not be called upon for military service. I may, therefore, emphasize that Indian participation in the war was wholly voluntary and not in any degree whatsoever subject to the influence of compulsory measures.[46]

When Canada's soldiers came home after the Armistice, they believed they were returning to an enlightened society for which many of them had fought and died. Many Indians hoped that their sacrifices would bring greater equality. For instance, Mark Steinhauer, from the Saddle Lake agency, wrote: "I have been wondering . . . whether we are going to get anything out of our country that we are going to fight for . . . What I want to find out is, is there a possible chance of us getting our franchise and our location in the reservation after the war is over? I do not think it would be fair not to get anything out of a country that we are fighting for."[47]

In reality, nothing really changed. When an Indian agent inquired, in 1922, about the legal status of Indian veterans, the assistant secretary of the department replied: "These returned Indian soldiers are subject to the provisions of the Indian Act and are in the same position as they were before enlisting."[48] Indian veterans continued to live at the bottom of the economic ladder and as the years passed their situation did not improve.

During the war, it appeared for a time that the legal status of Canada's Indians would change after Native soldiers were given the right to vote. Their franchise was officially confirmed in 1916. Member of Parliament William Chisholm asked the Minister of Justice: "Have Indians, 21 years of age and British subjects, who enlist as soldiers in the present war, the right to vote at a Dominion election held during the war?" The minister, Charles Doherty, responded by quoting Section 1 of the Canadian Soldiers on Active Military Service Act: "Every male British subject of 21 years of age or upwards serving in the military forces of Canada in the present war . . . is qualified to vote in any other electoral district in Canada he shall vote in such other district only. . . ." Doherty ended his statement by stating that the act "makes no exception of Indians."[49]

The vote had already been extended to the Indian soldiers when the Military Voters Bill was

Marker at gravesite of Lance Corporal Henry Norwest, Warvillers, France, n.d. Henry Louie "Ducky" Norwest was a sniper for the 50th Battalion, Canadian Expeditionary Force; his official record was 115 hits. He was killed at Fouquescourt, France, on 18 August 1918. Glenbow Archives, NA-4025-22. Copied from PA-2131-10.

introduced in late 1917. A provision was included that allowed Indian soldiers who had returned, or been discharged or released, to vote in a federal election.[50] Special arrangements were made for the 1917 election to set up polling stations on reserves, if it were not feasible for Indians to vote at the closest off-reserve polling station. During this election Indian veterans could vote without the fear of losing their Indian status.[51]

After the war, the legal status of Indians remained an unresolved question. Members of the public advocated giving the franchise to the entire Native population in recognition of their men's valiant performance on the battlefield.[52] However, while this idea appeared to many as a boon for the Indians, and a solution to the question of government wardship, the franchise also threatened to terminate their reserves and their Indian status.[53] This fear was well founded: Scott wanted the Indians' special status to be terminated when he believed they were ready, no matter the opposition.[54]

The "Greater Production" scheme was an indication of how easily the government overrode Native rights by arbitrarily amending the Indian Act. This project had originated in 1916, when feeding Britain had become a major priority. Although the Indian department sent out a circular in September 1914 asking Indians to produce as much wheat as possible, the first indication of their role in the program came in a circular from Scott in the autumn of 1916.[55] It stated that "the Indians should be encouraged to settle on their reserves, and, where feasible, to engage in farming, stockraising, etc. At any rate they should in most cases cultivate small gardens in which to raise potatoes, turnips, etc., for their own use."[56]

In January 1918, W.M. Graham outlined a plan to increase food production in order to assist with the war effort. It involved the use of "idle" Indian lands that he claimed amounted in the South Saskatchewan Inspectorate alone to 220,000 acres (just over 89,000 hectares). He argued that properly

using these lands could triple cattle production. The project became known as the Greater Production scheme, which Graham himself approved in February 1918 when he became commissioner for the western provinces.[57] By an order in council, he was given authority "to make proper arrangements with the Indians for the leasing of reserve lands" and to manage these lands for the Greater Production effort.[58]

The government endorsed Graham's plan, ignoring those who pointed to its deleterious impact on Indians. Minister of the Interior Arthur Meighen defended the commissioner when he stated in the House of Commons on 23 April 1918:

> We need not waste any time in sympathy for the Indian, for I am pretty sure his interests will be looked after by the Commissioner.... The Indian is a ward of the Government still. The presumption of the law is that he has not the capacity to decide what is for his ultimate benefit in the same degree as his guardian, the Government of Canada.[59]

To make the confiscation of reserve lands a simpler matter, the federal government amended the Indian Act in spring 1918 to eliminate the necessity of securing Indian consent.[60] Over 125,000 hectares of Indian land was leased to white farmers for up to five years, and a further 8,100 hectares on the Blood, Blackfoot, Muscowpetung, Crooked Lakes, and Assiniboine reserves were used for federal agricultural experiments.[61] The cabinet also quickly amended the Indian Act to make "idle" band funds available for investment in the Greater Production scheme.[62]

After the war, the Greater Production program continued to operate, which is surprising considering its limited financial success. Total expenditures far exceeded revenues from sales, and the balance of cash on hand was less than one-third of the initial investment of $362,000.[63] The project showed a profit only because of the leases of reserve lands. By April 1920, these leases had generated in excess of $200,000 and offset losses from the government farms.[64] Initially Scott saw the effort as a success,[65] but by 1922 he realized the project had no continued utility and terminated it.

The implementation of the scheme had greatly upset the Blood Indians. On 31 May 1920 they presented a memorandum to the Indian department outlining their complaints, which included gross mismanagement and the agent's high-handedness. They pointed out that, on 30 May 1918, after nearly 2,000 hectares of their reserve had been taken for the creation of a Greater Production farm, Indian labour was used at the expense of their own farms. In addition, the agent virtually took over all the Blood's farm machinery at great inconvenience to them. Scott tried to dismiss most of their complaints as being exaggerated, though he did concede that there had been some mismanagement.[66]

Generally speaking, the increased wartime food production had not bettered the Indians' economic conditions. Wartime technological innovations had, in fact, brought about changes in farm machinery that left the Indians further behind in economic development. Adding to the problem, the government failed to expand credit programs to them, thus preventing Indians from purchasing farm equipment to improve their own lands.[67] Initially, Indians benefited little from the Soldier Settlement Act (SSA), passed on 27 July 1917. It allowed veterans to obtain land and farming implements at a low rate of interest.[68] As the influx of immigrants at the turn of the century had taken most of the available Crown land, new land had to be found. W.A. Buchanan, the Member of Parliament from Medicine Hat, suggested during the debate over the bill that "there are lands occupied on lease and used as Indian reserves that would suit this particular purpose."[69] His suggestion was accepted. The revised SSA of 1919 made the following reference to Indian reserve land: "The Board may acquire from His Majesty by purchase, upon terms not inconsistent with those of the release or surrender, any Indian lands which, under the Indian Act, have been validly released or surrendered."[70]

The 1919 act gave veterans—including Indian veterans—who wished to farm an opportunity to obtain Dominion lands or to purchase farms.[71] Indian veterans in western Canada soon learned, however, that the act conflicted with an amendment to the Indian Act of 1906 that stated:

> No Indian or nontreaty Indian resident in the provinces of Manitoba, Saskatchewan, Alberta, or the Territories shall be held capable of having acquired or of acquiring a homestead or preemption right under any Act respecting Dominion lands, to a quarter section . . . in and surveyed or unsurveyed land in the said provinces or territories.[72]

The discrepancy was quickly brought to light when the majority of Indian veterans expressed an interest in farming under the act on their own reserves. Finally, the authorities, on W.M. Graham's suggestion, made arrangements allowing the Indian department to take over the administration of the Soldier Settlement Act for Indian veterans.[73] This led to other complications, as the reserve land could be given for personal use, but not owned by the

veteran. Although the Indian veterans now qualified for loans, a clause in the Indian Act remained
an obstacle to granting them land. Alexander Brass
attempted to avoid the problem by requesting land
outside of his reserve. In a letter to the department,
he stated:

> I hereby make application to leave the reserve
> and relinquish my rights therein. I have been
> living on the Peepeekesis Reserve for eight
> years before enlistment. Over three years I
> was working at the File Hills Indian Agency
> under Inspector Graham and over four years
> I was on a farm in the Colony, and I have the
> last three years served overseas in the Army.
> And I find that I'm not satisfied to resume
> work where I had left off before joining up. I
> wish to be exactly on the same footing as the
> settlers outside of Reserves. In this I have
> every confidence in myself, that I'm capable
> of handling my own affairs.[74]

Brass gained the opportunity to start a farm off the
reserve, and he made a success of it for 15 years, until
the Great Depression. Then, unable to repay his
loan, he was forced to return to his reserve.[75]

On the prairies, only one in ten Indians who
applied was granted a loan from the Soldier Settlement Board. The majority of those receiving them
did quite well. Using the department's list of payments by Indian soldier settlers for 1922 to 1923, it
is evident that of the 23 men documented from the
West, 10 paid off their loans, while 9 made payments
in 1923, leaving only 4 in arrears.[76] If the war did
little for the western Canadian Indians' economic
status, it did improve their political awareness.
Participation in the war had brought Indians from

across Canada into contact with one another and
created closer bonds among them while at the same
time promoting a new feeling of self-worth. Receiving decorations and commendations, and serving
alongside other Canadians, gave many Indians the
confidence to speak for themselves. Reflecting their
new awareness of nationhood, Indian veterans
worked, in 1919 and in the early 1920s, to help form
the League of Indians of Canada, in hopes of improving conditions on the reserves.[77] The league was the
first pan-Indian organization in the country.

Frederick Loft, a Mohawk Indian, drew up the
guiding principles of the league. He had served as
a lieutenant in the Forestry Corps, and had had the
opportunity to talk with many Indians from all over
Canada while in the service. He saw the need for a
national organization through which tribes might
be unified, and opinions on contemporary Indian
matters voiced.[78] The league's constitution recognized the authority of the Crown. It also emphasized
a need for "the perpetuation of the memory of those
who died in the War, and proper provision for their
dependents."[79] Also prominent in the league's objectives was a desire to cooperate with the federal government. Loft became the league's first president.
In September 1919, the league held its first meeting
at Sault Ste. Marie, Ontario, and the second in June
1920 at Elphinstone, Manitoba. A meeting for the
Saskatchewan Indians was held the following year.[80]
After 1922, the organization held its annual meetings in the West because western Canadian Indians
became the most active members.[81]

Scott saw the league as an annoyance and irrita-
tion as well as an impediment to efficient administration. Its proposals stood in direct opposition to
established departmental policy. Initially, the deputy
superintendent general felt that the league would

dissolve if the department refused to cooperate with it. To hasten its demise, Scott directed the agents to avoid all contact with it, and to pressure their wards to refrain from any correspondence with Loft.[82] The growth of the league in Western Canada particularly disturbed Commissioner W.M. Graham. He was concerned about the political implications of the movement, and also the fact that the league's rallies distracted the Indians from their farm work during the summer months.[83]

Although the league did not receive the cooperation it desired, it continued to pressure the federal government for changes to better the Indians' situation. In the area of education, many of its proposals would be achieved, but only two or three decades later. The league did, however, help to achieve the repeal of the federal bill of 1920 that had established compulsory enfranchisement.[84] This was indeed a victory, but in the 1930s the federal government simply reintroduced the clause into the Indian Act.

The league helped to bring Native problems to the forefront since the federal government did so little for Natives and, in particular, the Indian veterans. After the war, Native veterans and their families found that they were excluded from many of the regular war and postwar programs. They continued to be considered as wards of the government and, therefore, the responsibility of the Department of Indian Affairs.

When Scott concluded his essay on the Indians' participation in the Great War, he expressed his belief that the Indians were now "beginning a new era,"[85] and commented:

> The Indians themselves . . . cannot but feel an increased and renewed pride of race and selfrespect that should ensure the recovery of that ancient dignity and independence of spirit that were unfortunately lost to them in some measure through the depletion of the game supply, . . . and the ravages of vices . . . of the white man. The Indians deserve well of Canada, and the end of the war should mark the beginning of a new era for them wherein they shall play an increasingly honourable and useful part in the history of a country that was once the free and open hunting ground of their forefathers.[86]

Scott's statement held out the hope for Indians that changes would be forthcoming; however, these did not materialize. Instead, the Indians were relegated to their prewar status: wards of the federal government and dominated by the Indian Affairs department. It appeared that, in the postwar decade, Indian soldiers were good enough to fight and die for Canada, but they were not "civilized" enough to have the rights of a Canadian citizen.

Notes

1   John C. Ewers, "Primitive American Commandos," *The Masterkey Bi-Monthly* (Los Angeles: The Southwest Museum), 17, no. 4 (July 1943): 118.

2   Diamond Jenness, *Indians of Canada* (1932; repr., Ottawa: National Museum of Canada, 1955), 377–87, 308–26, 382–87.

3   Colin Taylor, *The Warriors of the Plains* (London, UK: Hamlyn Publishing Group, 1975), 38; Diamond Jenness, *The Ojibwa Indians of Parry Island, Their Social and Religious Life* (Ottawa: King's Printer, 1935), 53.

4   F.L. Barron, "A Summary of Federal Indian Policy in the Canadian West, 1867–1984," *Native Studies Review* 1, no. 1 (1984): 28.

5   John Leslie and Ron Maguire, *The Historical Develop-ment of the Indian Act* (Ottawa: Treaties and Historical Research Centre, 1978), 59.

6   Alexander Morris, *The Treaties of Canada with the Indi-ans of Manitoba and the Northwest Territories* (Toronto: Willing and Williamson, 1880), 69.

7   Ibid.

8   L.V. Kelly, *The Range Men* (1913; repr., Toronto: Coles Publishing, 1980), 369.

9   Duncan Campbell Scott, "The Canadian Indians and the Great World War," in *Canada in the Great War*, vol. 3, *Guarding the Channel Ports* (Toronto: United Publishing, 1919), 289. It is also known that there were additional numbers of Native enlistees for which the Department of Indian Affairs was unable to obtain any record.

10 *Macleod Spectator*, 25 November 1915.

11 Ibid.

12 Interview with Laurie Plume at his daughter's home on the Blood reserve on 20 June 1985.

13 Band letter from Blackfoot Indians to Department of Indian Affairs, Ottawa, September 1914, Library and Archives Canada (LAC), RG 10, vol. 6762, file 4522, 2.

14 *Calgary News-Telegram*, 3 October 1914; Form Letter, Sarcee Band Council, to Department of Indian Affairs, September 1914, LAC, RG 10, vol. 6762, file 4522, 2. Many of the other western tribes also contributed early in the war. Piegans – $1600. Form Letter, Piegan Indians, to Department of Indian Affairs, October 1914, LAC, RG 10, vol. 6762, file 4522, 2. Samson's Reserve – $1000. Letter, Hobbema Indian Agent, to J.D. McLean, January 1915, LAC, RG 10, vol. 6762, file 4522, 2. Carlton Agency – $50. Letter, Carlton Indian Agent, to J.D. McLean, February 1915, LAC, RG 10, vol. 6762, file 4522, 2.

15 Band Letter, Blood Council, to Department of Indian Affairs, August 1914, LAC, RG 10, vol. 6762, file 4522, 1; Letter, W.J. Dilworth, Blood Indian Agent, to J.D. McLean, 8 August 1914, LAC, RG 10, vol. 6762, file 4522, 2; and also found in Blood Agency Papers, Glenbow Archives, M1788, box 13, file 98; *Macleod Spectator*, 13 August 1914 and 12 November 1914;

Calgary News-Telegram, 18 May 1915; *Gleichen Call*, 24 June 1915.

16 *Calgary News-Telegram*, 14 August 1914.

17 In addition, at Treaty 3 negotiations, the commis-sioner promised Indians they did not need to fight in foreign wars. See Morris, *Treaties of Canada*, 69.

18 Letter, W.J. Dilworth, Blood Indian Agent, to Jose-phine Y. Cochrane, 12 August 1914, Blood Agency Papers, Glenbow Archives, M1788, box 13, file 98; *Calgary News-Telegram*, 19 August 1914.

19 Letter, J.D. McLean, to Charlie Tucker, Bella Coola Indian Agent, December 1914, LAC, RG 10, vol. 6762, file 452-2, 2; *Calgary News-Telegram*, 19 August 1914.

20 Letter, Eugène Fiset, Surgeon General Deputy Minister Department of Militia and Defence, to J.D. McLean, 9 December 1915, LAC, RG 24, vol. 1221, file HQ593-1-7; Letter, Brigadier General W.E. Hodgins, Acting Adjutant General, to the O.C.'s Divisions and Districts, and the Inspector General of Western Canada, 10 December 1915, LAC, RG 24, vol. 1221, file HQ593-1-7.

21 Scott, "Canadian Indians and the Great World War," 298–99; Marius Barbeau, "Charles A. Cooke, Mohawk Scholar," *Proceedings of the American Philosophical Society* 96, no. 4 (August 1952).

22 Harold Fryer, *Alberta, The Pioneer Years* (Langley, BC: Stagecoach Publishing, 1977), 89–90.

23 Ibid., LAC, RG 24, vol. 1221, file HQ593-1-7, mem-orandum, Lt. Maxwell Graham to Lt. Col. P.G.C. Campbell, 30 November 1916.

24 Memorandum, Lt. Maxwell Graham, to Lt. Col. P.G.C. Campbell, 4 December 1916, LAC, RG 24, vol. 1221, file HQ593-1-7.

25 *Lethbridge Daily Herald*, 15 July 1916.

26 Form Letter, J.D. McLean, to agents of Blackfoot, Blood, Sarcee, Peigan, and Stony bands, 10 December 1914, LAC, RG 10, vol. 6762, file 452-2, 1.

27 Letter, W.J. Dilworth, to J.D. McLean, 21 December 1914, Blood Agency Papers, Glenbow Archives, M1788, box 13, file 98. However, in July of 1915, Campbell did receive authorization to raise men for a corps of guides. *Calgary News-Telegram*, 20 July 1915.

28 Hugh A. Dempsey, *Red Crow, Warrior Chief* (Saskatoon: Western Producer Prairie Books, 1980), 152–53.

29 Form Letter, J.D. McLean, to agents of Blackfoot, Blood, Sarcee, Peigan, and Stony bands, 10 December 1914; Letter, J.D. McLean, to W.J. Dilworth, Blood Indian Agent, 10 December 1914, Blood Agency Papers, Glenbow Archives, M1788, box 13, file 98.

30 Letter, W.J. Dilworth, to Lt. Col. Bryan, O.C. 191st Btn, 19 February 1917, Blood Agency Papers, Glenbow Archives, M1788, box 16, file 121; Letter, James McDonald, Griswold Indian Agent, to D.C. Scott, 24 April 1917, LAC, RG 10, vol. 6771, file 45235, pt. 1.

31 Edward Ahenakew, *Voices of the Plains Cree* (Toronto: McClelland and Stewart, 1973), 120.

32 Night Lettergram, D.C. Scott, to J.H. Gooderham, 30 January 1917, LAC, RG 10, vol. 6766, file 45213.

33 *Calgary Herald*, 26 January 1917.

34 Letter, D.C. Scott, to Chiefs Iron Shield and Yellow Horse, 8 March 1917, LAC, RG 10, vol. 6767, file 45215, pt. 1.

35 Scott, "Canadian Indians and the Great World War," 318.

36 Ibid., 324.

37 LAC, RG 10, vol. 6768, file 452-20, pt. 1, letter, T.H. Carter, Fisher River Indian Agent, to J.D. McLean, 3 January 1918: file 452-2, 2, letter, Rev. Canon H.W. Gibbon Stocken to D.C. Scott, April 1916.

38 Notes on Registration, LAC, RG 10, vol. 6770, file 45226, pt. 1.

39 Ibid.

40 Ibid.

41 Letter, J.D. McLean, to Charles S. King, 1 February 1917, LAC, RG 10, vol. 6766, file 452-12.

42 Letter, W.J. Dilworth, to J.M. Carson, Registrar, Military Service Act, 5 September 1918, Blood Agency Papers, Glenbow Archives, M1788, box 16, file 121. In Dilworth's November 1917 report he noted that 8 Bloods reported for service, 21 claimed exemption, 15 were unreported, and 3 were in the United States. Letter, W.J. Dilworth to D.C. Scott, 16 November 1917, Blood Agency Papers, Glenbow Archives, M1788, box 16, file 121.

43 Letter, William Gordon, Acting Indian Agent Sarcee Agency, to D.C. Scott, 16 December 1917, LAC, RG 10, vol. 6768, file 452-20, pt. 1.

44 Letter, Capt. D.A.A.G., Secretary, Military Service Sub-Committee, to Ex-Chief Cornelius Logan, 26 February 1918, LAC, RG 24, vol. 6566, file HQ10643034, vol.1.

45 Letter, G.D. Robertson, Chairman Canada Registration Board, to D.C. Scott, 9 May 1918, LAC, RG 10, vol. 6770, file 452-26, pt. 1; Letter, G.D. Robertson, Chairman Canada Registration Board, to J.D. McLean, 27 May 1918, LAC, RG 10, vol. 6770, file 452-26, pt. 1.

46 Scott, "Canadian Indians and the Great World War," 289–90.

47 Letter, Mark Steinhauer, to D.C. Scott, 7 August 1916, LAC, RG 10, vol. 6767, file 452-15, pt. 1.

48 Letter, J.D. McLean, to Thomas Deasy, 8 September 1922, LAC, RG 10, vol. 3181, file 452, 124-1A.

49 Canadian Soldiers Active Military Services Act, 1916, s. 1.

50 Memorandum, General Returning Officer for Canada, to D.C. Scott, 13 December 1917, LAC, RG 10, vol. 6770, file 452-24. The government document can be found in Privy Council 5277, 27 November 1917.

51 Fred Gaffen, *Forgotten Soldiers* (Penticton, BC: Theytus Books, 1985), 31.

52 W. Everard Edmonds, "Canada's Red Army," *Canadian Magazine of Politics, Science, Art and Literature* 54, no. 4 (February 1921): 341–42.

53 Hana Samek, "Great Father and Great Mother: US and Canadian Indian Policy and the Blackfeet Confederation, 1880–1920" (PhD diss., University of New Mexico, 1985), 371–72; S.D. Grant, "Indian Affairs under Duncan Campbell Scott: The Plains Cree of Saskatchewan, 1913–1931," *Journal of Canadian Studies* 8, no. 3 (Fall 1983): 34.

54 Ahenakew, *Voices of the Plains Cree*, 122.

55 E. Brian Titley, *A Narrow Vision: Duncan Campbell Scott and the Administration of Indian Affairs in Canada* (Vancouver: UBC Press, 1986), 39.

56 Circular, D.C. Scott, to Agents, 14 September 1916, File Hills and Qu'Appelle Agency, General

Correspondence and Circulars, 1909–1922, LAC, RG 10, vol. 392.

57 Titley, *A Narrow Vision*, 29–30; John L. Taylor, *Canadian Indian Policy during the Inter-War Years* (Ottawa: Indian and Northern Affairs, Queen's Printer, 1984), 16–17.

58 Privy Council Order-in-Council 393, 16 February 1918.

59 Canada, *House of Commons Debates*, 1918, vol. 2 (Ottawa: King's Printer, 23 April 1918), 1049–50.

60 E. Brian Titley, "William Morris Graham: Indian Agent Extraordinaire," *Prairie Forum* 8, no. 1 (Spring 1983): 30; Titley, *A Narrow Vision*, 41–42; Taylor, *Canadian Indian Policy*, 17.

61 Titley, "William Morris Graham," 30.

62 Titley, *A Narrow Vision*, 41; Taylor, *Canadian Indian Policy*, 19.

63 Titley, "William Morris Graham," 31.

64 Titley, *A Narrow Vision*, 42–43, and Titley, "William Morris Graham," 30.

Summary of Receipts and Expenditures
Rez: Greater Production Farms, 23 March 1921

Amount advanced from war appropriation	$362,000.00
Revenue from sales as of 28 February 1921	$576,192.07
Total	$938,192.07
Expenditure	$826,838.93
Balance on hand	$111,353.13

65 Scott, "Canadian Indians and the Great World War," 326–27.

66 Titley, *A Narrow Vision*, 41–42; and L. James Dempsey, *Warriors of the King: Prairie Indians in World War I* (Regina: Canadian Plains Research Centre, 1999), 5–7.

67 Michael L. Tate, "From Scout to Doughboy: The National Debate over Integrating American Indians into the Military, 1891–1918," *Western Historical Quarterly* 17, no. 4 (October 1986): 434.

68 Glenn Wright, "Rifles to Ploughshares: Veterans and Land Settlement in Western Canada, 1917–1930" (paper presented to the Canadian Historical Association, June 1982), 8.

69 Taylor, *Canadian Indian Policy*, 28.

70 The Canadian Soldier Settlement Act, 1919, Section 10.

71 Taylor, *Canadian Indian Policy*, 34.

72 Revised Statutes of Canada, 1906, Clause 81, s. 164.

73 Letter, J.D. McLean, to James McDonald, Griswold Indian Agent, 28 March 1919, LAC, RG 10, vol. 7524, file 25, 102-1; Department of Indian Affairs Form Letter, to agents, 6 May 1919, Blood Agency Papers, Glenbow Archives, M1788, box 14, file 120. This document includes the conditions whereby an Indian veteran would be granted a loan.

74 Letter, Alexander Brass, to DIA, no date, LAC, RG 10, vol. 7524, file 25, 111-2, pt.1.

75 Letter, W.M. Graham, Indian Commissioner, to J.D. McLean, 19 January 1923, LAC, RG 10, vol. 7525, file 25, 111-6, pt. 1; Letter, G.A. Dodds, File Hills Indian Agent, to Secretary, Dept. of Mines and Resources, Indian Affairs Branch, 27 July 1938, LAC, RG 10, vol. 7524, file 25, 111-2, pt. 1.

76 Letter, D.C. Scott, to W.M. Graham, Indian Commissioner, 25 April 1923, LAC, RG 10, vol. 7484, file 25,000-101, pt. 1; Letter, D.C. Scott, to W.M. Graham, 5 February 1924, LAC, RG 10, vol. 7484, file 25,000-101, pt. 1.

77 Grant, "Indian Affairs under Duncan Campbell Scott," 34; Titley, *A Narrow Vision*, 101.

78 Grant, "Indian Affairs under Duncan Campbell Scott," 123.

79 Edmonds, "Canada's Red Army," 341.

80 Ahenakew, *Voices of the Plains Cree*, 124.

81 Titley, *A Narrow Vision*, 106.

82 Ibid., 104.

83 Ibid., 107.

84 *Calgary Albertan*, 26 June 1922.

85 Scott, "The Canadian Indians and the Great World War," 327–28.

86 Ibid.

Works Cited

PRIMARY SOURCES

Calgary Albertan
Calgary Herald
Calgary News-Telegram
Edmonton Bulletin
Gleichen Call
Lethbridge Daily Herald
Macleod Spectator
Saskatchewan Herald

Glenbow Archives, Calgary. Battleford Indian Agency Papers, 1904–1935, M1781, box 7, file 39.
———. Blood Agency Papers, M1788, box 13, file 98; box 14.
———. Graham, William Morris. Untitled, manuscript, ca. 1935.
Government of Canada. *Annual Report of the Department of Indian Affairs, 1914.*
———. Official Report of the Debates of the House of Commons of the Dominion of Canada, 6th Session, 12th Parliament, 4 May 1916.
———. "Report of the Indian Branch of the Department of the Secretary of State for the Provinces, 1871." Canada, *Sessional Papers*, no. 23, 1871, 4.
———. *Statutes of Canada* (31 Vic., cap. 42), 22 May 1868, 91–100.
Library and Archives Canada. RG 10, vol. 1392.
———. RG 10, vol. 3181, file 452.
———. RG 10, vol. 6762, file 452.
———. RG 10, vol. 6767, file 452, 453.
———. RG 10, vol. 6768, file 452.
———. RG 10, vol. 6770, file 452.
———. RG 10, vol. 6771, file 452.
———. RG 10, vol. 6786, file 452.
———. RG 10, vol. 7484, file 25.
———. RG 10, vol. 7524, file 25.
———. RG 10, vol. 7525, file 25.
———. RG 10, vol. 7527, file 25.
———. RG 24, vol. 1221, file HQ593.
———. RG 24, vol. 6566, file HQ1643034, HQ10643034.

SECONDARY SOURCES

Ahenakew, Edward. *Voices of the Plains Cree*. Toronto: McClelland and Stewart, 1973.
Barbeau, Marius. "Charles A. Cooke, Mohawk Scholar." *Proceedings of the American Philosophical Society* 96, no. 4 (August 1952).
Barron, F.L. "A Summary of Federal Indian Policy in the Canadian West, 1867–1984." *Native Studies Review* 1, no. 1 (1984): 28–39.
Dempsey, Hugh A. *Charcoal's World*. Saskatoon: Western Producer Prairie Books, 1978.
———. *Crowfoot, Chief of the Blackfeet*. Norman: University of Oklahoma Press, 1972.
———. "In the War the Indian Excelled But Peace Restored His Despair." In *Alberta in the 20th Century*. Vol. 4, *The Great War and Its Consequences, 1914–1920*, edited by Ted Byfield. Edmonton: United Western Communications, 1994.
———. *Red Crow, Warrior Chief*. Saskatoon: Western Producer Prairie Books, 1980.
Dempsey, L. James. "The Indians and World War One." *Alberta History* 31, no. 3 (1983): 1–8.
———. "Problems of Western Canadian Indian War Veterans after World War One." *Native Studies Review* 5, no. 2 (1989): 1–18.
———. *Warriors of the King: Prairie Indians in World War I*. Regina: Canadian Plains Research Centre, University of Regina, 1999.
———. "A Warrior's Robe." *Alberta History* 51, no. 4 (2003): 18–22.
Edmonds, W. Everard. "Canada's Red Army." *Canadian Magazine of Politics, Science, Art and Literature* 54, no. 4 (February 1921): 341–42.
Ewers, John C. "Primitive American Commandos." *The Masterkey Bi-Monthly* (Los Angeles, The Southwest Museum) 17, no. 4 (July 1943).
Forsberg, Roberta J. *Chief Mountain, The Story of Canon Middleton*. Whittier, CA: 1964.
Fryer, Harold. *Alberta, The Pioneer Years*. Langley, BC: Stagecoach Publishing Co. Ltd., 1977.

Gaffen, Fred. *Forgotten Soldiers*. Penticton, BC: Theytus Books Ltd., 1985.

Government of Canada. *Canadian Forces and Aboriginal Peoples (Les Forces canadiennes et les Peoples autochtones)*. Ottawa: Department of National Defence, 2003.

Graham, W. Roger. "Through the First War." In *The Canadians*, edited by J.M.S. Careless and R.C. Brown. Toronto: Macmillan, 1967.

Grant, S.D. "Indian Affairs under Duncan Campbell Scott: The Plains Cree of Saskatchewan, 1913–1931." *Journal of Canadian Studies* 8, no. 3 (Fall 1983): 21–39.

Hopkins, J. Castell. *The Canadian Annual Review: 1915*. Toronto: The Annual Review Publishing Co. Ltd.,1916.

Jenness, Diamond. *Indians of Canada*. Ottawa: National Museum of Canada, 1955. First published 1932.

———. *The Ojibwa Indians of Parry Island, Their Social and Religious Life*. Ottawa: King's Printer, 1935.

Kelly, L.V. *The Range Men*. Toronto: Coles Publishing Co. Ltd., 1980. First published 1913.

Kidd, Bruce. *Tom Longboat*. Don Mills, ON: Fitzhenry & Whiteside, 1980.

Lacendre, Barney. *The Bushman and the Spirits*. Boston and London: Horizon House Books, 1979.

Leslie, John, and Ron Maguire. *The Historical Development of the Indian Act*. Ottawa: Treaties and Historical Research Centre, 1978.

Littlechild, Wilton. "Tom Longboat: Canada's Outstanding Indian Athlete." MA thesis, University of Alberta, 1975.

McNaught, Kenneth. *The Pelican History of Canada*. Markham, ON: Penguin Books Canada, 1982.

Miller, James A. "The Alberta Press and the Conscription Issue in the First World War, 1914–1918." MA thesis, University of Alberta, 1974.

Morris, Alexander. *The Treaties of Canada with the Indians of Manitoba and the Northwest Territories*. Toronto: Willing and Williamson, 1880.

Samek, Hana. "Great Father and Great Mother: US and Canadian Indian Policy and the Blackfeet Confederation, 1880–1920." PhD diss., University of New Mexico, 1985.

Scott, Duncan Campbell. "The Canadian Indians and the Great World War." In *Canada in the Great War*. Vol. 3, *Guarding the Channel Ports*. Toronto: United Publishing of Canada Ltd., 1919.

Tate, Michael L. "From Scout to Doughboy: The National Debate over Integrating American Indians into the Military, 1891–1918." *The Western Historical Quarterly* 17, no. 4 (October 1986): 417–37.

Taylor, Colin. *The Warriors of the Plains*. London, UK: Hamlyn Publishing Group Ltd., 1975.

Thompson, John Herd. *The Harvests of War: The Prairie West, 1914–1918*. Toronto: McClelland and Stewart, 1983.

Titley, E. Brian. *A Narrow Vision: Duncan Campbell Scott and the Administration of Indian Affairs in Canada*. Vancouver: UBC Press, 1986.

———. "William Morris Graham: Indian Agent Extraordinaire." *Prairie Forum* 8, no. 1 (Spring 1983): 25–41.

Woodsworth, James S. *Strangers within Our Gates*. Toronto: F.C. Stephenson, Methodist Mission Rooms, 1909.

Wright, Glen T. "Rifles to Ploughshares: Veterans and Land Settlement in Western Canada, 1917–1930." Paper presented to the Canadian Historical Association, June 1982.

Zdunich, Darlene J. "Tuberculosis and the Canadian Veterans of World War One." MA thesis, University of Calgary, 1984.

Scattered by the Whirlwind:
Alberta Chaplains and the Great War

DUFF CRERAR

"Look here, Ball, you cut out this business about me being a miserable sinner," admonished the Colonel, "In the first place, it isn't true. In the second place, it is bad for discipline." —Lt. Col. W.A. Griesbach to Capt. the Rev. W.A.R. Ball, 49th Battalion, after an evangelistic service[1]

Clergy were not that thick on the ground in 1914 Alberta; yet, to the dismay of bishops, church presidents, moderators, and mission boards, many barely hesitated before joining the ranks and heading off to war. By mid-1916, dozens of clergy (ministers, priests, and even more theological students and probationers) left their church posts for military service, especially from denominations underrepresented in the Canadian Expeditionary Force. Home missionary and pastoral work was put on hold, or moved forward at a snail's pace, until the war was won. Most expected to return after the war, take up their vocations, and turn the lessons of the war—service, sacrifice, comradeship, and devotion to the highest causes—into an idealistic wave of Christian social reform. Once overseas, however, it became clear, both to soldiers and padres, that getting home to Alberta in one piece, or even at all, was far from certain. Most of Alberta's padres would never see the province again.[2]

Getting a chaplaincy was far from easy, as only a few units recruited in Alberta served at the front, while the rest were usually broken up to feed the unceasing demand for men. Despite glib promises and much political wrangling, most Alberta chaplains felt betrayed when the men of their unit disappeared into reserve battalions, and the unit's officers, including chaplains, were declared surplus and forced to accept reduction in rank or even to return home. A few, heeding home-country loyalties, sailed directly to Britain and joined the British Army, while others enlisted in the ranks as stretcher bearers, infantry privates, or junior officers. Throughout the war, seminary students and Methodist probationers provided a trickle of emergency chaplains from the ranks, which the Chaplain Service could call on for reinforcements.[3] Refused a chaplaincy in Calgary, Catholic missionary Adrian Beausoleil joined the French military as a soldier-priest (the French Army conscripted clergy, posting many to ambulance or

Chaplain (earnestly): "Believe me, comrades, hell is paved with Scotch whisky and ballet girls."
Irrepressible Canuck: "Oh death, *where* is thy sting?"

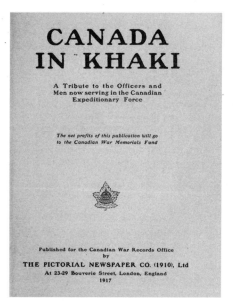

(left) A cartoon appearing in the booklet *Canada in Khaki* pokes fun at the tension between chaplains and soldiers with respect to temperance; (right) *Canada in Khaki*, in which the cartoon appears, was published as a tribute to the men who served.

combat units). Only at the end of the war would he don the Canadian chaplain's uniform, wearing the *Croix de Guerre* for his services to France.[4]

More often than not, a battalion from Alberta in any of the five Canadian divisions eventually formed did not have an Albertan padre.[5] Calgary's 10th Battalion sailed with Honorary Captain the Rev. W.H. Emsley, a Methodist clergyman from Ontario, as its chaplain, while Albertans in the 5th learned that their new padre was Anglican B.L. Whitaker from British Columbia. Thomas Bruce, a Trinity College graduate from Bowmanville, Ontario, was appointed to Edmonton's 9th Battalion, while others jockeyed for posts in the 2nd Division. Some found their way over in the 3rd Division, as did the 49th Battalion's Canon W.R. Ball from Edmonton, and the 51st somehow was given two chaplains, Father Iver Daniel,

an Oblate priest, and W.A. Carroll from the Calgary Salvation Army unit. Minister of Militia Sam Hughes (as usual, ignoring warnings) had decided to make the still-controversial evangelical organization an official Christian denomination in his army, and appoint its officers as chaplains. Carroll's appointment was controversial but beneficial to the troops, and his ministry as chaplain and social service worker to the troops gained him admission to the Order of the British Empire.[6] Edmonton's leading Baptist minister, John Campbell Bowen, a close friend of former Alberta premier and fellow Baptist A.C. Rutherford, joined the 63rd Battalion, though only about 60 of the troops were of his own denomination.

Severed from their units overseas, Alberta padres who stayed on were fitted into posts in the growing number of support units and hospitals spread across

England, and in the rear areas of France. From these posts many made their way to the front, as casualties pared away those with more seniority at the Corps. Thus William H. Davis, Anglican curate of St. Peter's church, Bonnie Doon, Edmonton, ended up with the 4th Canadian Mounted Rifles, a central Ontario unit. Thomas Augustine Wilson, a Methodist militia chaplain to the 35th Central Alberta Horse of Red Deer, reached England only to serve with other Canadian Mounted Rifles (CMR) units, while Webster Fanning-Harris, another Red Deer cleric, ended up serving with the 6th Brigade.[7] Other Alberta units were often ministered to by non-Albertans: Calgary's 31st Battalion mobilized with W.R. Walker as padre in Calgary, but its initial chaplain was Edward Appleyard, from outside the province, who won a Military Cross while with the battalion.

Alberta's Anglican clergy bore the brunt of the fatal casualties to the Canadian Chaplain Service. Webster Fanning-Harris from St. Luke's, Red Deer, eventually was posted to the 2nd Division serving with the 6th Brigade during the Battle of the Somme.

Grave of Reverend Webster Fanning-Harris, the first Canadian chaplain to be killed while on active service, 1917. Red Deer Archives, P5409.

On 25 September 1916 he was conducting a burial service when shrapnel severed his spine just above the waist. Surgeons in England confirmed that Harris was beyond treatment. His wife came from

Hon. Captain Reverend William Henry Davis MC. Born in King's County (now County Offaly), Ireland, in January 1883, William was a "Clerk in Holy Orders" with the Church of England at the time of his attestation into the 138th (Edmonton) Battalion, in Edmonton, in March 1916. Library Archives Canada, PA-002376.

Canada to sit by his bedside while his condition deteriorated. Three weeks after the Battle of Vimy Ridge, the end came. Anglicans in both Red Deer and Stettler mourned his passing. It seemed such a short time ago that he had resigned his parish, said his goodbyes, and gone to the war. [8]

William Davis soon achieved an admirable reputation at the front. During the battle of Vimy Ridge, he rescued wounded men and buried the dead while under fire. At Passchendaele, waving a Red Cross flag, he took out a large party of stretcher bearers to search for wounded in No Man's Land. His initiative may have triggered a spontaneous truce, for the Germans ceased firing and began to retrieve their own wounded. For his part in this strange interlude, Davis was awarded the Military Cross.[9] Davis embodied the athletic, cheerful courage that Sam Hughes and the Canadian public expected of chaplains. Whether good-naturedly playing cat-and-mouse games with officers trying (mostly in vain) to confiscate their pornographic prints, or kindly guiding them through dark days of heavy casualties, Davis was ready to cross sacrosanct boundaries to help his men. After a failed hunt-the-blasphemous-book game, Lieutenant Gregory Clarke found a rosary in Davis's tunic. As most of the officers were Ontario Orangemen, Davis's defence was that he kept it to assist his Catholic men who were dying without a priest. In fact, the brigade Catholic chaplain had provided him with the rosary. Six weeks later, at the Battle of Amiens, he was directing stretcher bearers going forward from the hospital at Le Quesnel when a shell killed him. He had just turned down his bishop's request to return to Edmonton so that he could stay with his men. Davis was buried in the communal cemetery at Le Quesnel by his brother officers. Clarke (previously coached by Davis on how to bury his own men when the padre was away) personally supervised the burial party; he made sure the crucifix was buried with him.[10]

Davis's heroism is well documented. S.G. Bennett, writing in the *4th CMR History*, published in 1926, commented of Davis at Vimy Ridge: "The first glimpse they had of their beloved Padre in action was seeing him in the twilight on the crest of the Ridge, his steel helmet hung over his arm, prayerbook in hand, burying the dead, regardless of shells dropping around him." Of the action around Lens in July 1917, Bennett wrote: "There were eighteen other casualties during this tour. Captain Davis, the Chaplain, was with the men as usual, in the front line, doing everything he could for their comfort. For three days he worked with a party of ten men, giving Christian burial to the dead who had been left unburied in the area; his courage and scorn of danger endeared him to all who knew him." Davis is also mentioned in the "Narrative of Events of the Action of October 26th, 1917," where it says of his actions at Passchendaele: "Scattered shelling and harassing fire persisted throughout the day and night but through the splendid efforts of the Battalion Chaplain, Capt. W.H. Davis, and the Stretcher Bearers, our ground was cleared of the wounded." And, finally, concerning his loss on 9 August 1918, in the taking of Le Quesnel and Folies, it was written:

> Every officer and man mourned for their beloved Padre. He came from Western Canada but he had retained his Irish heart and Celtic charm. If he knew what fear was he never showed it. His remarkable disregard for danger while carrying out what he considered his duty, became a regimental tradition. In the daily life of the Battalion, in billets or in

trenches he was always thinking of the men's welfare. On this day as on former occasions he was preparing to carry out his practical mission of mercy and was gathering around him his little band of stretcher-bearers when he and one of his men were hit by a shell. No officer was more loved for his character or more admired for his bravery than Padre Davis.[11]

The career of Parkland's circuit-riding probationer Sidney Lambert changed the lives of veterans, and eventually all Canadian amputees. He joined Calgary's 50th Battalion and served in the ranks. He was cut down by a shell in August 1916, and his left leg was amputated. In 1918, after receiving an artificial limb, Lambert was granted special ordination by the Methodist Church and joined the Canadian Chaplain Service. After the war, Lambert worked to support soldier amputees readjusting to civilian life. He served at Whitby Dominion Orthopedic Hospital, and helped to establish the Toronto Military Orthopaedic Hospital in 1919 (in 1936 it was renamed the Christie Street Veterans' Hospital). Lambert continued his service into the Second World War, assisting in the building of a new facility opened in 1948 as the Sunnybrook Hospital.[12] During his own struggles to find a proper-fitting prosthesis, he found a new calling as leader of the Toronto Amputees Association. Lambert eventually became the first president of the War Amputations of Canada. He served as chaplain to the Vimy Pilgrimage in 1936; initiated the famous key tag program to fund rehabilitation work; extended the association's outreach to children; and was principal mentor to the late Cliff Chadderton, the Second World War amputee who led the War Amps of Canada after Lambert's retirement.

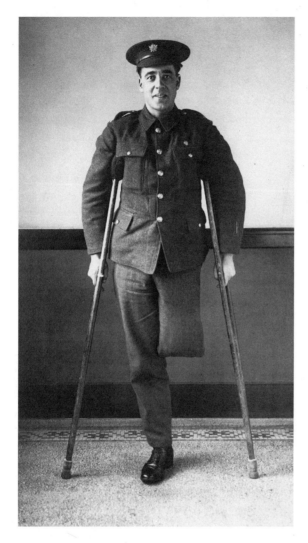

Reverend Sydney Lambert, Parkland, Alberta, 1918, Before the war, Reverend Lambert served as a probationary Methodist minister in Parkland. He joined the army in 1915, was wounded in action, and lost a leg. In Canada, he became a Lieutenant Colonel and served as chaplain at the Toronto Christie Street Hospital for wounded veterans, and was president of the War Amputee Association of Canada for 39 years. Glenbow Archives, NA-3535-162.

Famous for his sympathy with the bereaved, Lambert was also remembered by many veterans for his un-Methodist toleration of moderate drinking, quietly pouring a tot for those who needed a pick-me-up when life on the wards became unbearable.[13]

While most of Alberta's padres came late to the war and served primarily in support units until its latter days, Robert Thompson, a Presbyterian, became another "fighting padre." A missionary from Toronto's Knox College, he left the Peace Country region of Alberta in November 1914 and served with the 2nd Division Artillery. As chaplain to the 4th Brigade, Canadian Field Artillery, he saw the worst of the ugly conditions and bitter fighting that consumed many of the men he came over with. Chaplains often censored mail going back home as one of their duties, but that also provided a way to know soldiers. Many times Thompson wrote letters of condolence to families, breaking the news that their son, husband, brother, or father had been killed. One of the hardest was for Bombardier Ross Taylor, a divinity student from Victoria University (University of Toronto), who was killed while manning an observation post in Flanders. Thompson confided: "It was the hardest thing I have had to do since I have been in France, because I have known Ross so well ... Your boy like many another has given up his life for his friends."[14] Awarded a Military Cross for intrepid service under fire, Thompson also teamed up with Padre Davis when casualties were high. At Passchendaele, Davis found Thompson bandaged in a medical post behind the Canadian Mounted Rifles, temporarily blinded by mustard gas. Turning down two promotions in order to stay with his gunners, he left behind a reputation for courageous service, and a soldier's blunt contempt for those who sheltered themselves behind rank or curried favour with higher officers.

Though Thompson was somewhat contrary and shy of taking responsibility, Honorary Colonel the Reverend John Almond, director of the Canadian Chaplain Service, and Almond's staff respected Thompson and gave him the highest possible rating on his Confidential Report before he left the service. Later, however, when Ottawa asked him to return to work with restless veterans arriving home, Thompson promptly refused. He had taken a parish, was looking after his mother, and had gotten engaged. "I have had enough of chaplains' work," he wrote. During the Depression years, he became executive director of the Canadian National Institute for the Blind and welfare officer for the city of Toronto. During the Second World War, he led national veteran rehabilitation work through the Department of Labour and received membership in the Order of the British Empire for his contributions to veteran welfare.[15] Alberta's chaplain legacy meant that amputees of the Second World War would leave Padre Lambert's hospital (Toronto Military Orthopaedic, later, Sunnybrook) for retraining and rehabilitation with staff led by Thompson, a chaplain who, because of his own experience, had profound empathy for the blind.

Alberta's sole Baptist chaplain enjoyed, if such a word can be used of his postwar career, the most controversial public life of all the padres. John Campbell Bowen had gone from his Strathcona Baptist parish to serve overseas, where his strong character and ethical rigidity sometimes intimidated colleagues as well as the troops. Back in Canada, with a pragmatic and reforming nature that was strengthened by his war experiences, Bowen entered municipal politics. He served as an Edmonton alderman until 1921, after which he ran successfully to become a Liberal member of the Legislative Assembly of Alberta. In 1926 he became leader of the Alberta Liberal Party, leading the official opposition for a tumultuous year. Appointed lieutenant governor of the province (1937–1950), he ran afoul of the unbending Premier William Aberhart. Bowen refused to grant Royal Assent to the premier's legislation that would have had the provincial government take over banks and force newspapers to reveal confidential informants. A defender of liberty of the press, Bowen had no use for measures intended to force Alberta's newspapers to publish government propaganda either. The Social Credit government retaliated by cutting his budget, staff, and car allowance. This prompted Bowen to threaten to dismiss the Aberhart government in 1938, which would have been an extreme use of his reserve powers. Fortunately for him, if not for Premier Aberhart, the Supreme Court of Canada and the Judicial Committee of the Privy Council declared the laws unconstitutional.[16]

Counting the costs of the war for the Church in Alberta led to a solemn reckoning. By 1918, according to G.R. Stevens, 17 young Anglican clergy from the Edmonton area had volunteered, but only seven survived the war.[17] Ball had been crippled by shellfire with the 49th, and eventually retired in England.[18] Christopher Carruthers, already weakened by arthritis from militia days at Red Deer, came back almost crippled from his time overseas. Walter Fisher demobilized in England to care for ailing parents. Calgary's William Walker served bravely under fire, but in 1918 his supervisor had him admitted to the Canadian Convalescent Hospital in Matlock, Bath, for "nervous debility and insomnia."[19] Harold Shore, a Calgary Anglican priest, survived the hazards of 1917 at the front, but his time overseas was ended brutally by enemy shelling in 1918. He got back to Canada, on crutches, the day before the war ended.[20]

Banff's Ralph Harrison had similar hair-raising escapes in 1917, but demobilized in England where he completed correspondence courses through the Khaki University managed by Canada's YMCA.[21] Methodists such as R.J. Irwin, one of several who received special ordination and promotion from the ranks to the chaplaincy overseas, demobilized in Toronto, while Alexander Farrell needed a long vacation with his family before returning to play a leading role in the formation of the United Church of Canada.[22] One Methodist chaplain would never again minister in any capacity if the Alberta Conference had any say about it; he was deposed by the church for financial misdeeds and sent home in disgrace by the Chaplain Service.[23] John Watts, a Presbyterian academic ordained and taken on as a chaplain from the ranks, went on to a brilliant career as a popular professor at Queen's University in Ontario, while Coleman Presbyterian David Marshall demobilized in Guelph, Ontario.[24] The intrepid Father Beausoleil returned to his parish in High River, but a year later departed for another district.[25] The padres who had left Alberta rarely found their way back. Their experiences and influence with veterans were lost to the province.

Among the few clergy who returned, one became well known for his work between the wars. Father Archibald MacDonald, from Calgary, worked with Belgian refugees and investigated war crimes while with his troops in occupation. He also composed a guide on Vatican social teachings intended for Catholic social services in postwar Canada. Back home, he took over Catholic work at Sarcee Camp in Calgary, finding that returned men confided more openly to him than to civilian clerics. While overseas, he loudly opposed soldiers marrying British women who, he claimed, were only after their pay and postwar benefits but, in Calgary, he was widely known for his kindness, whether explaining a case of infidelity (or even bigamy) to bewildered wives and mothers-in-law, or getting a crippled officer addicted to cocaine into hospital while finding a home for the bankrupt family. Though forced to give up his uniform and military career in 1921 when the Chaplain Service was disbanded, MacDonald remained well known in Calgary as a soldier's friend.[26]

Although only 28 clergymen from Alberta became military chaplains (a small but respectable number for a young province), they paid a proportionately higher price for their enthusiasm. Harris and Davis were two of the four Canadian padres killed by enemy action, and several more Alberta padres who were wounded or burned out by arduous service never returned. Among those wounded were some who paved the way for better care for their own comrades and veterans yet to come, though living in Toronto or Ottawa, not Edmonton or Calgary. Other ex-padres would settle in the province helping the crippled, bereaved, and traumatized while nursing their own well-hidden wounds. Though the war had taken much, much still remained that was worth fighting for in a young and growing province. After all they had seen and done, the padres offered the same gifts they had during the conflict: encouragement and hope.

Notes

1   G.R. Stevens, *A City Goes to War* (Brampton, ON: Charters, 1964), 165.

2   In the fall of 1914, the Anglican Bishops of Calgary and Edmonton announced (in vain) that they would not permit very many clergy to abandon the real work of

the church to go to war. See *Canadian Churchman*, 8 and 17 September and 8 October 1914. According to G.R. Stevens, of 17 Anglican curates who had come as missionaries in 1910, all signed up, but only 7 survived the war, *City Goes to War*, 15.

3 One Anglican cleric, B.W. Pullinger, set out from Saskatoon to recruit a company of seminarians and probationers for the Princess Patricia's Canadian Light Infantry, and later served as a padre overseas. See *Canadian Churchman*, 24 June 1915.

4 LAC, RG9 IIIC15, CEF Chaplain Service Records (hereafter CCS Records), vols. 4617–4618, Beausoleil files.

5 As in the rest of English-speaking Canada, Anglican priests (six from the Diocese of Edmonton and seven from Calgary) made up the largest number of Albertan padres; many of them were newly arrived as missionaries. Two Roman Catholics, one French-speaking, were joined by seven Presbyterians from the Presbyteries of High River, Edmonton, and Calgary, and one Baptist from the Western Baptist Union. Despite their crusading zeal, the Methodists were permitted only four from the Alberta Conference. As with other young missions across the country, church leaders were both proud and perplexed by such clerical patriotism. None could be spared from mission work in the many isolated and virtually leaderless fields, especially to go rushing off after soldier souls in France and Flanders. A bishop or two made it clear that they were not impressed that home missions, where "the real work of the church" remained to be done, would languish, but they could hardly resist the argument that their churches would suffer public disapproval if the clergy did not play a leading role in the Dominion's greatest *rite de passage*.

6 Horace Singer, *History of the 31st Canadian Infantry Battalion CEF*, edited by Darrell Knight (Calgary: Detselig, 2006), 31, 198, 219, 281, 442.

7 *Red Deer News*, 12 January and 23 February 1916.

8 LAC, CCS Records, vol. 4626, Webster Henry Fanning-Harris file.

9 Gregory Clarke, "The Little Armistice," *The Legionary*, 1937, 17. See also LAC, CCS Records, vol. 4620, W.H. Davis file.

10 S.G. Bennett, *The 4th Canadian Mounted Rifles, 1914–1919* (Toronto: Murray, 1926), 123, also 85–86, 122–23. See also *Edmonton Bulletin*, 19 and 20 August 1918; Gregory Clarke, *A Bar'l of Apples* (Toronto: McGraw-Hill Ryerson, 1971), 162–63.

11 4th Canadian Mounted Rifles website, entry on Hon. Captain Rev. William Davis MC, URL: http://www.4cmr.com/daviswh.htm, retrieved 15 May 2014.

12 Victor Wheeler, *The 50th Battalion in No Man's Land* (Calgary: Alberta Historical Resources Foundation, 1980), 25, 53–69, 77.

13 Clifford Chadderton, in *The Fragment*, Summer 1971, 3–19. See also LAC, CCS Records, vol. 4630, Sidney E. Lambert file.

14 Western University, London, ON, Fred Landon Regional Archives, Letters of Bombardier Ross Malcolm Taylor, 1915–1916, Thompson to Mr. Taylor, 8 January 1916.

15 LAC, CCS Records, vol. 4644, R.F. Thompson file.

16 John Herd Thompson and Allan Seager, *Canada 1922–1939: Decades of Discord* (Toronto: McClelland and Stewart, 1985), 295–96.

17 One of these was Walter Fisher, LAC, CCS Records, vol. 4623, W.F.O. Fisher file.

18 LAC, CCS Records, vol. 4618, W. Ball file.

19 Ibid., vol. 4619, Carruthers file.

20 Ibid., vol. 4642, H.M. Shore file.

21 Ibid., vol. 4626, R.D. Harrison file. Dr. Henry Marshall Tory, founding president of the University of Alberta, was the leading force in the establishment of the Khaki University (initially Khaki College). It was set up during the First World War to provide courses to serving military and was managed by the general staff of the Canadian Army in Britain, 1917–19. Tory served as the president.

22 Ibid., vol. 4623, A.C. Farrell file; also vol. 4625, R.J. Irwin file.

23 Ibid., vol. 4618, Cameron file.
24 Ibid., vol. 4645, J.O. Watts file; also vol. 4632, D. Marshall file.
25 Ibid., vol. 4617, Adrian Beausoleil file.
26 Ibid., vol. 4634, A.B. MacDonald file.

Works Cited

PRIMARY SOURCES

Canadian Churchman
Edmonton Daily Bulletin
Red Deer News

Library and Archives Canada. Chaplain Service Records, RG9 IIIC15, CEF, vols. 4615–4675.
Western University, Fred Landon Regional Archives, London, ON. Letters of Bombardier Ross Malcolm Taylor, 1915–1916.

SECONDARY SOURCES

Bennett, S.G. *The 4th Canadian Mounted Rifles, 1914–1919*. Toronto: Murray, 1926.
Chadderton, Clifford. *The Fragment*. Summer 1971.
Clarke, Gregory. *A Bar'l of Apples*. Toronto: McGraw-Hill Ryerson, 1971.
———. "The Little Armistice." *The Legionary*. 1937.
Crerar, Duff. *Padres in No Man's Land: Canadian Chaplains and the Great War*. Montreal and Kingston: McGill-Queen's University Press, 1995 (2nd ed. revised 2014).
Singer, Horace. *History of the 31st Canadian Infantry Battalion CEF*. Edited by Darrell Knight. Calgary: Detselig, 2006.
Stevens, G.R. *A City Goes to War: History of the Loyal Edmonton Regiment*. Brampton, ON: Charters Publishing Company, 1964.
Thompson, John Herd, and Allan Seager. *Canada 1922–1939: Decades of Discord*. Toronto: McClelland and Stewart, 1985.
Wheeler, Victor. *The 50th Battalion in No Man's Land*. Calgary: Alberta Historical Resources Foundation, 1980.

The Experiences of Lethbridge Men Overseas, 1914–1918

BRETT CLIFTON

Canada's involvement in the Great War began on 4 August 1914 when the British Empire declared war on Germany. Canadians poured into the streets anxious to prove their loyalty to Canada and to the British Empire. Lethbridge, an unremarkable little prairie city, was as enthusiastic as any community across the nation. Since 1908 it had been home to the 25th Field Battery under the command of Major John Smith Stewart. The battery was disbanded shortly after the war began.[1] However, Lethbridge did go on to raise three fully active artillery batteries and a depot battery, in addition to an infantry battalion. Lethbridge men filled the ranks of these units, and also signed up for service with a variety of other batteries and regiments in the Canadian, British, and American expeditionary forces. By the war's end, Lethbridge had one of the highest enlistment rates of any city across Canada and, sadly, this was accompanied by the distinction of having one of the highest casualty rates as well.[2] As we look back a century later on some of Canada's most dramatic engagements in the First World War—including the battles for Ypres, the Somme, Vimy Ridge, Passchendaele, and the triumphant liberation of Mons—it will be found that, among those present on these historic occasions, were citizens of Lethbridge or members of Lethbridge-based units, whose experiences are documented in soldier correspondence, memoirs, diaries, unit histories, and local newspaper accounts.

Incorporated in 1906, Lethbridge then boasted a population of 2,313; by 1911 this had grown by a remarkable 248 percent, reaching 8,050.[3] When the first recruiting offices opened in August 1914, Lethbridge had many willing young men to choose from—since male citizens outnumbered females by an astounding ratio of 24:1—and there was no shortage of patriotic and adventurous individuals anxious to do their part.[4] John Chambers Kemsley MacKay, author of *The Diary of the 20th Battery C.F.A.*, documented the initial recruiting frenzy as follows: "All classes were represented: bookkeepers and farmers; cow-punchers and merchants; lumber-jacks and miners; from the office, the prairie, the bush and the mine they came; all eager to do their share in the big bid for freedom; for democracy; for very civilization."[5]

Among the first Lethbridge citizens to see action were a group of 50 British expatriates who in August 1914 returned to Britain to rejoin their former regiments or to fulfill their contracts as British army reservists.[6] Included in this group was Private Wilfrid Fletcher of the 2nd Battalion King's Own Yorkshire Light Infantry. Private Fletcher was to fight in the First Battle of Ypres and documented some of his experiences in a letter written to the folks at home in the fall of 1914:

> The Germans are retiring to strongly forti-
> fied positions which will take a lot of taking
> and some considerable loss of life before we
> can drive them back ... [T]here are thirteen
> of us from Canada in my regiment and we
> have kept together pretty well so far. We are
> divided up between Winnipeg, Calgary, Ham-
> ilton and Montreal and one chap from New
> York. They call us the Canadians. It is quite
> a distinction and so far has got us out of a lot
> of necessary duties such as soldiers are want
> [sic] to get. We have sung "The Maple Leaf
> Forever," "Casey Jones," "Red Wing," and
> "The Old Star Trail," until the whole garrison
> knows of the thirteen lucky Canucks.[7]

Private Fletcher may have felt like a lucky Canuck, but his good fortune was fleeting as, on 29 October 1914, he was killed in action in Belgium.[8] He is be-lieved to be the first man from Lethbridge to lose his life on the battlefields of the Great War.

On 23 November 1914, Major John Smith Stewart began recruiting members for the newly formed 20th Battery Canadian Field Artillery. Recruiting offices were opened in Lethbridge, Calgary, and Edmonton and in just 24 hours the offices were closed, having reached the goal of 140 men, with 70 coming from Lethbridge and 35 each from Calgary and Edmonton.[9] Similar results were achieved by the 39th Battery Canadian Field Artillery, which in Octo-ber 1915 was recruited under the command of Major Alexander Boswell Stafford;[10] and the following February, the 61st Battery Canadian Field Artillery, recruited under the command of Captain Colin Hood Collinson.[11]

The 78th Depot Battery Canadian Field Artillery was formed in Lethbridge in January 1916 to provide reinforcements to existing units in the Canadian Field Artillery.[12] At the same time, the 113th Battal-ion CEF (Lethbridge Highlanders), which had begun recruiting in the fall of 1915, was also busy snapping up men for the infantry.[13] By August 1916 the various units had attracted some 1,500 locals, or more than 15 percent of the city's population.[14] Citizens of Leth-bridge took great pride in these volunteers, affec-tionately calling them "Battery Boys" (for officers and men of artillery batteries) and "Kilties" (officers and men of the 113th Battalion CEF).

A 25-man contingent made up of members of the former 25th Field Battery left Lethbridge in Septem-ber 1914 under the command of Lieutenant Charles Magrath Godwin. By Christmas they were encamped on the infamous Salisbury Plain, the British training ground that was lamented for its harsh conditions, especially during inclement weather. Godwin's group was the first recipient of the thousands of Christ-mas parcels that were gathered and sent by service groups in Lethbridge. Reams of thank-you letters document the gratitude of local boys for the comfort packages and words of support they received from their hometown. In his letter dated 2 January 1915, Lieutenant Godwin wrote:

> That afternoon, I announced on stable parade
> to the boys that I had a small parcel from
> Lethbridge for them, and when I got down to

Members of the 113th Battalion CEF (Lethbridge Highlanders) parade with their Ross Rifles in the spring of 1916. Later that year, the Kilties were broken up, with the majority seeing service with the 16th, 43rd, and 85th battalions of the CEF. Galt Museum and Archives, 19861100009.

my tent they were lined up as if ready to buy tickets for a hockey match. . . . They asked me to thank you all for remembering them as best I could. It was more than thoughtful of you to say the least. I am sure you don't know what a dry pair of socks mean to a lot of men who have been trampling around in mud and rain, not all day, but every day.[15]

Although none of the Lethbridge-based units were on the Western Front at this time, there were several local men serving with other Canadian formations who were already in the trenches. Corporal Eustace Pritchard Churchill Chappelow had enlisted with the 10th Battalion CEF out of Calgary in the early days of the war, and by spring 1915 the 20-year-old bank clerk was on the frontlines in Belgium, serving in a machine gun section with several other recruits from Lethbridge. On 22 May 1915 the *Lethbridge Daily Herald* reported: "E.P. Chappelow, well known as 'The Count' in Lethbridge, is the second local man to lay down his life in the Empire's cause. He is in today's list of casualties as killed in action, having evidently fallen in the engagements following Lange-marck."[16] However, two weeks later the paper re-ported that Chappelow "is not dead, but is a prisoner in Germany, and has lost a leg. He lies in a German field hospital, according to a faintly scrawled post-card which has been received by his relatives in England." Chappelow had been released by the Ger-mans as part of the first wounded-prisoner exchange of the Great War.[17] When discussing the treatment he received at the hands of his German captors, Chap-pelow was conflicted. Ethel Conybeare, a Lethbridge woman who was a Red Cross nurse-in-training in Britain, related Chappelow's account of his capture as follows:

> So then Chappelow lay there all that night; and all the next day, and then the Germans came to pick up the wounded. He kept calling "Pick me up, pick me up," but no one could understand him. Then he called "Water," and they understood that and gave him some. Finally, one came along who spoke English, and told him he'd have to wait until all the Germans were picked up. He said all right, he didn't care if he was never picked up. So he became unconscious, and was finally picked up the next night. After that he spent 24 hours in a barn because he was overlooked. They carried him in a blanket with his wounded legs doubled up, and told him if he didn't keep quiet they would drop him.[18]

In a letter written 21 May 1916, Chappelow related a very different and much more humane experience once he reached a German field hospital. He described his treatment as follows:

> They are very kind to me, though, and I hope the people in England don't think we are badly treated here. The only thing I can't get used to is the black bread and lard. I am in a room with eight other Germans, all badly wounded, and they give me cigarettes and oranges. Just now, their paymaster came round and a fellow in the next bed to me told him that I had no money, and he gave me a mark out of his own pocket.[19]

There are many similar accounts from the locals regarding their perceptions of the behaviours and attitudes of the German forces. They range from descriptions of kind and civilized treatment to inhumane cruelty and outrageous atrocities. The now Lieutenant Colonel Stewart addressed the question-able veracity of some of the letters and stories writ-ten at the front. In a letter to his wife, he lamented the problem and noted: "The officers were very busy and were cussing pretty hard at some of the letters the men were writing about things over here. They, the men, mostly seem to be of the opinion that it is their duty to send along all the hot air they can get up, and they exaggerate things a lot. The officers cut some of it off and even tore up some of the letters, so you may know how bad the letters were."[20]

The 20th Battery Canadian Field Artillery, now under the command of Major Alvin Ripley, took up a firing position for the very first time on 4 February 1916. The next day Gunner Lennie Redmond fired the battery's first round of the war.[21] By summer 1916 the 20th was joined by the 39th Battery Canadian Field Artillery, and the two Lethbridge-based units prepared to do their part in the Somme campaign. The 20th Battery had been deployed in support of the Princess Patricia's Canadian Light Infantry and the Canadian Mounted Rifles at the Hooge front. The unit history of the battery records the actions at the Somme as being a baptism of fire, noting that they were shelled so frequently they became indifferent to the sights and sounds of war; however, they never disregarded the primitive instinct to make for cover. During the evening of 8 October 1916, the 39th Battery moved into a new position near Martinpuich under cover of darkness. As daylight dawned, they were greeted with a horrific sight, vividly described in their unit history as follows:

> When it was possible to view the field of battle next morning in daylight, it was an absolute desolation. Not a blade of grass could be seen, the ground having been turned over time and time again by the falling shells, not a living tree was standing though a few remained shattered about fifteen feet from the ground, but absolutely leafless. Martinpuich, the village to the right of the Battery position about a mile, was practically levelled, not a wall standing more than eight feet high. A few dead Germans lay around the position and one or two odd legs, which no one until then had thought fit to bury, but some of whom the men voluntarily buried about a week later.[22]

Around the same time, the 20th Battery was in the process of taking over a position from the 18th Battery Canadian Field Artillery when they found themselves occupying very unusual, if not morbid, accommodations. MacKay, author of the unit's history, relates the circumstances as follows: "A detail of 1 N.C.O. and 4 gunners proceeded to Pozieres Cemetery, where a 'sniping' gun was taken over from our 18th Battery. The gun position here was built of lumber and tombstones and the gunners not on duty at night slept in the vaults. Our friend the enemy had evidently been using these vaults as billets also, as we found no occupants when we gingerly entered."[23] There are varied accounts of the extent the local boys had to go to find shelter on the Western Front, and they certainly did what they had to do to stay as warm, dry, and safe as possible, sleeping in every imaginable location from country chateaus to pigsties.

Dealing with vermin was another ongoing concern for those fighting in France and Flanders. Members of the 39th Battery recalled their first encounter with rats when they woke up to find that their bone buttons had been chewed off, toothpaste eaten, and toothbrushes carried away.[24] Lice were also a constant irritant and almost impossible to avoid. The 39th Battery unit history includes a humorous story relating to lice infestations and the attitudes of one particularly intolerant officer:

> Here the majority got their "companions for the duration" and one officer made the unfortunate remark that if a man were "lousy" it was his own fault, as he was not, with the result that some who strongly objected to the remark—as he was living under entirely different and more favourable conditions than the men and was in possession of two or three grips of spare clothing which enabled him to change nightly, the Battery possessing a team and wagon for officers' baggage only, which

was later increased to two—caught some of the pests and when he was away, carefully carried them over to his tent and laid them in his blankets where no doubt they multiplied exceedingly as is their nature. From then on a man was never told it was his own fault if he were "crumby."[25]

By 1917 members of the 20th and 39th batteries had joined other units of the CEF, who were busy trading the muddy, rat-infested trenches of the Somme for the frosty, rat-infested trenches of the Vimy sector. Among the infantrymen making their way to the various locations along Vimy Ridge was a contingent of Lethbridge boys who had volunteered with the 113th Battalion CEF (Lethbridge Highlanders). They arrived in Britain in October 1916 and were promptly delivered a huge blow. Their hopes of fighting together and representing Lethbridge were dashed when the Kilties were disbanded and used as reinforcements for existing Canadian units, the largest number going to the 16th Battalion CEF (Canadian Scottish).[26] The 9 April 1917 attack on Vimy Ridge would prove to be the deadliest day of the war for the former Lethbridge battalion, as they lost 28 of the 905 members. Though celebrated as a nation-building event for Canada, it cost over 10,000 casualties, including more than 3,000 lives.[27] Lieutenant Cyril Beverly Ford Jones wrote to his former colleagues at the Canadian Imperial Bank of Commerce, stating that the "taking of Vimy Ridge by the Canadians will long remain a Red Letter day in Canadian history." He went on to proclaim: "the people of Canada have every reason to be proud of their boys out here; they did their work well, the only trouble was to keep them back when our objective

was reached." He vividly describes the taking of the ridge complete with all the sights, sounds, and smells of the day, but perhaps the most unusual part of his letter is his humorous account of an incident that occurred in the midst of battle, an aside that sheltered those at home from grisly details:

> One of the funniest things that occurred to me during the scrap was when I had just reached the last objective. I had got separated from my gallant gang of "Moppers-up," and the first thing I knew I found myself among a bunch of twenty Huns, who had just got out of a dugout and were beating it across towards us. They surrounded poor old "Jonesie" like a swarm of bees, each holding up his hands and shouting "Kamerad, Kamerad, mercy," and then began to pull out watches and other souvenirs. With my big frame glasses they probably took me for an enterprising curio hunter, and not a leader of His Majesty's Forces. They looked so damned funny, and so frightened, that I forgot there was a scrap on and howled with laughter. I simply pointed to our old lines and they beat it—couldn't get there fast enough.[28]

Although Lieutenant Jones did not partake in souvenir hunting, many from Lethbridge, like Canadian soldiers in general, delighted in the practice and often sent their treasures home along with notes describing the circumstances by which the souvenirs were acquired. Some were found items; others were confiscated from prisoners of war; but a large number were taken off the bodies of dead German soldiers, a practice that members of the 39th Battery called "going through." Attitudes towards the taking of items from corpses varied. Some individuals were indifferent, while others such as Sergeant Donald Patterson of the 39th Battery found it very distasteful. In his memoirs, Patterson recalled a particularly disturbing souvenir hunt as follows: "As an example of how good people get callous, one of our boys saw a ring on the finger of a corpse. He tried to get it off but it stuck so he just twisted the finger until it broke and he got the ring off. I hope he got a lot of pleasure from it because he himself was afterwards killed."[29]

In a letter written to his father in August 1918, Private Joe Mountain Horse, an enlistee from the Blood Indian Reserve near Lethbridge, provided a rare First Nations' perspective on the practice of souvenir hunting. Writing in response to a letter in which his father inquired as to the taking of scalps, he explained: "We did not scalp any dead Germans, as it is too dirty a thing to do, as it is too inhuman, it's bad enough to kill them."[30] His brother, Private Mike Mountain Horse, did manage to collect a few souvenirs, which he spoke of in a letter to their father at about the same time: "I could not bring any German's weapons as they don't allow us to bring them across the waters, but I got some small stuff from Germans I killed myself."[31]

It was during the Canadian action at Passchendaele that all three of the Lethbridge artillery batteries fought at the same time, with the 61st Battery Canadian Field Artillery having arrived in August 1917.[32] By the fall, they had taken up various positions near Passchendaele, a place still remembered for its swamp-like conditions. Canada suffered nearly 16,000 casualties there. On the morning of his death, 19 November 1917, Sergeant Harold Hamilton wrote to his father describing the fighting during the previous days from the perspective of an artillery gunner:

> The country was an awful sight. There was something in the air all the time, guns, planks from the road, motor lorries fiercely burning, men and horses blown to bits, ammunition going up—it was certainly an awful hammering. Was partially buried once, blown clean into a shell hole of water by an eight inch shell that lit not ten feet away, and covered with the mud and water from it and that's all. This mud which we so everlastingly curse has saved the lives of thousands of men, and it is a wonder how men escape, how we come through it all. But bad as our lot is, Fritz's must be worse for our heavies never let up and we sure send an awful lot of ammunition over there after him all the time.[33]

In the fall of 1917, at about the same time as the Passchendaele offensive, the matter of conscription was being decided in a federal election. The 39th Battery unit history notes that the unit's members, as well as members of the 10th Brigade, were "lined up in the square and told by a 'senior' officer exactly which way to vote and how later in the day the matter would be more fully explained by the Battery officers." Once a vote was secured that, in effect, said yes to conscription, the men of the battery were given a few drinks at a local estaminet where it was explained to them that more men would mean a quicker end to the war. The Battery Boys were not buying this argument: "heckling the officers and stating that if the authorities would cut out the shining up and harness cleaning and cut out the 'rest camps' and get on with the war, there were already plenty of men in France to win the same, and further that they did not mind voting their younger brothers into an army to fight but they were not going to vote them into a 'Brasso Brigade.'"[34]

By this time, almost everyone was war weary and missing those at home. Many letters reflect a sense of personal despair caused by isolation from loved ones. Gunner John Murray of the 20th Battery faithfully wrote to his mother every few days over the course of the war. In one letter, he expressed deep concern for his mother's health, which he had heard had taken a turn for the worse, saying "I feel so blame blue when things ain't just going good at home."[35] In a letter written to his father, Private Joe Mountain Horse noted: "I sincerely hope that you and mother and the rest of our people are all well and happy. Do not forget to see my family often as my children are not very strong, especially little Grace."[36]

The year 1918 did bring some hope for the end of the war, especially with the arrival of fresh troops from the United States. As the battles of the Last Hundred Days unfolded, Lethbridge boys fought at Amiens, Cambrai, Canal du Nord, and Drocourt-Queant, to name a few key battle sites. By November it was clear that it was not a matter of *if* they would win the war but *when*, and it was in the final days that the somewhat controversial decision to retake the Belgian town of Mons was made. The very first battles between the British and Germans had been fought there in 1914, with the British suffering a painful defeat. British military authorities were anxious to take Mons purely for its symbolic value. Among the artillery batteries near Mons was the 39th Battery Canadian Field Artillery of Lethbridge.

Of this final battle, Major Chris Kilford writes in his book *Lethbridge at War*:

Being the first battery into Mons had not been easy. Both the 39th and 33rd batteries were racing to see who would be first. The two were neck and neck on converging roads. The one that reached a key crossroads in time would cut the other off. Major Young, the Battery Commander, charged the 39th down the road at a full gallop and succeeded in cutting the passage of the 33rd, thus winning the honour of being the first to enter the main square in Mons . . . They were met by an excited populace who appeared to have a never ending quantity of coffee, cognac, and wine.[37]

The history of the 39th Battery notes that at 1530 hours on 10 November 1918, an official parade was presented to General Sir Arthur Currie, commander of the Canadian Corps, and that the parade was presided over by Lethbridge's own Brigadier General Stewart, who was the commander of the 3rd Divisional Canadian Field Artillery. Three days later the battery was officially represented at a Thanksgiving ceremony jointly held by the Prince of Wales and King Leopold of Belgium.[38]

The people of Lethbridge were eager to have their loved ones back as soon as possible, and though this took a while, they were without a doubt grateful and proud for all that the Lethbridge boys had accomplished. In his 1918 Christmas address, Mayor W.D.L. Hardie stated:

We cannot express the sentiments of appreciation and gratitude adequately, that are in

Members of the 39th Battery CFA pose for a photo in Mons, Belgium, in November 1918. They were the first artillery battery to enter the newly liberated city. Galt Museum and Archives, 19861018006.

our hearts and minds towards you who have done so much for us at home in Canada, and for the great British Empire. You have passed through the very jaws of death and gates of hell that the attributes of Righteousness might continue to be the rule of life, and that the high ideal of the Anglo-Saxon race might prevail. You have accomplished the almost impossible for which we devoutly thank you. For your gallant deeds the people of Canada shall enshrine upon their hearts the images of the noble men who saved the very soul of our country.[39]

A century ago the world went to war and stayed at war for more than four years. The toll to humanity was staggering, with more than 17 million combatants reported dead or missing. Grief and despair

To commemorate the diamond jubilee of the City of Lethbridge and, in honour of those from the community who served our nation in war and peace, an eternal flame was lit by Brigadier General Stewart at Mountain View Cemetery on 27 December 1966. Stewart is surely the most well-known Lethbridge soldier of the Great War. Galt Museum and Archives, 19760209012.

were felt in every corner of the world. In Lethbridge a cenotaph was erected to memorialize the dead and missing from the little prairie city. There are 262 names etched on the cenotaph. They had come from every walk of life—cowboys, railwaymen, bankers, clergymen, miners, and teachers. They filled the ranks of three artillery batteries and an infantry battalion, all raised from a community that boasted a population of less than 10,000. They served in nearly every major battle of the war. They saw action at the Dardanelles, the battles for Ypres, the Somme, Vimy Ridge, Passchendaele, Amiens, and the Last Hundred Days. Those who came home stoically bore the physical, mental, and emotional scars, and set to work raising families and building their community. They are gone now, but they have left behind the story of their war through letters, diaries, memoirs, photographs, and other artifacts, all of which are invaluable in helping us to recognize and appreciate their place in history.

Notes

1   Christopher R. Kilford, *Lethbridge at War: The Military History of Lethbridge from 1900 to 1996* (Lethbridge, AB: Battery Books & Publishing, 1996), 20–21.
2   Garry Allison, *The Prairie Boys: Southern Albertans Wartime Experiences* (Lethbridge, AB: Lethbridge Historical Society, 2006), 178.
3   City of Lethbridge website, "City of Lethbridge Population History," URL: http://www.lethbridge.ca, retrieved 7 May 2014.
4   Robert Rutherdale, *Hometown Horizons: Local Responses to Canada's Great War* (Vancouver: UBC Press, 2004), 28.

5 J.C.K. MacKay, *The Diary of the 20th Battery C.F.A.* (N.p.: privately printed, n.d.), "Organization and Early Training."

6 "George Bone, Callie Footballer, Missing," *Lethbridge Daily Herald*, 21 January 1915.

7 Letter from Wilfrid Fletcher to friends in Lethbridge, September 1914, *Lethbridge Daily Herald* Archives.

8 See Brett Clifton, *They Never Came Home—The Lethbridge Cenotaph Project*, vol. 1, for a complete biography and other relevant information relating to the life and service of Wilfrid Fletcher.

9 MacKay, *Diary of the 20th Battery*, "Organization and Early Training."

10 *The 39th: 1914–1918* (N.p.: privately printed, n.d.), 12.

11 *The Diary of the 61st Battery Canadian Field Artillery—1916 to 1919* (Uckfield, UK: Naval & Military Press, 2009), 5.

12 Kilford, *Lethbridge at War*, 50–51.

13 Ibid., 39.

14 Ibid., 27.

15 Quoted in the article "Our Boys at Salisbury Lines Up as at Hockey Game When Parcel From Lethbridge Arrived on Scene," *Lethbridge Daily Herald*, 23 January 1915.

16 "E.P. Chappelow is Killed in Action," *Lethbridge Daily Herald*, 22 May 1915.

17 "E.P. Chappelow, Wreck From Shells," *Lethbridge Daily Herald*, 17 July 1915.

18 "Local Boy Lay Three Days With Shattered Limbs," *Lethbridge Daily Herald*, 2 November 1915.

19 "E.P. Chappelow, Wreck From Shells," *Lethbridge Daily Herald*, 17 July 1915.

20 John Smith Stewart, *Memoirs of a Soldier* (Lethbridge, AB: Robins' Southern Printing Ltd., n.d.), 61.

21 MacKay, *Diary of the 20th Battery*, "The Ypres Salient."

22 *The 39th: 1914–1918*, 29.

23 MacKay, *Diary of the 20th Battery*, "The Somme."

24 *The 39th: 1914–1918*, 25.

25 Ibid., 26.

26 Upon the breakup of the 113th Battalion, the majority of men were divided among the following three battalions of the Canadian Expeditionary Force: 16th Battalion CEF (Canadian Scottish), 43rd Battalion CEF (Cameron Highlanders of Canada), and the 85th Battalion CEF (Nova Scotia Highlanders).

27 This figure was determined based on comparing the sailing list of the 113th Battalion CEF (Lethbridge Highlanders) with the death and burial registries available from Veterans Affairs Canada and the Commonwealth War Graves Commission.

28 Cyril Beverly Ford Jones, Officer of the 16th Battalion CEF, to colleagues at the Calgary Branch Canadian Imperial Bank of Commerce, 15 April 1917, Galt Museum and Archives, Lethbridge, AB.

29 Donald H. Patterson, *Autobiography of Donald H. Patterson* (Calgary: self-published, 1955), 45.

30 "Mountain Horse Boys Are Wounded," *Lethbridge Daily Herald*, 17 October 1918.

31 Ibid.

32 *The Diary of the 61st Battery Canadian Field Artillery—1916 to 1919*, 9.

33 "Harold Hamilton Killed Outright While in Action," *Lethbridge Daily Herald*, 12 January 1918.

34 *The 39th: 1914–1918*, 49.

35 Galt Museum and Archives, John Murray, Gunner of the 20th Battery CFA, to his mother, Lethbridge, 9 April 1917.

36 "Mountain Horse Boys Are Wounded," *Lethbridge Daily Herald*, 17 October 1918.

37 Kilford, *Lethbridge at War*, 58.

38 Ibid.

39 "Peace Greetings From Lethbridge & District," *Lethbridge Daily Herald*, 30 November 1918.

Works Cited

PRIMARY SOURCES

Lethbridge Daily Herald
Lethbridge Telegram

Galt Museum and Archives, Lethbridge, AB.
    Individual letters or collections of letters from the following Lethbridge men:

Wilfrid Fletcher
Sergeant Harold Henderson
Captain C.B.F. Jones (113th Battalion)
Gunner John Larson (39th Battery)
Gunner John Murray (20th Battery)
Warren Porter (113th Battalion)
Lieutenant Colonel A.W. Pryce-Jones (113th Battalion)
Major Alvin Ripley (20th Battery)
Norman Robison (10th Battalion)
Major Jack Ross (24th Battalion)
Andrew Russell
Frank Russell
Stewart Tuckwell (10th Battalion)

Individual letters or collections of letters written about the following Lethbridge men:

William Bartlett
George Bone
Alex Davidson
Herbert Goode
Fred Hewitt
William King
John Larson
Alex Martin
Ernest Meads
Jack Ross
Percy Scarth
Walter Short
Thomas Watt
Fred Whitcutt
John Wright
Claudius Young

SECONDARY SOURCES

The 39th: 1914–1918. N.p.: privately printed, n.d.

Allison, Garry. *The Prairie Boys: Southern Albertans Wartime Experiences*. Lethbridge, AB: Lethbridge Historical Society, 2006.

Clifton, Brett. "A Battalion of Our Own: The Story of the 113th Overseas Battalion CEF (Lethbridge Highlanders)." Unpublished manuscript, last modified 20 April 2013.

——. "From the Bridge to the Ridge: Lethbridge Volunteers and the Battle for Vimy Ridge." *Alberta History* 60, no. 1 (Winter 2012): 2–9.

——. *They Never Came Home—The Lethbridge Cenotaph Project*. Vol. 1. Lethbridge, AB: self-published, 2009.

The Diary of the 61st Battery Canadian Field Artillery—1916 to 1919. Uckfield, UK: Naval & Military Press Ltd., 2009.

Kilford, Christopher R. *Lethbridge at War: The Military History of Lethbridge from 1900 to 1996*. Lethbridge, AB: Battery Books & Publishing, 1996.

MacKay, J.C.K. *The Diary of the 20th Battery C.F.A.* N.p.: privately printed, n.d.

Patterson, Donald H. *Autobiography of Donald H. Patterson*. Calgary: self-published, 1955.

Rutherdale, Robert. *Hometown Horizons: Local Responses to Canada's Great War*. Vancouver: UBC Press, 2004.

Virtue, A.G. *Field Diary of Lieut. A.G. Virtue, 61st Battery, Canadian Field Artillery, 1918*. N.p.: privately printed, 1918.

Sid Unwin's War

MICHALE LANG

Like so many Alberta communities, Banff has a
memorial to those townspeople who died fighting
in the First World War. From a population of 1,000,
Banff lost 52 young men. "Unwin, S." appears among
the war casualties listed on Banff's cenotaph outside
the Royal Canadian Legion on Banff Avenue. Sidney
Joseph Unwin (1882–1917) led a life of adventure and
sacrifice. He inspired loyalty and love in those who
knew him. His family, friends, and fellow officers all
remembered him in different ways, and they help
us to remember him today through both words and
objects. His bravery on the battlefield, his stoicism,
and particularly his sense of humour in the face of
hardship move us today as they moved those who
knew him personally.

English-born adventurer Sid Unwin, like many
of those who served in the First World War, had
fought with distinction for three years in the South
African (Boer) War with the volunteer 1st City of
London Artillery. Returning to London following
that conflict, he worked as a survey clerk. In the fall
of 1904 he moved to Banff to pursue the life of a
guide, "having learned to love the life of the open as
he slept under the Southern Cross during the Boer

War."[1] He soon became known for his resourcefulness, horsemanship, marksmanship, and camp
skills, becoming one of the Canadian Rockies' legendary guides and outfitters in the years preceding
the war. He earned the name "Running Rabbit" from
local First Nations friends.

Unwin made a favourable impression on many
of the people he guided. "He drew aside the curtains
of conventional life and revealed to us the wonders
of the mountains and the pleasures of the trail,"
wrote Helen Tippin Ide of Philadelphia. In his book
Trail Life in the Canadian Rockies, B.W. Mitchell paid
a tribute to Unwin following several trips with him.
He noted: "Unsurpassed in woodcraft and resourcefulness, unequaled in thoughtful kindness to his
party, and with the charm of courteous manner
that adds the final touch of perfection to the little
self-centred microcosm that a party in the wilder-
ness constitutes."[2]

Unwin was also assigned to the famed expedi-
tions of Mary Schäffer and Molly Adams on their
quest for Maligne Lake in 1907 and 1908. Their
experiences were recounted in Schäffer's book *Old
Indian Trails of the Canadian Rockies*, still available as

Sid Unwin, ca. 1905, Sid Unwin Fonds, Whyte Museum of the Canadian Rockies, V25/PA-1.

A Hunter of Peace. Unwin, identified as "κ" in the account, was credited with uncanny abilities in locating the mystery lake and creating edible cuisine from trail-weary food supplies.[3] Not all of his culinary attempts were successful, however. Schäffer tells of a goat so tough that "though 'κ' pounded his steaks to jelly on the stones, and boiled and simmered his legs for hours, he (the goat) failed to be 'chewable' let alone digestible."[4]

Fortunately, Unwin had more success in locating the object of their search. During their 1908 trip, Schäffer and Adams set out with their guides on a quest for *Chaba Imne*, the elusive body of water that would later be named Maligne Lake. Stewardson Brown and his guide Reggie Holmes accompanied them. Sid Unwin's dog, Mr. Muggins, was the party's mascot. They had difficulty finding the trail over Poboktan Pass and were unsure which way to turn when they encountered a junction. The trail to the pass was challenging, with "quick changes from burnt timber to rock-climbing, muskeg, quicksand, scree slopes and mud-slides."[5] Schäffer described Poboktan Pass as a miserable route. Sampson Beaver's simple map (given to Mary by her Stony First Nation friend in 1907) was unclear, but they decided to take their chances on the northward route. They finally crossed Maligne Pass but still could not see the lake. Unwin decided to climb until he spotted it. Eight and a half hours later, he returned to inform the camp they were on the right path. The mountain he climbed in search of Maligne Lake was later named in his honour. Unwin accompanied Schäffer to Maligne Lake again in 1911 when she returned to map the lake.

Sadly, Unwin's adventurous but peaceful years in the Rockies were not only preceded but also followed by the horrors of war. When war broke out in 1914,

"Lake Maligne fr. [from] the summit of Mount Unwin," 1908. Photographer: Sid Unwin, Mary Schäffer Fonds, Whyte Museum of the Canadian Rockies, V527/ PS 1-61.

he asked his sister, Ethel, to take over his pack and saddle horse business, and enlisted in the Canadian Army. As a result, she was the first woman in Banff to become a licensed guide.

Unwin was assigned to the 20th Artillery Battery at Lethbridge (Regimental Number: 87113). In January 1916 the battery saw its first action in France. In May 1917, after surviving unscathed the Battle of Vimy Ridge, Unwin was severely wounded after single-handedly manning an artillery battery. Lieutenant E.K. Carmichael, his commanding officer, wrote: "I was so much pleased with, and admired his conduct, that I committed the circumstances to paper at once in case of accidents, so that if anything did happen to me, the paper would bear witness."[6]

These events and his day-to-day activities as an artilleryman are recorded in Unwin's 1917 diary, which was donated to the Whyte Museum of the Canadian Rockies Archives in 1998.[7] In it he provides short observations about duties at the front, gun positions, prisoners, and gas warfare. Unwin recounts the capture of Vimy Ridge, his injury, the amputation of his arm, and evacuation to England and convalescence. No days were without an entry, as he continued writing with his remaining hand, even scribbling poems and comic songs while in hospital. Unwin's diary also reflects the boredom and routine of life as an artilleryman. He complained frequently about the time spent polishing shoes and belt buckles, only to return to the filthy trench life of mud, rats, and lice. Despite his matter-of-fact delivery, it soon becomes clear from his entries that he and his fellow soldiers experienced long stretches of tedium punctuated by periods of sheer terror.

The following selected excerpts from Unwin's diary paint a vivid picture of an artilleryman's life on the Western Front.[8] Many of the diary entries not included here are either repetitive or simply say "Ditto." By the time Unwin started the surviving diary on 1 January 1917, he recorded having fired 13,028 rounds.

January 1, 1917:
In action at Bully-Grenay. This is a rather quiet part of the front. I went with Mr. Meikle to find forward positions. Quite a nice ride. Since the Battery has been in France, they have had the following casualties

Killed or died of wounds	14
Wounded or gassed	56
Invalided	15
Commissions (one killed)	2
Transfers	6
Home for Instructor	1
	94

January 10:
My birthday. Went to dentists. Quite a lot of firing, both day and night.

January 17:
Snow, 7:30 a.m. Our infantry again made a raid, which was very successful. Brought back about 100 prisoners and killed a lot, and destroyed dugouts, etc. We put up a barrage.

January 25:
On the march via Bruay to Pernes. We bivouacked in the market square. Very cold all day, about 15 degrees . . . Got a good billet, but very hard on horses and men.

February 1:
We are having a miserable time, not a minute to ourselves, inspections every five minutes. I think the general and colonels have all lost their reason, because no common sense is used at all.

February 17:
Weather has turned warmer and it is quite muddy again. Very foggy, therefore not much firing.

February 22:
Took part on another raid on trenches. Took 80 prisoners. Foggy.

February 27:
Today a German plane drove one of our scouts to the ground, and then turned his machine gun on men round about. He evidently caught sight of me, as he started shooting at me. I sure hopped for cover.

March 1:
March comes in like a lion. Stood to at 2 a.m. to repel a German attack. At 5 a.m., we discharged two waves of gas. At 5.40, our infantry attacked and remained in German trenches 1½ hours. But our men had terrible fighting as Fritz was waiting for them. Our casualties very heavy. A terrible stream of wounded passed our battery all day and night. We fired nearly 1,000 rounds.

March 2:
. . . from all accounts, our own gas killed a lot of our men, the wind changing.[9]

Sat. March 3:
Divine service in afternoon, in a little dugout by candlelight.

March 8:
Changed my assigned pay to $27 per month, commencing 1st April.

March 18:
Heard of the Russian Revolution. We wonder how it will affect the conduct of the war.

On April 8, Easter Sunday, Unwin realized that something big was about to happen. The following diary entries document the four-day battle of Vimy Ridge from a soldier's perspective.

April 8:
Easter Sunday. The eve of big events for Canadians. Enormous amount of traffic everywhere. Lots of tanks going up.

And so began the assault on Vimy Ridge. At 5:30 AM on 9 April 1917, Easter Monday, nearly 1,000 guns opened fire on the German positions, Sid Unwin's among them.

April 9:
Snow and rain. The big battle starts. We advance and take lots of prisoners . . . Heard later we took 9000 prisoners & 40 guns. Saw several big batches of prisoners going down.

An estimated 15,000 Canadians rose from the trenches and advanced towards the ridge in the first wave, with thousands more behind them. Despite hard fighting all across the front, the Canadians captured most of the ridge on April 9, and the remaining portions by the 12th.

April 10:
Moved our horse lines forward to Berthon vale in an open field, raining snowing wind blowing like hell. A hard day.

April 11:
Our guns moved forward to Thélus, [had] a very hard time getting through. Went up part way. A terrible day snowing & raining. Dr. Smith sent hospital. Prisoners reach over 11,000 & 70 guns.

April 12:
A terrible blizzard all day. A terrible day, like a bad nightmare. Lost several horses. Lots of dead men laying around.

April 13:
A slight improvement in the weather, packing ammunition. Two horses killed. Prisoners reach 13,000 & 166 guns.

April 16:
Terrible mess on Vimy Ridge, hard to explain.

April 18:
In the last nine days, we have taken 14,000 prisoners and 227 guns.

Unlike the nearly 10,600 Canadians killed and wounded, Unwin survived the bloody four-day battle unscathed. Shortly after, he was permitted a short leave in France (non-commissioned officers were entitled to 10 days a year).

May 1:
I got a holiday and went . . . to Bruay. A lovely day and a nice change . . . I became an uncle as Nellie gave birth to a daughter.

May 2:
I went up to guns in early morning. We were shelled all day & all night. We all had to beat it and lay in shell holes. No sleep at all. Fritz made several counter attacks. A nerve racking day.

May 3:
I got badly wounded at 6 p.m. Arm shattered and face badly cut open. I do not remember anything until next morning.

Here Unwin's handwriting changes. On May 4, he reports in a left-handed scrawl, "Came to about 8 a.m. at No. 6 Casualty Clearing Station at Barlin. I found my arm had been amputated, and head operated upon." It is remarkable that even the loss of his right arm, the side he used for writing, did not stop him from making his diary entries.

Sid Unwin's was just one of 42,000 Canadian amputations carried out in the war. The First World War "resulted in new types of wounds from high-velocity bullet and shrapnel injuries" that required more radical and timely medical intervention.[10] The more quickly the wounded could be moved to a Casualty Clearing Station, the higher were their chances of survival. Unwin's removal to No. 6 Casualty Clearing Station within 14 hours from the time of his injuries may have been a factor in his survival. Only four days after the amputation of his arm, Unwin wrote:

May 8:
Went on ambulance at 6 p.m. and went on board Pieter de Coninck and stayed all night. This hospital ship armed and painted like a warship.

May 9:
Sailed 11 a.m. Arrived Dover 1 p.m. Left 3 p.m. and went via London to Leeds, to M18 East Leeds War Hospital.

May 16:
Mother and Edith came to see me.[11]

May 18:
Had stitches taken out of arm.

Despite his injuries, Unwin did not lose his sense of humour. On May 27, he wrote this comic little poem.

> One spring day near Vimy Ridge
> I very nearly crossed the Bridge
> Which leads to Heaven or to Hell
> For I tried to stop a Fritz shell
> But now in Heaven I must be
> For around me angels do I see
> Protecting me from further harm
> For I am bruised and short one arm.

May 29:
Fine day. Visitor's day. I was allowed up and went into grounds.

May 31:
Had letter from Arthur [his brother, a bombardier with the 22nd Battery] to say I had been awarded the Military Medal.

June 4:
Went to a concert.

June 5:
Lovely day. I was allowed out for the first
time, and went with seven other Canadians to tea at Mrs. Boyle's, the Canadian Red
Cross representative. Had a very enjoyable
afternoon.

June 26:
They took two more pieces of shell out of my
face today. I went uptown to picture show.

June 27:
Went up town, and to tea with Miss Pushby.

This was Unwin's final diary entry. He died of complications from his injuries on June 29. Despite the
fact that blood transfusions with ABO compatibility
testing became available during the war, there were
no antibiotics to fight infections resulting from the
filthy battlefield conditions. It is little wonder that
Sid Unwin died of complications.

Unwin's last letter, written from the military
hospital shortly before his death, proved that his
spirit had not been broken: "Aside from having my
right arm blown off, being almost stone deafened
by shell fire, and having my head full of shrapnel
fragments, I'm fine and dandy." B.W. Mitchell writes
in *Trail Life in Canadian Rockies*:

> This was no affectation of courage; he meant
> it. When he was thus horribly wounded, he
> had just ordered his gun crew to leave the
> battery and go back to their dug-out because,

"it's too dangerous; the Boche has the range,"
and he was serving his gun alone. They got
him back to Blighty (England); and he was
listed as convalescent, when a hearty laugh
jarred one of the shell fragments into a vital
corner of his brain and all was over. God rest
a noble spirit.[12]

Despite his desire to serve his country, Unwin
must have longed for his time in the Rockies while
he lay in that hospital bed. His memory lives on in
Mount Unwin, 3,268 metres high, located between
Maligne Lake Valley and the Maligne River, in Jasper
National Park, Alberta. The mountain was named by
Mary Schäffer. In the text for a lantern slide presen-
tation sent to soldiers convalescing from wounds in
British hospitals during the war, Schäffer wrote:

> Such work as that great log-made raft took
> to drive it through the silent waters no one
> knows save those who did the work. As
> we slowly approached the double-headed
> peak here shown, Mr. Unwin, one of our
> co-workers suddenly exclaimed "That is the
> peak from which I first saw the lake." In jest
> someone said: "Let's name it for him." The
> name is there today, a beautiful monument
> to one of the finest men of Banff who gave his
> life in the Great War. It is thus lightly we place
> names on the monarchs of the hills but this
> one will never slightly be borne."[13]

When Mary Schäffer's nephew, Eric Sharples,
was killed in the war, Unwin asked for three days'
leave to search for the body. Although he was unsuccessful, and the body was never found, Schäffer

Stained glass window at St. George's-in-the-Pines Anglican Church, Banff, 2010, Whyte Museum of the Canadian Rockies, v500-166c-na.

demonstrated her appreciation for Unwin's efforts by dedicating the beautiful stained glass window at St. George's-in-the-Pines Anglican Church in Banff to her friend Unwin.

Memorials to soldiers such as Unwin not only help us remember their sacrifice but also serve as reminders of how we can face hardship in our own lives. Unwin's First World War diary provides a glimpse into his bravery and sense of humour. The mountain named in his honour is a poignant symbol of Unwin's ability to see beyond hardship to the final goal.

Notes

1 *The Canadian Great War Project* website, "CEF Soldier Detail, Sidney Joseph Unwin," URL: http://www.canadiangreatwarproject.com/searches/soldierDetail.asp?Id=19869, retrieved 10 December 2013.

2 B.W. Mitchell, *Trail Life in the Canadian Rockies* (New York: Macmillan, 1924).

3 E.J. Hart, *A Hunter of Peace: Mary T.S. Schaffer's Old Indian Trails of the Canadian Rockies* (Banff, AB: Whyte Museum of the Canadian Rockies, 1980), 16.

4 Ibid., 32.

5 Molly Adams, quoted in Mary T.S. Schäffer, *Old Indian Trails of the Canadian Rockies* (New York: G.P. Putnam's Sons, 1911), 232.

6 Peakfinder website, "Peaks of the Canadian Rockies: Mount Unwin," URL: http://www.peakfinder.com/peakfinder.ASP?PeakName=mount+unwin, retrieved 13 December 2013.

7 Josephine Parkinson (the daughter of Fredrick Unwin, Sid Unwin's older brother) donated the First World War diary of Sidney Joseph Unwin to the Whyte Museum of the Canadian Rockies in 1998.

8 Whyte Museum of the Canadian Rockies (Banff, AB), Sidney Unwin, "First World War Diary," excerpts from 1 January to 27 June 1917, M31/V25, Sid Unwin Fonds.

9 In the First World War, chemical agents came into use for the first time. By this stage of the war, Unwin could have been talking about either phosgene or mustard gas. Over the war, gas killed some 100,000 and injured an estimated 1 million soldiers and civilians.

10 Canadian War Museum website, "Canada and the Great War," URL: http://www.warmuseum.ca/cwm/exhibitions/guerre/cost-war-e.aspx, retrieved 8 December 2013.

11 Unwin's military records indicated that his next-of-kin was "Mrs. Julia Unwin (mother), 19 Ullswater Road, Southgate, London, England." Edith was his sister.

12 *The Canadian Great War Project* website, "Private Sidney Joseph Unwin," URL: http://www.canadiangreatwarproject.com/searches/soldierDetail.asp?Id=19869, retrieved 10 December 2013.

13 Mary S. Warren, "In the Heart of the Canadian Rockies with Horse and Camera, Parts I and II." (n.d.). Unpublished lantern slide presentation, M7189/7, Whyte Museum of the Canadian Rockies.

Works Cited

PRIMARY SOURCES

Whyte Museum of the Canadian Rockies, Banff, AB. Sid Unwin Fonds.

SECONDARY SOURCES

The Canadian Great War Project website. "CEF Soldier Detail, Sidney Joseph Unwin." URL: http://www.canadiangreatwarproject.com/searches/soldierDetail.asp?Id=19869, retrieved 10 December 2013.

Canadian War Museum website. "Canada and the First
World War: Vimy Ridge." URL: www.warmuseum.ca/
cwm/exhibitions/guerre/vimy-ridge-e.aspx, retrieved
8 December 2013.

Hart, E.J. *A Hunter of Peace: Mary T. S. Schaffer's Old Indian
Trails of the Canadian Rockies*. Banff, AB: Whyte
Museum of the Canadian Rockies, 1980.

Mitchell, Benjamin Wiestling. *Trail Life in the Canadian
Rockies*. New York: The Macmillan Company, 1924.

Murray, Clinton K., MD, Mary K. Hinkle, MD, and
Heather C. Yun. "History of Infections Associated
with Combat-Related Injuries." *The Journal of
Trauma, Injury, Infection, and Critical Care* 64,
no. 3, S223 Infections of Combat Casualties.
URL: http://afids.org/publications/PDF/CRI/
Prevention%20and%20Management%20of%20
CRI%20-4-%20-%20History.pdf, retrieved
11 December 2013.

Peakfinder website. "Peaks of the Canadian Rockies:
Mount Unwin." URL: http://www.peakfinder.com/
peakfinder.ASP?PeakName=mount+unwin, retrieved
13 December 2013.

Schäffer, Mary T.S. *Old Indian Trails of the Canadian
Rockies*. New York: G.P. Putnam's Sons, 1911.

Science Museum, London, website. "Brought to Life:
Exploring the History of Medicine: Amputation." URL:
http://www.sciencemuseum.org.uk/broughttolife/
techniques/amputation.aspx, retrieved
11 December 2013.

Singhal, Hemant, MD, MBBS, FRCSE, FRCS(C),
et al. "Medscape: Wound Infection." URL:
http://emedicine.medscape.com/article/188988-
overview, retrieved 8 December 2013.

Veterans Affairs Canada website. "The Battle of Vimy
Ridge—Fast Facts." URL:
http://www.veterans.gc.ca/eng/memorials/france/
vimy/battle, retrieved 8 December 2013.

Alberta Remittance Men in the Great War

RYAN FLAVELLE

Introduction: The Remittance Man as a Reflection of English Society

Armed with a public school education, an acculturation in English manners, a one-way ticket to Canada, and—often—more firearms and alcohol than would be good for their health, the "remittance men" were a group that became a fixture of the hotel bars and society functions on the sparsely populated prairies of Canada in the late nineteenth century. As the rancher historian L.V. Kelly put it, "no story of the early times in Alberta, of its cowmen and their lives, would be complete without a description of the remittance men . . . a remittance man was a rich Englishman who had proven a failure in his home land and had been shipped into the raw land to kill himself in quiet or to work out his own regeneration if possible."[1] In the prairies and foothills of southern Alberta many remittance men—so named because they received money (a remittance) from home, in some cases specifically to stay away—found that the wild and wide-open life of a rancher "gentleman" agreed with them. They set up shop by gaining title over vast tracts of land, often with no idea

whatsoever of how to manage it. In a remittance man's effects could generally be found the physical, intellectual, and cultural baggage of the British Empire as it existed in the "high" imperial period of the Second British Empire (roughly 1857–1914).[2]

It has long been believed that the First World War saw the end of the remittance man on the Canadian prairies. Historian Mark Zuehlke opens his study of remittance men in Canada with the "perhaps true, perhaps apocryphal," legend of their departure *en masse* for the war in 1914. "Hundreds of [them] struck a pact . . . On the morning they rode to war, each left his cabin without looking back. Instead he rode to the cabin of his nearest neighbour . . . dismounted, took his rifle, and shot the aged animals . . . he [then] spilled kerosene across the cabin's cracked floorboards and set the building ablaze."[3] The story, for which Zeulke can find no hard evidence, resonates more due to its emotional appeal than its factual accuracy. Although many remittance men did join the colours either in Canada or in Britain, the history of war is rarely as cut-and-dried as to eliminate an entire group of men without a trace. Some remittance men were killed during the war, but many others returned to Canada afterward. Often injured in body or spirit, some of these men seemed to have found no home to return to in the "mother country," and others preferred the life in the foothills of Alberta. The *idea* of Empire that the remittance men had represented before the war had been one of the ultimate casualties of the conflict, but, in many cases, the men themselves continued on, although greatly changed by their experiences on the Western Front.

The Life for the Remittance Man in Southern Alberta

Remittance men were, by definition, outsiders who willingly resided at the fringes of "good society"; in Alberta, the hotel bars and the shacks on the rolling foothills were the usual settings for the stories told

about them. Their dress, accent, and swagger were a source of amusement to the "men of the range," as evidenced by, for example, a piece of doggerel that emerged around 1900: "When the half-baked remittance man comes to the west / Arrayed in short pants which he thinks suit him best / He parades around town while he takes a short rest / 'Ere assuming the role of a rancher."[4] Two men, Charlie Sturrock and Eric Buckler, seemed to fit this description. After a few weeks drinking and outfitting themselves in Calgary, they set off south to take possession of a piece of land on which they planned to build adjoining cabins. They were in high spirits and, "after a breakfast of trout, coffee and Scotch to start the day well," Buckler exclaimed, "By Jove! This will be wizard."[5] The West afforded such men a new and exhilarating freedom compared to the severe strictures placed on life among the upper classes in England. "We have a picture of grown-ups playing in a dream world, a

'I NEVAH DRINK WITH STRANGAHS'

THE ENGLISHMAN IN CANADA—10.

(left) The Canadian author W.H.P. Jarvis's take on the remittance man as an overly cultured prig. W.H.P. Jarvis, *A Remittance Man's Letters to his Mother* (Toronto: The Musson Book Co., Ltd., 1908): (right) Weighed down with the accoutrements that he believes will be necessary for life in Canada, the Englishman arrives in Canada. First published in *The Montreal Daily Star* 1901. Reprinted in *Acres and Empires*, 28.

world which most had to leave in the end to return to the formality of upper-class life in England."[6]

Primarily as a result of the scarcity of population in relation to the wide-open spaces of the West, there was relative classlessness among the white settlers. These settlers, who made up an ever-larger proportion of the population of southern Alberta, did not accept a "noble" parentage as sufficient proof of merit. Actions spoke. As Freda Graham Bundy, a teacher arriving from Nova Scotia just before the war, wrote: "They did not care whether my grandparents were Archibalds or Blairs, it meant nothing to them that my ancestors had come to Nova Scotia in 1760. They were concerned solely with my own worth."[7] That being said, the settlers tended to be extremely social people; as Bundy remembers, "It therefore was a refreshing experience for me to be invited for supper or a weekend, upon such short acquaintance."[8]

In a world before radio, television, or even readily available books, sporting events were generally large community entertainments, and remittance men often set up sporting clubs of their own. Polo was all the rage among some of these men, combining as it did well-bred horses and a chivalric flare. Joseph Deane-Freeman became a fixture and organizer of the local polo scene, and the earliest matches in the region were played near his ranch, "Monea." Born in Ireland to an aristocratic Protestant family, Deane-Freeman left an unsuccessful naval career to marry and emigrate to Millarville. Similarly, the Critchley family, who emigrated to High River in the late nineteenth century, played with their team from High River in an international polo competition in Coronado near San Diego, winning the California Challenge Cup in December 1913. The team's captain, a veteran of the Boer War, Oswald A. Critchley,

Minister of the Interior Clifford Sifton's plan to people the west in the late nineteenth and early twentieth century had largely met with success. Among the flood of immigrants who responded to posters such as this could be found the remittance men. Pamphlet titled "Canada West: The Last Best West" published in 1909 by the Government of Canada to promote the provinces of Alberta, Saskatchewan, and Manitoba to prospective immigrants and settlers. The cover features a binder cutting grain and stooks in a field at sunset and the words "Homes for Millions." Glenbow Archives, 971-2-C212c-1909.

These pictures, which were published by Bob Edwards, show a tiny remittance man who is out of both luck and money, unable to get a drink "on jawbone." When his cheque arrives, however, the remittance man once again feels large and important. First published in *The High River Eye Opener*. Reprinted in Bob Edwards and Martin James, *Irresponsible Freaks, Highball Guzzlers and Unabashed Grafters: A Bob Edwards Chrestomathy*.

Bartender : "Oh, you're very dry and are expecting money from home and want a drink on jawbone, eh ? Well, there's nothing doin'. Scoot !"

"Aw, me cheque's arrived   Give me a brandy and soda and be demmed quick about it."

and his sons William and Jack would all make a name for themselves as polo players before the war broke out.[9]

Alberta was an expensive place to live in those early times. Coupled with the high cost of liquor, transportation and lodgings were also a constant drain on remittance money. As a guidebook for the prospective immigrant to western Canada noted, "Once the people are there, the railways have them at their mercy; and they exercise consummate skill in extracting from the established settler the uttermost farthing for the transportation of persons and goods."[10] Hotels also absorbed capital. In High River the Astoria tried to draw in "commercial men" who

could find "ample accommodation for the display of their wares to local merchants."[11] There was also to be found at the Astoria "our various assortment of Fine Liquors and Cigars." In Nanton, the Auditorium Hotel offered "First class accommodation for [the] travelling public. Ranchers and Cow Punchers warmly welcomed. Finest Wines, Liquors, Cigars. Every facility afforded guests to get a glad on."[12]

Simultaneously, remittance men tended to spread their capital around freely, often being bilked out of it by the "sharpsters" who abounded on the prairies. There was always someone with an eye to acquire some quick capital from an aristocratic Englishman fresh off the train. The doctor and MLA

George Douglas Stanley provides one such example, describing a remittance man in the Astoria hotel in High River:

> The first game of Black Jack I had ever seen had been in operation for twenty-four hours straight between a wealthy remittance Englishman and a high-grade, thoroughly qualified local poker player. The Englishman lost $21,600. However Sam Heslip as a responsible citizen interfered and warned both that if the transaction went through he would have both men placed under arrest. The game was called off—superficially only—for the Englishman delivered a pair of high class Clydesdale mares, a residence in High River and thirty acres within the townsite upon which is now located much of the residential section of one of Alberta's best towns. The really unforgettable part of this incident lay in the fact that the Englishman had staked the card shark the $50.00 with which he started the game.[13]

Some of the mythos surrounding these brash, outlandish, and overly cultured men makes it difficult to define who, exactly, was a remittance man. If an emigrant found success, started a family, or settled down to the life of a rancher, they were usually excluded from this derisively titled group. Prior to the war, many died or returned home. For example, Edward Melladew, a member of the Millarville polo team "accidently shot himself in the head at the Grand Central Hotel in Okotoks in 1911."[14] Richard Dale, another remittance man given to drink and debt, was living near Mayerthorpe, Alberta, when he was bludgeoned to death with an iron bar by his neighbour Ed Dickinson. Dickinson had lent him

$150, which he failed to pay back after receiving a remittance. The story created a small sensation, and Dickinson was confined to the Ponoka insane asylum, where he died in 1944.[15] Many others did join the Canadian Expeditionary Force (CEF), but the idea that they flocked *en masse* to the colours on the outbreak of war doesn't stand up to critical scrutiny. Some joined years after the war began, and, in at least one case, waited to be conscripted.

The Great War and the Albertan Remittance Man

One of the difficulties in tracing the lives and exploits of Albertan remittance men during the war is that very few of them left written accounts of their lives. Most of the information that we have about them is second-hand and often does not give adequate or accurate information about the identity of the man in question. Pseudonyms and nicknames such as "Coyote Jack," "Lord Dutton," "Kootenai Brown," or "Albert Buzzard-Cholomondeley of Skookingham Hall"[16] tend to obscure from critical enquiry the realities of these men's lives.

Those who remember the fate of the Albertan remittance men when the war broke out usually cite duty and patriotism as the driving factors in their enlistment. As Senator F.W. Gershaw wrote, "When . . . danger threatened the isles of Britain, they dropped everything and regardless of costs [how true to form] rushed to the defence of the beloved land of their birth. Many of them never returned. When the test came they proved to be true to the highest traditions of the race."[17] News of the war spread quickly throughout the settlements in Alberta, and "the talk of war was on everyone's lips." The mayor of Calgary, H.A. Sinnott, ordered the janitor at City Hall to "haul the Union Jack to the masthead." He told the *Calgary*

Herald that, now that the war was on, "let's have the flag up, say I."[18] Indeed, he also reported a shortage of flags, so many having been loaned out. While the mayor ruminated over the lack of flags, other men sought desperately to enlist. The unemployment problem was solved quickly, as unemployed men "rush[ed] to recruit." One young jobless Englishman, who probably would have been termed a remittance man had he received a remittance, was reliant on Calgary's Associated Charities, which provided him the basics of life. On Wednesday, 5 August 1914, the day after the British declared war, the unemployed one walked in the office of Superintendent McNicholl, and "thanked him for what the charities had done for him" and said goodbye, leaving for Esquimalt to join the crew of the HMCS *Rainbow*, one of the two cruisers that made up Canada's tiny navy.[19] Throughout the province, canvas villages sprouted up on the prairies to temporarily house men waiting to leave to join the CEF.

Many remittance men had served in the military prior to casting their lot on the prairies, and were thus all the more likely to join when news of the war reached them. "With a certain class of high-bred Englishmen there is only the twinkle of a star between the glory of a well-wined mess . . . and a shack on a western ranch."[20] Similarly, Grant McEwan relates that "ramrod-straight Col. James Walker might be found [in the Alberta Hotel] at almost any time—the old Colonel who was a member of the first troop of Mounted Police that trekked across the plains to build Fort Macleod . . . and a man who, according to General Sir Arthur Currie, 'breaks out every fifty years and goes to war.'"[21] These men were likely to rejoin their regiments as soon as possible after the start of the war. Men such as Captain Lionel Asquith would fall into this category. Having served

with the Royal Dragoons and East Kent Regiment during the Boer War, Asquith had settled down in Lethbridge and married Colia Alice. He remained an active member of the militia, serving as an officer with the 35th Battery of the Canadian Field Artillery based in Lethbridge. Asquith enlisted on Christmas Eve 1915 and survived the war; when asked to give his trade or calling, he responded that he was a "gentleman." Asquith returned to Canada with a "moderate general dibility [*sic*]," caused by a hernia sustained while training soldiers in bayonet fighting after a long route march in Bramshott, England.[22]

Asquith was not the only soldier who gave his trade or calling as "gentleman." Stanley Winther Caws, another Boer War veteran with tattoos covering both forearms, did as well. Despite being a remittance man, Caws had met relative success in Alberta, establishing a club and building a hall for the Legion of Frontiersmen in Alberta. He even paid the board for a newly arrived young Englishman who "couldn't manage the rough life of a pioneer."[23] Caws served first with the 19th Alberta Dragoons before transferring to the Royal Flying Corps (RFC). He was killed in action. Unlike Caws, most who enlisted as "gentleman" tended to use the word to indicate their genteel unemployment. Albert Edward Grimes was living at the YMCA in Lethbridge prior to enlisting in 1916. Herbert Cowell and John Graham Johnson, both of whom gave their calling as gentleman, resided in the Palliser hotel in Calgary and the Alexandra hotel in Lethbridge respectively. Robert Mansfield Fitzgerald, who lived the life of a day labourer and remittance man in Banff before the war, joined the Princess Patricia's Canadian Light Infantry as an original in 1914. Prior to the war he had fought the Zulus during the Natal Rebellion. He died in January 1916 while attempting to help a

Highland soldier lying in No Man's Land: "[He] had gone out between the two firing lines to ascertain if a Highlander lying there was past all help and, if so, to bring in his identification disc. As he was dropping to safety in the trench, disc in hand, a sniper's bullet pierced his brain. He was idolized by the men and a most gallant officer."[24] Another Patricia member described him as the "finest man and the most popular officer in the whole regiment. He was the British reservist, of good family, who went out to Calgary a couple of years ago, went broke, and finally had to go to work at manual labour for the government at Banff. When the war broke out he was among the first to offer his services." In the words of the *Crag and Canyon,* a newspaper in Banff, "those who knew him best recognized the gentleman born and bred under the guise of a working man."[25]

Perhaps surprisingly, those who self-identified as "gentleman" on their attestation papers were not all British. Charles McBride and Walker Lewis Taylor were both born in Alberta and gave their trade or calling as gentlemen. After being wounded in a German bombardment at Mount Sorrel in 1916, McBride wrote home to his sister that "One time when Nance was telling my fortune she said I was going on a long journey and going to be lucky; I am sure lucky to get out of that alive."[26] Taylor, who was made a sergeant based on his previous militia experience, rushed to enlist and signed his attestation papers at Valcartier in September 1914. He was eventually promoted to captain and survived the war. Perhaps Taylor was not being entirely honest when he gave his trade as gentleman, seeing as how he had contracted gonorrhea in 1912. Their use of the word "gentleman" at enlistment attests to the somewhat conflicted identities surrounding that word. Although Alberta was thought to be a classless

society in its early years, the word gentleman still had a large amount of *cachet* among Albertans prior to, during, and after the war. The word was not used as a determinant of class, as it was in the British context, but rather as a way of evoking a certain code of behaviour. It was also used as a way to indicate that a man did not have gainful employment.[27]

Both Eric Buckler, and Charlie Sturrock—those two rambling adventurers who, with bellies full of trout, coffee, and scotch, had exclaimed that their venture into ranching would "be wizard"—returned to England to enlist after the war broke out. Sturrock's wife, Irene, recalls their story: "When the 1914 war began, most of these would-be ranchers joined up and many lost their lives. Eric Buckler was killed, Charlie Sturrock, who had enlisted with the Lovat Scouts, transferred to the King's Own Scottish Borderers and returned from France late in 1917 with a disabled heart."[28] Irene Sturrock intimates that her husband—who had arrived in Alberta with a remittance in 1903—died young as a result of the war. Together with her two children, Joan and Bruce, Irene "carried on with the Ranch for a number of years after Charles' death, then decided to dispose of it and each go our own way in life." Note that Sturrock did return to Alberta, but as a changed man.

The High River Polo Club saw a large number of its members sign up after the outbreak of war. For men who had achieved such an excellent standard of horsemanship, to remain at home seemed unthinkable. Oswald A. Critchley became an officer in the Lord Strathcona's Horse, signing his attestation papers at the age of 50 on his farm. His sons, John Ashton and Alfred Cecil, also enlisted, Jack becoming an officer in the Strathconas and Alfred an officer in a machine gun battalion. Perhaps in those heady days of enlistment in the fall of 1914, they imagined

The war would not resemble the polo matches that the Critchleys excelled at. Jack did not survive the war, dying shortly before the Battle of Vimy Ridge. First published in *The Burlington Gazette*, 13 January 1915. Also published in A.C. Critchley, *Critch!: The Memoirs of Brigadier-General A.C. Critchley*.

that the war would be rather like a polo match; instead they would find that, in fact, barbed wire and trench warfare had all but eliminated the cavalry arm from the battlefield, at least until the very end of the war. Jack, who had played on the team at Coronado with his father, would not survive the war. He was mortally wounded during a heavy German bombardment near Equancourt in late March 1917 and died just prior to the battle of Vimy Ridge on 5 April 1917. He was 24. Alfred and Oswald both survived the war, but decided to remain in Britain after the Armistice.

Some remittance men chose to remain in Canada during the war. Coyote Charlie, who had had the

school in High River named the Union Jack, was an old man in 1914. He had "foresworn bathing and the use of any but profane language when he left his beautiful English home," and had fallen on hard times by the time the war broke out.[29] He rented a one-roomed shack on the outskirts of Calgary, and Stanley records that he was harassed by a drove of pigs owned by a German livestock operator. Finally he beseeched the doctor's aid, saying that "it's a *blankety-blank-blank* outrage that a German *blankety-blank-blank* should be allowed to corral his *blankety* dirty hogs on an English gentleman's lawn!"[30] Stanley also records that, prior to the war, Charlie had walked to the "nearest German neighbour's house" after finding the Union Jack on the local school replaced with a "dirty old gunny sack." "The neighbour was wise enough to know that discretion was the better part of valour," and was marched "in front of the gun, up the ladder and made to replace the Union Jack."[31] Charlie was too old to enlist despite his patriotic protestations.

Despite such overt protestations of patriotism (which, it seems possible, were slightly embellished in their reminiscence after the war), some remittance men of military age did not rush to join up. Neither of the Lusk brothers, Charlie and Harry—who were recorded as popular young bachelors whose family lived in a castle in Howell Kurkcubright, Scotland, and were much in demand in the Millarville social scene prior to the war's outbreak—seemed in any hurry to join the military. Charlie enlisted in February 1916 in Lethbridge and survived the war, whereas his brother Harry waited to be conscripted into the CEF, in August 1918. Harry would not survive the war, falling victim to the Spanish influenza that caused more casualties than the fighting itself.[32]

Conclusion: The Impact of the War on Remittance Men in Alberta

The Great War did not see the end of the British nobility, or the remittance man in Alberta. Some, like Coyote Charlie, never left the province during the war. Many more, like Harry Lusk, Charlie Sturrock, and Lionel Asquith, returned after the war. However, the Great War served as an opportunity for some of these "black sheep" to return to their families and their societies with whatever stain that existed on their characters wiped clean. Many returned to Canada after the war, but those who had served with the CEF no longer found it difficult to integrate into life in the foothills of Alberta. Remittance men continued to be a part of the cultural landscape of southern Alberta after the war; they were simply not as outlandishly apparelled or noticeable in the world that emerged from the war. There were no longer so many unemployed adventurers, and the whole landscape took on a more sober and mature countenance. The war did not see the end of the Albertan remittance man, but it did cause a significant drop in their numbers, and their adventurous spirit. And the country to which they returned was also different. The disappearance of the remittance man on the prairies has as much to do with a shift in Canadians' understanding of themselves as it does with the remittance men.

The war had changed those who fought in it, and the country that had sent them. This sentiment is perhaps best echoed by N.B. James, an Englishman who had emigrated to western Canada before the war (although he was careful to point out that "I was NOT a remittance man myself. I would have liked to have been but the one essential—the remittance—was lacking").[33]

Things had changed, and whether we really had saved the country or not, it didn't seem to be the same country we were told so effusively that we had rescued. By the same token we weren't quite the same. We had gone through things and they had left their mark. It wasn't altogether the nastiness of war . . . but also we had seen other countries and met and liked other peoples, and our vision had broadened, and our souls had hardened . . . I think perhaps we lost something that was infinitely more precious than the searing experience of bloodshed could teach us. But the change wasn't just in us. Canada, at least western Canada, had changed. We had come back with the idea of starting in where we had left off, and carrying on from there. Unfortunately, the place we had left off wasn't there anymore.[34]

James's experience was a common one. Many returning remittance men found that the world that they had left simply no longer existed; nor did the sort of young adventurers who had left it in the first place.

Perhaps the best demonstration of how the British nobility fared in Alberta after the war is provided by the case of Frederick Joseph Trevelyan Perceval and his son Frederick George Moore Perceval. Their story reads like something out of the television show *Downton Abbey*. From a minor branch of the Perceval family, Frederick and his first wife, Cecila, had emigrated to Alberta in 1900. He purchased a ranch, and they had a son in 1914. Cecilia died in 1916, and Frederick and his son became very close, raising livestock and living the ranching life in Alberta. In 1929 the childless Charles John Perceval, the ninth Earl of Egmont, died and his closest living relative

The 11th Earl of Egmont on his ranch near Priddis, Alberta. *The Calgary Herald* first published this photo in 1948; since published 28 April 2012.

was Frederick. Lord Beaverbrook, the Canadian Press Baron who owned the *Daily Express* in London, called the new earl to inform him of his good fortune. His son was not particularly enthusiastic about their change in station, saying, "You taught me to read and write and you taught me to ride and shoot . . . We've got a nice home here, and I don't want to leave it."[35] The pair never quite fit into English society. In 1932 Frederick Joseph died in a car crash. Eulogizing him, the *Sunday Express*'s theatre critic, James Agate, wrote that "doubtless the late earl's accent and manners may, like his boots, have been a shade too thick for the fine carpets of Hampshire. Doubtless he was no master of small talk, because on an Alberta ranch, if you talk at all, the subjects will probably be pretty big. They may be kittle cattle but they certainly won't be tittle tattle."[36] Frederick George, as the successor to the earldom and the eleventh Earl of Egmont, was also shy and retiring and did not care for the society in England or the media scrutiny that he lived under.

He put Avon Castle on the market and returned to Alberta. "What English people do not realise," he explained, "is that there is a greater spirit of freedom and generosity over here in Canada."[37] In 1932 he presented the prizes at the livestock review at the Calgary Stampede, married his childhood sweetheart, and continued to live in Alberta until dying at the age of 87 in 2002.[38]

What the Earl of Egmont's story demonstrates is that Alberta continued to be a place for upper-class Englishmen to escape the strictures that were placed on them by their own society. Just as before the war, so too after it, some Englishmen found a freedom in Alberta that they could not find in their own country. As for the individual remittance men who returned from the war, all had been changed by their experiences. They were no longer so numerous or innocent as they had once been, but Alberta continued as a place of refuge for them, just as Albertans continued to show an interest in their exploits.

Notes

1   L.V. Kelly, *The Range Men* (Toronto: William Briggs, 1913), 16–17.

2   Although no date serves as an accurate representation of the massive conglomeration of dependent states and "settler [White] Dominions" that made up the Second British Empire, the one normally given is that of the consolidation of British power in India and the cultural and psychological shift that occurred after the Indian Rebellion.

3   Mark Zuehlke, *Scoundrels, Dreamers and Second Sons: British Remittance Men in the Canadian West* (Toronto: Dundurn, 2001), 9.

4   Tracey Read, *Acres and Empires: A History of the Municipal District of Rocky View No. 44* (Irricana, AB: Tall-Taylor Publishing, 1983), 29.

5   Zuehlke, *Scoundrels, Dreamers and Second Sons,* 53.

6   Read, *Acres and Empires,* 31.

7   Glenbow Archives (Calgary), Freda Graham Bundy, "Go West Young Woman," Freda Graham Bundy Fonds.

8   Ibid.

9   *Our Foothills* (Calgary: Millarville, Kew, Priddis and Bragg Creek Historical Society, 1976), 110. A.C. Critchley, *Critch!: The Memoirs of Brigadier-General A.C. Critchley* (London, UK: Hutchinson, 1961). "Winter Polo in California," *The Polo Monthly* 10 (December 1913): 264, 354, 460–62.

10 H.R. Whates, *Canada the New Nation: A Book for the Settler, the Emigrant and the Politician* (London, UK: J.M. Dent and Co., 1906), 142.

11 Ad run in *High River Eye Opener,* July 1903.

12 Ibid.

13 Dr. G.D. Stanley, *A Roundup of Fun in the Foothills* (Calgary: G.D. Stanley, 1949), 9–10.

14 *Our Foothills,* 174.

15 *Three Trails Home: A History of Mayerthorpe and Districts, Alberta, Canada* (Mayerthorpe, AB: Intercollegiate Press, 1980), 56.

16 Newspaperman Bob Edwards's hilarious fictional character who has done so much to shape our perception of the English remittance man. Edwards's fictional "letters of a badly made son to his father in England" told the story of "Bertie," who had come to the prairies with a "love of liquor which I must have inherited either from yourself or my grandfather, made me a failure as a bartender and I soon got the bounce. So I packed my things in a large envelope and hit the blind baggage for the West where I went cow punching." Bob Edwards and Martin James, *Irresponsible Freaks, Highball Guzzlers and Unabashed Grafters: A Bob Edwards Chrestomathy* (Calgary: Brindle and Glass, 2004), 204–20. See also Grant MacEwan, *Eye Opener Bob: The Story of Bob Edwards* (Calgary: Brindle and Glass, 2004), 36–47.

17 F.W. Gershaw, *Medicine Hat: Early Days in Southern Alberta* (Medicine Hat, AB: F.W. Gershaw, 1954).

18 *Calgary Daily Herald,* 5 August 1914.

19 Ibid.

20 Grant McEwan, *Eye Opener Bob,* 36.

21 Ibid., 65.

22 "General Soldier Search," *The Canadian Great War Project,* URL: http://www.canadiangreatwarproject.com/searches/soldierSearch.asp, retrieved 1 July 2014. "Asquith, Lionel: Digitized Service File," *Library and Archives Canada,* URL: http://www.bac-lac.gc.ca/eng/discover/military-heritage/first-world-war/first-world-war-1914-1918-cef/, retrieved 1 July 2014.

23 "Lieutenant Stanley Winther Caws," *The Canadian Great War Project CEF Soldier Detail,* URL: http://www.canadiangreatwarproject.com/searches/soldierDetail.asp?ID=41627, retrieved 1 July 2014.

24 "Pte. Harry Horwood, PPCLI, Recounts Wartime Experiences," *Crag and Canyon* (Banff, AB), 23 October 1915, available on *The Canadian Great War Project* website, transcribed by M.I. Pirie, URL: http://www.canadiangreatwarproject.com/transcripts/transcriptDisplay.asp?Type=N&Id=823, retrieved 1 July 2014.

25 "A PPCLI Man First to be Killed from Banff, Alberta," *Crag and Canyon,* 6 February 1915, available on *The Canadian Great War Project* website, transcribed by M.I. Pirie, URL: http://www.canadiangreatwarproject.com/transcripts/transcriptDisplay.asp?Type=N&Id=817, retrieved 1 July 2014.

26 "Private Charles Dawson McBride: His Experience with the 2nd C.M.R. at Mount Sorrel, 1916," *The Canadian Great War Project CEF Letters from the Front,* URL: http://www.canadiangreatwarproject.com/transcripts/transcriptDisplay.asp?Type=L&id=35, retrieved 1 July 2014.

27 "Charles McBride," "Walker Lewis Taylor," *The Canadian Great War Project.*

28 *Our Foothills,* 213–15.

29 Stanley, *Fun in the Foothills,* 14.

30 Ibid.

31 Ibid.

32 Zuehlke, *Scoundrels, Dreamers and Second Sons,* 153–55; *Our Foothills,* 162.

33 N.B. James, *The Autobiography of a Nobody* (Toronto: J.M. Dent and Sons, 1947), 36–37.

34 Ibid., 101.

35 "The Earl of Egmont," *The Telegraph*, 3 January 2002, URL: http://www.telegraph.co.uk/news/obituaries/1380184/The-Earl-of-Egmont.html, retrieved 1 July 2014.

36 Ibid.

37 Ibid.

38 Ibid. See also "Stampede 100 Day Countdown: 1932 Rewind," *Calgary Herald,* 18 April 2012.

Works Cited

PRIMARY SOURCES

Calgary Daily Herald

Crag and Canyon (Banff, AB)

High River Eye Opener

Polo Monthly

The Canadian Great War Project CEF Letters from the Front.

The Canadian Great War Project CEF Soldier Detail.

Glenbow Archives, Calgary. Freda Graham Bundy Fonds.

Library and Archives Canada. "Asquith, Lionel: Digitized Service File." URL: http://www.bac-lac.gc.ca/eng/discover/military-heritage/first-world-war/first-world-war-1914-1918-cef/.

SECONDARY SOURCES

Critchley, A.C. *Critch!: The Memoirs of Brigadier-General A.C. Critchley*. London, UK: Hutchinson, 1961.

Edwards, Bob, and Martin James. *Irresponsible Freaks, Highball Guzzlers and Unabashed Grafters: A Bob Edwards Chrestomathy.* Calgary: Brindle and Glass, 2004.

Gershaw, F.W. *Medicine Hat: Early Days in Southern Alberta.* Medicine Hat, AB: F.W. Gershaw, 1954.

James, N.B. *The Autobiography of a Nobody*. Toronto: J.M. Dent and Sons, 1947.

Kelly, L.V. *The Range Men*. Toronto: William Briggs, 1913.

MacEwan, Grant. *Eye Opener Bob: The Story of Bob Edwards*. Calgary: Brindle and Glass, 2004.

Mayerthorpe and District History Society. *Three Trails Home: A History of Mayerthorpe and Districts, Alberta, Canada*. Mayerthorpe, AB: Intercollegiate Press, 1980.

Millarville, Kew, Priddis and Bragg Creek Historical Society. *Our Foothills*. Calgary: Millarville, Kew, Priddis, and Bragg Creek Historical Society, 1976.

Read, Tracey. *Acres and Empires: A History of the Municipal District of Rocky View No. 44.* Iricana, AB: Tall-Taylor Publishing, 1983.

Stanley, Dr. G.D. *A Roundup of Fun in the Foothills*. Calgary: G.D. Stanley, 1949.

Whates, H.R. *Canada the New Nation: A Book for the Settler the Emigrant and the Politician*. London, UK: J.M. Dent, 1906.

Zuehlke, Mark. *Scoundrels, Dreamers and Second Sons: British Remittance Men in the Canadian West*. Toronto: Dundurn, 2001.

BIBLIOGRAPHICAL NOTE

Information for individual soldiers is taken primarily from two excellent online databases which should form the foundation for any researcher undertaking a project dealing with soldiers of the First World War.

The first is Library and Archives Canada's database of digital attestation papers and service files, available at www.bac-lac.gc.ca/eng/discover/military-heritage/first-world-war/first-world-war-1914-1918-cef/Pages/search.aspx (or just google "attestation papers"). On it can be found the forms that soldiers filled out on enlistment for every one of the over 619,636 troops that made up the CEF. Furthermore, the digitization of service files is currently ongoing, and if you are lucky enough to be researching a soldier whose last name begins with a, b, or c, you stand a good chance of finding his complete digital service record.

The second resource is the privately run website *The Canadian Great War Project* (www.canadiangreatwarproject.com), which has a number of excellent tools. A "general soldier search" will give access to a digitally searchable form of the attestation paper (for example, using the keyword "gentleman" gives 127 hits), and cross references those files with known newspaper articles and letters.

The Effects of the First World War
on the Franco-European Immigrants of Alberta

JULIETTE CHAMPAGNE

In Alberta, little is remembered about the Franco-European immigrants to Canada who were called to their respective regiments with the outbreak of the war in August 1914. Yet there were approximately 10,000 French reservists in the country at the time.[1] Belgians and Swiss were also called up to their regiments. Although they fought in the war, these men are not counted as Canadian soldiers because they served under the flag of their country of origin. Some were killed; others were wounded or gassed and permanently debilitated from the effects. The lucky ones returned to pick up where they left off.

In Alberta, we do not find their names on memorials although many had become British citizens of Canada, or were in the process of becoming so, since eligibility consisted of three years of residence. For the Francophone community of Alberta, the consequences of the First World War were to bleed it of its Franco-European population. Regions that had a considerable population of these immigrants—farming communities, mining communities, towns and cities, ranching communities—lost almost all of these men and, often, their families as well. Some pieces of the story can be found in newspapers

from the period. Others can be told through a small collection of postcards that my mother, Germaine Champagne, has conserved. They were sent from the front to her parents by their compatriot, Jean Poilvé, who had rejoined his regiment in France. There are also two cards from relatives in France who were mobilized there. While there are a few mentions here and there in various publications about these members of the Francophone community who fought in the war, it is just a small part of the story of Franco-Europeans in Alberta; however, it is an interesting and significant one. The postcards form an important collection that provides insight into the way in which the war was depicted in France through this extremely popular art form. The images are iconic and frequently depict stereotypes of national heroes and heroines in a cartoon-like fashion. Wartime postcards in the Allied countries were everywhere and were a part of the propaganda war in which the Allies were always heroic and the enemy was depicted in the most unflattering light.

Sources readily available in Alberta on the subject of military service of recent immigrants from France are limited. Lists of names were published in the only French-language newspaper in Alberta at the time, *L'Union,* but these compilations from 1918 are mainly of "*pure-laine*" (that is, "virgin wool," or Canadian-born) men from the French-Canadian communities, although there are a few names of Franco-Europeans from central Alberta (Red Deer, Chauvin, Castor, etc.), where quite a few of them had also settled.[2] The list does not include Calgary or southern Alberta. It must be noted, however, that much of this newspaper has been lost over time, and it is possible that there were other lists published in the missing issues.

English-language newspapers also provide some information. For example, in 1916, a Stettler paper published a "Roll of Honor" of 100 local recruits, of which at least 19 are of known French, or Belgian, origin, but it is not specified in which army they enlisted.[3] There is also documentation from Library and Archives Canada about recruits who joined up with the Canadian Overseas Expeditionary Force, in 1916, coming from across Alberta: Sylvan Lake, Trochu, Edmonton, Calgary, St-Paul-des-Métis, Grande Prairie, Grandin, Legal, Beaverlodge, and so on.[4] Reviewing the enlistment records online requires exhaustive research and, as yet, has not been done. At the time, many members of the Missionary Oblates of Mary Immaculate in Canada were originally from France, and a considerable number of them returned to fight for their homeland. They served as interpreters, combatants, and as chaplains. Several of them had been based in Alberta, including Désiré Bocquené from Fort Vermilion, Laurent Legoff from Cold Lake, Jean-Marie Le Clainche from St-Paul-des-Métis, Émile Fabre from the Edmonton-based Juniorat St-Jean (a college run by the Oblates and now the Francophone Campus Saint-Jean of the University of Alberta), and several others.[5]

Canada had been recruiting settlers for many years from Europe but, as most of these countries had armies, many had undergone military training as young men and were obliged, as reservists, to rejoin their respective regiments if their country declared war. This applied to most Europeans, not only to the French, Belgians, or Swiss, but also to those from the Austro-Hungarian Empire, which, of course, led to the rapid internment of the latter group in camps created across Canada during the First World War. Rejoining their regiment was not just a patriotic duty, it was an obligation; not obeying was considered to be desertion and treason, which, of course, could mean imprisonment and even capital punishment upon returning to the home country. Given the great distances in the Canadian West, this was a concern, and the Canadian Belgian consulate, which began calling in its reservists at the beginning of August 1914, was informed by its minister of foreign affairs that Belgians in Canada could count on a period of amnesty until October 4 to come in.[6] As well, reservists who were homesteading, and had not yet completed the requirements for the title of their land, were concerned about retaining their rights, and, very quickly, the Lands and Titles Office in Ottawa made it clear that the time they spent in the service of their country would be counted as residence on their homestead.[7]

Early in August 1914, several newspapers in Alberta mentioned the sudden departure of French reservists accompanied to the train stations by large crowds singing *La Marseillaise* and waving French flags. Going-away dinners and parades were also the norm. On August 6, the *Bassano Mail* reported hundreds of French reservists leaving Calgary on the train bound for Montreal to embark for the Atlantic crossing, and particularly noted the sudden departure of local resident "Charlie" (Charles) De

Bourboule, who for several years had been the chauffeur for the director of the large irrigation project in Bassano.[8]

The number of French reservists in Alberta is not specified in the papers, but in a news release in the *Patriote de l'Ouest* of Prince Albert, Saskatchewan, the French vice-consul of Saskatchewan stated that there were over 4,000 in Saskatchewan alone.[9] The number may not have been as high in Alberta, but it seems to have been considerable nonetheless. The "French" population of Alberta in the 1911 census results was listed as 20,600; this included all Francophones in the province, not just those from France or elsewhere in Europe. The French could be found in large numbers working in the mines owned by the French and Belgian conglomerate of West Canadian Collieries in the Bellevue and Frank regions of southern Alberta. They were also on ranches, the Trochu group being the best known today, but many others were located in Edmonton and Calgary, and there were a great number who had taken homesteads across the province.

Those who had the financial means could report to their regiment immediately, and some did. The mobilization order had been issued in Canada on August 2, after the invasion of France by Germany.[10] Within days, the French consuls were able to give train tickets to the reservists departing from Calgary as well as Edmonton.[11] At Trochu, they received a telegram from the French consul, and a dozen Frenchmen, along with Belgians from the area, left the next day for Calgary.[12] The consuls were aware of the considerable isolation of many of their reservists, and fully expected that it would take some of them at least a month before they could clear up their affairs and answer the call.[13] It was, after all, August, time for farmers to be haying or tilling fallow fields, and harvest time was near. Arrangements also had to be made for livestock. It is said that one man departed in such haste that he left his plow in the middle of the field.[14]

According to another family's oral tradition, Jean-Louis Sévère, a Breton who was then in Ouelletteville, near Cluny in southern Alberta, left within a week of the declaration of war, but closer examination revealed that it was September 12 before he entrained at Calgary.[15] It was estimated that there were over 200 French reservists north of Edmonton, and on August 10, according to the *Courrier de l'Ouest*, more than 50 left Edmonton for France. They left from Montreal on the 15th.[16] Transportation across the Atlantic from Montreal had been held up as early as August 4, as rumours were flying that British ships were being attacked by German ships in the gulf of the St. Lawrence.[17] But, according to the *Courrier de l'Ouest*, the *Royal Edward* left on August 10 with 600 reservists and was accompanied across the Atlantic by French and British warships.[18]

My grandfather, Alexandre Mahé, was homesteading near St. Vincent, about 20 kilometres north of St-Paul-des-Métis, having come from France in 1909. He would have gone to fight if he had been able, but in 1912 he came down with a severe case of pleurisy that required surgery. He was still in the process of regaining his health when war broke out. His two brothers in France, as well as several of his brothers-in-law, were called up, but here in Canada, Alex obtained a dispensation from his doctor and was officially invalidated.[19]

Contrary to the French Canadians originally from eastern Canada, most of whom had come to take homesteads in western Canada with their families, many of the Frenchmen and Belgians were bachelors, and they tended to socialize and help each other out since they had much in common culturally. There were quite a few French and Belgians established a few kilometres north of St. Vincent, in the Thérien and St. Lina area. When the war broke out, Jean Poilvé and his nephew, Jules Sancenot, who were both farming nearby, decided to leave for France. The date of their departure is not known, but they arrived by September, so travel across the Atlantic was possible at that time, although other soldiers experienced delays. Alex, along with Charles Marthoz, a neighbour of Belgian origin, agreed to help them by managing their farms while they were away. Alex was to sell Poilvé's livestock and grain, while Marthoz would rent the land. The correspondence that has survived about Poilvé and Sancenot is only in the form of postcards, all of which are in French. There were letters, but they were not preserved.

The earliest card, dated 19 September 1914, is from Poilvé. It shows Kaiser William depicted as a pig. The boot prints on its behind illustrate the commonly held belief that the Germans would be quickly

Kaiser William as a pig. Germaine Mahé Champagne postcard collection.

booted out of France and Belgium, as mentioned in the message on the second postcard. The stamp has been deliberately positioned as if "Marianne," the young woman used as an emblem of France, is preparing to kick the pig. The text "S.M. Guillaume II" is, of course, "His Majesty William," with the cartoon pig wearing the Prussian helmet, sword, and riding boots, typical items of military dress of the Kaiser and the officer class. The pig's large tusks mimic the large, pointed moustache that the Kaiser was known to wear. It was common in cartoons of the period in the various western countries to use animal images to represent the values of different countries and their citizenry.

Poilvé wrote "Vive la France" on the face of the card and signed his name. On the back of the card he wrote:

> My dear friends:
> Everything went well on the voyage. I sailed on the *Espagne*. The news is very good and we think we will be going to Berlin. I have seen many who are very lightly wounded and wish to return to the fighting. The Germans are still retreating. I hope it will not be long now. I will give you more ample news next week in a letter. Sancenot went to London, while I went to St. Malo.
> Your friend, Jean Poilvé.[20]

From the mention of London and St. Malo, it can be presumed that the two men sailed on different ships. We do not know when they left, but we can assume it was late August, if not early September, as this card is dated the 15th. No newspapers mention the departure of these two from Alberta. If the promised letter was received, it was not preserved. It is possible that

An Italian soldier bearing the national flag. Germaine Mahé Champagne postcard collection

you are as well. We are convinced we will be victorious and afterwards will have a very well deserved peace." Touchingly, his note ends with: "Your friend, who never ceases thinking of his Canada." It is clear that he was committed to his land, his friends, and Canada.

On 28 May 1915 he sent five cards at once. Two of the postcards are the same, that of two women holding the French flag aloft and wearing the traditional costumes of Alsace and Lorraine. The Franco-Prussian War, in 1870, was a deep wound to the French nation. The Imperial Territory of Alsace-Lorraine was established in 1871, after the French loss, when the Germans annexed the majority of Alsace and part of Lorraine. This image was an incendiary one for the French and intended to arouse patriotic feelings and the desire to obtain revenge on the Germans. The text on the first card reads: "I send you these five cards to amuse you and please let me know when you have received them. I will then send you some others. Your old friend, Jean Poilvé, sergeant, 24 7-34 postal sector 1051, France." On the back of the second card, he wrote: "My dear friends, I send you this card to give you and show you my valiant Lorraine and Alsace, my future fiancées of a coming day. Dear friends, I had answered your last letter. I do not know if you have received it. I hope so, and if you write back please let me know if you have sold my cattle. If not, please do your utmost to sell them, Jean." While he was already in the military, he still worried about his Alberta homestead and the investment that it represented.

The loss of almost the entire department of Alsace and the Moselle portion of Lorraine had been a long-standing sore point with the French. Reintegrating these two departments back into the fold was a national dream shared by Poilvé. One can

not all the postcards were saved either, but the next one in the collection is from January 1915; Italy was then an ally of France and Britain.

On 10 January 1915, Poilvé asked about the disposal of the effects from his farm: "Give me some news of my livestock. Have you sold them along with my machinery? At this time I am very well and I hope

only suppose that with his mention of his "future fiancées" Poilvé, a single man at the time, was also expressing the hope that the day would come when he too could settle down with a wife. Again, he voices his concern that his livestock be sold, as he had evidently learned that they had been overwintered, and this was an unnecessary expense for him. It is likely that Alex was trying to sell the cattle; however, they were probably thin after the winter and needed

(above) Two young women in the regional dress of Alsace and Lorraine appear to be embraced by the French flag, and the slogan "Vive la France" appears below. The rising sun behind the church spire suggests hope that France will regain the territories it lost in the Franco-Prussian War. Germaine Mahé Champagne postcard collection; (right) Postcards depicting soldiers were extremely popular. *Poilu* was the French popular term for the ordinary soldier. The ruined church and houses in the background suggest what he is fighting for. Germaine Mahé Champagne postcard collection.

to be fattened up before they could be sold. Driving them on the hoof to the nearest railhead was a two-day journey and hard on the cattle; a local sale would have been more reasonable, but money was very tight for everyone in these isolated rural areas.

The third card of the five, dated May 28, is of a "*Poilu*" (from *poil*, or hair), the popular term for French soldiers in First World War, surely having to do with the fact that they did not have much opportunity to shave and were, therefore, "shaggy" or "hairy." The equivalent British term for the common soldier was "Tommy" (and, later on for the Americans, "Doughboy"). The soldier represented is heavily bearded and bravely standing at attention, holding his bayonet in front of a ruined country church. Poilvé wrote: "This shows you the work of the *bochemen*, our valiant Poilu is guarding the ruins—many are the cities like this. Fortunately all this will soon end. If you see some of the old friends say hello to them for me, Jean."

The fourth card depicts the uniformed French, Belgian and British allies with their respective flags. No doubt, Poilvé was missing his friends and his home in Canada, and he knew that they too were hungry for news of the war. On this card Poilvé wrote: "Dear friends, Do not forget to give our good news to neighbours and friends of the region and that we hope for a final victory and a prompt return home (*au pays*). In the meantime, I shake your hand. Put these cards in your store window, they will attract customers." My grandfather had opened a general store soon after his arrival to the area in 1909, and this had enabled him to manage financially until the arrival of the railroad.

The last card is titled "For France, for the homeland, for God," and Poilvé writes: "Dear Friends, Jules has gone towards Notre-Dame-de-Lorette, he

Allied soldiers depicted with their national flags and the slogan "Towards Victory." The sun is shown breaking through the clouds to herald a new day. Traditional age-old rivalries are forgotten as they fight together to defeat Germany. Germaine Mahé Champagne postcard collection.

This postcard juxtaposes a praying nun with young soldiers on the front. Since most combatants were Christians, it was commonly believed that the deity was on their side; thus, the slogan, "For France, for the homeland, for God." Germaine Mahé Champagne postcard collection.

is very well at this time as am I. This card shows some of the effects of the bombardments and the devotion of our good Sisters." Two vignettes are depicted:

uppermost is the image of two French soldiers on the battlefield with bombs exploding around them and nearby buildings. In the bottom half, a nun is seen half rising from a kneeling position. A large rosary hangs from her belt and she is raising her right hand to her right ear as if she is listening to the sounds of battle and has been interrupted in her prayers. A peaceful little town is seen in the background. In France, nuns from religious communities were often the nurses, from which the term "sisters" for nurses arose. That his nephew Jules Sancenot had gone to Notre-Dame-de-Lorette and returned safely was good news, as this was a very hotly contested part of the front.

Sent on 19 June 1915, Poilvé's next card is a photo of General Joffre, commemorating three battles of 1914: La Marne, L'Aigne, and L'Yger. A battle scene with a large army is in the background. Poilvé noted that he hadn't received any mail from Alex. Far away on the battlefields of France, he is thinking of the farming conditions in Alberta and of his friends and neighbours. He also sends news of Sancenot:

Dear friends, Tell me what's happening with you? I had sent you five cards, did you receive them? You did not answer me; tell me what is going on there. The seeding must be done by now and must be coming up nicely. Jules has gone to the north to Pas de Calais. He tells me the action is very hot there right now. I am looking forward to receiving news from you. Hello to the neighbours and a cordial handshake, Jean.

Poilvé sent two cards on 30 July 1915. On the first one, he wrote to Alex and his wife:

(left) General Joffre is depicted with the slogan that France's destiny is entrusted to him. The flowers surrounding his image are of the poppy, the marguerite, and cornflower, representing the colours of the French flag. Germaine Mahé Champagne postcard collection; (right) A charming young girl depicts a martial goddess of victory. The Arc de Triomphe is in the background and the slogan "Glory and Immortality!" below. The monument is incredibly important to the French and was designed by Jean Chalgrin in 1806. It depicts classically nude French youths pitted against Germanic warriors in chain mail. It was one of a series of monuments stretching from the Louvre to the Grande Arche de la Défense. In subtext appears another slogan: "We salute the flag!" Germaine Mahé Champagne postcard collection.

My dear friends, I have just received your letter of the 7th of July and I am glad you have sold some of my belongings. For the money you can manage it for now. For the rest of the livestock to be sold, do your best to sell everything this fall, as I do not wish to have to pay to over winter the livestock again this year. Write to me when you have received these two cards and you can let me know if Marthoz has had a good crop on my land. I have written to him at the same time as I wrote to you, but I still do not have an answer. We are encouraged by the thought that we will be victorious, but we must be patient.

Poilvé continued to be concerned about developments on his farm. As the war dragged on, he indicated that he preferred to cut his losses and sell all of his livestock, rather than maintain them. The choice of the card depicting the goddess of victory with a triumphal arch in the background suggests that he still hoped for the end of the conflict.

On the second card of July 30, Poilvé gave news of Sancenot to his friends back in Canada. The illustration is again of Alsace, showing how important regaining this territory was for the French. This may not have been very clear to French Canadians, but to those from France in the Canadian hinterland, it was accepted without question. Poilvé wrote:

Jules has written to me a few days ago and he is still in good health. I think he even has gone on leave a few days ago. My health is still holding up, thank God. You will be so kind as

Alsace was a deeply contested area and this postcard's slogan, "In Alsace—long live France," is provocative. The young woman on the left is depicted pouring a glass of wine for the French victors. Germaine Mahé Champagne postcard collection.

to tell the friends and neighbours that I say hello and wish a prompt return in your midst. The day when we manage to get them out of the trenches it will be a hard chase, but we have much hope that they will no longer stop on their way. You know with how much courage we will march. Finally, dear comrade, I leave you while thanking you and your wife as well for all you are doing for me. Jean Poilvé.

Two more cards are sent on 28 December 1915. From the cards, we see that that Poilvé's letters were not always getting through: "I had written two or three letters some time ago. I don't think you have received them as the military censors are very strict, even the letters that I receive from you have been opened by the military authorities. I beg of you to say hello to all the friends and neighbours." My grandparents' reaction to letters being censored has long been forgotten—it was war, after all, and that sort of thing was to be expected. At least some communication was still taking place. The Alsatian card is a scene of convivial socializing between the French soldiers and the women of the town who are pouring wine and raising their glasses in a toast, again reiterating the dream of regaining Alsace for France once and for all.

On the second card, "Fishing for the Boche," the *poilu* fishes a German soldier out of the trench. The term *boche* means "hard head" (blockhead) and is definitely derogatory. It is thought to have originated during the Franco-Prussian war as a common term for German soldiers. Poilvé writes:

My dear friends,
A few words to answer your letter, yes, I have received the money order as well as the tally, which I find to be correct. Please continue to

42   Le " Poilu " pêche à la ligne de fond

The French soldier is depicted "fishing" for Germans—an example of the black humour evident in some popular art. Germaine Mahé Champagne postcard collection.

sell the rest of what you have in your possession, if you can, do your best to sell the oats. Best wishes for the New Year, good health and good luck in your commerce, etc. Jean.

There are three more cards from Poilvé. The first shows a statue of Joan of Arc and women and

Bienheureuse Jeanne d'Arc, protégez-les

Jeanne d'Arc had been beatified, one of the steps toward sainthood, on 18 April 1909 at Notre-Dame Cathedral in Paris by Pope Pius X. In this scene, women and children are praying for the protection of soldiers on the front, and the slogan reads "Blessed Jeanne d'Arc, protect us." Germaine Mahé Champagne postcard collection.

children at prayer. From their homes, there was little that women and children could do other than call upon heaven for help in this period of hard times and danger for their menfolk. Who better than the French feminine warrior saint? The second is titled "The Vision." It has no date and just one line from Poilvé: "My dream always, Jean." A bachelor, Poilvé is clearly expressing his longing for a wife and companion. While caught in the throes of war, it was certainly a dream to cherish in the hope of normalcy and better times.

A third card with a rescue dog is blank except for the date—1 November 1916—pencilled on the illustration. Belgian sheepdogs were used for war work, and it seems the breed almost died out in the First World War.[21] German shepherds have a distinctive saddle; this is a Belgian sheepdog, typical of the Tervuren breed, with a double coat with varying shades of brown or fawn. He has a distinctive mask and pointed ears. The dog was used for search and rescue work and has found a collapsed soldier in a foxhole.

The last card is from Jules Sancenot to Poilvé, with an illustration of an aviator flying above a young Alsatian woman holding flowers. It is undated; presumably Poilvé forwarded it along at some point. The note reveals little about Sancenot's work as a soldier; note even the phrase "the job is going marvellously" is very much a generalization, necessary due to the censorship of correspondence.

Dear Uncle,

For the last few days I have been putting off writing to you to let you know that the job is going marvellously and for the time being the weather is beautiful. I went on leave last Sunday for the first time and I went to the Laborde family. They are all well, as am I and (above) A soldier looking at a vision of his sweetheart. Germaine Mahé Champagne postcard collection; (below) The horrors of the battlefield are suggested in this picture, and the dog wears a Red Cross emblem as a collar. Germaine Mahé Champagne postcard collection.

Paul and I hope my card will find you well too.
Many of my things are at my uncle Deloy's.
Receive dear uncle, my utmost friendship.
M. Jules Sancenot, bachelor at Longehay,
Côte Doré (?)

Also included in my grandparents' card collection
is a photo of their friend Jean Poilvé in uniform,
wearing the decorations that were awarded to him by
the French government for bravery during the conflict. He wears a Croix de Guerre and a citation for

(above) An Alsatian girl in regional dress holds a flower posy
with colours of the French flag. A French aviator appears to be
about to drop a floral bouquet for her. French aviation pioneers
Henri Farman and Louis Blériot suggested that the airplane could
be used for reconnaissance. As early as 1909, the French War
Department promoted pilot training for army officers; on 22
October 1910 the *Aéronautique Militaire* was created as a branch of
the army, later becoming the French Air Force; (right) Jean Poilvé
depicted in uniform with the French Croix de Guerre, the medal of
bravery, and an additional citation. Germaine Mahé Champagne
postcard collection.

The card depicts the flags of the Allies with the slogan "In homage to the Allies!" Germaine Mahé Champagne postcard collection.

bravery. After the war, he returned to Canada to sell his farm, as he had been gassed and the after-effects did not permit him to continue farming. His brother had been killed, and on his return to France, Poilvé married his brother's widow, who had been left with three young children. Jules Sancenot was killed in the conflict, but we do not know more of him, other than that Poilvé helped with the sale of his farm, which my grandfather purchased. The proceeds went to Sancenot's family in France, who were in need.

There are two other cards in my grandparents' collection from this time. My grandmother received cards from her sister, Nenette, who was married to Gustave Boutteny: The first card is hand painted and is titled: "In homage to the Allies," "with kisses from a brother and sister, Vive la France!"

The last card, a promotional card for French war bonds for 1917, was addressed to the Mahés' eldest child, Jean, godchild of Nenette and Gustave, and is a calendar of saint days. Nenette has written on the back of it, "Two kisses for little Jean and René Mahé." In France, Gustave was also a combatant, and on this card, below the image of the soldier blowing a horn, Nenette has written "Godfather who is killing

French war bond postcard. Germaine Mahé Champagne postcard collection.

the Boches." Although it is a pretty strong statement to make to a five-year-old, this was the common sentiment of the day. My grandmother thought much the same about the Boches, as they called the Germans. This feeling went back to 1870, many years before she was born, but relatives had been killed in the Franco-Prussian war, and she bore a great deal of resentment toward them.

Alex's brother Louis received a medal for his part in the conflict, in which he was wounded and lost an eye. In my mother's photo collection, there is a photo of him receiving his medal in front of the French military hospital "Les Invalides" in Paris; although he did send a few cards during the war, none had the warlike illustrations of those Poilvé sent.

Little is known of the settlers of St. Vincent and Thérien at the time of the First World War; however, it is unlikely that Sancenot was the only Frenchman

of the area to die in the war. For example, the brothers Le Jeloux farmed in the Thérien region. Julien, who had arrived in 1909, had been joined by his brother Étienne a few years later. Julien was able to remain in Canada and manage both of their farms, while Étienne rejoined his regiment. He was killed in battle in 1918. Both men had been single, and Julien continued to live by himself for a few years. Loneliness finally got to him, and he went back to Brittany and married. He returned to his farm with his wife and founded a family whose descendants still live in Alberta and contribute to the cultural diversity of the province. Mathurin Guevello, who had come to Canada with the Le Jeloux brothers and had homesteaded near them, is presumed to have been lost in action as he was never heard from again. Two other pairs of brothers of French origin who homesteaded in the area also returned to serve their country: Pierre and Paul Oyenart, and Armand and Pierre Duholde. It is not known if they returned or not.

Further research is required to establish conclusively how many Franco-Europeans joined up with their regiments in their homelands, or with Canadian battalions. There is a list of over 250 Franco-Albertans who enrolled in the armed forces, but neither the French nor Belgians are included in that group.[23] If we are to judge by the numbers recounted in the papers, there could have been at least 300. One thing is certain, however: the loss of these men, including many of their families who followed them back to France, was significant to Alberta's French community, and to Albertans in general. As my grandfather Alex wrote in the weekly paper, *La Survivance*, a few years later concerning the naming of a new railway station of the Canadian National Railways, there were plenty of choices to be found locally as "several young men of the region had sacrificed their life full of youth and hope in the trenches of France so that life and the youth could continue to prosper here without interruption."[24]

Notes

1   *Edmonton Daily Capital*, 3 August 1914, URL: http://peel.library.ualberta.ca/newspapers/EDC/1914/08/03/8/Ar00809.html, retrieved 16 June 2014.

2   *L'Union*, 1 November 1918, 3, and 14 November 1918, 2. My thanks go to Éloi De Grâce for bringing these pages and the list from Stettler's *Independent* to my attention.

3   *The Independent*, 3 February 1916, 7.

4   John Matthews, a volunteer with the Loyal Edmonton Regiment Museum, provided me with a sampling of the file, for which I am grateful. In it, of 27 names of Franco-Europeans in Alberta, 15 were from France, 10 from Belgium, and two were Swiss. Library and Archives Canada, URL: https://www.collectionscanada.gc.ca/databases/cef/001042-100.01-e.php, retrieved 16 June 2014.

5   Gaston Carrière, o.m.i., *Dictionnaire biographique des Oblats de Marie Immaculée au Canada*, vols. I–IV (Ottawa: Éditions de l'Université d'Ottawa, 1977, 1984); J. Le Falher, *Les Oblats de Marie-Immaculée au service de la France, 1914–1918* (Vannes: La Foyle Frères, éditeurs, 1920).

6   *Le Patriote de l'Ouest (PDO)*, 3 September 1914, URL: http://peel.library.ualberta.ca/newspapers/PDW/1914/09/03/8/Ar00802.html, retrieved 16 June 2014.

7   "Position of Homesteaders Who Are Called to the Front," *Bellevue Times*, 7 August 1914, URL: http://peel.library.ualberta.ca/newspapers/BVT/1914/08/07/4/Ar00406.html, retrieved 16 June 2014; "Pour les reservists homesteaders," *Le Courier de l'Ouest (CDO)*, URL: http://peel.library.ualberta.ca/newspapers/CDW/1914/08/20/8, retrieved 16 June 2014.

8   *Bassano Mail*, 6 August 1914, URL: http://peel.library.ualberta.ca/newspapers/BSM/1914/08/06/1/Ar00111.html, retrieved 16 June 2014.

9   *PDO*, 6 August 1914, URL: http://peel.library.ualberta.ca/newspapers/PDW/1914/08/06/8/Ar00800.html, retrieved 16 June 2014.

10   *CDO*, 6 August 1914, URL: http://peel.library.ualberta.ca/newspapers/CDW/1914/08/06/1/Ar00103.html, retrieved 16 June 2014; *Edmonton Bulletin*, 4 August 1914, URL: http://peel.library.ualberta.ca/newspapers/EDB/1914/08/04/5, retrieved 16 June 2014.

11   "En route pour la France," *CDO*, 13 August 1914, URL: http://peel.library.ualberta.ca/newspapers/CDW/1914/08/13/8/Ar00800.html.

12   *Stettler Independent*, 19 March 1920, 3.

13   Fr. Dominique Bocquené, who was posted at the isolated Oblate mission at Fond-du-lac, Saskatchewan, left as soon as he received the news, but it was

1915 before he finally arrived to rejoin his regiment at Vannes. J. Le Falher, *Au service de la France, les Oblats de Marie-Immaculée* (Vannes: La Folye Frères, éditeurs, 1920), 14–15; "Désiré Louis Marie Bocquené," *Dictionnaire biographique des Oblats*, vol. IV, 33–34.

14 As told to the author by Eugène Trottier.

15 As told to the author by Denise Rougeau-Kent, Sévère's niece.

16 "En route pour la France," *CDO*, 13 August 1914, URL: http://peel.library.ualberta.ca/newspapers/ CDW/1914/08/13/8/Ar00800.html, retrieved 16 June 2014.

17 Dominique and Jacques Baylaucq, *Brutinel, 1882–1964, Le remarquable destin d'un Français brigadier-général de l'Armée canadienne* (St. Albert, AB: Musée Héritage Museum, 2014), 20.

18 "Le Docteur Valery," *CDO*, 13 August 1914, 8.

19 Juliette Marthe Champagne, *De la Bretagne aux plaines de l'Ouest canadien, lettres d'un défricheur franco-albertain, Alexandre Mahé (1880–1968)* (Quebec City: Les Presses de l'Université Laval, 2003), 104–5; Carnet militaire, Alexandre Mahé, Fonds Juliette Champagne, Provincial Archives of Alberta, PR 2014.2051.

20 All translations are by the author.

21 "Belgian Tervuren," *On the Nature of Dogs*, photographs by Mary Ludington, foreword by Patricia Hampl (New York: Simon and Schuster, 2007), 84–85; Patricia Sylvester, ed., *The Reader's Digest Illustrated Book of Dogs*, 2nd rev. ed. (New York: Reader's Digest Publishing Co., 1993), 66–67.

22 Wikipedia, "The *Armée de l'Air* (1909–1942)," URL: http://en.wikipedia.org/wiki/History_of_the_Arm %C3%A9e_de_l%27Air_%281909%E2%80% 9342%29, retrieved 17 June 2014.

23 *L'Union*, 1 and 14 November 1918.

24 Champagne, *De la Bretagne aux plaines de l'Ouest*, 168.

Works Cited

PRIMARY SOURCES

Bassano Mail
Bellevue Times
Le Courrier de l'Ouest
Edmonton Bulletin
Edmonton Daily Capital
The Independent
Le Patriote de l'Ouest
Stettler Independent

Library and Archives Canada. URL: https://www.collectionscanada.gc.ca/databases/ cef/001042-100.01-e.php.

SECONDARY SOURCES

Baylaucq, Dominique, and Jacques Baylaucq. *Brutinel, 1882–1964, Le remarquable destin d'un Français brigadier-général de l'Armée canadienne*. St. Albert, AB: Musée Héritage Museum, 2014.

Carrière, Gaston, o.m.i., ed. *Dictionnaire biographique des Oblats de Marie Immaculée au Canada*, Tome I–IV. Ottawa: Éditions de l'Université d'Ottawa, 1977, 1984.

Champagne, Juliette Marthe. *De la Bretagne aux plaines de l'Ouest canadien, lettres d'un défricheur franco-albertain, Alexandre Mahé (1880–1968)*. Quebec City: Les Presses de l'Université Laval, 2003.

Le Falher, J. *Les Oblats de Marie-Immaculée au service de la France, 1914–1918*. Vannes: La Foyle Frères, éditeurs, 1920.

Ludington, Mary, photographer. *On the Nature of Dogs*. Foreword by Patricia Hampl. New York: Simon and Schuster, 2007.

Sylvester, Patricia, ed. *The Reader's Digest Illustrated Book of Dogs*. 2nd rev. ed. New York: Reader's Digest Publishing Co., 1993.

The Little Institution that Could:
The University of Alberta and the First World War

DAVID BORYS

"The common patriotic impulse which stirred the whole of Canada and which found a voice in all the Universities of the country found expression amongst us," wrote University of Alberta President H.M. Tory, when reflecting on his institution's contribution to Canada's First World War effort.[1] In August 1914, the University of Alberta was one of the youngest educational institutions in Canada; however, its support of the war at home and abroad was one of dedication and commitment far beyond what could have been expected.

Although the university had only 439 registered students and a small staff when war broke out, by the end of the conflict, in 1918, 4,484 staff and students had served in some capacity in the armed forces, 82 of whom died. Reacting to this toll, Tory maintained: "Certainly civilization is asking a terrible price, but a price which is worth paying, if liberty and honour are to be conserved in the world."[2] The number of University of Alberta students registered per academic year between 1914 and 1918 was less than the overall number of students and staff serving overseas. For example, in 1914, the university rugby team won the provincial championship; by 1916, all members

were serving on the Western Front. By 1916, roughly 50 percent of the U of A staff and student body were serving in some capacity overseas in various units throughout the Canadian and British military forces. In May 1915, Herbert Joseph Ball of the Faculty of Arts became the first student killed in action. Of this, the university's newspaper, *The Gateway*, proclaimed: "The blood of 'Bert' Ball has baptized the University of Alberta to her share in the great battle for freedom."[3]

One of the first units overseas with a significant contingent of U of A students was the 11th Field Ambulance, a unit also containing students from British Columbia, Saskatchewan, and Manitoba. The commanding officer of the 32-person U of A section was Major Heber Moshier, professor of physiology, later promoted to colonel and commanding officer. While in Canada, the men were billeted at the Manitoba Agricultural College (MAC), where they went through basic training. Reginald Lister was one of the U of A boys who joined up and wrote about his first impression at the MAC: "We were lined up, told to get to the stores and receive our uniforms, be dressed as soldiers and be ready to parade for supper.... Well, you can guess what kind of soldiers we looked like. Half of the uniforms didn't fit and the way the boys had their puttees on they looked fine!"[4]

The unit embarked for France in May 1916, where they undertook a range of tasks including medical treatment, removal and retrieval of wounded and dead soldiers, and ferrying of supplies. It was dangerous work, and the official history of the 11th Field Ambulance remarked: "The green infantry man might refer to the ambulance man as a trench dodger, but once let him be carried out wounded or tended behind the line for sickness and his estimation underwent a change."[5]

Although life on the front was dangerous, bouts of mischievousness broke up the monotony and danger of the day to day. The men of the 11th Field Ambulance were key figures in one of these events.

In May 1917, when Colonel Moshier was to take over as commanding officer of the 11th, the officers decided to stage a large dinner in his honour and that of his predecessor Colonel MacQueen. Captain Turnbull was placed in charge of obtaining the liquor for the dinner, and did so late the night before. Turnbull acquired the liquor but, with the officer's mess closed, he decided to store the spirits under his bed. The next morning, Captain Turnbull, to his shock and dismay, discovered that all the liquor had been stolen while he slept. The officers searched high and low but could not find the alcohol, and were forced to have a dry dinner. After the war, Reginald (Reg) Lister reported that several U of A students confessed to stealing the liquor right out from under Captain Turnbull's bed "and had sunk it in a small river at the back of the camp, suspending the bottles by string

University of Alberta, 11th Field Ambulance, 1916, Smith Co., photographer. University of Alberta Archives, 69-12-73, *Gateway* newspaper.

The first University of Alberta draft, 1915, unknown photographer. Back row (left to right): G.T. Riley, J.A. Carswell, Dr. H.M. Tory, J.S. Kerr; middle row (left to right): A. McQueen, E. Parsons, C. Beck; front row (left to right): N. McArthur, R. Stevens, Capt. H.J. MacLeod, A.T. Glanville. University of Alberta Archives, AN 87-78-0002.

around the necks. And for months they would go and bring in a bottle or two and have a party."[6]

The single largest contribution by the U of A came with the creation of the 196th battalion, otherwise known as the Western Universities Battalion. The presidents of the four provincial universities (British Columbia, Alberta, Saskatchewan, and Manitoba) proposed to the government of Canada that each university raise one company (roughly 150 to 200 men) to form a battalion for front line service. However, not all enlisted men came directly from the institution as the "conditions of eligibility are . . . professional and business men of education;

graduates of any university; undergraduates; high school students of suitable age; students of various schools and colleges, students and junior members of the learned professions in the provinces; and friends of these various groups."[7]

It would have been extremely difficult for a school whose enrollment stood at just under 400 students to raise a company nearly half that size. Therefore, Tory expanded the eligibility for recruitment. Similar action was taken by all four of the western Canadian universities.[8] Although designed so that all four companies would fight alongside each other, the 196th would not see action as a unit, as it

University of Alberta Company—196th Battalion, Edmonton, June 1916, unknown photographer. University of Alberta Archives, AN 69-12-75.

96TH D(W.U.) BRTTN. C.E.F.
APRIL 7TH 1916

was made into a reinforcement battalion to supply fresh troops to units already in combat. University pride was evidenced in the song "The 196th Forever: The Good Old U of A,"[9] written to the tune of 'The Maple Leaf Forever."

The university also made plans to recruit a company for a Canadian universities tank battalion. In 1916, tanks had made their first appearance on the Western Front. The British high command began promoting their use so that, by 1918, tanks proliferated throughout the British Army and the Canadian Corps. The Canadian militia department requested that the 1st Canadian Tank Battalion be formed from all the universities across Canada. William A.R. Kerr, interim president (President Tory was involved with the Khaki University at the time), actively pushed for a company to be made up of U of A students, and was adamant that the entire battalion be comprised of Canadian university students. Writing to the judge advocate general of the Canadian forces, Lieutenant Colonel Biggar, Kerr stated: "We do not wish students to be mixed indiscriminately with regular recruits. If we had assurance that University men would serve together under our own officers we could get satisfactory enrolment."[10] This concern was also shared by Professor W.H. Alexander, who, applying for a captaincy in the tank battalion, wrote: "Can you advise re proposed Tanks battalion whether unit is genuinely of university character in officering and organization? Good prospects locally if such is case."[11]

It was obvious that those involved in the recruiting process at the university were concerned that the battalion be made up primarily of university students in order to keep its unique character. In July 1918, while the tank battalion was training in England, President Kerr received a letter from the Department of Militia and Defence stating: "As you are aware the unit was raised for the most part, through the instrumentality of Canadian universities; and it should be reinforced by men of the same type and standing as those who joined it on formation."[12] This letter alleviated the concerns of both Kerr and Alexander.

U of A staff also committed themselves to the war effort by serving as commissioned officers. A graduate of the University of Toronto medical school,

Professor Moshier was 27 when he enlisted in 1916, and started as second in command of the 11th Field Ambulance Unit (commanding the U of A contingent that included nearly the entire medical class of 1914); Professor MacEachran, a philosophy professor, became a captain in the 196th Battalion; and Professor Macleod, lecturer in electrical engineering, accepted a commission as commanding officer of "C" company of the 196th Battalion. Not all were directly involved in combat units. Professor Robert Boyle, head of the Department of Physics, went to the United Kingdom and undertook pivotal research on sonar technology and detection of submarines. Boyle was born in Newfoundland and attended McGill University, studying under Sir Ernest Rutherford in the area of radioactivity. In 1909, he had gone to work with Rutherford at the University of Manchester, and in 1912 was recruited by President Tory to set up the physics department at the U of A. There he shifted his research interest to ultrasonics. After his wartime work in Britain, he returned to the U of A in 1919.

Several pieces of information highlight the fact that soldiers and staff were cognizant of their university attachments even when on the Western Front and fighting in various units. In spring 1917, Reg Lister described how the 11th Field Ambulance staged a mock convocation, as several of the unit's members would have graduated that year. The men of the 11th were billeted in an old barn, and that was used as an interim convocation hall. Lister records: "Our academic procession was quite a sight, with hoods and gowns made of everything from a sand bag to a canvas water bucket."[13] Obviously, the men were well aware of the interruption that the war had caused to both their educational and personal lives.

One of the more remarkable moments highlighting the young men's university ties took place in

Third University Company Overseas, 1915, unknown photographer. Front row (left to right): F. Philip Galbraith, Harvey Beecroft, G. Stanley Fife, Robert M. Martin, A. Earl F. Robinson, F. Reg Henry; middle row (left to right): Salteau, E.C. Peters, Earl German, J.B. McCubbin, Larry H. Crawford; back row (left to right): Donald S. Edwards, A. Hutchinson. University of Alberta Archives, AN 71-197.

June 1917 when a reunion of sorts was held involving many U of A students fighting on the front. By this time, all four divisions of the Canadian Corps were fighting together, and this made it possible for a significant number of the students serving in the corps to come together in the sector surrounding Vimy Ridge. Lister wrote: "It was a very nice affair and I believe it was the only time so many from the U of A got together; and many who were there that night did not return to Canada."[14] The jovial atmosphere contrasted sharply with the stark realities of life on the front, where nearly 3,600 lives were lost to capture the ridge.

The constant threat of death and danger could seriously affect the attitudes of the men. Thus, staying connected to home was a crucial component of fighting against a drop in morale. One of the most important methods of connecting back home was through the Soldiers Comfort Club letters. These were, simply, newsletters sent to all the students and staff from the U of A serving in Europe. During the academic year, they were also published in *The Gateway*, the student newspaper, for all to read. The letters discussed local Edmonton and university news, as well as information concerning U of A staff and students serving overseas. For example, in November 1917 the paper discussed the withdrawal of Russia from the war after the Bolshevik revolution, as well as the death of Lieutenant J.E. Van Petten, a pivotal player on both the university wrestling and football teams.[15]

Some of the students recruited from the U of A were products of the university's Canadian Officers Training Corps (COTC) program, established in

January 1915 with the approval of the Canadian Department of Militia and Defence. Male staff and students received military training and obtained university credit. The COTC also had a professor's platoon where, for a brief period, President Tory held the rank of private. His commanding officer was Professor Killam, with the rank of lieutenant. While Tory accepted the lowly rank of private, he never forgot his own civilian position, as noted in an anecdote recounted by Professor Alexander. Lieutenant Killam was lecturing on proper marching order and, in the middle of his talk, Private Tory piped up and stated, "Lt Killam, there's a bad draught through the Convocation Hall: would you mind shutting the east door?" Alexander noted, "The foundations of the Empire and every last sacred tradition of the British Army rocked violently to and fro, and it was even thought that Jove's thunderbolt might descend upon him who had sinned beyond all redemption, but Professor Killam shut the door as required, and then Lieutenant Killam resumed the drill."[16] By 1916, the COTC had over 150 registered students and was the main recruitment pool for the university.

Artillery Army Group, University of Alberta, August 1914. University of Alberta Archives, AN 69-97-251.

As in most Canadian academic institutions, male enrollment steadily declined during the war years as enlistments increased. This resulted in a rise in the enrollment of women. The board of governors' reports for the 1915–16 academic year showed 57 women enrolled. The next academic year, 85 women were enrolled, and for the first time the position of president of the student union went to a woman. For the 1917–18 academic year, 118 women were registered, and in the final year of the war 187 female students were enrolled. As Professor Alexander wrote, "Much of the duty of keeping alive university tradition and carrying on university societies rested with the girls, and they rose to the occasion."[17]

The campus continued to act as a centre of recruiting, training, and supporting the war effort. In early 1915, President Tory and the board of governors offered up the university hospital for military use. The federal government rejected this because it had enough facilities for the care of the sick and wounded. However, by 1916, the increasing number of casualties resulted in the government rescinding the rejection and using the hospital for sick and wounded military personnel. The government continued to operate the hospital until 1922, when its control was handed back to the university. During that period, its bacteriological department was managed by the Department of Militia and Defence, and played a significant role in production and administration of an anti-typhoid vaccine that was administered to all men recruited from Alberta.

Although university life revolved around the war effort, this did not prevent some other developments. In October 1915, the Arts building, home of the faculties of Arts and Sciences, was officially opened and became the largest building on campus. This was the first building to be built on campus

solely for the use of the university. It was the only major physical addition to the campus during the war. The curriculum, however, continued to expand. In 1915, the College of Agriculture was established (later to be the Faculty of Agriculture) with E.A. Howes as the first dean. The university now had five faculties, the other four being Law, Applied Science, Arts, and Medicine. That same year the Committee of Graduate Studies was established. Pharmacy was taught at the university since 1914, and was officially recognized as the School of Pharmacy in 1917. The teaching of dentistry began that same year and was considered a department within the Faculty of Medicine. The Department of Accountancy was established in 1916 and later became the School of Commerce. In 1918, the Department of Household Economics was established. The war may have occupied the minds and the actions of the majority of those on campus; however, under President Tory, the educational opportunities offered continued to expand in a variety of areas. As John Macdonald wrote: "With these beginnings . . . the shape of things to come was already clearly foreshadowed when peace broke out."[18]

When the war began, the University of Alberta was a small institution attempting to forge its identity and prove its worth. The dedication of staff and students to the war effort resulted in a stronger, more focused institution by war's end that was poised to play a leading role in post-secondary education in western Canada. Enrollment sharply increased in the years following the cessation of hostilities. Yet, 82 men paid the supreme price, and many more came back physically and emotionally damaged. Nonetheless, the development of the University of Alberta during the war years was marked with maturation and growth, paralleling the country's development. The university, like the country that came out of 1918, had grown rapidly and in unforeseen ways. Its following decades would be guided by the institutional and cultural foundation laid during the formative years of 1914–18.

Notes

1 H.M. Tory, Report of 1915 on University's Contribution to the War, date unknown, University of Alberta Archives [hereafter UAA] 68-9, box 37.
2 Letter, H.M. Tory to Private Carswell, 21 January 1916, UAA 68-9, box 41, file 506.
3 *The Gateway* 6, no. 1 (1 November 1915).
4 Reginald Lister, *My 45 Years on Campus* (Edmonton: University of Alberta Printing Department, 1958), 23.
5 A.E. Johnson, A. Roland Hall, C.T. Best, J.M. Roe, *Diary of the Eleventh: Being a Record of the XI Field Ambulance, February 1916–May 1919* ([Winnipeg]: n.p., 1919), 70.
6 Lister, *My 45 Years on Campus*, 25.
7 H.M. Tory, Western Universities Battalion CEF, UAA, Tory Fonds 68-9, box 38, file 463.
8 For example, see pages 143–49 of William C. Gibson's *Wesbrook and His University* (Vancouver: UBC Press, 1973).
9 C. Burbidge. *The 196th Forever: The Good Old University of Alberta*, UAA Tory Fonds 68-9, box 38, file 463.
10 Letter, W.A.R. Kerr to Lt. Col. Biggar, date unknown, UAA Tory Fonds 68-9, box 38, file 476.
11 Letter to Captain Wallace, date unknown, UAA Tory Fonds 68-9, box 38, file 476.
12 Letter, Maj. Gen. Gwatkin to President Kerr, 29 July 1918, UAA Tory Fonds 68-9, box 38, file 467.
13 Lister, *My 45 Years on Campus*, 25.
14 Ibid., 26.
15 *The Gateway* 7, no. 3 (15 November 1917).
16 W.H. Alexander, *The University of Alberta: A Retrospect 1908–1929* (Edmonton: publisher unknown, 1929), 18–19.
17 Ibid., 20.
18 John Macdonald, *The History of the University of Alberta: 1908–1958* (Toronto: W.J. Gage, 1958), 21.

Works Cited

PRIMARY SOURCES

The Gateway

University of Alberta Archives, Edmonton. St. Stephen's College Fonds, 88-66-70.
——. Tory Fonds, 68-9, box 37.
——. Tory Fonds, 68-9, box 38, files 463, 467, 476.
——. Tory Fonds, 68-9, box 41, file 506.

SECONDARY SOURCES

Alexander, W.H. *The University of Alberta: A Retrospect 1908–1929*. Edmonton University Printing Press, 1929.
Friedland, Martin L. *The University of Toronto: A History*. Toronto: University of Toronto Press, 2002.
Gibson, William C. *Wesbrook and His University*. Victoria: Morris Printing Company, 1973.
Johnson, A.E., A. Roland Hall, C.T. Best, and J.M. Roe. *Diary of the Eleventh: Being a Record of the XI Field Ambulance, February 1916–May 1919*. n.p., 1919.
Lister, Reginald. *My 45 Years on Campus*. Edmonton: University of Alberta Printing Department, 1958.
Macdonald, John. *The History of the University of Alberta: 1908–1958*. Toronto: W.J. Gage Ltd., 1958.
Macmillan, Cyrus. *McGill and Its Story: 1821–1921*. Toronto: Oxford University Press, 1921.
Neatby, Hilda. *Queen's University*. Vol. 1, *1841–1917: And Not to Yield*. Montreal and Kingston: McGill-Queen's University Press, 1978.
Reid, John G. *Mount Allison University: A History, to 1963*. Vol. 2, *1914–1963*. Toronto: University of Toronto Press, 1984.
Waite, P.B. *The Lives of Dalhousie University*. Vol. 1, *1818–1925*. Montreal and Kingston: McGill-Queen's University Press, 1994.

The Gospel of Sacrifice:
Lady Principal Nettie Burkholder and Her Boys at the Front

ADRIANA A. DAVIES

The University of Alberta Archives is the repository of the Alberta College South Fonds.[1] Among these are 302 letters and cards written by students from the First World War battlefront to Lady Principal Nettie Burkholder, and four of her returned letters. The letters are largely handwritten on both sides of very thin paper, mostly in pencil; some are on letterhead (YMCA, regimental, and Royal Flying Corps). They recount the experiences of the writers, most "probationers," or individuals studying for the ministry at the theological college of the Methodist Church in Alberta. Their survival indicates that Miss Burkholder believed the correspondence was historically significant. The demographic represented at the college was that of the British ruling elite, whether immigrants from the United Kingdom, or arrivals from Ontario and the Atlantic region. A memorial service was held at the college in December 1919, and a newspaper article observed:

> A tribute to the fallen was offered by Dr. D.E. Thomas which was followed by a silent tribute. Addresses of Welcome were extended by Dr. H.R. Smith, on behalf of the governors of the college, and by Miss Nettie Burkholder, B.A., on behalf of the faculty. Dean Kerr also tendered a welcome on behalf of the university and the affiliated colleges. Messrs. Johnson [probationer Ralph E.] and Pinder [probationer Charles S.] responded to the addresses.[2]

The article noted that 85 students enlisted initially, followed by another 32 after the war began. Nineteen were killed, among them letter writers J. Crawford Anglin, John R. Barker, Arthur M. Hummel, and Clement Beck Wilson.

The letters are unexpected in that male students were writing to the "Lady Principal," rather than to Principal J.H. Riddell or other male staff. They reveal the astounding network established by Burkholder that provided not only moral support, friendship, and encouragement but also comfort packages. Fifty letter writers are represented, with the number of letters and cards per individual ranging from one to 66. Keeping up with this correspondence required amazing commitment from Burkholder, particularly during term time when she performed the duties of

Miss Nettie Burkholder in academic dress, ca. 1885, C. Larves, photographer. Whitby Public Library Collection, public domain.

lady principal and instructor. Burkholder nurtured a sense of camaraderie and mutual support that bound the group together as she passed on news received in letters around the writing circle. Who was the lady principal, and who were the letter writers?

The Lady Principal

Nettie Burkholder was born in Hamilton, Ontario, on 1 January 1863 and died in Edmonton on 16 September 1950.[3] She was of a Swiss Mennonite family, and her ancestor Jacob Burkholder immigrated to Pennsylvania in 1765. As a United Empire Loyalist, in 1794, he chose to settle in Canada, taking up a land grant near Hamilton, Barton Township. The family converted to Methodism and established Burkholder Methodist Church in 1886.[4] Miss Burkholder's educational aspirations were supported by her family, and made possible by the growing movement within the Methodist Church that allowed women to seek higher education for self-improvement, and to better accomplish their duties as homemakers and church workers. Johanna M. Selles in *Methodists and Women's Education in Ontario 1836–1925* explores social change regarding women, linking it with the growth in dedicated "women's colleges." She observes that in the 1880s women were allowed to study at Victoria College, which had been established in 1831 by the Wesleyan Methodist Church and notes that this was a reversal of the policy set in 1842 by Principal Egerton Ryerson.[5]

Burkholder attended Wesleyan Ladies College in Hamilton, receiving a solid education that nurtured a "Christian feminist sensibility." Selles writes: "Another student, Nettie Burkholder, argued in the same issue of the *Portfolio* [the student newspaper], that a woman who had taken a college course could not become a butterfly of fashion. Women could continue to develop their minds or work for the elevation of humanity."[6] In 1891, Burkholder obtained a Bachelor of Arts degree from Victoria College and joined the staff of the Ontario Ladies College, Whitby, as instructor of English and chemistry. In 1901, she became Lady Principal and served in that capacity until 1912, when she was lured to Edmonton by the founders of Alberta College South.[7]

Alberta College was established in 1903, on the north bank of the North Saskatchewan River, with the Reverend John Riddell as principal. The college was coeducational and offered matriculation courses as well as arts and business courses. University of Alberta founding president Henry Marshall Tory encouraged the establishment of a Methodist College on the University of Alberta grounds, and, thus, Alberta College South (ACS) was born in 1910 (the college was located on the south side of the North Saskatchewan River). It was also known as Methodist Theological.

At the outbreak of the war, Burkholder was an established and beloved figure ready to do whatever was required to support the war effort. On 28 October 1915, according to the student newspaper *The Gateway*, the students' union set up a new society, "The University Soldiers' Comfort Club," to send "articles of luxury or comfort" to soldiers. At ACS, Miss Burkholder took charge. The "Alberta College" column, in the December 7 issue, noted:

> The ladies have just mailed Xmas boxes to 12 of the college boys who are serving in overseas regiments. The boxes are 8" × 8" × 8", and contain a varied assortment of goods useful to the soldier on active services, such as shortbread, cookies, hankys [sic], shoe laces, chocolate, soap, powder (vermin), sharing materials, etc. The college students feel grateful to Miss Burkholder and the ladies for their activity in this matter, thus showing the boys at the front that they are not forgotten.[8]

While the boxes provided bodily comfort, the hundreds of letters that she sent were, for the recipients, a tangible token of home. Their responses allowed them to share their experiences with someone who would not sit in judgment. The letters are a powerful outpouring of hopes, dreams, and experiences from the perspective of those who lived the war.[9]

Paul Fussell's *The Great War and Modern Memory* contextualized the war through the writings of established authors and intellectuals. Jonathan F. Vance in *Death So Noble: Memory, Meaning, and the First World War* focused on the perceptions of Canadians and discussed battles such as Vimy Ridge as foundational to nationhood. Both point out the way in which the war was "mythologized" and communicate an anti-war sentiment that became prevalent in the Western democracies as opposition grew to the Vietnam war in the 1970s. While placing wartime experiences into larger historical and social contexts is important, this kind of interpretation downplays what the letter writers and diarists desired to communicate. With the range of war centenaries coming up, it is perhaps time to let them speak in their own voices.

Miss Burkholder's Returned Letters

Of the hundreds of missives that Miss Burkholder sent off, five letters and one postcard have survived because they were returned to sender. The earliest were written to George North (30 January and 15 October 1916). In the first, she began with an apology:

Your interesting letter to me was read eagerly by all your friends, and we feel very proud of you, for your heroic courage through all these dangerous times. But I feel I have no right even to offer words of encouragement to you, when I have done so little myself. It seems that I have hardly changed my mode of living—going daily to classes, and attending to the little round of duties, while you are enduring so much hardship. But then your reward will be greater because you have suffered much for your fellow-men.[10]

She recounted that more recruits had left and were currently in Montreal, and included a report on how the boys abroad were faring:

Dr. Riddell's son, Harold now in France is dangerously ill with spinal meningitis. Mrs. Riddell left immediately and is now probably in France. Harold is in St. Omer hospital, and the last cablegram Friday said he was very low. Dr. Riddell has aged considerably since Harold left but this last stroke has been very hard to bear. Dr. and Mrs. Dyde [Samuel Dyde was the first principal of Robertson College, the Presbyterian Theological College] have looked much worried lately because their eldest son, who was a Rhodes' Scholar at Oxford is now commanding an artillery unit and is constantly exposed to danger. Their second son leaves in the spring.[11]

The Canadian Expeditionary Force (CEF) experienced 399 cases of cerebrospinal meningitis, of which 219 resulted in death.[12]

She continued: "Dr. Tory and the Presidents of the other Western Universities are now at Ottawa planning to send a full company of men in the spring." This account is juxtaposed with news about plans for the spring convocation, descriptions of college activities, as well as talk of the weather. The letter continued with news about the boys:

I wonder if you knew Mr. J.C. Anglin. He is now at Shorncliffe expecting to cross to France. He is in the 4th Company P.P.C.L.I. and his home in war Dublin. Also Margaret Anglin, the actress is his cousin. Mr. McCubbin [Jesse B.] is in France "Somewhere", and also Mr. A.L. Smith, men from Alberta College. Is it possible that some time you may meet. We have 35 names on our Honor Roll now, which hangs in the Main Hall near the entrance to the Assembly Hall.[13]

Burkholder was conscious of the paradox in their respective situations and, after describing her Sunday activities, noted: "It seems a quiet, protected life and apparently unconscious of the terrible shrieks of shot and shell that you hear. It seems so unfair that you and others should endure so much and we so little."[14] She also mentioned a disturbing trend:

A strange feature about the war is that crime is on the increase, and papers report many dreadful murders. It is going to be difficult to keep up the morals and also the religious tone of the country. We feel we are nearing a religious revival, and to that end, a series of services were held in the University for all the students and the city. These services came early in January and lasted three days. We feel that the students were given a deeper insight into life and that whether they go to the Front or stay at home, they will do "their bit" with better understanding.[15]

These observations reflect the sense shared by many that the war meant the end of civilization as they knew it.

The October 15 letter noted that the January letter had been returned to her, and she wonders whether she has the correct address. She reported that Mr. Pinder had assured her that North was well, but, subsequently, Pinder himself had been badly injured. She continued:

> I think you would not know Mr. Anglin, and Mr. McInnes. We hear they have paid the Great Sacrifice, also Albert Robertson, nephew of Dr. Tory is thought to be dead as he cannot be found. Mr. McCubbin is wounded, also Mr. Hummel and Mr. Roy Taylor.
>
> Mr. Sydney Bainbridge wrote a short time ago that he and his brother were stretcher-bearers, a very dangerous work. They expected another charge and dreaded the result when picking up the wounded. Mr. [unreadable] and Mr. Cooke are also with the Ambulance Corps.[16]

The letters reveal that she kept track of the battalions in which her boys served, and their progress through newspaper accounts. She refers specifically to the University Battalion (196th) and the 151st.

There are no letters from North to Miss Burkholder. Corporal North (19903, 10th Battalion) died on 11 August 1916, and his gravesite is at Transport Farm, Zillebeke, southeast of Ypres.[17] The battles fought at Ypres over a three-year period claimed a number of ACS students.[18] Herbert Joseph Ball, the first ACS and University of Alberta student to be killed, is noted in an article in the 1 November 1915 issue of *The Gateway* titled "Dead on the Field of Honour." His profile is typical of that of many of the ACS students. He was born 11 February 1887 in Coventry, England, and registered at the university in 1912 in the arts faculty, studying theology and living at ACS. He was killed 8 May 1915 during the Second Battle of Ypres where the Germans first made extensive use of poison gas on the Western Front. This did not prevent a victory by the 1st Canadian Division.[19]

The envelope of the letter Miss Burkholder wrote to Arthur M. Hummel (48740.9) dated 18 November 1917 has "Missing" on it as well as "wounded in hosp."[20] A letter from Hummel dated 26 September 1917 began by apologizing for not writing to her sooner and also thanked her for the "liberal parcel" sent by her "kind brother."[21] She had been visiting her brother in Chicago and enlisted him in sending comforts to her boys. Hummel mentioned sharing the parcel's contents with other soldiers because there were no ACS boys nearby to benefit from it. He provided a status report:

> You have heard Sammie won the Military Medal to represent A.C. in this old game.
>
> We regret the sad fact that Girtl[e] Baker was taken prisoner. Five of his comrades were wounded in the trench near Girt and he being nearest to Fritz and a few long paces from them was surprised and carried away by

a Hun officer and six men so I was informed.
McCubbin, Cook, Ball, Pinder, Musto and
Mason are in England as far as I know now.
Harding I believe is there also. Sid Bain-
bridge is no doubt within range of you most
of the time so can tell you all about it.[22]

Campbell was a bit of a joker as evidenced in
a quote that Sid Bainbridge attributed to him in
a letter dated 12 September 1916, "somewhere in
France": "Well, Sid you know swotting Latin would
be not too bad now, after a few of the grim experiences out here."[23] Hummel mentioned that he had
been away from the battalion at a training school
for the last couple of weeks and speculated that
they would "clean up on the Hun before 1918."[24]
Burkholder's letter of 18 November 1917 provided
Christmas greetings and reported that they were
based at Pembina Hall because the college building
was being used as a convalescent home for returning
soldiers. She also referred to Dr. Tory's commission
from the Canadian government and the YMCA for the
further education of Canadian soldiers during their
rest periods and demobilization. Private Hummel
(487409, PPCLI) died on 17 November 1917, a casualty of the Third Battle of Ypres at Passchendaele,
where he was buried.[25]

The returned letter to John R. Barker (911346,
Canadian Infantry, Saskatchewan Regiment, 46th
Battalion and 196th Battalion), dated 28 October
1917, is stamped "Killed in action." Burkholder
mentioned that they had heard that he was wounded
and enquired about the nature of the wounds.[26] She
noted an increase in enrollment in the faculty of
agriculture, and observed that it was for this reason
that they were exempted from enlisting. She tells
him that Bainbridge and Clarke are back taking

courses (both were wounded and invalided out),
and continued: "Mr. Hustler writes of his good days
in London while yet in a hospital. He may be in that
city until the New Year. We hear that Mr. Pinder and
Mr. McCubbin have gone to France again with much
less enthusiasm than when they first went. It is so
hard to pluck up courage to go again into the horrors
that they have escaped from for a time."[27] The cycle
of injury, hospitalization, and return to the front
appears repeatedly in the letters.

There are two letters from Barker. The first,
dated 31 December 1916, was from Seaford, Sussex,
and recounted the joy with which her Christmas
parcel and the college news were received. He also
reported an outbreak of measles:

Our battalion is still in quarantine but we
are expecting our release in a few days. We
have been confined to our line for over three
weeks now. Measles have been very prevalent
throughout the camp and few battalions have
escaped quarantine. I had the pleasure of
six days' leave shortly after we arrived here,
and I spent the time at home with my people
in Yorkshire. I enjoyed the short holiday
immensely.[28]

Measles, a disease affecting the young, spread
like wildfire in barracks. Among the CEF, it saw
2,186 men hospitalized, with 30 deaths.[29] Barker
mentioned that he, Upton, and Chapman were
taking Officers Training Corps courses and were
recommended by Major Macleod and interviewed
by Major Eaton.[30] Barker discussed the possibility of
advancement: "If one does not get a chance to take a
commission, the training and insight one receives in
this course must be invaluable. We study everything

from the officer's point of view. There is a lot of work to do, but I prefer this to the humdrum life we have been living."[31] The next letter, dated 2 August 1917 from "Somewhere in France," is written in pencil, and the envelope has on it "opened by censor."[32] Barker thanked Burkholder for her letters and mentioned that they were "particularly welcome" since he was on the front lines:

> You will be interested to know that we had a Varsity Reunion here about four weeks ago, and about fifty of us gathered for the evening. We had a very pleasant time and it was surely fine to see the old faces again.
>
> J. Bainbridge was there and looked well. V. Hummell too was present. I understand that Baker [Gyrtle] was taken prisoner just three nights before we had the Reunion. He came across to France a short time ago. Hustler is in Blighty having been gassed while in the line. C.B. Wilson was killed in action. I have come through safely so far and except for a touch of "nyralgia" [*sic*] am feeling quite well. I am with the 46th Battalion, Canadians, B.E.F. France.[33]

Barker died aged 35 on 25 October 1917 at Passchendaele.

The Ultimate Sacrifice

It is not only the men whose letters were returned who made "the ultimate sacrifice." There are three letters from Private Clement Beck Wilson (487389). He was born in Dundee, Scotland, on 31 December 1886 and grew up in Toronto before going to ACS

to study for the ministry. He enlisted 12 December 1915 in Montreal with the PPCLI (Eastern Ontario Regiment) and indicated in his attestation papers that he had prior military experience, likely with the Canadian Officers Training Corps (COTC) at the university. Wilson wrote on 1 January 1916 from McGill where the 5th University Company was based before going overseas.[34] He had already received his first comfort package, including a "hussif" made by the "young ladies" of the college. The "Alberta College" column in *The Gateway* of 16 December 1915 explained what the mysterious "hussif" was. College Principal Dr. Riddell had given a banquet in honour of the boys who had enlisted in the 5th Universities Contingent and were about to depart: "Mrs. Riddell, on behalf of the student body, presented each recruit with a small testament, and Miss Burkholder, on behalf of the ladies of the faculty, presented a 'hussif' complete with outfits necessary for mending clothes." The Middle English term for housewife clearly was still in common usage and, in this instance, described a basic sewing kit.

The next letter is dated 27 November 1916. Wilson thanked her for her postcard and, with a touch of black humour, noted: "My friends out here tell me that I am getting fat. I think Mr. Peters is judging from a photograph which I sent him after a long hard trip in the trenches, before I recuperated from it."[35] He catalogued the boys who were with him on the French front and noted that they reminisced about the "good old days" at the college. He cheerfully observed that "the war will not last much longer and the prices will return to normal when the men return to their homes." The inevitable tally of injuries and deaths is made, including the death of Bert Ball buried in "one of the towns in France" and the wounding of "Pinder, Clark [Giles H.], Hummel,

Bainsbridge [Joseph W.].... How different from a year ago when we were starting out for our training for real. Now we have seen six months of service and will be willing to see peace declared any day."[36] Wilson's last letter is dated 14 February 1917, and he teased Burkholder about putting 1916 in her letter and then crossing it out.[37]

The soldiers appear to be well informed about the war effort, including the American vacillation as to whether to enter the conflict. A column in *The Gateway* indicates that this was debated at ACS and the opinion that the US should not enter the war won. Wilson wrote: "I do not fully understand the situation in the States, but I expect a break of a definite nature now. The U-boat campaign of Fritz is not meeting with very favourable treatment from the neutral nations. I hope it will tend to shorten the war, and bring a permanent peace. I expect Peace soon and then for a big reunion at A.C. with all the boys and the ladies too." Wilson died on 26 April 1917 at the Battle of Méricourt (one of the series of battles around Vimy Ridge). An obituary in the *Toronto Star* of 26 May 1917 noted:

> Signaller C.B. Wilson, a former resident of Toronto, is reported killed in action. A letter from Corp. J.W. Bainbridge, a fellow-student and probationer for the Methodist ministry, states that Signaller Wilson was instantly killed on April 26th by shell explosion while carrying out his duty in the trenches. He enlisted in Calgary with an infantry battalion eighteen months ago, and had been in France over a year. He lived in Toronto about three years, being a member of Epworth Methodist Church.

A Crisis of Faith

In all of the letters, there are a number of set phrases about the dead, such as "they paid the Great Sacrifice" and "a true hero fighting for a noble cause." For the Christian population in Alberta, in particular the students of ACS, the war was between God and Satan, good and evil. In a letter dated 12 September 1916 from France, Sid Bainbridge indicated a shift from the role of combatant:

> My brother and I have just recently handed in our rifles and ammunition in exchange for a First Aid kit and Stretcher. It is our duty to give First Aid treatment to the wounded in the trenches, and superintend their removal to the nearest dressing-station. This work is very strenuous and entails much exposure to shells etc. but we both like it fine as it is more suited to our conscience to heal rather than destroy.[38]

He also talked about the ACS men's ability to adapt to hardships and compared them to Saint Paul: "That whatsoever state we are in, therewith to be content." For Bainbridge, their war service was comparable to being a missionary: "In a short time we expect to be once more in the thick of the fray, and it is very uncertain as to how many of us will see this thing through. But whatever it means we feel we are here under Divine Guidance, and I feel quite satisfied that if my Father has still a work for me to do He will bring me safely through."[39]

Resignation to divine will provided Bainbridge with comfort and is evidence of his commitment to the ministry. He was born in Carlisle, Scotland,

and received his early education there acting as a Sunday school teacher and local preacher. He came to Alberta in 1913 and received his probation in 1914. He entered ACS in 1916 working as a summer supply preacher and also teaching school in the "Ruthenian" (Ukrainian) settlement area. He was invalided out (his brother Joe bandaged his wounds in the trenches) and ended up at the Edinburgh War Hospital in Bangor, Scotland. By 13 August 1917 he was in the Strathcona Military Hospital in Edmonton and writing to Miss Burkholder in Chicago anticipating the start of term.[40]

In an article in the 13 December 1917 issue of *The Gateway*, Bainbridge noted that, at the request of the editor, he was "presenting the impressions of a returned soldier regarding the attitude of our boys in khaki to the Christian Church as it exists today. A 'Theologue' in the rank and file of the army, needless to say, has a glorious opportunity of gaining first-hand knowledge of what the average man of the world is thinking about, and of course more particularly what he thinks of the Church." He asserted: "In a word, it can be said without much fear of contradiction, although with much regret and shame, that the average soldier in our army today has very little use for our Church." Bainbridge had little time for the comfortable Christians at home prognosticating about the war:

> Our soldiers shun the Church, but not the Christ, whom the churches claim to represent. Why are our boys ready to tolerate such frightful conditions as exist in the trenches? Why do they make such tremendous sacrifice, and are so determined "to see this thing through?" It is because like Jesus Christ,

they want to give mankind a chance; they are ready to die out yonder in France that we at home might live in the best sense. Our President tells us that the soldier at his best is the most wonderful thing in the world. What gives to him this spirit of greatness? It is because he is living a life of sacrifice, and like St. Paul of old, he counts everything but loss that he might win the goal of democracy and freedom.[41]

The article echoes a letter to Miss Burkholder, with whom he had had this discussion initially. In part two of the article in the issue of 20 December 1917, he continued his attack on the church by targeting the "wolves in sheep's clothing": "How many of the men in our churches who are holding the most important offices are also living double lives, one scene being enacted in the church on Sunday, and the other in business during the remaining six days of the week?" Bainbridge summarized his own experience at the front as follows:

> It is under conditions such as these that a man proves his true worth, and the fellows see each other as they are. The value of different individuals has often been radically changed in France from what it was back here at home. Many of the boys who were despised at home on account of their outward wickedness have now proved themselves to be true men. They have shown that although on the surface they may be rough and wild, they nevertheless have great big hearts, and are ready if necessary to share their last biscuit with a fellow in need. Great numbers of these

same fellows have given up life itself to save a comrade in distress.[42]

Finally, he attacked "denominationalism," stating: "There is no denominationalism in the trenches, but a man is judged by his daily life. We are all being urged to unite to win the war. Surely the Church also needs to bury her little party strifes and unite in a great common campaign to win the world."[43] It would be this thinking that would result in the creation of the United Church in 1925.

The struggle between believing and not believing is summarized in a letter by Harry Clark dated 2 January 1916. He wrote from Montreal before shipping out:

I suppose that I have adopted the fatalistic viewpoint—that is characteristic of the soldier, but there does not seem to be any other to take. We are all whether soldiers or not in the hands of what some call chance and others Providence. I suppose that in the case of the soldier the human element which makes us to a certain extent masters of our destinies is more or less eliminated. But I am afraid that I would be a great coward if I could not believe that even the life of a soldier is in God's hands.[44]

He was wounded in France, and, in two subsequent letters to Miss Burkholder, did not reveal any change of perspective.[45]

Thomas Musto gave a sense of battle "somewhere in Belgium" in a letter dated 30 April 1916 from London. He described the shell fire and contrasted the destruction with the beauty of the trees coming into leaf and observed: "What a pity it is that God's beautiful creation should be destroyed by the devices of man! Let us hope that this is a 'war to end war.'"[46] He described the fighting that they had gone through as "a horrible nightmare" in a letter dated 28 October 1916 and observed:

As we think of these men who paid the supreme sacrifice facing death in a manly way our hearts are saddened not so much on their account but for those who have been robbed (or rather I should say have given) for a great cause. This recalls a short inscription I saw on the tombstone of one of our fallen heroes. "How could a man die better than by facing terrible odds. For the ashes of his Fathers and the temples of his God." Which I think is fine.[47]

Richard Upton (911426)—who enlisted on 14 March 1916 with the 196th Western Universities Battalion, listing his "Trade or Calling" as "The Ministry"—was there for the duration.[48] He was born in Shropshire, England, on 27 December 1894 and must have been a relative newcomer in Edmonton when he registered at ACS. His letters are chatty and, like the others, he tells Miss Burkholder of the wounding and deaths of fellow students. In a letter dated March 1917, he tackled moral issues, writing: "I suppose the temptations one encounters as you mention in your letter, but none of us that have left A.C. should find this life an unbearable one. If one has been out on our fields [the theology studies involved mission work], directing men & women how to withstand evil—to prove this in our own lives should not be so very difficult, yet I fear that to some perhaps our own, it may mean defeat."[49]

Luck saw him attached to the machine gun section in Crowborough, Sussex, and he did not actually

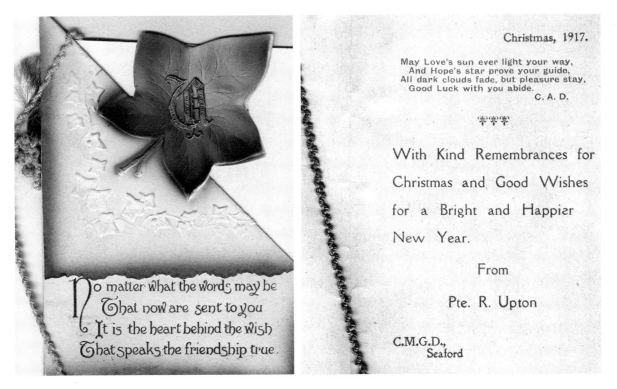

Christmas, 1917.

May Love's sun ever light your way,
And Hope's star prove your guide,
All dark clouds fade, but pleasure stay,
Good Luck with you abide.

C. A. D.

❀❀❀

With Kind Remembrances for Christmas and Good Wishes for a Bright and Happier New Year.

From

Pte. R. Upton

C.M.G.D.,
Seaford

No matter what the words may be
That now are sent to you
It is the heart behind the wish
That speaks the friendship true.

A printed Christmas card send to Miss Burkholder by Private Upton, 1917. University of Alberta Archives, 88-66-67.

get to France until sometime in early 1918. A letter dated November 30 from Wellington is barely legible, and it becomes clear why. The letter described his participation in the Battle of Amiens (also known as the Third Battle of Picardy). It began on 8 August 1918 and was part of the famous Allied Hundred Days Offensive resulting in the end of the war. The letter is lengthy, and it is as if Upton wanted to unburden himself of the experience, and also somehow seek her blessing. He described events at Canal De Nord, Bourlon Wood, and the fall of Cambrai. He wrote of the march through Mons to Denain, where he mentioned that the population of 25,000 treated them

as heroes and opened their homes. On October 27, they had a "thanksgiving service" and a march past. He wrote: "There was something significant about it, that men of a far distant country should be the liberators of those heroic, downtrodden people of Denain. Time & space will not permit me to unfold to you the stories of hardships enforced by the iron fist of Prussianism during those last years of invasion but they were cheerful & brave every one of them."[50] Upton's personal war ended in the next battle, at Valenciennes, on November 1 when he received a dose of gas and was blinded, ending up at the Ford House Military Hospital, in Devonport, England. The

Upton writes: "But I agree with you Miss Burkholder, that our message must be concern because Christ in all his great work, never preached but what even the humblest could understand him. I must conclude with every good wish for Xmas. I hope you will have an enjoyable time." Private Upton letter, University of Alberta Archives, 88-66-67.

temporary blindness accounts for the poor quality of his writing. According to Canadian government figures, 11,356 soldiers suffered from the effects of gas fumes, or 7.85 percent of the wounded total.[51]

Some soldiers had the sense of a personal god or providence that protected them from harm. A.V. Houghton wrote a letter dated 27 February 1917 from "Somewhere in France" where he served as a stretcher bearer and at times was called upon to treat German prisoners. He wrote about the Battle of the Somme as follows: "It is a peculiar feeling one experiences when he is called upon to bandage the wounds of a Fritz. As I did, I felt after all they are men, 'a man's a man for a' that.'" He then went on to discuss the few "narrow escapes" that he had in France, concluding:

> On one occasion a Fritz shell exploded about 15 feet in front of me. I was at the front end of the stretcher, which two of us were carrying with an old dead civilian on it; he had been killed by a bursting shell about 150 yds from our Headquarters. We were running back with him when the shell fell & exploded in front of me. Another half a minute later would have been fatal for me & my partner, as we would have reached this death-spot. I helped to pick up many dead soldiers, being badly blown to pieces. When I think of this and other similar experiences I feel as if there was a special Providence guarding my life.... With these escapades, can I be blamed if I feel that I will be granted special Divine Protection to come through safely?[52]

Another correspondent, Oswald W. Whitford, joined the Royal Naval Canadian Volunteer Reserve and was based initially at Keyham, Devonport, Plymouth.[53] Whitford was born in Gunnislake, Cornwall, and came to Canada in 1912. He took his matriculation at ACS and served as a preacher at Grace Church in Edmonton. His first letter (dated 25 October 1917) revealed that he was in hospital recovering from the mumps; he contrasted this with the battle casualties, observing that one hospital was full of wounded Canadian soldiers.[54] There is an inherent irony in the juxtaposition of a childhood illness with the war injuries. There were 9,644 cases of mumps among Canadian soldiers.[55]

Whitford knew that he was much safer at sea than in the trenches and almost apologizes for this in his letters. The letter written on 13 November 1918 is full of jubilation but also reflection on the war and its costs expressed in quasi-Biblical language:

> This week is one of the most important in the world's history. We see the ambitions of

Oswald W. Whitford with the HMS *Royal Oak* insignia and flags. University of Alberta Archives, 88-66-69.

Lieutenant P.E.Smith.
(Age 18)

~ His ~
~ Spouse ~

—THE—
—ARMY-LIFE-OF—
—P.E·SMITH—

Colonel P.E·Smith.
(Age 38)

General P.E.Smith.
(Age 58)

~ -The End.- ~

An original drawing by soldier Jack Taylor sent by Sam Laycock to Miss Burkholder in a letter dated 17 January 1918 from France. University of Alberta Archives, 88-66-5.

a worldly Emperor dashed to the ground in ruins, never more to rise again, except as an emblem of despotic rule, brutal force and untold and unimaginable outrages. A more proud Emperor than the Kaiser there never was therefore a more humiliated one never lived. It is hard for one's mind to imagine him, as he read his own death warrant and a warrant for millions of others in 1914, and compared him as he is today, not a foot of soil can he call his own.[56]

He experienced the surrender of the German fleet on 11 November 1918 to Admiral Sir David Beatty.

Conclusion

Miss Burkholder's boys ranged in age from their late teens to their mid-thirties. They were part of a faith community and envisioned spending their lives in the ministry. Instead, a number lost their lives; some were wounded and lost limbs; and all who came back were changed. The most complex view of the impact of the war is found in the letters of Sam R. Laycock, Miss Burkholder's most prolific correspondent with 66 letters and cards. He was older and had been teaching and preaching around Alberta before enlisting with the Signal Company of the Canadian Engineers in October 1916. Laycock was born in Marmora, Ontario, in 1891, and obtained a BA degree from the University of Toronto. He had a particularly close relationship with Miss Burkholder and addressed her as "Dear Sister."[57] He revealed to her that he had enlisted, in the end, because he believed that it was the thing to do. On 14 October 1917, he wrote from France:

I've changed mightily in the army and especially in France. In fact so fast of late that I've had growing pains. And I've seen others grow too. Empires are being made & unmade over here but one thing certain, men [the underlining is his] are being made too. I used to think I was a Christian but I doubt if I was one for I hadn't learned the essential gospel of sacrifice. I gave myself largely to those I liked to those who didn't need me so much and I did not give myself to the unlovable or to those who need my comradeship most.[58]

This letter was written after the Battle of Passchendaele (31 July to 6 November 1917). Clearly, doing what he had to do to survive and help others in the process was an experience that the insular life he had led in Canada had not prepared him for.

The war challenged the belief systems of the probationers; indeed, some probationers did not continue their theological studies after the war. However, a few did. Oswald Whitford returned to ACS and graduated in Arts in 1923 and in Theology in 1925, and became a Presbyterian minister in the United States. Sidney Bainbridge obtained an Arts degree with a Theology major in 1921; his brother Joe did take holy orders. G.H. [Harrison] Villett (Royal Air Force, Muster Roll 1917, 277051) had an illustrious career as both a minister and educator.[59] He completed his studies at ACS and served as pastor for various churches. From 1947 until his death in 1959, he served as the Principal of Alberta College in a great era of postwar expansion. Laycock obtained a Bachelor of Education degree from the University of Alberta and lectured in philosophy and psychology of education. He obtained a doctorate in education from the University of London in 1927 and taught at the University of Saskatchewan for 27 years, the last seven serving as dean of the School of Education.[60] Thomas Musto also pursued a career in education.

Miss Burkholder remained the lady principal of ACS until her retirement in 1925. Her strength of character and service were recognized by Laycock, if not the male establishment at ACS. In a letter from France dated 4 July 1918, Laycock playfully referred to her as "the Reverend Miss B." and continued, "I think you're great to do pioneer work for your sex in the ministry. . . . You musn't worry about Theology. The church has had too much of it & that is exactly what is wrong with her. The war has shown that up & if the church wants to succeed or even to continue she must lay emphasis not on creeds but on plain Christian living, sympathy, brotherhood & fellowship."[61]

The letters between Miss Burkholder and her boys on the front, at one and the same time, are deeply personal and also representative of the thoughts and feelings of the many young men who fought in the war, and those who waited, safe at home, for their return. They provide an insight into the way in which the "horrors of history" marked and shaped the participants.

Notes

1   Alberta College South materials are contained within the larger St. Stephen's College Fonds, 1903–1971, AN 88-66, University of Alberta Archives [hereafter UAA]. In 1925 with church union, Alberta College South and the Presbyterian Robertson College merged to become United Theological College, and in 1927 the name was changed to St. Stephen's College.

2   "Reception at Alberta College So.: Welcome Home Extended to Returned Soldiers . . ." The photocopy does not include article source or date.

3   Whitby Public Library, "Nettie Burkholder," URL: http://images.ourontario.ca/whitby/43023/data, retrieved 14 February 2014.

4   Burkholder family history, URL: http://billbuchanan.byethost17.com/ourfamily/pafg691.htm, retrieved 17 February 2014. This notes that Nettie Burkholder helped to compile the early family history.

5   Johanna M. Selles, *Methodists and Women's Education in Ontario, 1836–1925* (Montreal and Kingston: McGill-Queen's University Press, 1996), 7.

6   Ibid., 111.

7   Gayle Simonson, *Ever-Widening Circles: A History of St. Stephen's College* (Edmonton: St. Stephen's College, 2008), 10–18, provides a comprehensive description of the early period of the college.

8   ACS column, *The Gateway*, 7 December 1915, 3.

9   Tim Cook in "Tools of Memory," *Archivaria* 45 (Spring 1998), 195 notes the importance of archives not only with respect to their war-specific content but also in their connection to "the broader concept of the construction of memory." He believes this work still has to be done in Canada. The article is a review of the following books: Jonathan Vance, *Death So Noble: Memory, Meaning, and the First World War* (Vancouver: UBC Press, 1997); Geoff Dyer, *The Missing of the Somme* (London, UK: Penguin, 1995); and Michael McKernan, *Here Is Their Spirit: A History of the Australian War Memorial 1917–1990* (St. Lucia, AU: University of Queensland Press, 1991).

10 Burkholder to George North, 30 January 1916, UAA, AN 88-66, 22.

11 Ibid.

12 The Regimental Rogue website, "Researching Canadian Soldiers of the First World War," Part 14: The Wounded and Sick, URL: http://regimentalrogue.com/misc/researching_first_world_war_soldiers_part14.htm, retrieved 14 May 2014.

13 Burkholder to North, 30 January 1916.

14 Ibid.

15 Ibid.

16 Burkholder to George North, 15 October 1916, UAA, AN 88-66-22.

17 Canadian War Graves, Ancestry.ca, URL: http://www.ancestry.ca/genealogy/canadian-war-graves/North.html, retrieved 3 March 2014.

18 These were the First Battle of Ypres: 19 October to 22 November 1914; Second Battles of Ypres: 22 April to 15 May 1915; Third Battle of Ypres: fought at Passchendaele, 31 July to 6 November 1917; the Fourth Battle of Ypres: fought at Lys, 9 April to 29 April 1918; and the Fifth Battle of Ypres: 2 September to 2 October 1918.

19 "Dead on the Field of Honour," *The Gateway*, 1 November 1915, 1.

20 Burkholder to Arthur M. Hummel, 18 November 1917, UAA, AN 88-66-22.

21 Hummel to Burkholder, 26 September 1917, UAA, AN 88-66-50.

22 Ibid.

23 Sid Bainbridge to Burkholder, 12 September 1916, UAA, AN 88-66-27-28.

24 Hummel to Burkholder, 26 September 1917.

25 Burkholder apparently wrote to Mrs. J.C. Hummel, Chesterville, Ontario, to inquire about him, and Mrs. Hummel responds on 24 March 1918 thanking her for her thoughtful letter.

26 Burkholder to John R. Barker, 28 October 1917, UAA, AN 88-66-22.

27 Ibid.

28 Barker to Burkholder, 31 December 1916, UAA, AN 88-66-30.

29 Regimental Rogue.

30 Major General Malcolm N. Macleod was the commander of the 145th Anti-Tank Company, Royal Engineers. Major General Herbert Francis Eaton, 3rd Baron Cheylesmore, was commandant of the School of Musketry at Bisley Camp.

31 Barker to Burkholder, 31 December 1916.

32 Barker to Burkholder, 2 August 1917, UAA, AN 88-66-30.

33 Ibid.

34 Clement Beck Wilson to Burkholder, 1 January 1916, UAA, AN 88-66-70.

35 Wilson to Burkholder, 27 November 1916, UAA, AN 88-66-70.

36 Ibid.

37 Wilson to Burkholder, 14 February 1917, UAA, AN 88-66-70.

38 Sidney Bainbridge to Burkholder, 12 September 1916, UAA, AN 88-66-27-28.

39 Ibid.

40 Bainbridge to Burkholder, 13 August 1917, UAA, AN 88-66-27-28.

41 Ibid.

42 Ibid.

43 Ibid.

44 Clark to Burkholder, 2 January 1916, UAA, AN 88-66-34.

45 Clark to Burkholder, 27 December 1916, UAA, AN 88-66-34, and 3 February 1917.

46 Musto to Burkholder, 30 April 1916, UAA, AN 88-66-60.

47 Musto to Burkholder, 28 October 1916, UAA, AN 88-66-60.

48 Upton writes five letters to Miss Burkholder as well as sending her two printed Christmas cards (1917 and 1918).

49 Upton to Burkholder, March 1917, UAA, AN 88-66-67.

50 Ibid.

51 Regimental Rogue.

52 Houghton to Burkholder, 27 February 1917, UAA, AN 88-66-49.

53 Eight letters written to Miss Burkholder by Oswald W. Whitford survived.

54 Whitford to Burkholder, 25 October 1917, UAA, AN 88-66-69.

55 Regimental Rogue.

56 Whitford to Burkholder, 13 November 1918, UAA, AN 88-66-69.

57 Laycock to Burkholder, 22 June 1917, UAA, AN 88-66-55.

58 Laycock to Burkholder, 14 October 1917, UAA, AN 88-66-55.

59 The G. Harrison Villett Fonds PR2856 are located in the Provincial Archives of Alberta, Edmonton.

60 Sam Laycock biography, University of British Columbia, URL: http://www.library.ubc.ca/archives/u_arch/laycock.pdf, retrieved 10 March 2014.

61 Laycock to Burkholder, 4 July 1918, UAA, AN 88-66-56.

Works Cited

PRIMARY SOURCES

The Gateway, University of Alberta student newspaper, Peel's Prairie Provinces. URL: http://peel.library.ualberta.ca/newspapers/GAT/.

University of Alberta Archives, Edmonton. Alberta College South Fonds, within the larger St. Stephen's College Fonds, 1903–1971, AN 88-66.

SECONDARY SOURCES

Bill Buchanan Family Genealogy (includes Burkholder relations). URL: http://billbuchanan.byethost17.com/ourfamily/pafg691.htm, retrieved 17 February 2014.

Burkholder Family Genealogy, Papers and Records of the Wentworth Historical Society, Upper Canada. URL: http://archive.org/stream/papersrecordsof191920went/papersrecordsof191920went_djvu.txt.

Cook, Tim. "Tools of Memory." *Archivaria* 45 (Spring 1998): 195.

Elson, D.J.C. "Faith, Labour, and Dreams." University of Alberta Alumni Association History Trails. URL: http://www.ualberta.ca/~alumni/history/affiliate/51winfaith.htm, retrieved 24 February 2014.

Fussell, Paul. *The Great War and Modern Memory*. London, UK: Oxford University Press, 1975.

The Regimental Rogue website. "Researching Canadian Soldiers of the First World War," Part 14: The Wounded and Sick. URL: http://regimentalrogue.com/misc/

researching_first_world_war_soldiers_part14.htm, retrieved 14 May 2014.

Reid, John G. "Mary Electa Adams." Dictionary of Canadian Biography. URL: http://www.biographi.ca/en/bio.php?id_nbr=5922, retrieved 3 March 2014. Adams retired from OLC in 1892 aged 70.

Selles, Johanna M. *Methodists and Women's Education in Ontario, 1836–1925*. Montreal and Kingston: McGill-Queen's University Press, 1996.

Simonson, Gayle. *Ever-Widening Circles: A History of St. Stephen's College*. Edmonton: St. Stephen's College, 2008.

University of British Columbia Archives. Sam Laycock biography. URL: http://www.library.ubc.ca/archives/u_arch/laycock.pdf, retrieved 10 March 2014.

Vance, Jonathan. *Death So Noble: Memory, Meaning, and the First World War*. Vancouver: UBC Press, 1997.

Whitby Public Library. "Nettie Burkholder." URL: http://images.ourontario.ca/whitby/43023/data, retrieved 14 February 2014.

Medical Contributions of Albertans in the First World War: Rising to the Challenge

J. ROBERT LAMPARD

Introduction

The impact of the First World War on medical care in Alberta has received little attention for almost 100 years. The vacuum is surprising because in 1914 Alberta and Saskatchewan faced the greatest challenges of any provinces. They were only nine years old; experiencing an economic downturn following the prewar boom; and filling rapidly with rural immigrants. While they had Northwest Territories–created medical associations, the University of Alberta's three-year medical school program had just started the year before, and the faculty's primary teaching hospital (the Strathcona) had only been open for a year and would be taken over by the military for six years starting in 1916.

The 1914 call to arms was widely heard and responded to by a patriotic but relatively young prairie population. In Alberta, the enlistment response to the armed services and to the medical corps exceeded the Canadian norms. The high physician enlistment rate left many rural communities without a doctor. When the Spanish Flu arrived with returning soldiers in early October 1918, it rapidly spread throughout a province that was under-doctored and under-bedded. Care was literally rationed. All institutions—the medical school, hospitals, and public health services—rose to the challenge. Healthcare changes accelerated after the war, at a rate not equalled in any other province. Alberta would become the informal leader of healthcare changes in Canada until the next war.

The Canadian Army Medical Corps

To appreciate the contributions of Alberta doctors and other medical personnel in the First World War, it is necessary to have an understanding of the state of military medicine in Canada in August 1914. The Canadian Army Medical Corps (CAMC) was established in 1896, formed by Minister of Militia Frederick Borden, MD. Nurses were added starting in 1906 as officers, and dentists in 1914. Both were British Empire precedents.[1] The organization of the medical armed services was based on the British model with the appointment of regimental or battalion medical officers (RMOs) and the establishment of field ambulances (FAs) to triage and transfer injured soldiers to Casualty Clearing Stations (CCS) and general hospitals.[2] RMOs had existed prior to the Riel Rebellion in 1885. FAs were created in eastern Canada as part of a voluntary reserve, about 1899.

In August 1914, the permanent CAMC consisted of 20 doctors, 5 nurses, and 102 field ambulance stretcher bearers and care givers.[3] The total would rise to 19,053 before 11 November 1918. A few physicians held American or British fellowships, as specialist recognition did not exist in Canada at the time. Ranking usually was determined by the institution that formed the medical unit. Historian G.W.L. Nicholson noted that younger physicians were more willing to work closer to the frontlines as RMOs; older and more senior physicians (department heads and teachers) tended to join the hospital medical staff.[4]

Anticipating a short war, the British government requested a contingent (division) of troops from Canada in August 1914. Canada's legal position was that it could not refuse war entry, but it could determine the size of the response. In October, 33,000 Canadians went overseas, medically supported by the just-created, fully staffed #1 Canadian General Hospital from Montreal.[5] Because the CAMC (and other Empire medical corps) were organized along British lines, the medical units were easily integrated with existing British units.[6] The second medical call came in 1915, after battle losses increased dramatically. Subsequently the call became continuous, leading in 1917 to a contentious conscription order for soldiers. Medical, dental, and nursing recruitment remained voluntary throughout the war, although medical conscription was introduced in Britain and the United States.

The first, unanticipated call for more medical staff came after the Second Battle of Ypres on 22 April 1915, when the German army released chlorine gas on French Colonial and nearby Canadian troops. The 3rd FA triaged 1,800 casualties in 24 hours.[7] There were 700 gas casualties in the 1st Canadian Division, of which 478 were hospitalized.[8] The government responded at home by appointing the Military Hospitals Commission (MHC) in June 1915, under Senator James Lougheed (future Premier Peter Lougheed's grandfather).[9] Lougheed was charged with preparing Canada to receive not just the war wounded with amputations and other such disabilities but also those who had been gassed, had contracted tuberculosis (TB) or venereal disease (VD), or required long-term care. The returning convoys were augmented by more than 9,000 soldiers who had developed the "shell-shock" syndrome.[10] Lougheed would be knighted a year later for his work.

A second, unexpected challenge came from the poor assessment of recruits sent overseas. They required reassessments and quarantining once in England. The commonest "unfit" diagnosis was flat feet with foot pain on marching. Up to 40 percent of the new arrivals overseas were sent back. The next challenge came in 1916 when Minister of Militia and Defence Sir Sam Hughes appointed the Bruce and Mawson Inquiries to study, respectively, the organization of the CAMC overseas and the Military Hospital Commission (MHC) in Canada. Although most of the Bruce Inquiry's 23 recommendations would be implemented, the inquiry was critical of the non-alignment of Canadian hospitals with Canadian troops. As a result, the top medical officers were fired. They were then rehired when the alignment

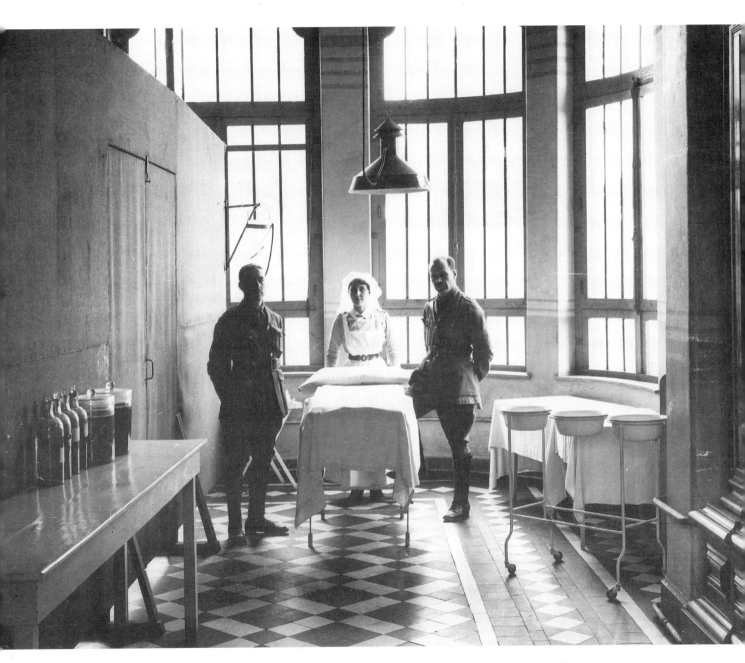

"Small Operating Room. 1st Cdn CCS" [Casualty Clearing Station]. Lt. Col. E.R. Selby Photo Album. The Military Museums, Calgary.

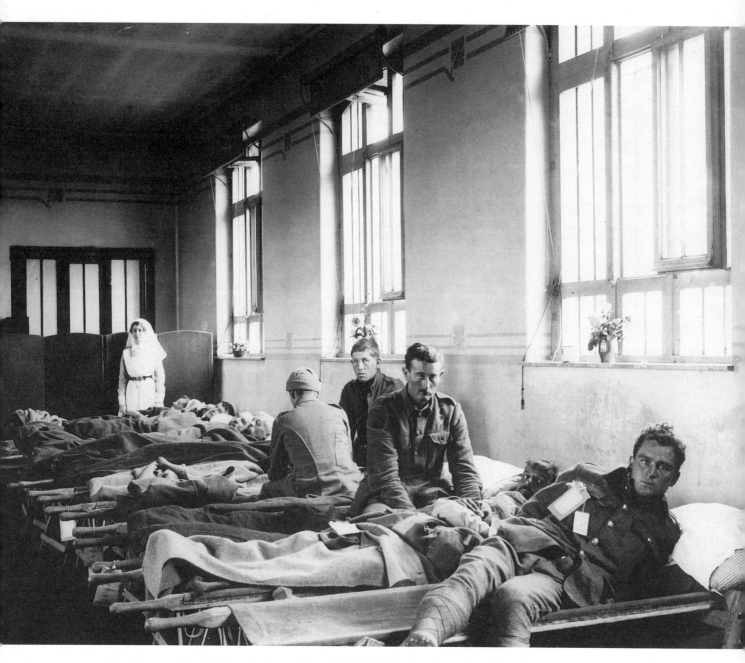

"Ward 1 Cases. 1st Cdn CCS" [Casualty Clearing Station]. Lt. Col. E.R. Selby Photo Album. The Military Museums, Calgary.

recommendation was set aside as impossible to implement, after it became apparent that one-half of the wounded Canadian troops were already being cared for in British hospitals. That ratio would continue throughout the war.[11] The prime minister replaced Hughes.

Andrew Macphail's *Official History of the Canadian Forces in the Great War 1914–19: The Medical Services* was released by the King's Printer in 1924–25. He reported that of the 418,000 Canadian men who went overseas, 56,638 were killed, 144,606 were hospitalized with battle injuries, and 395,084 were hospitalized (some repeatedly) with acquired diseases.[12] An estimate of the comparable Alberta figures is 6,140 killed and 20,000 wounded from a population of 500,000.[13]

In the Canadian medical services, 30 doctors were killed and 31 died of diseases; a further 99 were wounded. As of October 1918, 1,528 physician positions had been created overseas and 836 in Canada for a medical establishment of 2,364. Thirty-eight registered nurses (RNs) were killed or died of diseases. Six nurses were wounded from a total nursing establishment of 1,901 overseas and 385 in Canada. Of the 223 who went overseas, seven dentists died from acquired diseases.[14]

In the military, physicians had many different roles both within Canada and overseas. They were responsible for assessing the fitness of recruits, supervising their transport, caring for them in camps and hospitals, maintaining hygiene and sanitation, and preventing and treating diseases.[15] At the front, the ailments most commonly seen were scabies, trench foot, trench fever, VD, and shell shock.[16] Shell- and shrapnel-fire injuries required IVs, blood transfusions, debridement (surgical removal of dead tissue), and surgery, particularly to avoid infection.

Most diseases that affected frontline soldiers were treated locally (in France) and the soldiers returned to the front.[17] The death rate from diseases versus battlefield wounds was 1:27.[18] This was a major reversal from the Boer War, when the rate was 2:1.

Casualties from the Western Front came in waves, following each major battle. The triage and treatment process started with the RMO who, with his up to six stretcher bearers, identified, stabilized, and moved the injured to advanced dressing stations. There, they were triaged to the nearest FA, which typically had some 10 doctors who reassessed, categorized (red was most urgent), and sent the wounded to the CCS, slightly behind the lines. It had 20 or more doctors and an operating room (OR) capability. From there, the wounded were sent to a Stationary Hospital and, if the rehabilitation was going to be long-term (more than a month), to a general hospital with 40 or more doctors at Étaples (Étaples-sur-Mer) or Le Touquet in France, or to one of the Specialty Hospitals in Britain, such as for orthopedic, rehabilitative, and neurological/mental problems.[19] Canadian physicians also staffed two French-speaking hospitals near Paris. As the war progressed, transfers back to Canada increased to free up overseas beds.

Developments in Alberta

In the fall of 1914, a discussion about the impact the war might have on the medical profession in Alberta led to the first winter training program. More than 50 doctors signed up for it.[20] The number of Alberta doctors who answered the call remains an approximate figure. In 1916, Dr. William Whitelaw, president of the Alberta Medical Association, estimated that a third of Alberta's physicians had enlisted. In 1917, his figure was closer to 40 percent, with 42 of 118 Edmonton and 45 of 90 Calgary physicians having volunteered for military service.[21] The Medical List for District 13 (Alberta) in October 1918 gives a total of 216 of the estimated 400 physicians in active practice in Alberta as having enlisted.[22] At least three physicians died: Captain H.S. Monkman and Lieutenant Colonels H.H. Moshier and S.W. Hewetson. The Canadian average was 36 percent of the estimated 7,800 physicians in Canada having enlisted by the end of war.[23]

The impact of the first call for doctors in August 1914 was more a function of who left than how many. Two "non-Alberta" enlistments were significant. The new director of the provincial laboratory based in Edmonton, Dr. Allan Rankin, who had arrived three months before from Bangkok, enlisted immediately. He was one of four full-time faculty members who were to give the first medical lectures at the University of Alberta, starting in September 1914. Rankin was joined by Dr. J.C. Fyshe, who was the superintendent of the Royal Alexandra, Strathcona (named the University of Alberta Hospital in 1922), and Isolation Hospitals. Both joined the No. 1 Canadian General Hospital from Montreal.[24]

University of Alberta President Henry Marshall Tory took advantage of Fyshe's departure to assume control over the Strathcona Hospital. He appointed Dr. Moshier as its superintendent. Moshier would also teach the physiology and pharmacology courses to the students and start the Faculty of Pharmacy in 1915. He joined the reserve Canadian Officers Training Corps (COTC) and was appointed second in command of the 1915-formed 11th (Western Universities) Field Ambulance. In March 1916 the unit was mobilized and Moshier left with 15 medical students

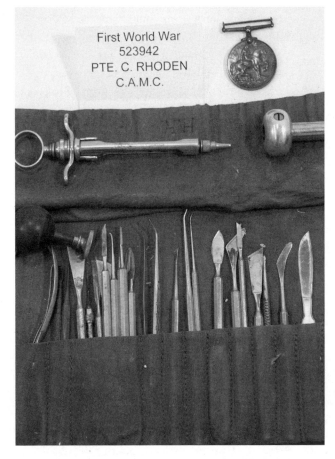

Instruments carried by Private C. Rhoden, Canadian Army Medical Corps. He was born on 17 August 1894 in Saskatoon and enlisted in Winnipeg on 30 April 1916. His brother Harry was born 31 January 1899 and enlisted on 5 April 1916. Their father, John Rhoden (born 21 June 1874 in England) enlisted on 30 March 1916 and also served with the CAMC, achieving the rank of sergeant. They served with the 11th Field Ambulance in which Dr. H. Moshier, Reg Lister, and a number of University of Alberta medical students served. In the spring of 1916, the 11th Field Ambulance assembled for training at the Manitoba Agricultural College in Winnipeg. On May 14, they left for Halifax to go overseas. Kerr Collection, Canadian Militaria Preservation Society Museum, Edmonton.

and six theology students from the university, as well as his batman, Reg Lister, who became a well-known University of Alberta personality.[25]

Fortunately, J.B. Collip, PhD, had arrived in September 1915 and took over Dr. Moshier's courses at the university. Dr. H.C. Jamieson assumed Rankin's provincial lab responsibilities and lectures. With Dr. D.G. Revell, several part-timers, and volunteers, the program kept going although enrollment dropped significantly to a dozen students per year.[26] At the September 1915 Alberta Medical Association meeting, it was announced that President Tory had offered a fully equipped hospital of 1,040 beds to be sent overseas. The federal government declined the offer.[27] The requirement for 40 physicians to staff the field hospital would have put in jeopardy the two-year-old Faculty of Medicine.

In 1917, Dr. Tory suggested expanding the YMCA idea of giving overseas presentations and lectures by professors who had enlisted. He recommended that university-level and other educational courses be offered to soldiers, who could receive credit for them in Canada. This proposal was accepted, and Tory went overseas for two years to create and operate the

(left) Tools from medical kit carried by Private C. Rhoden, Canadian Army Medical Corps. Kerr Collection, Canadian Militaria Preservation Society Museum, Edmonton; (right) Scalpels from medical kit carried by Private C. Rhoden, Canadian Army Medical Corps. Kerr Collection, Canadian Militaria Preservation Society Museum, Edmonton.

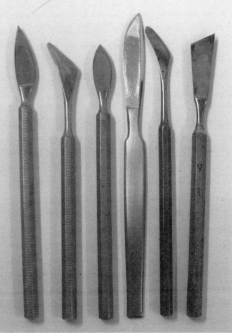

Khaki University during the last year of the war and the first year following it.[28] A number of overseas medical students took advantage of the program and enrolled in courses in England; in some cases, they earned a British fellowship.

The exact number of Alberta nurses who enlisted is unknown.[29] Marjorie Norris, in *Sister Heroines: The Roseate Glow of Wartime Nursing 1914–1918*, has explored the First World War contributions of Calgary nurses. She lists 77 as having served, of whom 40 graduated from the Calgary General and Holy Cross Hospitals. Some joined the Queen Alexandra nurses, others the British Red Cross and Volunteer Aid Detachments, but the majority joined the CAMC as lieutenants and received $730 per year. The Calgary nurses were awarded six medals. In 1916 the Alberta government unanimously passed the Nursing Act, the fourth one in Canada. In 1920, 39 Edmonton nurses formed the first Overseas Nurses Association.[30]

The Military Hospitals Commission

The need for and value of the Military Hospitals Commission (MHC) in Canada was apparent as soon as it was appointed in June 1915. In Alberta, A.E. Cross, owner of the Calgary Brewing and Malting Co., offered the Ogden Hotel in October 1915 for use as a hospital; it would house 200 patients.[31] In December 1916 the MHC took control of the Strathcona Hospital (190 beds) and added the nearby Alberta College South-Methodist Theological (350 beds) in Edmonton, the Alberta Ladies College in Red Deer (106 beds), the Edmonton Convalescent Hospital, a small (14-bed) hospital in Wetaskiwin, the Calgary Soldiers hospital, and a 10-bed "Sanitorium" attached

to "Sarcee City." The bed total would reach 918.[32] The MHC also paid hospitals that treated veterans on a fee-for-service basis. Most rural hospitals were unprepared to treat injured veterans, let alone meet their long rehabilitation requirements, so they took few of them.

Another serious problem arose over the 3,123 cases of tuberculosis discovered among troops both in Canada and in Europe. Alberta was the only province without a sanatorium. The MHC leased the CPR hotel in the town of Frank in the Crowsnest Pass, in 1916, to create one.[33]

In 1918 the MHC transferred the responsibility for the care of discharged veterans to the newly established Soldiers Civil Rehabilitation Commission (SCR), again under Senator Lougheed. That change met the Geneva Convention requirement that MHC hospitals be under military control.[34]

Political Change and Medicine: The Creation of Rural Hospital Districts

In April 1916, Alberta gave females the right to vote, the third province in Canada, after Manitoba and Saskatchewan, to do so. The impact of the 1915-formed United Farm Women of Alberta was soon felt. Louise McKinney and Nursing Sister Roberta MacAdams (from the CAMC) were elected to the provincial legislature in 1917. The UFWA president, Irene Parlby, was appointed by the Liberal government to a 1916 committee to create rural hospital districts. Under the 1917 Municipal Hospital Act, approved hospital districts could tax landowners to support their services. The act was revised in 1918 to match hospital districts with municipal boundaries; a similar act was passed the same year in Saskatchewan.[35]

The first municipally funded hospital in Canada was on the Saskatchewan side of the boundary town of Lloydminster, with funding coming from both provinces. The first municipal hospital built in Alberta under the act was approved for Mannville, in 1918. It declared itself to be the first one built in the British Empire.[36] The idea spread rapidly across Saskatchewan, Alberta, Manitoba, and throughout the Empire. It helped meet the needs of returning veterans. By 1921 there were 15 of a planned 30 municipal hospitals in the province.[37]

In 1917 Alberta's healthcare sensitive Liberal government took another step to form the second public health department in the country (after New Brunswick). The government passed 17 public health acts in 1918.[38] A.G. MacKay became the first health minister in Canada (1919) and established the second District Nurse program, to serve sparsely populated northern communities using returning wartime nurses. The three Prairie provinces also retained J.S. Woodsworth to conduct a "social services" review in 1916, which led to an expansion of psychiatric facilities, the building of the Oliver Mental Hospital in Edmonton, and the transfer of mentally handicapped persons to the vacated Red Deer facility in 1923.[39]

The War Service of Individual Alberta Medical Personnel

Insight into physician experiences can be gathered from letters, manuscripts, and several recently published First World War biographies and histories.[40] Collectively, Alberta physicians earned 16 medals. Twelve were demobilized as lieutenant colonels, and one as a colonel.[41] The lone colonel was Dr. George Macdonald, the CPSA registrar from 1911 to 1915. The lieutenant colonels were Doctors Moshier, Mason, Gunn, Selby, Hewetson, Mewburn, Hepburn, Harwood, Ferris, McGuffin, Rankin, and Orr.

Dr. H.W. McGill joined the 31st Battalion from Calgary in November 1914 and went overseas, as an RMO, in May 1915.[42] He had fixed views on both courage and cowards, which he strongly communicated to his staff. Courage was described as "doing the job in spite of being afraid."[43] While moving a soldier on a stretcher into a dugout, a shell landed between McGill and one of the stretcher bearers. McGill was thrown into the dugout, the soldier was unscathed, but McGill's stretcher partner was killed. On another occasion, McGill left his dugout, turned around, and saw a shell directly hit it. Later, he was unnerved when the chlorine gas containers that were being prepared for firing at the German lines were stored in his dugout.

McGill recorded in his near-daily diary how wounded soldiers could be gritty and even euphoric after they had lost an arm or a leg, perhaps from the morphine they received. Their greatest fear was death from hemorrhage. He could not rationalize the shock of the violence that he faced.[44] His attitude was fatalistic, and he realized that tragedy and comedy were not far apart. During leaves, he attended plays and theatre productions in London. He remained remarkably loyal to his unit and men, refusing to leave until 26 September 1917. McGill's determination to make the most of a potentially short life led to a secret engagement and marriage to a Calgary RN, Emma Griffis, in 1917, in London. She remained overseas and, unknown to McGill, had a miscarriage, which he only learned about shortly before their return to Calgary and his discharge in June 1919.

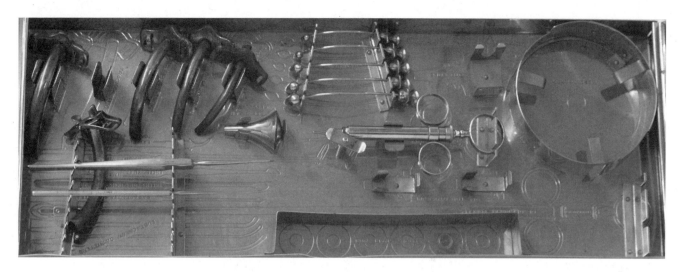

Trachea instruments contained in a Field Medical Kit made in Philadelphia, USA. Kerr Collection.

Dr. Harry Wallace from Ontario was assigned to Edmonton's 49th Battalion as its RMO, succeeding Captain L.C. Harris. Wallace enlisted in January 1916 and was wounded on Vimy Ridge on 24 April 1917, two weeks after the main battle. Wallace and several members of his unit were returning to the frontlines when a shell landed beside them. Two were killed; Wallace was injured. He returned to Edmonton, moving in 1919 to Wainwright, where he became the town's leading physician and mayor.[45]

Captain Ashley Cooper C. Johnston graduated from the University of Toronto before the war. Originally from High River and Lundbreck, he was assigned to the 50th Battalion and went overseas with it in August 1916. His inflexible rule was "paint the spot giving trouble with Iodine, give him a No 9 pill [a placebo] and order the man back to duty."[46] After many months with the battalion, Johnston was gassed badly enough to be sent to England. Once recovered, he remained in England until after the end

of the war. He met his wife there and they had three children before the family returned to Calgary. Each summer his family moved to Sarcee, where he was a medical officer for the recruits.[47]

Edward Heller was a farm boy from Grande Prairie who became a stretcher bearer in Calgary's 31st battalion.[48] He undertook several risky evacuations. One was to retrieve an injured officer who had led a charge on Vimy Ridge. Although successful, Heller was soon exhausted when there were only two to carry the officer back to the Regimental Aid Post. Another soldier Heller retrieved was within hearing distance of the German lines. Heller had to slide through the mud to reach the soldier, and crawl back to his unit's trench with his wounded comrade on his back. When advances occurred, stretcher bearing became a problem. Six men were required to carry a soldier for up to four miles. Many wounded soldiers did not make it and Heller wrote that they are "now sleeping beneath their crosses with the poppies in silent splendor standing watch over them." When Heller hand-wrote his memoir in 1976, he recorded how one of his own near misses came when a bullet severed the water-bottle strap hanging between his arm and body. At Passchendaele, a shell exploded just behind him. Dug out and dazed, he was sent in severe pain to the CCS. The next day, he realized he had a fractured foot, which was successfully operated on. He avoided being (as he described those who died) "another mother's prayer that wasn't answered."

The 8th Field Ambulance was drafted in April 1915 in Calgary.[49] It left a year later for France. Major J.N. Gunn of Calgary was transferred to it in November 1916 and became the CO in January 1917, just before the battle for Vimy Ridge on April 9–12. The 8th was the primary FA for the 3rd Division. Gunn's closest call came while on duty. A shell narrowly missed his helmet; however, some of the shrapnel fragments penetrated it. Over-taxed at Vimy, Gunn's unit used German prisoners as stretcher bearers, expediting the moving of more

Soldiers of the 8th Canadian Field Ambulance leaving Calgary, Alberta, ca. 1915. Glenbow Archives, NA-4617-5. Copied from PA-2579-10.

"Huns carrying wounded Canadian in improvised stretcher." Lt. Col. E.R. Selby Photo Album. The Military Museums, Calgary.

than 700 injured soldiers to the nearby narrow-gauge railway. The biggest problem was the stretcher shortage, which occurred because the German prisoners did not understand the stretchers were to be sent back. The 8th handled 2,000 casualties that day. Their work was disrupted when a snowstorm hit the next day. The FA was relieved after 48 hours of continuous duty. Following Vimy, Gunn began an eye clinic, as he was an EENT (Eye Ear Nose Throat) surgeon. He could fit glasses, make diagnoses, and bandage and irrigate eyes. It wasn't long before the whole Canadian Corps were coming to his clinic, pleased that they didn't have to travel 70 kilometres to the nearest eye clinic behind the lines. Lieutenant

Colonel Gunn developed trench fever while at Vimy; he suffered a relapse that led to a convalescent break in November and then a permanent leave and return to Canada on 27 February 1918. He was replaced by another Calgary physician, Lieutenant Colonel E.R. Selby.

During the war, the 8th Field Ambulance suffered 9 killed in action, 10 who died of wounds, 3 who died of illness, and 79 who were wounded, out of a total of 200 men. In October alone, the FA handled 3,255 sick and wounded. The 11th FA's most significant casualty came when Lieutenant Colonel Moshier, who had assumed command in August 1917, was looking for a better location at Drocourt-Queant. His vehicle was struck by a shell and he was killed on 26 August 1918 at the age of 29.[50]

"Officers of 8th Canadian Field Ambulance at the time of Vimy Ridge." Lt. Col. E.R. Selby Photo Album. The Military Museums, Calgary.

"Loading an ambulance on the field." Lt. Col. E.R. Selby Photo Album. The Military Museums, Calgary.

Fred Miller was a young Vermilion farmer who decided to study medicine at McGill in 1912.[51] After three years of study, he joined the #3 Canadian (McGill) General Hospital as a private, along with 100 other medical students. In France, one of the

staff members was Lieutenant Revere Osler, the son of Sir William Osler, the McGill-trained physician who came to be widely regarded as a "father of modern medicine" (Osler was one of four founding professors at the Johns Hopkins Hospital in

Baltimore, Maryland, and the Regius Professor of Medicine at Oxford). Miller designed a card-and-pin system to record each patient's arrival and departure, an idea which led to his promotion; simply put, medical data was written onto an index card and it was pinned to the soldier's tunic. After becoming the regiment's sergeant major, Miller was allowed to give chloroform and administer dressing changes, as well as remove shrapnel under local anesthetic. Disconcertingly, two of his first three patients were dead on arrival. The two typhoid cases he saw were both men who had skipped their vaccination. During the war, his hospital's capacity increased from 500 to more than 2,200, even before the battle at Vimy Ridge. In December 1917, Miller, along with 230 other Canadian medical and dental students, returned to their universities to enter the accelerated medical training programs and receive their degrees. Each academic year was compressed into six months and taught continuously, as it would be in the Second World War.

Lieutenant Colonel H.H. Hepburn was 21 when he entered the McGill medical class of 1906.[52] After interning, in December 1912 he accepted a two-year post as the chief of surgery at the Bangkok Police Hospital. There he worked with Dr. Allan Rankin on his beriberi research. Hepburn moved to Berlin to begin neurosurgical studies in June 1914. With the declaration of war, he was placed under house arrest as a British citizen. Portraying himself and his colleague as Americans led to a laxity in their surveillance. The two escaped by joining a recruitment parade as it went by. They exited from it at the railway station, where passengers were being loaded onto the last train to Amsterdam. They caught the train and were then transported by submarine to Britain, where they joined the RAMC and were back

in France on August 24, 10 days after leaving the continent, this time as British RAMC surgeons.

One of Hepburn's clinical tricks was to boil seawater each day for IVs and irrigations. For surgery, he wore five pairs of gloves and took off one pair after each operation. He conducted a number of direct blood transfusions using universal, or 0-negative, blood. As the war continued, he served with several FAs, becoming an RMO, before being transferred to the No. 24 General Hospital as the chief of surgery, with 1,800 beds under his charge. He wrote three articles for the *British Medical Journal*: on splinting after performing arthrotomies (creating an opening in a joint for drainage), on delayed primary closure of wounds, and on 100 beriberi patients in Thailand. One soldier he found had a shrapnel wound to his frontal sinus and a natural pneumo-encephalogram, with air outlining the brain.

Pneumoencephalography was a medical procedure in which cerebrospinal fluid was drained from around the brain and oxygen was injected by means of a lumbar puncture so that the structure of the brain could be seen better on an X-ray image. Personally, Hepburn suffered a wound to his biceps (1917) and was exposed to chlorine gas. For his war effort, Lieutenant Colonel Hepburn received four medals. He earned a Fellowship in the Royal College of Surgeons of Edinburgh (1919), and a Fellowship in the American College of Surgeons (1920).

In his late fifties in 1914, Dr. F.H. Mewburn tried to enlist.[53] He had already served in the Riel Rebellion of 1885. Refused by Minister Sam Hughes, he approached his nephew Brigadier General Stanley Mewburn and Sir William Osler for advice, and then paid his own way to Europe. He was accepted into the CAMC before leaving Halifax. As he already was a Fellow of the Alberta College of Surgeons,

Dr. Mewburn was soon appointed lieutenant colonel and named chief of surgery at the hospital established at Lord Astor's estate at Cliveden, in Taplow, England. He remained there for the rest of the war. After his return to Calgary, he was called upon by Dean Rankin to become the first professor and head of surgery at the University of Alberta in 1922.

University of Alberta professor Dr. A.C. Rankin's military career took many turns.[54] After dealing with the 1914 cerebrospinal encephalitis outbreak at the Salisbury Plain encampment, the largest military training camp in England, he was transferred to one of the first mobile lab units in France. In April 1915 he confirmed, with Lieutenant Colonel G.G. Nasmith, the first German chlorine gas attack. He was the first to describe the Trench Fever Syndrome in the medical journal *The Lancet*, proved that troops from India brought malaria with them, and prevented the 1914 typhoid outbreak from recurring by vaccinating Belgian citizens on a house-to-house search. He was assigned to do research on respirators and gas masks in England, before being injured while serving as the commanding officer of a field ambulance in France. Rankin stayed behind after the war and managed an officer's convalescent hospital. He was presented to the King, and was honoured as a Companion of the Order of St. Michael and St. George (CMG), before returning to Edmonton in the spring of 1919. In 1920, President Tory appointed him to be the first University of Alberta dean of medicine, a position he held until 1945.

Dr. J.J. Ower joined the 5th Field Ambulance in Montreal during his undergraduate years.[55] He likely met Rankin there, as they were in the same unit; if not, they met when he was assigned to the No. 1 Canadian General Hospital at Christmas 1914 under Rankin. Ower assisted him in investigating and treating the encephalitis outbreak. A trained pathologist, he was transferred to France where he worked in the pathology departments of No. 3 and then the No. 1 General Hospital. His specialty was Wasserman testing for diagnosing soldiers with suspected venereal disease (VD).[56] On his return, in September 1919, Ower was seconded for a year to the new Ste. Anne de Bellevue Military Hospital to do the same, before he could take up his position as the provincial seropathologist (a pathologist with a specialty in serum testing) and faculty member at the University of Alberta. He became acting dean of medicine at the University of Alberta (1939–1943) and the second dean (1945–1949), succeeding Dr. Rankin.

Dr. H.H. Orr had a prewar interest in sanitation and hygiene and had implemented a system for the daily removal of human wastes in Medicine Hat, thereby avoiding typhoid outbreaks. Overseas, he became the head of the No. 3 Sanitation Unit. He designed the "Orr hut," which was used to decontaminate soldier's clothing of lice that caused trench fever. For that he received an Order of the British Empire (OBE) and a Médaille d'Honneur des Epidemies (French Medal of Honour for Epidemics).[57] Dr. Orr became the CMA president in 1952.

Dr. E.G. Mason joined the militia in Hamilton and rejoined it when he moved to Calgary in 1903.[58] Although it was unusual for an MD, he was offered the lieutenant colonel and CO position with the 50th Battalion when it was formed in 1915 in Calgary. He was the only Canadian MD to command an overseas battalion in France. He was gassed in November 1916, and returned to England. Following his recovery, he was appointed the CO of the Canadian Medical Depot at Shorncliffe. The start of his appointment coincided with the battle of Vimy Ridge, in April 1917, where his battalion was

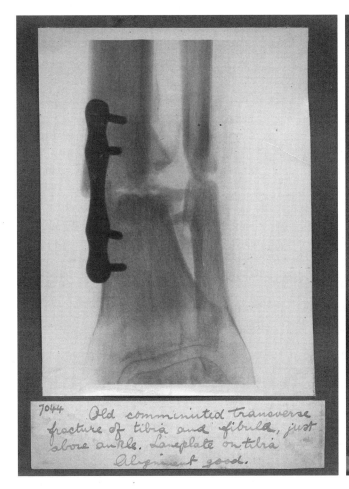

7044 Old comminuted transverse fracture of tibia and fibula, just above ankle. Laneplate on tibia Alignment good.

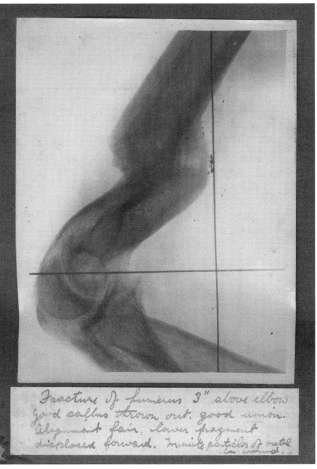

Fracture of humerus 3" above elbow good callus thrown out. good union. Alignment fair, lower fragment displaced forward. Minute particles of metal in wound.

(left) Field X-ray – "7044 – Old comminuted transverse fracture of tibia and fibula, just above ankle. Laneplate on tibia Alignment good." Taken by Private C. Rhoden, Canadian Army Medical Corps; (right) Field X-ray: "Fracture of humerus 3 above elbow good callus thrown out, good union. Alignment fair, lower fragment displaced forward. Minute particles of metal in wound." Taken by Private C. Rhoden, Canadian Army Medical Corps. Kerr Collection, Canadian Militaria Preservation Society Museum, Edmonton.

involved in the capture of the two highest points on the ridge. Through his efforts, the work of the supply depot was dramatically improved, as recommended by the Bruce Inquiry. He was joined overseas by his wife, who worked with the British Red Cross. On his return, he joined the staff of the Colonel Belcher Hospital in Calgary.

Dr. Reginald de Lotbiniere-Harwood, a member of an aristocratic Quebec family, graduated in medicine from McGill University and moved to Pincher

Creek, Alberta, where he practised medicine for several years. He then took postgraduate training in France before moving to Edmonton to set up a surgical practice. In 1914 he was asked to form the 51st Battalion in Edmonton. Before arriving in France, the battalion was dispersed to fill vacancies in the continuing Alberta battalions (the 31st, 49th, 50th). Bilingual and from a long-standing military family, Lieutenant Colonel Harwood was appointed the head of surgery and then the CO of the 1,800-bed No. 8 Canadian General Hospital at St. Cloud, near Paris.[59] The hospital treated 900 gas cases. For his services, he was made a Chevalier of the Legion of Honour of France and was awarded the Order of the White Elephant of Siam.

Dr. G. Macdonald was the CPSA registrar from 1911 to 1915. That year, he mobilized with the 12th Calgary Mounted Rifles, and went overseas as its

Amputation kit made by C.H. Petch & Sons Ltd. Manufacturers, Ottawa, Canada. Kerr Collection, Canadian Militaria Preservation Society Museum, Edmonton.

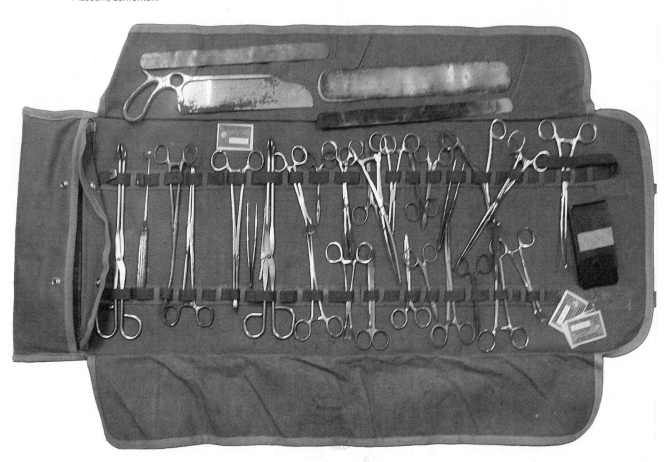

"Dental Corps going into action," 4th Canadian Field Ambulance, ca. 1915–18. This First World War sketch was drawn by Harry Howell. Written on the back of sketch: "Dr. Blair – Bob Hardwick" [Sergeant Hardwicke?]. Glenbow Archives, M-6811-2-9.

lieutenant colonel. The 12th was broken up and he became the CO of the Royal Canadian Dragoons and then the Fort Garry Horse. He was subsequently asked to organize the Bramshott Military Hospital in England before being recalled to Calgary as the colonel and CO of Military District No. 13 in Calgary (1917–1919).[60]

Dr. J.W. Richardson, after graduating with a fellowship from Edinburgh in 1915, served briefly as head of surgery at a British hospital.[61] Then he joined the Royal Army Medical Corps, and was assigned to ambulance trains as their physician. Quickly tiring of that duty, he returned to Canada and was demobilized. Back in Calgary, he rejoined the CAMC and worked as a surgeon at the Ogden hospital.

Dr. Walter Morrish graduated with first-class honours from the University of Alberta in 1915, and finished his medical training at the University of Toronto in 1918.[62] He enlisted and was assigned as a physician to accompany ships carrying troops to and from Europe. On one crossing, he acted as a peacemaker to quell a potential mutiny; soldiers on board felt that two-thirds of the ship was too much to be assigned only to the officers. Back in Edmonton, he became a successful physician and politician.

John W. Scott was in the third University of Alberta medical class.[63] He went overseas as a private in 1918 with his lifelong friend and the future CMA president Morley Young. Although they signed up with a tank battalion, they saw no action and never left England. After the war, they knew they would be slow returning to Canada because of the "last in, last out" rule, so they audited medical classes at the University of Edinburgh. Dr. Scott finished his medical training at McGill. He returned to Alberta working under Dr. J.B. Collip and then completed his fellowship in internal medicine. He became the first clinician to be the dean of medicine at the university, from 1948 to 1959.

The 25th Artillery battery was formed in Lethbridge in 1907, in Dr. George deVeber's office. Dr. J.S. Stewart, a doctor of dental surgery, offered to head it, although the appointment was subject to his passing a training course at the Royal Military College. Successful in doing this, he was promoted to lieutenant colonel and CO of the 7th Artillery Brigade at the start of the war. He headed overseas in August 1915, and was promoted to brigadier general in command of the Canadian 3rd Division Artillery. He was the highest-ranking officer of any Alberta dentist or physician during the war.[64] Although he did not practice dentistry during the war, dental care was a high priority for the Canadian military. Seventy percent of all soldiers were seen by a dentist, and 100 percent were checked before they were discharged. One-quarter of Canada's dentists enlisted, with an estimated 35 coming from Alberta.[65] In support of their colleagues, in 1917 Alberta's dentists raised funds to purchase a car for their colleagues at Sarcee.

Roberta MacAdams, probably Alberta's best-known "nursing sister," was born in Ontario and graduated in 1911 with a degree in domestic science from the Macdonald Institute (now the University of Guelph). She was invited to come to Edmonton by her brother William, who was the publisher of the *Edmonton Daily Capital* newspaper. In 1912 she began work for the government of Alberta travelling throughout the province teaching home economics. Her report prompted the government to provide funding for the establishment of the Alberta Women's Institutes to support rural women. In 1916 she enlisted in the Canadian Army Medical Corps with the rank of lieutenant and was assigned as a dietician to the Ontario Military Hospital in Orpington, England, where she oversaw production of more than 6,000 meals per day for patients and staff.[66] Using the winning slogan "Give your other Vote to the Sister," MacAdams was elected as one of two non-partisan Alberta military MLAs in 1917. During her term, she strongly supported establishment of a veterans department, programs for returning soldiers, greater access to healthcare, an improved school curriculum, and urban-based normal schools.

After the War

The war served as a catalyst for development of medical education in Alberta and, eventually, expansion of hospital facilities. Although overseas, University of Alberta President Tory requested that the medical program be extended to a full five years. There were several reasons for this. The shortage of physicians in Alberta during the war continued into 1919 because of their delayed return from overseas. The shortage became a crisis during the 1918 flu epidemic. There was also the perception that doctors with three years of training were leaving the province to complete their medical studies and were not returning. That made it easy for the government to approve Tory's request, in 1919. The government also approved the building of a medical school as part of a 1920–21 winter works project. It relieved the university space problem that was compounded by a high postwar veteran enrollment.

Then came a remarkable opportunity: J.D. Rockefeller allocated $5 million of his second Rockefeller Foundation donation to Canada.[67] To secure Alberta's $500,000 grant, the foundation required that the medical school be completed. No sooner was the conditional grant approved than Tory requested the interest on it. He also secured a travelling fellowship for Professor J.B. Collip, during which time Collip isolated insulin at the University of Toronto.

Fortuitously, President Tory had secured and transferred the provincial lab to the university in 1910. By the early 1920s it had four pathologists on staff. Dr. Rankin, the lab director, was appointed the first dean of medicine in 1920. Tory had more difficulty returning the Strathcona Hospital to the university. This did not occur until November 1922; it reopened as the University of Alberta Hospital. The members of the first medical class commenced their clinical training in 1923, the same year both RN and BSc RN programs were started. The faculty secured American Medical Association accreditation in 1922. The conditional Rockefeller grant was approved and released in 1923, before the hospital received the American College of Surgeon's approval in 1924.[68] The first MDs and dentists graduated in 1925 and 1927, respectively.

The hospitalized veterans in the MHC facilities in Alberta were placed under SCR control in 1918. In July 1920 the Strathcona Hospital was operating with two medical and four surgical full-time staff.[69] The federal government built an 84-bed annex next to it in 1922 for soldiers who were still hospitalized. It also funded the building of the second wing on the Royal Alexandra Hospital. The warehouse that was converted into the Colonel Belcher Hospital opened in 1919 and received the remaining Calgary veterans. The Keith Sanitorium west of Calgary opened with 185 TB beds in 1920.[70]

The 39,208 hospital beds overseas, staffed by British and Canadian medical personnel, were closed by September 1919.[71] Two years after the war, the MHC/SCR beds in Canada were down to 6,500 from their high of 12,283. Extrapolating the SCR figure, there probably were 650 veterans left in Alberta hospitals. In 1923 the mental or "shell-shocked" patients were moved to the new Oliver Mental Hospital that opened in Edmonton.[72]

Postwar control and treatment of VD was a problem because of the high rate of cases contracted overseas (about 66,000). Dr. Harold Orr was appointed to head the VD surveillance program in 1918. In the same year, Alberta became the first province to take advantage of the offer of federal funding to provide follow-up care, treatment, and case finding. Dr. Orr then went overseas to study Salvarsan treatment (for syphilis), fever therapy, and other forms of VD treatment before returning to manage the Alberta program.[73]

The province was desirous of more rapid health-care changes after the war. The United Farmers of Alberta government replaced the Liberals in 1921. Its strongest healthcare petitioner was Irene Parlby, who publicly announced that "health care was a right" (1919). She had already raised the need for upgrading physician competence at the 1918 AMA meeting.[74] As minister without portfolio, she worked closely with the minister of health, George Hoadley (appointed in 1923), to introduce summer travelling clinics in northern and rural communities. With the municipal hospital system becoming so successful, Hoadley capped the number of beds at 6/1,000, a ceiling that would last for decades. He introduced the first specialist recognition system in 1926, three years before the Royal College of Physicians and Surgeons of Canada was chartered. Public health initiatives included building the first polio hospital (1927), passing the second free TB care act in Canada, introducing the first Polio Rehabilitation Act, and passing the first free cancer care and maternity care acts in Canada.

Notes

1 G.W.L. Nicholson, *70 Years of Service* (Ottawa: Borealis Press, 1977), 68–113.

2 A.E. Snell, *The CAMC and the Canadian Corps during the last One Hundred Days of the Great* War (Ottawa: King's Printer, 1924), 1–11.

3 Andrew MacPhail, *The History of the Canadian Forces 1918–19, The Medical Services* (Ottawa: King's Printer, 1925), 6, 250.

4 Nicholson, *70 Years of Service*, 71–72.

5 Canadian Fields Comforts Commission, *With the First Canadian Contingent* (London, UK: Hodder and Stoughton, 1917), 19.

6 Nicholson, *70 Years of Service*, assorted pages; see also MacPhail, *Medical Services*.

7 Tim Cook, *No Place to Run* (Vancouver: UBC Press, 1999), 17–33. G.B. Peat described "The Effects of Gassing as seen at a Casualty Creating Station," *Canadian Medical Association Journal* [*CMAJ*] 8, no. 1 (January 1918): 17–24; Dr. W. Boyd gives a frontline perspective in "With a Field Ambulance at Ypres" (Toronto: The Musson Book Company Limited, 1916), 60–68; and Dr. J.J. Ower in "Pictures on Memory's Wall," *Calgary Historical Society Bulletin* 19, no. 2 (1954): 42, 53.

8 J.C. Meakins, "The After-Effects of Chlorine Gas Poisoning," *CMAJ* 9, no. 11 (1919): 968–74. Meakins and Priestley followed up 700 consecutive gas poisoning cases from the 1st Canadian Division, gassed in late April/early May 1915 and found that 478 were evacuated to hospitals in France. Of these, 332 were sent to Britain, 204 were invalided to Canada. Four years later, 134 still had appreciable ailments and 5 had died.

9 James A. Lougheed, *Report on the Work of the Military Hospitals Commission* (Ottawa: King's Printer, 1917).

10 Tom Brown, "Shell Shock in the Canadian Expeditionary Force 1914–1928," in *Health, Disease and Medicine: Essays in Canadian History* (Toronto: McClelland and Stewart, 1988).

11 MacPhail, *Medical Services*, 156–69. He also wrote editorials on the Bruce and Mason Commissions in the *CMAJ* 7, no. 2 (February 1917): 137–42, 252–54.

12 Ibid., 5–6, 247–50, 329–33, 365.

13 Janice Tyrwhitt, "49,000 Albertans flocked to a war whose horror none could imagine," in *Alberta in the 20th Century*, vol. 4, *The Great War and Its Consequences, 1914–1920* (Edmonton: United Western Communications, 1994), 4–5. See also John Blue, *Alberta Past and Present: Historical and Biographical* (Chicago: Pioneer Historical Publishing, 1924), 400.

14 Macphail, *Medical Services*, 400.

15 Snell, *The CAMC and the Canadian Corps*, 4–6.

16 P.H. Bryce, "Why Federal Legislation Is Necessary in Order That Venereal Diseases May Be Effectively Dealt with in Canada," *CMAJ* 8, no. 11 (November 1917): 1005–1009. It was a follow up to the editorial on "The Venereal Disease Problem," *CMAJ* 7, no. 8 (August 1917): 740.

17 Snell, *The CAMC and the Canadian Corps*, 1–10.

18 Bill Rawling, *Death Their Enemy: Canadian Medical Practitioners and the War* (Ottawa: self-published, 2001), 73–74.

19 MacPhail, *Medical Services*, 246–54.

20 Lorne Drum, "The Medical Profession of Alberta and the Defense of the Country," *CMAJ* 4, no. 10 (October 1914): 881–85. The article was followed by "Lieutenant Colonel S.W. Hewetson's National Defense and the (Alberta) Medical Profession," *CMAJ* 4, no. 10 (October 1914): 886–89.

21 William Whitelaw, "Presidential Address," *CMAJ* 6, no. 11 (November 1916): 961–68. Whitelaw's figures are similar to the enlistment figures of the Manitoba Medical College (36 percent) as recorded in Ian Carr and Robert Beamish's *Manitoba Medicine—Interruption in Hell* (Winnipeg: University of Manitoba Press, 1999), 75. Eight Manitoba doctors and two MMC medical students died, 29 were wounded, and eight were gassed.

22 The estimate of 216 comes from a count of all the CAMC medical officers who enlisted in District 13 (Alberta) to January 1918, as reported in the Canadian Army Medical Corps Militia lists, January–July 1918, 482–572. Forty-eight percent of the enlistees went overseas. The estimated number of physicians in Alberta (400) is based on Whitelaw's figures and the number of College of Physicians and Surgeons of Alberta registered and practicing physicians of 925 (October 1928), less the number of NWT physicians in Saskatchewan included in that figure (an estimated 285), less the number of physicians who had moved, returned or died to 1918 (an estimated 200), and the ratio of physicians to the population of 500,000, which was slightly less than one per 1,000.

23 Deadman, "Canada's Supply of Army Doctors," CMAJ 46, no. 1 (January 1942): 60–62.

24 Robert Lampard, Deans, Dreams and a President: The Deans of Medicine at the University of Alberta 1913 to 2009 (Red Deer, AB: self-published, 2011), 23–31.

25 Canadian Army, 11th Canadian Field Ambulance: Diary of the Eleventh: Being a Record of the XIth Canadian Field Ambulance (Western Universities), February 1916–May 1919 (Winnipeg?: [1919?]), 4.

26 Elise A. Corbet, Frontiers of Medicine (Edmonton: University of Alberta Press, 1990), 14–17. It is also highlighted in Walter Johns, A History of the University of Alberta 1980–1969 (Edmonton: University of Alberta Press, 1981).

27 Corbet, Frontiers of Medicine.

28 Johns, History of the University of Alberta, and also E.A. Corbet, Henry Marshall Tory (Toronto: Ryerson Press, 1954), 138–56.

29 The Canadian Army Medical Military List to January 1918 lists 147 nurses from District 13 as having enlisted.

30 Marjorie Norris, Sister Heroines: The Roseate Glow of Wartime Nursing 1914–1918 (Calgary: Bunker to Bunker Publishing, 2002). See also G.W.L. Nicholson, Canada's Nursing Sisters, Canadian Museum of Civilization (now Canadian Museum of History) historical publication no. 13 (Toronto: Samuel Stevens Hakkert and Company, 1975).

31 Hobart Reed, "End Results of the Various Disabilities of the Returned Soldier," CMAJ 7, no. 30 (March 1917): 208–12; and the Military Hospitals Commission's 1917 Report, May 1917, 29.

32 Lougheed, The Military Hospitals Commission, 29, 31; and MacPhail, Medical Services, 331.

33 Robert Lampard, Alberta's Medical History, Young and Lusty and Full of Life (Red Deer, AB: self-published, 2008), 291–93.

34 J.J. Heagerty, 400 Years of Medical History in Canada (Toronto: Macmillan, 1928), vol. 1, 313.

35 David Tuckwell, "Helping to Solve a Prairie Problem," CMAJ 7, no. 9 (September 1917): 800–3. Tuckwell was the former mayor of Lloydminster and the organizer of municipal hospitals in Saskatchewan.

36 Alice MacKinnon, Margaret Fulkerth, and T. Bryan Campbell-Hope, Hospitals of Alberta—Their Stories 1890–2000 (Edmonton: Edmonton Colour Press, 2006). The Municipal Hospital District including Mannville was approved 14 June 1918 and the 10-bed hospital was opened 7 October 1919.

37 Tyrwhitt, "49,000 Albertans flocked to a war," 336.

38 A.G. MacKay, Edmonton Bulletin, 26 October 1918.

39 Lampard, Alberta's Medical History, 8–10, 350.

40 These include two books by Marjorie Norris, Sister Heroines (2002) and Medicine and Duty: The World War I Memoir of Captain Harold W. McGill, Medical Officer, 31st Battalion C.E.F. (Calgary: University of Calgary Press, 2007); a reprint of Major Horace Singer, The History of the 31st Battalion, edited by Edward Darrell Knight (Calgary: Detselig Enterprises, 2006); and Reginald Roy, ed., The Journal of Private Fraser, 1914–1919: Canadian Expeditionary Force (Nepean, ON: CEF Books, 1998).

41 Macphail, Medical Services.

42 Norris, Medicine and Duty, 16.

43 John Hillsman, Eleven Men and a Scalpel (Winnipeg: Columbia Press, 1948).

44 Norris, Medicine and Duty, 21, 231.

45 G.H. Stevens, *A City Goes to War: History of the Loyal Edmonton Regiment (3 PPCLI)* (Brampton, ON: Charters Publishing Company, 1964).

46 Victor Wheeler, *The 50th Battalion in No Man's Land* (Edmonton: Alberta Historical Resources Foundation, 1980), 66.

47 William Johnston, personal communication with the author, 5 September 2013.

48 Edward Heller produced a handwritten manuscript, which was deposited on November 1976 in the Grande Prairie Archives.

49 J.N. Gunn and E.E. Dutton, *Historical Records of No. 8 Canadian Field Ambulance: Canada, England, France, Belgium, 1915–1918* (Toronto: Ryerson Press, 1920). Gunn presented a lecture on "A Field Ambulance in France" to the Alberta Military Institute on April 7, which was published in the *Alberta Military Journal*, 1922, 82–85. He also addressed the Edmonton Rotary Club on "War Weapons" as reported by the *Edmonton Bulletin* of 27 September 1918.

50 *Diary of the 11th Field Ambulance*, 113.

51 Frederick Miller, *A Pioneer Doctor: Elk Point's F.G. Miller* (Elk Point, AB: Elk Point Historical Society, 2003).

52 A.L. Hepburn, "A Biographical Sketch of a Pioneer Neuro Surgeon: Life and Times of Howard Havelock Hepburn, 4 Nov 1885 to 31 Jan 1972," 24 August 1997.

53 Lampard, *Alberta's Medical History*, 100–13.

54 Lampard, *Deans, Dreams and a President*, 17–43.

55 Ibid., 44–66.

56 John Ower, "The Complement Fixation Test in Gonorrhea," *CMAJ* 4, no. 12 (December 1914): 1074–80.

57 MacPhail, *Medical Services*, 275. See also Lampard, *Deans, Dreams and a President*, 29–30.

58 Lampard, *Alberta's Medical History*, 215–22.

59 "Third of City's Medical Men on Military Duty: Edmonton Has 112 Doctors," *Edmonton Journal*, 31 May 1916. The article lists 39 doctors who had enlisted and adds a note on Dr. Harwood, a surgeon, whose sister had married Sam Steele, and whose Quebec ancestors had fought on the Plains of Abraham.

60 Blue, *Alberta Past and Present*, vol. 3, 412–14.

61 James Richardson, "The Prairie Doctor," 1973, unpublished manuscript in the possession of his son, Dr. Tom Richardson.

62 Walter Morrish, "Memoirs," unpublished manuscript, University of Alberta Archives #81-109, 81-109.

63 Lampard, *Deans, Dreams and a President*, 67–87.

64 D.W. Gullett, *A History of Dentistry in Canada* (Toronto: University of Toronto Press, 1971), 157–58. See also Christopher Kilford, *Lethbridge at War: The Military History of Lethbridge from 1900 to 1996* (Lethbridge, AB: Battery Books, 1996), 20–25, 27–30, 58–62.

65 Hector MacLean, *History of Dentistry in Alberta 1880–1980* (Edmonton: Alberta Dental Association, 1987), 98. The Canadian Military List for January 1918 gives 27 dentists as having enlisted in Alberta.

66 Debbie Marshall, *Give Your Other Vote to the Sister: A Woman's Journey into the Great War* (Calgary: University of Calgary Press, 2007).

67 Marianne Fedunkiw, "The University of Alberta and The Rockefeller Foundation 1920–1923," in Lampard, *Alberta's Medical History*, 545–57.

68 Lampard, *Deans, Dreams and a President*, 9–10.

69 Macdougall Acheson, *Edmonton Bulletin*, 27 July 1920. The hospital had 144 beds available with a large outpatient service.

70 Lampard, *Alberta's Medical History*, 293.

71 Desmond Morton, *A Military History of Canada* (Edmonton: Hurtig Publishers, 1985), 167.

72 Lampard, *Alberta's Medical History*, 346–47.

73 Donald R. Wilson and Paul Rentiers, "Evolution of the Venereal Disease Program in the Province of Alberta," in *Medicine in Alberta: Historical Reflections*, 92–96. 4. Salvarsan was an arsenic-based drug (discovered by Paul Erhlich in Germany) used to treat syphilis. It was unstable in air and produced significant nausea and vomiting, making the treatment worse than the disease. It was not replaced until penicillin was discovered.

74 *Edmonton Bulletin*, 26 September 1918.

Works Cited

PRIMARY SOURCES

Edmonton Journal

Grande Prairie Archives, AB. Heller, Edward. Handwritten manuscript.

Richardson, James. "The Prairie Doctor." Unpublished manuscript, 1973. Family.

University of Alberta Archives, Edmonton. Morrish, Walter. "Memoirs."

SECONDARY SOURCES

Blue, John. *Alberta Past and Present*. 3 vols. Chicago: Pioneer Historical Publishing, 1924.

Boyd, William. "With a Field Ambulance at Ypres." Toronto: The Musson Book Company Limited, 1916.

Bright, David. "1919: A Year of Extraordinary Difficulty." In *Alberta Formed, Alberta Transformed*, edited by Michael Payne, Donald Wetherell, and Catherine Cavanaugh. Vol. 2. Calgary: University of Calgary Press, 2006.

Brown, Tom. "Shell Shock in the Canadian Expeditionary Force 1914–1918." In *Health, Disease and Medicine: Essays in Canadian History*. Toronto: McClelland and Stewart, 1988.

Bryce, P.H. "Why Federal Legislation Is Necessary in Order That Venereal Diseases May Be Effectively Dealt with in Canada." *Canadian Medical Association Journal* [*CMAJ*] 8, no. 11 (November 1917): 1005–90.

Canadian Field Comforts Commission. *With the First Canadian Contingent*. London, UK: Hodder and Stoughton, May 1917.

Carney, Bill. "The Hospital's Story: The History of the Alberta Hospital Association." Unpublished AHA manuscript, April 1987.

Carr, Ian, and Robert Beamish. *Manitoba Medicine*. Winnipeg: University of Manitoba Press, 1999.

Cook, Tim. *No Place to Run: The Canadian Corps and Gas Warfare in the First World War*. Vancouver: UBC Press, 1999.

Corbet, Elise A. *Frontiers of Medicine: A History of Medical Education and Research at the University of Alberta*. Edmonton: University of Alberta Press, 1990.

Corbett, E.A. *Henry Marshall Tory*. Toronto: Ryerson Press, 1954.

Deadman, William. "Canada's Supply of Army Doctors." *CMAJ* 46, no. 1 (January 1942): 60–62.

Drum, Lorne. "The Medical Profession of Alberta and the Defense of the Country." *CMAJ* 4, no. 10 (October 1914): 881–85.

Gullett, D.W. *A History of Dentistry in Canada*. Toronto: University of Toronto Press, 1971.

Gunn, J.N., and E.E. Dutton. *Historical Records of No. 8 Canadian Field Ambulance: Canada, England, France, Belgium, 1915–1918*. Toronto: Ryerson Press, 1920.

Heagerty, J.J. *400 Years of Medical History in Canada*. Toronto: Macmillan, 1928.

Hepburn. A.L. "A Biographical Sketch of a Pioneer Neuro Surgeon: Life and Times of Howard Havelock Hepburn, 4 Nov 1885 to Jan 1972." 1997.

Hewetson, Lt. Col. S.W. "National Defense and the (Alberta) Medical Profession." *CMAJ* 4, no. 10 (October 1914): 886–89.

Hillsman, John. *Eleven Men and a Scalpel*. Winnipeg: Columbia Press, 1948.

Johns, Walter. *A History of the University of Alberta, 1908–1969*. Edmonton: University of Alberta Press, 1981.

Kilford, Major Christopher R. *Lethbridge at War: The Military History of Lethbridge from 1900 to 1996*. Lethbridge, AB: Battery Books, 1996.

Lampard, Robert. *Alberta's Medical History, Young and Lusty and Full of Life*. Red Deer, AB: self-published, 2008.

———. *Deans, Dreams and a President: The Deans of Medicine at the University of Alberta 1913 to 2009*. Red Deer, AB: self-published, 2011.

———. "The Hoadley Commission (1932–34) and Health Insurance in Alberta." In *Making Medicare*, edited by Greg Marchildon. Toronto: University of Toronto Press, 2013.

Lougheed, James A. *Report of the Work of the Military Hospitals Commission, May 1917*. Ottawa: King's Printer, 1917.

MacKinnon, Alice, Margaret Fulkerth, and T. Bryan Campbell-Hope. *Hospitals of Alberta—Their Stories 1890–2000*. Edmonton: Edmonton Colour Press, 2006.

MacLean, Hector. *History of Dentistry in Alberta 1880–1980*. Edmonton: Alberta Dental Association, 1987.

MacPhail, John Andrew. *Official History of the Canadian Forces in the Great War 1914–1918—The Medical Services*. Ottawa: King's Printer, 1925.

Marshall, Debbie. *Give Your Other Vote to the Sister: A Woman's Journey into the Great War*. Calgary: University of Calgary Press, 2007.

McGinnis, Janice P. "A City Faces an Epidemic." *Alberta History* 24 (Autumn 1976): 1–2.

——. "Impact of Epidemic Influenza: Canada 1918–1919." In *Medicine in Canadian Society: Historical Perspectives*, edited by S.E. Shortt. Montreal and Kingston: McGill-Queen's University Press, 1981.

Meakins, J.C., and J.G. Priestley. "The After-Effects of Chlorine Gas Poisoning." *CMAJ* 11 (1919): 968–74.

Miller, Frederick. *A Pioneer Doctor: Elk Point's F.G. Miller*. Elk Point, AB: Elk Point Historical Society, 2003.

Morton, Desmond. *A Military History of Canada*. Edmonton: Hurtig Publishers, 1985.

Nicholson, G.W.L. *Canada's Nursing Sisters*. Canadian Museum of Civilization (now Canadian Museum of History) historical publication no. 13. Toronto: Samuel Stevens Hakkert and Company, 1975.

——. *Seventy Years of Service: A History of the Royal Canadian Army Medical Corps*. Ottawa: Borealis Press, 1977.

Norris, Marjorie, ed. *Medicine and Duty: The World War I Memoir of Captain Harold W. McGill, Medical Officer, 31st Battalion C.E.F.* Calgary: University of Calgary Press, 2007.

——. *Sister Heroines: The Roseate Glow of Wartime Nursing 1914–1918*. Calgary: Bunker to Bunker Publishing, 2002.

Ower, John. "The Complement Fixation Test in Gonorrhea." *CMAJ* 4, no. 12 (December 1914): 1074–80.

Pettigrew, Eileen. *The Silent Enemy: Canada and the Deadly Flu of 1918*. Saskatoon: Western Producer Prairie Books, 1983.

Rawling, Bill. *Death Their Enemy: Canadian Medical Practitioners and the War*. Ottawa: self-published, 2001.

Reed, Hobart. "End Results of the Various Disabilities of the Returned Soldier." *CMAJ* 7, no. 3 (March 1917): 208–12.

Roe, J.M., et al. *Diary of the 11th Field Ambulance, February 1916–May 14, 1919*. N.p., n.d. [1919].

Roy, Reginald, ed. *The Journal of Private Fraser, 1914–1919: Canadian Expeditionary Force*. Nepean, ON: CEF Books, 1998.

Singer, Marjorie Horace. *The History of the 31st Battalion*. Reprint, edited by Edward Darrell Knight. Calgary: Detselig Enterprises, 2006.

Snell, A.E. *The CAMC and the Canadian Corps during the Last One Hundred Days of the Great War*. Ottawa: King's Printer, 1924.

Stevens, G.H. *A City Goes to War: History of the Loyal Edmonton Regiment (3 PPCLI)*. Brampton, ON: Charters Publishing Company, 1964.

Tuckwell, David. "Helping to Solve a Prairie Problem." *CMAJ* 7, no. 9 (September 1917): 800–3.

Tyrwhitt, Janice. "49,000 Albertans flocked to a war whose horror none could imagine." In *Alberta in the 20th Century*. Vol. 4, *The Great War and Its Consequences, 1914–1920*, edited by Ted Byfield, 4–23. Edmonton: Western Canadian Communications, 1994.

Wheeler, Victor W. *The 50th Battalion in No Man's Land*. Edmonton: Alberta Historical Resources Foundation, 1980.

Whitelaw, William. "Presidential Address." *CMAJ* 6, no. 11 (November 1916): 857–961.

Wilson, Don, and Paul Rentiers. "Evolution of the Venereal Disease Program in the Province of Alberta." In *Medicine in Alberta: Historical Reflections, 75th Anniversary*, edited by Carl Betke. Edmonton: Alberta Medical Foundation, 1993.

Harold and Emma McGill: A War-Front Love Story

ANTONELLA FANELLA

In today's world of digital media, handwritten letters have become an antiquated and, in some instances, obsolete form of communication. Yet 100 years ago during the First World War, letters from servicemen to loved ones at home provided first-hand accounts of one of the most brutal and deadly wars.

Harold McGill was a medical officer (MO) with the 31st Battalion. Emma Griffis was a nurse. They had been acquaintances in Calgary. On 12 May 1915 Harold departed for the war. On May 30, Emma wrote him a friendly letter, and so began a most re-markable correspondence. Harold's letters chronicle not only his and Emma's wartime medical experi-ences but also the beautiful love story that developed between them. In the beginning Harold addressed his letters to "Dear Miss Griffis"; as their love affair blossomed, it was "Dearest Emma" and finally "Dear Sweetheart."

The letters describe life in the trenches, his medical duties at the front, his views on the war, and their plans for the future. Harold's descriptions of the horrors of war were very frank and were not censored for Emma's feminine eyes. Perhaps be-cause she was a nurse, he knew that descriptions of

blood and death would not shock her. Fortunately for historians, Emma kept Harold's letters (he destroyed hers). The letters, along with Harold's diaries, were later donated to Calgary's Glenbow Museum.

Harold Wigmore McGill was born on 21 Decem-ber 1879 in Norwood, Ontario. The son of an Irish immigrant, Harold grew up in Manitoba. Harold's father, Edward, had gone to Manitoba to take up farming at Minnedosa. He was later joined by his wife, Henrietta, and their children. Edward became an active citizen in the young community of Harri-son, first as a councillor, then as reeve, and later as a secretary-treasurer of the school board. Edward's dedication to public service no doubt inspired Harold to also be active in community affairs and politics after he returned from the war.

In 1900 both of Harold's parents died of ty-phoid fever. In 1905 Harold graduated with a degree in medicine from the University of Manitoba. He worked at the Winnipeg General Hospital as the house surgeon until 1907. Harold came out West and opened an office in Exshaw, Alberta. He stayed there for a year before leaving to do graduate work at the Universities of Chicago and Philadelphia. In 1910 he

Major H.W. McGill, Calgary, Alberta, 1914. Glenbow Archives, NA-4938-15.

Emma Griffis, nurse outside the old General Hospital, Calgary ca. 1910. Glenbow Archives, NA-4938-10.

returned to Canada and settled in Calgary. From 1912 he served as the physician in charge of the Sarcee (Tsuu T'ina) First Nation reserve, located southwest of Calgary. Harold joined the 31st Alberta Battalion on the day of its official formation—14 November 1914. He was almost 35 years old. Most of the men who enlisted in the 31st were, like Harold, gainfully employed and of British birth or descent.

Emma Mildred Griffis was born in Kansas in 1884 and raised in Ontario. She graduated from the Calgary General Hospital School of Nursing in 1910, and was placed in charge of the typhoid ward. During the First World War, she served at the Bramshott Military Hospital in Sussex, England. In his first letter to Emma, Harold, ever the gentleman, kept the tone formal, yet it was obvious he was smitten with her. Unfortunately for Harold, Emma did not reciprocate his feelings. On the surface, they were an unlikely couple. As his letters reveal, Harold was a shy, quiet man who preferred books to people. Emma was a social butterfly. Yet Harold remained undeterred. He continued to pursue her through his letters and eventually won her over.

Shorncliffe, England, June 16, 1915.

Dear Miss Griffis:

Your very nice letter of May 30 reached me yesterday and to say I was delighted would be putting it too mildly. Yours was the first and only letter from Calgary, or indeed from Canada, that I have had since we landed over two weeks ago. I hope your health has come quite up to the normal by this time.

We had a very nice trip all the way across. We did not have any leave at Quebec but embarked aboard the S. S. Carpathia at once May 17 sailing about 3 P.M. There was scarcely any rough weather on the ocean trip and I never missed a meal. The land lubbers fared better than the old travellers very few of the former being seasick. I never felt even a twinge, but then I was too busy most of the time to indulge in any such frivolities. We never got a glimpse of a submarine although we kept a sharp lookout. There were over 2200 troops aboard and the last part of the journey was run with lights all shut off at night, or at least with portholes all blanketed. For the last two days we had two machine guns mounted on deck and 100 men on guard with loaded rifles. We came in sight of Plymouth Harbour on the afternoon of May

28 and docked at Devonport – a few miles up the river that evening. The scene coming into Plymouth was most beautiful and I am very glad we arrived during daylight. We had not got any leave from the boat to see Plymouth as I should like to have done for it is a most interesting city. The people gave us a royal welcome and the boys on the training ship cheered themselves hoarse. The Jackies certainly know how to cheer.

We spent the night on the ship and entrained next morning for Shorncliffe. On the way down we passed through some of the most interesting parts of England including London.

Our camp is on a hill overlooking the sea about four miles from Folkestone. The ships are passing up and down all day and on clear days we can make out the French coast quite distinctly. With Field glasses we can see the towns and villages. We are about 50 minutes by flying machine from the scene of the fighting. We see their machines nearly every day and this evening a big airship (British) flew right over the camp. It was only a few hundred feet up and we got a fine view of it. The men in the car were dressed in naval uniform. Torpedo boat destroyers are patrolling up and down the coast all day.

Dr. Gunn is at present at Canadian Shorncliffe Hospital about two miles away from here. Dr. McGuffin is here in the Fourth Field Ambulance attached to our brigade. Dr. Charlie Stewart is in charge of the hospital at Beachborough a few miles away. I went out to see him on Sunday. The hospital is an old country seat and is very beautiful – I had the pleasure of meeting the donors, Sir Arthur and Lady Markham who gave up their home for hospital purposes. Tommy Costello came down from London to see us on Sunday. I heard his voice in the next tent to mine and could hardly believe my ears. Upon investigation I found it was Tommy sure enough. He keeps asking everybody if there is so much danger connected with their M.O.s work. I was able to assure him that most of the medical officers with the first division were either killed wounded or driven insane. Dr. Morris called at the camp yesterday but I did not have much time to talk to him as I had to go down to Folkestone.

A few of us drove down to Dover the other evening. It was a most interesting trip. The harbor was full of warships. I shall try to go to Canterbury next Saturday and see the Cathedral. It is only a few miles away. I have not been up to London yet.

Was very interested to know that the family responsibilities of Drs. Follett and Johnson had increased. Is Geo. Johnson out at the Reserve?

Give my kind regards to Miss Murphy and all others and do write again soon.

Yours very sincerely,

Harold W. McGill Capt. C.A.M.C.

Like many young men of this generation, Harold believed strongly enough in the war effort to risk his life. His sense of honour and duty was so profound that it led him to behave in an almost reckless manner. Harold regularly toured the trenches, and "while a practical thing to do, given his responsibilities, it was nonetheless fraught with risks and required courage."[1] The risk of death was very real. Over a period of four years, the 31st Battalion suffered heavy causalities: of the 941 who died, 708 were killed in action.[2] Harold's thoughts of Emma provided much comfort while war raged on all around him. In his first letters of 1916, Harold, despite the ongoing horrors of war, continued to charm his beloved Emma:

Jan 1, 1916.

Dear Miss Griffis;

What do you think of this stationary! Isn't it pretty fine to come from the firing line? I feel quite civilized writing on this paper instead of using a leaf out of my field message book. Please accept my warmest thanks for the very kind manner in which you remembered me at Christmas . . . Try to write more frequently if you can find the time; I am always so pleased to hear from you.

Sincerely yours,

Harold W McGill

Feb 5 / 1916

Dear Miss Griffis;

Your very interesting letter of Jan 2 came to hand some days ago when we were out in divisional reserve. In your letter you asked a number of questions which I shall try to answer before my superfine paper runs out. Usually my stationary is a field message book but for very special correspondence with particular people I use envelopes & paper that came in a Christmas box. However—to get on with my answers. I may be court-martialed for giving you this information but shall risk being sent home. We do six day shifts in the trenches. During that time we sleep in our clothes and in the fire trenches the men are not allowed to take off their boots except to change socks. At the end of the six days we move out to billets just behind the firing line and are then what is known as brigade reserve. At the end of six days we again relieve in the trenches and after another tour of duty

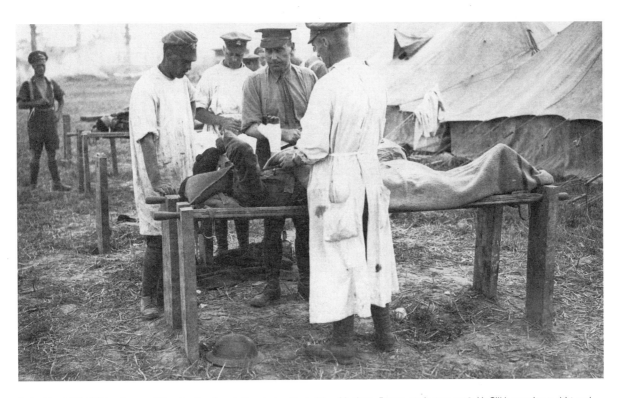

Major Harold McGill treating a soldier at a dressing station during the battle of Amiens, France, 10 August 1918. McGill is wearing a shirt and tie. Glenbow Archives, NA-4938-17.

go back to divisional reserve. The divisional reserve billets are pretty well out of the shelled area and everybody feels pretty safe there. Besides the men have practically no fatigues to do and get rested up a bit. After 6 days in divisional reserve the whole program begins again . . .

You ask about our rations and I must say they are very good. I do not think that ever before an army has been fed like this one. Now and then of course there will be a shortage in certain articles but on the whole very little complaint is heard. When the battalion is in the trenches my two orderlies and I have our rations come together and one of the orderlies does

the cooking. About the only extra I buy is oatmeal to make porridge in the mornings. In the way of luxuries we get a daily ration of rum apiece when in the trenches. In addition to my duties as M.O. I help to issue the rum. Each company issues its own rum, but some of the extra detachments such as bombers, snipers, signallers, M. Gun men, and wiremen get their issue at the dressing room dugout. My corporal measures it out in a teapot. The wiremen I mention are the chaps that go out between our own and the German trenches at night repairing old and erecting new barbed wire defences. They sometimes work within a few yards of the German parapet and are certainly entitled to get a drink of rum when they come in.

I saw for the first time a real live Hun a few days ago. He was a prisoner who had just been brought in wounded. The other two battalions of our brigade who occupied the trenches at the time made a raid into Fritz's lines and captured four prisoners besides doing a lot of damage. Unfortunately one of the prisoners was killed by the German fire when the party was coming back. The German I saw was in a Field Ambulance and had received a bayonet thrust to make him come along with his captors. He was a big fine looking chap and very capable looking. He had the rank of sergeant and wore the iron cross with two bars. He was a Prussian and had been here only a few days, having come from the Russian front . . .

From Calgary papers that have just come to hand you must have been led to believe that we had been roughing it up with Fritz in capital shape. The whole story was a pure hoax and somebody should be put in jail for that sort of thing. Just let me thank you for your many kind offers of assistance and also for the papers and magazines which are much appreciated. Goodbye.

Sincerely yours,

Harold W McGill

P.S. That bovril was fine.
H.W.McG.

April 15 / 1916.

Dear Miss Griffis:

Your letter of March 23 came to hand two days ago. A couple of big bundles of papers also arrived but I do not know by whom they were sent. Do not think the papers you send are not appreciated even if I am discourteous enough to fail thanking you.

We are now out in divisional reserve but expect to go back into the trenches in a few days. The men are getting well rested up and they needed it for our last trip in was a very trying ordeal as you would probably read in the papers. It was in fact our first real action and the battalion behaved splendidly. Anything we had hitherto experienced in the way of war was a pink tea compared with what we were up against those few days. The Germans made several attacks after frightful artillery bombardments in each case. One bombardment began about 3 in the morning and lasted for 18 hours without a break. Hundreds of shells per minute must have exploded in our lines during that time. Our artillery sent back just as good as we got and perhaps a little more. A number of Germans came over and surrendered to get out of the shell fire. A lot of the German infantry coming over to attack seemed half dazed, probably by the terrible shell fire, and were shot down like sheep in front of our trenches, or at least what had been our trenches. In many places both our own and the enemy trenches were wiped completely out of existence. Most of us got scarcely any sleep for four days and nights. We were in five days but the last one was comparatively quiet. You will be pleased to know that our battalion did not lose an inch of ground. In one case four bombers broke up an enemy infantry attack after shooting the German officer. I used to wonder why men went insane under shell fire but understand it perfectly now. However, we had very few cases of nervous breakdown.

Now I must stop giving you war news or the censor will take a notion to hold up the letter. Besides you will probably be able to read that sort of thing *told in a better way in the papers. When one is in action he sees only the very small part that comes under his individual notice and is liable to give a wrong impression . . .*

Yours sincerely,

Harold W. McGill

In early 1917, Emma travelled to England to serve as a nurse at the Bramshott Military Hospital. She and Harold continued their correspondence and occasionally met in person when Harold had a chance to return to England from the trenches. The relationship continued to blossom, and a mere five days after meeting her in England during his July 1917 leave, they secretly became engaged. Yet, as the next letter reveals, despite having corresponded for two years, they knew very little about each other's families. While the decision to marry so quickly may seem rash by today's standards, this was the generation that lived for today. They did not worry about tomorrow because tomorrow might not come. Having seen so many of their friends and fellow soldiers killed in battle, they truly understood that life was precious and could end without warning. The fact that they were both in their thirties probably added to the sense of urgency to get on with their lives.

France,
July 22, 1917.

My dearest Emma;

I have your letter of July 16 containing your gentle reproach for me because of my tardiness in writing. I wrote you a few minutes after reaching my dugout on the night of July 12. I was kept fairly well hustled up until that time. I am afraid though that it was some

time before you received the letter if indeed it reached you at all.

You ask me why I did not give you a hint of what I was thinking—when I thought. I do not exactly get your meaning but I have thought of you every day since I first came to the war, and surely my dear girl you know I cared for you before I told you so. No, I am grieved to say my dear mother is not alive, and I think it was perfectly lovely of you to ask me about her. I have a brother older than myself and two sisters younger. Our father and mother both died within 10 days of each other many years ago. Margaret was 15 years of age at the time. Ever since the four of us have always maintained a strong family relationship although we have been much scattered most of the time. We are indeed I am afraid inclined to be "clannish". My brother who has been married for years hardly ever lets a week go by without writing to me, and his wife has been a third sister. They have 3 children.

We don't know much about each other's family relationships do we? But I know that you are a good lovely girl with a keen sense of humour. Did you ever think what a terrible thing it would be for two people, neither with the sense of humour, to live together? Small jolts would be detonated into mine explosions. As for myself—a few unimportant particulars. I was born in Peterborough County, Ont. on the twenty first day of December 1879 A.D. So you see I am no longer in the first flush of youth. During the past few years indeed I have been alarmed and discouraged at the speed with which the old gentleman with the scythe has been tearing down the road. So far as I know, apart from the hazards of my present occupation, I am a first class risk for a life insurance company, I have never served a term in prison, and my religious belief is very unorthodox. And lastly as I think I warned you I do not belong to the class of predatory rich . . .

Yours lovingly,

Harold W McGill

France, Aug 5, 1917.

Dearest Emma;

I think I made a promise to write you a nice letter when we came out of the line but am afraid I am hardly in form to day. I have your letter of July 28 and am very pleased to know that you are away from the Tb. patients. I had been worried ever since you first told me you were detailed for that duty . . .

The horrible rain seems to have relented a little and it is fine to day. I walked out to the village where we are billeted early this morning with Lt. Irwin of Calgary. It was a fine moonlight night but rather warm for walking in full kit. A team of six mules on a G.S. [General Service] wagon caught up to us and we were not too proud to ride behind the lowly but useful mules. We reached our billets about 1:30 A.M. and had a cup of tea and something to eat before going to bed. I drew a very nice billet with the most comfortable bed I have seen in France. My batman had a bath ready for me and it was certainly a luxury to have a wash and get into clean sheets. I hadn't had my clothes off for 13 days. I trust we have no more rain for a time.

I got the gramophone going right after breakfast (which by the way was not very early) this morning and ran over a lot of our old records. One of our officers now on leave is getting a new instrument. Did I tell you that Col. Bell did not have a chance to hear "Irish Eyes"? The day we had the gramophone

brought up from the horse lines the Colonel went off to take temporary command of the brigade and has not been back since.

Your information concerning weddings covered all I had previously known and a little more. I did not know anything about a short service, but if there is one we shall have it, the shorter the better. We shall also indulge in the luxury of a special license. The idea of some low brow curate getting up on three successive Sundays, or whatever the number of times it is, and yapping out our intentions to a crowd of people that never heard of us and don't give a damn does not appeal to me. Are you in favor of as quiet a wedding as possible? I hope so. Have you told anybody of our engagement yet? . . . I have not told a soul yet but am anxiously waiting your unqualified permission to give the glad tidings to my immediate relatives.

Yours lovingly Harold W McGill

While on a two-week leave in England, Harold and Emma married on 9 December 1917, a mere five months after they became engaged. They enjoyed a brief yet frenzied honeymoon in London before Harold returned to duty on December 25. During this time, Harold was promoted to acting major and was placed in charge of the 5th Canadian Field Ambulance Corps.

After their marriage, Emma went through a difficult period; she became ill with influenza, was unemployed, and later suffered a miscarriage. Her mood was dark and, on occasion, she questioned the wisdom of the decision to marry so quickly. But, if Emma had doubts, Harold did not. As his correspondence revealed, he did not regret his decision and longed to be with woman he loved.

Belgium, March 16/19. Dear Emma;

Your two letters of March 10 & 11 respectively brought a bright ray of sunshine into my life this afternoon. It is a dull cold miserable day, and I do not remember ever having been more "Fed up" with things in general than just before the mail came in . . .

I have heard nothing further of my application for recall to England for the purpose of proceeding to Canada with my dependent, the latter being your dear self. A brigade staff officer was into our mess this afternoon and informed us that our group would likely be moved to England on or about April 5. This will not be too bad if the information turns out to be correct.

Whatever made you ask me if I were sorry that we were married? The only question that ever concerned me was whether we should be married during the war or wait until it was finished. If I had decided upon the latter alternative I should not have mentioned the matter to you until the end of the war, and the Lord only knows where you would have been by this time; married to someone else perhaps. That might have been well for you but would most certainly have been bad for me.

Your loving husband Harold W. McGill

Belgium

March 28/19 Dear Emma;

Your letter of March 22 came to hand this afternoon. I am so very sorry you have been ill, and shall be most anxious until I hear from you again. And I fear that I shall not have any more letters from you until after our unit reaches England, for we go on the road the

day after to-morrow. Our last mail from "The Field" goes out to-morrow morning. Unless I get a letter from you in to-morrow's mail I shall not get any more on this side of the Channel.

What in the world brought on your trouble? It was the last thing that I should have expected. Well, so long as you get around alright again I shall be thankful enough.

I have had dreams about you during each of the past few nights and in all my dreams you were lovely and in the best of health. There has never been any suggestion of illness on your part. Two nights ago I dreamed that we were together in the "State Apartment" which you had engaged in expectation of my homecoming.

We have at last received our definite entraining orders. Our unit goes on the first train of the division, which leaves here at noon on Sunday March 30. We should be in Bramshott within a week from our date of starting. I shall try to phone you from there when we arrive.

I must close now. I shall look for a letter from you to-morrow. I am glad that Col. Gunn is looking after you.

Your loving husband,

Harold W. McGill

On 7 April 1919, Harold arrived for dispersal at Bramshott. Emma was waiting for him in London. In total, Harold served three years with the 31st battalion. He was awarded the Military Cross for his service in France. Harold's recollections of his wartime experiences were recorded in a manuscript titled "Reminiscences of a Battalion M.O." In 1935 he submitted the manuscript to Macmillan of Canada, hoping to have it published. He wrote: "Although the editors who reviewed the memoir considered it a work of merit, Macmillan declined for economic reasons."[3] As the country was in the middle of the Great Depression, Macmillan's decision was understandable. The manuscript was finally published in 2007, edited by Marjorie Norris, and titled *Medicine and Duty: The World War I Memoir of Captain Harold W. McGill, Medical Officer, 31st Battalion C.E.F.* Norris had previously explored the experiences of Calgary nurses serving on the front in *Sister Heroines: The Roseate Glow of Wartime Nursing 1914–1918*, published in 2002.[4]

Emma and Harold returned to Calgary in spring 1919. Harold resumed his position as the Sarcee (Tsuu T'ina) Reservation medical officer. He became a prominent physician and, in 1920, was elected president of the Calgary Medical Society. Two years later, he was elected as the Calgary member of the Council of the College of Physicians and Surgeons of Alberta. He also became active in politics and, in 1926, was elected to Calgary city council, where he served two terms as alderman. In June 1930 he was elected as a Conservative member of the Legislative Assembly of Alberta to represent Calgary, but resigned in October 1932 when he was appointed deputy superintendent general of Indian Affairs in Ottawa by his long-time friend Prime Minister R.B. Bennett. Four years later, he was promoted to director of Indian Affairs, which entitled him to a seat in the Northwest Territories government. He was appointed to the 2nd Council of the Northwest Territories and served as a member until 1947. Emma was also active in local politics. She sat on the executive of the Women's Canadian Club and the Women's Conservative Association.

The McGills eventually moved to the west coast to live out the remainder of their lives. Harold died on 3 July 1961 in Vancouver, British Columbia. Emma died 10 years later. The McGills had two daughters, Kathleen (Odell) and Doris (McNab).

Notes

1   The Harold William McGill and Emma Griffis McGill Fonds are in the Glenbow Archives, Calgary, and a description can be found at http://www.glenbow.org/collections/search/findingaids/archhtm/mcgill.cfm. Marjorie Norris has edited his memoir as *Medicine and Duty: The World War I Memoir of Captain Harold W. McGill, Medical Officer, 31st Battalion C.E.F.* (Calgary: University of Calgary Press, 2007), xi.

2   *Medicine and Duty*, xv.

3   Ibid., xiv.

4   Marjorie Norris, *Sister Heroines: The Roseate Glow of Wartime Nursing 1914–1918* (Calgary: Bunker to Bunker Publishing, 2002).

Works Cited

PRIMARY SOURCES

Glenbow Archives, Calgary. The Harold William McGill and Emma Griffis McGill Fonds. A description can be found at URL: http://www.glenbow.org/collections/search/findingaids/archhtm/mcgill.cfm.

SECONDARY SOURCES

Norris, Marjorie, ed. *Medicine and Duty: The World War I Memoir of Captain Harold W. McGill, Medical Officer, 31st Battalion C.E.F.* Calgary: University of Calgary Press, 2007.

——. *Sister Heroines: The Roseate Glow of Wartime Nursing 1914–1918.* Calgary: Bunker to Bunker Publishing, 2002.

Private Stephen Smith and His Trench Art Belts

ALLAN KERR AND DOUG STYLES

Since human beings are naturally collectors or souvenir hunters, it is inevitable that soldiers in the First World War would collect or make items for the purpose of remembrance or as trophies. These artifacts are described as "trench art" and can include decorated shell and bullet casings, items carved from wood or bone, and others with buttons or similar elements of uniforms, whether from enemy or allied sources. While any conflict resulted in such production, the First World War saw a proliferation, and it was not only soldiers, prisoners of war, and internees who made them, but also, after a market developed, commercial enterprises. Items made by soldiers are the most personal and can serve to tell their own wartime story.

Private Stephen Smith was born on 6 September 1872 in Uxbridge, Ontario, and, before joining the 12th Canadian Mounted Rifles at the Sarcee Camp in Calgary on 20 August 1915, worked as a saddler. He had served for a year with the 23rd Alberta Rangers. After training in Canada, he was sent overseas aboard the SS *Missanabie*, arriving in England on 9 October 1915. Smith was transferred to the 2nd Canadian Mounted Rifles and sent to France on

January 20, arriving at his unit on 10 February 1916. He was diagnosed with myalgia on April 17, and as a result he was moved from one medical facility to another, including No. 3 Canadian General Hospital in Boulogne (18 April 1916) and #18 Ambulance Train, No. 17 Casualty Clearing Station, ending up at the Marlborough Detail Camp in England on 20 May 1916. Since he could not be on active service, he was loaned to the 9th Reserve Battalion in Folkestone on 6 June 1916, and then transferred to the Garrison Depot at Hastings on 27 November 1916. On 5 March 1917, he was returned to Canada, and by March 17, he was in a convalescent home in Calgary. Smith was discharged from the army as "medically unfit" due to rheumatism on 13 October 1917. Still anxious to serve, he rejoined the Canadian Army on 1 August 1919 in Edmonton, where he worked in the Edmonton Military Hospital until his discharge on 15 November 1919. For his service, he received the British War Medal and the Victory Medal.

In 1916 or 1917, Private Stephen Smith sent a belt covered with badges and buttons home to his wife Evelyn with a note scrawled in a pocket of the belt that stated: "These are the names of the Badges &

Private Stephen Smith framed his two souvenir belts together with his picture, cap badge, and collars. Kerr Collection, Canadian Militaria Preservation Society, Edmonton, Alberta.

Buttons on my Belt all Came from the Front Except 82nd 89th & 66 Numerals. I have another one about twice as Wide or Wider and have it over half filled but there are not many of there [*sic*] Imperial." Private Smith's two souvenirs from the front came to be popularly known as "hate belts," since some of the buttons and badges were collected from enemy soldiers. Smith's service records indicate that he served less than three months at the front with the balance of his service being on light duty in the rear and in hospital. His service indicates that at least some of the items on his belts were obtained at the front.

Jane A Kimball in *Trench Art: An Illustrated History* classifies these belts as trench art and prefers to call

them "souvenir belts."[1] The French word "souvenir" (literally, "a remembrance") came into everyday English usage during the Great War, and largely replaced the word "keepsake" to describe objects made or collected as tangible reminders of places and events. Nicholas J. Saunders in *Trench Art: A Brief History and Guide* defines trench art as "any object made by soldiers, prisoners of war and civilians, from war material, as long as the object and maker are associated in time and space with an armed conflict or its consequences."[2]

Most cap and collar badges, buttons, and insignia were obtained on or near the battle front. Items removed from the uniforms of the deceased, from

(above) The small belt (6.5 cm wide, 96 cm long) contains 68 items. The original list was found in the pocket near the belt buckle and is shown left of the picture in the photograph on page 198. Kerr Collection, Canadian Militaria Preservation Society, Edmonton, Alberta; (below) The large belt (14 cm wide, 93 cm long) contains 95 items. Kerr Collection, Canadian Militaria Preservation Society, Edmonton, Alberta.

The commercially produced memorial picture frame and backing illustrates another type of trench art. Families were contacted, whenever a son or father's name appeared in a newspaper, and offered such products. The backing to Smith's picture frame is marked "COPYRIGHTED BY CHAS E NEVILLE." Kerr Collection, Canadian Militaria Preservation Society, Edmonton, Alberta.

prisoners, or traded with comrades were retained as souvenirs, to keep as personal remembrances or to sell/trade to those away from the front. The currency of trade between combat and support soldiers was mainly cigarettes and liquor. It was difficult to manufacture and maintain belts, specifically large belts, at the front due to the cramped and dirty living conditions. The care that is evident in the production of the belts, and later the professional framing, reveal Smith's pride in serving and his desire to share this with not only his wife but also his friends and the community at large.

Notes

1   Jane A. Kimball, *Trench Art: An Illustrated History* (Davis, CA: Silverpenny Press, 2004).

2   Nicholas J. Saunders, *Trench Art: A Brief History and Guide* (South Yorkshire, UK: Pen & Sword Books Limited, 2001), 20.

Works Cited

Kimball, Jane A. *Trench Art: An Illustrated History*. Davis, CA: Silverpenny Press, 2004.

Saunders, Nicholas J. *Trench Art: A Brief History and Guide*. South Yorkshire, UK: Pen & Sword Books Limited, 2001.

SECTION TWO

The Home Front: Context and Meaning

In 1914, Alberta had been a province of the Dominion of Canada for only nine years. Both the federal and provincial governments were enticing immigrants to settle the wide open stretches of what was described as "the last, best West." While life in Alberta was viewed as "on the margins" of the civilized world, it was by no means primitive. Settlement went hand-in-hand with economic modernization and the creation of civil society. The early part of the twentieth century saw the people of Alberta dealing with a whole range of issues, including women's suffrage, the rights of the working class, and challenges to established religion. The life-and-death experience on the battle front heightened the sense that somehow life in the homeland must be improved for those returning. The Social Gospel movement that influenced Protestant churches of Canada and the United States from the end of the nineteenth century to the early part of the twentieth century focused attention on social ills, including the link between alcoholism, poverty, unemployment, crime, and family violence. This was an age of belief, and the Protestant churches – Presbyterian, Methodist, Unitarian, and Anglican – dominated. In 1911, Presbyterianism was the largest denomination in Alberta.[1] The Protestant churches shared a belief that it was incumbent on Christians of goodwill to address social problems. While the war was seen by most as a just one and in defence of Christian values, there were some who came to question this.

Section Two: The Home Front – Context and Meaning features essays that take a thematic approach to elucidating the home front experience. Duff Crerar's essay provides an overview of the year 1916, the war's midpoint, which brought soaring demand for Alberta products, declining enlistment, mounting inflation, labour shortages, and more powerful temperance and women's suffrage campaigns. Aritha van Herk shows that, for Albertans at home, the effects of war varied greatly: for some, routines changed little, while for others the war brought excitement, purpose, pride, and even fun, or at the other extreme, despair and devastation. Norman Knowles demonstrates the significance of religion in framing how Albertans understood the war and coped with the sacrifices it exacted. Adriana Davies examines the growing influence of women of British descent in Alberta and how this was wielded through charitable organizations to support key causes including women's suffrage and the war effort.

Newspapers became a powerful tool not only for providing news of battles lost and won but also for discussing notions of heroism and Canada's role in an international conflict. While members of some of Alberta's militias had participated in the Boer War, the First World War was the first time that Canadians fought as a Dominion within the British Empire. David Gallant examines war coverage in Alberta newspapers, especially during the conflict's early stages, when, contrary to standard interpretations, fear and trepidation vied with patriotism and optimism. Stephen Greenhalgh focuses on the war service of Edmonton men whom the media highlighted to create symbols of local heroes. Jeff Keshen's two chapters assess the degree to which patriotism, censorship, and propaganda shaped perceptions of the war in Alberta.

Alvin Finkel shows that despite efforts to manage public opinion, Alberta's labour movement grew disenchanted over rapidly increasing inflation, emphasis on the conscription of men before wealth, and the ongoing lack of collective bargaining rights. Finally, Catherine Cole shows that despite gripes from western Canada about war industry congregating in southern Ontario and Quebec, Edmonton's Great Western Garment Company played a major role in producing military uniforms, while Peter McKenzie-Brown explains how a little-known wartime survey pointed to future areas of petroleum development in Alberta, including the oil sands.

The wartime years in Alberta were thus a period of intellectual ferment leading to change. In fact, the ideas forged at the time through hardship and suffering would help to shape modern Alberta.

Notes

1 Ken Munro in *First Presbyterian Church, Edmonton: A History* (Bloomington, IN: Trafford Publishing, 2004), iv–v.

Enthusiasm Embattled: Alberta 1916

DUFF CRERAR

In 1915 Jeannie Alexander, a young girl living in the Peace River Block with her pioneering family, received an embroidered postcard from France: a shamrock with the flags of the Allies on the leaves. The motto, stitched in gold, said, "Right is Might." But in 1916 a shadow crossed her path. Her brother's best friend, the cheerful young man who had tramped cross-country to Athabasca Landing in 1914, had been killed on the Somme.[1] Someone had to explain that her hero was not coming back.

Little Jeannie was by no means the only Albertan whose world grew darker in 1916. Two years before, war had been something of a relief: Alberta was weathering a major depression and drought. Enlistment substituted one immigrant strategy gone sour with a better one, when many Albertans, much like Westerners in general, were far from "placid and prosperous."[2] For those down on their luck, enlistment meant a free trip to England and a little adventure, as everyone believed the war would be both short and victorious. Those with British military origins tried to fill the vacancies in the first Canadian Contingent. The retired French Army officers who had founded the town of Trochu, Alberta, packed up and returned to fight for France. Of those who survived the war, almost none returned. The well-bred,

middle-class Britishers who populated Millarville, Okotoks, and many other stock-and-ranch operations, flocked back to join cavalry units. Some would never see Alberta again, or would find their way back as broken men.[3]

By mid-war, 1916, wheat prices were high and the land seemed generously productive. This was the year when it was easier for some to pay the bills, put food on the table, and plan for the prosperity that was supposed to come with the peace. But for many others, it was a year that undermined hope with grief, frustration, and apprehension. A culture war that had started long before 1914 reached a fever pitch in 1916. Amidst the bustle and bluster of Alberta public life emerged a growing unease that the war could not be won by voluntarism alone. By year's end, most Albertans' fiery determination to win at any cost was tainted with anxiety that the costs of victory were spiralling out of control.

A Wave of Militant Idealism

The first few days of August 1914 produced a swarm of volunteers. Wesleyan Methodist Rev. G.H. Cobbledick of Lethbridge spoke for most clergy when he

This postcard was sent to Jeannie Alexander in Spirit River, Alberta from Jack Pringle in France in 1916. A pencilled note on the back adds that in October word reached Spirit River of his death in action. South Peace Regional Archives.

pronounced: "Our hearts and hands are with our boys who will go to the front."[4] The province seemed dominated by an infectious blend of enthusiasm and militant idealism. Recruiting continued in every community. Even prewar pacifism was not much of a barrier. But when a Red Deer MP, Liberal Michael Clark, called for an immediate war income tax, fellow Albertans thought this was going a bit too far. Very few were prepared to entertain the thought of conscription of men, and those calling for conscription of wealth could be ignored.[5] It was assumed that the war would be won on the voluntary principle.

Meanwhile the Protestant churches sustained the crusade. At the June 1916 Methodist Conference in Lethbridge, Dr. W.L. Armstrong of Edmonton proclaimed that the war was leavening the world for the coming Kingdom of God on Earth.[6] The crusade overseas must be matched and the war redeemed by another crusade at home. Though Presbyterians were somewhat distracted by the Church Union debate (Red Deer's Rev. W.G. Brown led the Presbyterian Church Association, a bastion of anti-Union sentiment), and the Anglicans got most of the military chaplaincies, Methodists had the highest profile on the provincial home front.[7] Alberta College South, the Methodist theological college in Edmonton, donated facilities for military training, put its female students to work sewing for soldiers, and sent its male students to the front, nearly suspending operations for lack of students. By 1917 more than 50 ministers and probationers were in uniform, mostly as combatants. Prominent Methodist laymen such as Calgary's R.B. Bennett, Lethbridge's W.A. Buchanan, George Stanley of High River, and women such as Nellie McClung, Louise McKinney, and Mrs. George Kerby (whose husband was principal of Calgary's Mount Royal College) stumped the province,

This cartoon appeared in the *Grain Grower's Guide* in 1914. Glenbow Archives, NA-3818-14.

THE VOTE GIRL

I WANT THE VOTE, AND I MEAN TO HAVE THE VOTE, THATS THE SORT OF GIRL I AM

marshalling support for the war effort as a mission to stamp out social ills both at home and overseas. In Methodist churches, women's circles sent (mostly cigarette-free) packages to soldiers, and raised funds for war relief.[8]

To militant social progressives, Ottawa's neglect and betrayal of Western prewar farm grievances and nativist anxieties could now be resolved by the war-induced consensus. Thus, two of the great progressive causes that had emerged before the war gained critical momentum and won their greatest victories in 1916. Rural and small-town elites had supported prohibition by provincial plebiscite in 1915.[9] While French Canadians, a portion of the soldier vote, and perhaps some Ukrainian voters east and north of Edmonton kept four districts temporarily wet, the powerful Women's Christian Temperance Union (WCTU) and United Farm Women of Alberta (UFWA) were not to be denied. Prohibition in Alberta became the law on 1 July 1916. Supporters

cheered the decreasing number of arrests for drunkenness, and set their sights on nonpartisan politics, and votes for women. Through the Women's Institute and other organisations, sewing circles from the town of Vulcan in the south to the hamlet of Glen Leslie in the north discussed politics, promoted war work, sent chocolates to the boys in uniform, or read aloud letters from the front. In most of rural Alberta it was women's work that supported the local Patriotic Fund.[10]

The Alberta Women's Institute campaigned for war and women's votes in its *Farm and Ranch Review* (although Irene Parlby, Alberta's leading United Farmers of Alberta feminist, complained that Institute women still talked too much housekeeping and not enough politics). Along with the WCTU, the Imperial Order Daughters of the Empire (IODE), UFWA, Victorian Order of Nurses, and the host of church women (whose members often belonged to several of these organizations simultaneously), the Institute demanded the attention of politicians.[11] Even R.B. Bennett, Calgary's notorious bachelor millionaire and Conservative pillar, was converted to the cause of women's suffrage. On 19 April 1916, Alberta granted the female franchise.[12]

War and Its Social Discontents

The triumph of prohibition and women's suffrage both rewarded the largest and most active proportions of the population, but there were many other Albertans who were either indifferent to or alienated by these and other wartime causes. The war made English sacred: other languages were to be banned from the schools. This was preached by educators criss-crossing the province, inspired by H.M. Tory, president of the University of Alberta, and by its Department of Extension.[13] Ukrainians and German-speaking or French Canadians prudently kept their opinions to themselves, as war-enhanced nativism peaked. Roberta MacAdams, destined by the soldier vote to become a member of the legislature, blasted "enemy foreigners" for getting rich on the land while Anglo-Saxon Alberta boys were dying overseas.[14] Patriotism blended with paranoia. In Lethbridge, rumours spread that German sympathizers were sabotaging threshing machines with rocks and metal in wheat stooks.[15] In Vulcan, hard-working Germans were viewed as brutal, ruthless, and militaristic, while stories went round that they might set fire to the crops.

The non-British tried to prove their loyalty with donations to patriotic funds, by flying Union Jacks, by cooperating with the police, and sometimes by enlisting, but harassment, internment, and loss of civil rights plagued them. Lethbridge and Banff-Castle Mountain enemy alien internment camps locked up German and Austrian reservists, and unwelcome immigrants. Many Ukrainians—former subjects of Austria and no friends of Russia—were concentrated at Banff, while Germans and Austrians ended up in the converted hen barns at the Lethbridge Exhibition grounds. There, successful escapes raised suspicions that enemy sympathizers populated southern Alberta. The internment camp became the focus of controversy, bigotry, and brutality. Increased enlistment resulted in labour shortages that made it harder to hire guards for the camps, and this resulted in closure of the camps on 2 November 1916. Some enemy aliens had also been paroled so long as they agreed to work in certain areas.[16] Germans changed their names, trying to sound Scandinavian, for instance, to limit persecution. Two German newspapers, Calgary's *Deutsch Kanadier* and the *Alberta Herold*, ceased publication. On 10–11 February 1916 a mob of veterans in Calgary smashed German shops and restaurants. Anti-German hysteria ruined Martin Nordegg's plans to found a model coal-mining community; the government seized his property and he fled to the United States.

On the farms, however, 1916 brought new optimism. The cycles of drought and depressed prices seemed cured by the war. In 1915 there had been a bumper harvest, thanks to heavy rains that made even Palliser's Triangle bloom.[17] Prices had risen from the depressed rates of 1914 to 91 cents a bushel. The following summer, wheat prices were at their highest, over $1.30 a bushel, though yields were lower. During 1916 many farmers made up their minds. The war had confirmed the nostrum that a farmer who wanted to profit grew wheat.[18] The number of homesteads and acreage under cultivation increased for the first time in years.[19] Cattle- and horse-raising became profitable, owing to the demand for beef and draft animals for the military. High River saw prosperity again.[20] But the war took too many experienced men away to the front, raising the cost of labour, while farmers rented more expensive fields and cultivated without soil conservation measures, stressing both their credit and their land.[21]

Attempts to get the 1916 crop seeded early failed because the soil was too cold. Dry weather and stem rust also reduced yields. Still, there was almost an embarrassment of wealth by the end of the year, though the high prices of 1916 came partly from scarcity. Extra cash in farmers' pockets did not always translate into buying better equipment, as tariffs on them kept costs high. The only noticeable outcome of the 1916 boom was perhaps the larger number of farmers driving automobiles.[22] When drought-afflicted crop yields dropped even lower and prices bottomed out after the war, too many farmers were left with dust, weeds, and bad debts.[23] Less damaged by the false dawn were the immigrants who, though persecuted, made enough money in 1915 and 1916 to secure a better economic foothold on their smaller holdings. Often discouraged from over-expansion by hostile social and economic conditions, these farmers had lower debt loads, and their traditional farming techniques made them better stewards of the land.[24]

In the Peace and Athabasca watersheds the war brought disaster for some but, with the arrival of the railway in 1916, prosperity for others. Here the war years accelerated the marginalization of the indigenous peoples in the economy and on the land. Already caught between the promises of Treaty 8 and the reality of the Indian Act, provincial game laws, and boarding schools, the fur economy collapsed in 1914 when Britain suspended all such trading for the duration of the war. Coinciding with a shortage of game (except moose in the western districts), trappers and their families were near starvation by spring 1915.[25] Restrictions on cash-crop agriculture delayed reserve surveys (allowing squatters to claim traditional lands), and exclusion from commercial fishing on Lesser Slave Lake furthered the government prewar agenda of letting Aboriginal development slide until white settlement depleted or appropriated traditional resources, forcing Indians to adopt modern ways of living.[26] The fur trade recovered in 1916 when the United States took up the business, but new regulations and railway access opened up the land to white trappers and free market competition, which killed the old relationship between Aboriginal people and the Hudson's Bay Company, and eventually ended the traditional economy.

In 1916, the long-heralded railway finally arrived, and the dreamed-of transformation of Alberta's north became feasible. By summer 1916, the end-of-steel for the Edmonton, Dunvegan, and British Columbia railway reached Grande Prairie. A few months later, the Athabasca and Great Waterways approached Fort McMurray. Both of these railways were already sliding towards bankruptcy, as the war diverted capital from Great Britain, the United States, and the rest of Canada. Propped up by the ingenuity of its owners, provincial assistance, and ruthless cutting of corners (endangering passengers and crews), the railways destroyed the riverboat network that had supplied the north for decades, and ended the harrowing necessity of migrating overland by the Edson Trail. Farmers now had access to the wheat market, though the 1916 harvest virtually failed in the Peace region, perhaps because of all the young men gone to war.[27] With the railway came commercial fishing on Lesser Slave Lake, which soon supplied most of Alberta's fish, some being put on tables as far away as Chicago. But as the railway gave, it also took away. The end of the land boom in most northern towns was followed by near-death sentences for communities such as Grouard, Athabasca, Dunvegan, and Bezanson, when the lines bypassed them, and trains sparked devastating forest fires. In the end even the railways had to wait for the war to finish before the population and agricultural growth could swamp indigenous peoples with immigrants. Population growth actually declined early in the war, as the Peace River Block had high enlistment rates, and immigration slowed.[28] The delayed frontier would have to wait a little longer.

Scraping the Bottom of the Barrel: Boosterism and Recruiting Fade

As summer 1916 went on, Alberta reached the peak of its manpower contribution to the army. As soon as war broke out, businessmen and politicians began lobbying for regiments to be recruited and trained locally, bringing barracks construction, production contracts, and other economic benefits to cities and towns with flat economies. Alberta became "Militia District No. 13," based in Edmonton, which, along with Calgary, Lethbridge, and Medicine Hat, benefited most from the military's budget.[29] City recruiting, where the patriotic well-to-do sought recruits from among the poor, unemployed, and ne'er-do-well, kept the numbers up a little longer. Small-town businessmen and newspaper editors did their bit by telling itinerant peddlers to join the army.[30] But 1916 saw more than 20 different units recruiting against each other in MD No. 13.[31] Calgary

was a hive of activity, with recruiters for the American Legion buttonholing US citizens to enlist (Sam Hughes had authorized creation of a CEF battalion for Americans willing to violate their own country's neutrality), while two other Battalions, the 82nd and 56th, prepared for departure. Lethbridge, along with its artillery batteries, raised a Highland Battalion, the 113th "Kilties."[32] Once in England, however, the 113th learned that it would be broken up to reinforce battalions already at the front.[33] The same fate awaited Red Deer's 187th, Blairmore's 192nd, and Edmonton's 51st.[34] Edmonton's 63rd had men to spare, and a galaxy of well-connected officers, yet it too became fodder for other units. Those still left behind would follow the same path from hurrahs to oblivion; even "Peace River" Jim Cornwall's notorious Irish Guards—wild men from the north so undisciplined, rumours said, that the *Edmonton Bulletin* sent a reporter to their makeshift headquarters in the old Rubber Co. warehouse to reassure the public. Already in smaller towns such as Camrose and High River, while efforts to raise funds for the Patriotic Fund and Red Cross were helped by high grain prices, men were hard to come by. Edmonton merchants wondered if the drain of departing men would hurt business.

The hunt went on. Although Ottawa decreed, and many Albertans agreed, that the conflict was a "White Man's War," recruiters turned to the Indian and Métis population. Native Albertans across the province made contributions out of all proportion to their numbers. Jim Cornwall's Irish Guards included more than 50 Indians, Métis, and even some Inuit. Henry J. Bury, who helped negotiate Treaty 8, went back north to find another 250 recruits around Whitefish Lake.[35] But southern reserves were divided over volunteering. Traditionalists worried that the dead could not lie in their native soil, and that soldiers would die of tuberculosis, like Albert Mountain Horse, who survived poison gas at Ypres only to die back in Canada. Relatives and band leaders feared losing more young men and demanded that Indian agents ban recruiting on reserves. Things came to a head when, at the end of 1916, the National Registration cards came around to be signed. In the traditional warrior code, conscription both insulted and repelled Aboriginal recruits, who honoured their treaty with the King, not the government in Ottawa.[36] Reserves nevertheless made substantial and self-sacrificing financial contributions to the Red Cross and Canadian Patriotic Fund.[37] What they did not know was that large tracts of their land would be expropriated and exploited by outsiders in the Greater Production Program of 1917–18. In a 1916 letter, Saddle Lake Cree soldier Mark Steinhauer reflected: "I have been wondering whether we are going to get anything out of our country that we going to fight for." When he and other veterans returned, the obvious answer was, nothing more than the Indian Act already stipulated.[38]

Society Under Strain: Home-Front Woes and Anxieties

A troubling problem for home-front enthusiasts concerned what to do for families who had given up their breadwinners to the war. Like the rest of the nation, most Albertan military families received bonuses from the Patriotic Fund, an organization commissioned by the Canadian government under Montreal manufacturer and Conservative MP Sir Herbert Ames. At least 55,000 families across Canada depended on the Canadian Patriotic Fund,

This poster for the Patriotic Fund was based on the story of an Onion Lake man who donated twenty-five cents for every member of his family to the fund. He wanted to contribute to the war effort but, given his age and near-blindness, money was all he could offer. Glenbow Museum, Poster Collection number 14.

but each province was tasked with raising its own support. A practical example of voluntarism, the fund seemed to have the capacity to care for soldier dependents while casualties and recruitment numbers were low, but the strain was showing by the beginning of 1916. Edmonton had granted free streetcar tickets to soldiers and half-cost tickets to families of city employees who enlisted.[39] The offer seemed practical in 1915, but a year later the growing number of families without breadwinners became an alarming drain on city resources. Edmontonians called on the Patriotic Fund, while leaders pondered whether the provincial or federal governments would have to take over its work. While organizations such as the Red Cross, IODE, Canadian Women's Club, St. John's Ambulance, and others did their best for dependants, the job was exhausting Albertans. Lethbridge had created an Overseas Club pledged to support soldier families but by 1916 its funds and energy were drying up. Stunts like Calgary's 56th Battalion "Follies," a concert show with proceeds going to the Patriotic Fund, could not raise enough.[40] Civic leaders grew uneasy that voluntarism could no longer keep up with the need.

Patriotic Fund procedures also revealed the prejudices and anxieties of the "haves" regarding the "have-nots." Rumours spread that "undeserving" soldiers' wives were wasting donors' hard-earned money. Patriotic Fund investigators went to great lengths to judge the "worthiness" of cases, noting "many impudent and fraudulent claims were entered and certification rested with the local committee." Sometimes committees threatened to deprive mothers they judged unfit, for things such as letting their children go unaccompanied to the cinema.[41] Embittered by the officiousness they encountered

in mid-war Alberta, it seemed the sacrifices many women made were costing them more dearly than they ever had imagined.[42]

Veterans often felt the same way. By 1916 more and more "returned" (wounded and disabled) men were evident in Alberta cities, hamlets, and rural areas. Edmonton set up a Returned Soldiers Bureau in December 1915, and talks began about a convalescent home. However, the Municipal Committee called for Provincial and Dominion governments to take on the burden. It was one thing to offer Christmas dinner to returned men and military staff in 1916, but for the city to handle the welfare of all returned men was too much.[43]

Lethbridge had one of the most enthusiastic and well-organized Patriotic Fund canvasses. The local Red Cross solicited a percentage of local business profits on 29 February 1916 as a "leap day" donation.[44] With help from smaller groups such as the Lethbridge Tennis Club, the city contribution to the Patriotic Fund was over $88,000 (worth $1.7 million in 2015) by war's end, a decidedly impressive figure from a population of some 11,000. But, by 1916, the bulk of that amount had already been given, and subsequent contributions had dropped so dramatically that a frustrated *Lethbridge Herald* threatened to publish the names of those with the money but unwilling to donate. By 1918 the city would be levying a *tax* to keep the Patriotic Fund alive.[45] Led by Mayor W. Hardie, Lethbridge became a leading promoter of equal federal pensions for all veterans, regardless of military rank.[46] This was only a few months before the phrase "Conscription of Wealth" polarized Lethbridge, a province, and a nation.[47]

Manpower problems at home also created anxiety, for it was in 1916 that complaints first arose

One of the major changes on the home front was that women entered the work force in increasing numbers. They also took on non-traditional roles, including factory work. These women were photographed in 1917, working in the W.H. Clark lumber company, which produced sash, doors, and interior furnishings including church furniture in Edmonton. McDermid Studio. Glenbow Archives, NC-6-3311.

about too many men going overseas. Prime Minister Borden's New Year 1916 commitment to raise an army of 500,000 men added to the interest in Alberta newspapers covering Britain's controversial edging towards conscription.[48] As newspapers hectored the "slacker" who had not yet done his duty, the

president of the Lethbridge Board of Trade warned that the year's harvest could not be gathered nor enough coal mined for the winter unless recruiting slowed. Many farmers had little sympathy with the prospect of either leaving their farms or having sons taken away from the fields.[49] The obvious remedy

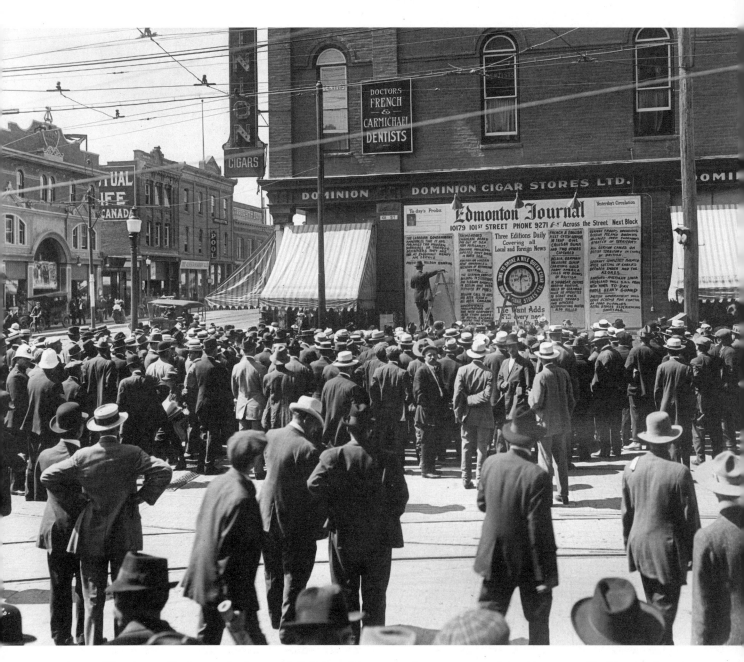

Although many Albertans remained preoccupied with immediate concerns, there was enormous interest in war news. *The Edmonton Journal* posted the latest news on Jasper Avenue for all to read. McDermid Studio, 3 August 1914. City of Edmonton Archives, EA-10-3184.

was for the Canadian government to begin a national registration for selective service.[50] However, registration made workers and miners uneasy; to them it looked like a prelude to conscription, and they were right.

Other dark clouds hung on the horizon. After the initial bustle and optimism about military camps, recruiting, and trying to get shell contracts, Edmonton and Calgary discovered their money and population woes were not cured. War contracts west of Winnipeg were too few and far between.[51] After 1914, Edmonton actually lost 16,000 people, as its prewar economic sag continued into 1916, and Red Deer and Lethbridge experienced only slight growth. Even the wheat prices did not help, as farmers took their business to eastern mail-order houses.[52] At the end of 1916, most small Alberta towns were still financially floundering and cities just getting by. Calgary basked in the grand summer review of troops at Sarcee Camp by the Duke of Connaught, the Governor General, but there seemed little capital or interest in its newly discovered oil and natural gas in Turner Valley.[53]

Then came trouble in the mines. Under intensified wartime demand, coal production more than tripled in Alberta during the Great War.[54] Steady work, though, did not make mining safer or living conditions better. While there had not been much protest in Lethbridge against National Registration after all, miners were on the verge of striking. Galloping wartime inflation depressed the standard of living for everyone, admitted the Lethbridge Board of Trade. As the mayor and civic leaders across Alberta called on the State to control the problem, miners could not wait. The United Mineworkers, supported by the Lethbridge miners, walked out on November 27. Outrage over the demand for a 25

percent increase (while inflation stood at just over 8 percent) waned as descriptions of the appalling living conditions in most camps leaked out. Promised a toothless federal cost-of-living inquiry, the miners grew restless again in 1917.[55] Farmers, too, were becoming impatient, as were representatives for the urban underprivileged in Calgary. Usually willing to cooperate with the Liberals but now radicalized by the war, prohibition, and women's suffrage—and goaded by firebrands such as William Irvine (Calgary's minister to the poor, editor of The Nutcracker, and spokesman for nonpartisan politics)—Henry Wise Wood of the United Farmers of Alberta reluctantly edged towards running for office. Calgary labour, some women's groups, and Southern Alberta's more radical farmers could not wait, joining the Non-Partisan League. In 1917 the League elected two members to the legislature.[56] Wood knew by then that farmers would have to enter politics.

Problems also emerged on the prohibition front. The Mounted Police flatly refused to enforce the heavily loopholed law, and bowed out of policing the province. The new Alberta Provincial Police—which were not even fully mobilized by the end of the year and, in 1917, undermanned, underpaid, and easily corrupted—could not stem the tide of interprovincial or cross-border smuggling.[57] The battle to stop the sale of 2 percent beer also provoked determined legal challenges from bar owners and their supporters.[58] The war against "John Barleycorn" was not over, as ministers of religion and progressives learned that the Social Gospel consensus did not hold sway in every rural community. Much of northern Alberta was both Catholic and populated by persecuted minorities who had little interest in or sympathy with moral crusading. Even Vulcan and High River shunned prohibition. To the dismay and even the fury of the underpaid and overworked clergy, farmers asserted that pragmatic church union and community social cohesion, with a good Sunday school for the children—not crusading idealism—was the basis of their religion, even in wartime.[59] Methodist leader Rev. S.D. Chown, speaking to a Lethbridge meeting of churchmen, proclaimed that the war had convicted, but not yet converted, the country to a life of service and sacrifice. Chown was being unfair: proportionately, more Albertans volunteered to fight than did the residents of nearly every other province, and they suffered accordingly with a high casualty rate.[60] People dreaded the arrival of a telegram, a clergyman, or Red Cross volunteer.[61] There was no place in Alberta where the shadow of death did not fall.

Albertans from Jeannie Alexander, the little Spirit River girl, to Henry Wise Wood crossed a watershed in 1916. While the war heightened pre-existing crusades for social and political regeneration, and many Albertans would have said by the end of 1916 that the ultimate goals and benefits of the wartime crusade were achievable, the costs already had generated the anxiety, unease, and rebellion that surged in 1917. By New Year's 1917, signs were already evident that the war would not solve any of Alberta's problems. In the north, it cemented divisions between Native and settler, farmer and trapper, and contributed to the resource exploitation that deepened the gulf between have and have-not. The war made many farmers both affluent and unwilling to sacrifice their sons, while, culturally and ethnically, the walls between Albertans were raised higher as social reform and majoritarian democracy linked up with nativism and repression. Labour and farm protest hinted, too, that the war was doing anything but unite the province. On the battlefield,

Alberta fighting units had been emptied and refilled two or three times with fresh recruits, and volunteers were drying up. More and more crippled and disabled men—many strangely restless, impatient, unnaturally sensitive to loud noises, and too-often reaching for the only medication they knew, now illegal—arrived back in the province's villages, towns, and cities. Finally, 1916 brought bereavement to the private and public world of the province, and the first signs that reckoning the price of victory would be almost unbearable. And still no victory was in sight. Now was the time for sober, determined, and angry persistence. After 1916 many Albertans were willing to stop at nothing to win. It would be left to the survivors to judge whether or not it was worth it. Little Jeannie Alexander learned that freedom had a high price.

Notes

A longer version of this article was previously published as "Enthusiasm Embattled: 1916 and the Great War," in *Alberta Formed Alberta Transformed*, vol. 2, edited by Michael Payne, Donald Wetherell, and Catherine Cavanaugh (Calgary and Edmonton: University of Calgary Press and University of Alberta Press, 2006), 386–411. The co-editors wish to thank the author and the University of Calgary and University of Alberta presses for permission to republish.

1   Grande Prairie Pioneer Museum and Archives (AB), Jean (Alexander) O'Brien papers.

2   John Herd Thompson, *The Harvests of War: The Prairie West, 1914–1918* (Toronto: McClelland and Stewart, 1978), 13, 45–49, 56. See also James G. MacGregor, *A History of Alberta* (Edmonton: Hurtig, 1981 [1972]), 219–26. Another group of men prone to enlistment were underpaid and overtaxed teachers in many isolated rural schools. See Paul Voisey, *Vulcan: The Making*

of a Prairie Community (Toronto: University of Toronto Press, 1988), 179.

3   On Trochu, see Donald B. Smith, "A History of French-Speaking Albertans," in *Peoples of Alberta: Portraits of Cultural Diversity*, edited by Howard Palmer and Tamara Palmer (Saskatoon: Western Producer Prairie Books, 1985), 93–94. On the British elite in the Foothills and their war, see Patrick A. Dunae, ed., *Rancher's Legacy: Alberta Essays by Lewis G. Thomas* (Edmonton: University of Alberta Press, 1986), 46, 57, 83, 92–94, 107, 165–66. On the war ending the era of the "remittance man" in Alberta, see Howard Palmer and Tamara Palmer, *Alberta: A New History* (Edmonton: Hurtig, 1990), 55.

4   *Lethbridge Daily Herald*, 18 August 1914, 6. See also Robert MacDonald, "The Methodist Church in Alberta during the First World War," *Canadian Methodist Historical Society Papers, 1993–1994*, 146–49.

5   Thompson, *Harvests of War*, 14–23.

6   *Lethbridge Daily Herald*, 5 June 1916. See also 3–6 June 1916, passim.

7   Peter Bush, *Western Challenge: The Presbyterian Church in Canada's Mission on the Prairies and in the North, 1885–1925* (Winnipeg: Watson Dwyer, 2002), 226–28, 231, 235–36. The merger of Protestant denominations was hotly debated in Canada in the early years of the twentieth century. In 1925, the United Church was founded merging four Protestant congregations: the Methodist Church of Canada, the Congregational Union of Ontario and Quebec, two-thirds of the congregations of the Presbyterian Church in Canada, and the Association of Local Union Churches. The total membership was about 600,000.

8   MacDonald, "The Methodist Church in Alberta," 150–62.

9   Voisey, *Vulcan*, 163, 227, 232, and Paul Voisey, *High River and the Times, 1901–1966: An Alberta Community and Its Weekly Newspaper* (Edmonton: University of Alberta Press, 2004), 57.

10 Grande Prairie Pioneer Museum and Archives (AB), Minutes of the Agnes Forbes Women's Auxiliary, Glen Leslie Presbyterian Church, 1914–1921. See also Voisey, *Vulcan*, 171, 240–41, and "The 'Votes for Women' Movement," *Alberta History* 23, no. 3 (1975): 10–23. Near Foremost, one of the most ingenious schemes involved a woman whose crippled chicken laid enough eggs for the chicks to be sold to buy a piglet. When it was raised, the woman raffled it for $25, and the new owner raffled it again for the same amount. As a result, cheered the local paper, the crippled hen contributed $50 to the Red Cross. See David C. Jones, *Empire of Dust* (Calgary: University of Calgary Press, 1987), 84.

11 Ibid., 39–44, 87–94.

12 John Herd Thompson, "'The Beginning of Our Regeneration': The Great War and Western Canadian Reform Movements," in *Prophecy and Protest: Social Movements in Twentieth Century Canada*, edited by S.D. Clark, Paul Grayson, and Linda Grayson (Toronto: Gage, 1975), 91, 96–101, and Thompson, *Harvests of War*, 97–105. On the Women's Institute and the 1917 Dower Act, see Catherine Cole and Judy Larmour, *Many and Remarkable: The Story of Alberta Women's Institutes* (Edmonton: Alberta Women's Institutes, 1997), 11.

13 Ibid., 39–44, 87–94.

14 J.L. Granatstein and Desmond Morton, *Marching to Armageddon: Canadians and the Great War, 1914–1919* (Toronto: Lester & Orpen Denys, 1988), 184.

15 See Robert Rutherdale's excellent study of the Great War's effect on Lethbridge, Guelph, and Three Rivers, *Hometown Horizons: Local Responses to Canada's Great War* (Vancouver: UBC Press, 2004). On demonization of the "enemy alien," see chapter 4. See also Robert Allen Rutherdale, "The Home Front: Consensus and Conflict in Lethbridge, Guelph and Trois-Rivieres during the Great War" (PhD diss., York University, 1993), 145.

16 On the Lethbridge Home Guard and its anxiety over the CPR, see Rutherdale, *Hometown Horizons*, 192–93, 219–22; also Rutherdale, "The Home Front," 145–50. On the internment camp, see *Hometown Horizons*, 143–53. Rutherdale provides an informative and detailed discussion of the topic in his dissertation, chapter 3.

17 Jones, *Empire of Dust*, 88.

18 Voisey, *Vulcan*, 65, 85, 97, 116–17, 117–18.

19 Jones, *Empire of Dust*, 88–91.

20 Voisey, *High River and the Times*, 81–82.

21 Thompson, *Harvests of War*, 45–46, 69–70.

22 Ibid., 56–62.

23 Voisey, *Vulcan*, 106, 111, 114, 133, 148–49, 215, and Jones, *Empire of Dust*, 88, 87–102. On farmers' higher incomes but resistance to conscription, see Voisey, *Vulcan*, 243–44, and Jones, *Empire of Dust*, 86.

24 Jones, *Empire of Dust*, 85–86; also Palmer and Palmer, *Alberta: A New History*, 107.

25 Donald G. Wetherell and Irene R.A. Kmet, *Alberta's North: A History, 1890–1950* (Edmonton: University of Alberta, Circumpolar Institute, and Alberta Community Development, 2000), 98–103, 120–21, 174.

26 Ibid., 137–44, 172, 175–79.

27 Ibid., 92–95, 132–33, 151. Significantly, the federal government–amalgamated Canadian National Railway showed no interest in the two shaky firms, leaving the CPR and other groups to salvage the lines.

28 Ibid., 133, 154–73, 242–43.

29 Ibid., 50–51. On Lethbridge's successful lobby and the economic benefits of local recruiting, see Rutherdale, "The Home Front," 80–82.

30 Donald Wetherell and Irene Kmet, *Town Life: Main Street and the Evolution of Small Town Alberta, 1880–1947* (Edmonton: University of Alberta Press, 1995), 133.

31 MacGregor, *History of Alberta*, 230.

32 Rutherdale, *Hometown Horizons*, 193–214.

33 C.R. Kilford, *Lethbridge at War: 1900–1996* (Lethbridge, AB: Battery Books and Publishing, 1996), 42–44; and *Lethbridge Daily Herald*, 28 October 1916, 1.

34 Kilford, *Lethbridge at War*, 45–47. Also see *Lethbridge Daily Herald*, 26 June 1916, 1; and James McWilliams and K. James Steele, *The Suicide Battalion* (Edmonton: Hurtig, 1978), 26.

35 James L. Dempsey, *Warriors of the King* (Regina: Canadian Plains Research Centre, 1999), 25–28, 47–52, 55–56.

36 Ibid., 19, 26–29, 35–37, 55.

37 Ibid., 104, 106; also *Lethbridge Daily Herald*, 11 August 1914, 1, and 27 February 1917, 1.

38 Dempsey, *Warriors of the King*, 73–79, 80.

39 G.R. Stevens, *A City Goes to War: History of the Loyal Edmonton Regiment* (Brampton, ON: Charters Publishing Company, 1964), 18, 152.

40 *Calgary Daily Herald*, 3 January 1916. On Lethbridge, see Rutherdale, *Hometown Horizons*, 59–60. Rutherdale's detailed and illuminating discussion of soldier "relief, not charity" by the Patriotic Fund and other organizations in Lethbridge shows how the volunteer effort was more about keeping the social order at home intact than about fulfilling its own rhetoric. See *Hometown Horizons*, 91–98, 102–3, 106–11.

41 Granatstein and Morton, *Marching to Armageddon*, 23. Also see Stevens, *A City Goes to War*, 151–52.

42 Thompson, *Harvests of War*, 165.

43 Stevens, *A City Goes to War*, 152.

44 Galt Museum and Archives (Lethbridge, AB), Red Cross Minute Book, 1914–1921.

45 Rutherdale, *Hometown Horizons*, 116–17. Also see Rutherdale, "The Home Front," 39, 94–126, 128, 157–58, and Kilford, *Lethbridge at War*, 52.

46 Rutherdale, *Hometown Horizons*, 234–239. Also see Rutherdale, "The Home Front," 12–13, 372–75, 379–81.

47 Rutherdale, "The Home Front," 158–59. On the divisive 1917 election and the conscription of wealth issue in Lethbridge, see Rutherdale, *Hometown Horizons*, 166–77.

48 *Calgary Daily Herald*, 5 January 1916.

49 Rutherdale, "The Home Front," 88–89, 151–52, 273–74. Vulcan and Carmangay farmers were also distressed at the lack of harvesters owing to recruiting at this stage of the war, and had little sympathy with conscription. See Voisey, *Vulcan*, 145, 242.

50 Granatstein and Morton, *Marching to Armageddon*, 34.

51 Ibid., 50–56.

52 Ibid., 56–59.

53 James G. MacGregor, *Edmonton: A History* (Edmonton: Hurtig, 1967), 215–19, and *History of Alberta*, 234.

54 MacGregor, *History of Alberta*, 232.

55 Rutherdale, "The Home Front," 279–87.

56 Palmer and Palmer, *Alberta: A New History*, 182–85.

57 Janice Tyrwhitt, et al., *Alberta in the 20th Century*, vol. 4, *The Great War and Its Consequences, 1914–1920* (Edmonton: Western Canadian Communications, 1994), 265–67. Rutherdale, "The Home Front," 240.

58 *Lethbridge Daily Herald*, 6 June 1916.

59 Voisey, *Vulcan*, 185.

60 On Alberta's enlistments and casualties, see Palmer and Palmer, *Alberta: A New History*, 167.

61 Some of the most trenchant observations on the impact of the war on the climate of opinion in Alberta are found in Palmer and Palmer, *Alberta: A New History*, 185–92, and Gerald Friesen, *The Canadian Prairies: A History* (Toronto: University of Toronto Press, 1987), 347–55.

Works Cited

PRIMARY SOURCES

Calgary Herald
Edmonton Bulletin
Lethbridge Daily Herald

Galt Museum and Archives, Lethbridge, AB. Red Cross Minute Book, 1914–1921.

Grande Prairie Pioneer Museum and Archives, AB. Jean (Alexander) O'Brien papers.

——. Minutes of the Agnes Forbes Women's Auxiliary, Glen Leslie Presbyterian Church, 1914–1921.

Library and Archives Canada. RG9 Militia and Defence, Series IIIC15, CEF, Canadian Chaplain Service.

SECONDARY SOURCES

Babcock, D.R. *Alexander Cameron Rutherford: A Gentleman of Strathcona*. Calgary: Friends of Rutherford House and the University of Calgary, 1989.

Bennett, S.G. *The 4th Canadian Mounted Rifles, 1914–1919*. Toronto: Murray, 1926.

Bercuson, David J. *The Patricias: The Proud History of a Fighting Regiment*. Toronto: Stoddart, 2001.

Bush, Peter. *Western Challenge: The Presbyterian Church in Canada's Mission on the Prairies and in the North, 1885–1925*. Winnipeg: Watson Dwyer, 2002.

Chadderton, Cliff. *The Fragment*. Summer 1971, 3–19.

Clark, Gregory. *A Bar'l of Apples: A Gregory Clark Omnibus*. Toronto: McGraw-Hill Ryerson [1971].

Cole, Catherine, and Judy Larmour. *Many and Remarkable: The Story of Alberta Women's Institutes*. Edmonton: Alberta Women's Institutes, 1997.

Dancocks, Daniel. *Gallant Canadians: The Story of the Tenth Canadian Infantry Battalion, 1914–1919*. Calgary: Calgary Highlanders Regimental Fund Foundation, 1990.

Dempsey, L. James. *Warriors of the King*. Regina: Canadian Plains Research Centre, 1999.

Duguid, A.F. *Official History of the Canadian Forces in the Great War 1914–1919*. Vol. 1, *Chronology, Appendices and Maps*. Ottawa: King's Printer, 1938.

Dunae, Patrick, ed. *Ranchers' Legacy: Alberta Essays by Lewis G. Thomas*. Edmonton: University of Alberta Press, 1986.

Friesen, Gerald. *The Canadian Prairies: A History*. Toronto: University of Toronto Press, 1987.

Granatstein, J.L., and Desmond Morton. *Marching to Armageddon: Canadians and the Great War, 1914–1919*. Toronto: Lester & Orpen Denys, 1988.

Jones, David C. *Empire of Dust*. Calgary: University of Calgary Press, 1987.

Kilford, C.R. *Lethbridge at War*. Lethbridge, AB: Battery Books and Publishing, 1996.

MacDonald, Robert. "The Methodist Church in Alberta during the First World War." *Canadian Methodist Historical Papers, 1993–1994*, 145–69.

MacEwan, Grant. *Eye-Opener Bob*. Saskatoon: Western Producer Book Service, 1974.

MacGregor, James G. *Edmonton: A History*. Edmonton: Hurtig, 1967.

——. *A History of Alberta*. Edmonton: Hurtig, 1981. First published 1972.

McWilliams, James, and K. James Steele. *The Suicide Battalion*. Edmonton: Hurtig, 1978.

Palmer, Howard, and Tamara Palmer. *Alberta: A New History*. Edmonton: Hurtig, 1990.

Rutherdale, Robert Allen. "The Home Front: Consensus and Conflict in Lethbridge, Guelph and Trois-Rivieres during the Great War." PhD diss., York University, 1993.

———. *Hometown Horizons: Local Responses to Canada's Great War*. Vancouver: UBC Press, 2004.

Stevens, G.R. *A City Goes to War: History of the Loyal Edmonton Regiment*. Brampton, ON: Charters Publishing Company, 1964.

Thompson, John Herd. "'The Beginning of Our Regeneration': The Great War and Western Canadian Reform Movements." In *Prophecy and Protest: Social Movements in Twentieth Century Canada*, edited by S.D. Clark, Paul Grayson, and Linda Grayson, 87–104. Toronto: Gage, 1975.

———. *The Harvests of War: The Prairie West, 1914–1918*. Toronto: McClelland and Stewart, 1978.

Tyrwhitt, Janice, et al. *Alberta in the 20th Century*. Vol. 4, *The Great War and Its Consequences, 1914–1920*. Edmonton: Western Canadian Communications, 1994.

Voisey, Paul. *High River and the Times, 1901–1966: An Alberta Community and Its Weekly Newspaper*. Edmonton: University of Alberta Press, 2004.

———. "The 'Votes for Women' Movement." *Alberta History* 23, no. 3 (1975): 10–23.

———. *Vulcan: The Making of a Prairie Community*. Toronto: University of Toronto Press, 1988.

Wetherell, Donald G., and Irene R.A. Kmet. *Alberta's North: A History, 1890–1950*. Edmonton: University of Alberta and Canadian Circumpolar Press, and Alberta Community Development, 2000.

Wheeler, Victor. *The 50th Battalion in No Man's Land*. Calgary: Alberta Historical Resources Foundation, 1980.

Ordinary Life in Alberta in the First World War

ARITHA VAN HERK

The nascent towns and cities of Alberta could not have imagined how the experience of the First World War would affect them. Far away from the centres of culture and conflict, the people of Alberta pulled themselves through the four years of the war with a mixture of pragmatism and resilience, to some extent responding to world events but, in other ways, practising a blinkered focus concerned with matters close to home and the context of day-to-day life.

In one photograph that speaks volumes about this divide between home and the conflict in Europe, two battalions march south on 9th Street in Calgary, visible behind them Grace Presbyterian Church and the Devenish Apartments. In the road stands a child watching their progress. It is impossible to reconstruct what the child might have thought, although he has clearly interrupted his play. It is, with hindsight, even more difficult to contemplate the soldiers' good cheer: they are smiling, energized, and healthy. The city behind them is clustered low to the ground—a young city, optimistic, if inexperienced. The column of men forms a solid, heavy line on the road while the people on the sidewalk observe them from a cautious distance, with an interested and yet strangely

detached curiosity. The gap between what the bodies of those men would endure and what the people of Alberta would encounter in the four years of the war is enormous. At home, daily life was altered but not interrupted; it was disturbed but not curtailed. That rift between the two experiences would be a fracture that altered Alberta as it knew itself.

It is, one hundred years later, easy to recite the statistics, the dates, and names that toll behind the vague geography of "over there." But how can today's Albertan worm into the mindset of the average citizen between 1914 and 1918, living in a province enjoying the boom of new immigration, the optimism of the West, and agrarian wealth? We can measure certain events: in August 1913 a grand new Hudson's Bay Company store opened in Calgary; in May 1914 the Dingman Well blew in; in June 1914 the Hillcrest Mine Disaster happened. Government documents tell us that the average monthly wage of a farm labourer in the summer of 1914 was $40.26 with board, while a female could earn $23.63.[1] The essentials of life are work, food, and sleep. That has not changed. But larger events ignore the significance of the diurnal. Social interaction and neighbourly

The 50th and 31st Battalions, Canadian Expeditionary Force, marching up 9th Street SW hill in winter, Calgary, Alberta, 1915. Glenbow Archives, NC-44-39.

connection measure the foundations of private character and public engagement. Day-to-day requirements and desires articulate routine but reveal as well the invisible pressures of the outside world on individuals in what was considered a remote corner of the Empire.

But how to taste what ordinary people tasted? What were their joys and disappointments? The

50th Battalion, Calgary Regiment, parading on 1st Street SW, Calgary, Alberta, October 1915. Glenbow Archives, NA 4218-1.

private grief of losing a husband, a son, or a father is untranslatable; casualty lists without context are bare and almost sterile. Men in war partake of a structured narrative: recruitment, enlistment, training and fighting, repatriation, and then, once war is over, re-assimilation into daily life. Their needs are attended to by military organization and management, and they must work together in a cooperative system. Family and community, who have sent their youngest and strongest off to fight in another country, face as well unpredictable challenges, a different set of contingencies. How did ordinary life—here in Alberta—continue its practical and necessary course?

It is said that if you want to do research on a historical person, or a time, it is better not to read about the subject but to read what that person, or what one in that milieu, would have read. Accordingly, to tease out just a few elements of life in Alberta between 1914 and 1918, I have sifted through the newspapers of the day, not in search of the names of battles or heroes, but for the quotidian, the commonplace, the marvellously revelatory advertisement asking for a girl able to candle eggs.

Does the trepidation that families felt when they saw the telegraph boy or girl (for women too served as bicycle messengers) turning into their lane carry over to the bicycle itself? Were the dreaded words "killed in action," and "regret to inform you," made more or less painful by the fact that the bicycle, that almost playful vehicle, was touted as a way to save carfare and shoe leather? An ad in the *Calgary Daily Herald* on 8 May 1918 claimed that "Bicycles are coming into general favor now ... The bike is handy for city work, and men, women, boys and girls can use it to advantage."[2] Did such an item sting more deeply for its personal etching of grief?

Certainly, communities shared sorrows and losses brought about by the war. And, while there was grieving, it was leavened by celebration and humour, chores and structure. Knitting, for example, offers a traceable pattern. In general accounts of activities of the time, knitting is one of the occupations that women undertook; the hands that wielded needles and wool made more than the socks that were sent to men whose feet rotted in the muck of the trenches. Advertisements were filled with offerings of yarn comforts for "sailors and soldiers." The metaphysical comfort of knitting could be read as a war weapon; knitting became a part of the structure of at-home memory. The knitting songs that proliferated were certainly heard in Alberta, words articulating the connection between hand and heart and waiting. Thousands of women contributed to the war by knitting socks for men overseas, memorialized in popular tunes called "I Wonder Who's Knitting for Me," "Each Stitch Is a Thought of You," and "Knitting All the Day."[3] The knitting craze was a concrete physical behaviour; through knitting, the "Soldier Girls at Home" could feel themselves an integral part of the war effort. Notices in the paper emphasized the habit, which became as normal as breathing: "Major Fitz. Horrigan has been informed by the Military Chapter of the I.O.D.E. [Imperial Order Daughters of the Empire] that they are sending 100 pairs of socks to the late members of the force that left here recently in connection with the overseas draft. This gift, the major states, will be much appreciated by the men."[4] Women knitted so much that on 4 January 1915 the *Calgary Daily Herald* included an item that asked, tongue-in-cheek, "At the rate the women are going at it, isn't there a danger that some of them will be going knitty before the war ends?"[5] As might have been the case, since knitting was both social and patriotic.

This combination of the practical and the charitable argues for a community structure that merged responsibility with entertainment. The newspapers of the day identified dances and whist drives and teas, with proceeds going to the Red Cross Society or the Princess Patricia Red Cross Hospital fund. The outreach of formal Red Cross groups was augmented by the activities of organizations such as the Loyal True Blue Friends, the American Woman's Club, the Daughters and Maids of England Benevolent Society, along with various church groups. The Women's Canadian Club held tag days—days on which money was collected on the street and donors given "tags" to show they had contributed— in support of the club's war service. During one year at the end of the war it gave $1,000 to the YMCA for its work among soldiers and to assist in local activities for the comfort of the returned men. All entertainment needed to have a useful outcome related to the war.

And such support was work, blurring the line between labour and pleasure. The *Calgary Daily Herald* reported on 6 November 1916 that:

> Two hundred and forty-nine jars of fruit and one dollar were received by the Samaritan club at the shower held on Saturday afternoon

Red Cross tea, Fort Macleod, Alberta, 1915. Glenbow Archives, NA-2883-4.

Group outside Ogden Military Hospital, Calgary, Alberta, ca. 1915–18. Glenbow Archives, NA-1616-2.

and evening for the Soldiers' Convalescent Home at Ogden. In view of the high price of living this year, and especially the increased price of sugar the ladies consider the response to their appeal very gratifying. The contributions consisted of jams, jellies, preserved fruit and home-made pickles. There have been a number of jam showers this season and owing to the many demands for patriotic causes the response could scarcely be expected to come up to that of last year, which was 1,200 jars.[6]

The idea of feeding veterans with what could be made pragmatically linked the needs of the men with the provisioning skills of the women. The "boys" in the Ogden Military Convalescent Hospital (formerly the Ogden Hotel owned by the Calgary Brewing and Malting Company and during the war donated by the company to the Alberta Red Cross) were tangible reminders of the war's injured, and immediate recipients of charity and entertainment. Organizations would visit to perform songs, solos and duets, and the ladies to distribute "smokes" to the men.

Civilian or soldier, the tension between those who had been in the war and those who watched from a distance was evident. On one hand, there was definite pride taken in supporting the military; mixed social events usually declared, "Veterans half price." In 1915 it was reported that "Miss Forsythe, of the Blue Moon tea-room in Edmonton, has generously offered to supply free of charge a cup of tea during the afternoon to all officers and men of the third contingent stationed in Edmonton during the month of April."[7] But, by the end of the war, some churches took to questioning the morals of soldiers, and sermons were preached about girls talking to soldiers too much (talking apparently being a dangerous occupation that could lead to other activities). Letters to the editor decried equally the loosening of morals and any disapproval of soldiers. One read, "Glad to see someone has taken up the subject in favor of our soldier boys . . . think there has been too much criticizing of the boys by the churches. Where is the harm in a girl talking to a soldier any more than a civilian? If a girl is getting into trouble or that way inclined she don't [sic] have to go with a soldier to do so. Why try to disgrace the uniform?"[8] Private Bowie from the 21st Battalion responded rather bitterly: "On behalf of myself and other men of the 21st battalion, I wish to say that we are sorry that we have stayed in Calgary so long to be bombarded by the parsons and their clique. We would rather be bombed by German shells. It would be more to our liking."[9] The attempt to assert moral order may have been a result of the length of time that the war had dragged on, or it may have been an indication of how women's roles were changing, and their lives beginning to assume different contours. After all, suffrage had been granted in 1916, and women were flexing their right to speak, vote, and behave without the strictures of the past.

For while the men were away, women undertook jobs traditionally associated with men—farm work and physical labour. In tandem with increased activity, women began to insist on clothing that enhanced their freedom. Trouserettes came into vogue, and although there was still advice about what "well-dressed" women were wearing (smart little coats and jackets), other advertisements spoke to the wave of the future:

New Togs For The War Farmerette
The young woman on the step-ladder in the picture herewith, with a feather duster rampant is not pursuing a fugitive fly, nor is she dusting down the wall paper in housecleaning. She is demonstrating how much easier it is for women to work in these war times in a new garment called 'womanalls' than in the skirts to which women have been accustomed many years. They are just like the gardener's overalls, only they are more commodious where necessary, and, it will be observed, each pantaloon buttons snugly about the ankle. Obviously, the idea of the snug fitting anklets is to defeat any inquisitive mouse in exercising its time honoured and probably constitutional right of frightening girls. As many young women are doing farm work as their 'bit,' and as they have heard that field mice are quite inquisitive, 'womanalls' seems to have relieved one condition that threatened the very structure and foundation of farmerettes.[10]

The ad's tone is condescending, but women were doing farm work, and heavier work than they had done in the past.

Although women were physically engaged, there was still a patronizing desire to shield them from too much knowledge. An advertisement for the "Magic and Mystery Show, CUNNING, to commence at the Grand Theatre on July 9, 1917," indicates one

"Matinee for Ladies only," but "Girls under 16 not admitted."[11] And the steady advertising of Lydia Pinkham's Vegetable Compound (a herbal-alcohol mixture), to "ease nervousness and indigestion," suggests that the sensitivities of women were assumed and marketed to with a deliberate pitch.[12]

The casualty lists recorded names of men whom the community knew, remarked on, mourned, and remembered. Despite that threnody, throughout the war forms of play persisted, another means by which the tenor of the age can be deciphered. Old country soccer leagues continued, and there were holiday sports, skating, roller skating, curling, and football, with matches held between soldiers and civilians. Albertans' energetic embrace of sports persisted despite the hovering shadow of war, evidenced by the annoyance when a golf tournament at Banff was cancelled in September 1918:

> Banff, Sept. 4—The local golf man are [sic] much disappointed at the action of the Ottawa authorities in withdrawing their support of the championship tournament which was booked for September 14. A wire was received this morning saying that it would be undesirable to have a tournament owing to the war. The local committee therefore, have [sic] no option but to cancel all arrangements.[13]

The tone of such deliberations suggests that, whatever Ottawa authorities might decree, the games would go on, and the distant thunder in Europe had worn everyone's patience thin. Horse racing in Alberta persisted as a popular sport with a long pedigree going back to Chief Factor John Rowand's having built a two-mile racetrack at Fort Edmonton in 1825. The Millarville Races, west of Calgary,

begun in 1905, were discontinued in 1916 and 1917, but resumed in 1918, with proceeds donated to the Red Cross. In 1915, races at the Calgary Exhibition included a "green pony race; ½-mile dash, open only to Alberta-bred ponies that have never won money." At "Calgary's Big Fair," the Industrial Exhibition of July 1917, attendance figures were high, with auto speed racing the strongest attraction.[14]

Cars were the wave of the future, machines full of possibility. Accidents received notice because they were unusual ("Seven Motor Car Accidents Cause Loss To Owners: No One Hurt—Woman, Boy, and Man Are Knocked Down by Other Cars But Are Unhurt"), and the siren song of the automobile had begun to increase in decibels.[15] Auto Clubs arranged drives as outings, with a "pathfinder" familiar with the roads to lead the motoring parties, who would be entertained at various stops along the way. Part of the goal of these jaunts was to promote the organization of clubs, which would lobby for the improvement of road conditions in Alberta. Of course, the "proceeds" always went to patriotic funds, so the war was acknowledged, even if it was left behind in the dust.

Daredevil Auto Driving was a key attraction on the last day of the Calgary Industrial Exhibition in 1917. The *Calgary Daily Herald* of July 5 noted: "One of the largest crowds that ever turned out for any grandstand attraction packed the seating capacity and swarmed the front space during the entire afternoon in order to catch a fleeting glimpse of the dust-dogs as they tore around, lap after lap. No one was disappointed, for the boys gave a high class performance and showed up remarkably well on the half-mile speedway, which is not really suited to auto racing."[16] On the final night, a local driver's car skidded around one of the turns and crashed through a fence; the driver died at midnight in the General

Hospital as a result of his injuries. But the races were nevertheless considered a great success.

To top that, there was to be a race between an airplane "driven" by "young woman aviator" Miss Katherine Stinson (the "Flying Schoolgirl") and a speed automobile driven by George Clark, the Texas speed king. The race did not come off, as high winds prevented Stinson from keeping to the circuit; she was blown off course. A barnstormer, Stinson visited Edmonton and Calgary for the 1916, 1917, and 1918 exhibitions. But she contributed to the war effort too by providing the prize for a Red Cross aviation contest: "Mrs. Stoney and Miss Halliday were winners: Mrs. Stoney sold the largest number of tickets and Miss Halliday drew the lucky number entitling her to a ride with the aviatrix."[17] Stinson was an even bigger attraction when she returned in 1918, flying her new Curtiss Stinson Special biplane in a series of demonstration flights. She performed at the Edmonton and Lethbridge Exhibitions; on 9 July 1918 she flew a sack with 259 items of mail from Calgary to Edmonton, marking western Canada's first airmail flight with an actual flying time of 2 hours, 5 minutes. Even though the audience knew that flight was one of the means by which the war was waged, it had irresistible excursion appeal.

But locomotion and travel were to face curtailment by the push to end the war. In September 1918 a request was made to all service stations and garages in Canada to discontinue the sale of gasoline for use in pleasure cars on Sundays, so as to conserve the supply of gasoline for war purposes. Sunday joy riding came to an end.

Pleasure and forgetting were both manifest in the live entertainments and "photo plays" offered at the theatres, from gripping detective stories to the antics of the Keystone Kops to rag-time tunes sung in a snappy fashion. Bills listed plays and comedies, and occasionally noted that "none of the shows refer to the war!" although, by September 1918, *To Hell With The Kaiser* and *The Claws of the Hun*, as well as a six-reel war picture titled SMASHING THE HINDENBURG LINE, the "Last Official British War Film To Date," were shown.[18] That mingling of information and entertainment, support and pleasure culminated in a war character that invisibly shaped the province of Alberta.

Women's increased responsibilities marked both the extension of suffrage and the introduction of prohibition. Drinking and smoking were part of the male world, with men hosting a "smoker" as a means of relaxation. Even Premier Sifton, in April 1915, refused to agree that all hotel bars in the province should be closed at 7 p.m. instead of 10 p.m. for the period of the war. He based his refusal on the argument it would not be right to alter the current law in view of the fact that the people of the province were to vote on the prohibition question. When the amendment came into full force on 5 July 1916, it was not permissible for any person to keep more than one quart of spirits and two gallons of malt, and there could be no advertising of liquor. But by 1918 recipes for dandelion wine were published, as if homemade alcohol was exempt. By then, after four years of war, even teetotallers could dream of a drink. A typical recipe was as follows:

Pour one gallon of boiling water over three quarts of dandelion flowers. Let stand 24 hours. Strain and add five pounds of light brown sugar, juice and rind of two lemons and of two oranges. Let boil ten minutes and strain. When cold add half a cake of any good yeast, put in crock and let stand until it commences to work. Bottle, putting corks in loose to allow working. In each bottle put one raisin after it stops working. Cork tight.[19]

What effect the raisin had is a mystery, but a good housekeeper knew about such kitchen tricks.

The price of food, along with the availability of sugar and flour, was always a concern. The outbreak of the war initiated a higher demand for agricultural products, and shortages were noticeable. A housewife might typically do her marketing three times a week, but now market days were reduced because farm produce did not come in sufficient quantity to make that many trips worthwhile. Sales of cooking and baking products were a popular way to raise funds for the Red Cross, and markets always had a Red Cross booth, run on donations of homemade cakes, bread, and pies. In 1918 the big flour mills in western Canada were told by the Canada Food Board to ship all wheat on hand, over and above 10 days' supply, meaning that local flour mills could not plan to run continuously until the new crop of grain arrived. An indication of the shortage of dairy meant that "all cows in the city from which milk is sold will be given a tuberculin test free of charge," which would now enable the owners to sell unpasteurized milk to anyone.[20] Vacant lots were used for gardens so as not to waste arable space. The Food Board, which was established in 1917, brought in more than 38 food regulations, especially to do with flour and sugar; icing and the making of candies became illegal; and the hoarding of flour or sugar, punishable with fines or imprisonment. Domestic support of the war effort was obviously serious business.

The need to support not only the men who had gone overseas to fight but also the families they left behind continued to inform the character of the province, and dual expectations of work and productivity. Yet Alberta was also becoming aware of the necessity of larger talents and skills. The University of Alberta had been accepting students since 1908 and in May 1916 celebrated its sixth annual convocation, reporting that "The affair was essentially a khaki one, many of the graduates attached to local regiments appearing in khaki, while the Alberta company of the Universities battalion were present in a body and formed a guard of honor to the lieutenant-governor. Twenty-seven students received the degree of B.A., eight the degree of Bachelor of Science, ten the degree of Bachelor of Laws, one the degree of Bachelor of Divinity, seven the degree of Master of Arts and three the degree of Master of Science."[21] Later the newspaper reported that eight students, three from Calgary, were entitled to scholarships at the University of Alberta on the basis of their matriculation examinations, worth $25 and payable to the student upon registration. Alberta was clearly beginning to recognize that, war or no war, the population of the province needed to grow and educate itself in order to take its place in the larger world.

Meanwhile, there was a sharp rise in the number of children between six and ten, so much so that schools were crowded and inadequate, and deputations of citizens visited the school board arguing that conditions needed to be improved. There was the predictable problem of boys working instead of attending school. While one might assume that children would be oblivious to the conflict in Europe, the repeated stories of children starving in Belgium had an effect. The *Calgary Daily Herald* reported: "Little Miss Cecilia Fendall, of Okotoks, decided that she wanted to raise money to give to the 'poor Belgian babies and the soldiers held captive by the Germans' [*sic*] . . . She took her most cherished doll and proceeded to raffle it off. The results of the splendid sacrifice on the part of the dollie's young mother amounted to $7.50, which has been divided between the Belgian relief and the Allied prisoners of war."[22] Stories of the deprivations of war had found their way into everyone's home.

The account of Little Miss Cecilia Fendall suggests that patriotism can be tracked by its manifestation in small and unlikely corners. But the same feeling had an opposite side: intolerance. People complained that, while some were sacrificing luxuries in order to swell the coffers of the Canadian Patriotic Fund, it was galling to see neighbouring districts contributing nothing. There were complaints of settlements almost entirely populated by "Germans" taking advantage of the times to become more and more wealthy, attending sales where young men sold land and equipment at a sacrifice in order to enlist, of profiteers buying implements and stock at a bargain, but donating nothing to the Patriotic Fund. The starving Belgians and the Belgian Relief Fund too raised questions. Did the money go to deserving recipients or was it simply drained from those at home? The war required investment and belief, but the cost of living did not go down, and some asked whether all those deaths in an unimaginable land were worth it. Only a handful of the men who had enlisted were coming home. Reality and loss had crossed the ocean, and ghosts haunted the optimism that had accompanied 1914.

Thus, when the ear-splitting screeching of a whistle on a CPR locomotive, at 1:30 in the morning on Monday, 11 November 1918, announced the end of the debacle, it is unsurprising that Albertans were relieved. The weather for Alberta that day was fair and cool. The evil Kaiser had been vanquished.

When the news that Germany had accepted the terms of surrender was confirmed, the fire chief in Calgary threw open the doors to the fire hall and sounded the bells on the fire-fighting equipment—for a full 15 minutes. The noise drew people into town, and soon the veterans had started a parade, which grew in magnitude as the day progressed. Everyone partied, some all day and night long. The *Calgary Daily Herald* noted that the "alarm raised over the alleged shortage of liquor in the province was somewhat premature, not to say unnecessary," for the revellers had no trouble finding spirits to fuel their jubilation.[23] The official events took place the next day, November 12, when people threw over the traces of decorum, and celebrated having survived four long years of anxiety and deprivation. And, if the joy of victory was interspersed with articles about the severity of the influenza outbreak and the need for volunteer nurses, on that day at least, hearts and minds united across the distance between Europe and Alberta.

What then to conclude about the gap between the official sombreness of war and the tedious but necessary ritual of day-to-day life? This divide was lived by those who grew gardens and chopped wood and tried to make cookies with less sugar, as much as by those men who saw the carnage of the trenches. Their experiences are not comparable, but the home front's desire to continue life's pleasures and necessities might have been what that lost generation sacrificed so much to ensure.

Notes

1   Statistics Canada, Table: "Average wages of farm help in Canada, by province, 1909, 1910 and 1914 to 1916," URL: http://www65.statcan.gc.ca/acybo2/1917/ acybo2_191702028-eng.htm, retrieved 13 April 2014.

2   "Canada's Cycle Week, May 4th to 11th – Buy A Bicycle, It Will Save Health, Wealth And Time," *Calgary Daily Herald*, 8 May 1918.

3   The Knitmore Podcast, URL: http://www.cdbaby.com/AlbumDetails.aspx?AlbumID=melaniegall2, retrieved 13 April 2014.

4   "Send Socks to R.N.W.M.P.," *Calgary Daily Herald*, 16 May 1918.

5   "Pertinent and Impertinent," *Calgary Daily Herald*, 4 January 1915.

6   "Shower Brings 249 Jars Fruit For Home," *Calgary Daily Herald*, 6 November 1916.

7   "Calgary Society," *Calgary Daily Herald*, 9 April 1915.

8   J.A. McCaw, letter, "Soldiers and Girls: A Very Sensible Letter From a Woman With a Heart," *Calgary Daily Herald*, 9 April 1915.

9   Private Bowie, letter, "States His Preference." *Calgary Daily Herald*, 9 April 1915.

10 *Calgary Daily Herald*, 4 July 4 1917.

11 Cunning, advertisement, *Calgary Daily Herald*, 5 July 1917.

12 Lydia E. Pinkham's Vegetable Compound, advertisement, *Calgary Daily Herald*, 2 January 1915.

13 "Golf Tournament At Banff Cancelled," *Calgary Daily Herald*, 4 September 1918.

14 "Races At The Fair This Year; Clip 'Em Out," *Calgary Daily Herald*, 9 April 1915.

15 *Calgary Daily Herald*, 4 September 1918.

16 "Thrilling Exhibition of Daredevil Auto Driving At the Fair Yesterday: Fred Horey Drove Sensational Three-Mile Race Against George Clark and Won by Half a Length—Koetzla Captured the First Heat of the Five-Mile Free-for-all in Hard Run with Horey and Willard—Record Grand Stand Crowd Witnessed the Performance by Speed Demons," *Calgary Daily Herald*, 5 July 1917.

17 "Social and Personal," *Calgary Daily Herald*, 5 July 1917.

18 Allen Theatre, advertisement, *Calgary Daily Herald*, 4 July 1917.

19 "Tried Recipe—Dandelion Wine," *Calgary Daily Herald*, 8 May 1918.

20 "Council Would Let Down Bars on City Herds: City Solicitor to Write to Province for Modification of Rules—Ald. F.J. Marshall Sees Peril in Move—Thinks Outside Producers Might Begin to Slaughter Cattle," *Calgary Daily Herald*, 4 September 1918.

21 "Alberta University Gives Sheepskins: Sixth Annual Convocation of Provincial University Was Held Yesterday," *Calgary Daily Herald*, 11 May 1916.

22 "Cecilia Fendall Raffles Her Doll For War Relief," *Calgary Daily Herald*, 8 May 1918.

23 "Calgarians in Celebration of Huns' Surrender—Screeching Whistle of C.P.R. Locomotive First Signal of event—Crowds Gather Quickly to Cheer Good News—Flash Over C.P.R. News Stirs Canada From Coast to Coast," *Calgary Daily Herald*, 11 November 1918.

Works Cited

PRIMARY SOURCES

Calgary Daily Herald

SECONDARY SOURCES

Calgary Public Library. Community Heritage and Family History blog. URL: http://calgarypubliclibrary.com/blogs/community-heritage-and-family-history?p=486, retrieved 13 May 2014. [site discontinued].

"O valiant hearts who to your glory came": Protestant Responses to Alberta's Great War

NORMAN KNOWLES

On the morning of Sunday, 2 January 1921, the congregation of Knox Presbyterian Church in Calgary gathered to witness the unveiling and dedication of a stained glass memorial window honouring the 53 members of that church who fell in the Great War.[1] As the window was unveiled, the congregation sang "O Valiant Hearts," a hymn based on the words of a poem by Sir John Stanhope Arkwright honouring the supreme sacrifice of the fallen.[2] The hymn, like the window, portrayed the soldier as crusading knight who, like Christ, suffered and died for the redemption of the world. The centre panel shows suffering humanity looking up from a strife-torn world to the risen Christ as the hope of humanity. In one hand, Christ carries the banner of "Triumph over Death," while the other is raised in benediction. In the tracery above the central panel, two angels with scrolls are pictured. One scroll reads: "The Armies of Heaven followed Him"; the other is inscribed: "He hath Prepared for them a City." In the upper tiers (to the left and right of the central pane) four torches sit above shields representing hope, peace, charity, and love. Below stand knights clad in armour of light representing the virtues of fidelity (bearing

the Union Jack and crowned with laurels), nobility, honour, humility, devotion, patience, sincerity, charity (bearing a banner of St. George's Cross), and brotherly love.

The horrors of war are depicted at the foot of each knight along with figures representing a wounded Canadian soldier beholding the heavenly vision; a soldier dying in the arms of a nursing sister bearing an expression of faithful resignation; a dying soldier looking up to the welcoming Christ; and a soldier bowed in penitence. In the distance are seen wounded, dying, and dead soldiers of both contending armies; a village church in flames; a smoking artillery piece; and a wayside shrine that has escaped the ravages of war. Patriotic shields are found at the base of each panel: the beaver and the maple leaf for Canada, the English rose, the crown of Britannia, the shamrock and thistle, and Alberta's coat of arms. The imagery and iconography contained within this "sermon in glass" evocatively captures the faith and beliefs, virtues and values, hopes and expectations, patriotism and pride that shaped how Protestant Albertans responded to the Great War and wished to remember it.[3]

Knox Presbyterian Church in Calgary, Alberta, unveiled on Sunday, 2 January 1921, a stained glass memorial window to its war dead. It was designed by A.J. Larshchild of the Pittsburgh Glass Company in Minneapolis.

St. Paul's Methodist Church, Calgary, Alberta, ca. 1920–25, with an inset of Rev. W.B. Cobbledick. Glenbow Archives, NA-385-1.

In the days following the outbreak of war on 4 August 1914, Protestant preachers throughout Alberta mounted their pulpits and reflected on the meaning of the conflict.[4] Caught up in the patriotic fervour that swept the province, many clergy called upon Albertans to rise up and fulfill their duty to "God, King, and Country." At an open-air church parade at Mewata Park in Calgary, the Rev. C.W.E. Horne, the rector of Christ Church, Elbow Park, praised the "high ideals of the British Empire," and lauded the "spirit of sacrifice" exhibited by the men assembled before him who had courageously volunteered to take up this "glorious work" and "uphold the honor of the flag." Horne believed that the future of Canada was inevitably tied up with that of the British Empire. The Empire, Horne insisted, had a providential mission to uphold and protect Christian virtues of truth, liberty, and justice. Horne maintained that, unlike previous empires, the British

Empire was not brought into this conflict by any desire for gain, but rather by the need to confront unwarranted aggression. As it was a just and necessary war, all Albertans were thus summoned to rally in defence of the right.[5]

Similar views were expressed in Lethbridge by the Rev. W.B. Cobbledick of Wesley Methodist Church. Cobbledick characterized the war as "one of principles" with "liberty and democracy pitted against despotism and autocracy." "Honor," Cobbledick continued, "bade Britain to take her stand and she took it without fear," and "Canada's duty is plainly to assist the Motherland to the utmost of her power." The Rev. Canon Murrell-Wright of St. Augustine's praised the "true patriotism" of the people of Lethbridge for displaying such "unselfishness and sacrifice" in taking up "the Cross and the Flag" against the foe.[6] At McDougall Methodist Church in Edmonton, the Rev. Dr. W.L. Armstrong characterized the war as a regrettable but necessary struggle to defend the weak against the strong, and justice against oppression. Armstrong appealed to notions of Christian manhood, and examples from

Tablet commemorating soldiers who died in the Great War, ca. 1945–65, Photographer/Illustrator: Rosettis Studio, Calgary, Alberta. Glenbow Archives, NA-2575-47. Copied from PA-1444-135.

British history, to rouse his congregation to take up the torches of liberty and righteousness.[7] Such heady appeals to faith and fidelity, to country and empire inspired many Albertans to join in the war effort.

While the language of patriotism and just war certainly prevailed in the pulpit, a few voices offered an alternative perspective during the early months of the war.[8] Vulcan's Presbyterian minister, the Rev. R.W. Glover, questioned the outpouring of patriotic sentiment and war fever, and called upon the church to be a champion of peace. "Let the Church," Glover urged, "but set some word, some example, for wandering humanity to follow. Let her teach them not only the doctrines, but the ways of peace."[9] Such reservations about the war and pleas for peace quickly faded. As the conflict continued, and reports of German atrocities spread, the war was increasingly viewed as a holy crusade against the forces of evil. Nellie McClung, a committed Methodist, long-time peace advocate, and critic of militarism, overcame her opposition to the war when her son Jack enlisted.[10] "When I saw the first troops going away," she recalled in her wartime memoir, *The Next of Kin*, "I wondered how their mothers let them go, and I made up my mind that I would not let my boy go." The sinking of the *Lusitania* opened McClung's eyes "to see the whole truth . . . I saw that we were waging war on the very Prince of Darkness, and I knew that it would be better—a thousand times better—to be dead than to live under the rule of people whose hearts were so utterly black and . . . so stupidly brutal. I knew that no man could die better than in defending civilization from this ghastly thing which threatened her."[11] Most Albertans understood the war as a providential struggle fought for a just cause against an evil enemy, and in support of Christian values embodied by the empire around which they rallied. Like the knights depicted in the memorial window at Knox Presbyterian, Canada's young men were now engaged in a sacred mission to defend not only their country and heritage but Christian civilization itself.

For many Albertans, this great crusade promised to bring about a lasting peace, and the emergence of a "brave new world" based on principles of brotherhood, equality, and justice. Victory, however, required that the battle to redeem humanity be fought on the home front with the same vigour and commitment displayed by the brave men overseas. Inspired by wartime sacrifices, clergy and the champions of social and moral reform urged Albertans to take up the torches of hope, peace, charity, and love and dedicate themselves to building the Kingdom of God by improving the quality of human relations on earth.[12] In a June 1916 address to Methodists meeting in Lethbridge, the Rev. Dr. Armstrong of Edmonton's McDougall Church described the war as "leaven in the world" that promised to give rise to "a much needed reformation." To achieve this "better world," Armstrong insisted that the churches must take the lead in bringing about a "social revival" that would "quicken the public conscience" and "purify politics, industry and labor and capital."[13] These objectives could only be achieved, however, by acknowledging and repenting for the sins that infected society. Citing Christ's own life and witness, Nellie McClung urged those who remained on the home front to "declare war" on "all forms of injustice, all forms of special privilege, all selfishness and all greed," "recast their values," and embrace a "fair deal" for everyone. It is "not wealth or cleverness or skill or power which makes a nation or individual great," she argued, but rather "goodness, gentleness, kindness, the sense of brotherhood, which alone maketh rich and addeth no sorrow."[14]

Knox Presbyterian Church, Calgary, Alberta, ca. 1890s. Photographer/Illustrator: W.E. Wing, Calgary, Alberta. Glenbow Archives, NA-1075-6.

To Henry Wise Wood, the president of the United Farmers of Alberta (UFA) and a devout member of the Disciples of Christ, wartime sacrifices required that Albertans commit themselves to a model of social development grounded in the teachings and example of Jesus Christ.[15] In an address to the UFA Convention of 1917, Wood asserted: "Christ promises us that if we follow his word of Life in the service of God, the great Spirit of Love, we may establish a world-wide Kingdom over which the great force of love will reign supreme, the nations of the earth will bring their glory into it, the force of evil will cease from troubling, and the people be at rest."[16] Cooperation, not competition, Wood insisted, was the basis of a genuinely Christian social order, and true democracy. At a 21 May 1917 Sunday forum organized by the former Methodist minister turned Unitarian activist William Irvine, the Rev. J. Austin Huntley of Calgary's First Baptist Church condemned wartime profiteering, and called upon the churches to assume a more active political role in creating a just society. "Our national and industrial life is unchristian," Huntley argued and "a man is guilty of treason who make great profits in time of war." "When the Church is told to keep out of politics," he concluded, "politics must be rank."[17] Throughout the duration of the war, Protestant Albertans were repeatedly reminded that they could not look only to their own salvation but must work for the salvation of the world as well, if they were to atone for their personal sins, and the collective ills of society, and enjoy the benefits of the Kingdom of God both in this life and the next.

The language of repentance and redemption also informed the movements for prohibition and women's suffrage.[18] Consumption of spirits, prohibition advocates insisted, was a great sin that threatened the physical and moral health of young Albertans who had enlisted, and everything possible must be done to ensure that veterans returned to a society purged of the social ills produced by alcohol. To dedicated church women and prohibitionists such as Irene Parlby, Louise McKinney, Emily Spencer Kerby, and Nellie McClung, alcohol was a foe every bit as dangerous as the Kaiser. If "we despise the army of the Kaiser for dropping bombs on defenceless people, and shooting down women and children," McClung argued that Canadians should also despise the "liquor traffic which has waged war on women and children all down the centuries."[19] A coalition of clergy, women's organizations, and farm groups successfully petitioned for a referendum on prohibition. Prodded from the pulpit to join the soldiers resisting evil overseas by opposing vice at home, 61 percent of Albertans voted for prohibition on 21 July 1915. Empowered by the successful crusade against alcohol, women's groups in Alberta insisted that the enfranchisement of women was also essential to the moral reform and uplift of society.[20] The war, Nellie McClung observed, has "made us hate all forms of tyranny and oppression and autocracy," and "all forms of hypocrisy and deceit." But, McClung continued, "There have been some forms of kaiserism dwelling among us for many years, so veneered with respectability and custom that some were deceived by them; but the lid is off now—the veneer has cracked—the veil is torn, and we see things as they are."[21]

If the war was really a fight for liberty and justice, Alberta suffragists like McClung concluded that justice must begin at home by recognizing women's claims to the same rights for which their husbands and sons fought and died overseas. Equality between men and women, McClung argued, was an essential part of the campaign unleashed by the war to redeem society and build the Kingdom of God. "It is no wonder," she asserted, "that the teachings of Christ make a special appeal to women, for Christ was a true democrat. He made no discrimination between men and women. They were all human beings to Him, with souls to save and lives to live, and He applied to men and women the same rule of conduct."[22] In taking up the torch of social and moral reform during the Great War, Albertans believed that they were keeping faith with the soldiers at the front and doing their part in the great crusade to redeem humanity.

The Social Gospel's commitment to building the Kingdom of God has sometimes been interpreted as representing a drift away from traditional Protestant preoccupations with personal sin and salvation.[23] Such a dichotomy, however, does not really appear to have existed in Alberta during the war. The subject of sin, both personal and corporate, continued to be at the forefront of the thinking of those Albertans committed to the cause of social and moral reform. Most clergy and reformers remained equally convinced that salvation could only be achieved through a commitment to Christ. Deliverance, however, required not only a personal faith but also a translation of that faith into social action. If there was a shift from earlier Protestant teaching, it was in the recognition that the atonement for sin that was needed for salvation must occur at both an individual and a collective level. While many Albertans were convinced that society could be redeemed through social action, their optimism did not rest on an idealistic understanding of human nature, or a naive faith in progress, but rather in their belief in a God of providence whose plans for humanity were revealed in the course of history. God's purposes could only be fulfilled, however, through a response of faith that required both repentance and a willingness to offer oneself up to God's saving purposes.

The view of the war as crusade, both to defend Christian civilization as embodied by the Empire and to redeem society and contribute to the building of God's Kingdom here on earth, was grounded in an understanding of suffering and sacrifice that centred on the death and resurrection of Jesus Christ. This focus is clearly evident in the central panel of the memorial window erected at Knox Presbyterian, which pictures suffering humanity looking up from

a war-ravaged world to the risen Christ. In countless sermons preached at memorial services for the fallen, clergy stressed the relationship between Christ's sacrificial death on the cross and the noble sacrifice of the soldier in the field. At Calgary's Anglican Pro-Cathedral, the Rev. Canon A.P. Hayes addressed a congregation that included many of the officers and men of Calgary's regiments shortly after news was received of the great losses inflicted at the Second Battle of Ypres. Hayes took as his text "all things work together for good." In his sermon, he acknowledged that the tragic news from overseas had shaken the faith of many, and given cause for doubt among those overwhelmed by sorrow at this difficult time. Hayes assured the congregation that the sacrifice had not been in vain, and that the souls of the fallen men were even now committed to "the care and keeping of their Father, that they might have the perpetual love of His presence shining upon them." "If their hearts were fixed aright," Hayes asserted, "what did it matter for shot or shell. The soul, which nothing could destroy, went to the God which gave it to fulfill His purpose in a brighter world where there would be no more sorrow and where all tears would be wiped away."[24] The manner in which one lived one's life, Hayes insisted, prepared a person for death. So long as these noble warriors conducted themselves with honour, sincerity, devotion, humility, and charity, and repented for their sins, they had nothing to fear from death and could trust in the promise of resurrection and a more rewarding life with Christ.

The dean of the Pro-Cathedral, E.C. Paget, emphasized the connection between the fallen soldier and Christ at an evening service that same day. Quoting from John 15:13—"greater love hath no man than this, that a man lay down his life for his friends"—Paget insisted that, just as Jesus had sacrificed his life for the sake of humanity, the fallen at the front had willingly laid down their lives in the service of freedom and justice. Alberta's brave soldiers, Paget asserted, had courageously taken up the cross, "suffering that others may not suffer, dying that others may live," confident in the "sure and certain hope of Christ's resurrection."[25] In a sympathy letter, the Rev. J. Macartney Wilson of Knox Presbyterian in Calgary assured bereaved mothers that their sons had fallen in a righteous cause. "It is," he wrote, "the cause of truth and chivalry and honour; it is the cause of Christ against Satan."[26] Clinton Ford, the City of Calgary's solicitor, wrote a moving tribute to his fallen friend, Private Stanley Albright, for the *Christian Guardian.* In praising "the nobility of his sacrifice," Ford described Albright as "A True Soldier of Jesus Christ."[27] By insisting that a community of suffering and sacrifice existed between Christ, those who had given their lives overseas, and those who mourned at home, Albertans invested the war with a higher meaning, and provided comfort and consolation to all those afflicted by the war's heavy toll.

A number of historians have suggested that the representation of the war as a noble crusade that would redeem society, and the oft-repeated message that the suffering and sacrifice endured at the front would be rewarded by a loving and merciful God, meant very little to soldiers in the field, who confronted the cruel realities of war on a daily basis. As the war continued and casualties mounted, David Marshall argues that confident proclamations of the coming Kingdom of God, and the redemption of humanity, became not only increasingly implausible but offensive to those who toiled in the trenches. The result, according to Marshall, was a growing indifference, scepticism, and even hostility towards religion as the men at the front struggled to find any

divine purpose or presence in the carnage they witnessed. Questioning how an omnipotent God of love could permit such horrors to occur, Marshall concludes that many abandoned their faith altogether.[28]

That such feelings existed among some of the men is undoubtedly true, but there is no way to quantify the extent of this. It is also true, however, that the faith of some remained resilient, and an important source of comfort and meaning, throughout the duration of the war.[29] One individual for which this was true was Victor Wheeler, a signaller in Calgary's 50th Battalion. Wheeler kept a diary while serving on the Western Front that provided the basis for his memoir, *The 50th Battalion in No Man's Land*, published by the Alberta Historical Resources Foundation shortly after his death in 1980. Wheeler's memoir is notable for its particularly candid discussion of his spiritual state and religious views while serving at the front.

Wheeler was a devout Presbyterian who found great solace in his faith throughout the war. He treasured the pocket New Testament issued when he was deployed to France, and took the message from Field Marshal Roberts printed in the front to heart. Following Roberts' advice, Wheeler strove to "trust in God," and to find comfort and strength "in this little Book."[30] Once, when he discovered that his New Testament was missing, a distraught Wheeler sought permission from his commanding officer to return to a farm where he had been billeted to make a search. He wrote, movingly, of the relief he experienced when he retrieved the bible that had provided him with so much assurance. Wheeler often prayed for God's guidance and protection, and found that "communing with God . . . lessened the tension of the tightly coiled spring within me."[31] The Communion services that preceded battle also provided him with great comfort. "Observance of the Lord's Supper," Wheeler wrote, "was always a heart-searching personal experience, preparatory of being thrown into battle."[32] Although other men sometimes scoffed at his piety, and often complained about attending church services, Wheeler observed that most of the men were in fact quietly "God fearing" and spent "considerable time looking spiritually inward."[33] Wheeler often frequented the Soldiers Clubs Association (SCA) Huts run by the chaplains. The bible classes, wholesome recreation, library and lounge offered at the huts provided "a calm refuge" where Wheeler could forget the front, and where "others who had not yet gone through their baptism of fire" could find reassurance and hope. While Wheeler welcomed the hut's "positive programs of moral maintenance," he acknowledged that many men scoffed at their restrictions on gambling, drinking, and swearing and sought recreation and release elsewhere.[34]

Unlike some of the chaplains sent to the front, Wheeler was slow to judge the behaviour and moral lapses of his comrades. The most effective chaplains, he contended, were those who were able to talk with the men on their level and focused on their inner spirit rather than their outward foibles and flaws. Despite his faith and commitment to the church, Wheeler had little time for chaplains who doled out platitudes in the face of the "the madness and misery" that pressed upon the men.[35] On Christmas Day 1916, Wheeler scathingly wrote in his diary about a Salvation Army chaplain who cheerily traipsed through the trenches wishing the men a Merry Christmas, and was summarily told to go to hell.[36] He also had little patience for domineering commanders who used mandatory church parades to impose discipline rather than provide spiritual

sustenance. Wheeler was equally critical of the sermons preached by the chaplains who visited the front. In July 1917, Wheeler expected to be "uplifted" when he attended a service conducted by the Rev. Major Charles Gordon, the celebrated author of the Ralph Connor novels. He wrote in his diary: "Went to service conducted by Ralph Conner [sic] tonight—and was very disappointed in him. He can't speak easily; neither does he express himself with any conviction. He seemed to be lackadaisical and very tired."[37] While Wheeler was unimpressed by moralizers and trippers to the trenches, he expressed great admiration for those servants of God who shared in the perils and privations of the front lines.

Wheeler often wrote about his own struggles with faith and temptation. In his diary, he records an encounter with a scared and lonely French maiden who sidled up against him while he was sleeping in a barn. He admits that only his fear of displeasing God preserved his virtue that night. Although Wheeler never lost his faith, it was sorely tested by the horrors of war. Distressed by "the inhuman cruelty and death" meted out "by unwilling men in khaki against other equally reluctant men in the hated grey-green of les Allemandes," Wheeler struggled to find some higher meaning and purpose in a conflict that pitted Christian against Christian.[38] At first he was convinced that he was doing only what God and country required to defend "human right and dignity, justice and freedom" from unwarranted aggression.

After a night mission on 17 March 1916 in which the Allies deployed chlorine gas against the enemy, Wheeler found himself "troubled and confused," and "earnestly prayed for man's forgiveness."[39] In September 1918 a tormented Wheeler recorded in his diary the anguish he felt when he turned his back on a young, critically wounded German soldier pleading for mercy on the Drocourt-Quéant Line. He writes: "It's as if in denying one of the least of these my brethren, I had denied Him, the Prince of Peace."[40] For all his doubts, Wheeler continued to yearn "for a new day of peace and man's return to brotherhood," and remained convinced that the war would ultimately produce a better world in which God's Kingdom of justice, charity, hope, and peace reigned.[41] On 18 November 1917 Wheeler recounted in his diary the service held to remember the anniversary of the 50th Battalion's fight for the Regina Trench during the Battle of the Somme: "We solemnly recalled the supreme sacrifice made by so many of our comrades there and along the way since, pledged our lives to God and prayed we would continue to be spared from the withering fire of the enemy. Having entrusted ourselves to Him, we genuinely felt He would preserve 'our going out and our coming in' according to His will."[42] While many men hid their faith, complained about attending church parade, bristled at the restrictive morality preached by many of the chaplains, and questioned where God was to be found amid the slaughter of the front, Wheeler's wartime journal suggests that their Christian heritage nonetheless proved to be a source of comfort and consolation for many.

In this, Wheeler was an exception. Most wartime diaries and letters home contain few references to religious or spiritual matters. The absence of any sustained discussion of religion in the personal writings of men at the front could be interpreted as a sign of their indifference to matters of faith. Virtually all of the men enlisted in Alberta, however, reported some church affiliation. While affiliation is certainly not an indication of active belief or participation in the life of the church, it does suggest that membership in the church continued to be

an important part of self-identification. That few wartime diarists wrote about their faith, the impact belief had on their lives, or their thoughts about God and religion may simply have reflected the norms of masculinity and middle-class restraint. According to the "separate spheres" ideology that dominated the discourse on gender in the late nineteenth and early twentieth centuries, matters of morality and piety and the care and nurture of others were regarded as innately feminine qualities. Such beliefs contributed to what historian Ann Douglas has described as the feminization of religion. With its emphasis on love, gentleness, and submission to God's will, Christianity appeared to stand in opposition to the manly ideals of strength, independence, and autonomy. Consequently, few men spoke or wrote about their faith. Reticence about religion was reinforced by an Anglo-Protestant middle-class temperament that viewed religion as a personal and private matter.

When Canada went to war in 1914, most Protestant Albertans viewed the conflict through the lens of their religious values and worldview. Christian duty, as much as patriotism, required Alberta's Protestants to answer the call to defend justice against aggression, and to create a true and lasting peace rooted in the Christian values they believed were incarnate within the British Empire. The men and women who rallied to the cause were widely hailed as Christian knights on a crusade to uphold the right as they emulated Christ's example in their willingness to sacrifice all for a higher cause. Preachers praised the fidelity, nobility, honour, devotion, and sincerity of the volunteers, and urged that they conduct themselves with humility, patience, charity, and love. To keep trust with those at the front, Albertans rededicated themselves to building the Kingdom of God by campaigning against moral and social sins at home. Contrary to the assertions of some historians, the cause of reform was firmly rooted in notions of repentance and a commitment to salvation by following Christ's example. Only by acknowledging the sins that afflicted society, and responding to Christ's call to service, would a society founded upon the Christian principles of brotherly love, peace, and charity be possible. Throughout the duration of the war, Albertans found hope and consolation in the redeeming sacrifice of Christ on the cross, and the promise of eternal life. In countless funeral sermons and addresses, the bereaved were assured that the loss of their loved ones had not been in vain, that the deceased had served a higher cause, and that they now rested in sure and certain peace of the promise of the resurrection. While the evidence is limited, there is little reason to doubt that many of the men serving overseas shared these views and values and held on to their faith in the face of the Great War's waste and desolation. The memorial window unveiled at Calgary's Presbyterian Church in 1921 demonstrates that these beliefs and hopes had not been, as some have suggested, eroded by the war but rather continued to define how many Albertan's understood the war.

Notes

1   *Calgary Herald*, 3 January 1921; Charles W. Ross, *Calgary Knox, 1883–1983* (Altona, MB: D.W. Friesen, 1983), 42–45. The window was designed by A.J. Larshchild of the Pittsburgh Glass Company in Minneapolis.

2   John Stanhope Arkwright, *The Supreme Sacrifice and Other Poems in Time of War* (London, UK: Skeffington, 1919), 18–19. The poem was set to music by the Rev. Dr. Charles Harris, the Vicar of Colwall, Herefordshire.

3   Dozens of similar windows were erected in churches across Canada following the war. On stained glass memorials to the Great War, see Jonathan Vance, "Sacrifice in Stained Glass: Memorial Windows of the Great War," *Canadian Military History* 5, no. 2 (Autumn 1996): 16–24.

4   On the response of Canada's Protestant churches to the Great War, see Murray E. Angus, "King Jesus and King George: The Manly Christian Patriot and the Great War," *Canadian Methodist Historical Society Papers* 12 (1997–98): 15–31; J.M. Bliss, "The Methodist Church and World War I," *Canadian Historical Review* 49 (1968): 213–33; Melissa Davidson, "Private Sorrow Becomes Private Property: Canadian Anglican Sermons and the Second Battle of Ypres, May 1915," *Canadian Society of Church History Papers* (2011); Michelle Fowler, "Keeping the Faith: The Presbyterian Press in Peace and War" (MA thesis, Wilfrid Laurier University, 2005); Robert Macdonald, "The Methodist Church in Alberta during the First World War," *Canadian Methodist Historical Society Papers* (1993–94): 146–69; Stuart MacDonald, "The War-Time Sermons of the Rev. Thomas Eakin," *Canadian Society of Church History Papers* (1985): 58–78; David Marshall, "Methodism Embattled: A Reconsideration of the Methodist Church and World War I," *Canadian Historical Review* 66 (1985): 48–64; Trevor Powell, "The Church on the Home Front: The Church of England and the Diocese of Qu'Appelle and the Great War," *Saskatchewan History* 64, no. 2 (Fall/Winter 2012): 24–33; Beth Profit, "'The Making of a Nation': Nationalism and World War I in the Social Gospel Literature of Ralph Connor," *Canadian Society of Church History Papers* (1992): 127–38; Samuel J. Reynolds, "Ministry of Propaganda: Canadian Methodists, Empire and Loyalty in the World War I" (MA thesis, Salisbury University, 2007); and Richard Ruggle, "Some Canadian Anglican Attitudes to War and Peace, 1890–1930," *Journal of the Canadian Church Historical Society* (1993): 65–74.

5   *Calgary Herald*, 17 August 1914.

6   *Lethbridge Daily Herald*, 19 August 1914.

7   *Edmonton Bulletin* 17 August 1914.

8   Opposition to war was a matter of faith for pacifist Protestant religious sects such as the Hutterites and Mennonites. Attracted by promises of exemption from military service and the right to live communally, Hutterites migrated to Alberta from the United States during the First World War. Their arrival was opposed by some politicians, the press, and patriotic groups suspicious of their German language, offended by their pacifism, and convinced that they prospered at the expense of the men serving overseas. Some Hutterite colonies experienced vandalism and harassment during the war, and a number of Hutterite men found themselves interred in camps for conscientious objectors. Mennonites had a similar experience. A number of Mennonites enlisted, however, despite opposition from their community. Both communities responded to public criticism by donating to organizations that supported soldiers in uniform and their families. On the experience of the Hutterites and Mennonites, see Howard Palmer, *Patterns of Prejudice: A History of Nativism in Alberta* (Toronto: McClelland and Stewart: 1982), 50–53.

9   *The Presbyterian*, 15 October 1915.

10 McClung was not unique in her change in view. Emily Spencer Kerby, a prominent Calgary reformer and the wife of the Rev. William Kerby, the principal of Mount Royal College, experienced a similar shift in attitude when her own son enlisted. See Anne White, *A New Day for Women: Life and Writings of Emily Spencer Kerby* (Calgary: Historical Society of Alberta, 2004).

11 Nellie McClung, *The Next of Kin: Those Who Wait and Wonder* (Toronto: T. Allen, 1917), 45.

12 On the Social Gospel and its influence in the causes of social and moral reform, see Richard Allen, *The Social Passion: Religion and Social Reform in Canada, 1914–1918* (Toronto: University of Toronto Press, 1971); Nancy Christie and Michael Gauvreau, *A Full-Orbed Christianity: The Protestant Churches and Social Welfare in Canada, 1900–1940* (Montreal and Kingston: McGill-Queen's University Press, 1996); Ramsay Cook, *The Regenerators: Social Criticism in Late Victorian Canada* (Toronto: University of Toronto Press, 1985); Paul T. Philips, *A Kingdom on Earth: Anglo-American Social Christianity, 1880–1940* (University Park: Pennsylvania State University Press, 1996); and John Herd Thompson, "'The Beginning of Our Regeneration': The Great War and Western Canadian Reform Movements" in *Prophecy and Protest: Social Movements in Twentieth Century Canada*, edited by S.D. Clark, Paul Grayson, and Linda Grayson (Toronto: Gage, 1975).

13 Nellie McClung, *In Times Like These* (1915; repr., Toronto: University of Toronto Press, 1972), 5.

14 Ibid., 98–99.

15 On religious influences within the UFA, see Bradford James Rennie, *The Rise of Agrarian Democracy: The United Farmers and United Farm Women of Alberta, 1909–1921* (Toronto: University of Toronto Press, 2000), 57–58, 83–84, 122–23.

16 *Grain Growers' Guide*, 29 January 1917.

17 Anthony Madiros, *William Irvine: The Life of a Prairie Radical* (Toronto: Lorimer, 1979), 40.

18 On the prohibition movement, see: J.P. Bates, "Prohibition and the UFA," *Alberta Historical Review* 18, no. 4 (Autumn 1970): 3–4; Robert Irwin McLean, "A Most Effectual Remedy: Temperance and Prohibition in Alberta, 1875–1915" (MA thesis, University of Calgary, 1969); Diane Katherine Stretch, "From Prohibition to Government Control: The Liquor Question in Alberta, 1909–1929" (MA thesis, University of Alberta, 1979); Thompson, "'The Beginning of Our Regeneration': The Great War and Western Canadian Reform Movements," Canadian Historical Association, *Historical Papers*, 1972, 227–245.

19 McClung, *In Times Like These*, 165.

20 On women's involvement in moral and social reform and the campaign for suffrage in Alberta, see Catherine C. Cole and Judy Larmour, *Many and Remarkable: The Story of the Alberta Women's Institutes* (Edmonton: Alberta Women's Institutes, 1997); Nanci Langford, "The Political Apprenticeship of Alberta Women," in *Standing New Ground: Women in Alberta*, edited by Catherine A. Cavanaugh and Randi R. Warne

(Edmonton: University of Alberta Press, 1993), 71–86;
Paul Voisey, "The 'Votes for Women' Movement,"
Alberta History 23, no. 3 (1975): 10–23.

21 McClung, *In Times Like These*, 162.

22 Ibid., 104.

23 See David Marshall, *Secularizing the Faith: Canadian
Protestant Clergy and the Crisis of Belief, 1850–1940*
(Toronto: University of Toronto Press, 1992), 156–60.

24 *Calgary Herald*, 3 May 1915.

25 Ibid.

26 Knox United Church Archives, Macartney Wilson,
"Letter to Bereaved Mothers," 1918.

27 Quoted in Donald B. Smith, *Calgary's Grand Story:
The Making of a Prairie Metropolis from the Viewpoint of
Two Heritage Buildings* (Calgary: University of Calgary
Press, 2005), 135.

28 Marshall, *Secularizing the Faith*, 157–58.

29 Marshall's interpretation is challenged by Duff Crerar
in *Padres in No Man's Land: Canadian Chaplains and the
Great War* (Montreal and Kingston: McGill-Queen's
University Press, 1995), and Nancy Christie and
Michael Gauvreau in *The Evangelical Century: College
and Creed in English Canada from the Great Revival
to the Great Depression* (Montreal and Kingston:
McGill-Queen's University Press, 1991).

30 Victor W. Wheeler, *The 50th Battalion in No Man's Land*
(Calgary: Alberta Historical Resources Foundation,
1980), 33.

31 Ibid., 212.

32 Ibid., 33.

33 Ibid., 145.

34 Ibid., 205, 209.

35 Ibid., 45.

36 Ibid., 80.

37 Ibid., 179.

38 Ibid., 45.

39 Ibid., 102.

40 Ibid., 337.

41 Ibid., 354.

42 Ibid., 234–35.

Works Cited

PRIMARY SOURCES

Calgary Herald
Edmonton Bulletin
Grain Growers' Guide
Lethbridge Daily Herald
The Presbyterian

Knox United Church Archives, Calgary. Wilson, Macartney,
    "Letter to Bereaved Mothers," 1918.

SECONDARY SOURCES

Allen, Richard. *The Social Passion: Religion and Social
    Reform in Canada, 1914–1918*. Toronto: University of
    Toronto Press, 1971.

Angus, Murray E. "King Jesus and King George: The
    Manly Christian Patriot and the Great War." *Canadian
    Methodist Historical Society Papers* 12 (1997–98): 15–31.

Arkwright, John Stanhope. *The Supreme Sacrifice and Other
    Poems in Time of War*. London, UK: Skeffington, 1919.

Bates, J.P. "Prohibition and the UFA." *Alberta Historical
    Review* 18, no. 4 (Autumn 1970): 3–4.

Bliss, J.M. "The Methodist Church and World War I."
    Canadian Historical Review 49 (1968): 213–33.

Christie, Nancy, and Michael Gauvreau. *The Evangelical
    Century: College and Creed in English Canada from the
    Great Revival to the Great Depression*. Montreal and
    Kingston: McGill-Queen's University Press, 1991.

———. *A Full-Orbed Christianity: The Protestant Churches and
    Social Welfare in Canada, 1900–1940*. Montreal and
    Kingston: McGill-Queen's University Press, 1996.

Cole, Catherine C., and Judy Larmour, eds. *Many and
    Remarkable: The Story of the Alberta Women's Institutes*.
    Edmonton: Alberta Women's Institutes, 1997.

Cook, Ramsay. *The Regenerators: Social Criticism in Late
    Victorian Canada*. Toronto: University of Toronto
    Press, 1985.

Crerar, Duff. *Padres in No Man's Land: Canadian Chaplains
    and the Great War*. Montreal and Kingston: McGill-
    Queen's University Press, 1995.

Davidson, Melissa. "Private Sorrow Becomes Private Property: Canadian Anglican Sermons and the Second Battle of Ypres, May 1915." *Canadian Society of Church History Papers*, 2011.

Fowler, Michelle. "Keeping the Faith: The Presbyterian Press in Peace and War." MA thesis, Wilfrid Laurier University, 2005.

Langford, Nanci. "The Political Apprenticeship of Alberta Women." In *Standing on New Ground: Women in Alberta*, edited by Catherine A. Cavanaugh and Randi R. Warne. Edmonton: University of Alberta Press, 1993.

Macdonald, Robert. "The Methodist Church in Alberta during the First World War." *Canadian Methodist Historical Society Papers* (1993–94): 146–69.

MacDonald, Stuart. "The War-Time Sermons of the Rev. Thomas Eakin." *Canadian Society of Church History Papers* (1985): 58–78.

Mardiros, Anthony. *William Irvine: The Life of a Prairie Radical*. Toronto: Lorimer, 1979.

Marshall, David. "Methodism Embattled: A Reconsideration of the Methodist Church and World War I." *Canadian Historical Review* 66 (1985): 48–64.

——. *Secularizing the Faith: Canadian Protestant Clergy and the Crisis of Belief, 1850–1940*. Toronto: University of Toronto Press, 1992.

McClung, Nellie. *In Times Like These*. Toronto: McLeod & Allen, 1915. Reprint, Toronto: University of Toronto Press, 1972.

——. *The Next of Kin: Those Who Wait and Wonder*. Toronto: T. Allen, 1917.

McLean, Robert Irwin. "A Most Effectual Remedy: Temperance and Prohibition in Alberta, 1875–1915." MA thesis, University of Calgary, 1969.

Palmer, Howard. *Patterns of Prejudice: A History of Nativism in Alberta*. Toronto: McClelland and Stewart, 1982.

Philips, Paul T. *A Kingdom on Earth: Anglo-American Social Christianity, 1880–1940*. University Park: Pennsylvania State University Press, 1996.

Powell, Trevor. "The Church on the Home Front: The Church of England and the Diocese of Qu'Appelle and the Great War." *Saskatchewan History* 64, no. 2 (Fall/Winter 2012): 24–33.

Profit, Beth. "'The Making of a Nation': Nationalism and World War I in the Social Gospel Literature of Ralph Conner." *Canadian Society of Church History Papers* (1992): 127–38.

Rennie, Bradford James. *The Rise of Agrarian Democracy: The United Farmers and United Farm Women of Alberta, 1909–1921*. Toronto: University of Toronto Press, 2000.

Reynolds, Samuel J. "Ministry of Propaganda: Canadian Methodists, Empire and Loyalty in the World War." MA thesis, Salisbury University, 2007.

Ross, Charles W. *Calgary Knox, 1883–1983*. Altona, MB: D.W. Friesen, 1983.

Ruggle, Richard. "Some Canadian Anglican Attitudes to War and Peace, 1890–1930." *Journal of the Canadian Church Historical Society* (1993): 65–74.

Smith, Donald B. *Calgary's Grand Story: The Making of a Prairie Metropolis from the Viewpoint of Two Heritage Buildings*. Calgary: University of Calgary Press, 2005.

Stretch, Diane Katherine. "From Prohibition to Government Control: The Liquor Question in Alberta, 1909–1929." MA thesis, University of Alberta, 1979.

Thompson, John Herd. "'The Beginning of Our Regeneration': The Great War and Western Canadian Reform Movements." In *Prophecy and Protest: Social Movements in Twentieth Century Canada*, edited by S.D. Clark, Paul Grayson, and Linda Grayson. Toronto: Gage, 1975.

Vance, Jonathan. "Sacrifice in Stained Glass: Memorial Windows of the Great War." *Canadian Military History* 5, no. 2 (Autumn 1996): 16–24.

Voisey, Paul. "The 'Votes for Women' Movement." *Alberta History* 23, no. 3 (1975): 10–23.

Wheeler, Victor W. *The 50th Battalion in No Man's Land*. Calgary: Alberta Historical Resources Foundation, 1980.

White, Anne. *A New Day for Women: Life and Writings of Emily Spencer Kerby*. Calgary: Historical Society of Alberta, 2004.

Alberta Women in the First World War: A Genius for Organization

ADRIANA A. DAVIES

The home front contributions of Alberta women in the First World War occurred through a range of volunteer activities, and were impressive in nature and scope. Many of the organizations that were created to further women's causes, including promoting the rights of women, were patriotic in nature, and there was a seamless shift to wartime volunteer work. The war itself, and the perceived threat to democracy and Anglo-Canadian values, also spurred the desire for suffrage, and put additional pressure on the Alberta government to approve it. None of these achievements could have been made without the "army" of powerful women and the societies that they created for collective action and mutual support in the early part of the twentieth century.

According to the Women's Press Club of Calgary, in 1913, 42 women's societies had a total of about 3,000 members. In 1916 the Edmonton Women's Press Club reported 61 societies and more than 7,000 members. The growth evidenced in Edmonton is significant, and can be partly attributed to the onset of the war and opportunities that it created for women's involvement. Two key publications provide information about these societies. The Calgary

Women's Press Club on 12 June 1913 published *Calgary: The Gateway to the Women's West*.[1] In 1916 the Edmonton Women's Press Club produced a booklet titled *Club Women's Records: Women's Institutes of Alberta, United Farm Women of Alberta*.[2] The former contains spirited articles proclaiming women's achievements, while the latter is a compendium of Edmonton's women's societies with entries on the provincial Women's Institutes [WIS] and United Farm Women of Alberta [UFWA].[3] The document is invaluable for studies of feminist issues in Alberta, and is a blend of "women's magazine" ads and club histories.

The year 1916 is significant because on April 19 Alberta women won the right to vote and hold provincial office. On June 13 Emily Murphy was appointed the first woman magistrate in the British Empire, and on July 1 Murphy had her first day in court. The booklet thus serves a commemorative function as well as trumpeting women's achievements in the 11 years since the province's creation. It is a "year in the life" of powerful and influential women—an Albertan women's "who's who." The year was also the midpoint of the war, and the booklet

A group portrait of the Edmonton Women's Press Club. Miriam Green Ellis is at the far right, 1913. Ellis is a lesser-known member of the Press Club. Of an Ontario family, she was well-educated, graduating from the Toronto Conservatory of Music. In 1904, she married George Edward Ellis and they moved to Edmonton in 1906 so that he could become Provincial Inspector of Schools. Ellis was hired by Frank Oliver to cover business affairs and agriculture in *The Bulletin*. Miriam Green Ellis, "Edmonton Women's Press Club," *Bruce Peel Special Collections Library Online Exhibits*, accessed 21 January 2014, http://omeka.library.ualberta.ca/items/show/507.

includes the wartime activities of the societies, demonstrating how engaged they were in the war effort. It is, thus, evidence of the shift from involvement in a range of social causes to ones targeted to assisting "the boys at the Front."

The origins of charitable organizations in the Western democracies have been well documented, from the charity schools in the reign of Henry VIII to the proliferation of women's societies in the nineteenth century. In Alberta, as in other provinces except Quebec, the women who formed these organizations were largely of British origin, reflecting Canada's status as a British colony and its selective immigration policy. Alberta's population reached 375,000 by 1911; 57 percent were immigrants.[4] In 1916 it reached 496,000. There were 119,510 families, 277,256 males, and 219,269 females.[5] More than half of the population was of British origin, and these people dominated government, industry, and the church.

Letters, newspaper articles, and books of the time reveal the excitement felt by women desiring to participate fully in building the new province. The leaders, in many cases, were "literary" women who took pride in their intellectual powers and communications skills. The press clubs became the vehicle for forging feminist agendas.[6] Successful and socially engaged women shared a common characteristic: in many instances they had male figures—fathers and husbands—who enabled their development. Emily Murphy is a case in point. Her father, Isaac Ferguson, a successful businessman in Cookstown, Ontario, did not differentiate between his only daughter and two sons with respect to education. The family included leaders of the Ontario political and legal establishment. Murphy understood the power of the pen in enabling social change and created a pen name—"Janey Canuck"—that asserted her patriotism and served as an "alter ego." Her publications were vehicles for public education.

Nellie McClung (née Nellie Letitia Mooney, 1873–1951), another Edmonton Women's Press Club member, was born in Sudbury, Ontario. She did not share Murphy's privileged background or education, receiving only six years of formal education then qualifying for a teaching certificate. This did not deter her from pursuing a writing career, and in 1908 she published her first novel, *Sowing Seeds in Danny*, which became a national bestseller. With her husband, pharmacist Wesley McClung, she made her home from 1911 in Winnipeg, where she was quickly drawn into suffrage and temperance causes. In 1916, she continued this work in Edmonton.

May L. Armitage Smith (d. 1965), an established journalist, was president of the Edmonton Women's Press Club in 1916 and coedited the *Club Women's Records*. In her report, she noted that the club was established in 1908 and unabashedly acknowledges the high-profile members—Murphy and McClung: "The membership of the club is necessarily small as the qualifications for good standing call for active work along newspaper, magazine, or other literary lines."[7] The ambitions of the group are evident: in June 1913 it hosted the national organization's triennial meeting in Edmonton with the support of city council, the railways, and Alberta newspapers. The guests travelled to Calgary, Banff, and Lake Louise. At the end of the event, three members of the Edmonton club were placed on the Dominion executive: Mrs. Murphy as president; Mrs. Ambrose Dickins, secretary; and Mrs. Reginald Smith [the report's author], honorary treasurer.[8]

The Women's Press Club of Calgary included Elizabeth Bailey Price (1886–1944) and Ethel Heydon (d. 1969). Price, a teacher, grew up in Calgary and turned to journalism, joining the *Calgary Albertan* in 1911 and becoming the women's editor. She chaired the local branch and, eventually, the Canadian Women's Press Club, as well as helping to set up the Calgary Branch of the WI in 1918 and becoming its first president.[9] Her husband, Josiah Price, was sports editor of the *Albertan*. Ethel Heydon joined the *Albertan* in January 1911 and was the first women's pages editor. Under her leadership, the women's pages not only covered social events and provided housekeeping advice but also became the voice of the women's club movement in Calgary.[10] She used the pseudonym "Alberta West." In 1913 she married William M. Davidson, the founder and publisher of the paper. She was succeeded by Elizabeth Price as women's editor.

Finally, there is Emily Spencer Kerby (1860–1938), an Ontario-born Methodist and gifted teacher. In 1903 she arrived in Calgary with her husband, George Kerby, who was appointed minister at Grace Methodist Church. In 1911 he became the first principal of Mount Royal College, set up by the Methodist Alberta Conference. Locals considered them "joint principals" and she taught there. In 1912 she helped to re-establish the Calgary Local Council of Women and led it in support of a whole range of women's causes, which she promoted as an author. These women writers were the documentarians of not only the women's societies but also the women's movement in Alberta.[11]

The Societies: A Tale of Two Cities

While women's organizations with provincial reach, such as the WI and the UFWA, played important roles in causes such as enfranchisement, temperance, and the war effort, the Alberta stage was dominated by Calgary and Edmonton. The rivalry between the two cities that has flourished for over one hundred years is evident in the records of their respective women's societies.

The Calgary Women's Press Club on 12 June 1913, as part of the *Western Standard Illustrated Weekly*, published a "souvenir edition" or "Opportunity Number." The magazine was edited by Ethel Heydon and is a blend of stories and ads. It commemorated the triennial convention of the Canadian Women's Press Club in Alberta.[12] Heydon affirmed that "Calgary is now the fifth city in importance in the Dominion of Canada" and noted that from 1905 to 1913 more than 27,000 women had come to make their homes there.[13] She appropriated the "last best West" slogan and gave it a feminist twist: "The Last West is the woman's west. Nowhere else in the world is the evolution worked by the great feminist

movement of the last century, demonstrated more strikingly." For Heydon, the model of the modern woman is American, and she allied Calgary women's suffrage endeavours to those in the United States.[14] This is significant because it confirms the commonly held notion that Calgary is more American than any other part of the province.[15] Heydon's language is direct and has none of the coyness found in the writing of Murphy.

Mabel Hutton addressed the extent of women's volunteer work in an article titled "Three Thousand Club Women: Forty-two Women's Clubs spend $50,000 annually." In it she linked economics, charity, education, and industry, and asserted that they are women's spheres of action. Hutton also played with Calgary's iconic image as "cow town" and the change that women had wrought: "This western woman is a distinct type. She may have been but six months or a year in the west, but that short period is sufficient to convert her into the enthusiastic, aggressive, breezy democratic woman who 'does things.'"[16] The one-page article is a "brag sheet" of women's society achievements. One initiative could have been devised by a contemporary marketing company: the Women's Alliance of the Unitarian Church of Calgary created a "Made in Calgary" exhibition, the second of the kind in Canada.[17] Hutton also rejected the notion of women as victims: "The self-supporting women of western Canada do not regard themselves as the unfortunate victims of unusual industrial conditions; they have come out here with the frank intention of making money, and finding happiness, and they assert, with considerable spirit those rights which should be the inalienable rights of womankind." She noted the existence of the Business Women's Club—the first in western Canada. This theme of the business woman is explored further in an article by Margaret Forbes called "Making Good in the West: Business Women find the Golden Gate wide open in Calgary, where Opportunity waits for Clever Girls."

Suffrage is given a separate article—"When Alberta Women Vote: Calgary Women having Equal Voting Privileges With Men for 20 Years Have Created A Well Governed City—Extension of Franchise Sought"—written by Price and Ingram. The observation is made that "Women's rights are recognized in Calgary" and that women have been active in municipal affairs and are informed about civic issues.[18] There appears to be no one publication that charts women's wartime work for Calgary.

While *The Gateway to the Woman's West* expressed the aspirations of Calgary women in fiery language, it is the Women's Press Club of Edmonton *Club Women's Records* that provides a comprehensive view of women's organizations. The character of the two cities emerges: Edmonton, the seat of government, civil service, and University of Alberta, versus the business-oriented Calgary. The *Records* are reminiscent of government reports and the allegiance manifested is to Britain and Empire. The introduction, by "Mrs. Arthur Murphy," pictured wearing the insignia of the "Lady of Grace of the Order of St. John of Jerusalem," noted that the first women's societies in Edmonton were those connected with churches. The first of an "interdenominational character" was the Order of King's Daughters (established by Mrs. J.T. Blowey in 1894). The officers were Mrs. Alex Taylor, president; Mrs. N.D. Beck, recording secretary; and Mrs. W. Johnstone Walker, corresponding secretary. These are wives of important Edmonton founders; respectively, an entrepreneur and politician, a member of the Supreme Court of Alberta, and a high-end retailer. In 1908, the first chapter

in Alberta of the Imperial Order Daughters of the Empire—the "Westward Ho" Chapter in Edmonton—was set up with Mrs. H.C. Wilson as regent. Murphy began her discussion with patriotic organizations and underscored her vision of the role of women:

It is not necessary to dwell upon the work of the women of today in that a resume of this is given in the pages which follow. It is easy to predicate, however, that its future work must largely concern itself with the nationalizing of the foreigners who have trekked across this land of Alberta in long and lustful lines. It is not only desirable that we should do this, but necessary in order that we may protect the rights we have secured by enfranchisement. I heard, the other day, of a foreigner in this province who wrote home to Italy: "Come to Canada all of you, they give you a vote out here, and then give you $2.00 for it."[19]

The preeminent organization was the Local Council of Women of Edmonton, a local of the National Council of Women. It served a coordinating role, and in 1916 had 61 "affiliated" societies, of which 15 had joined that year.[20]

Edmonton's population in 1916 was just under 54,000 (a significant decrease from the 1914 number of 72,615, this being a result of enlistment and the economic downturn). The number of women's societies with a combined membership of 7,000 is, therefore, staggering (compared to the 3,000 reported in Calgary in 1913). The significant difference in numbers between Edmonton and Calgary is, no doubt, due to the former being the provincial capital and, therefore, the seat of provincial organizations. The account was written by

Lily Forbes Reid, the recording secretary, who noted that Mrs. O.C. Edwards (Henrietta Muir Edwards, 1849–1931) of Fort Macleod had convened a meeting in Edmonton on 21 February 1908 to establish the Edmonton Council. Ten societies were involved. Edwards had served as the vice-president of Alberta for the National Council as well as the convenor of the Standing Committee on Laws. The 1916 report noted that the important issues studied by the Provincial Law Committee were property rights, parental rights, and the widows' pension act. It flagged an achievement: the Equal Moral Standard Committee "was successful in having Mrs. Arthur Murphy 'Janey Canuck,' appointed police magistrate with a full

The National Council of Women on the steps of the First Presbyterian Church in Edmonton, Alberta. Mrs. B.J. Saunders is third from the right in the third row from the back, PAA, A5605.

women's court."[21] The council met at First Presbyterian Church, reinforcing the nature of the woman's movement in Alberta as led and supported by establishment structures such as the church. Ken Munro, in *First Presbyterian Church, Edmonton: A History*, notes that in 1911 Presbyterianism was the largest denomination in Alberta and also in Edmonton.[22]

The powerful women of the Edmonton establishment—the wives and daughters of provincial politicians and other elected officials, entrepreneurs, and university professors as well as the army of churchwomen—decided to create a dedicated suffrage society. On 4 February 1914 the Edmonton's Equal Franchise League was born. Secretary Helen Nichols provided an explanation in the *Club Women's Records*: "it being deemed expedient that some society should have the one object in view of bringing the question of women's suffrage before the legislature."[23] The women understood their advantage in residing in the capital city and quickly set up a series of public meetings and launched a petition drive, obtaining signatures via house-to-house calls. The first annual meeting, in 1915, created a media stir. A meeting with Premier Sifton was requested and he indicated that he would meet a deputation later in the month. The group put out the call and 1,100 men and women responded. Nichols observed: "The Premier heard all delegates, acknowledged that they had a very strong case, but objected that the farming population of the province should be better represented. The league then arranged a series of public meetings to be held in all parts of the province, to create interest; a local speaker was selected where possible."[24]

The 1,100 delegates drawn from Edmonton and district is significant, however, Sifton wanted to ensure that it wasn't just the urban political elites that wanted women's suffrage. Nichols noted that this condition was addressed when the UFA voted unanimously in favour of women's suffrage. Nichols could afford to be generous with Sifton because women's suffrage prevailed. Historian David Hall provides a less-flattering view of Sifton, noting that he asked the 1913 delegation: "Did you ladies wash up your luncheon dishes before you came down here to ask me for the vote? If you haven't you'd better go home because you're not going to get any votes from me."[25] It took a second delegation in October 1914 with a 40,000-name petition (Calgary's Emily Spencer Kerby was part of the delegation), and a third even larger delegation in February 1915 that occupied MLAs' seats in the legislature for Sifton to finally capitulate. In spring 1916 he introduced legislation to give women the vote in all provincial and municipal elections. The League also successfully promoted the *Married Woman's Home Protection Act*.[26]

Women's suffrage was also supported by the Women's Canadian Club of Edmonton, established on 30 October 1911 with Mrs. Arthur Murphy as president and with a membership of 265 in the first year. In 1916 the club had six honorary presidents, all matriarchs of the British establishment in Alberta: Mrs. R.G. Brett (née Helen M. Fleming), Mrs. A.L. Sifton (née Mary Deering), Mrs. G.H.V. Bulyea (née Annie Blanche Babbit), Mrs. Arthur Murphy, Mrs. A.F. Ewing, and Mrs. E.V. Hardisty (née Eliza Victoria McDougall). Arthur Sifton was the former chief justice of Alberta and became premier in 1913, serving for only one term (before moving to the federal Union government in late 1917), and was viewed as a reformer. Ewing was elected to the Legislative Assembly representing an Edmonton riding in 1913. Eliza Victoria Hardisty was the daughter of the Rev. George McDougall and, at the time, the widow of Hudson's Bay Company Chief Factor Richard Charles

Women's Canadian Club Officers, 1912, The majority of the women were married to establishment figures. Back row (left to right), Mme. Cauchon, Mrs. F.C. Jamieson, Mrs. J.H. Riddell, Mrs. A.F. Ewing, Mrs. Duncan Marshall, Mrs. H.M. Tory, Mrs. G.S. Armstrong, and Mrs. W.A. Griesbach. Front row (left to right), Mrs. D.G. McQueen, Mrs. G.H.V. Bulyea, Mrs. Murphy, Mrs. A.L. Sifton, and Mrs. Gray. McDermid Collection #19354. City of Edmonton Archives, EA-10-2191.

Hardisty, who in 1888 became the first senator for the District of Alberta. Richard's sister Isabella Hardisty was married to Lord Strathcona (Donald Smith), philanthropist and builder of the Canadian Pacific Railway. Their niece, Isabella Clarke Hardisty, married Senator James Lougheed, whose extensive Calgary legal practice was based on work for the CPR. Richard Hardisty was considered the wealthiest man in the North-West Territories, and Lord Strathcona would become one of the wealthiest men in Canada. Were these women "token" representatives of their influential families, or did they really support women's causes? While in some instances the commitment might not have been full-hearted, women such as Eliza Hardisty who came from missionary families were used to assisting in caring for their parishioners and considered their calling equal to that of fathers or husbands. They were not simply society matrons interested in the round of social activities.

Patriotism and the War Effort

The recording secretary of the Local Council of Edmonton Women had noted a growth of 15 societies in 1916 alone. It is likely that these were all related to the war effort, at the centre of which was the Imperial Order Daughters of the Empire (IODE). In 1914 Edmonton had a total of 500 Daughters of the Empire. The IODE entry is written by Secretary Margaret L. Osborne, who noted that the chapter was begun in 1911 with Mrs. Percy Barnes as regent; the 1916 regent was Mrs. J.D. Hyndman (Ethel Davies).[27] Even before the war, the group passed a resolution to establish a municipally owned convalescent home. With the coming of war, supporting soldiers and their families became the focus. A staffed office was set up in the McLeod Building where soldier's wives could come for assistance. It remained open for a year. In November 1915 the group established a Soldier's Club (including a cafeteria) to provide a gathering place for servicemen stationed in the city. By the end of the year there were 27 primary chapters of the IODE.[28]

A full description of the primary chapters was provided, including the names of officers and the wartime work accomplished. Kate M. Smith, secretary of the Mistanusk Chapter (formed January 1908) reported that the number of working members had

declined to 25 because wives had gone overseas to Britain to be near to husbands on active service. E.M. Hyndman (Ethel M. Davies, born ca. 1878), secretary of the Beaver House Branch, clarified the work of the IODE, noting that it was not primarily a philanthropic organization but rather one that promoted patriotism and the bond of women and children with Empire. The group, in addition, provided support to various societies and hospitals. Hyndman noted: "We have also had the honor of presenting the colours to one of the first battalions, of our city, to leave for the front. Our chapter has also presented each of the public schools with a Union Jack and flag staff and have sent many country schools flags and patriotic pictures. These have been especially appreciated by the teachers in schools among the foreign population."[29] The "foreign population" reference reveals that members viewed immigration, particularly from non-British countries, with distrust, a view commonly held among the elites. Hyndman was the wife of Mr. Justice James D. Hyndman and grandmother of Albertan politician Lou Hyndman.

But it was not all serious work. "A Masque of Empire," with a large orchestra and a chorus of 50 conducted by Vernon Barford, attracted a large audience to the Empire Theatre in Edmonton on 4–6 June 1914. Mrs. Hyndman directed the production and portrayed "Britannia." These performances, based on readings from famous English authors, were presented around the Empire to raise awareness and funds. In the Edmonton show, the principal roles were taken by "society people."[30]

Osborne concluded:

All of whom have taken a full share of the work brought on by war conditions, and all of whom when in the wisdom of Providence this dreadful struggle shall end, will deem it a privilege to cherish the memory of the brave and heroic deeds performed by our soldiers "Somewhere in France" and the last resting places of our heroes and heroines, especially those in distant and solitary places; and to erect memorial stones on spots which have become sacred to the nation in this great struggle for freedom.[31]

The Canadian Red Cross was also important to the war effort. Julia Ponton, honorary secretary of the Edmonton Branch, contributed the entry to the *Club Women's Records*. The Canadian Pacific Railway helped to set it up in November 1914, and it was operational by January 1915 in the CPR building. The initial work involved purchasing material for garments, and Ponton noted that the Great Western Garment Co. and Emery Manufacturing Ltd. cut the garments and bandages free of charge. City Red Cross Sewing Circles crafted bandages, bags, slings, operation stockings, etc. Some sewing was also sent out to individual workers. This "cottage industry" extended beyond Edmonton to volunteer auxiliaries in the district and northern towns. Ponton noted the existence of 161 city circles nationwide—averaging about 3,000 workers each. In addition, 350 local women undertook such work on their own. In the first seven months of 1916, 100 boxes per month were packed with an average of 125 women working per week. She continued: "At the end of the year, September 1915, there were 40 outside auxiliaries. There are to date nearly four times that number, the last recorded being 154."[32]

The production was outstanding and provided an enormous saving for the government of Canada.

Ponton assigned a cash value, figuring that "From the date of inception to the end of October, 1915, there have been 18 shipments to headquarters, totalling 325 boxes, and 76,325 articles, [with] the approximate value being $19,110.20," and "From the date of inception to the end of October, 1915, there was sent from Edmonton a total of 976 boxes and 215,440 articles, the approximate value being $63,464.10." She calculated the value of the 293,771 articles shipped at approximately $82,574.30 (worth some $1.6 million in 2015).[33]

Another society that played a crucial role in war work was the St. John's Ambulance Association, a department of the Order of St. John of Jerusalem. Secretary of the Edmonton Branch, Margaret L. Osborne, provided a short history of the order, noting that the Canadian association was established in 1877, and the Canadian Branch with Ottawa headquarters in 1910. The Alberta council, headed by University of Alberta President H.M. Tory, had existed for a number of years. The Edmonton branch was established on 29 August 1914 with the aim of supplying auxiliary aid to those on active service at home and abroad.[34] The IODE Westward Ho! Chapter contributed the first funds ($50). Since there were several organizations involved in this type of relief work, the St. John's Ambulance Branch collaborated with the Red Cross Society, which was started four months later. A division of labour was agreed—the Red Cross Society was to focus on the sick, wounded, and prisoners of war while the St. John's Ambulance Association dealt with "Field Comforts for our fighting men." It quickly collected an impressive 2,000 pairs of socks and 500 shirts for the Edmonton boys at Valcartier.[35] It went on to provide scarves, wristlets, handkerchiefs, cups, soap, candles, towels,

Knitted goods and soldier comforts piled against John A. McDougall's fence, September 1914. The packages were destined for the 101st Edmonton Fusiliers stationed at Valcartier, Quebec, and were sent care of Col. Saunders. McDougall was a successful retailer who had served as a municipal councilor and mayor of Edmonton as well as an MLA. Provincial Archives of Alberta, A5603.

paper, envelopes, pencils, gum, toffee, chocolate, pipes, tobacco, and cigarettes (despite some members not approving of smoking).

Women's organizations, thus, made up a domestic "army" providing creature comforts to soldiers. This effort cannot be underestimated. When they discovered that these supplies could be delayed because of congestion of traffic and shortage of boats, they packaged "comforts" in seven-pound parcels and mailed them to individual Edmonton soldiers requesting that they share them with their fellows.[36] It would appear that small parcels directed to individuals were given preference over larger

shipments of goods. Aid was also provided to the people of Belgium and their military reserves as well as their Italian Army supporters. When the organizers discovered that they did not have enough knitters because, in their opinion, it was "a dying art," they appealed to the superintendent of schools, who arranged for knitting classes in the schools, thereby augmenting the number of workers. Prizes for knitting were offered to the children at the Edmonton exhibition in July.[37]

Just as charities today experience "compassion fatigue," Osborne noted that this was the case by 1915. As the calls for support for "different patriotic objects" increased, voluntary contributions declined. The St. John's Ambulance Association redoubled its efforts and used monies raised to purchase wool for the knitting of socks. She concluded: "Edmonton has taken a magnificent part in sending overseas her very best, to fight for Freedom, King, and Empire, and with so many gallant lads in the trenches watching for parcels from home, the sympathy, interest and help of every individual is needed in order that they may not watch in vain."[38]

Rural Organizations: Country Cousins

From the foregoing, it would appear that power was concentrated solely in the hands of urban women; however, this assumption would be misleading. The fact that the *Club Women's Records* publication included WIs and the UFWA is significant. They were not only provincial organizations with enormous reach but also were incredibly active and successful in their endeavours. In the entry, the reason given for the formation of the UFWA was the need for "social intercourse" to alleviate the isolation of farm life, but the article quickly focused on the "true needs" of women. The entry, written by Leona R. Barrett, the provincial secretary, noted:

> Wide awake women realized that back of their social problems—the efficient management of the home and the training and care of children—lay the economic problem. Labour-saving devices, conservation of health, better rural schools and higher education were directly connected with better markets, co-operative buying and selling, and better agricultural credit. In other words, the

farmer's problem was his wife's problem also. What could be more logical than for them to assist the former's movement? And that is exactly what happened.[39]

The statement affirmed that women's contributions to the growth of rural society equalled those of men. Thus, in 1913 the constitution of the UFA was changed to admit women with the same privileges as men. In 1915 the women met in a separate but parallel convention, organized as an auxiliary of the UFA, and elected directors. The meeting, attended by 58 women, took place at McDougall Church in Edmonton, and Miss Jean C. Reed was elected the auxiliary's first president.[40]

A permanent provincial society was established in January 1916 at a meeting in Calgary. In the first year, the number of clubs increased to 23 with 500 members. From this group emerged some of the leaders of the "political wing," as it were, of Alberta's women's movement. Mrs. Walter Parlby (Irene Marryat, 1868–1965) of Alix became the first president; Mrs. H.E. Spencer of Edgerton, the vice-president; and Mrs. R.W. Barrett of Mirror, the secretary-treasurer. Irene and her husband Walter both became involved with the UFA and, in 1913, she was the founding secretary of the Alix Country Women's Club. This became the first local of the UFWA. Parlby, with Henrietta Muir Edwards, Emily Murphy, Nellie McClung, and Louise Crummy McKinney, in the 1920s, would lead the movement to see women recognized as "persons" at law. In 1921, as a UFA candidate, Parlby was elected MLA for Lacombe and served as a minister without portfolio from 1921 to 1935, the second female to serve in cabinet in the British Commonwealth.[41] The political flexing of muscles is clear in Reporting Secretary Barrett's conclusion:

Behind us is the fighting force of the thirty thousand or more voters of the farmers' organization who will support us in any sane and just movement for the public good. What we need most is far-sighted and devoted men and women as rural leaders. Given these, who will accuse us of being too optimistic when we say that the rural life of Alberta may be made the best in the world!

She also took pride in the fact that not only women's suffrage but also prohibition was approved in 1916.[42]

Women's Institutes of Alberta

Women's Institutes were first established in Canada in 1897; an Ontario woman, Martha Graham, began the first in Alberta in 1909 at Lea Park. A principal aim of the movement was social betterment through the education of individuals. With respect to rural women, they focused on courses to improve household management and other skills. They also focused on the creation of social networks to strengthen communities. In Alberta, short courses were initiated in 1907. The WI thus emerged as a model for providing practical courses and also networking opportunities for rural women.

The enormous strides made required that talented women work together with government to achieve their ends to further social good. The government of Alberta understood the importance of agriculture and the need for specialized training for both men and women in rural communities. As early as 1912, wishing to make training more applied, the government hired Ontario home economist Roberta MacAdams (1881–1959) to determine the needs of rural women. She graduated in 1911 from the MacDonald Institute, Ontario Agricultural College at Guelph. As a result of her recommendations, the Alberta government came to see the value of a province-wide system of institutes. In the period 1912–1914, MacAdams and another OAC graduate, Georgina Stiven, helped to establish WI branches throughout the province.[43]

The entry on the WIs in the *Club Women's Records* focused on the change in the organization's legal status, which in 1915 was set out in provincial legislation, receiving Royal Assent on 19 April 1916. The move from a new, volunteer organization to a provincial entity in a matter of a few years is a testament to the power of the women promoting the betterment of rural women and related causes. Thus, in one banner year—1916—three important women's causes were enshrined in legislation and/or given royal assent: suffrage, prohibition, and the support of rural women. The entry provided the objects of the organization and the constitution. The provincial superintendent was Miss Mary MacIsaac. In 1915 the number of branch institutes grew from 40 to 107, and membership from 1,400 to 3,000. In 1916 there were 132 branches with 3,700 members. This growth was staggering, as was the provincial reach evidenced in the list of branches with the names of their secretaries. A section titled "Sociological Outlook" indicated a shift from improving cooking, sewing, sanitation, etc.: "The demands of the war have been instrumental in calling out a fine type of community work. In fact, this larger type of work has, to a considerable extent, monopolized the interest and activity of the women of the country just as it has in the case of the men."[44]

Roberta MacAdams emerged as a visionary and leader. Once her work in establishing WI branches was accomplished, she moved to Edmonton in 1914 and established the Department of Domestic Economy for the Edmonton Public School Board, another first. Her next big adventure would involve enlisting, in 1916, and serving with the Medical Corps. On 7 June 1917, a general election was held in Alberta and soldiers fighting overseas were allowed to vote and elect two members-at-large. This was the first election in which women could not only vote but also stand for office. The spirited MacAdams ran with the slogan "Give your other vote to the Sister." The slogan referenced not only "sister" as in the familial relationship, but also the important role of the nursing "sister" in the war. On voting day, she and Captain Robert Pearson (1879–1956) were elected.[45]

He received only 263 more votes than she did (4,286 versus 4,023). This victory can be viewed as symbolic of how far women had come during the war in their fight for equality.

Women and the Labour Force

While the assumption can be made that women entered the workforce as men enlisted, women's records for this period in Alberta's labour history are sketchy. Alberta was largely an agrarian society and women were already part of the unacknowledged agricultural work force, as pointed out strongly by the UFWA. Numeric statements—such as "In Great

Superior Laundry interior in Edmonton showing female workers, ca. 1920. City of Edmonton Archives, EA-10-2264.

Britain the number of women employed in industry rose from 3.3 million in July 1914 to 4.9 million in July 1918"—cannot be provided for Alberta.[46]

An anonymous article titled "Women's Industrial Opportunities" in *Calgary: The Gateway to the Woman's West* provides valuable information on industrial development and women's employment in the city. The subhead noted: "Calgary Pays Professional and Tradeswomen the Highest Rate of Wages in Canada." Wage levels are provided for school teachers, nurses, milliners, stenographers, saleswomen, waitresses, domestics, housekeepers, dressmakers, reporters, clerks, and cashiers. According to the article, Calgary had 96 manufacturers employing 4,600 people with an annual output of $22 million. The items produced ranged from household goods and foodstuffs to building materials, drugs, and other chemicals. The observation is made that these industries provided little employment for women but that this was expected to change in the next year. The population of Calgary at that time was about 75,000.

The McDermid Photographic Studio in 1914 created a pictorial history titled *Edmonton: Alberta's Capital City*.[47] It includes a series of economic indicators for the city, which in that year had a population of 72,615. There were 26 banks and branches, 21 public school buildings, 53 churches, 150 factories, 90 wholesale houses, 3 abattoirs, 3 theatres, 4 colleges, and 30 coal mines. Bank clearings totalled $213,053,319. The city also prided itself on being the "gateway to the North." It can be assumed that women would have continued in the occupations noted in *The Gateway to the Woman's West* in both cities, and that some may have moved into light manufacturing jobs vacated by men. It was, however, women's unpaid labour that made the far greater contribution to the war effort.

Conclusion

While women's organizations of various types had begun to form with the establishment of the province of Alberta, the start of the First World War gave them a focus. The *Club Women's Records* reveal a spirit of collaboration and cooperation that helped to forge the solidarity required to fight an external enemy. The executive of the societies are a veritable "roll call" of establishment figures in Edmonton and Alberta society, and almost exclusively Protestant and of British descent. What is surprising is the extent to which they espoused key reform issues—women's suffrage, women's property rights, temperance, and the needs of rural women. The new century; the new province; opportunities for women to play new roles in the workplace and also in support of the war effort—all played a role. The war on the battlefront and at the ballot box won, Alberta suffrage leaders would continue to strive for Senate seats and to be acknowledged as "persons" before the law, but women's issues would cease to have the broad support evidenced in the wartime years.

Notes

1   Calgary Women's Press Club, *Calgary: Gateway to the Woman's West*, *Western Standard Illustrated Weekly* 3, no. 13 (12 June 1913), Calgary, Alberta. It was priced at 25 cents.

2   Canadian Women's Press Club of Edmonton, *Club Women's Records: Women's Institutes of Alberta, United Farm Women of Alberta*, edited by May L. Armitage Smith and Elizabeth Barry Price (Edmonton: Canadian Women's Press Club, Edmonton Branch, 1916).

3   Provincial Librarian John Blue, in the three-volume work *Alberta Past and Present, Historical and*

Biographical, published in 1924, provides a comprehensive history of the new province. He includes a
chapter titled "Women's Organization's and Activities." He attributes women's achievements, including
the franchise, to their "genius for organization" and
views them as an example of the remarkable development of the province. Blue's chapter was based on the
Club Women's Records booklet.

4   Howard Palmer and Tamara Palmer, eds., *Peoples of Al-
    berta: Portraits of Cultural Diversity* (Saskatoon: Western
    Producer Prairie Books, 1985), 6–7. This is a bench-
    mark book that mapped Alberta's cultural diversity.

5   Ibid., 217.

6   The Canadian Women's Press Club was established in
    1904 by Ottawa journalist Margaret Graham with the
    support of Colonel George Ham, the publicity agent
    for the Canadian Pacific Railway. Influential mem-
    bers included Lucy Maud Montgomery and Emmeline
    Pankhurst.

7   *Club Women's Records*, 90.

8   Ibid., 89.

9   Elizabeth Bailey Price Fonds, Glenbow Archives,
    M-1000, M-1002. See Catherine C. Cole, "Elizabeth
    Bailey Price: A Brilliant and Unusual Woman," *Legacy*
    2, no. 2 (May–July 1997): 36–37.

10 Jim Bradley, "Alberta West: A Pioneer Journalist,"
    Alberta History 57, no. 3 (Summer 2009): 10–14.

11 Anne White, "Emily Spencer (Kerby)" entry,
    Dictionary of Canadian Biography online, URL:
    http://biographi.ca/en/bio/spencer_emily_16E.html,
    retrieved 21 May 2014.

12 In it, she mentions that their first meeting in Alberta
    was in 1905.

13 Ibid., n.p.

14 Ibid., n.p.

15 Eva Langley Jacobs provides the lead article trum-
    peting Calgary achievements: "Thirty Thousand New
    Houses: Homes are built in Calgary to accommodate
    1,000 new arrivals each month."

16 Calgary Women's Press Club, *Calgary: Gateway to the
    Woman's West*, n.p.

17 Ibid., n.p.

18 Ibid., n.p.

19 Ibid., 16.

20 Ibid., 17; National Council of Women, Edmonton Local
    Fonds, Provincial Archives of Alberta, PR0457.

21 *Club Women's Record*, 18.

22 Ken Munro, *First Presbyterian Church, Edmonton: A
    History* (Bloomington, IN: Trafford Publishing, 2004),
    iv–v.

23 *Club Women's Records*, 19.

24 Ibid., 20.

25 David Hall, "Arthur L. Sifton," in *Alberta Premiers of
    the Twentieth Century*, edited by Bradford J. Rennie,
    (Regina: Canadian Plains Research Centre, 2004),
    34–35.

26 Ibid., 20. The *Married Woman's Home Protection Act*
    allowed a married woman to file a caveat to preclude
    her husband from transferring or encumbering the
    "homestead" or matrimonial home.

27 The provincial Imperial Order Daughters of the
    Empire Fonds, Provincial Archives of Alberta,
    PR0267, 1905–2000.

28 Ibid., 60.

29 *Club Women's Records*, 58.

30 Anon., "New Theatre Likely for Edmonton—Winni-
    peg Manager Negotiates for Sherman Interests," *The
    New York Dramatic Mirror*, 24 June 1914, 17. Vernon
    Barford was an English-trained musician who arrived
    in Edmonton where he became the choirmaster and
    organist of All Saints Anglican Church.

31 Ibid., 55.

32 *Club Women's Records*, 30.

33 Ibid., 31.

34 Ibid.

35 Ibid., 32.

36 Ibid., 33.

37 Ibid.

38 Ibid., 34.

39 Ibid., 52.

40 United Farm Women of Alberta Fonds, Provincial
    Archives of Alberta, PR0363.014.SF.

41 The Irene and Walter Parlby Fonds, Glenbow Archives, GLEN glen-1818.

42 Ibid., 55.

43 Athabasca University has created the Alberta Women's Institute website, URL: http://awi.athabascau.ca/, retrieved 8 January 2014. .

44 *Club Women's Records*, 105.

45 Debbie Marshall imaginatively recounts MacAdams's wartime adventure in *Give Your Other Vote to the Sister: A Woman's Journey into the Great War* (Calgary: University of Calgary Press, 2007).

46 Mildred A. Joiner and Clarence M. Welner, "Employment of Women in War Production," *Social Security Bulletin* 5, no. 7 (July 1942). This is an American publication that focuses on the US and British experiences.

47 Anon., *Edmonton: Alberta's Capital City* (Edmonton: Esdale Press and McDermid Engraving, 1914).

Works Cited

SECONDARY SOURCES

Anon. *Edmonton: Alberta's Capital City*. Edmonton: Esdale Press Limited and McDermid Engraving Co. Ltd., 1914.

Athabasca University. Alberta Women's Institute website. URL: http://awi.athabascau.ca/, retrieved 8 January 2014.

Blue, John. *Alberta Past and Present: Historical and Biographical*. Chicago: Pioneer Publishing Co., 1924.

Bosetti, Shelley Anne Marie. "The Rural Women's University: Women's Institutes in Alberta from 1909 to 1940." MEd thesis, University of Alberta, 1983.

Bradley, Jim. "Alberta West: A Pioneer Journalist." *Alberta History* 57, no. 3 (Summer 2009): 10–14. URL: http://www.thefreelibrary.com/ Alberta+West%3A+a+pioneer+journalist.- a0233502971.

Canadian Women's Press Club of Edmonton. *Club Women's Records: Women's Institutes of Alberta, United Farm Women of Alberta*, edited by May L. Armitage Smith and Elizabeth Barry Price. Edmonton: Canadian Women's Press Club, Edmonton Branch, 1916.

Cavanaugh, Catherine A., and Randi R. Warne, eds. *Standing on New Ground: Women in Alberta*. Edmonton: University of Alberta Press, 1993.

Cole, Catherine C. "Elizabeth Bailey Price: A Brilliant and Unusual Woman." *Legacy* 2, no. 2 (May–July 1997): 36–37.

Cole, Catherine C., and Ann Milovic. "The Alberta Women's Institute and Rural Families." In *Standing on New Ground: Women in Alberta,* edited by Catherine A. Cavanaugh and Randi R. Warne, 19–31. Edmonton: University of Alberta Press, 1993.

Demers, Patricia. *Miriam Green Ellis: Champion of the West*. Edmonton: University of Alberta Press, 2013.

Dominey, Erna. "Les Girls." In *Edmonton: The Life of a City*, edited by Bob Hesketh and Frances Swyripa, 226–33. Edmonton: NeWest Press, 1995.

Glassford, Sarah, and Amy J. Shaw, eds. *A Sisterhood of Suffering and Service: Women and Girls of Canada and Newfoundland during the First World War*. Vancouver: UBC Press, 2012.

Hall, David. "Arthur L. Sifton." In *Alberta Premiers of the Twentieth Century*, edited by Bradford J. Rennie, 34–35. Regina: Canadian Plains Research Centre, 2004.

Holt, Faye Reineberg. "Magistrate Emily Ferguson Murphy." In *Edmonton: The Life of a City*, edited by Bob Hesketh and Frances Swyripa, 142–49. Edmonton: NeWest Press, 1995.

Howes, Ruth (Mrs. T.H.). *Adelaide Hoodles—Women with a Vision*. Millet, AB: 1965.

Joiner, Mildred A., and Clarence M. Welner. "Employment of Women in War Production." *Social Security Bulletin* 5, no. 7 (July 1942): 4–15.

Langford, Nanci. "'All That Glitters': The Political Apprenticeship of Alberta Women, 1916–1930." In *Standing on New Ground: Women in Alberta*, edited by Catherine A. Cavanaugh and Randi R. Warne, 71–85. Edmonton: University of Alberta Press, 1993.

———. *Politics, Pitchforks, and Pickle Jars: 75 Years of Organized Farm Women in Alberta*. Calgary: Detselig Enterprises, 1997.

Macpherson, M.A. *Nellie McClung: Voice for the Voiceless*. Montreal: XYZ Publishing, 2003.

Marshall, Debbie. *Give Your Other Vote to the Sister: A Woman's Journey into the Great War*. Calgary: University of Calgary Press, 2007.

Munro, Ken. *First Presbyterian Church, Edmonton: A History*. Bloomington, IN: Trafford Publishing, 2004.

Palmer, Howard, and Tamara Palmer, eds. *Peoples of Alberta: Portraits of Cultural Diversity*. Saskatoon: Western Producer Prairie Book, 1985.

Peel's Prairie Provinces, University of Alberta. *Miriam Green Ellis: Pioneer Journalist of the Canadian West*, virtual exhibit. URL: http://omeka.library.ualberta.ca/exhibits/show/ellis/intro, retrieved 22 January 2014.

Penney, Sheila M. *A Century of Caring, 1897–1997: The History of the Victorian Order of Nurses for Canada*. Ottawa: VON, 1996.

Pickles, Katie. *Female Imperialism and National Identity: The Imperial Order Daughters of the Empire*. Manchester, UK: Manchester University Press, 2002.

Prentice, Alison, et al. *Canadian Women: A History*. Toronto: Harcourt Brace Jovanovich, 1988.

Rennie, B.J. *The Rise of Agrarian Democracy: The United Farmers and Farm Women of Alberta, 1909–1921*. Toronto: University of Toronto Press, 2000.

Savage, Candace. *Our Nell: A Scrapbook Biography of Nellie L. McClung*. Saskatoon: Western Producer Prairie Books, 1979. Reprint, Halifax: Formac Publishing, 1985.

Strong-Boag, Veronica. *The Parliament of Women: The National Council of Women of Canada, 1893–1929*. Ottawa: National Museum, 1976.

Western Standard Weekly. *Calgary: The Gateway to the Woman's West*. Calgary: Women's Press Club, 1913. URL: http://peel.library.ualberta.ca/bibliography/3871/1.html, retrieved 24 January 2014.

White, Anne. "Emily Spencer (Kerby)" entry. *Dictionary of Canadian Biography*. URL: http://biographi.ca/en/bio/spencer_emily_16E.html, retrieved 21 May 2014.

Armageddon: Alberta Newspapers and the Outbreak of the Great War, 1914

DAVID JOSEPH GALLANT

Introduction: Voices of 1914

On 30 July 1914, five days before Great Britain declared war on Germany for its invasion of Belgium, the Liberal *Edmonton Daily Bulletin* warned its readers of the "possibility of a vast catastrophe."[1] On the same day, the Conservative *Calgary Daily Herald* carried chilling words from London: "Should international war come, it would mean a new story in the history of civilization—a kind of death grapple in the darkness: a cosmic catastrophe."[2] As the fearsome military machines of the Triple Entente

(Russia, Britain, and France) and the Triple Alliance (Germany, Austria-Hungary, and Italy) began to mobilize for war in late July and early August 1914, Alberta's newspapers avidly followed their movements, cognizant that they were witnessing the most momentous events in history. The small-town *Lethbridge Daily Herald*, surveying the size of the armies preparing for war, wrote of a "world war" in which "Armies of 20,000,000 May Clash."[3] The *Medicine Hat News* reported attempts by British Prime Minister H.H. Asquith and Foreign Secretary Sir Edward Grey to localize the war among the

Lethbridge Daily Herald banner heading – "WORLD WAR ONLY MATTER OF HOURS," Saturday, 1 August 1914.

ARMAGEDDON HAS ARRIVED

Great Britain has spoken and Armageddon is upon us.

A mad Servian took the life of the Austrian crown prince less than a month ago. Austria's ruler at once determined to make war upon Servia, on the pretext that it was the duty of the house of Hapsburg to avenge the murder. As the Austrian emperor put it, the Servians were keeping alive "a flame of hatred for myself and my house," and this flame had to be subdued.

Russia, blood relation to Servia, and fearful of the result of a conflict in which a big dog proposed to worry a little one, urged Germany to intervene for peace, knowing that Germany had power with Austria. Great Britain, too, made representations to Germany of a peacemaking nature. Germany showed by its replies a desire to see the unequal fight proceed.

To protect herself against possible Austrian aggression, Russia began mobilization. Germany noted the fact and protested. The protest was so worded as to constitute a demand, with punishment proposed in the event of non-compliance. Russia explained that her mobilization was merely protective and in no sense aggressive. Germany's answer was a declaration of war against Russia.

"ARMAGEDDON HAS ARRIVED," *Calgary Daily Herald* editorial, Wednesday, 5 August 1914.

original combatants, Austria-Hungary and Serbia, amid "Reports of the massing of armies in strategic positions" across Europe.[4]

As Austria-Hungary declared war on Serbia in late July, and Germany invaded France and Belgium in early August, Alberta's newspapers struggled to make sense of the terrible events unfolding in Europe. In a predominantly Christian province, Alberta's editors, journalists, and ordinary citizens used their religious imaginations to make sense of this gigantic, novel conflict. On August 5, the morning after Great Britain declared war on Germany, bringing the British Empire, including the Dominion of Canada to war, the *Calgary Daily Herald* announced that "Armageddon Has Arrived."[5] The *Sedgewick Sentinel*, a small rural weekly, relayed news from London that "the empire is on the brink of the greatest war in the history of the world."[6] Armageddon was upon the Empire, including Alberta.

Newspapers: The Medium of the Age

From June 28, when the Austrian Archduke Franz Ferdinand was assassinated by Bosnian-Serb radicals, to August 4, when the British Empire declared war against Germany for its invasion of Belgium, Albertans avidly followed events in Europe through the ubiquitous newspaper, the central medium of the age. Liberal or Conservative, urban or rural, newspapers in Alberta belonged to a transatlantic telegraphic news network, the world's original "information superhighway." Toronto's six dailies had a combined circulation of 433,023 by 1914, while the *Calgary Daily Herald* regularly topped 21,000 readers when war broke out.[7] Financially well-endowed newspapers had their own correspondents to supply them with international news, yet a handful of major telegraphic news networks—Reuters, Wolff, Havas, and the Associated Press—mostly controlled the flow of international news from major world capitals to colonial outposts.[8] London, the world's financial centre, also controlled many of the world's major cable companies, and Canada, as part of the British Empire, shared a common telegraphic communication network, language, culture, and political sensibility with Great Britain, Australia, and New Zealand.

Although Canadians drew much of their international news from the American-owned Associated Press (AP),[9] the dominance of London as a world news centre ensured that "papers in each of the Dominions would continue to share the same basic perspective on international events, even if editorial opinions varied."[10] Most importantly, Canadians received instantaneous domestic and international news via a global system of overland and undersea telegraphic cables, from the 1860s forward. As historian Simon Potter has argued, from the mid-nineteenth century, "information could now travel around the Empire in hours or even minutes."[11] For example, in late July and early August 1914, the *Edmonton Daily Bulletin* carried international news via telegram from London, Berlin, Belgrade, Vienna, Paris, and St. Petersburg, as well as domestic news from Toronto, Ottawa, Winnipeg, and Vancouver. Much smaller newspapers, such as the *Claresholm Advertiser*, an Alberta rural weekly, would not be denied coverage as the threat of war grew. The *Advertiser* secured a "Special Bulletin Service" with a bigger newspaper, in its case "courtesy of the *Calgary News-Telegram*," immediately posting news bulletins on its office windows.[12] Alberta was part of a worldwide newspaper web, and every newspaper wanted to be as current as possible as citizens devoured war coverage in 1914. As historian Ian Miller has argued, "Waking up with a morning paper, or relaxing after work with the news, was part of the daily routine."[13]

Most Canadian newspapers reported the assassination of the Austrian heir to the throne, Franz Ferdinand, at the hands of Gavrilo Princip on June 28 in Sarajevo. The news dominated the front page of the *Lethbridge Daily Herald* with the headline

"ASSASSIN'S BULLETS KILL AUSTRIAN PRINCE."[14] However, Canadian newspapers viewed the assassination as part of an ancient quarrel between Serbia and German-dominated Austria-Hungary, or "Slavs versus Teutons." It was not until Austria-Hungary sent a powerful and diplomatically irreconcilable ultimatum to Serbia on July 23, seeking redress for its dead prince, that Alberta newspapers began to take the brewing storm in Europe seriously. From that day forward, news coverage adopted an ominous tone, with the *Lethbridge Daily Herald* warning readers on its front page that "SERVIA[15] AND AUSTRIA MAY LOOSE THE DOGS OF WAR" upon Europe.[16] To the *Edmonton Daily Bulletin*, there was the possibility that "Europe will be plunged into the great international struggle which for fifty years has been her nightmare."[17] Western Canadians, like their eastern counterparts, were well informed in 1914, reacting to the outbreak of war with profound maturity, patriotism, courage, and determination.

As Russia and Germany moved closer to entering the war between Serbia and Austria-Hungary in late July, Alberta newspapers focused their attention on both the events themselves and the public responses to those events. From the beginning of the July crisis, contemporaries believed that they were in the midst of something grand, unique, tragic, and potentially catastrophic. On July 29, the *Edmonton Daily Bulletin*, carrying a story from London, wrote of how "newspapers [there] fully realize the gravity of the menace threatening Europe." The *Bulletin* made it clear that there was "absolutely no enthusiasm in England for war," and that they faced the prospect of a conflict with the "deepest gloom."[18] The next day, a *Bulletin* editorial demonstrated the depth of the contemporary understanding of the catastrophe that could erupt in Europe: "The armies of Alexander, Caesar or Napoleon would not constitute an advance guard for the armies which any one of the five of the great nations will have in the field within a fortnight."[19] On July 31, a *Calgary Daily Herald* editorial shared the anxiety of their Edmonton counterparts: "Out in the open and at close range war is horrid—a plague far-reaching in its effects and debasing to those who participate in it."[20]

This is not to say that there were no reports of "enthusiasm" in Europe or Canada in late July and early August 1914. For example, on July 30, after Austria had declared war on Serbia, the *Edmonton Daily Bulletin* reported from Vienna that "the war spirit in the Austrian capital is hourly increasing," while in Russia a "great patriotic demonstration" was unfolding in St. Petersburg.[21] On August 3, the *Bulletin* wrote of "a scene of great enthusiasm outside Buckingham Palace," while closer to home, in Edmonton, "Never were there such wildly exciting scenes in all sections of the city."[22] When Great Britain's declaration of war was announced in Lethbridge on August 4, the *Daily Herald* reported "excitement which baffles description" as "bulletins were megaphoned out the window" of the newspaper's beleaguered offices.[23] In Calgary, as thousands gathered in front of the *Herald* offices to catch the latest news, people "went wild with excitement" as war was announced "shortly after 7 o'clock" on the evening of August 4.[24] In multiple cities across Canada, newspapers commented on patriotic displays of enthusiasm at the outbreak of war.[25]

However, reports of "enthusiasm" were always contextualized and downplayed by stories of more complex, mature, and serious public responses. For example, on August 3, in the same article in which the *Edmonton Daily Bulletin* spoke of "excited crowds on Jasper [Ave.]," the story continued with a deeper, more nuanced analysis: "Citizens realised the gravity of the situation, and the awful catastrophe that a general European war would mean." Such a conflict would "eclipse in horror anything that the world has ever known."[26] In Calgary, as pictures of King George V, French President Raymond Poincaré, and British Foreign Secretary Grey were flashed on bulletin boards by projectors, "relief" and "anxiety" overtook the brief excitement of the declaration of war: "The tenor of the crowds was one of grim exultation not unmixed with a sense of what serious results the war into which the world is being plunged will entail."[27]

On August 22, as thousands of Calgarians said goodbye to loved ones departing for war, the *Daily Herald* wrote of a "silent grief" behind the veneer of patriotic zeal: "Beneath the general buoyant spirits and enthusiasm was nevertheless a good deal of deeper and more sentimental feeling, which in many instances was difficult to conceal."[28] An examination of a single newspaper on August 5, the *Calgary Daily Herald*, reports a multitude of intellectual and emotional responses to the outbreak of war: *shock, serious faces, great gravity, cheering, flag waving, suspense, enthusiasm, patriotism, loyalty, silence, anxiety, grim exultation, relief, eagerness*, and *determination*. Canadian author J. Castell Hopkins, writing in 1919, understood the complex emotions at work in August 1914: "It is difficult to describe one man's state of mind at a time of war-crisis; it is a thousand-fold more difficult to analyze the soul of a nation."[29] There was no uniform reaction to the outbreak of war in Alberta in 1914. An article titled "The Omen in the Sky," which ran in the *Calgary Daily Herald* after war was declared, poignantly captures the complex mood of the August crowds:

Away over in the southeast, across the roofs of buildings, and above the heads of the cheering crowds, the round summer moon, blood red, formed an ominous symbol in the sky. To the onlooker gazing in that direction, the emblematic touch could not fail to be striking. It was symbolic of war clouds that had been slowly gathered over Europe and were now hanging luridly in the firmament. It was as if a reflection from the centre of the turmoil had been thrown across the world, shedding its lurid glow over Canada's life, and rousing the patriotism of Canadians to a common pitch. The smoke of our forest fires seemed to be the smoke of battlefields, in which Canadians too shall take their place by the side of their brothers across the sea in the defence of liberty and in opposition to tyrannic [sic] domination. It was a symbol horrible yet stimulating.[30]

Horrified yet stimulated, afraid and excited, relieved and worried, Albertans faced an uncertain future. Yet what kind of war did newspapers envision in the summer of 1914?

A World War

On July 27, nine days before Britain declared war, the *Toronto Daily Star* published "Forces for European War." It contained a chart estimating the military strength at the disposal of the two power blocs to be 10.4 million for the Triple Entente (including Serbia) and 8.4 million for the Triple Alliance.[31] This chart was also published in the *Lethbridge Daily*

Herald on July 30, with the proviso that the inclusion of allies on either side could result in a "world war" of more than 20 million men, not including "the greatest fleets ever engaged in an international struggle."[32] The chart was utilized again, with modified figures for the British and Russians, by the *Edmonton Daily Bulletin* on August 3, with headlines blaring "20,000,000 MEN MAY FIGHT 14,000,000 IN THE WORLD'S WAR." The *Bulletin* estimated

"WILL IT LAST LONG," *Calgary Daily Herald* editorial, 6 August 1914.

WILL IT LAST LONG

There has been and will likely be much speculation as to the probable length of the European war just started.

Because of the close proximity to each other of the warring fleets at the beginning of hostilities, an impression has gained ground that the war will be a short one, the destruction of one or the other of the great fleets being only a matter of weeks.

But it must be remembered that while big fleets are engaged, this is really not a war in which the fleets stand first. More than a million and a half of men are, or will soon be, engaged in land fighting, and as many more are ready to jump in at a moment's notice. Moreover, the territory over which the war is spread is so vast that every facility offers for continuing the fight for an indefinite time.

Another factor in determining the length of conflict is race pride. Neither the Germans, French or British are likely to give up easily with the tide of battle turned against them. They are fighting for national existence, which to any of them means everything worth while.

Indications are that the war will be both long and sanguinary—just how long time alone can tell, and how sanguinary may be imagined when it is remembered what the nations are fighting for.

9.8 million Triple Entente forces (not including Serbia) could face 8.4 million Triple Alliance forces, with the numbers swelling to 20 and 14 million, respectively, if "unorganized men of military age" (neither professional soldiers nor reservists) were drawn into the conflict.[33] The *Camrose Canadian*, a rural Alberta weekly, printed an expanded version of the same chart on August 13, replete with several outstanding subsections on the population and naval strength of the major powers. "The World's Great Wars," listing "Loss of Life" from the Napoleonic Wars (1.9 million) to the recent Balkan Wars (145,500), followed by a chart outlining the millions of troops available to the great powers in 1914, suggested to the reader the enormous casualties that would ensue in a general European war.[34]

Similar military charts appeared in newspapers across Canada. The weekly *Grain Growers' Guide*, the influential voice of the Western farmer,[35] with its large circulation of 35,000, believed that unprecedented armies of more than eight million per side would soon face each other, with untold consequences: "A war between such forces would, if carried on for a year, lay Europe in waste beside which that of the Napoleonic wars would be child's play."[36]

These contemporary estimates were remarkably accurate. Historian Hew Strachan has calculated that 2 million Frenchmen (1,108 battalions) faced 1.7 million Germans (1,077 battalions) on the Western Front in August 1914, with approximately 2 million men per side available as reinforcements should the need arise—not far from the 4 million French and 4.3 million Germans imagined by the *Edmonton Daily Bulletin*.[37] The important point to remember is that contemporaries believed they were engaged in the greatest conflagration in human history. The *Grain Growers' Guide* understood this well: "Never

before in the history of the world has it been possible to organize armies of such enormous size."[38]

Alberta newspapers often analyzed recent major wars in order to better understand the novel but much larger conflict of 1914. For example, Alberta newspapers used their institutional memory of the South African War, in which Canada had been a combatant,[39] to warn readers of the dangers of the war at hand. On August 13, the *Camrose Canadian* calculated the cost of the South African War to be one billion dollars, with 90,890 dead on all sides.[40] On August 12, the *Grain Growers' Guide* published an article out of London by the "Peace Society" that calculated the "Cost of the Boer War." With 75,000 men in the field, the Dutch settlers had suffered 3,700 dead, with 32,000 taken prisoner, while the British, with 450,000 men in the field, had suffered nearly 100,000 casualties. The war, costing Britain £223 million, could have built 50,000 "model houses" and 500 "cottage hospitals." With an additional 20,000 South African men, women, and children dying in British concentration camps, the "moral damage" ensured that there were no victors in the South African War.[41]

On August 5, the *Calgary Daily Herald* carried a prescient news story from Chicago, titled "Glory and Romance of War is Dead; Now a Matter of Science." A "Special Dispatch [telegram] to the Herald," the article recalled the bloody Battle of Mukden during the Russo-Japanese War of 1904–05. Modern long-range artillery, battle lines "150 miles long," generals miles from the front, and heavy casualties led to entrenchment on both sides and one inescapable conclusion: "To the present day soldier the spade is almost as important as the gun." The glory and romance of war was dead. It was now "a matter of cold calculation, a bloody business of long distance slaughter, with no

GLORY AND ROMANCE OF WAR IS DEAD; NOW MATTER OF SCIENCE

Special Dispatch to The Herald.

CHICAGO, Ill. Aug. 4.—The glory and the romance of war is dead. It has become chiefly a matter of cold calculation, a bloody business of long distance slaughter, with no longer any opportunity for dashing personal heroism.

Never again can a Napoleon, looking down from a hill top, direct the movements of his army of 50,000 men as it manoeuvres under his eye on the plain below. The modern general, directing a battle line 150 miles long—such as the Japanese had at Mukden—will never be within sight of his troops. Oyama, the Japanese chief of staff, was fifteen miles to the rear when that great battle was fought.

Never again will a courier bearing orders from headquarters to division and corps commanders, have two horses shot under him as he dashes across the battle front. Orders go out today from headquarters over the field which reached every brigadier-general, as he also sits in safety far back of the line of fire.

Never again will a battery of field guns gallop madly into action, with the gunners sitting with crossed arms on the caissons and the infantry cheering the rescuers.

Located Out of Sight.

Modern field guns are located out of sight over the shoulder of a hill, three miles or more away. The gunners never even get a sight of the army they are firing at. Their fire is guided by calculations carefully made by an expert mathematician, who sits down in a hole in the ground and figures trajectories and curves and makes allowances for wind and pressure.

Hold your fire until you see the whites of the enemy's eyes, is an ancient command that will never be given in a modern battle.

Modern infantry dig themselves a nice deep ditch in the ground about two miles away from the first of the enemy's line. To the present-day soldier the spade is almost as important as the gun. He gets down into his ditch so that only his eyes and the top of his head are in sight at all. And he looks across an apparently perfectly empty plain to where in the dim distance he is told the hostile entrenchments lie.

Never in a modern battle picture will a solid column of charging men be shown, rallying round their cherished battle flag, which can be seen but dimly through the clouds of black smoke.

In Modern Battlefields.

There are no battle flags to shoot, and no charging columns in modern battlefields. The presence of a flag on the battle line would instantly reveal its location to the enemy. Smokeless powder has taken the place of the old cloud-belt, and one may look over a modern battlefield with a hundred field guns in action and not be able to locate one of them. As for solid columns of charging men, a modern infantry attack is a far different affair.

Perhaps by the time the infantry is within close striking distance of the enemy, its field guns may have silenced his artillery. Then it may be possible to order a charge with bayonets over the last few yards, which will finally drive the foe from his trenches.

On the other hand, the enemy's gun fire may prove superior and the infantry may be driven back across the field it has crossed. But the centrifugal commander will have figured out the chances and weighed the cost beforehand.

War is Business

At Mukden, Oyama, the chief, who was never closer than fifteen miles to the battlefield, telephoned to Kiroki, commanding the first corps of the Japanese army, who was also never under fire, and asked how many men it would cost to capture a line of entrenchments. Three thousand, was the instant answer. "Too much," said the field-marshal, as if refusing the offer of a certain bill of goods. The attack was not ordered. War is business nowadays, and the price asked for this particular bargain was not attractive to the purchasing agent.

"GLORY AND ROMANCE OF WAR IS DEAD; NOW MATTER OF SCIENCE," *Calgary Daily Herald*, 5 August 1914.

longer any opportunity for dashing personal heroism."[42] On August 12, a *Calgary Daily Herald* editorial used calculations by a French professor, a surgeon for the Bulgarians in the Second Balkan War of 1913, to analyze that conflict and extrapolate the casualties that would occur in a larger, general European war. According to the professor, the war pitting Bulgaria against the Ottoman Empire, Serbia, Romania, Montenegro, and Greece cost 150,000 deaths in a single month. Bulgaria lost one-third of its forces in the two Balkan wars. The editorial concluded that casualties in the first month of a great power war would be horrendous: "There would be not less than 1,500,000 wounded and killed in a month once the forces were fully in the field."[43] According to historian Holger Herwig, in one major battle, the First Battle of the Marne in early September 1914, Germany suffered nearly 100,000 casualties, while French historians have calculated that their armies lost 206,515 in August and 213,445 in September.[44] By the end of 1914, France and Germany had suffered nearly 800,000 casualties each on the Western Front, while the British Expeditionary Force, 110,000 strong in August, had lost 86,237 men.[45]

Armageddon

Clearly, many Albertans were anticipating a brutal and costly war in 1914. Attempting to understand the magnitude of an industrial war involving millions of troops on both sides, Albertans, like many other Canadians, used their religious imagination to make sense of events. Fearing the debilitating effects of urbanization and industrialization on a growing Canadian population, Methodist minister J.S. Woodsworth and other prairie ministers were at the forefront of the Social Gospel movement in the prewar years, seeking social change so that "Heaven may be brought to earth."[46] Just as Western Canadians had used their religious imagination to seek solutions to urban slums and rampant secularism,

"THE ANGEL OF DEATH IS ABROAD IN EUROPE," *Grain Grower's Guide*, 12 August 1914, page 4.

they would use the same imaginative framework to understand the conflagration of 1914. On August 5, a *Calgary Daily Herald* editorial proclaimed that "ARMAGEDDON HAS ARRIVED." Editors evoked the greatest calamity their Christian imaginations could conceive, the place where the demonic kings of earth would wage war on God's forces at the end of time.[47] To the *Calgary Daily Herald*, the German emperor, Wilhelm II, personified the forces of darkness: "The German emperor seems to be blinded with war lust, and at any moment he may force into the carnage other European nations ... The Teuton ruling house must be once and for all checked if human progress is to continue as it should."[48] The small-town *Crag and Canyon*, Banff's weekly, also blamed "the war lord" Wilhelm II for causing the conflict. Germany had not attempted to halt the aggression of its ally Austria-Hungary, rejected Britain's peace offers to end or localize the Austro-Serbian conflict, invaded France, and violated international treaties by invading Belgium, "forcing the war declaration of the Motherland [England]."[49]

On August 3, a *Calgary Daily Herald* correspondent in London reported "anxiety and apprehension" on the streets of the capital, as the "great Armageddon" engulfed Europe. In London, as in Alberta, few doubted that England's course was clear and its cause just: "In England itself there is a feeling of unrest and intense anxiety for all feel that this country is duty bound to protect France from the aggression of Germany and to prevent the latter country gaining the ascendancy on the very frontier of our shores. England will not tolerate for one instant a German hegemony in Europe."[50] To Albertans, the Empire's stance was both defensive and just.

Along with coverage from Europe of the approach of Armageddon, Alberta newspapers carried many American news reports and poems in August, particularly the *Calgary Daily Herald*. On August 1, the *Herald* published a poem from *Life* magazine in the United States by James Logan Mosby. Speaking in the "voice" of War, the poem reveals much about the contemporary religious attitude towards war: "I was conceived in passion, hatred, envy and greed, born in the morning of antiquity ... I paint the midnight skies a lurid glow from the burning homes I have ravaged, and I turn peaceful scenes of rural beauty, where God's own creatures dwell together in amity, into a raging hell. Famine, want, and misery follow in my path!"[51] On August 8 came a poem by Frank Emerich of the *Chicago Herald*, "The Wail of the Mothers." It spoke of the horrors of war, of "widowed wives behind, and babies unborn ... Of marshal'd millions trampling on the dead ... And dying mothers wail—'Oh, give me back my son!'"[52] On August 12, in an editorial section titled "American Press on the War," a report from the *Baltimore Sun* spoke of the "European Armageddon," followed by ominous words from the *Buffalo Enquirer*: "The greatest calamity in the history of the world is at hand. What sickens the thoughtful is that it is man-made calamity."[53] Visions of Armageddon from Europe and America were being published in Alberta newspapers in August 1914.

The subject of Armageddon raged most fiercely in Alberta churches. On August 10, a Monday, the *Herald* reported Armageddon as the subject of Sunday sermons in Calgary churches. In "Armageddon," Hillhurst Presbyterian Church's Reverend P.A. Walker lamented the lack of Christianity in the world, but made it clear that Canada was on the righteous side in the developing world war:

> One frequently meets those who are shocked that such a thing as this gigantic war could happen in what we speak of with a tang of pride as the 'twentieth century.' The trouble does not lie in the failure of Christianity after it has been tried. It lies the other way. The nations are but partially Christianized. The Kingdom of Christ has been spread widely, but it has not gone deep enough ... The bright spot in this cloud's silver lining is that we are not engaged in a war of conquest or oppression. If war can be righteous we are righteously warring.[54]

In Lethbridge, on August 11, the *Daily Herald* published a sermon from Reverend Cameron of Knox Presbyterian Church. In "Blessed are the Peacemakers," the reverend declared that a "veritable Armageddon is upon us." He praised England for fighting "so earnestly to maintain peace," and insisted that only a turn to Christ could calm the passions of war lust: "Above the awful din and roar of battle let us hear the voice of the great Prince of Peace. He came to earth as the angelic choir sang of peace and His last word to His disciples was 'Peace I leave with you.'"[55]

"War From Its Inglorious Side," *Calgary Daily Herald*, 1 August 1914.

On September 3, the *Medicine Hat News* published a sermon by Methodist Reverend A.S. Tuttle, "The Present War and the Second Coming of Christ." While debating the idea of whether human beings could ever know the exact time of the Second Coming, he believed that the war, paradoxically, would herald the coming of a new age and a new nation, through the fires of Armageddon:

Every religious awakening, every struggle for freedom, every struggle by a social democracy is a still further coming of Christ to the world. And now, the destruction of military despotism which will end in the triumph of the people, their forward march industrially and socially, the laying aside of armaments and the turning to Christ of all people, will be another evidence that He has come. Sometimes it requires a fearful shaking up, a shock to cause men to think and act aright. If Christ comes as He will come by spiritual presence and instills into the hearts and minds of men His spirit, war will be inconceivable and the outcome should be such a reign of peace as has never been known in the world. We are seeing the birth pangs of a new nation. May we have grace and patience and endurance and by faith and sacrifice and toil make crooked places straight and cast up a highway for the coming of the King.[56]

Albertans realized that they had a vital role to play in this great unfolding world drama. In the *Edmonton Daily Bulletin* on August 15, a *Daily Telegraph* war correspondent in Brussels described the carnage of war using the traditional poetic imagery of Dante.

In "Vision of Hell Which Only Dante Could Describe," a story picked up by other Alberta newspapers, came horrific news of the plight of Belgium:

A two hours' motor ride from Belgium's capital takes one to a world of grim realities and sinister contrasts . . . Everywhere is the loathsome squalor of war. Horrible wounds were inflicted at a distance of a couple of inches from the mouth or breast. One could see masses of soldiers—a vision of hell which only Dante could describe . . . the maimed warriors, homeless families, destitute women and orphaned children who are receiving attention remind one of the harvest of misery yet to be garnered. Thirty thousand inhabitants fled when the shells began to fall. The remaining inhabitants buried themselves in cellars. Havoc marks the city everywhere. Gaping bridges, demolished houses, fallen roofs and smouldering ruins are seen on all sides . . . Newly made graves protrude in unexpected places."[57]

With such horrifying news coming from the front, most Canadians had no doubt that the British declaration of war was honourable and just, a defensive response to German aggression. The belief that the British Empire was on the right side of history, that war could usher in a new era after Armageddon had cleansed the world, led many to call for a vigorous response from Albertans, and their fellow Canadians. On August 12, the *Grain Growers' Guide*, under the bold front-page headline "BRITISH IDEALS MUST TRIUMPH," insisted that the British Empire, in fighting for the rights of small nations like Belgium, must prevail if the forces of peace were to survive. The passage also suggests that Canada, as a nation, was struggling to discern a vital role for itself in the early days of the war:

British Civilization and British manhood is now on trial. In the great struggle which now convulses Europe Anglo-Saxonism again has been challenged and again has been told 'Thus far shalt thou go.' The mighty issue now to be settled on the field of blood is whether British justice can be upheld by British might. Whether democracy or autocracy shall triumph, whether the smaller nations shall be free or whether they shall bow and yield to the brute force of military maniacs. In this fight Canada has everything at stake and must stand by Britain to the very limit of its resources. In self-defence we must do our utmost in the struggle in which Britishers everywhere are now engaged.[58]

Reluctantly to War

Thus armed with a legion of news stories from the global telegraphic network of 1914, Albertans sent their sons into this righteous war of "self-defence."[59] On August 12, the *Claresholm Advertiser* proudly announced the send-off of six of its sons to the war, all with previous military experience. The little newspaper recognized the enormity of the event in tones that suggest, again, the seminal importance of the year 1914 to Canada's national consciousness: "For the first time in the history of the town, war was brought home to her. The motherland was engaged in a titanic struggle for the welfare of the world and Claresholm boys were going to her assistance . . .

Canada, a nation within a nation was the definition of Principal Stephen and as a heartbeat within a heart Canada responds to the call of the mother."[60] Stephen was principal of the recently established Claresholm School of Agriculture. The rest of the passage reveals the complex emotions and noble intentions of Albertans in 1914, and demonstrates understanding of the dangers of the European war to which their young men were being sent:

Reverend McNichol spoke of the clean lives of the young men who were going to represent Claresholm and emphasized the fact that the greatest obligation rested upon the young men upon whom in times of stress the country must depend to keep themselves clean and strong and pure that they be not wanting when the nation needed them for its defence. On Sunday morning the population of Claresholm turned out en masse to see the boys off for Edmonton . . . Smiles which belied the eyes bright with unshed tears and handshakes with words of parting in suspiciously husky tones told that underneath all was the consciousness that war means death, that the shadow of the grim reaper falls athwart the gayest trappings and to the multi-colored bunting [draped-fabric building decoration] will be added the funeral pall for some mother's son.[61]

On August 24, a contingent of the 101st Fusiliers prepared to leave the CPR station in Edmonton, receiving a great send-off from an estimated 15,000 citizens. Captured on the front page of the *Edmonton Daily Bulletin*, the passage speaks of the outward enthusiasm and cheerfulness, but the inner maturity, anxiety, dread, and resolve of Albertans as they sent their sons to war:

> Over the surface there was a spirit of cheerfulness and optimism. But when the time for the last good-bye came, the sending of a thousand men—of a thousand husbands, sons, sweethearts and brothers . . . perhaps even to make the ultimate sacrifice for King and country—then the sending away of a thousand men from Edmonton became suddenly a solemn duty . . . there was a brave youth in G company. His mother was there to see him off. Both were calm until the order came to the ranks to "fall in." "Don't feel badly mother," cried the boy, who did not look over nineteen. "I'll be all right, I guess." As the mother turned away, she broke down, and women near sobbed openly in sympathy. The boy took his place in the khaki line . . . He refused to look once more at his mother. But his fingers were trembling as he tried to loosen the collar of his uniform, and something kept rising in his throat, trying to choke him. Such scenes as these all round set the on-looker all atremble with pity . . . Here and there a cheer was smothered in a sob, or a good-bye became of a sudden a trembling whisper.[62]

Conclusion: Armageddon and Hope

From the assassination of the Austrian Archduke Franz Ferdinand on June 28 to the first days of war in August 1914, Alberta newspapers, part of a global telegraphic news network, provided extensive

coverage of international affairs for their readers. News from across Canada, as well as American and European telegraphic reports, was printed in Alberta newspapers and posted on their office bulletin boards to satisfy a news-thirsty, literate public. As historian Hew Strachan has explained, the generation of 1914 was "a literate generation, and the big press barons responded to their education with cheap papers, often publishing several editions a day."[63] While some reports indicated "enthusiasm" as war approached and especially with Britain's declaration of war on Germany, most Albertans reacted with a solemn, patriotic, mature, and calm determination to the events unfolding in Europe. On August 1, an *Edmonton Daily Bulletin* report from London spoke of the absence of flag-waving "music hall patriotism," with Londoners united in a "sober and grim determination" to the great threat of European war.[64] On the same day, the sense of dread was palpable in Alberta: "Like the human blood which will be wantonly shed, the millions that will be spent will

"WAR," a poem by John Stephen that appeared in the *Calgary Daily Herald*, 4 August 1914.

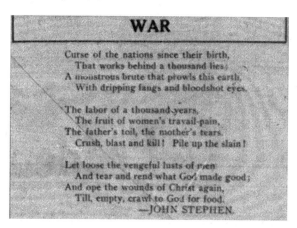

WAR

Curse of the nations since their birth,
  That works behind a thousand lies;
A monstrous brute that prowls this earth,
  With dripping fangs and bloodshot eyes.

The labor of a thousand years,
  The fruit of women's travail-pain,
The father's toil, the mother's tears,
  Crush, blast and kill! Pile up the slain!

Let loose the vengeful lusts of men
  And tear and rend what God made good;
And ope the wounds of Christ again,
  Till, empty, crawl to God for food.
    —JOHN STEPHEN

be practically wasted, bringing an aftermath which will leave its mark long after all conflict ceases," wrote the *Lethbridge Daily Herald*.[65] The opening lines of a poem called "War" on the front page of the *Calgary Daily Herald* on August 4 reveals much about the contemporary attitude towards war: "Curse of the nations since their birth, that works behind a thousand lies, a monstrous brute that prowls this earth, with dripping fangs and bloodshot eyes."[66]

Fear and anxiety were prevalent at the outbreak of war; nonetheless, Albertans and their fellow Canadians were courageously united in the belief that their cause was both defensive and just. An August 11 editorial from Lethbridge, quoting a local reverend's sermon, speaks to the certainty of purpose in 1914 Alberta: "If any nation has a shred of justification [for war], it is our own nation, for she is fighting in defence of the weak."[67] The duration of the conflict was uncertain, yet many Alberta newspapers, attempting to make sense of the greatest conflict in world history, evoked the spectre of Armageddon, the final conflagration and the Second Coming, to understand the approaching catastrophe. Albertans and their fellow Canadians believed that they had a vital part to play in this great drama—through the provision of men, food, charitable aid, and moral support to Belgium, Great Britain, France, and Serbia. Before Canada was legally involved in war on August 4, newspapers such as the *Lethbridge Daily Herald* reported from Ottawa that "Canada Issues Wholehearted Offer of Aid"[68] in the form of thousands of soldiers.[69] It is here, in late July and early August 1914, *before* war was declared, that we can discern the awakening of a Canadian national consciousness. We see the nation, fully cognizant of the great dangers involved, prepare for a war of great intensity, involving monumental principles,

for nothing less than the future of the world. Anxious, fearful, brave, and patriotic Albertans hoped and prayed that this war would lead to a rebirth of Alberta, Canada, and the world. On August 3, an Edmonton reverend prayed that, through war, a new world might be reborn: "It may be that the hour for war has come, in order that the nations may learn that the greater glory is not in armaments, but in a nobler brotherhood and a larger humanity."[70] Armageddon *and* hope coexisted in the hearts and minds of Albertans in 1914.

Notes

1   *Edmonton Daily Bulletin*, 30 July 1914, 1.
2   *Calgary Daily Herald*, 30 July 1914, 8.
3   *Lethbridge Daily Herald*, 30 July 1914, 1.
4   *Medicine Hat News*, 30 July 1914, 1.
5   *Calgary Daily Herald*, 5 August 1914, 6.
6   *Sedgewick Sentinel*, 6 August 1914, 5.
7   Paul Rutherford, *A Victorian Authority: The Daily Press in Late Nineteenth-Century Canada* (Toronto: University of Toronto Press, 1982), 3–5; Ian Miller, *Our Glory and Our Grief: Torontonians and the Great War* (Toronto: University of Toronto Press, 2002), 9; *Calgary Daily Herald*, 8 August 1914. As historian Paul Rutherford has demonstrated, there was tremendous growth in the press in the late nineteenth century. In 1872 the Canadian press had a combined yearly circulation of 24.5 million, which grew to 100 million by 1900. In 1872, 600,000 Canadian families received 276,000 daily newspapers; by 1900 one million Canadian families received 1.23 million daily newspapers.
8   Gordon Winder, "London's Global Reach?: Reuters News and Network, 1865, 1881, and 1914," *Journal of World History* 21, no. 2 (June 2010): 276.
9   In 1893 the Associated Press signed a contract with Reuters giving it the exclusive right to treat Canada as a subsidiary territory under the cartel's system of

territorial exclusivity. The Associated Press received an enormous bundle of international news via telegram from Havas, Wolff, and Reuters, which they then sold to Canadian newspapers. By 1909, 48 Canadian dailies paid for the AP service, receiving between 2,000 and 12,000 words of US and international news per day. See Gene Allen, *Making National News: A History of Canadian Press* (Toronto: University of Toronto Press, 2013), 18–26.

10 Simon J. Potter, *News and the British World: The Emergence of an Imperial Press System, 1876–1922* (Oxford, UK: Clarendon Press, 2003), 15, 28–29, 33–35, 212.

11 Ibid., 27–28.

12 *Claresholm Advertiser*, 12 August 1914, 1.

13 Miller, *Our Glory and Our Grief*, 9.

14 *Lethbridge Daily Herald*, 29 June 1914, 1. For an example of coverage in other Canadian cities, see *Quebec Chronicle*, 29 June 1914, 1; Toronto *Globe*, 29 June 1914, 1; *Halifax Herald*, 29 June 1914, 3.

15 Serbia was commonly spelled "Servia" by English-Canadian newspapers in 1914.

16 *Lethbridge Daily Herald*, 24 July 1914, 1.

17 *Edmonton Daily Bulletin*, 25 July 1914, 1.

18 Ibid., 29 July 1914, 1.

19 Ibid., 30 July 1914, 4.

20 *Calgary Daily Herald*, 31 July 1914, 6.

21 *Edmonton Daily Bulletin*, 30 July 1914, 1.

22 Ibid., 3 August 1914, 1–2.

23 *Lethbridge Daily Herald*, 5 August 1914, 1.

24 *Calgary Daily Herald*, 5 August 1914, 7–9.

25 For example, see *Toronto Daily Star*, 5 August 1914, 5.

26 *Edmonton Daily Bulletin*, 3 August 1914, 5.

27 *Calgary Daily Herald*, 5 August 1914, 7, 9.

28 Ibid., 22 August 1914, 9.

29 J. Castell Hopkins, *Canada at War: A Record of Heroism and Achievement 1914–1918* (Toronto: The Canadian Annual Review Limited, 1919), 22.

30 *Calgary Daily Herald*, 5 August 1914, 9.

31 *Toronto Daily Star*, 27 July 1914, 4. The status of Italy as a combatant had yet to be determined in early August 1914, but military estimates included Italian forces

with those of Germany and Austria-Hungary. Italy would not fight with Germany and the Central Powers, joining the British side in 1915.

32 *Lethbridge Daily Herald*, 30 July 1914, 1.

33 *Edmonton Daily Bulletin*, 3 August 1914, 5.

34 *Camrose Canadian*, 13 August 1914, 6.

35 Published in Winnipeg, the *Grain Growers' Guide* declared itself "the Official Organ of the Manitoba Grain Growers' Association, the Saskatchewan Grain Growers' Association, and the United Farmers of Alberta." Thus for our purposes the GGG can be considered an "Alberta" newspaper.

36 *Grain Growers' Guide*, 5 August 1914, 26.

37 Strachan, *The First World War*, vol. I, *To Arms* (Oxford, UK: Oxford University Press, 2001), 207; *Edmonton Daily Bulletin*, 3 August 1914, 5.

38 *Grain Growers' Guide*, 5 August 1914, 26.

39 Canada sent 7,368 men to South Africa to fight on the British side from 1899 to 1902, suffering 270 deaths, mostly from diseases. Carman Miller, *Painting the Map Red: Canada and the South African War, 1899–1902* (Montreal and Kingston: McGill-Queen's University Press, 1993), xi, 429.

40 *Camrose Canadian*, 13 August 1914, 6.

41 *Grain Growers' Guide*, 12 August 1914, 7.

42 *Calgary Daily Herald*, 5 August 1914, 13.

43 Ibid., 12 August 1914, 6.

44 Holger H. Herwig, *The Marne, 1914: The Opening of World War I and the Battle That Changed the World* (New York: Random House Trade Paperback Edition, 2011), 315.

45 Holger H. Herwig, "War in the West, 1914–16," in *A Companion to World War I*, edited by John Horne (Chichester, UK: Wiley-Blackwell, 2012), 54.

46 James M. Pitsula, *For All We Have and Are: Regina and the Experience of the Great War* (Winnipeg: University of Manitoba Press, 2008), 13; Robert Craig Brown and Ramsay Cook, *Canada 1896–1921: A Nation Transformed* (Toronto: McClelland and Stewart, 1974), 3.

47 The idea of Armageddon, the site of the final battle between the forces of God and Satan, is from a vision of St. John in the Book of Revelation, the last book of the

Christian New Testament. Historian Eric Reisenauer, in his study of Britain in the Great War, has argued that Armageddon was a ubiquitous term in the war years, and that the "war was often presented as an expression of the will of God, a judgment upon the nation, a new crusade, a call for redemption of both self and nation, and even a war between Christ and the devil." See "A World in Crisis and Transition: The Millennial and the Modern in Britain, 1914–1918," *First World War Studies* 2, no. 2 (2011): 218–19.

48 *Calgary Daily Herald*, 5 August 1914, 6.

49 *Crag and Canyon*, 8 August 1914, 1. Among the most vitriolic attacks on the German emperor in the early days of the war came from the *Grand Prairie Herald*, which denounced "King William the Murderer" on the front page of its 25 August 1914 edition.

50 *Calgary Daily Herald*, 19 August 1914, 9.

51 Ibid., 1 August 1914, 6.

52 Ibid., 8 August 1914, 5.

53 Ibid., 12 August 1914, 6.

54 Ibid., 10 August 1914, 8.

55 *Lethbridge Daily Herald*, 11 August 1914, 5.

56 *Medicine Hat News*, 3 September 1914, 8.

57 *Edmonton Daily Bulletin*, 15 August 1914, 1; *Calgary Daily Herald*, 15 August 1914, 7.

58 *Grain Growers' Guide*, 12 August 1914, 1.

59 The first troops began to arrive for training at Valcartier, Quebec, on August 18. Canada's First Contingent, 30,617 strong, left for England on 30 ships on 3 October 1914. Tim Cook, *At the Sharp End: Canadians Fighting the Great War, 1914–1916* (Toronto: Penguin Canada, 2007), 35–54.

60 *Claresholm Advertiser*, 12 August 1914.

61 Ibid., 1, 4.

62 *Edmonton Daily Bulletin*, 24 August 1914, 1, 8.

63 Jay Winter, *The Legacy of the Great War: Ninety Years On* (Columbia: University of Missouri Press, 2009), 185.

64 *Edmonton Daily Bulletin*, 1 August 1914, 1.

65 *Lethbridge Daily Herald*, 1 August 1914, 4.

66 *Calgary Daily Herald*, 4 August 1914, 1.

67 *Lethbridge Daily Herald*, 11 August 1914, 5.

68 Ibid., 3 August 1914, 3.

69 For instance, on August 1, the *Edmonton Daily Bulletin* confirmed reports from Ottawa of the mobilization of 21,000 men for overseas service.

70 *Edmonton Daily Bulletin*, 3 August 1914, 2.

Works Cited

PRIMARY SOURCES

Calgary Daily Herald
Camrose Canadian
Claresholm Advertiser
Crag and Canyon (Banff, AB)
Edmonton Daily Bulletin
Grain Growers' Guide
Grand Prairie Herald
Halifax Herald
Lethbridge Daily Herald
Medicine Hat News
Quebec Chronicle
Sedgewick Sentinel
Toronto Daily Star
Toronto Globe

SECONDARY SOURCES

Allen, Gene. *Making National News: A History of Canadian Press*. Toronto: University of Toronto Press, 2013.

Brown, Robert Craig, and Ramsay Cook. *Canada 1896–1921: A Nation Transformed*. Toronto: McClelland and Stewart, 1974.

Cook, Tim. *At the Sharp End: Canadians Fighting the Great War, 1914–1916*. Toronto: Penguin, 2007.

Herwig, Holger H. *The Marne, 1914: The Opening of World War I and the Battle That Changed the World*. New York: Random House Trade Paperback Edition, 2011.

———. "War in the West, 1914–16." In *A Companion to World War I*, edited by John Horne. Chichester, UK: Wiley-Blackwell, 2012.

Hopkins, J. Castell. *Canada at War: A Record of Heroism and Achievement 1914–1918*. Toronto: The Canadian Annual Review, 1919.

Miller, Carman. *Painting the Map Red: Canada and the South African War, 1899–1902*. Montreal and Kingston: McGill-Queen's University Press, 1993.

Miller, Ian. *Our Glory and Our Grief: Torontonians and the Great War*. Toronto: University of Toronto Press, 2002.

Pitsula, James. *For All We Have and Are: Regina and the Experience of the Great War*. Winnipeg: University of Manitoba Press, 2008.

Potter, Simon J. *News and the British World: The Emergence of an Imperial Press System, 1876–1922*. Oxford, UK: Clarendon Press, 2003.

Reisenauer, Eric. "A World in Crisis and Transition: The Millennial and the Modern in Britain, 1914–1918." *First World War Studies* 2, no. 2 (2011): 217–32.

Rutherford, Paul. *A Victorian Authority: The Daily Press in Late Nineteenth-Century Canada*. Toronto: University of Toronto Press, 1982.

Strachan, Hew. *The First World War*. Vol. 1, *To Arms*. Oxford, UK: Oxford University Press, 2001.

Winder, Gordon. "London's Global Reach? Reuters News and Network, 1865, 1881, and 1914." *Journal of World History* 21, no. 2 (June 2010): 271–96.

Winter, Jay. *The Legacy of the Great War: Ninety Years On*. Columbia: University of Missouri Press, 2009.

Edmonton's Local Heroes

STEPHEN GREENHALGH

During the First World War, numerous Albertans responded to the call to volunteer with the Canadian Expeditionary Force (CEF). Alberta was among the leaders in provincial enlistment: out of 374,663 residents (according to the 1911 census), 25,871 enlisted as of April 1916. This number amounted to almost 7 percent of Alberta's population.[1] This continued to climb: by 21 June 1916, the figure reached 30,764, or approximately 8.2 percent of the province's population.[2]

One possible reason for Alberta's large contribution to the war effort, relative to its size, was the province's recent formation in 1905. Unlike in other regions of Canada, Alberta's population yet lacked a long history of settlement, and still maintained a bit of its pre-provincial frontier heritage. In fact, many men residing in Alberta by 1914 were either immigrants from overseas or had been born in eastern Canada before migrating westward. The fact that they were relatively new residents, many searching for adventure on the frontier, and largely unmarried, presumably with fewer responsibilities, may have accounted for the high enlistment rate.[3]

Throughout the war, the press celebrated local lads who were overseas, often with very personal stories. Lester J. Collins was an Edmonton soldier left almost speechless and completely deaf as a result of a gas attack while stationed in Europe. Edmontonians were kept aware of the events surrounding his journey home through the *Edmonton Bulletin* so that he could be officially welcomed on his return to the city at the end of September 1915. The *Bulletin* reported that Collins had been on the military ship *Hesperian* when it was torpedoed crossing from Glasgow to Montreal, on 4 September 1915.[4] His encounters in the war were of great interest to readers, and the media was keen to provide details. On 22 July 1915 Collins had been gassed on the frontline, and also received shrapnel in his back at St. Julien.[5] In the weeks and months that followed the battle, Edmontonians read that Collins had been unable to taste solid food, and had survived on soups and nourishing drinks. His gratitude for having survived his experiences was noted: "Yes, I have been gassed, but thank God I came out alive."[6] Collins' story and his experiences are just one example of many

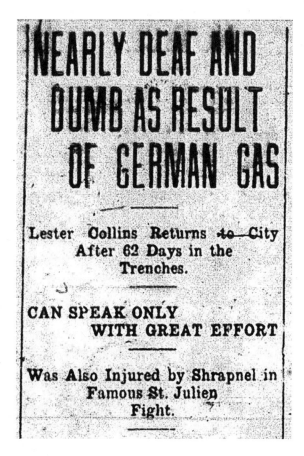

NEARLY DEAF AND DUMB AS RESULT OF GERMAN GAS

Lester Collins Returns to City After 62 Days in the Trenches.

CAN SPEAK ONLY WITH GREAT EFFORT

Was Also Injured by Shrapnel in Famous St. Julien Fight.

Many Edmonton soldiers would return home permanently disfigured from their encounters on the front. Sometimes they would be invited to address fellow Edmontonians about their wartime experiences. "Nearly Deaf and Dumb as Result of German Gas," *Edmonton Bulletin*, 30 September 1915.

such accounts appearing in the pages of the *Bulletin* during the course of the war years.

Privates Walter Guild and H. Wolfe were two other local soldiers who returned to Edmonton early on in the war after experiences on the battlefront. The *Bulletin* alerted readers about their arrival by

train at 9:05 p.m. on 30 December 1915. The account noted that Private Guild had left Edmonton the previous year with the 101st Fusiliers, and had been wounded in the left shoulder and struck with shrapnel in his wrist. The *Bulletin* reported that Guild was met by his father, who boarded the train on the south side of the city, while the rest of his family greeted him at the Jasper Avenue train depot.

Private H. Wolfe, like Guild, had left Edmonton the previous year, and spent six months in France before he was invalided out due to severe rheumatism. Even though his time in the war had been cut short, he was given the honour and respect deserved by a soldier fighting for his country.[7] The article notes that, in Quebec, Wolfe was honoured at a Christmas tree reception event and, on his return to Edmonton, children danced and bestowed him with kisses.

Besides being welcomed by their respective families, both men were also met by a special reception committee of the local chapter of the Returned Soldiers' Bureau.[8] Greeting soldiers returning from the war became commonplace for Edmontonians. Train staff alerted Edmonton officials who, in turn, notified the media.[9] The desire to acknowledge, honour, and respect soldiers is evidence of a sense of community that existed in the city in spite of its relative youth.

Another Edmontonian who made headlines in the *Bulletin* was Major Pete Anderson. He left Edmonton with the 101st regiment in fall 1914 and was captured by the Germans on 24 April 1915. While stationed in France, he had been placed in command of a brigade of sharpshooters and charged with putting German snipers out of business.[10] At the time of his capture, he was a member of the Canadian 3rd Battalion and was taken prisoner at the Second

Battle of Ypres in late April 1915.[11] Although thought dead by his battalion, Anderson was able to escape from Bischofswerda, an allied prisoner of war camp located not far from Germany's border with Austria, some 160 kilometres south of Berlin.[12]

The major did not want to go into details about his place of captivity, or how he was able to escape; however, he was eventually able to return to freedom via Denmark, his home country prior to immigrating to Canada.[13] As the *Bulletin* reported, the fact that he

For several months in the fall of 1915, Edmontonians could read about the daring escape of Major Pete Anderson from a German prisoner of war camp and his 700-kilometre journey back to freedom. Despite this experience, Major Anderson was still eager to return to the front. "700 Kilometres through Germany in His Uniform," *Edmonton Bulletin*, 12 November 1915.

700 Kilometres Through Germany in His Uniform

Major Pete Anderson in Letter From Copenhagen Tells of His Escape.

TRAVELLED AT NIGHT; EVADED ALL SENTRIES

Promises to Give Details in Subsequent Letter—Lived on Biscuits and Chocolate.

Out of the maze of superhuman endeavor and unparalled bravery which merges into the vast make-up of the world's greatest war, there is one deed of daring and determination which will undoubtedly place the name of an Edmonton man in a unique and honored chapter of the history of the struggle. This man is Major Pete Anderson, whose escape from the rigid confines of a German military prison was the sensation of a continent a few days ago.

How the rugged pioneer of Edmonton took the chances of sheer desperation, how he grimly made his way across 700 kilometres (about 500 miles) of hostile territory, how he faced starvation and suffered the most unfavorable climatic conditions, these alone in a multitude of incidents, would make a story of enthralling in-

MAJOR PETE ANDERSON.

had a good knowledge of German, and spoke English with a noticeable Danish accent, probably aided his escape. On leaving the prison camp, Anderson discarded his Canadian uniform and travelled at night through the enemy territory, seeking to evade sentries.[14] On 18 October 1915 he wrote to his wife from Copenhagen telling her how, during his escape across German territory, it had rained day and night, and that he had survived on meat lozenges, biscuits, and chocolate, all of which had been soaked due to the rain. He further stated that, as he made his way over the 700 kilometres to Denmark, he rarely slept as he often passed armed German camps.[15]

While Major Anderson's experiences were not typical of most Edmonton soldiers, the attention that he received back home was. The *Bulletin* featured his picture (in the October 26 edition) and provided readers with his background in Edmonton prior to enlistment. The paper, thus, actively created the notion of local heroes, and demonstrated that the men were not exceptional or extraordinary but simply ordinary Edmontonians. Anderson had come to Edmonton 25 years previously (ca. 1890) as a poor boy, and had worked as a bricklayer before eventually owning his own company.[16] His daring escape was featured in the paper on three separate occasions, from late October to mid-November 1915, including once on the front page. The multiple publications of Anderson's wartime experiences fed the public's appetite to read about the heroism of local soldiers.

Stanley McCuaig, the future son-in-law of A.C. Rutherford, the first premier of Alberta, provides another example. He spent 1917 training in Canada at Lethbridge and Calgary (Sarcee Camp), Alberta, and Petawawa, Ontario.[17] He initially shipped out to eastern Canada where he stopped to visit his family in Montreal before Christmas.[18] He then passed through a devastated Halifax only three weeks after the munitions explosion that occurred in the harbour on December 6 killing more than 2,000 people.[19] After spending a few months training in England in early 1918, he was shipped across the channel to France and reached the frontline by the end of March 1918.[20]

McCuaig wrote frequently to his sweetheart, Hazel Rutherford, in Edmonton. His letters in some instances were quite detailed, sparing Hazel little in terms of what he witnessed and experienced. For example, McCuaig sometimes described the countryside where he was stationed, including that it was marked by massive shell holes and craters. He also informed her about how the French peasants walked around wearing gas masks.[21] Enemy planes, captured prisoners of war, and the noise and lights of battle were further topics in his letters home.[22] Rats were yet another problem that he complained about, describing them in one letter as being as big and sly as cats.[23]

McCuaig experienced a few close calls. In a letter dated 14 April 1918 he related an encounter that he and several others soldiers had with the enemy. For five days he was required to be up all hours of the day and night to carry messages along the front. During one trip in which he and four other soldiers were en route to brigade headquarters, there was a sudden whistling through the air, followed by a shell landing and a hail of debris. McCuaig and the four soldiers with him immediately dropped flat to the ground before getting up and making a run for it. Thirty seconds passed before another shell exploded next to them, and they again dropped flat. They made another dash over the terrain as fast as they could go, before yet another shell exploded next to them. This scenario went on about ten times with the enemy

increasing their range each time, as McCuaig and his fellow soldiers equally increased their distance. He told Hazel how all of them ran until they were winded and laughing about their close call, once they reached safety. It was only later, when he was reflecting on the experience and writing about it in a letter, that he considered how the event was truly no joke and that he could have been injured or killed.[24]

McCuaig's openness in his letters to his future wife is, perhaps at first, surprising; however, it is evident that writing about these experiences was likely a means to come to terms with what he was doing in the war. Other letters to Hazel reflect his need to understand his experiences so far from home. For example, a few months before the war's end, he wrote Hazel wondering when peace would come after all the hardships endured by the soldiers. He also questioned why some soldiers had been taken while others were left unharmed. Was divine providence behind it all, or was it all just luck? McCuaig believed it to be the latter.[25] After arriving in England, he further wrote that he loathed the war and hated the idea of killing another human being. Despite having spent 1917 in military training in Canada, McCuaig had trouble viewing himself as a soldier, as did his mother whom he quoted in a letter to Hazel: "I never thought of you a soldier."[26]

Correspondence home allowed McCuaig and other Edmonton soldiers to reflect on their experiences, what they had encountered and continued to encounter, the hardships they endured, as well as the sacrifices they were each willingly making. Some would make the ultimate sacrifice and never return to Edmonton. McCuaig was fortunate, returning home in 1919 and marrying Hazel that same year.[27] His letters home were not published in the newspapers of the day; however, that did not stop his

Wednesday 2:30 pm Feb 13/18

My dearest Hazel,

I am in very excellent form this afternoon and I may add since yesterday, the reason being that I am in receipt of six more letters from you. When mail does come here, it comes with a rush. The letters I received yesterday and this morning are dated as follows:— Jan 5th, 7th, 9th, 11th, 13th and 15th. I also received one from my father written on the 14th. Doesn't it take a long time for mail to reach its destination now? I was most assuredly under the impression that it would only be a matter of three weeks but it is longer than that in most cases. You are the dearest and most considerate girl that ever lived; your letters are so full of just the news that I want to hear about, and you are always so cheerful. The mail you addressed to the Camp, Canadian Reserve Artillery, reached me yesterday while the mail sent to the Commissioner's Office did not get here until this morning, just a day's delay. I think taking it all through it will be more satisfactory to have my letters forwarded

8.

I cannot help but think of your thoughts while knitting — you know what you said — well my dear an hour — I was going to say a minute — never passes without my mind wandering back to you. It is the thought of you that makes life bearable in this far-off country, and it will be the same in France, I carry in my tunic your picture always and your ring on my finger, I never realized quite as much until now that life after the war would be unbearable if a boy so circumstanced as I was, hadn't been in it. Frankly, I confess, I loathe war; I hate the thought of killing fellow human beings; I was never before subjected to discipline. I recall my mother's words a year ago when she said 'I never thought of you a soldier! Well I am glad to say, I have conquered my own feelings in this respect largely through your influence and I hope that I shall fight a good fight!

Col Sharton, the Commandant of the C.R.A. sent a young lieutenant for me at noon today. I was rather flustered for a moment but on arriving at the Colonel's office I was soon at ease. It appears that Col Cameron

(left) Lieutenant Stanley McCuaig wrote frequently—every other day or every two days—to his sweetheart, Hazel Rutherford. Subject matter varied widely from the local weather to close calls on the battlefield. In this letter, dated 13 February 1918, Stanley questioned whether or not he could kill another human being. RAM, CN H92.137: (right) Stanley's opinion on killing another human being. Same letter.

Stanley McCuaig returned to Edmonton in January 1919 via the Panama Canal. Later that year, he and Hazel Rutherford were wed. Wedding photo, 1919. Courtesy of Rutherford House, Provincial Historic Site.

experiences, or those of other local soldiers, from entering the collective memory. Loved ones who received letters from soldiers likely spoke about their experiences to friends and coworkers. The war was, thus, a shared experience. Edmontonians were also confronted with the war through recruitment ads, displays of war trophies, and the appearance of returning soldiers.[28] This shared experience contributed to Edmonton's sense of community, strengthening it further and helping to solidify its identity in light of Alberta's recent founding and the city's incorporation in 1904.

Harry Campbell was one local soldier who, unlike McCuaig, did not return from the war. His passing was noted in the *Bulletin*. Campbell had come to Edmonton at the age of five, and had attended school in Strathcona and was a member of Knox Presbyterian Church. He was a member of the 19th Alberta Dragoons prior to the outbreak of war. In fact, he had just returned from camp in Calgary when the war broke out and, despite having suffered two severe accidents during the course of his military training, remained determined to do his part and fight as part of the CEF. He was on active service in France for most of the war except when he suffered from a short bout of trench fever.[29] His platoon commander, Lieutenant W.H. Williams, wrote to Harry's parents conveying word of their son's passing. The letter found its way into the 18 May 1918 morning edition of the *Bulletin*:

Harry Campbell

Details regarding the death in action of Harry Campbell have just been received by his parents, Mr. and Mrs D. L. Campbell, 8304 99th street South Side. The letter comes from his platoon commander, Lieut. W H. Williams, with whom he had been serving since his transfer in England from the Sportsmen's battalion, and is as follows:

"Somewhere in France,"
18-4-18

Dear Sir—It is with heartfelt sympathy that I, his platoon commander, write you these few words of condolence in the loss of your dear son, who was killed on the 16th instant. It was while "holding the line" that a hostile shell fell amongst the Lewis Gun Crew, of which your son was a member, killing him instantly. Thank God he did not suffer!

I can assure you that his loss will be keenly felt by all his comrades, with whom he was ever popular—he always looked on the bright side and trusted in God. His cheerfulness at all times helped to keep up the spirits of others, and it is such men as these, that makes the Canadian corps what it is today. Harry has been under my command since November, 1917, and I have always found him a keen, obedient soldier.

While his loss will be a great blow to you, I pray that God will give you strength to sustain it, knowing that he died for his country, facing the enemy in the fight for freedom and right.

His body was laid to rest today.

His personal effects will be forwarded to you through the paymaster.

God bless you.

Sincerely yours,
W. H. WILLIAMS,
Lieutenant.

Harry Campbell was just one of many Edmonton soldiers who did not return home from the war and whom Edmontonians read about in local newspapers. "Harry Campbell," *Morning Bulletin*, 18 May 1918.

Dear Sir—It is with heartfelt sympathy that I, his platoon commander, write to you these few words of condolence in the loss of your dear son who was killed on the 16th instant.

It was while "holding the line" that a hostile shell fell amongst the Lewis Gun Crew, of which your son was a member, killing him instantly. Thank God he did not suffer.

I can assure you that his loss will be keenly felt by all his comrades, with whom he was ever popular—he always looked on the bright side and trusted in God. His cheerfulness at all times helped to keep up the spirits of others, and it is such men as these, that makes the Canadian corps what it is today.[30]

The publication of the letter in the *Bulletin*, along with a photo of Harry, allowed all Edmontonians, and not just his parents, to reflect on his contributions to the war, to take pride in his deeds, and to collectively mourn his passing. The publication of Lieutenant Williams' letter personalized the soldier's death for all Edmontonians. Soldiers such as Harry Campbell, Stanley McCuaig, Pete Anderson, and others demonstrated the fact that ordinary men could do extraordinary things and that all Edmontonians could share and take pride in their suffering and sacrifice.

Notes

The research for this essay was part of a larger project undertaken for the Rutherford House Provincial Historic Site. I would like to thank Alberta Culture and Tourism and the staff of Rutherford House for their support of the project and the writing of this essay.

1 "Alberta Leads in Recruiting," *Edmonton Bulletin*, 25 March 1916, 7.

2 "Enlistment in Alberta 30,764 Canada 340,128," *Edmonton Bulletin*, 1 June 1916, 5.

3 "Alberta Leads in Recruiting."

4 "Nearly Deaf and Dumb as Result of German Gas," *Edmonton Bulletin*, 30 September 1915, 8.

5 Ibid.

6 "Edmonton Man Victim of Gas," *Edmonton Bulletin*, 27 September 1915, front page.

7 "Two Soldiers Back from the War," *Edmonton Bulletin*, 31 December 1915, front page.

8 Ibid.

9 "Discuss Questions of Providing for Soldiers Returning to City," *Edmonton Bulletin*, 4 December 1915, front page.

10 "Edmonton Officer is Now Safe in London," *Edmonton Bulletin*, 26 October 1915, 5.

11 Ibid.; "Major P. Anderson Has Grown Heavy Beard: Aided Escape," *Edmonton Bulletin*, 13 November 1915, front page.

12 "Edmonton Officer is Now Safe in London."

13 Ibid.; "Major P. Anderson Has Grown Heavy Beard: Aided Escape."

14 "Edmonton Officer is Now Safe in London."

15 "700 Kilometres through Germany in His Uniform," *Edmonton Bulletin*, 12 November 1915, 5.

16 "Edmonton Officer is Now Safe in London."

17 Royal Alberta Museum (Edmonton), Stanley McCuaig Fonds, Letters to Hazel Rutherford, 19 April 1917, CN H92.137; 2 May 1917, CN H92.137; 5 May 1917, CN H92.137; 22 May 1917, CN H92.137; 27 May 1917, CN H92.137.

18 Ibid., Telegram to Hazel Rutherford, 12 December 1917, CN H92.137; and Letter to Hazel Rutherford, 16 December 1917, CN H92.137.

19 Ibid., Letter to Hazel Rutherford, 20 December 1917, CN H92.137; and "The Halifax Explosion," cbc.ca, 28 October 2013, URL: http://www.cbc.ca/halifaxexplosion/, retrieved 29 May 2014.

20 Royal Alberta Museum (Edmonton), Stanley McCuaig Fonds, Telegram to Hazel Rutherford, 2 January 1918, CN H92.137; and Letter to Hazel Rutherford, 29 March 1918, CN H92.137.

21 Ibid., Letter to Hazel Rutherford, 14 July 1918, CN H92.137.

22 Ibid., Letters to Hazel Rutherford, 16 June 1918, CN H92.137; 3 July 1918, CN H92.137; and 8 July 1918, CN H92.137.

23 Ibid., Letter to Hazel Rutherford, 3 July 1918, CN H92.137.

24 Ibid., Letter to Hazel Rutherford, 14 April 1918, CN H92.137.

25 Ibid., Letter to Hazel Rutherford, 15 September 1918, CN H92.137.

26 Ibid., Letter to Hazel Rutherford, 13 February 1918, CN H92.137.

27 Ibid., Letter to Hazel Rutherford, 14 January 1919, CN H92.137.

28 Ad recruiting for the Edmonton Highlands Battalion (194th), *Edmonton Bulletin*, 5 February 1916, 16; "Big Display of War Trophies Brings the Conflict Nearer," *Edmonton Bulletin*, 28 April 1916, front page, 3.

29 "Harry Campbell," *The Morning Bulletin*, 18 May 1918, 2.

30 Ibid.

Works Cited

PRIMARY SOURCES

Edmonton Bulletin
Morning Bulletin (Edmonton)

Royal Alberta Museum, Edmonton. Stanley McCuaig Fonds, CN H92.137.

Voices of War: The Press and the Personal

JEFF KESHEN

Canadians, particularly those living in the prairies, remained far removed from the battles raging in Europe. This was not only the result of geography. Civilians received filtered information about events overseas. True, long casualty lists printed in newspapers and telegraphs, or letters bearing soul-destroying news, brought home the ugly realities of war. Still, those living in Alberta's cities, towns, and in rural domains remained sheltered from the gruesome realities that so often dominated the experiences of those from the province who went overseas to fight in France and Flanders.

News stories destined for Canada from the front were first perused by military personnel in France and often again in London. There was no means of circumventing this process. To prevent the spread of German propaganda to a neutral United States, transatlantic cables were cut at the beginning of August 1914. Reliable wireless service and the beginning of radio broadcasts were still a decade away.

Britain's war minister, Lord Kitchener, did not trust the press, considering journalists as having been too critical of Britain's performance in the 1899–1902 Boer War. Not until March 1915 did Britain's War Office officially accept journalists near the front. Before that, a large proportion of war reports came from Colonel Ernest Swinton, formally of the *London Daily Chronicle*, who was given the title of official *eye-witness*. His dispatches, termed "eyewash" by many newsmen, described war in terms of "plucky cavalry charges."[1]

The drive for frontline Canadian press representation mounted after the country's troops saw action in March 1915 at Neuve Chapelle. Canada's federal government responded by appointing William Maxwell Aitken, later honoured in Britain as Lord Beaverbrook, as *eye-witness*. Information for his dispatches came from military-unit war diaries and designated soldier correspondents, whose words Aitken twisted into inspirational tales of triumph. For example, in early 1916 military records from St. Eloi disclosed that many of Canada's 1,500 casualties (approximately three times those suffered by the enemy) were due to poor air reconnaissance that incorrectly claimed that the Allies controlled certain craters, the result being misdirected artillery support for advancing Canadian troops. For public consumption, however, Aitken told Canadians at home of the "endurance, courage, and cheerfulness" of their troops whose "attacks were delivered with an unabated fury."[2]

By 1916, Canada's journalistic community noted that even the neutral United States had nongovernment press representation in France. One of Aitken's principal assistants advised his boss that this would change newspaper content little, if at all, for besides being subject to censorship laws, it was noted that English and Australian correspondents had demonstrated "a keen sense of patriotism."[3] Likely Aitken had reached a similar conclusion from his role, starting in September 1915, in bringing over small parties of Canadian reporters for brief visits to France. To obtain frontline access, many Canadian publishers wrote to Aitken to assure him that patriotism, not desire for sensationalism, would guide their reporters.

Not only did press reports pass through military censors, but so too did personal correspondence from soldiers. Each company designated an officer as a field censor. Military authorities said the reason was to prevent the leakage of sensitive information. Although regulations did not prohibit men from sending home grisly accounts, one soldier remarked in his diary that "in writing [home] we were supposed to be very cheerful . . . [and] only tell the people . . . how well pleased we were."[4] Many soldiers sought to avoid upsetting or worrying loved ones or, in an age that celebrated courage and chivalry, did not want to appear weak. Countless men also remained fervent in their belief that no matter its costs, the war was essential to the survival of democracy, freedom, and civilization.

Still, this aspect of censorship was not airtight. Censors, often working in dimly lit trench dugouts, examined hundreds of letters. Fatigue and boredom produced lapses. Also, if not sharing the despair that overwhelmed many soldiers, censors sometimes passed gruesome accounts as a result of becoming desensitized to such matter.

Information was also filtered in Canada. On 22 August 1914, Canada's Parliament passed the War Measures Act. Made retroactive to August 4, the beginning of the war for Canada, this statute, among other restrictions, provided for "censorship and control and suppression of publications, writings, maps, plans, photographs, communication and means of communication."[5] Those contravening the act were liable to receive a $5,000 fine (equivalent to $106,000 in 2015[6]), five years in jail, or both. In June 1915, Canada's federal government appointed a Chief Press Censor. The man chosen for the job was Ernest J. Chambers. A former journalist, militia commander, and officer with the Corps of Guides (forerunner to Canada's army intelligence service), Chambers received authority to ban sources "assisting or encouraging the enemy, or preventing . . . or hindering the successful prosecution of the war."[7] In western Canada, J.F. Livesay, former president of the Western Canadian Press Association, assisted Chambers.

In late April 1915, Canadian soldiers experienced their first major clash at the Second Battle of Ypres. Some 18,000 were in the line. Suddenly they saw French colonial soldiers retreating in panic, many collapsing, gasping for air as this fight witnessed the first large-scale use of poison gas. As the deadly mist floated toward Canadian lines, soldiers, without gas masks, were told to urinate onto a piece of clothing and place it over their mouth and nose, as the ammonia acted as a neutralizing agent. Many who could not were soon turning blue. Others desperately tried to get their Ross Rifle to fire, kicking wildly at its bolt, which, unlike the British-made Lee Enfield, jammed from imperfectly made .303 ammunition or when encountering dirt. Canadian forces suffered a one-third casualty rate at Second Ypres—just over 6,000 killed, wounded, or taken prisoner—the highest rate among major battles in which the country's soldiers participated. But they held the line, preventing a major German breakthrough. Typical in its coverage was the *Edmonton Bulletin*, whose front page proclaimed:

> Tried in the crucible of the most intense heat they have not been found wanting . . . Wounded Canadians who came down to the base today . . . were in high spirits, though many of them assuredly will never fight again . . . The Canadians broke all conventional rules of warfare in their amazing operations . . . They found the Germans wheeling all around them, both behind and in front of their trenches. Instantly they adapted themselves to the situation and fitted up a double-ended trench to meet the trouble. They were surrounded . . . and hemmed in on all sides, but it did not avail the enemy. Yelling their war cry they rallied and fought back with infinite courage and dash, giving the Germans behind them, as well as in front of them, most terrible punishment.[8]

Among those fighting at Ypres was Albert Walter Bennett. In the opening weeks of the war, he enlisted in Calgary with the 10th Battalion, and arrived in France in February 1915. A half-century later, he wrote about his experiences in an unpublished memoir. Part of a machine gun crew helping to hold the left flank at Ypres, he and a few comrades were holed up in a farmhouse some 75 metres in advance of the Allied trenches, where he recalled:

> Rifle fire was opening up on all sides of us—and over to our right we could see our men lying out on top of their trenches, firing into the Germans, who we could see two or three fields away . . . Gas fumes were still drifting through our positions . . . Our orders were "To hold the house at all costs" . . . We waited anxiously in the left, watching through both shell-holes. We still had our gun mounted behind the barricade—and decided to leave it there, in case they rushed the house from the side. We knew the gun below would be ready to take care of any attack coming from the front. It was up to us in the loft to do what we thought best. Allen opened fire again at the Germans on the other side of the hedge. Then the gun jammed! Hell broke loose outside with the bullets coming in through the opening. We soon fixed the jam—and just as Allen was ready to fire the gun again—he got his! A bullet clean through the top of his head. He dropped dead on top of me . . . One more gone . . . Who was the next to go? . . . We had been holding the house up to this time for about 60 hours—yet, it seemed like a week. It looked hopeless for us to keep the gun in the loft any longer. The fire from their machine gun, coming through the shell-hole, was cutting down our barricade, in front of our gun. Soon we wouldn't have any cover left at all. We decided to bring the gun down—but, before doing so, I took the handle of the gun and fired into the corner of the hedge until the belt was empty. That would hold them

for a while! Then, without showing ourselves above the barricade, Foss and I immediately dismounted the gun. He took that down while I dragged the tripod along the floor with me . . . It was no use our waiting any longer for the firing to let up, so out we crawled. There was no other way as the manure hole was full of slimy water. We made a quick move, one after the other. The Germans in the ditch opened fire on us—the bullets hitting the cobblestones around us. We got by—dragging the gun, tripod and ammunition behind us. Back into the house again, and what a place! Just a handful of men left—no water to drink, and nothing to eat—and Hell let loose outside. All the same, Foss and I were glad to get out of that loft with our gun—as if we had got trapped up there with a jammed machine-gun—it would have been "all up" with us—as I couldn't imagine them taking us prisoners, with so many of their dead lying out there by the hedges.[9]

On 1 July 1916, British forces launched the long-awaited "Big Push" to end stalemate along the Western Front. Known as the Somme offensive, its first day brought the British 60,000 casualties for nothing of advantage. Into the summer and autumn, the push continued, now involving the Canadians, who took 24,000 casualties for incremental gains at places such as Courcelette and Regina Trench. For many, this part of the war came to symbolize its wanton waste as waves of men poured forth from trenches in massed linear assaults, cut into pieces by shells and machine gun fire.

Describing the attack on Regina Trench, the *Edmonton Bulletin* quoted extensively from a Private Winter, a local lad who insisted that "I could ask for no better or nobler place than beside the men I have seen fall out there." Referring to the night of the attack, he said it "was most horrible, and yet the most magnificent in my lifetime . . . While the Germans had no lack of ammunition . . . they had lack of pluck. When it came to hand to hand encounter, they prayed for mercy and were glad to be sent to the rear in charge of the wounded."[10]

Around the same time, Private Victor Wheeler experienced his baptism of fire. Some six decades later, he wrote of that period in a memoir titled *The 50th Battalion in No Man's Land*. A deeply religious man whose faith sustained him through the misery of war, Wheeler told of the chaos of battle and revealed a rather callous perspective on death, recalling:

On returning to our lines, our inexperienced Patrol Officer mistook the movements of one chap, who had become separated from us in the darkness, as being those of a German. The Officer instantly reacted, tossing a Mills bomb at the shadow. The lagging member of our patrol party found himself on the receiving end of a five-seconds high-explosive bomb and was severely wounded. In the nervous confusion that followed, our Patrol Officer, not giving the "enemy" a chance to identify himself as Comrade K.C., fatally bayoneted him as he tried to crawl away. C'est la guerre![11]

Canada's most celebrated victory of the First World War was at Vimy Ridge. The attack, from 9 to 12 April 1917, saw Canada's four divisions capture an objective that the British and French had formerly failed to take. Though the costs were steep—more than 10,300 casualties, including some

3,700 dead—Vimy became a source for celebration as news of Canada's victory was splashed across the front page of newspapers in England and America. Soon it was a common refrain that Vimy was a nation-building experience for a young Dominion that had shown itself as an equal of Britain, with a right to consultation in shaping the war effort. Typical in its coverage was the *Calgary Herald*, which, like many newspapers across the province and the country, carried a story from Canadian correspondent Roland Hill, who declared:

> The Canadians today are perched well over the top of the Vimy Ridge, thousands of prisoners have been taken, and, according to the first summing up of our casualties, it has been the cheapest victory the troops from the Dominion have won . . . Canada's division started the attack just as a rainy, stormy dawn was breaking. It followed what, one of my informants who has been through three great bombardments, describes as "the Somme's most terrific day multiplied by five." The Huns' first three lines with which the Canadians were well acquainted after many raids were gained with slight casualties. The Bavarian garrisons were dazed into surrender and, in the first hour, over a thousand prisoners were hustled back and five machine guns captured.[12]

Emmanuel "Gus" Lambert was among those killed at Vimy. In 1913, at the age of 17, he and his twin brother, Tony, emigrated from England to Saskatchewan. Gus worked on a farm for a year and then moved to Calgary, where he attended the Mercer school to specialize in art. In October 1914, he enlisted with the 1st Canadian Mounted Rifles,

and went overseas in November 1915. The day before his death, he scrawled a note to his parents and older sister from "France à la mud," reassuring them that "in case old Fritz gets my number don't worry. After all, I had a good run out here—more than most of the boys."[13] His note was enclosed with a letter from Corporal E.M. Hallowsmith to Gus's mother conveying the bad news, but also celebrating her "gallant son," who was killed while trying to help an officer who had been fatally shot by a sniper. "We were all proud of him for his continued pluck and I know his officers thought highly of him," wrote Hallowsmith. "I know what a mother must feel at such a time, but one must be frank and remember that it is a great thing to give one's son to one's country."[14]

Eric Harvie also saw significant action in 1917, particularly shortly after the battle at Vimy Ridge. He had enlisted in 1915 with the 15th Alberta Light Horse; was commissioned as a second lieutenant in the 103rd Regiment, Calgary Rifles, Non-Permanent Active Militia; then a month later was transferred to the 56th Battalion of the Canadian Expeditionary Force. In April 1916, he embarked for England, and in June was commissioned as an officer in the Edmonton-raised 49th Regiment. To his family, Harvie, though maintaining an upbeat and even humorous disposition, still provided insights into the strains of combat:

> Well it's a pretty good war today. Fritz seems tired out and hasn't put a [shell] . . . within 75 yds of us all day. So as a consequence all the boys think we are winning today; in a few hours he'll probably open up again and everybody will confine himself to the depth of the lower regions and everyone will begin to wonder if we are winning or not. It's funny to hear the boys curse when something

comes extra near. I always thought that I had least had a very fair vocabulary even if I never utilized it, but I find that compared with some of the fellows in my section I am a babe unborn. I think if Fritz heard what he was called sometimes he'd give up the war. I was awfully glad Alan [Eric's brother] got out before the big scrap as I was right beside his Bn [battalion] through it all and I can tell you it was a big relief to me to know that he wasn't there as they suffered terrifically. It was a horrible scrap but I must say I wouldn't have missed it for the worlds [*sic*]. I suppose you want to know what I think of the war. Well it is hard just to say it is actually more terrible (at least this last bit was) than I ever dreamt of, but then again the attitude you take toward it is also different than I ever anticipated. It is the attitude that saved everybody from going bug-house; combined with a sense of humour under all conditions. For instance, if a shell drops beside you and covers you with mud and corruption you don't say to yourself my gosh that nearly killed me, but shucks the beggars haven't got anything with my number on it. Well as I read this over you'd think I was morbid or something but nothing is farther from the truth, as I never felt better in my life nor weighed so much. And talking it all through although I can't or no sane person would say that they liked it or that it isn't horrible in a sense, still I must say I wouldn't miss it for anything in the world.[15]

While most soldiers downplayed dangers, discomforts, and fears in their correspondence, this was not the case with Noel Adair Farrow, at least in an August 1917 letter to his mother shortly after being wounded. Born in Summerside, Prince Edward Island, Farrow obtained a diploma from the Ohio Institute of Pharmacy, moved to Alberta in 1912 at age 20, and worked for a pharmacist in Innisfail. Serving with the Canadian Army Medical Corps, he appeared afflicted with battle fatigue following a particularly intense period coping with dead and gruesomely disfigured men, and his own efforts to stay alive.

First I shall ask you to pardon my nervous writing as I am not quite recovered from the shock as of yet. It was on the night of the 14th. I was ordered up with about thirty other men to one of our advance aid posts where we remained all night. Just before dawn our bombardment started. I have been here for two years but the artillery of the 15th was the worst I ever heard. About 4.30 we were ordered out of our dugouts to proceed to our old front line aid post at least 30 yards rear of our front line . . . We had to cross from our trench over an open space of 50 yds. The sgt and four men first then I and my squad. Here one may say Fritz was bombing our trenches and lines of communication like the old nick himself and our task was by no means a pleasant one but we had to reach our post . . . I was within the five [indecipherable] of the sgt. Oh, will I ever forget it the sgt and three men down and I standing there. All I remember was the boys fall. A shower of bricks and mud . . . It was hell Mother right here on earth. I stepped to the sgt's side. There he was with his head held in place by a piece of flesh. His arm torn off the shoulder and a large wound in the chest.

He never knew what hit him poor boy. One of the other boys was wounded through both legs and a third in the chest and face and I in both thighs. The wound was not open but the legs were black and very badly swollen. Our wounded comrades and I started back for our dugouts. All the wounded boys went down the line except myself. I continued to carry stretchers all day and had many close calls but that was one time I stepped from the Valley of Death a reward for the earnest prayers of a loving mother. I am quite well now except a little shaky but shall be all right in a day or so.[16]

The battle of Passchendaele in late October 1917 also came to exemplify the horrors and slaughter of the First World War. The British had launched an offensive in the area, in late July, to drive the Germans from the channel ports and diminish their U-Boat campaign, then wreaking havoc on shipping to and from Britain. Weeks of rain and unrelenting artillery fire had churned the ground into a bog. The Germans held the high ground, namely Passchendaele Ridge. Britain's commander-in-chief, Sir Douglas Haig, turned to the Canadians, 100,000 strong in the area, to take the ridge and the town of Passchendaele. General Arthur Currie, who commanded the Canadian forces, opposed the plan, considering the objectives nonessential, and the offensive as certain to bring massive casualties, but Haig, the supreme commander, insisted. The Canadians arrived at the front in mid-October to relieve ANZAC (Australian and New Zealand Army Corps) forces; they were shocked at the terrain over which they were expected to attack. Still, under a creeping barrage, the Canadians poured out of their trenches on October 26. Several men, especially those wounded, drowned in the

Conditions at Passchendaele, October 1917. Library and Archives Canada, PA-040139.

muck and water. The Canadians eventually reached their objectives, but at the cost of 15,654 casualties, only 346 less than Currie had eerily predicted, though this paled in comparison to 275,000 British and 220,000 German casualties since the campaign had started in July.

Robert Borden, meeting with British Prime Minister Lloyd George in London, threatened that he would not allow another Canadian soldier to leave Canada should there be a repetition of Passchendaele. However, the story Albertans read in the press was much different. The *Calgary Herald* wrote of "bayonet charges that broke the heart of German troops," and that the "best of the Kaiser's troops were sent reeling before an onslaught of cold steel."[17] By contrast, Victor Wheeler's memoir spoke of "unmitigated hell . . . as veterans and recent reinforcements alike fell with every yard of mud gained . . . Approximately two hundred of us were ripped and shredded into bloody pieces that trailed and stained the battlefield."[18]

Despite being in the thick of things, soldiers often commented that they had little idea of the progress of the war beyond their immediate surroundings. Indeed, though often scoffing at the sanitized and upbeat accounts in civilian newspapers, still they asked family and friends to send them copies to better understand the general flow of events and to try to catch up on news from home.

Newspapers of a different sort were published for those in uniform. Produced by all militaries, they were meant to entertain as much as to inform, and were often characterized by satire. The *Wipers Times* was printed for the British Army, its title reflecting the sardonic nickname men gave to Ypres. Canada's military newspapers were battalion-based. They typically contained some war-related news,

inspirational messages from commanding officers, stories of bravery, and, perhaps most appealing, a healthy dose of humour to better enable men to cope with the strains and fierceness of life at the front.

The *Forty-Niner* was printed for those with the 49th Regiment. Its first edition, published in England in early 1917, expressed optimism over what lay ahead, even to the point of offering "sympathy . . . to all members of the Battalion . . . who through

Making sarcastic reference to the upbeat reports about front-line conditions that came from Lord Beaverbrook, or Max Aitken. *Forty-Niner*, vol. 1, no. 6, 7.

various causes has had the misfortune to be left behind . . . on our first trip across the water."[19] In one of its first editions printed in France, it carried a full-page photograph of Private C.J. Kinross, who was awarded a Victoria Cross for his bravery at Passchendaele. The accompanying story spoke of his "most remarkable . . . gallantry . . . [as] on the morning of October 30 . . . Private Kinross, making a careful survey of the situation, deliberately divested himself of all his equipment save his rifle and bandolier, and, regardless of his personal safety, advanced alone over open ground in broad daylight, charged the enemy machine-gun crew of six, killing every member and seized and destroyed the gun."[20]

However, the *Forty-Niner* also poked fun at the vagaries of military life. Sometimes this was done through poetry and song. One entry, "Ode to Brasso," meant to be sung to the tune of "Bonnie Dundee," went in part: "I'm no good in trenches, no use in attack/I can't hit a target, I'm blind as a bat/If a whizz-bang dropped near me I'd die in a fright/But I'm still a good soldier if my buttons are bright."[21] In "Regulations for the Trenches," the *Forty-Niner* quoted from the fictitious "Daily Orders, part 77, subsection 129 X.V.Z., paragraph 33, quarter section 19, range 56, meridian 23 W," to decree that "it is to be distinctly understood that on no account is anyone to swim in the trenches unless clothed in the regulation bathing-dress."[22] Cartoons were also utilized to help soldiers cope with difficult and distressing situations, such as dreadful conditions at the front that made many men hope for a *blighty*, namely a wound not horribly debilitating or disfiguring, but serious enough to send them back to England.

Albertans perceived the war in starkly different ways. The degree to which civilians understood the experiences of those in uniform was distorted by

THE WRITING ON THE WALL.

Celebrating a Blighty, or a non-disfiguring wound, serious enough to send a soldier to England to recuperate. *Forty-Niner*, vol. 1, no. 7, 23.

propagandistic press accounts, censorship, and the willingness and ability of soldiers to share their feelings. Clearly, some soldiers conveyed gritty truths and press accounts did speak of the intensity of battles. However, even when compared to regimental newspapers, information meant for civilians held more closely to romanticized ideals stressing the bravery, pluck, and superiority of Canada's fighting men. Wartime accounts did not prevent war weariness that, in Alberta, became evident in declining voluntary enlistment, rising labour strife, and increased rural discontent. Still, they did maintain a perceptual gulf between civilians and soldiers, who eventually encountered many difficulties reconnecting with one another once the fighting stopped.

Notes

1   Kevin Fewster, "Expression and Suppression: Aspects of Military Censorship in Australia during World War I" (PhD diss., University of New South Wales, 1980), 88.

2   Library and Archives Canada, RG9, Records of the Department of Militia and Defence, vol. 4676, file H.S. 27-1-2, Dispatch, 29 March 1916.

3   House of Lords Record Office, Lord Beaverbrook papers, E/1/16, Beckles Willson to Aitken, 28 June 1916.

4   J.A. Fournier papers, Metropolitan Toronto Library, Baldwin Room, Series A, Diary, 52.

5   House of Commons, *Statutes*, 5 George V, Chapter 22, 22 August 1914.

6   See http://www.bankofcanada.ca/rates/related/inflation-calculator/.

7   Order-in-Council PC 1330, 10 June 1915.

8   *Edmonton Bulletin*, 27 April 1915, 1.

9   Glenbow Archives (Calgary), Albert Walter Bennett Fonds, M7912, unpublished memoir, "The Second Battle of Ypres," 9–18.

10 *Edmonton Bulletin*, 21 October 1916, 15.

11 Victor Wheeler, *The 50th Battalion in No Man's Land* (Edmonton: Alberta Historical Resources Foundation, 1980), 3–7.

12 *Calgary Herald*, 10 April 1917, 1.

13 Glenbow Archives, Gus Lambert Fonds, M467, Gus Lambert to his family, 7 April 1917.

14 Ibid., Corporal E.M. Hallowsmith to Mrs. Lambert, 12 April 1917.

15 Glenbow Archives, Eric Harvie Fonds, G1/1123, Eric Harvie to his family, 17 September 1917.

16 Glenbow Archives, Noel Adair Fonds, M639, file 4, Noel Adair to his mother, 22 August 1917.

17 *Calgary Herald*, 31 October 1917, 1.

18 Wheeler, *50th Battalion*, 166–70.

19 *Forty-Niner* 1, no. 1, 4.

20 Ibid., no. 6, 3.

21 Ibid., no. 6, 10.

22 Ibid., no. 4, 10.

Works Cited

PRIMARY SOURCES

Edmonton Bulletin

Calgary Herald

Forty-Niner (newspaper of the 49th Regiment)

Glenbow Archives, Calgary. Albert Walter Bennett Fonds, M7912. "The Second Battle of Ypres." Unpublished memoir.

———. Eric Harvie Fonds, G1/1123.

———. Gus Lambert Fonds, M467.

———. Noel Adair Fonds, M639.

House of Commons. *Statutes*, 5 George V, Chapter 22, 22 August 1914.

House of Lords Record Office. Lord Beaverbrook papers, E/1/16.

Library and Archives Canada. RG9, Records of the Department of Militia and Defence, vol. 4676, file H.S. 27-1-2.

Metropolitan Toronto Library, Baldwin Room. J.A. Fournier papers, Series A, Diary, 52.

PC Order in Council 1330, 10 June 1915.

SECONDARY SOURCES

Fewster, Kevin. "Expression and Suppression: Aspects of Military Censorship in Australia during World War I." PhD diss., University of New South Wales, 1980.

Wheeler, Victor. *The 50th Battalion in No Man's Land*. Edmonton: Alberta Historical Resources Foundation, 1980.

From Local to National:
Pictorial Propaganda in Alberta during the First World War

JEFF KESHEN

The First World War was fought not only on battle-fields but also for the hearts and minds of those at home. It was the first war in which organized propaganda played a major role. However, in Canada, this developed more slowly than in Britain, France, and, despite its late entry into the war, the United States, where large, centralized government-directed operations were established.

This pattern is evident in pictorial propaganda, namely posters and display advertising, which gained a pervasive wartime presence. The poster had become a legitimate art form by the time of the First World War. Its coming of age was linked to the end of the Art Nouveau period (1895–1915) and advanced by well-known artists, most notably Henri de Toulouse-Lautrec in France. Because of their ability to evoke emotions and quickly convey essential information, posters were used by political parties and labour unions to advance social movements (such as women's suffrage), to publicize entertainment events, and to bolster the war effort.

Britain established an extensive propaganda system early in the war. In late 1914 it created a Parliamentary Recruiting Committee to meet the challenge of quickly raising a massive army. Chaired by Prime Minister Herbert Asquith, it mobilized advertisers, commercial artists, and printing houses to generate some 200 distinct posters, with print runs typically in the thousands.

In Canada, the process of generating propaganda was slower to develop, and was initially highly decentralized. This reflected what historian Paul Maroney, in his analysis of wartime recruiting in Ontario, identified as the locally focused and voluntary nature of Canada.[1] At the time, governments played a very modest role in daily life compared to Britain where rudimentary social policies existed.

For the first half of the war, most posters were locally generated and had very small print runs, typically a few hundred. In Alberta there were a number of commercial printing houses capable of producing such material. An example is the Esdale Press based in Edmonton, which in 1914 released a 180-page, large-format book titled *Edmonton: Alberta's Capital 1914*, with lavish illustrations by McDermid Studios. Newspapers flourished and they were printed by local presses.

Douglas Printing Company, Edmonton, Alberta, 1918. Glenbow Archives, NC-6-3486.

With Canada's military initially overwhelmed with volunteers, the national government did not see the need for a major propaganda effort. Sam Hughes, Canada's minister of militia and defence, boasted to Parliament in early 1915 that he "could raise three more contingents inside of three weeks."[2] He allowed a decentralized and, at times, chaotic approach to recruitment. Rather than recruiting through existing formations, all manner of new regiments were permitted. Some, based upon heritage, stressed the need to make a good showing to maintain the pride of that ethnic group. Chums battalions were established, such as from a particular workplace, university, or even from fans of the Hamilton Tigers Football Club. Hughes also provided no geographic boundaries in which recruiters were to concentrate their efforts. Consequently, some locales were denuded of essential labour while others remained virtually untouched. Reflecting the belief in the boundless willingness of Canadian lads to volunteer, the Department of Militia and Defence provided virtually no funds for recruitment propaganda. Compensating for Ottawa's miserly approach, commanding officers dipped into regimental funds and their own pockets. Even with newspapers charging pennies per line for advertising, most battalions shunned this option. Alberta newspapers contain no reprints of regimental poster propaganda.

There are few surviving recruitment posters from Alberta. Besides having tiny advertising budgets, most formations raised in the province had short life spans, being absorbed into larger configurations overseas. While Calgary's 10th and Edmonton's 49th retained their identity throughout the war, this was not the case with Edmonton's 9th, 51st, 63rd, 66th, 194th, and 202nd; Calgary's 11th, 32nd, 56th, 82nd, and 89th; Lethbridge's 113th; Red Deer's 187th; and Medicine Hat's 175th.

Recruitment propaganda in Alberta mirrored themes established elsewhere but also had distinct qualities grounded in the local market. Some material identified the commanding officer, as such figures were typically well known and considered inspirational. One was W. A. Griesbach, commander of "A" squadron in the 19th Alberta Dragoons, who later played a key role in raising Edmonton's 49th Regiment. Griesbach was also a decorated veteran of the Boer War, a prominent lawyer, and former Edmonton mayor. Recruitment material for Edmonton's 202nd Overseas Battalion not only identified its commanding officer but also conveyed duty to the Mother Country (potential recruits were told to carry the Union Jack forward to victory); the adventure of combat (young men were told that this was "the life for you"); and that war was a manly sport (the battalion presented itself as comprising those with athletic qualities). The 233rd, the West's only French-Canadian formation, expressed loyalty to the Crown but also emphasized practical concerns such as good living quarters, something of appeal given a recession that extended into the first year of the war. Such campaigns helped raise over 45,000 volunteers from among a provincial population of

Recruitment poster from Edmonton's 49th Regiment, 1915.
Kerr Collection, Canadian Militaria Preservation Society, Edmonton, Alberta.

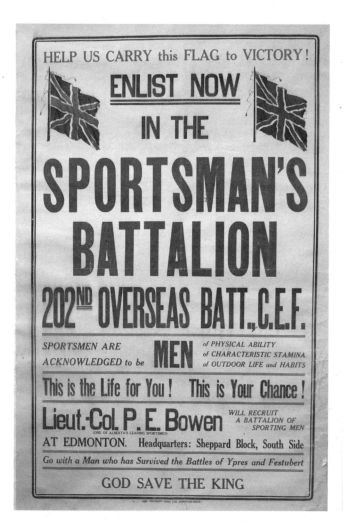

(left) Edmonton's 202nd Battalion promotes itself as a formation for athletic men. Kerr Collection, Canadian Militaria Preservation Society, Edmonton, Alberta; (right) Recruitment poster from the 233rd Battalion targets francophones from across Western Canada. Kerr Collection, Canadian Militaria Preservation Society, Edmonton, Alberta.

nearly 500,000, one of the highest enlistment rates in Canada.

Nationally distributed recruitment propaganda appeared in the latter half of the war. It advanced

familiar themes such as the adventure and comradeship of military service, the need to demonstrate loyalty to Britain, and the glory earned by Canada on the battlefield. Increased government involvement reflected growing difficulty in attracting adequate numbers of recruits, something compounded by rising casualties overseas, and Prime Minister Robert Borden's pledge of 1 January 1916 to raise a 500,000-man volunteer army when little more than 300,000 had enlisted.

The last 18 months of the war also brought nationally distributed, though decidedly modest,

The adventure of war was portrayed to potential recruits. LAC online MIKAN no. 2894452.

newspaper ads for the navy and air force.[3] The ads were informational rather than inspirational. These service branches were small-scale operations in Canada; most of those who enlisted ended up with Britain's Royal Air Force and Royal Navy. Much more significant were government advertisements relating to compulsory military service. These ads commenced at the end of 1916 with the call for Canadians to complete the National Service Board's survey to gauge available human resources, and by autumn 1917 moved to outlining the terms of the Military Service Act and deadlines to apply for an exemption.

Although government was slow in developing propaganda, still, throughout the war, Alberta newspapers contained propagandistic editorial cartoons, company advertisements, and appeals from privately run war-related charitable organizations. Editorial cartoons commonly presented the archetypal militaristic German, often using caricatures of the Kaiser. Under the caption of "Civilized Germany," the front page of the *Edmonton Journal* depicted the Kaiser holding a large knife to a doll representing Belgium.[4] The *Calgary Eye Opener*, a weekly newspaper with a decidedly satirical side (which sometimes landed it in trouble with censorship authorities), was clear about what it saw as the issues at stake. Under the heading "Back to the Jungle," it portrayed a gorilla-type character representing Germany tearing apart books symbolizing "civilization."[5] Conveying a naive, positive, depiction of conflict, another cartoon in the *Journal* depicted soldiers firing at each other having a "fine ole' time" as the caption read that the "sportsman's time has come."[6]

Many companies linked private enterprise to patriotism. Department stores in Calgary and Edmonton advertised "Victory Sales."[7] In High River,

Eversfield & Blair Chemists proudly told of a new germicidal soap it stocked that was ideal to send to soldiers overseas because it "destroys insects, ringworm, and skin disease."[8] In nationally distributed advertising campaigns, the Gillette Razor Company told Canadians to carry their "patriotism into buying" by purchasing its product because its "superior durability" would save them money that could be used to support the war effort.[9]

Starting in late 1914, the privately administered Canadian Patriotic Fund launched a nationwide campaign to raise money to provide an allowance to soldiers' immediate families. Alberta newspapers carried the message that, if one could not fight overseas, then one had an obligation to "pay" to support soldiers and their dependants. Beginning in mid-1915, promotional campaigns for Belgian Relief began filling Alberta newspapers. Based on Britain's Bryce Commission, which used fabricated testimony, propaganda emphasized German savagery, such as the wholesale murder of women and children. The *Calgary Herald* carried an illustration of a dishevelled Belgian woman and her two children desperately fleeing their ravaged homeland.[10] Other major propaganda campaigns included those of the Red Cross, YMCA, Salvation Army, and Knights of Columbus that were geared to easing the plight of Canadian soldiers, allied POWs, and civilians overseas. One advertisement portrayed two weary soldiers, one with a bandage on his head, pointing with hope to a YMCA hut off in the distance.[11]

Government-directed propaganda that further immersed Albertans into a common national discourse got underway in earnest in mid-1917, especially focussed on the need for food control and in support of massive, nationwide Victory Bond drives. In June 1917, Ottawa established a Food Controller's Office, which in February 1918 expanded to become the Canada Food Board. The situation overseas was critical. Between 1913 and 1917, France's wheat crop plunged by 57 percent while Germany's unrestricted U-Boat campaign necessitated the implementation of coupon rationing in Britain.

Propaganda stressing public participation in conservation and production campaigns, and eventually "Meatless Mondays," became a key ingredient in generating success. Between the inauguration of food control and the end of the war, more than $500,000 (worth $8 million in 2015) was spent on promotional activities.[12] Most of this went into nationally distributed posters and newspaper display advertising. Portrayed as guardians of the kitchen, women were beseeched to practice thrift, both by decreasing the quantity of food prepared and by using those items that were in greater supply. "THE WOMEN OF WESTERN CANADA," proclaimed one advertisement, "are more important than ever . . . Theirs will be the making of victory in the Great War."[13] In another gender-based appeal, a boy holding a spade brings his father into the backyard to begin the tough physical work of establishing a "War Garden."[14] Also emphasized was the need to send more food to Britain, something presented as bringing economic benefits, as propaganda spoke of Canada's egg, pork, and beef "opportunity."

Overshadowing all other propaganda campaigns, however, were those to convince Canadians to purchase Victory Bonds. Between 1915 and 1917, the daily costs for Canada to fight the war doubled to $1 million. Prior to 1917 the first three Victory Bond drives were low-key, securing funds from financial institutions. For the fourth loan, in November 1917, the national target doubled to $400 million and the propaganda floodgates opened. Through every conceivable means of communication, citizens were told that duty, national pride, and self-interest demanded a patriotic response. That November, 820,035 people subscribed to securities worth $413.6 million, while in November 1918, 1.067 million citizens loaned Ottawa $660 million, an extraordinary tally in a country whose population barely topped eight million.

A Dominion Publicity Committee within the Department of Finance orchestrated the national campaign. For the fourth and fifth loans, it spent three-quarters of a million dollars. Utilizing the services of public relations firms in Toronto and Montreal, display advertising appeared in more than 1,000 sources, including in every Alberta news publication and magazine. Publicity commenced six weeks prior to the Victory Bond issue date and, during the three-week campaign, the federal government prohibited any other organized appeal for money. Much of the material focused on Victory Bond's favourable terms, namely, that at 5.5 percent interest, it was a percentage point higher than what had been customary to receive before the war. Canadians were told that their money was desperately needed to ensure economic stability. Relating the situation to farmers, one appeal in the *Grande Prairie Herald* explained, "Canada's own producers, who need a market, will have one," as without the ability to extend credit, Britain would be unable to purchase Canadian produce.[15] *Calgary Herald* readers were confronted with an illustration of a man looking in a shop window, while over his shoulder hovered a shadow in the shape of the devil, with the message being "Selfishness and self-indulgence are . . . allies of the Hun."[16] To those who might balk at buying a bond, an illustration of a mother with a son at the front declared: "I know in my own heart that my

Protecting the freedom of future generations through Victory Bond purchases. LAC online MIKAN no. 2894498.

boy's chances of life are in exact proportion to the length of time he stays in France . . . I am told that when those boys go over the top they run less risk if the artillery protection is good. And bonds buy guns

Western images were used to sell Victory Bonds. LAC online MIKAN no. 3635517

and shells."[17] Humour was also used: an appeal in the *High River Times* showed the Kaiser thrown from a bucking horse representing Victory Bonds.[18]

Some nationally distributed poster propaganda expressed a Western theme. One linked the ability to market wheat to providing the government with funds to extend credit, including to Britain. Most material advanced well-established tropes, namely the need to buy bonds to back Canadian soldiers; to set an example and ensure freedom for young Canadians; to vanquish German fiendishness; and, as the war ended, to fund reestablishment programs for veterans.

Not all appeals were national. As with food control, local businesses linked themselves to this campaign. As Christmas approached, a Medicine Hat jewellery shop advertised that though its products made wonderful gifts, a better one was a Victory Bond.[19] A Studebaker dealership in Lethbridge said it would take Victory Bonds at face value for auto- mobile purchases, something it cast as patriotic for "keep[ing] the wheels of industry turning."[20] Also in Lethbridge, advertisements from the local 2-M Clothing Store and the nationally syndicated Hudson's Bay Company told shoppers that their low prices would enable people to make their "dollars fight" by saving them money to purchase Victory Bonds.[21]

Pictorial propaganda played a very significant role in the First World War, especially given the absence of radio and television, and with motion pictures still being a new form of communication. However, in Canada, government mobilization of the public mind was slow to develop. During the first half of the war, recruitment propaganda was locally driven with regiments and battalions sell- ing themselves on factors such as the reputation of their commanding officer, while war-related display advertising came from businesses promoting their patriotism and from privately controlled charities.

Increasingly, however, the war demanded far more resources. In mid-1917, the federal govern- ment appointed a food controller; that office, and its successor, the Canada Food Board, had a healthy advertising budget to rally Canadians behind cam- paigns to practice thrift and enhance production. The move towards centrally and professionally administered government propaganda peaked with later Victory Bond campaigns that inundated com- munities, including across Alberta.

Although the First World War brought consid- erable strain to, and fuelled regional sentiment, in parts of the country including in the prairie West, pictorial propaganda ultimately acted as a galvaniz- ing force. As the Alberta story shows, its develop- ment replaced a local perspective with a national one underlining shared commitment, sacrifice, accom- plishments, and pride.

Notes

1   Paul Maroney, "'The Great Adventure': The Context and Ideology of Recruiting in Ontario," *Canadian Historical Review* 77 (1996): 62–98.

2   Library and Archives Canada (LAC), Records of the Department of National Defence, RG 24, vol. 856, file 54-21-12-5, Extract from House of Commons Debates, 25 February 1915.

3   *Edmonton Bulletin*, 9 August 1917, second section; *High River Times*, 6 November 1917, n.p.

4   *Edmonton Journal*, 29 August 1914, 1.

5   *Calgary Eye Opener*, 28 November 1914, 1.

6   *Edmonton Journal*, 3 September 1914, 1.

7   See, for example, *Calgary Herald*, 27 September 1917, 17.

8   *High River Times*, 19 September 1918, n.p.

9   *Calgary Herald*, 4 October 1918, 5.

10 Ibid., 3 October 1918, 5.

11 Canadian Militaria Preservation Society Collection, Edmonton, AB.

12 Records of the Department of Agriculture, LAC RG 17, vol. 1987, Report of the Food Controller, 26 October 1917.

13 *Edmonton Bulletin*, 27 November 1917, 11

14 Canadian Militaria Preservation Society Collection.

15 *Grande Prairie Herald*, 22 November 1917, n.p.

16 *Calgary Herald*, 1 October 1918, 6.

17 *Edmonton Bulletin*, 27 November 1917, 15.

18 *High River Times*, 14 November 1918, 1.

19 *Medicine Hat News*, 10 November 1917, 7.

20 *Lethbridge Herald*, 10 November 1917, 11.

Works Cited

PRIMARY SOURCES

Calgary Eye Opener
Calgary Herald
Edmonton Bulletin
Edmonton Journal
Grande Prairie Herald
High River Times
Lethbridge Herald
Medicine Hat News

SECONDARY SOURCES

Choko, Marc H. *Canadian War Posters: Posters from the First and Second World Wars*. Cambridge, UK: Worth Press, 2012.

Darracott, Joseph, and Belinda Loftus. *First World War Posters*. London, UK: Imperial War Museum, 1981.

Doll, Maurice F.V. *The Poster War: Allied Propaganda Art of the First World War*. Edmonton: Alberta Community Development, Cultural Facilities and Historical Resources Division, 1993.

Keshen, Jeff. *Propaganda and Censorship during Canada's Great War*. Edmonton: University of Alberta Press, 1996.

Rickards, Maurice. *Posters of the First World War*. London, UK: Evelyn, Adams & Mackay, 1968.

The Great War and Labour in Alberta

ALVIN FINKEL

"We are the producers and we are not getting what we produce"; so protested Grand Trunk Railway machinist E.J. Johnson before the Mathers Commission during its Edmonton hearing on 6 May 1919.[1] Three days earlier, Calgary laundry worker organizer Jean McWilliams commented: "Are we in favour of a bloody revolution? Why, any kind of revolution would be better than conditions as they are now."[2]

The Mathers Commission had been established in March 1919 by the federal government to enquire into the causes of industrial unrest during the First World War and its immediate aftermath, and to report on potential means for creating greater harmony between capital and labour.[3] This chapter explores why many, perhaps a majority, of Alberta urban and industrial workers became disenchanted with the organization of the war effort, even though the mobilization for war gradually ended a nasty recession that began in 1913, and created virtually full employment in the province for a time. It also looks at the consequences of that disenchantment as the war wound down, ending whatever war-induced prosperity many individuals and families had enjoyed.

Some politically conscious workers opposed the war effort from the start. Charles O'Brien, for example, who served as the Socialist Party MLA for the Rocky Mountain constituency from 1909 until his narrow defeat in 1913, argued in a speech in November 1914 that "the master class, in order to avert impending disaster . . . had to do something to divert the attention of the workers. They chose war."[4] A majority of United Mine Workers of America (UMWA) members in Alberta had voted to make the Socialist Party their official voice shortly after O'Brien's electoral defeat, demonstrating miner antipathy with the pro-capitalist thinking of their neighbours. Miners, who had struck often in efforts to get better wages and safer working conditions, had much cause to be disillusioned. There had been repeated mine disasters in the province, and the worst occurred less than two months before the declaration of war when an explosion at the Hillcrest Coal and Coke Company cost 189 miners' lives. The coroner's inquest report noted that "the jury desire to add that they do not think the regulations of the Coal Mines Act have been strictly adhered to."[5]

In the cities, as well, many workers believed that the political and economic systems ignored

Aftermath of the Hillcrest Mining disaster. Glenbow Archives, NA-1767-1.

their interests. The Industrial Workers of the World (IWW), an organization with origins in the US, sparked interest in western Canada with its syndicalist campaign for general strikes—sympathy strikes by all workers to ensure victories for striking workers—and for the right to free speech, and free assembly. Though there were no general strikes of Alberta workers before the war, the IWW message of worker resistance had a particular resonance for the unemployed in Calgary and Edmonton during the recession of 1913–14, and the "Wobblies" (as the IWW became known) successfully enjoined the unemployed to occupy churches for a place to sleep, to eat in restaurants without paying the bill, and to demonstrate to demand that the authorities create work with wages for the unemployed.[6]

The crafts unions, far more conservative than the IWW, were nonetheless angry as the pre-1913 boom in Alberta ended, leaving many of their members unemployed and with little state provision for help. In the context of their increasing alienation from the system, it was unsurprising that on 3 August 1914, the day the war started, the Edmonton Trades and Labour Council (ETLC) passed a motion brought forward by carpenters' representative Joseph Knight, a Socialist, that "the sympathies of the Edmonton Trades and Labour Council are entirely with the working class, irrespective of nationality, who will, as they always have in the past, bear the burden of misery and privation which will be the inevitable result of the war being waged at the present in Europe."[7]

Marxist analyses of the causes and beneficiaries of warfare notwithstanding, working people, including trade union members, enlisted in droves to fight for Britain, if only, for some, as a welcome alternative to devastating unemployment that persisted until the early months of 1916. Edmonton was home to between 3,000 and 6,000 unemployed workers at most times between the beginning of 1913 and the end of 1915. The city organized a relief camp on its fair grounds, then closed it in response to IWW organization of the ground's inmates. Calgary and Lethbridge also reported that their civic charities were overwhelmed by the demands of the unemployed.[8]

About 60 percent of Calgary's tradesmen signed up to fight.[9] In 1912 and 1913, the Trades and Labour Congress of Canada (TLC) had adopted resolutions favouring a general strike should the Canadian government declare war. It shelved such militancy when the declaration actually occurred, rejecting radicals' analysis that the conflict was a war of rival imperialisms in favour of an argument that it was a war of British democracy against continental European despots.[10]

Sufficient antipathy to the war remained to make it unacceptable to the leadership of labour in the province, both radical and moderate, that any working people be conscripted into the fight. In 1916 the Calgary Trades and Labour Council (CTLC) joined other western city and town labour councils in denouncing the federal government's announcement that it would conduct a national registration of manpower resources. The CTLC suspected, correctly, that the registration was the prelude to conscription, and warned that conscription of labour was only acceptable to its members if it was accompanied by "conscription of wealth," by which it meant the suspension of profit-making by industry while the war lasted.

Soaring inflation—which began in earnest in 1916, and reached the national rate of 18 percent in 1917 and 13.5 percent in 1918—angered workers, few of whom proved able to win wage increases that matched rising prices. Food and fuel price increases were particularly dramatic. By July 1920 the cost of a sample food basket used in cost-of-living surveys had jumped 128 percent since the war began in August 1914. The CTLC, however, did not follow the example of Winnipeg and Vancouver in threatening

Alex Ross was Labour's first elected member in the Alberta legislature. In 1917, he defeated Conservative Thomas Tweedie running as a member of the Labor Representation League, which later merged with the Dominion Labor Party of Alberta. The cartoon plays on his trade as a stonemason working with the building blocks of labour issues including "Minimum Wage, Workmen's Compensation, Amended Factories Act, Taxation and the Patriotic Fund." From *The Albertan Non-Partisan*, Calgary, 8 February 1918. Glenbow Archives.

Alex. Ross through years of service has earned the confidence of the workers in this community. He will now fight labor's battle in the Provincial Legislature, where his practical mind and wide knowledge of labor problems will be able to exert a strong influence on provincial legislation in the interest of the workers.

to engage in a general strike if the federal government implemented conscription of labour without conscripting wealth.[11] Instead, two moderate Alberta labour leaders, Alf Farmilo, an Edmonton stonemason, and Alex Ross, Calgary stonemason and MLA, moved at the September 1917 TLC convention that the national labour organization should oppose conscription of men unless there was also conscription of wealth. The motion was defeated, adding to a long-standing rift between western and eastern Canadian trade unionists about whether labour should assert tough political positions and then follow them up with action.[12]

Opposition to conscription in the provincial labour movement provided the major spur for the Calgary and Edmonton labour councils to create Labour Representation Leagues in 1917, on March 19 and May 4, respectively, dedicated to preventing forced recruitment into the armed forces.[13] The Calgary League joined with the farm-based Non-Partisan League (NPL) to nominate William Irvine, preacher, sometime railway worker, and NPL activist, as its candidate in Calgary East. The Labour League declared itself "for the most courageous and democratic and the most adequate policy ever advanced in Canada, i.e. Universal Conscription. It stands for conscription carried to the logical conclusion and not a class conscription imposed by a class government to save its wealth while it takes human life."[14]

The labour candidates, like all of the Alberta candidates opposed to conscription, lost to Unionist, meaning pro-conscription, candidates. Irvine won just short of a third of the votes in Calgary East, a shade better than average for the anti-conscription candidates in the province.[15] That result, no doubt, understated his real support. Anti-conscription

sentiment in the province and the country was systematically underreported electorally thanks to the combination of the Military Voters Act and the War-Time Elections Act, passed by the federal government in the months before the election. Between them, these laws removed the right to vote from citizens whose origins were in "enemy" countries and who had been Canadian citizens for less than 15 years (which, effectively, disenfranchised almost all of them because large-scale immigration from the Austro-Hungarian Empire had begun only in 1897). Even the early immigrants would not have been resident long enough to receive citizenship before 1902. These pieces of legislation also created a female franchise restricted to women serving in the armed forces, or having close relatives who had enlisted. The votes of soldiers who did not list their constituency of origin could be assigned by the government to whatever constituency it chose, which allowed government supporters to win seats where a majority of resident voters had actually voted for the opposition.[16]

Workers, both pro-conscription and anti-conscription, took advantage of the shortage of labour that prevailed in the province beginning in 1916 to join trade unions in record numbers, and to strike, when necessary, to force employers to yield to their demands, or at least to bargain. There were no protections in law at the time anywhere in Canada of the right to join a union, to bargain collectively, or to strike.[17] So the knowledge that employers would have a hard time replacing them encouraged workers, who may have been intimidated to accept what employers offered in the period when unemployment was high. If an employer had the audacity to fire them or to refuse to negotiate, there were many other employers who would be eager to hire them. Calgary had 1,769 unionists at the end of 1915, and 3,000 by the beginning of 1917. Service industry workers, including even domestic workers whose dispersal in private homes made them virtually unorganizeable before the war, began to unionize.[18] In both Edmonton and Calgary, as well as in various towns, civic workers who had been without union representation before the war—including firefighters, police, and city hall employees—took advantage of the new economic conditions to organize.[19] The provincial government workers waited till just after the war and created the Civil Service Association in 1919.[20]

Teachers, who had been unorganized before the war, were frustrated that many school boards, continuing a long tradition of imposing conditions and pay on their teachers, docked teacher pay unilaterally to make contributions to the war effort. Led by Edmonton and Calgary teachers, a large percentage of Alberta teachers formed the Alberta Teachers' Alliance (now the Alberta Teachers' Association) in 1917. The new organization hired John Barnett as a full-time secretary-treasurer in 1918, a position that he held until 1946. Despite the antipathy of rural school trustees, the ATA had signed up two-thirds of the province's teachers by 1921.[21] It remained a voluntary organization until 1936 when Premier William Aberhart made membership for teachers in the ATA compulsory.[22]

Strikes became more common as labour scarcity increased. Only 500 workers had been involved in strikes in Alberta in 1916. In 1917 the figure was 11,000, with miners in southern Alberta accounting for the majority. Crowsnest Pass miners were on strike for better wages and safer working conditions for much of the period from November 1916 to July 1917. Their leaders having been critics of the war from the beginning, the miners were largely unconcerned with the claims of the government and the mine owners that they were serving the interests of the Kaiser against the Canadian people. The government eventually conceded some of their wage demands, and named a Dominion Fuel Controller and a Director of Coal Operations to take charge of the mines from the mine owners for the duration of the war.[23]

The strike wave went well beyond the miners to include such sectors as the post office, railways, Edmonton firefighters, and Calgary flour and cereal workers. From 1 January 1917 to 30 June 1919, 600,000 work days were lost to strikes in the province.[24] In part, the big increase in strikes was a result of a new focus on sympathy strikes. The IWW philosophy, viewed as impractical by most workers when jobs were scarce, appeared a realistic tactic in the context of labour shortages. In September 1918, as the federal government threatened to legislate freight handlers in Calgary back to work, half of the city's unionized workers obeyed a call for a general strike from the city's Trades and Labour Council. This forced the federal government to make concessions to the freight handlers. Similarly, the following month, Edmonton's Trades and Labour Council helped to win a labour settlement when it endorsed a sympathy strike with members of the Canadian Brotherhood of Railway Employees.[25] Eight months earlier, a dispute between the newly organized Edmonton firefighters and the city council over the naming of the new fire chief had been enough to cause a strike of the firefighters and a threat of a general sympathy strike. Twenty-six locals held plebiscites to determine whether their members were prepared to strike their own employers in solidarity with the firefighters' demand that the seniority clause in their contract be respected in the naming of the fire chief. Seventeen locals voted to strike. The previously recalcitrant city council rescinded its selection of the chief and acceded to the union's demand to respect the contract in naming a new chief. The willingness of workers in different occupations to act collectively to assert workers' rights as superior to management rights represented a dramatic shift in class-consciousness in wartime-created conditions.[26]

The federal government responded to the wave of strikes and sympathy strikes across the country, along with growing radicalism, with a series of orders-in-council that, in the guise of defending the war effort, attempted to eliminate the threats that the ruling class perceived to the social order. In September 1918, PC 2381 prohibited the use of "enemy languages" in all publications within Canada, while PC 2384, promulgated simultaneously, banned outright 14 organizations deemed radical, including the IWW and a variety of socialist/ethnic organizations. Even having been a past member of the banned organizations became a crime, along with any favourable mention of them or their publications. On 11 October 1918 the government declared, via PC 2525, that all strikes and lockouts in Canada were illegal until further notice; all issues in dispute between unions and management were to go to compulsory arbitration. All of this legislation threatened stiff fines and jail sentences for violators.[27]

Spying that had been conducted throughout the war by the Dominion Police (Canada's paramilitary police and security force for provinces east of Manitoba) and the Royal North-West Mounted Police (the two were combined to create the Royal Canadian Mounted Police in 1920) had identified a large number of alleged subversives. Thus, arrests under the various orders-in-council occurred swiftly, and

caused a bitter reaction among labour and socialist activists that would long outlast the war. In Alberta, the RNWMP had been spying in the Crowsnest Pass since 1915. Frank Zanetti, operating under the name Harry Blask, had infiltrated the IWW and then the Socialist Party in Alberta, starting in Drumheller and Canmore, afterwards moving to Calgary in 1918. Blask provided information to the RNWMP about all radical activities within the city, and his insider claims would become part of the state's evidence at the trial of R.B. Russell, one of the leaders of the Winnipeg General Strike of 1919.[28]

The state crackdown on labour and political radicals, in the last months of the war, contributed to militancy among working people that wartime inflation, unchecked by state action, and conscription, had also helped to incite. Prompted by the Socialist Party, and by the remnants of the IWW, radicals within the labour movement, by war's end, were promoting the idea of "One Big Union." The OBU would go beyond organization of workers by industry to organization of all workers in one union with an "each for all" philosophy that would make general strikes the main economic weapon of the working class. The Socialist promoters of the OBU largely rejected the old IWW notion that such class economic warfare would produce socialist revolution. They viewed it more as a tactic to educate workers to see their collective power and encourage them to then use parliamentary means to create a workers' government in Canada.[29]

The "one big union" approach was endorsed overwhelmingly by the Western Labour Conference, called in Calgary in March 1919 to draft western proposals to counter the perceived conservative approach of the TLC to the federal government's pro-capitalist and repressive policies. Influenced by

Strikers belonging to the One Big Union at Drumheller, Alberta, 1919. Glenbow Archives, NA-2513-1.

the success of the Bolshevik Revolution in Russia, the conference passed a resolution that included such fighting words as "This convention declares its full acceptance of this principle of 'Proletarian Dictatorship' as being absolute and efficient for the transformation of capitalist private property to public or communal wealth."[30]

Proposals for radical socialist responses to repression and to economic inequalities were met with division within the labour movement. Much of the labour establishment insisted on continuing organization of the labour force by craft, rather than supporting the industry-wide unions with no distinction between crafts and day labourers that socialists and the IWW favoured. In April 1919 the Edmonton Trades and Labour Council expelled member unions that openly supported the call for an OBU to replace existing craft organizations. That included Edmonton's Carpenters, Federated Labour Union No. 49, and UMWA Local 4070. Machinists

and street railway workers quit the council in sympathy with the expelled locals.[31]

Many of the unions that expelled the OBU supporters, however, proved ambivalent about securing change purely through traditional collective bargaining. During the war, craft unions had often combined to negotiate with groups of employers. When Winnipeg employers, in both the machine trades and building trades, declared that they would only negotiate one craft at a time, their intransigence, added to a radical atmosphere created by wartime discontent and the excitement created by the OBU idea, produced a general strike in that city that began on 15 May 1919. ETLC members, fearful of the employer counter-offensive suggested by the attitude of Winnipeg's employers, decided to stage a sympathy strike with the Winnipeg workers. Thirty-eight of 49 remaining locals voted on whether to strike, and 34 elected to join the sympathy action, which was led by a strike committee that included the locals that had been expelled or had left.[32] The ETLC tried to retain the whip hand among unions on strike through its newspaper, the *Edmonton Free Press*. The paper denounced the OBU, and attempted to focus the strikers' demands on the strengthening of the bargaining power of trade unions and away from socialist calls for a new economic order from which private capital would be largely removed.[33]

In Calgary as well, splits in the labour movement over the OBU did not prevent a large number of union locals from joining a sympathy strike. In both cities, over half of all unionized workers were on strike at least part of the time from May 26 to June 25, with only essential services spared from the civic workers' shutdown of services. In all, there were about 2,000 Edmonton workers and 1,500 Calgary workers on strike in cities with populations of 66,000 and 75,000, respectively.[34] Workers in Lethbridge also joined the sympathy strike.[35]

A few days before the sympathy strikes in Edmonton and Calgary began, 6,500 miners belonging to District 18 of the UMWA, which had organized most of the miners in the south of the province, closed the mines to demand that the industry recognize the OBU as their representative, rather than the UMWA which the miners believed had become too comfortable with the bosses. Ninety-five percent of the miners had voted to join the OBU, with only 5 percent preferring to remain in the UMWA. The companies hired goons to attack strikers physically, and received reinforcements from the newly formed Alberta Provincial Police. The showdown between the two sides lasted more than two months. While the companies made concessions to the workers regarding wages, they refused to recognize the

OBU over the compliant UMWA. Their resolve was supported by the federal government's appointee as director of coal operations, W.H. Armstrong. Effectively, the federal government opposed the right of workers to choose their own representatives in favour of maintaining the privileges of the mine owners of Alberta.[36]

Government actions suggested an unwillingness to give greater economic power to working people and the trade union representatives, whom they chose. For the most part, the federal government ignored the findings of its own creation, the Mathers Commission, which, while its majority report was vague in its recommendations, was clear that the chief causes of continuing unrest included "unemployment and the fear of unemployment"; the high cost of living, and the desire of the worker for a larger share of the product of their labour; a

The 26 May 1919 edition of the *Edmonton Bulletin* announces the impending Edmonton general strike.

desire for shorter work hours; and denial of rights to organize and to bargain collectively. Further, the commissioners noted as contributing factors a "lack of confidence in constituted government," "insufficient and poor housing," restrictions on freedom of speech and freedom of the press, "ostentatious displays of wealth," and a "lack of equal educational opportunities."[37]

Alberta's coal mine owners had nonetheless impressed two of the commission members, who chose to write a minority report. They claimed:

> In the Province of Alberta this "One Big Union" was in part recruited by Austrians and other aliens who, owing to the scarcity of labour in the local mines and other industries throughout this province, had been fully employed during the war. These aliens, for their own protection, are 100 per cent organized; and any organization willing to include them in its membership found it easy to do so. War conditions created such demand for production that when highly organized bodies of this character made demands upon the operators they were obliged to grant them rather than have curtailment in production.[38]

The effort to portray the divisions within Alberta as between people of British descent and "aliens," as opposed to workers versus employers, was mined effectively by employers' groups across western Canada in the wake of all prewar, wartime, and postwar radicalism.[39]

State repression, along with state and employer intervention on the side of more conservative unionists, damaged the prospects of the OBU and of radicals more generally. Still, the Labour Representation Leagues, formed initially to oppose conscription, became the seed of Alberta labour's fruitful postwar entry into municipal, provincial, and federal politics. That included labour representation in the first United Farmers of Alberta (UFA) government, in 1921, and a de facto alliance between the Canadian Labour Party's Alberta section and the UFA throughout the latter's period of government from 1921 to 1935. Although labour's political clout was severely restricted after Social Credit swept the province in the provincial and federal elections of 1935, wartime organization had paved the way for more than a decade and a half of effective labour political action in Alberta. That labour political action would play a major role in creating the national Co-Operative Commonwealth Federation (CCF), forerunner of the NDP.[40]

For several generations, Alberta has been viewed by political commentators as a bastion of conservatism. A focus on working people and the First World War helps us understand why Alberta's organized workers were poised, at the end of the war, to be a major progressive contributor to provincial political life for some time, and to have a lasting impact on labour's political importance within Canada for generations to come. A focus on labour and the war, much like a focus on the treatment of "aliens," raises questions about whether Canada fought in the war to uphold democratic rights as opposed to simply defending British imperialism. While working people made some advances during the war thanks to wartime labour shortages, those gains occurred in spite of state policies of censorship, spying, manipulating the right to vote, supporting management against labour, and ignoring workers' choices for union representation. As the war ended, and unemployment mounted, the continuation of many of these anti-democratic policies proved harmful to working people's interests.

Notes

1 Gregory S. Kealey, "1919: The Canadian Labour Revolt," *Labour/Le Travail* 13 (Spring 1984): 12.

2 Ibid., 15.

3 Royal Commission on Industrial Relations, *Report of Commission*, appointed under Order-in-Council (PC 670) to enquire into Industrial Relations in Canada, together with a Minority Report and Supplementary Report (printed as a supplement to the *Labour Gazette*, July 1919). For background on Thomas Graham Mathers, the chair of the Commission, see Dale Brawn, *The Court of Queen's Bench of Manitoba: 1870–1950: A Biographical History* (Toronto: University of Toronto Press, 2006), 185–199.

4 Alan Seager, "Socialists and Workers: The Western Canadian Coal Miners, 1900–21," *Labour/Le Travail* 16 (1985): 45.

5 Steve Hanon, *The Devil's Breath: The Story of the Hillcrest Mine Disaster of 1914* (Edmonton: NeWest Press, 2013), 237.

6 Jim Selby, "One Step Forward: Alberta Workers 1885–1914," in *Working People in Alberta: A History*, edited by Alvin Finkel et al. (Edmonton: Athabasca University Press, 2012), 70–71.

7 Warren Caragata, *Alberta Labour: A Heritage Untold* (Toronto: James Lorimer, 1979), 55–56.

8 Eric Strikwerda and Alvin Finkel, "War, Repression, and Depression, 1914–1939," in *Working People in Alberta: A History*, edited by Alvin Finkel et al. (Edmonton: Athabasca University Press, 2012), 81.

9 David Bright, *The Limits of Labour: Class Formation and the Labour Movement in Calgary, 1883–1929* (Vancouver: UBC Press, 1998), 110; David Bright, "'We Are All Kin': Reconsidering Labour and Class in Calgary, 1919," *Labour/Le Travail* 29 (Spring 1992): 70.

10 Craig Heron and Myer Siemiatycki, "The Great War, the State, and Working Class Canada," in *The Workers' Revolt in Canada, 1917–1925*, edited by Craig Heron (Toronto: University of Toronto Press, 1998), 13; Judy Fudge and Eric Tucker, *Labour Before the Law: The Regulation of Workers' Collective Action in Canada, 1900–1948* (Toronto: University of Toronto Press, 2004), 91.

11 Bright, *The Limits of Labour*, 116–17; Robert Bothwell, Ian Drummond, and John English, *Canada, 1900–1945* (Toronto: University of Toronto Press, 1987), 162; Paul Michael Boothe and Heather Edwards, eds., *Eric J. Hanson's Financial History of Alberta, 1905–1950* (Calgary: University of Calgary Press, 2003), 63; Heron and Siemiatyick, "The Great War," 20; and Caragata, *Alberta Labour*, 61.

12 Caragata, *Alberta Labour*.

13 Alvin Finkel, "The Rise and Fall of the Labour Party in Alberta, 1917–42," *Labour/Le Travail* 16 (1985): 68.

14 William Mardiros, *William Irvine: The Life of a Prairie Radical* (Toronto: Lorimer, 1979), 65.

15 Ibid.

16 J.L. Granatstein and J.M. Hitsman, *Broken Promises: A History of Conscription in Canada* (Toronto: Oxford University Press, 1977), 71.

17 Trade unions were provided with legal recognition under the law by John A. Macdonald's Trade Unions Act of 1872. That recognition, while preventing employers from taking union leaders who registered their union under the provisions of the act to court for the mere fact of organizing a union or a strike, did not either prevent employers from firing workers for unionizing or require employers to bargain with a union created by their employees. In any case, a registered union was responsible for paying fines for any damages caused by their members, with the result that few unions registered. The first legislation to provide protection for the right to bargain collectively in Alberta was not passed until 1937. Bryan Palmer, *Working Class Experience: Rethinking the History of Canadian*

Labour, 1800–1991, 2nd ed. (Toronto: McClelland and Stewart, 1992), 111; Fudge and Tucker, *Labour Before the Law*, 220.

18 Bright, *The Limits of Labour*, 111.

19 David Bright, "1919: A Year of Extraordinary Difficulty," in *Alberta Formed, Alberta Transformed*, vol. 2, edited by Michael Payne, Donald Wetherell, and Catherine Cavanaugh (Calgary: University of Calgary Press, 2006), 424; Tom Monto, *Old Strathcona Before the Great Depression* (Edmonton: Crang Publishing, 2008), 387.

20 Strikwerda and Finkel, "War, Repression, and Depression," 86.

21 John West Chalmers, *Teachers of the Foothills Province: The Story of the Alberta Teachers' Association* (Toronto: University of Toronto Press, 1968), 3.

22 Alvin Finkel, *The Social Credit Phenomenon in Alberta* (Toronto: University of Toronto Press, 1989), 43.

23 Strikwerda and Finkel, "War, Repression, and Depression," 83–84.

24 Ibid., 84; Caragata, *Alberta Labour*, 61.

25 Bright, *The Limits of Labour*, 148–49; Kealey, "1919: The Canadian Labour Revolt," 30.

26 Strikwerda and Finkel, "War, Repression, and Depression," 77.

27 Gregory S. Kealey, "State Repression of Labour and the Left in Canada, 1914–1920: The Impact of the First World War," *Canadian Historical Review* 73, no. 3 (September 1992): 294, 299; Barbara Roberts, *Whence They Came: Deportation from Canada, 1900–1935* (Ottawa: University of Ottawa Press, 1988), 81; Reg Whitaker, Gregory S. Kealey, and Andrew Parnaby, *Secret Service: Political Policing in Canada from the Fenians to Fortress America* (Toronto: University of Toronto Press, 2012), 68–69.

28 Whitaker, Kealey, and Parnaby, *Secret Service*, 60, 71, 84.

29 Gerald Friesen, "'Yours in Revolt': The Socialist Party of Canada and the Western Labour Movement," *Labour/Le Travailleur* 1, no. 1 (1976): 139–57; Tom Mitchell and James Naylor, "The Prairies: In the Eye of the Storm," in *The Workers' Revolt in Canada, 1917–1925*, edited by Craig Heron (Toronto: University of Toronto Press, 1998), 194–95.

30 Strikwerda and Finkel, "War, Repression, and Depression," 77.

31 Kealey, "1919: The Canadian Labour Revolt," 30.

32 Ibid.

33 The ETLC began publishing the *Edmonton Free Press* on 12 April 1919, and from the first issue, the paper was as dedicated to blasting the OBU as to promoting an agenda for labour. Finkel, "The Rise and Fall," 67.

34 Strikwerda and Finkel, "War, Repression, and Depression," 91.

35 Ibid.

36 Bright, "1919: A Year of Extraordinary Difficulty," 430–31; A.B. Woywitka, "The Drumheller Strike of 1919," *Alberta Historical Review* 21, no. 1 (Winter 1973): 1–7; Caragata, *Alberta Labour*, 77–81.

37 Royal Commission on Industrial Relations, *Report of Commission*, 6.

38 Ibid., 21.

39 See Donald Avery, *Dangerous Foreigners: European Immigrant Workers and Labour Radicalism in Canada, 1896–1932* (Toronto: McClelland and Stewart, 1979).

40 Finkel, "The Rise and Fall."

Works Cited

PRIMARY SOURCES

Royal Commission on Industrial Relations. *Report of Commission*, PC 670 together with a Minority Report and Supplementary Report printed as a supplement to the *Labour Gazette*, July 1919.

SECONDARY SOURCES

Avery, Donald. *Dangerous Foreigners: European Immigrant Workers and Labour Radicalism in Canada, 1896–1932*. Toronto: McClelland and Stewart, 1979.

Boothe, Paul Michael, and Heather Edwards, eds. *Eric J. Hanson's Financial History of Alberta, 1905–1950.* Calgary: University of Calgary Press, 2003.

Bothwell, Robert, Ian Drummond, and John English. *Canada, 1900–1945.* Toronto: University of Toronto Press, 1987.

Bright, David. "1919: A Year of Extraordinary Difficulty." In *Alberta Formed, Alberta Transformed*, edited by Michael Payne, Donald Wetherell, and Catherine Cavanaugh. Vol. 2. Calgary: University of Calgary Press, 2006.

——. *The Limits of Labour: Class Formation and the Labour Movement in Calgary, 1883–1929.* Vancouver: UBC Press, 1998.

——. "'We Are All Kin': Reconsidering Labour and Class in Calgary, 1919." *Labour/Le Travail* 29 (Spring 1992).

Caragata, Warren. *Alberta Labour: A Heritage Untold.* Toronto: James Lorimer, 1979.

Chalmers, John West. *Teachers of the Foothills Province: The Story of the Alberta Teachers' Association.* Toronto: University of Toronto Press, 1968.

Finkel, Alvin. "The Rise and Fall of the Labour Party in Alberta, 1917–42." *Labour/Le Travail* 16 (1985).

——. *The Social Credit Phenomenon in Alberta.* Toronto: University of Toronto Press, 1989.

Friesen, Gerald. "'Yours in Revolt': The Socialist Party of Canada and the Western Labour Movement." *Labour/Le Travailleur* 1, no. 1 (1976).

Fudge, Judy, and Eric Tucker. *Labour Before the Law: The Regulation of Workers' Collective Action in Canada, 1900–1948.* Toronto: University of Toronto Press, 2004.

Granatstein, J.L., and J.M. Hitsman. *Broken Promises: A History of Conscription in Canada.* Toronto: Oxford University Press, 1977.

Hanon, Steve. *The Devil's Breath: The Story of the Hillcrest Mine Disaster of 1914.* Edmonton: NeWest Press, 2013.

Heron, Craig, and Myer Siemiatycki. "The Great War, the State, and Working Class Canada." In *The Workers' Revolt in Canada, 1917–1925*, edited by Craig Heron. Toronto: University of Toronto Press, 1998.

Kealey, Gregory S.K. "1919: The Canadian Labour Revolt." *Labour/Le Travail* 13 (Spring 1984).

——. "State Repression of Labour and the Left in Canada, 1914–1920: The Impact of the First World War." *Canadian Historical Review* 73, no. 3 (September 1992): 294, 299.

Mardiros, William. *William Irvine: The Life of a Prairie Radical.* Toronto: Lorimer, 1979.

Mitchell, Tom, and James Naylor. "The Prairies: In the Eye of the Storm." In *The Workers' Revolt in Canada, 1917–1925*, edited by Craig Heron, 194–95. Toronto: University of Toronto Press, 1998.

Monto, Tom. *Old Strathcona Before the Great Depression.* Edmonton: Crang, 2008.

Palmer, Bryan. *Working Class Experience: Rethinking the History of Canadian Labour, 1800–1991.* 2nd ed. Toronto: McClelland and Stewart, 1992.

Roberts, Barbara. *Whence They Came: Deportation from Canada, 1900–1935.* Ottawa: University of Ottawa Press, 1988.

Seager, Alan. "Socialists and Workers: The Western Canadian Coal Miners, 1900–21." *Labour/Le Travail* 16 (1985).

Selby, Jim. "One Step Forward: Alberta Workers 1885–1914." In *Working People in Alberta: A History*, edited by Alvin Finkel et al. Edmonton: Athabasca University Press, 2012.

Strikwerda, Eric, and Alvin Finkel. "War, Repression, and Depression, 1914–1939." In *Working People in Alberta: A History*, edited by Alvin Finkel et al. Edmonton: Athabasca University Press, 2012.

Whitaker, Reg, Gregory S. Kealey, and Andrew Parnaby. *Secret Service: Political Policing in Canada from the Fenians to Fortress America.* Toronto: University of Toronto Press, 2012.

The Great Western Garment Company during the First World War

CATHERINE C. COLE

The Great Western Garment Company (GWG) contributed to the war effort by producing military uniforms. GWG had been established in 1911 by Alexander C. Rutherford, Alfred E. Jackson, and Charles A. Graham to provide functional, hard-wearing clothing initially marketed to agricultural, railway, mining, and other industrial workers. The company was founded at a time when Edmonton's economy was booming and the future looked bright; however, the boom ended the next year and work was not always steady.

Garment manufacturing required a relatively small capital investment. Before assembly-line methods and automated machinery were introduced, the overhead cost was primarily wages, which most manufacturers kept to a minimum. However, GWG paid slightly higher rates than other garment manufacturing firms, as it had been unionized, within months of being established, as Local 120 of the United Garment Workers of America (UGWA). This was done to develop an affinity with working people through use of the union label and promotion of workers' wages and working conditions.

Although orders ebbed and flowed, and workers were laid off when there was not enough business, overall demand was high, and GWG expanded rapidly. The workforce increased from an initial seven to more than 100 in its first year of operations, and to 150 by 1914. The plant doubled in size, taking over the adjacent building on Namayo Street (now called 97th Street) between 104th and 105th Avenues through an additional investment of $150,000. When the war broke out, GWG was only a few years old but was already a significant local enterprise.

Workers were paid on a piecework basis, with the price for each operation set through negotiations between the union local and management. When new styles or fabrics were introduced, new prices had to be determined. In the summer of 1914, workers at the plant were in negotiations with management for a new contract and discussed the strategy of withholding the union label if they could not come to terms on a new price list. UGWA representatives from Toronto, or headquarters in New York, rarely visited. If necessary, Alfred Farmilo, head of the Edmonton Trades and Labour Council (ETLC), whose wife worked at GWG, occasionally supported the union's position.[1]

GWG quickly built a reputation for quality goods suitable for hard-working men developing the West. In 1915 the company began to fill war contracts. The *Edmonton Journal* reported that GWG had manufactured 3,000 shirts for the Canadian government, and received a contract (valued at $70,000) to produce 20,000 pairs of British Army service trousers, allowing the plant to run at full capacity for two to three months with a promise of more wartime contracts to follow.[2]

However, labourers complained about low prices being paid for their work on army pants, and the ETLC suggested that they take the matter up with the government rather than wait for direction from UGWA headquarters.[3] The UGWA union organizer took the recommended price list to Graham for approval, and he accepted it right away, placing GWG workers on the same pay scale as those doing similar work in Winnipeg, rather than being comparable to the lower rates paid in Ontario.[4] The union negotiated time-and-a-half for the overtime necessary to meet wartime demands.

The First World War led GWG to hire women to meet increased demand, including from government war orders. Lillian Morris, who started work at GWG in 1916, remembered that married women were allowed to apply for jobs for the first time. They worked 10-hour days and a half-day on Saturday.[5]

Graham became manager in 1916 and continued to expand the company with the cooperation of labour. The union was able to negotiate a number of improvements.[6] It also arranged social events

The Great Western Garment Company with a horse-drawn delivery wagon, Edmonton, Alberta, 1918. McDermid Studio, Glenbow Archives, NC-6-3267.

GWG plant, Edmonton, interior, 1911. Glenbow Archives, NC-6-62221.

GWG factory, November 1917. Photographer: McDermid Studios, City of Edmonton Archives, EA-64-186.

for workers such as biweekly dances and an annual Labour Day picnic.

The company relocated to much larger premises in 1917 and, until 1953, the factory was located in a former department store at the corner of 97th Street and 103rd Avenue. The plant was considered "one of the finest on the continent from the standpoint of the worker."[7] Sewing-machine operators at GWG worked fewer hours than other workers in the province. By 1917 the company had become, if not the

first, then certainly one of the first in North America to institute the 8-hour day and 44-hour week. GWG's letterhead proudly stated: "Where the eight hour day and fair wages prevail."[8]

When the province's Factories Act was introduced in 1917, followed by the Minimum Wage Act in 1922, Local 120 influenced the hours, wages, and working conditions of other women working in Alberta through the participation of union member Lillian Morris on the Minimum Wage

Board.[9] Alberta's Factories Act was intended to protect "homeless girls" and prevent home-based piece work (an arrangement that, although not an issue locally, had led to sweatshop conditions in other cities), and was based on measures in other provinces.[10] The ETLC and the Alberta Federation of Labour (AFL) continued to lobby the provincial government to legislate an 8-hour day and 44-hour week into the 1920s.

The 8-hour day at GWG was a significant breakthrough. However, the piecework system continued to put pressure on women to work additional time to finish more work, to clean their machines, or to do repairs for which they were not paid. Operators who worked faster and completed more work earned more than minimum wage—in some cases, significantly more—and complained about delays from machinists in repairing machines. The union could fine operators for working through their breaks. In November 1917 the union "decided to have three girls to watch that no member worked during noon hour."[11]

By the end of the war, GWG employed 375 workers. Although the local economy continued to pose challenges through the 1920s and 1930s, by the Second World War the company was positioned to take on a much larger role. In 1939 two-thirds of the plant's production was dedicated to government contracts, and the company had become a major employer of women in Edmonton. The workforce climbed to 500 and GWG was reputed to be the largest garment manufacturing company in the British Empire. Up to 25,000 pieces of military clothing a week were produced for the armed forces, including prisoner-of-war uniforms and military uniforms for other countries.

Notes

1   Special Meeting, 21 March 1914; 19 February 1915; 12 May 1915; 11 August 1915; 10 February 1949; 8 June 1956, Local 120 UGWA Minutes 1913–1918 and February 1943–December 1962, Provincial Archives of Alberta (PAA).

2   *Edmonton Journal*, 3 February 1915.

3   19 March 1915, Local 120 UGWA Minutes 1913–1918, PAA.

4   11 August 1915, Local 120 UGWA Minutes 1913–1918, PAA.

5   From an interview with Lillian Morris, operator and union representative, 1988.

6   Edmonton Trades and Labour Council Minutes, 1911–1958, PAA, 70.394/1-11.

7   *Farmer's Advocate and Home Journal*, 7 July 1920; and *Farm and Ranch Review*, 21 June 1920.

8   Noted on a statement from Glenn B. Chadwick, Secretary, to the Office of the Registrar of Joint Stock Companies, 17 November 1917, Consumer and Corporate Affairs, Government of Alberta.

9   *Minimum Wage Act*, Correspondence with Members of the Board. PAA 75.409, box 1-1-06-04; Annual Report of the Commissioner of Labour, 1926–1928, PAA 70.414.952.

10 *Statutes of Alberta*, 1917, chapter 20, and *Edmonton Journal*, 6 April 1917.

11 12 September 1917; 10 October 1917; November, n.d., 1917, Local 120 UGWA Minutes 1913–1918, PAA.

Works Cited

PRIMARY SOURCES

Edmonton Journal
Farm and Ranch Review
Farmer's Advocate and Home Journal

Provincial Archives of Alberta, Edmonton. The Annual Report of the Commissioner of Labour, 1926–1928, 70.414.952.

———. Edmonton Trades and Labour Council Minutes, 1911–1958, 70.394/1-11.

———. *Minimum Wage Act*, Correspondence with Members of the Board, 75.409, box 1-1-06-04.

———. Minutes of the Local 120 United Garment Workers of America, 1913–1918, 1943–1962.

Statutes of Alberta, 1917.

SECONDARY SOURCES

Cole, Catherine C. *GWG: Piece by Piece*. Fredericton, NB: Goose Lane Editions, 2012.

Royal Alberta Museum. *Piece by Piece: The GWG Story* website. URL: http://www.royalalbertamuseum.ca/virtualexhibit/gwg/en/history/edmonton.html, retrieved 26 March 2014.

The Bosworth Expedition: An Early Petroleum Survey

PETER MCKENZIE-BROWN

In early 1914, oil fever swept Calgary. Investors lined up outside makeshift brokerage houses to get in on exploration activity triggered by a wet-gas discovery at Turner Valley. So great was the excitement that, in one 24-hour period, promoters formed more than 500 "oil companies." The Calgary Stock Exchange, established the previous year, was unable to control the unscrupulous practices that robbed many Albertans of their savings.

Calgary Petroleum Products drilled Calgary Petroleum Products #1 (or Dingman #1), the well behind this speculative flurry, near the crest of the great geological structure that underlies Turner Valley. On an American-style cable-tool drilling rig, the tools hung from the longest manila drilling line ever used. Spudded in January 1913, the well came in with a roar on 14 May 1914. It found the reservoir at 664 metres and soon produced four million cubic feet of gas per day from the Cretaceous sandstone horizon. The gas dripped with smelly naphtha, a light oil condensate, pure enough to burn in automobiles without further refining. Fame and success greeted Bill Herron, William Elder, and Archibald Dingman, as well as the other partners in the syndicate that created the Calgary Petroleum Products Company.

While the Dingman well and its successors established the first commercial oilfield in western Canada, the high expectations raised by the discovery did not last. The few wells from the ensuing boom that struck gas in the Cretaceous sandstone produced only small volumes of naphtha. By 1917 the Calgary City Directory listed only 21 "oil mining companies," compared to 226 in 1914.[1]

At the time, the Athabasca oil sands were already well known; in fact, the first recorded mention of Canada's bitumen deposits goes back to a Hudson's Bay Company record of 12 June 1719.[2] Hoping to find light oil beneath the sands, in the late nineteenth century the Dominion government undertook a drilling program to help define the region's resources. Using a rig taken north by river, in 1893 contractor A.W. Fraser began drilling for liquid oil at Athabasca, where the oil sands had been known for centuries. In 1897 he moved the rig to Pelican Rapids, also in northern Alberta; there it struck natural gas at 250 metres. However, the well blew wild, flowing huge volumes of gas for 21 years. It was not until 1918 that a crew succeeded in killing the flow.

Ask any of Canada's exploration professionals when western Canada's oil industry began, and you will get one of two answers: the first is the Dingman #1 discovery; the second is Imperial's 1947 discovery at Leduc. The more thoughtful industrial historian would probably say Dingman was the critical event for the industry's early years, while the modern era began at Leduc. But a largely unknown expedition at the beginning of the First World War was equally pivotal. In 1914, British geologist Dr. T.O. Bosworth went down the Mackenzie River. His findings would be critical to the modern industry's birth.

The Bosworth Expedition

Two Calgary businessmen, F.C. Lowes and J.K. Cornwall, commissioned Bosworth's journey. They wanted to investigate the petroleum potential of northern Alberta and beyond, and to stake the most promising claims. Bosworth did not disappoint. His confidence that the north had high potential for oil prospecting is apparent on almost every page of his 69-page report. Bosworth's own words suggest how ambitious the expedition was:

> The undertaking was planned in March 1914 ... In April I consulted with the officers of the Government Geological Survey and other Departments in Ottawa and gathered from them all available information: maps and literature bearing on the subject.
>
> At the beginning of May, I journeyed from London to Canada accompanied by three assistant geologists and surveyors, and on May 19th, the expedition set out from Edmonton to travel northwards in the Guidance of the Northern Trading Company. We returned to Edmonton September 24th.[3]

The Bosworth expedition covered huge distances and, according to the report, there were excellent exploration prospects in three general regions: the Mackenzie River between Old Fort Good Hope and Fort Norman, the Tar Springs District on Great Slave Lake, and the Tar Sand District on the Athabasca River.[4]

Bosworth's report offered concise, well-written geological descriptions of rocks, formations, and structures. It also included chemical reports on both rocks and oil from the numerous seepages in the area. Some of his highest expectations came from investigations north of Norman Wells, areas that to this day have not yielded a major oil discovery. He wrote:

> Near Old Fort Good Hope (lat 67 30') in the banks of a tributary stream, the shales are well exposed ... from the fossils it is evident that the shales are of Upper Paleozoic Age and probably belong to the Upper Devonian. This remarkable series of Bituminous Shales and Limestones, of such thickness and of such richness contains the material from which a vast amount of petroleum might be generated and might pass into an overlying porous rock. It is admirable as an oil generating formation.[5] [emphasis in the original].

In a discussion of the evidence of good reservoir rock, Bosworth pointed to a nearby occurrence of grey clay shales and shaley sandstone, and to another of greenish, shaley sandstone containing occasional fossils—corals, chenetes, and rhynconella.[6] Bosworth speculated that both of the reservoir rocks lay above the Devonian shales. He was looking, specifically, for overlying porous rock to form the reservoir. It did not seem to have occurred to him that reefs within the shales could have served as reservoirs, even though he specifically noted the presence of Devonian corals. In the conclusion, Bosworth instructed his clients as follows:

> To avoid all competition, I strongly advise that you form a controlling company or syndicate containing the most influential men. I recommend particularly that you arrange matters in such a way that it would be to the obvious advantage of every oilman to join you, and that you freely provide the opportunity so that the Company may include every man who wishes to venture anything in the exploitation of the oilfields of the North. By this means alone can you hope to avoid competition and the unfortunate results which must follow.[7]

Bosworth noted that he had investigated the discovery at Turner Valley that had come in on 14 May 1914, 15 months into the drilling (this was just before Bosworth left Edmonton on his expedition). Within 20 years, that discovery would be recognized as the largest oilfield in the British Empire. Bosworth, however, was not impressed. In his view, the real

In 1914, a Geological Survey of Canada party let by mining engineer Sidney Ells studied the tar sands deposits along the Athabasca River and its tributaries. The first shipment was taken on a scow that was tracked up the Athabasca River for over 240 miles. The Government of Canada considered the work so important that Ells was not allowed to enlist, which he wished to do. Glenbow Archives, NA-711-187.

Visit of Duke and Duchess of Connaught to see the Dingman Well in Turner Valley on 28 July 1914. The duke had been sworn in on 13 October 1911 as Governor General of Canada and took a great interest in the mobilization of Canada for the First World War. Glenbow Archives, PA-3670-22.

potential was in the North. Believing Turner Valley was doomed to disappoint explorers, he noted that

> there are a number of oil companies in Western Canada who have capital in hand which must be spent on drilling wells. At this moment they are faced with failure [at Turner Valley], and might gladly turn to any region where there is a genuine reason to expect oil. Any such companies might become associated with your controlling company to the obvious advantage of all parties, on terms which can be mutually arranged.[8]

Bosworth did not confine his recommendations to the drilling site. After further commentary, he advised his clients as follows:

> You would also provide for the transportation; the necessary railroads; the pipe lines, the refineries, and, what is more important than all the rest, and which would give you complete command of the whole situation, all of the oil produced in the region would pass through your hands to be marketed by you.
>
> If you could succeed in promoting a great scheme on some such lines as these, no smaller rival group could hope to compete against you, and you might eventually be in the position to control the great oil fields of the North.[9]

One of the great ironies, of course, is that these comments came barely three years after the Standard Oil Trust was dismantled for just such anti-competitive practices. In addition, Bosworth completely misread the importance of Turner Valley and the petroleum potential of Alberta, so smitten was he by the North. The practical value of his advice may be seen in the fact that seven decades elapsed before oil from the Norman Wells oilfield actually began flowing to southern markets.

Impact on Two Wars

Bosworth does not remark on the coming of the First World War. When he and his men left, the world was at peace; when he returned, Europe and the British Empire had become embroiled in that terrible conflict. He was probably totally unaware of those developments while in the north. The demands of war postponed exploration of Bosworth's claims, as did the Dingman discovery. The petroleum industry, by this time, was focused on the development of the Turner Valley field, where standard practice was to strip naphtha from the gas stream and flare the gas itself.

A copy of Bosworth's study clearly made it to London during the war, where it raised eyebrows. In 1917 Canada's interior minister, William James Roche, received an imperious, eight-page letter from London-based Shell Transport. As Mary Janigan notes in *Let the Eastern Bastards Freeze in the Dark: The West Versus the Rest Since Confederation:* "The firm wanted exclusive oil and natural gas rights over an enormous swath of the West for the duration of the war and for five years after Armistice."[10] The company wanted rights to a 328,000-square-mile parcel (849,516 square kilometres); for practical purposes, the land Bosworth had recommended. Along with other demands, Shell wanted "right-of-way over all Crown lands for pipelines, telegraph and telephone lines, railways and highways" and "land for factories, storehouses, refineries and reservoirs."[11] The demands went even further. Shell executive R.N. Benjamin said the company "would not pay taxes

A feature story by W.A. McRae appeared in the Toronto-based magazine *Saturday Night* on 15 March 1919 titled: "Open your mouth and shut your eyes and we'll take your oil land, wherever it lies." It attacked the deal that the Shell oil company proposed noting: "Shell Transport and Trading Company boldly asks Canadian government for monopoly which might, if granted, make millions of profit for the promoters, and little or nothing for the government."

"Open Your Mouth and Shut Your Eyes And We'll Take Your Oil Land, Wherever it Lies"

Shell Transport and Trading Company Boldly Asks Canadian Government for Monopoly Which Might, if Granted, Make Millions of Profit for the Promoters, and Little or Nothing for the Government. Applicants Want 250,000 Miles of Potential Oil Lands in the Far West and North.

By W. A. McRae, M.P.P., Alberta.

IN TWO PARTS— PART ONE.

THERE is on file at Ottawa, on behalf of the Shell Transport and Trading Company, an application for an exclusive right to explore "during the war and for five years after the declaration of peace," two hundred and fifty thousand square miles of the area of Alberta and Northwestern Canada, out of which the applicant company may, at the termination of the five years after declaration of peace, select twenty-five thousand square miles of territory for its own purposes.

remains sufficiently intact as to act as a reservoir for oil to any great extent.

So by process of elimination, the geologic possibility of oil in Canada reduces itself to a small part of Western Ontario, now producing 2 per cent. of Canada's consumption, to a part of New Brunswick, to a small and unlikely territory south of James Bay, and to that country lying between the Red River and Lake Winnipeg on the east, the Rocky Mountains on the west extending to a little beyond the Saskatchewan on the north plus so much of for the first fifteen years of exploration," and would not begin paying royalties (of three cents per barrel) until 1 January 1930.[12] The federal government did not cede those rights to Shell; indeed, it did not even reply to the request.

If Shell's missive rankled in Ottawa, the following year it sparked downright outrage in western Canada. This is evidenced in an article in the *Winnipeg Telegram*, dated 21 November 1918, which covered the story, followed by equally inflammatory stories in the Edmonton and Calgary media. The Alberta legislature promptly passed a resolution describing "the terms of the concession as being oppressive to the people of the province." It continued by passing a resolution stating: "In the opinion of this House no such deposition of Petroleum and or any other Natural Resources should be made."[13] As Joyce E. Hunt observes in *Local Push—Global Pull: The Untold History of the Athabasca Oil Sands 1900 to 1930*, if the federal government had dealt openly with the proposal and its rejection, there would have been no protests.[14]

What probably triggered the news story was a meeting of Canada's premiers, the same month, in Ottawa to discuss land settlement and resource ownership. The occasion was not auspicious; Germany had just signed its Armistice with the Allied Powers, and Prime Minister Robert Borden was in Europe.[15] The issue of resource ownership would not be resolved for another dozen years.

Shell did not acquire the lands Bosworth explored. By 1918 an Imperial Oil subsidiary, the Northwest Company, had obtained the properties Bosworth had staked. Imperial hired Bosworth as chief geologist, and the company decided to drill on one of those claims. Imperial Oil Limited's legendary exploration geologist Ted Link led the drilling expedition.[16] By train, scow, and riverboat,

he and his crew followed Bosworth's route north to Fort Norman, just south of the Arctic Circle. They had taken with them the wherewithal to assemble a cable-tool drilling rig, and they soon set to work. One valuable member of the party was an ox, which provided heavy labour during the summer. As the autumn cold began killing off the forage, he delivered steaks and stew.

In 1920, Imperial brought in the great Norman Wells discovery, but there was no practical way to get the oil to market. Because demand in the Northwest Territories was marginal, Imperial had little reason to develop the field. However, later in the decade, the company constructed a tiny refinery at Norman Wells to supply gasoline and other products to missions, mines, riverboats, and other local customers. The company did not need many wells to meet local needs, and did little investigation of the geology of the reservoir. That changed after the 1941 attack on Pearl Harbor. When the Americans came into the Second World War, they were extremely concerned about securing local fuel supplies in the North, especially after Japan took control of a couple of Alaska's Aleutian islands. They, therefore, worked with Canada to develop Norman Wells into a source of local oil supply for a refining and distribution complex. This was the beginning of the Canol Project. The name supposedly came from the contraction of "Canadian" and "oil," the second syllable likely "oil" said with a Texan accent.

Construction crews built a 950-kilometre oil pipeline over the Mackenzie Mountains to a newly constructed refinery in Whitehorse, Yukon Territory. The pipeline was built over some of the most difficult terrain in the country, and much of the work had to be done in bitter cold. Crews also laid product pipelines to Skagway, Alaska. In total, they

Experimental asphalt paving in Edmonton, Alberta, in 1915 using tar sands from Fort McMurray. McDermid Studio, Glenbow Archives, NC-6-1522.

constructed 2,560 kilometres of pipeline.[17] By any standard, those lines were terrible; they ran on top of the ground, alongside the road, and often without supports. The Canol pipelines were not designed for extreme cold and, as a result, were vulnerable to frost heaving, snowstorms, and flooding. They were neither installed nor handled properly, and they failed frequently. The crude oil pipeline leaked onto the permafrost. So did the product pipelines, which delivered diesel and gasoline to a fuelling station in Skagway, Alaska.

To meet the needs of the refinery, Imperial drilled more wells, and began to better understand the Norman Wells reservoir. Of particular note, the company discovered that it was a Devonian reef—of earlier vintage than the Leduc and Redwater fields, soon to be discovered in Alberta, but still a Devonian reef. That turned out to be the geological key. By the time the refinery was ready to begin operations, the company had drilled 60 productive wells out of 67 project wells in total. The test for the field came on 16 February 1944, when the pipeline began operating. As a producer of good-quality oil (39° to 41° API), the field surpassed expectations.[18] By October 1944, Norman Wells was producing 4,600 barrels per day by natural pressure. Later studies of the project's environmental impact in Whitehorse were revealing. The Canol legacy included the creation of an environmental horror known locally as the Maxwell Tar Pit. Appalling disposal and cleanup practices during the Canol debacle had created an oily mess that was declared an environmentally contaminated site in 1998.

Leduc

Although Canol had little impact on affairs of state, it had a huge impact on oil development in western Canada. As a result of wartime field development at Norman Wells, Imperial learned that the field's reservoir rock was Devonian reef. Armed with this knowledge, the company's geologists—led by Ted Link, who by this time was in charge of Imperial's exploration efforts—rethought their approach to western Canada's petroleum resources. Other oilmen at the time were on the hunt for big plays like that in Turner Valley—they would be roughly 340 million years old, and they would be thrusted anticlines of Paleozoic age in a Mississippian formation. Much fruitless drilling in the foothills sought the next Turner Valley.

Perhaps not all credit should be given to Imperial Oil for the geological idea that there might be Devonian reefs in Alberta. Geological Survey of Canada mapping of the Rockies west of Edmonton—work undertaken by Helen Belyea, Digby Maclaren, and others—influenced Imperial's thinking. Before the Leduc discovery, Charles Stelck, at the University of Alberta, also gave thought to the question of Devonian reefs in Alberta. Imperial arrived at its revolutionary idea, and the importance of its decision to

drill for a reef cannot be understated. That geological idea resulted in a series of great discoveries. The first came with the aid of primitive seismic technology, and it was a big one—the famous Leduc #1 discovery well. When it came in to much fanfare on 21 February 1947, Leduc laid the groundwork for one of the world's great postwar oil booms.

There is another important connection between postwar oil development in Alberta and the Canol Project. The refinery built in Whitehorse played an important role in Alberta's industrial development. Imperial bought the mothballed refinery for one dollar, dismantled it, and moved it to Strathcona, near Edmonton. There the company reassembled it to handle production from Leduc and other postwar discoveries. That refinery was the starting site for one of Canada's biggest refining complexes.

If not for the Bosworth report, Canada's petroleum industry would have had quite a different history. Imperial Oil's efforts were heroic—indeed the stuff of legend. Enormously frustrated with its unbroken string of 133 dry holes, Imperial planned the program that yielded Leduc as its last major wildcat play in Alberta. If Leduc had not come in, it is easy to imagine the Devonian oil fields lying fallow for many, many years. No other big players were exploring the prairies. As a result of the coming in of the Leduc well, oilmen around the world became aware of this important new discovery, and began to bring expertise and investment into the province. They created one of the first great postwar oil booms, and helped lay the foundation for one of the world's most diverse and technically advanced petroleum industries. With respect to its long-term impact, T.O. Bosworth's 1914 report may have been the most influential geological document in Canadian history.

Notes

1   Peter McKenzie-Brown, Gordon Jaremko, and David Finch, *The Great Oil Age: The Petroleum Industry in Canada* (Calgary: Detselig, 1993), 36.

2   Ibid., 71.

3   T.O. Bosworth, *The Mackenzie River between Old Fort Good Hope and Fort Norman; the Tar Springs District on the Great Slave Lake; and in the Tar Sand District on the Athabasca River*, 1914, Glenbow Archives (Calgary), M-8656, 1.

4   Ibid., 5.

5   Ibid., 9–10.

6   Ibid., 11.

7   Ibid., 67.

8   Ibid., 68.

9   Ibid., 69.

10 Mary Janigan, *Let the Eastern Bastards Freeze in the Dark: The West versus the Rest since Confederation* (Toronto: Knopf Canada, 2012), 202–3.

11 Ibid.

12 Ibid.

13 Joyce E. Hunt, *Local Push—Global Pull: The Untold History of the Athabasca Oil Sands, 1900 to 1930* (Calgary: Pushpull, 2011), 261–62.

14 Ibid., 263.

15 Janigan, *Let the Eastern Bastards Freeze in the Dark*, 3.

16 It is worth noting that the most important early geological work at Norman Wells, including the location of the discovery well, needs to be attributed to Ted Link—not to T.O. Bosworth. In an important 1947 presentation to the American Association of Petroleum Geologists, J.S. Stewart of the Geological Survey of Canada was adamant on this point (J.S. Stewart, "Norman Wells Oil Field, Northwest Territories, Canada," in Anonymous, *Structure of Typical American Oil Fields*, vol. 3, [1948]: 86–109 [Original paper read before an American Association of Petroleum Geologists meeting in Wichita, Kansas, on 18 January 1947]).

17 McKenzie-Brown, Jaremko, and Finch, *The Great Oil Age*, 43

18 API gravity is an American Petroleum Institute measure of liquid gravity. Water is 10 degrees API, and light crude is typically from 35 to 40. Heavy oil is, by convention, typically from 9.0 to 11 degrees API, while bitumen is 7.5 to 8.5.

Works Cited

PRIMARY SOURCES

Glenbow Archives, Calgary. Bosworth, T.O. *The Mackenzie River between Old Fort Good Hope and Fort Norman; the Tar Springs District on the Great Slave Lake; and in the Tar Sand District on the Athabasca River*, 1914, M-8656.

SECONDARY SOURCES

Hunt, Joyce E. *Local Push—Global Pull: The Untold History of the Athabasca Oil Sands, 1900 to 1930*. Calgary: Pushpull, 2011.

Janigan, Mary. *Let the Eastern Bastards Freeze in the Dark: The West versus the Rest since Confederation*. Toronto: Knopf Canada, 2012.

McKenzie-Brown, Peter, Gordon Jaremko, and David Finch. *The Great Oil Age: The Petroleum Industry in Canada*. Calgary: Detselig, 1993.

Stewart, J.S. "Norman Wells Oil Field, Northwest Territories, Canada." In Anonymous, *Structure of Typical American Oil Fields*. Vol. 3 (1948): 86–109. Original paper read before an American Association of Petroleum Geologists meeting in Wichita, Kansas, on 18 January 1947.

SECTION THREE

Communities at War

The 1911 Canadian census revealed that Alberta was a diverse society. Of a total population of 374,295, those of British descent numbered 215,174 (about 57 percent). Other significant groups were: 41,656 of German descent; 29,547 of Scandinavian descent; 20,600 of French descent; 17,584 of Ukrainian descent; and 8,033 of Russian descent. Also present were people of Dutch, Italian, Jewish, Polish, and Asian descent, although in much lower numbers (2,000–3,000). These patterns of settlement were established from the late 1880s onward.

Of particular significance during the First World War was German immigration. In 1911, German settlers were the largest ethno-cultural group next to the British. The first German settlers arrived in the Pincher Creek area of southwestern Alberta in 1883. In 1889, 100 families settled near Medicine Hat. They came from two German settlements in eastern Galicia, which was then part of the Austro-Hungarian Empire and today part of southern Poland and western Ukraine. While these particular settlements did not survive, they began a trend that resulted in the area around Medicine Hat becoming a major location for German settlement in Canada.[1] The next focus of settlement centered on the communities of Leduc and Stony Plain located west of Edmonton; in 1892, 13 German Protestant communities were established in the region. Germans from Galicia settled around Fort Saskatchewan at Josephburg, and some of their former Ukrainian and Polish neighbours also came to that area.

While Alberta's population was diverse, the establishment that dominated government, the law, education, the church, and other aspects of civil society was unquestionably of British descent. Immigration policy favoured British and American settlers, with other ethnic groups, particularly southern Europeans and Asians, being considered less desirable. A large number of American immigrants were Scandinavians who had come from the Midwestern states. This is why people of Scandinavian descent were third largest in the 1911 census (after British and German). People of French descent, from France and Belgium, comprised the fourth-ranking group. They settled near Edmonton, in particular in St. Albert, and in the Peace country. Ukrainian settlement was encouraged because they were viewed as strong farmers who could meet the challenges of prairie agriculture. A large group formed the Ukrainian block settlement east of Edmonton around what is now Elk Island National Park. As historian Frances Swyripa noted: "Ukrainian peasants gladly exchanged their tiny plots for 160 acres, 'free' for a $10 registration fee. In spite of Minister of Interior Clifford Sifton's enthusiastic endorsement of the 'men in sheepskin coats,' however, Ukrainian immigrants were greeted with mixed emotions by the dominant Anglo-Celtic society in Canada."[2]

The War Measures Act, passed on 22 August 1914, gave the federal government full powers for the security, defence, peace, order, and welfare of Canada. The order in council made these measures retroactive to the outset of the conflict, thus establishing ex post facto guilt. Whether immigrants from enemy nations espoused the values of their homelands or not, they came under suspicion. The act enabled the registration and internment of so-called "enemy aliens." Major General Sir William Otter, director of internment operations for the Government of Canada, viewed individuals from suspect communities as a potential source of civil unrest. The most affected were the 80,000 Canadians who were former citizens of the Austro-Hungarian Empire. While most had to report to local authorities on a regular basis, some were sent to 24 internment camps established across the country. Eight were in British Columbia and three in Alberta (Banff/Castle Mountain, Jasper, and Lethbridge). While many were interned based on their citizenship and ethnicity, some indigent poor deemed "undesirable" were also interned. Between 1914 and 1920, 8,579 men were interned: 5,954 of Austro-Hungarian origin (which included 5,000 Ukrainians), 2,009 Germans, 205 Turks, and 99 Bulgarians.[3]

The Castle Mountain Internment Camp was built in Banff National Park in July 1915 and, in November, moved to the Cave and Basin in Banff. Over its life, it housed over 600 immigrant prisoners.[4] It closed in July 1917. The Jasper internment camp was established at Old Fort Point, about a mile from Jasper, in February 1916 and was closed in August 1917. In 1920, it became a tuberculosis treatment facility. The camp housed 200 prisoners of Austro-Hungarian descent, who were moved there from the camp in Brandon, Manitoba.[5] The camp commanders reported to Brigadier General E.A. Cruikshank, Commanding Officer Military District No. 13, based in Calgary. The two camps were located in beauty spots in the Rockies because these were important sites for tourism development by the federal government. The budget for national parks had been cut due to wartime priorities, and Parks Commissioner J.B. Harkin requested that enemy aliens be used as a temporary work force. The majority of internees were thus used as conscript labour for government projects, the most important being development of park infrastructure in the Banff–Lake Louise corridor and Jasper. Conditions at the camps were poor and were condemned by neutral observers. The Alberta Dragoons served as camp guards.

The Lethbridge camp was situated in the fairgrounds and operated from 30 September 1914 to 11 November 1916. The Lethbridge 20th Battery provided 60 guards for the camp. It housed a maximum of 300 individuals, some of whom were military reservists (German, Austrian, and Turkish) interned as prisoners of war. As with the other two Alberta camps, prisoners did escape, and many were helped by friends who had settled in neighbouring communities. When the camp closed, the inmates were sent to other camps.

Section Three: Communities at War examines the ways in which the war mobilized, and divided, Alberta communities. Enlistment, the changing economic landscape, population shifts, women's issues, patriotic fundraising campaigns, prohibition, labour unrest, reintegration of veterans, and memorialization of local sacrifice are among issues covered by Ken Tingley for Edmonton, Robert Rutherdale for Lethbridge, and Michael Dawe for Red Deer. Adriana Davies, Sean Moir, and Anthony Worman use one artifact—the Waskatenau Red Cross Quilt—to demonstrate how women raised funds to provide comforts for local soldiers overseas. In addition, the names of soldiers embroidered on the quilt reveal the high price the war exacted on the community. Donald Smith details the ways that Calgary's Grand Theatre became a focal point for local patriotic events. Universities, as Chris Hyland and Paul Stortz show for the University of Alberta and Jarett Henderson for Mount Royal College, were also communities profoundly affected by the war in areas that include gender composition, academic programs, finances, infrastructure, and student and faculty activities. Providing a much different perspective, P. Whitney Lackenbauer shows that soldiers training in Alberta not only generated local enthusiasm, pride, and significant extra business but also over-strained local facilities and engaged in drunk, disorderly, and even violent conduct, as demonstrated by the destruction of Calgary businesses run by suspected enemy sympathizers. Nativism manifested itself strongly in wartime Alberta, given its significant non-British population. Kassandra Luciuk details the Ukrainian experience before, during, and after the war, focusing on how Canada's first national internment program fractured Alberta's Ukrainian community. Amy Shaw covers the harsh treatment meted out to conscientious objectors in Alberta, including religious groups that the federal government had pledged exemption from military service.

The war generated patriotic outpourings but also suspicion, nativism, and discrimination that fell hard on certain groups because of their ethnicity and beliefs. Alberta thus became a microcosm of the European conflict as race and nationality came into play at the local level.

Notes

1   Howard Palmer and Tamara Palmer, eds., *Peoples of Alberta: Portraits of Cultural Diversity* (Saskatoon: Western Producer Prairie Books, 1985), 5.

2   Frances Swyripa, "The Ukrainians in Alberta," in *Peoples of Alberta*, edited by Palmer and Palmer, 215. Also see Swyripa and John Herd Thompson, eds., *Loyalties in Conflict: Ukrainians in Canada during the Great War* (Edmonton: Canadian Institute of Ukrainian Studies/University of Alberta Press, 1983).

3   "Internment" entry, *The Canadian Encyclopedia* online, URL: http://www.thecanadianencyclopedia.ca/en/article/internment/, retrieved 13 May 2015.

4   Parks Canada has created an interactive internment exhibit adjacent to the Cave and Basin Historic Site in Banff as part of First World War commemorations.

5   For additional information about the use of enemy aliens as conscript labour in the western mountain parks, see Bill Waiser, *Park Prisoners: The Untold Story of Western Canada's National Parks, 1915–1946* (Saskatoon: Fifth House, 1995).

Edmonton and the Great War

KEN TINGLEY

The Declaration of War

Edmonton seemed to be taken by surprise when war was declared on 4 August 1914. Crowds gathered at the corner of Jasper Avenue and 101st Street, where the *Edmonton Journal* had installed a giant billboard on which were posted the latest developments received by telegraph from England, Europe, and Ottawa. The Archduke Franz Ferdinand, heir to the throne of Austria-Hungary, and his wife were assassinated in Sarajevo, Bosnia-Herzegovina, on 28 June 1914. Local newspapers reported the event, but most seemed unaware that in coming months it would prove the important turning point. A tangled complex of treaties would soon enmesh Europe and its overseas dependencies in a maelstrom, but, at first, the story did not attract much attention in Edmonton.

The *Edmonton Bulletin* ran its first headline warning of the impending war on 25 July 1914. Events moved rapidly after this, and on August 5 local newspapers reported that Canada had commenced formal mobilization for the war effort.

Edmonton's men hastened to serve King and Empire. Many of the city's organizations and influential leaders were of recent British stock, or the inheritors of the patriotic traditions still strong in Ontario and the Maritime provinces, from which so many westerners had arrived during the boom years. They still felt strong ties with the imperial motherland.

Rushing to the Colours

Minister of Militia and Defence Sam Hughes announced plans to raise a division of 21,000 men. Hughes was a strong advocate for militia involvement, and he resisted plans to upgrade existing professional troops for the first overseas force. As a result, confusion reigned during the beginning of Canadian recruitment.[1] For example, the 19th Alberta Dragoons was notified on August 8 that it would be contributing a 200-man squadron to the first Canadian contingent. These orders were cancelled within three days, but two weeks later the plan was reconstituted.[2] Confusion increased when plans to train at Petawawa, Ontario, were replaced by Hughes's order to build an entirely new camp at Valcartier, Quebec.

Edmonton had a strong militia tradition to build on. In 1908 the federal government began to look toward the burgeoning Prairie Provinces as a source of militia strength. Edmonton's population had multiplied more than six-fold between its incorporation as a city in 1904 and amalgamation with Strathcona in 1912. In fact, with its new Legislature Building, High Level Bridge, street railway, and university, it considered itself a modern metropolis. Still, support for the militia remained fairly low until war overtook

Edmonton men rushed to the colours when war was declared in August 1914. Many were recent immigrants from the British Isles, and felt a deep loyalty to the Empire. McDermid Studio, Glenbow Archives, NC-6-1287.

planning. What preparedness existed in Edmonton by 1914 owed its existence to a handful of local men committed to the idea of militia organization.

W.A. Griesbach, a civic leader with deep local roots, came to the Edmonton district in 1883 while still a boy. His father, Inspector Arthur H. Griesbach, commanded the North-West Mounted Police at Fort Saskatchewan during its first days. William Griesbach studied at St. John's School in Winnipeg, and later enlisted for service in the South African War. He practised law and served in civic politics after returning to Edmonton in January 1901.

In early 1908, the 19th Alberta Dragoons and 101st Regiment were established in Edmonton, although their training would remain intermittent until the First World War. Competitive marksmanship and sporadic drilling, complemented by annual June training camps in Calgary, were its most common activities. With the declaration of war, the 19th and the 101st continued to recruit from among the thousands of eager young men hoping to get to Europe before the war ended. The 19th Alberta Dragoons was the first off the mark, and its men among the first Edmonton soldiers to see active service in France, on 11 February 1915. In addition, the Princess Patricia's Canadian Light Infantry (PPCLI) was recruiting in Edmonton during August and, by February 14, 200 men from Edmonton and northern Alberta were ready to leave for Valcartier with the PPCLI. Some men also joined the Patricia's from the 101st Regiment ranks.[3]

In early September 1914, the 9th Battalion, Canadian Expeditionary Force (CEF), was formed largely from the 101st Regiment (Edmonton Fusiliers), originally established as Edmonton's reserve militia in 1908. In early November 1914, a contingent of 100 Edmonton men left for Calgary en route

Men from the 19th Alberta Dragoons were the first from the city to go into action in Europe. They wave farewell to family and friends as they head south on a CPR train from the Strathcona station in late 1914. McDermid Studio, Glenbow Archives, NC-6-1210.

to Montreal to enlist; among them were many former 101st and 19th Alberta Dragoons, too eager to wait for a second local recruitment. Recruiting for the 51st Battalion began on 2 January 1915, and it was up to strength by the end of the month. The 151st Battalion began recruiting in the Edmonton district in November 1915. In June 1915, the 63rd and 66th Battalions began their recruitment drives. The 138th

Battalion then was organized and began recruitment in December 1915. The 194th Highland Battalion began recruitment on 4 February 1916, while the famous 202nd Sportsman's Battalion began recruitment a week later. When it was announced at the end of the month that Lieutenant Colonel J.W. McKinery would raise the 218th Battalion Irish Guards, it brought the total number of Edmonton battalions to eight. Several drafts of "bantam" recruits, under the minimum height for the other battalions, would also begin leaving the city to join the Vancouver regiment. The *Edmonton Morning Bulletin* reported on 25 November 1915 that 12,000 men already had enlisted in Edmonton district.

Many Edmontonians would serve in other units that recruited in the city. In September 1915, a group of Chinese volunteers who were members of the Chinese National Party were preparing to form a unit; lack of fluency in English was mentioned as the main reason they did not enlist in other regiments. At the beginning of January 1916, 71 French-Canadian recruits left Edmonton for St Boniface, Manitoba, where a French-Canadian battalion was being raised. In March 1916, Captain Edward Leprohon was offered command of a French-Canadian battalion to be raised in Edmonton after a long local campaign to raise one; this would become the 233rd Battalion. Several Italian reserves also left for the front, to serve with the Italian forces. Specialized units such as the 1st Battalion Canadian Pioneers, Canadian Army Medical Corps, and Canadian Dental Corps also actively recruited in the city and district. In late April 1915, twenty "mechanics" were recruited in Edmonton and sent to work in Newcastle-on-Tyne, England. In 1915, the Women's Volunteer Reserve was formed and enlisted hundreds of Edmonton women.

Enlistment in Edmonton and across Alberta was very high. There were several reasons for this, the first being that wheat prices had declined during 1912 and 1913, although the *Edmonton Capital* proclaimed "a record yield of wheat in Canada for this year, and probably for all time" in September 1914. Such a decline affected every aspect of life in a predominantly agricultural community.[4] In addition to the international economic downturn of 1913, many labourers had lost their jobs after the explosive surge in transcontinental railway construction came to an end. Another aspect of the rapid recruitment was the hardship imposed on many families whose breadwinner had left. In September 1914, the Edmonton civic relief officer forwarded the first instalment for the month to the families of soldiers who had gone to the front.[5]

Many men enlisted on the spur of the moment. Harold Peat, a young Edmontonian, was discussing the war situation in his kitchen with two friends shortly after the commencement of hostilities in Europe. "If I was old enough to go, boys, I'd go," one young friend said. Bill Ravenscroft, who had served in the South African War, at first expressed his reluctance to get involved in another conflict. But, after the young friend expressed his support of the noble cause, Ravenscroft changed his tune. Peat said, "Well, Bill, I'm game to go if you will." Peat and Ravenscroft then went to enlist in the 101st Edmonton Fusiliers, soon to be absorbed into the 9th Battalion CEF at Valcartier camp.[6]

During the war, Alberta supplied 45,136 men to the armed forces. The University of Alberta alone saw 484 of its staff and students join the war effort, and, of those, 82 died in service or in action. Returned men began to show up in Edmonton quite early in the war, many of them wounded. In late 1915, the Edmonton Returned Soldiers Bureau set up in a municipal building located on the northeast corner of 101A Avenue and 100th Street; in January 1916 alone, G.H. Hensley, chairman of the bureau, reported that 86 veterans "had been provided with work or maintenance."[7]

Of the many battalions raised in Edmonton, that most associated with the city during the First World

War was the 49th Battalion, CEF. Heavy enlistment of 49ers began on 4 January 1915; this unit was one of very few that retained a connection to its city of origin throughout the war.

As fall approached, the Legion of Frontiersmen, the Edmonton Home Defence Corps, the University of Alberta Battalion, and a planned Highland regiment absorbed many more recruits. The *Edmonton Capital* called on all Scotsmen to raise a "kiltie regiment." A public meeting to promote this end was presided over by John A. McDougall, Colonel E.B. Edwards, A.C. Rutherford, Frank Oliver, and other local notables.[8]

On 3 September 1914, 1,200 men, recruited by the 101st Regiment, had left Edmonton for Valcartier. This became the occasion for splitting up the 101st, preventing it from maintaining its Edmonton identity as the 49th would succeed in accomplishing. It was decided that the 1st Division, CEF, would consist of new battalions created at Valcartier. Therefore, most of the Edmonton men were taken into the new 9th Battalion under Colonel Maynard Rogers.

A second contingent was announced in October 1915, to be recruited and organized locally. Alberta was allocated one battalion, the 31st, which went to Calgary. In November 1915, hundreds of Edmonton recruits enlisted in the new battalion in Calgary. Edmonton's sense of civic pride received a boost when it was announced on December 1 that the very popular William Griesbach would return to the city to command a new regiment. Griesbach was elected to the first city council in 1904 and, in 1907, as "the boy mayor." His popularity would enable him to defeat the virtually indestructible Frank Oliver for a federal seat in 1917.

The 51st Battalion was authorized on 16 December 1915. Its commanding officer, Lieutenant Colonel Reginald de Lotbiniere-Harwood, was a previous commanding officer of the 101st Regiment, and brought a number of his officers with him to the 51st. This battalion became the first to use the newly constructed Edmonton Drill Hall. Its marching song, written by Harwood's wife, proclaimed:

> They are gathered from all corners
> Of Alberta fair and blessed,
> And they're Colonel Harwood's huskies
> Who are out to do their best.[9]

At the beginning of 1915, Edmonton already had raised about 2,400 men for the CEF, but most of these had served to bolster other battalions. It was hoped that, now, Edmonton would have its own battalion. Griesbach's energetic efforts seem to have ensured that the 49th would become the representative unit for Edmonton. Local Scots, who had been organizing the Highland regiment, enlisted as a company in the 49th, and, perhaps, were responsible for the unit embracing "Bonnie Dundee" for its quick march. The battalion reached full complement on 21 January 1915. Until the 49ers left for Europe, they continued to play an important part in city life. The Exhibition Grounds were converted to a training base and, in April, were the site of a display of military drill and equipment for those attending the Spring Horse Show.

At this time, with the popularity of the 49ers at its height, the unit almost lost its connection with the city when it looked like both the 49th and 51st would be relegated to a reinforcement draft. Loud protests quickly led to the cancellation of this plan, and the Edmonton boys were soon ready to leave for the war.[10] On May 11, Lieutenant Governor George H.V. Bulyea reviewed both city regiments and presented them with their colours, embroidered by women of the Borden Club, established in the city in early November 1914. The following day, an announcement was made that the 49th would leave for England in a few days, but the 51st would go to Calgary for further training.[11] On May 29, the 49th

boarded two trains without fanfare or ceremony; Edmontonians did not even know it had departed until June 2. Shortly after the departure, an *Edmonton Bulletin* editorial expressed the hope that the 49ers would remain intact. "A man enlisting for active service naturally prefers to go to the front with men he

Thousands of Edmontonians turned out at the CPR station to see the 49th Battalion return. G.D. Clark, Glenbow Archives, NA-1337-10.

has known, and as part of a battalion whose fortunes may be watched by the relatives and friends he leaves behind," it declared.[12]

Before the 49th Battalion returned to Edmonton on 22 March 1919, it would fight through many of the major battles of the war with the 7th Brigade, 3rd Division, of the Canadian Corps, winning numerous honours, including two Victoria Crosses. In early 1916, the 49ers fought in the Ypres Salient, including the battles at Sanctuary Wood, Mount Sorrel, and Passchendaele. At the Somme, during the summer and early fall, they were at the battles for Courcelette and the Regina Trench, and then in 1917 at Vimy Ridge and then back at Passchendaele. During the Last Hundred Days in the summer and fall of 1918, they were at Amiens, Arras, the Canal du Nord, and Cambrai, ending the war at Mons, near which hostilities had begun in 1914.

Lieutenant Colonel Griesbach, who took the battalion to France, ended the war as a brigadier general, being promoted in 1917. He had proclaimed on 4 January 1915 that his ambition was to take an Edmonton regiment to serve as "the finest in the second Canadian contingent," noting: "My regiment will be commanded by Edmonton officers and pride in this city will be one of the predominating features in it."[13] When the battalion returned to Edmonton at the end of the war, this ambition had been fully realized.

War Heroes

Edmonton proudly recognized its own heroes, maintaining its focus on the war in a very personal way. One of the more colourful was Major Pete Anderson, well known to the city for his mansion and his large brickworks located in Gallagher's Flats. Anderson personally led the first contingent of Edmonton recruits down Jasper Avenue on 22 August 1914. By April 1915, he was with the 3rd Battalion, assigned as a scout and sniper to roam the battlefield during the defence of St. Julien. After accounting for many German dead, he was captured and became a prisoner of war. When asked by his captors where his other men were, while standing surrounded by German dead, he famously replied: "These are all the men we have here including the dead ones." The German officer was reported to have exclaimed, "You do not mean to tell me that you did all this damage with these few men?" Of such accounts wartime lore was forged.

Anderson's fortunes as a prisoner of war were followed carefully in his hometown. After a spectacular escape, he made his way home, only to find his brick business destroyed by a June 1915 flood, as well as rumours that he had struck a deal with his captors. Partly to counter these suspicions, he wrote an account of his adventures titled *I, That's Me*.[14]

Corporal William Freemont "Deacon" White, very well-known as a professional baseball player and sports organizer, was with the 49th Battalion when it made its first trench raid on 28 January 1915. He is reputed to have said, as he led three German prisoners into camp, "Boys, this beats baseball all to hell."

Lieutenant Allen Oliver (26th Battery, 7th Brigade, Canadian Field Artillery) was a graduate of McGill University, enlisted in Kingston, Ontario, on 3 April 1915, and began serving with the 26th Battery on 17 January 1916. Edmontonians recognized Allen as the son of Frank Oliver, the prominent newspaper editor and influential politician. Lieutenant Oliver was reported injured on 3 April 1916 but returned to active service. He was reported killed in action on November 18, having been awarded the Military Cross for bravery in the field at St. Eloi and the Somme on the day before his death.[15]

Not all Edmonton men served with "Edmonton" units. Lieutenant George Burdon McKean was a city recruit who won a Victoria Cross. He was serving in the 14th Battalion (Royal Montreal Regiment) when he dramatically led the attack on a communications trench near Vimy Ridge on 27 April 1917. When he enlisted in the 51st Battalion in January 1915, he was a University of Alberta student and assistant minister at Robertson Presbyterian Church. In short, he was the perfect gallant and faithful young hero for the war.

Thousands of Edmonton citizens gathered to welcome another hero home at the end of the war. John Chipman Kerr, a Spirit River man who had enlisted in Edmonton, was claimed by the city when, in autumn 1916, he received a Victoria Cross for capturing 62 Germans in his attack on an enemy trench at Courcelette.

Edmonton also took pride in its Métis and Aboriginal soldiers. Among the most famous was Corporal Henry Norwest, a Cree sniper from Fort Saskatchewan, who was killed shortly before the Armistice, having 115 observed kills. The most famous was Alexander Decoteau, a Saskatchewan Cree who had moved to Edmonton, where he became the city's first Aboriginal police officer. He also was a local celebrity who competed in the many semi-professional marathon races of the day in which Aboriginal runners such as Moosewa became stars. Decoteau attended the Olympics in 1912, although he was prevented from competing due to an injury. In 1916, he joined the 202nd (Sportsman's) Battalion, and was killed at Passchendaele the following year.

Two air force recruits assumed special significance during the war. Lieutenant R.A. Logan, a Nova Scotia science student from the University of Alberta, and Lieutenant Reg Henry, a classmate of Logan's and son of Mayor W.T. Henry, piloted a plane near Vimy Ridge during the offensive in April 1917. The plane sported the Cree name for Beaver Hills House, the original Native name for the fur trade post Edmonton House. Both men died while serving with the Royal Flying Corps. "The City of Edmonton," the JN4 biplane piloted by "Wop" May, became a sort of city mascot as well, playing a part in the postwar establishment of commercial aviation in Edmonton.[16]

The Home Front

While the grim reality of the war began to permeate the home front fairly quickly, thousands of advertisements appeared in newspapers, taking advantage of the war where possible. In July 1915, W.H. Chillman ran one such advertisement for the Shoe Hospital located on Whyte Avenue. "Your King and Country Need You to keep fit, but you can't keep fit with bad shoes, let us fix them today,"[17] it proclaimed. Many other such advertisements would appear in Edmonton in the next three years.

Despite the generally high level of civic moral support for its recruits, Edmonton was not always so eager to provide financial support. This was partly due to the reduced financial conditions in the city and partly to the habitual bureaucratic reluctance to loosen the purse strings. The commissioner of operations for the Department of Water and Light recommended that no policy be established to provide relief for the cost of utilities, but that each petition for hardship relief should be taken up individually. "No doubt in certain cases this contention [difficulty paying utilities for families whose heads had gone overseas] is correct," the newly established Board of Commissioners reported, "still, it is also possible that it might be abused to the disadvantage of the City."[18] Requests for free tickets for servicemen to ride the Edmonton Radial Railway (ERR) also met with only very cautious support. The commissioner of operations added a long section outlining the financial problems with the ERR to his recommendation that only two tickets be doled out to each enlisted man at every drill, allowing only one round trip. This would be "the best way to avoid abuse of the privilege."[19] Labour unrest emerged early in the war but, constrained by the demands of the war itself, would only break out in any significant way after the Armistice. However, the issue of "enemy

The Edmonton Exhibition built this display to demonstrate the kind of trenches where local men were serving overseas. Needless to say, such nice clean trenches, in which children played, hardly did justice to the gruesome reality experienced by Edmonton soldiers at the front. McDermid Studio, Glenbow Archives, NC-6-2394.

The war touched every aspect of life in Edmonton. Tales of atrocities against Belgium flooded the newspapers during the first months of the war, and Edmonton rushed to provide relief, along with many other communities. This car is preparing to leave Edmonton for shipment of its cargo to Europe in 1914. McDermid Studio, Glenbow Archives, NC-6-1307.

alien" labour was raised as early as July 1915, when the Edmonton Trades and Labor Council (ETLC) led a protest against the Grand Trunk Pacific Railway's practice of importing such labour from central Canada and the United States for its recently opened Macdonald Hotel.[20]

Wartime profiteering also grew despite efforts by the federal government to check this trend. Aside from the impact on morale, profiteering led to inflation, which in turn made it more difficult for the average worker to make a living. The demand for increased wages meant that the trade union movement grew rapidly during the First World War. Skilled and semi-skilled workers had found employment during the prewar boom in construction and railway building across the West, but demands for better wages or working conditions were hampered

by the fear of being fired or blacklisted when there was surplus labour.

With increasing wartime labour shortages, workers and unions gained more power. While a brief strike by city labourers had failed in 1912, by 1916 the municipal inside workers were able to mount a successful protest of their work conditions. They were issued a charter by the Trades and Labour Congress of Canada (TLCC) on May Day, 1917. The newly organized Civic Employees Federal Union No. 30 inspired other local municipal workers to follow suit, including city hall staff, labourers, police, firefighters, teamsters, electricians, and Edmonton Radial Railway street railway employees.

By 1917, the newly organized Edmonton and District Labour Council (EDLC) established the Labour Representation League (LRL) to nominate working-class candidates to carry its banner to all levels of the electoral process. It opposed the rising demand for universal conscription, arguing for "the conscription of wealth" before conscription for overseas service. The EDLC also supported the broadening of the municipal franchise to include tenants, and not just property owners. The league further insisted that city contracts be awarded to contractors that had been unionized and paid union rates. Its voice became more demanding, pointing to the inequitable provision of municipal services to working-class neighbourhoods. At the provincial level, demands were made for more inspectors to enforce labour laws. Federally, the EDLC opposed immigration, fearing that a labour surplus would diminish its growing influence, and because of the belief that foreign workers would accept low wages.[21]

Elmer Roper, a future mayor of Edmonton and a printer who had influenced the Calgary Labour Council to establish the LRL in 1917, later that year moved to Edmonton. Roper spearheaded the establishment by the EDLC of a similar representative league. The LRLs were influential in drafting political platforms for candidates, and endorsed those who accepted these demands. The LRL in Edmonton unsuccessfully ran anti-conscription candidates in the December 1917 federal election, struggling against the overwhelming tide of patriotic fervor set loose by the wider national conscription campaign.

Women had already established many social and political organizations advocating reform at all levels of government by the outbreak of the war. Bess H. Nichols became the first woman elected to public office in Canada when she became a member of the Edmonton Public School Board in 1912. In Edmonton, Emily Murphy was regarded as the personification of the reform impulse among women's groups.

Settling in Edmonton in 1910, where her reputation as a novelist and journalist grew, she championed a wide range of reform causes. When the war came, "Janey Canuck," as she became known by her pen name, worked to register women volunteers for patriotic work on the home front, including through a new national War Council of Women.

Edmonton women gave early indications that they planned to take an active role in the war effort. Ten offered to serve as nurses as soon as war was declared. Flora Kathleen Willson, a decorated army nurse who was a veteran of the South African War, was foremost among them. She was the wife of Major Justus Willson, commanding officer of "D" Company in the 49th Battalion. Roberta MacAdams, who enlisted in the Canadian Army Medical Corps and was assigned as a dietician to the Ontario Military Hospital in Orpington, England, launched a political career during the war. The Voluntary Aid Detachments and Victorian Order of Nurses absorbed other women eager to serve.

Many Edmonton women became heads of their families when their husbands put on their country's uniform. Aside from the hardships associated with this situation, many were widowed by the war, or struggled when severely injured husbands returned to Edmonton. At the beginning of the war, married men required their wife's permission to enlist. Not until 1919 did Alberta enact the Mothers Allowance Act, which provided some consistent support for such women and their children. Government pensions for military personnel, or their families, were almost unknown when the war began. In Edmonton, such people relied upon private charities such as the Edmonton Patriotic Fund. The Military Hospitals Commission took the federal initiative to aid injured soldiers in 1915, and the disabled were among the first to receive aid through pensions and training for civilian life. The Board of Pension Commissioners was established under an Order in Council (3 June 1916), and a district office was located in Edmonton. Widows would receive a pension of $480, with children receiving between $96 and $144. This varied considerably; for example, Private William Reid, 14th Battalion, left a widow, Robina Reid, and seven children when he was killed in action in September 1916. The board granted her an annual pension of $384, with $6 monthly for each child.[22] Another federal initiative was the Soldier Settlement Act (1917), which helped veterans obtain farms. The Department of Soldiers' Civil Re-establishment, formed in 1918, set pensions among its other responsibilities. However, it required energetic advocacy by the Great War Veterans' Association to obtain even marginally better pensions for veterans or war widows.

As early as October 1914, two months into the war, a number of men and women presented a petition to the Alberta legislature signed by 1,200 people, insisting that "male" be changed to "person" in the Alberta Election Act, giving women equal voting rights with men. Another delegation went to Alberta's legislature to petition for women's right to vote the following year. Alberta women won the municipal and provincial vote in 1916. The war also saw the greater involvement of women in the workplace. For example, in western Canada, the number of women doing clerical work doubled in the decade between 1911 and 1921. Most of this reflected a growing labour shortage caused by the war.[23]

Prohibition became law in Alberta during July 1916 and would last until 1923. Groups such as the Women's Canadian Temperance Union played a significant role in this development. Success was claimed for prohibition across the Canadian West.

For example, arrests for drunkenness in Alberta declined by 90 percent during 1917 and 1918.[24]

While the war created conditions that encouraged many "women's causes," it also created a rift among the various groups linked to the suffrage movement. Nellie McClung, at her cottage on Lake Winnipeg, wrote that the outbreak of war was "like a troubled dream." Some of the women in the prewar movement were strong pacifists, one being Cora Hind, who McClung said "saw only one side of the question and there were times when I envied her, though I resented her denunciations of those who thought otherwise." McClung continued, lamenting that "the old crowd began to break up, and our good times were over."[25]

Female suffrage was generally regarded as the foremost legacy of wartime women's activities. These contributions were central to the gaining of the federal vote for most Canadian women with the Women's Franchise Act in May 1918. The federal franchise had been achieved in stages in the year prior to this with the Military Voters Act, which gave the franchise to military nurses, and the Wartime Elections Act, which enfranchised wives, widows, mothers, sisters, and daughters of men serving in the Canadian or British military. Women such as Murphy and McClung were instrumental in these developments.

End of War and Postwar Edmonton

Rationing was a daily issue in Edmonton as the war entered its final stage. Under Order in Council 3214, introduced on 15 November 1917, the Food Controller could prohibit the manufacture or distribution of any food without a federal licence, and could cancel such licences for any violation of the regulations.

Regular statements of changes to rationing regulations appeared in the *Canada Gazette*. For example, on 15 February 1918, Order No. 16 proclaimed that in Alberta and Saskatchewan bread could only be sold in loaves to a maximum of 21 ounces.[26]

Despite wartime stringency, the community pulled together and staged many patriotic events. On 1 May 1918, the 49th Regiment Chapter of the Imperial Order Daughters of the Empire (IODE) sponsored a concert by schoolchildren in All Saint's Schoolroom; Vernon Barford, co-founder of the Alberta Music Festival, provided the music, and all proceeds went to the Edmonton Prisoners of War Fund.[27] Influential local organizations such as the United Commercial Travellers (Edmonton Council 447) also staged such events, including a Patriotic Street Carnival to raise funds for war-related causes. City Council granted permission for the carnival to be held near Jasper Avenue and 102nd Street in September 1918.[28]

As soon as the war ended, the city began to consider how to deal with its returned men. A commissioner's report noted a recent case in which a fireman had returned to Edmonton and was re-engaged by the fire department. He felt that he should receive the wage increases that he would have realized if he had worked through the war years. The Finance Committee took the view that each case should be decided on its merits. On the issue of re-employment, separate from wages, the case was clearer. A special committee struck a month after the Armistice recommended that all department superintendents be instructed to give preference to returned men or their dependents.[29]

In October 1918, Lieutenant Colonel E.G. May, Militia Headquarters No. 13, Calgary, began negotiations with Howard Stutchbury, Commissioner for Returned Soldiers in Edmonton, hoping to have separate sections for deceased soldiers who had been receiving treatment in Military Hospitals, or through the Soldiers' Civil Re-establishment Commission. "In view of possible 'Decoration Days' in the future it would be desirable to have the graves [of service personnel] together," May added. The City Safety and Health Committee took this forward, and today such sections are to be found in all the municipal cemeteries.[30]

The Great War Veterans' Association commenced negotiations with the city in May 1918, hoping to obtain access to the old College Avenue High School site near Alberta College for its planned veterans' hall. This hall would be built, and remained the centre of veterans' activities for decades.[31]

As the hostilities finally ceased near Mons in November 1918, Private F.R. Hasse of the 49th Battalion is reputed to have declared: "The only road worth taking from here is to Jasper Avenue." When the 49ers returned home, in March 1919, it was to a city just beginning to recover from the devastating effects of the Spanish influenza pandemic that killed 614 Edmontonians among millions worldwide. As they marched down Jasper Avenue, greeted by crowds still wearing their white cotton "flu masks," it was clear that a bond had been forged with Edmonton that has never faded.

Conclusion

On 11 October 1919, two years after claiming at the enlistment office to be 19 years of age, Frank Burstrom returned to his hometown of Edmonton with his father. The younger Burstrom joined the 77th Battalion, Canadian Field Artillery, in September

1917, just after his fifteenth birthday. He was one of the youngest soldiers to serve in the British forces during the Great War, although it was impossible at the time to confirm this claim, since all the under-age recruits lied about their ages in order to enlist. Burstrom first saw the front on 22 September 1917 as a driver for his battalion in France. Interestingly, his father Frank Sr. also served in France with the 197th Infantry Battalion (Winnipeg). In June 1919 the younger Burstrom admitted his real age, but the discharge officer refused to record it. After the war, both father and son went to British Colum-bia, where Frank Sr. worked for the Grand Trunk Pacific Railway.[32]

In many ways, the Edmonton to which the Bur-stroms, *pere et fils*, returned in 1919 was very much, but not entirely, as Frank had left it in 1917. There were a few more cars on the streets; more railway connections reached out to the north; women's styles and attitudes changed; women's suffrage had been achieved; prohibition had been adopted in July 1916; and more sophisticated "movies" now entertained enthusiastic audiences at nickelodeons and palatial movie houses. But such things perhaps obscured the more fundamental malaise that would continue to trouble the city intermittently but consistently until the Second World War again initiated extensive development.

Edmonton had been successfully racing headlong toward its goals of growth and prosperity for almost two decades, until stalled abruptly and unexpectedly by the international financial decline in 1913. It became a city in 1904; the capital of the new prov-ince of Alberta in 1906; and gained the provincial university in 1908. Its population mushroomed during the decade before the war. But, over the next decade, Edmonton suffered the terrible sacrifices of a global war and the Spanish influenza pandemic of 1918–19. A June 1915 flood also destroyed much of its industrial core as brickyards, lumber mills, and other businesses were washed away, devastating the commercial developments in the North Saskatche-wan River Valley flats.

Unlike the situation some two decades later during the Second World War, the city's popula-tion decreased dramatically between 1914 and 1918. Edmonton's population in 1914 was 72,516. A significant number of local men enlisted and soon were serving on the battlefields of Europe. By 1917, Edmonton's population had declined to about 56,000.

Virtually no construction occurred in the city during the Great War. After the opening, in 1915, of several landmark projects such as the Macdonald Hotel and Princess Theatre, on which construction had commenced before the war, both residential and commercial building stagnated. The labour shortage resulting from extensive enlistment ensured that only a few significant building projects were under-taken for years following 1914. Wartime resources, which would otherwise be used in construction, also were largely diverted to military use.

The longer-term impact of the war on Edmonton is difficult to assess. The contributions from those who never returned can only be guessed at. There were many such as prominent Edmonton architect Roland Lines, killed in 1916, whose commissions survive as a reminder of his missing role in postwar Edmonton, and the lost possibilities of his talent. His is one of many such losses to the city. But the real effect, in the end, would be felt at a deeper, personal level by the families left to deal with their missing fathers, sons, and husbands.

Notes

1 Loyal Edmonton Regiment website, URL: http://www.lermuseum.org/en/regimental-history/edmonton-and-the-49th/outbreak-of-war/, retrieved 28 May 2014.

2 *Edmonton Bulletin*, 8, 12, and 26 August 1914.

3 Ibid., 12 August 1914.

4 *Edmonton Capital*, 29 September 1914.

5 Ibid., 28 September 1914.

6 Harold R. Peat, *Private Peat* (New York: Grosset & Dunlap, 1917), 1–2.

7 City of Edmonton Archives, RG 8.10, box 8, file 53, City Clerk, Special Committee Reports 1916, Finance Committee: G.H. Hensley to Mayor W.T. Henry, 1 February 1916.

8 *Edmonton Capital*, 28 September 1914.

9 City of Edmonton Archives, Clipping File: "51st Battalion."

10 *Edmonton Bulletin*, 7 May 1915.

11 Ibid., 12 May 1915.

12 Ibid., 10 June 1915.

13 Ibid., 4 January 1915.

14 Lt. Col. P. Anderson DSO, *I, That's Me: Escape from German Prison Camp and Other Adventures* (Edmonton: Bradburn Printers, n.d.).

15 *Edmonton Morning Bulletin*, 11 April 1916, 24 November 1916.

16 "Cree Legend Is Painted on Body of Aeroplane Driven by Edmonton Boys," *Edmonton Morning Bulletin*, 18 April 1917; "Edmonton Boys in Great Air Fight," *Edmonton Morning Bulletin*, 28 May 1918.

17 *Edmonton News-Advertiser*, 19 July 1915.

18 City of Edmonton Archives, RG 8.10, box 4, file 29, City Clerk, Special Committee Reports 1914, Operations, Commissioners Reports Nos. 640, 649, 18/31 August 1914.

19 Ibid., No. 665, 26 October 1914.

20 Ibid., Report No. 12, 13 July 1915.

21 Edmonton and District Labour Council, Northern Alberta and NWT (District of Mackenzie), and Building and Construction Trades Council, *Then, Now and Next 100 Years of Edmonton Labour* (Edmonton: n.p., 2006), 1–5.

22 Proceedings of the Advisory Board of Pension Commissioners decision on the Reid case, URL: http://www.warmuseum.ca/firstworldwar/wp-content/mcme-uploads/2014/08/2-f-2-a-pension.pdf, retrieved 19 August 2015.

23 Graham S. Lowe, "Women, Work, and the Office: The Feminization of Clerical Occupations in Canada, 1901–1931," in *Rethinking Canada: The Promise of Women's History,* edited by Veronica Strong-Boag and Anita Clair Fellman (Toronto: Copp Clark Pittman, 1986), 109–14.

24 John Herd Thompson, *The Harvests of War: The Prairie West, 1914–1918* (Toronto: McClelland and Stewart, 1978), 98–106.

25 Candace Savage, *Our Nell: A Scrapbook Biography of Nellie L. McClung* (Saskatoon: Western Producer Prairie Books, 1979), 109–10.

26 Canada, Office of the Food Controller, Extract from the *Canada Gazette*, Order No. 16, 15 February 1918.

27 City of Edmonton Archives, RG 8.10, box 10, file 72: "Display BY the Pupils of Mrs. and Miss Lotta Boucher," program.

28 City of Edmonton Archives, RG 8.10, box 10, file 72: C.J. Davidson, Chairman, UCT Council 447, to Mayor and Council, 30 July 1918; Alderman Grant, Chairman Safety and Health Committee, to Mayor and Council, 13 August 1918.

29 City of Edmonton Archives, RG 8.10, box 9, file 67, City Clerk, Special Committee Reports 1918, Finance Committee Report No. 61, 21 November 1918; file 80, "Meeting No. 1," 17 December 1918.

30 City of Edmonton Archives, RG 8.10, box 10, file 72, City Clerk, Special Committee Reports 1918, Safety and Health Committee.

31 City of Edmonton Archives, RG 8.10, box 10, file 69, City Clerk, Special Committee Reports 1918, Parks and Markets Committee.

32 *Edmonton Journal*, 11 October 1919.

Works Cited

PRIMARY SOURCES

Edmonton Bulletin
Edmonton Capital
Edmonton Journal
Edmonton Morning Bulletin
Edmonton News-Advertiser

City of Edmonton Archives
  RG 8.10, box 4, file 29, City Clerk, Special Committee Reports 1914.
  RG 8.10, box 7, file 50, City Clerk, Special Committee Reports 1915.
  RG 8.10, box 8, file 53, City Clerk, Special Committee Reports 1916.
  RG 8.10, box 9, file 67, City Clerk, Special Committee Reports 1918.
  RG 8.10, box 10, file 69, City Clerk, Special Committee Reports 1918.
  RG 8.10, box 10, file 72, City Clerk, Special Committee Reports 1918.
  RG 8.10, box 10, file 72, C.J. Davidson, Chairman, UCT Council 447.
  RG 8.10, file 80, Commissioners Report No. 48, 10 February 1919.

SECONDARY SOURCES

Anderson, Lt. Col. P. DSO. *I, That's Me: Escape from German Prison Camp and Other Adventures*. Edmonton: Bradburn Printers Ltd., n.d.

Edmonton and District Labour Council, Northern Alberta and NWT (District of Mackenzie), and Building and Construction Trades Council. *Then, Now and Next 100 Years of Edmonton Labour*. N.p., 2006.

Lowe, Graham S. "Women, Work, and the Office: The Feminization of Clerical Occupations in Canada, 1901–1931." In *Rethinking Canada: The Promise of Women's History*, edited by Veronica Strong-Boag and Anita Clair Fellman. Toronto: Copp Clark Pittman, 1986.

Loyal Edmonton Regiment website. URL: http://www.lermuseum.org/en/regimental-history/edmonton-and-the-49th/outbreak-of-war/, retrieved 28 May 2014.

Morton, Desmond. "Dissolving Canada's Great War Army." Images of a Forgotten War: Films of the Canadian Expeditionary Force in the Great War website, National Film Board. URL: http://www3.nfb.ca/ww1/dissolving.php, retrieved 21 July 2014.

Peat, Harold R. *Private Peat*. New York: Grosset & Dunlap, 1917.

Proceedings of the Advisory Board of Pension Commissioners decision on the Reid case. URL: http://www.warmuseum.ca/firstworldwar/wp-content/mcme-uploads/2014/08/2-f-2-a-pension.pdf, retrieved 19 August 2015.

Savage, Candace. *Our Nell: A Scrapbook Biography of Nellie L. McClung*. Saskatoon: Western Producer Prairie Books, 1979.

Thompson, John Herd. *The Harvests of War: The Prairie West, 1914–1918*. Toronto: McClelland and Stewart, 1978.

The First World War as a Local Experience: Mobilization, Citizen Voluntary Support, and Memorializing the Sacrifice in Lethbridge, Alberta

ROBERT RUTHERDALE

Canada entered the Great War both as part of the British Empire and as a confederated Dominion of provinces, territories, and, especially in Alberta, rapidly growing rural and urban settlements in agricultural districts. The city of Lethbridge had a resource-based economy, largely coal production, as well as being the agricultural service centre in the southern region of the province. With a population of just over 8,000 in 1914, Lethbridge's diversity—its gendered, age-based, class, and ethnic divisions—would increasingly play a significant role in complicating local responses to the war. This situation allows historians to probe the complexities of a great event by contrasting what drew people together, on a local level, in a shared purpose of a final victory, and what drove them apart, as the war dragged on for some 54 months, with a considerable period of post-war adjustment following the veterans' return. This essay focuses on three aspects of war and societal relations: recruitment and send-offs, patriotic fund appeal drives, and, with the end of the war, memorializing the sacrifice.

Lethbridge as a Prairie City at the Outbreak of the War

Lethbridge entered the war as a prairie city incorporated in 1905 that had been largely transformed by peoples transplanted from eastern Canada and central Europe. Growth was rapid, often disjointed in terms of planning based on economic goals alone, and aimed to bring local lands and resources into a web of exchanges that met the interests of a national economy. The city's accelerated development since the mid-1880s reflected the goods, services, and demographic changes that were expected as part of Canada's National Policy.[1] This should, of course, be construed as a *re*-settlement history in an area long occupied by Aboriginal peoples. In 1877, just three years after the arrival of the North-West Mounted Police, the Mik-kwee-ye-ne-wak (Blood) First Nation, who had wintered on the nearby Belly (Oldman, after 1915) and St. Mary's Rivers, were absorbed within the colonial administration of Treaty 7, a large territory that included the Sarcee, Blackfoot, Blood, Stoney, and Peigan peoples.

Coal was first exploited, even before the arrival of the Canadian Pacific Railway in 1874, when Frank Sherman, a prospector and whisky trader, hand dug a rich, black seam from the upper banks of the Belly River, near Fort Whoop-Up. This was used for heating fuel by the North-West Mounted Police at Fort Macleod and by merchants across the Missouri at Fort Benton. An assistant Indian commissioner for Treaty 7, Elliott Torrance Galt, son of Sir Alexander Tilloch Galt, a father of Confederation, had informed his father, then serving as the Dominion's high commissioner to Britain and actively seeking to use his position to secure capital for investment in western Canada, of the promising coal deposits Sherman had uncovered. Surveys completed by mining engineers from the Maritimes confirmed the coal potential, and a land concession was granted to start what proved to be a profitable operation at the newly constituted Coalbanks mines, connecting the CPR main line to a narrow-gauge rail line. The line was built by London-based capital under the aegis of the North-West Coal and Navigation Company (NWC&NCo), established in 1882, three years before the completion of Canada's transcontinental railway. Some 400 miners, carpenters, engineers, and saloonkeepers, in a male-dominated work context, arrived at Coalbanks. The CPR monopoly would be repealed in 1889, and the NWC&NCo would be recapitalized as the Alberta Railway and Coal Company (AR&CCo), under the management of Charles A. Magrath, the first mayor of Lethbridge.

The development of the frost-resistant Marquis wheat strain and the attractiveness of dryland farming opportunities as well as irrigation farming to the south led to a significant influx of farming families at the beginning of the Laurier-era economic boom in western Canada. As Lethbridge grew in tandem with southern Alberta, so did its comparatively diverse resource operations, with the establishment of the Alberta Railway and Irrigation Company (AR&ICo) led by Elliott Galt in 1906, the year in which grain production edged out coal as the city's primary commodity.

Since 1885, when the CPR was completed, the sudden rise of coal and wheat had transformed Galt's investments and the city's social geography into a subordinate, yet prosperous, locale within the framework of Canada's National Policy. Some 570 kilometres of railways and 240 kilometres of irrigation canals had been laid or dug in the local area, and mines produced up to 2,000 tons of coal per day. Up to 1914, outside capital investment maintained tight control over local growth, despite the best efforts of leading citizens who saw themselves as competitors. In 1907, Lethbridge's boosterism took on a formal organizational impetus with the creation of the "25,000 Club," a network of local merchants, professionals, and managers who strove to intensify population growth. The target of 25,000 was set for 1912, the year the city prepared for the Seventh International Dry Land Farming Conference in October, which brought over 5,000 delegates from around the world.

Some setbacks followed. Boosters fell significantly short of their goals for population growth, as the city reached just 8,050 inhabitants in 1911, with no significant boom thereafter. According to the census that year, Lethbridge, compared to the provincial population, had a higher percentage of respondents claiming "English" (over 35 percent versus 25 percent for the province) or "Scot" (over 20 percent compared to less than 15 percent provincially) ancestry. With respect to peoples soon to be classified as enemy aliens, 385 residents claimed German heritage and 362 claimed Austro-Hungarian heritage. Anglicans, Presbyterians, and Methodists led Protestant religious affiliations, with Catholics at approximately 12 percent. Reflecting a fading predominance of males over females from the Coalbanks days, the gender ratio had fallen to about one-quarter more men than women at the war's outbreak. The year before, real estate prices had suddenly collapsed on the heels of a speculative bubble, which left municipal debt at a crippling $2,515,676. As a result, on 1 January 1914, William Duncan Livingston Hardie, a former Galt mine manager, took over a commission style of government through an amendment of the city's charter.

The past decade of rapid in-migration, business establishment, and the creation of social and cultural institutions, from churches and schools to voluntary associations, could be best construed as indicating an "emergent society." This can be defined as a locale encompassing diverse occupations, social classes, and ethnicities that reflects, overall, western Canada's great experiment of transplanting, grafting, mixing, and transforming towns, cities, and district landscapes into a regional quilt of two new provinces. Proportionally, Lethbridge was to play a significant role both in recruitment and voluntary support for the war that exceeded its place in Alberta's urban hierarchies measured by population alone.

Lethbridge and the Canadian Expeditionary Force's Voluntary Wartime Mobilization

Raising troops for the Canadian Expeditionary Force was a huge undertaking. It began amid a great outpouring of enthusiasm for a war most thought would be short and victorious for the British Empire, signalling the triumph of democracy over autocracy. As First World War British historian Dan Todman suggests, wartime mobilization reflected a crucial connection between local communities and national mobilization efforts.[2] Essentially, the Canadian experience of voluntary recruitment up until conscription was imposed in 1917 passed through three fairly distinct phases. Lethbridge was a part of the initial "Valcartier" phase that led to the formation of Canada's First Contingent, trained principally at a massively revamped training centre located at Valcartier, Quebec, at which Lethbridge's 25th Battery, Canadian Field Artillery arrived in August 1914. The subsequent "militia regiment" phase used local facilities across Canada's six military districts (Lethbridge was located in Military District No. 13 with headquarters in Calgary) and three divisions. During this phase, Lethbridge trained and dispatched the 20th and 39th Batteries throughout 1915. The final, so-called "community regiment," phase lasted from late 1915 onward and was, ultimately, displaced by Canada's divisive approach to compulsory military service.

In general, as the fighting overseas dragged on, voluntary recruitment drives were increasingly localized and drew on the networks and resources of individual communities. The final "community regiment" phase of recruitment emerged as a last resort across Canada and depended on an assortment of local initiatives from county battalions to those defined by invented ethnic identities (i.e., Scottish highlanders), physical stature (the "Bantam" regiments), or various "pals" affiliations such as "Sportsmen," or explicit "pals" regimental units. Lethbridge's "Kiltie" battalion, the 113th Highlanders, which initially trained at a militia camp in nearby Sarcee, was created in the winter of 1915–16 during the concluding phase of voluntary recruitment.

In October 1915, following lobbying efforts by city solicitor W.S. Ball and E.C. Mackenzie—both lawyers who had ties to the Conservative party—Ottawa authorized a Highlanders battalion for Lethbridge. The city's two papers, the *Telegram* and the *Daily Herald*, featured prominent coverage throughout its training and final send-off. Both papers complained, however, that the battalion was rarely seen on parade.[3] Its commander, Lieutenant Colonel A.W. Pryce-Jones, a Welsh-born militia officer who had settled in Calgary four years before, had taken charge in December 1915 with his junior officers receiving their appointments the following month. Recruitment was slow, and by the spring of 1916, the unit could only attract 900 of the 1,100 men normally required for a complete battalion.

Nonetheless, from the start, local leaders had been fully behind the effort as a local initiative, highlighting the fact that recruitment from the city had been, according to press reports, stronger from Lethbridge than anywhere else in Canada—a remarkable achievement. Being awarded local procurement contracts for raising new regiments was also an inducement for this. If the city supplied men, it should receive tenders and contracts. Mayor Hardie and the Lethbridge Board of Trade were quoted by the *Daily Herald* as stating that the city had already supplied more than its fair allotment of "brawn and muscle" of over 1,000 men and, yet, at that time, as part of the "militia regiment" phase, was only provisioning some 140 trainees as part of the 39th Battery.[4]

From the dramatic outbreak of the war onward, intimate connections between cities such as Lethbridge and their overseas-bound troops remained intense. This could be as direct as a loved family

This photograph of the first trainload of volunteers for Lethbridge's 25th Field Battery, Canadian Field Artillery, was taken in August 1914. Courtesy of Galt Museum and Archives, Lethbridge, 19831018000.

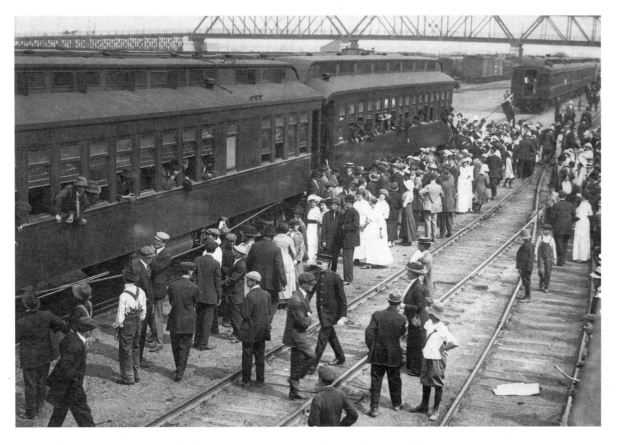

First World War soldiers entraining, Lethbridge, Alberta, September 1914. Glenbow Archives, NA-1111-1.

member departing—too often forever—or as imagined as the conceptual framework through which the distant war was envisioned and understood. The largest crowds ever assembled in urban centres across Canada were mirrored in front of the Lethbridge *Daily Herald*'s office on 5 August 1914 when Britain's ultimatum to Germany expired, and "the despatch stating that Germany had declared war on Great Britain was megaphoned to the eagerly awaiting crowd," the *Daily Herald* reported.[5] "The vast assemblage in front of the Herald Office was enthused

to the breaking point," its front page declared in a special edition, continuing: "The people listened in tense silence until the despatch was finished and then one yell—you could not describe it as a cheer—rent the air, hats were thrown, sky high and for [a] moment the people went mad." Then, "[c]heer after cheer arose amid the greatest of excitement." The city's Citizen Band "was vociferously cheered with each contribution to the general uproar." Then they played "Rule Britannia," "The Red, White and Blue," "Bonnie Dundee," "Men of Harlech," "Cock of the North," "The 81st Regimental March," "The Maple Leaf," "O Canada," and "God Save the King."[6] Mayor Hardie addressed the crowd, stating, "You are assembled now at the most momentous moment in the history of the British Empire, to which it is our proud privilege to belong. The war has been thrust on us, we have not sought it. But now it has come we are ready and I know that every citizen of the City of Lethbridge is ready to do his duty at any sacrifice to himself."[7] This marked the climax of several days of tense waiting and local celebration. The *Herald* had already reported, for example, that the bandstand of the city's Galt Gardens in the late afternoon of August 3 had held "the largest crowd ever" that had gathered in the city, which in their cheering and calls for more patriotic music "testified beyond the shadow of a doubt that if the sentiment was as strong all over the Dominion as it is in Lethbridge, Canada is ready to

meet any emergency into which the Motherland may be precipitated."[8]

Of course the war was not over by Christmas; and, during the Valcartier and militia regiment phases, when the 25th and, then, the 20th Field Batteries were raised and dispatched, the initial enthusiasm died down and even waned altogether when it came to recruiting for the 113th Highlanders in the winter of 1915–16. This was despite the fact that Lethbridge had, indeed, contributed proportionally higher numbers of men than any other locale across the country. The send-offs were much-publicized affairs that took shape with considerable planning by local officials and volunteers. "Members of the battery were carried aloft of the shoulders of their comrades, and cheer after cheer followed them down the platform," the *Daily Herald* reported as the 25th Battery made their way down the CPR platform.[9]

Sergeants, 113th Overseas Battalion (Lethbridge Highlanders), Calgary, Alberta, ca. 1914–18. Photographer/Illustrator: W.J. Oliver, Calgary, Alberta. Glenbow Archives, PB-427-2.

"Three cheers and the singing of 'God Save the King,' led by the city band, accompanied the music of the moving wheels, and the Lethbridge contingent of the Overseas forces had a last look at the home town that will remain with them throughout their campaign, no matter where it may take them."[10] This had followed a formal dinner in which the unit's commander, Major J.S. Stewart, a city dentist and experienced militia officer, delivered a rousing farewell address, which gave family and friends a chance to salute each member of the local battery. Stewart was reported to have spoken "mostly of the boys, their loyalty, their willingness to sacrifice, and the zeal for the Motherland."[11]

Between this moment, not a fortnight after the outbreak of the war, and the departure of the 113th Highlanders, intense bonds were fostered between the volunteers preparing to go overseas and the local citizens—friends, family, and onlookers—who would remain behind. Imperial Order Daughters of the Empire women in Lethbridge's Galt chapter, as elsewhere, played a particular role in cementing bonds between hometown and regimental units. On the Saturday afternoon that preceded the 113th's departure, the Galt chapter, led by its president, Mrs. G.W. Robinson, organized a formal presentation of a set of pipe drums, each suitably engraved to commemorate the occasion for the regiment, which had formed a hollow square in front of the same bandstand at the war's onset nearly two years before. Both the *Daily Herald* and *Telegram* reprinted Robinson's speech in full, which concluded with her reassurance of what came next with respect to local support for the war and the families left behind. "To those of you in the ranks leaving families behind," she assured the men, "I can safely promise for the Order, which I have the honor and pleasure to represent, that we will at all times and in all ways do our best to help them and 'keep the home fires burning' in anticipation of the time when the enemy shall be vanquished and you will return covered with glory and honor."[12]

The considerable extent to which communities expressed a deep sense of pride and connection to *their* boys was mirrored in the efforts of local volunteers to provide support for the families left behind. These efforts were, almost by definition, local. They depended on pre-existing networks of citizens bound by class and ethnicity. And they operated most effectively, even if each fed into a broad nationwide war effort, on local levels in terms of basic organization and administration. The Canadian Patriotic Fund (CPF), established as a voluntary effort to raise and distribute monies to families of soldiers in service during the war, is the best example of this. Understanding how, as Todman puts it, "the nature of the voluntary effort . . . was in many ways a local one" necessitates incorporating local case study approaches. As with recruitment and early mobilization, Lethbridge's history as part of the CPF serves as a particularly apt example of intimate connection between local civilians and an imperial/national war effort.

Local Volunteerism: Lethbridge Responds to the Canadian Patriotic Fund

The CPF was created at the beginning of the war by federal statute as a private fundraising organization for soldier's families, headed by Sir Herbert B. Ames, a Montreal businessman and Conservative MP. It extended considerably a tradition of fundraising for soldiers and their families in British North America dating back to the War of 1812.[13] With

Phillip Morris serving as the executive director, and Canada's Governor General, the Duke of Connaught, serving as its honorary president, the history of the fund displayed a bottom-up, decentralized, voluntary, and fundamentally locally based approach to branch organization, fundraising, and wartime dependant reimbursement. Second, the CPF operated as a top-down expression of a conservative ethos (by both national and local business and political leaders) to maintain, through a voluntary system of relief rather than charity, the status quo in state/societal relations. Locally controlled, citizen-based initiatives were pursued, as opposed to relying on nationwide and federal social welfare. CPF efforts throughout its history were based not on taxing and spending on a national level but on canvassing donations and redistributing relief in every region across the country. The fund maintained a consistent approach on this from the beginning. "I sincerely hope," Governor General Connaught declared at the outset, "that in every town and city throughout the Dominion branches of this organization may be formed." And, indeed they were. Morris later noted that this announcement and appeal was reprinted in newspapers across Canada as "the first shot fired in the campaign to stir up local action."[14]

In mid-October 1914, acting in his capacity as a member of the Alberta legislature, Lieutenant Colonel J.S. Stewart asked city commissioner A.M. Grace to assemble an executive committee for a newly formed Lethbridge chapter of the Canadian Patriotic Fund. The task was done that same day, with board of trade president G.M. Marnoch and Lethbridge MP and *Daily Herald* publisher William A. Buchanan serving on the committee. L.M. Johnstone, a Lethbridge lawyer, was named chapter vice-president (Stewart served as president), and pharmacist J.D.

Higinbotham was appointed honorary treasurer.[15] Within two years, overseas service had taken two: Stewart joined the active force and was promoted to the rank of brigadier general for Canada's 3rd Division, the highest rank obtained by anyone from the province during the war. Johnstone departed with the 113th Highlanders, and Higinbotham eventually stepped down, though many branches across the country had two or more treasurers during their histories.

Lethbridge followed many branches in receiving start-up donations from city officials; Mayor Hardie and Commissioner Grace both donated 10 percent of their salaries and, in so doing, followed the example set by all members of the Alberta legislature. The fund's early, door-to-door fundraising canvasses depended solely on the close connection between locale and contributory commitment. Following a pattern displayed in communities across the country, the city was divided into 17 districts, each led by a male "district captain." Though women played leading roles in organizing wartime chapters of the Canadian Red Cross, the CPF's fundraising efforts tended to be male dominated. Lethbridge's first canvassing drive was organized as a joint CPF–Canadian Red Cross steering committee that met in late November 1914. "The joint committee," the *Daily Herald* reported, "has made a comprehensive survey of the city, so that every nook and corner will be covered in the effort to raise money for these splendid causes." Prospective donors could choose between giving to the CPF or the Canadian Red Cross or, if no preference was expressed, the monies would be evenly divided between the two.[16] "At noon today," the *Daily Herald* announced in its report on 2 December 1914, "the captains of the campaign had lunch together at the Hudson's Bay and reported the progress they had made in the first day's canvass. "Lunch will be taken tomorrow and Friday at the same place."[17] Gatherings like these offered citizen-volunteers an opportunity to socialize, signify their importance to the local community, and demonstrate their own willingness to contribute time as well as money.

Historian Duff Crerar asserts with considerable evidence that "Lethbridge had one of the most enthusiastic and well-organized welfare efforts in the province." Local canvassing campaigns were well underway by Christmas 1914 "with the help from the middle-class women of the elite Galt chapter of the IODE."[18] Contributors included the tribal chiefs of Alberta's Blood Nation; the Chinese National League; Lethbridge coal miners, many of whom were enemy aliens; and the Lethbridge Tennis Club. Local schoolteachers donated 5 percent of their small salaries each month. Donations eventually reached $88,000, but with such a high proportion of the city's male population serving overseas, this fell far short of the disbursements that, at $167,639, totalled nearly twice as much. Crerar noted that by 1916, the bulk of that amount had been given and contributions dropped so dramatically that the *Daily Herald* threatened to publish the names of those who had money but were unwilling to donate. The city would be forced to impose a tax to keep the Patriotic Fund alive.[19]

By that time, Mrs. Frank Colpman played the most significant role, not in collecting funds but in supervising their disbursement. In his final report, the national fund's executive director Phillip Morris describes Colpman, who was married to one of the city's leading merchants, as someone who "the bulk of the work . . . fell upon," with a rather unusual title compared to other branches: "Dependants Secretary." Her volunteer efforts were no doubt enormous. She, personally, and with many home visits, handled a caseload of some 450 families, obviously a full-time commitment, until the end of the war and well into the postwar years. Colpman, the Galt chapter of the IODE, and the Lethbridge branch of the Red Cross were part of a large and powerful segment of mostly white, middle-class volunteers who exerted their authority over the war primarily through their efforts in both supporting recruitment and the families left behind.

Early Commemorations of the Great War in Lethbridge

The end of the war came officially with the Armistice of 11 November 1918 but, given the enormous human cost borne by every belligerent country and across their empires, it was clear that finding meaning, merit, purpose, and nobility in what some might call a senseless slaughter became a vast, national project. Canada's sacrifice was 60,000 men killed in action or later dying of their wounds, and many others returning wounded, physically and psychologically. In his significant study of the meaning and memory of the First World War in Canada, Jonathan Vance writes that "paying due tribute to the sacrifice required more than donating a few dollars to the war memorial fund or turning up at the cenotaph every November. The only way to render adequate tribute was to complete the task the soldiers had gone to Flanders to begin, by ensuring the war was indeed the progenitor of good. Failure to do so reduced the deaths of 60,000 Canadians and the suffering of untold others to utter meaninglessness."[20] As with other wartime enterprises, local communities played crucial roles. Lethbridge citizens mobilized local resources to commemorate the war long beyond the Armistice and, after the Second World War, Remembrance Day ceremonies. As Todman argues, despite the fact that commemorating the war can be approached as a national, even nation-*building* project, the "pattern of memorialization" is generated, first and foremost, by families closely connected to war, specifically what might be referred to as communities of families.

Beginning in this way, with home front communities meeting the huge postwar necessity of memorializing the war, it is also important to recognize that the inventions of social memory that took place through cenotaphs, ceremonies, and other commemorative acts turned the real men and real experiences of war into a "usable" past that could, as Vance suggests, advance a meaningful, purposive, even positive meaning to the enormous sacrifices that were made. While social memories, in the most general terms, reflect the motivations and aims of whomever seeks to invent them, an idealized sense of the past—what the war has come to *mean*, as a *noble* sacrifice, a just cause for fighting, dying, or returning as veterans to reintegrate into civil society—had been sought across Canada, including in Lethbridge. Indeed, despite the widespread disillusionment felt by many veterans, this has been a consistent feature of how local commemoration across Canada has fed into national expression of unity of purpose to the present day.

The earliest history hitherto found in Lethbridge of a local commemorative project appeared in the pages of W.A. Buchanan's *Daily Herald*, which ran a series of articles shortly after the Armistice that reflected the city's pattern of memorialization. Opinions were put forth by municipal leaders, local businessmen, labour leaders, service groups,

schoolteachers, and women's voluntary organizations. They had one common feature: the suggestions reflected the perspectives, interests, and social aims of whomever forwarded them. They did not, however, coalesce around any specific proposal. Largely, the calls were rooted in what John Bodnar's work on public commemoration suggests were the diverse, "vernacular" elements of the local community. For Bodnar, any successful—that is, lasting and well-received—public commemorative project depends crucially on a convergence between multiple, *vernacular* elements (popular groups and social factions defined by ethnicity, class, gender, and age, from students to business elites) and an "official culture" defined by broad hegemonic interests, typically falling under the rubric of a national government. If both forces within any public commemoration project—from a poem to a monument—come together in terms of critical responses, the effort succeeds. If, however, significant tensions develop between or within the nexus of vernacular and official cultures when it is performed or displayed, it fails.[21] Following a direct call for proposals that appeared in the *Herald* on 21 November 1918, a revealing cross-section of Lethbridge's varied vernacular elements appeared. What should the city do? Captain E.C. McKenzie, reported to be "in close touch with the needs of returned men," recommended a veterans' convalescent hospital be built with Ottawa's support.[22] This impulse was part of the broad struggle veterans came to engage in throughout the interwar period to re-establish returned soldiers within civil society across the country. Other options from the returned men also surfaced. After "considerable discussion," as the *Herald* put it, the Lethbridge chapter of the Great War Veterans' Association favoured a statue of British Prime Minister Lloyd George, engraved with the names, serial numbers, and battalions of all local soldiers who had served, whether returned or killed in action.[23] Lloyd George's strong pro-war policy and comparatively plebeian appeal, as compared to Field Marshals Sir Douglas Haig or Sir William Robertson, may have inspired this.

However, what the men wanted was quickly overshadowed by other ideas from a variety of civilians. Pharmacist J.D. Higinbotham, "one of the leaders for years of public movements in Lethbridge," as the *Daily Herald* portrayed him, was one of the first to suggest construction of a war memorial public library.[24] He advocated that space be set aside within it for a museum display as a well as a gallery to present material artifacts and artistic expressions reflecting local participation and sacrifice. Building a war memorial library became the most popular project proposed. Among his many public roles, Higinbotham had twice served as a school board trustee, and the educational benefits of a public library and museum building stood uppermost in his choice, as it did with several others including another school trustee, H.P. Wallace.[25] Wallace, who spoke explicitly about a new war memorial library supporting the value of education, echoed the views of Principal R. Howard Dobson of the Lethbridge Collegiate Institute. "A monument," Dobson opined as an educator, "is a very fine thing to look at, but it fills very little further purpose than filling the eye with architectural beauty."[26] A former 113th Regiment and Khaki League organizer, W.S. Ball, supported Dobson's idea, as did Lethbridge school board secretary J.H. Fleetwood.[27]

While the library and museum idea proved the most popular, its many advocates differed in precisely how and why it should be pursued. G.R. Marnoch, president of the Lethbridge Board of Trade, for example, claimed that a sum of $35,600

was available through the Carnegie Public Library Trust, a famous trust established by American industrial magnate Andrew Carnegie.[28] The project, he added, would help to put unemployed veterans in the city to work. However, Lethbridge Trades and Labour Council president Fred Smeed strongly opposed any project that would draw on Carnegie's endowment. He endorsed the library idea in principle, but only if it was funded municipally, and he wanted nothing to do with a Lloyd George statue.[29]

A veritable chorus of opinion gathered that reflected vernacular perspectives. While International Brotherhood of Electrical Workers' William Symonds acknowledged that an appropriate statue, erected with the "support from some wealthy citizen who desires to show his appreciation of the sacrifices made," could be considered, nothing could be better than a public library built to support the ideals of democracy for which the war had been fought. "What better idea," added the Reverend J.E. Murrel-Wright of St. Cyprian's Anglican Church, "than that the people go to a building associated with the memory of our fallen heroes in order to keep abreast with the civilization which they fought to maintain?"[30] Public Works Commissioner W.H. Meech, a man of substantial "architectural experience," the *Daily Herald* related, suggested a highly ornate monument without providing details. Fred W. Downer, who had served as recruiting campaign speaker during the militia and community regiment phases, also wanted a monument that included a sizable pedestal for public addresses.[31] From the city's Women's Civic Club, J.F. Simpson called for a memorial fountain, placed at the centre of Galt Gardens.[32] Apart from Captain McKenzie's call for a military hospital, the only proposal that seemed to reflect the most pressing needs of soldiers' families came from the Lethbridge branch of the Great War Next-of-Kin

Association, established throughout Canada in 1917 to aid soldier's dependants. This group called for a war memorial children's home for infant or school-aged children.[33] Louis Moore, identified as a ratepayer, worried that any sort of war memorial edifice might pose an additional annual tax burden for the city.[34] As opinions mounted, one *Daily Herald* editorial called for a permanent war museum, under the title, "Why Not a War Museum for Lethbridge?" Probably spurred by the Department of Militia and Defence's recent announcement to all municipalities that battlefield war trophies, mostly artillery guns, were available for public display, Buchanan's paper cottoned on to the idea that some form of permanent exhibit that included captured enemy weapons could be constructed in the city.[35] In fact, Mayor Hardie did follow up with a formal request, in July 1920, for two German cannons, which were placed conspicuously in front of city hall. They remained there for nearly a decade.

No one else advanced proposals, and none resulted in action; the varied suggestions for a war memorial project received no official backing. Only Lethbridge Rotarians were able to forward a sum of $500 toward a memorial at that time. A "start has been made," the *Daily Herald* declared on the last day of 1918, "and it remains now for the citizens of Lethbridge and district to organize without delay to carry the project to completion."[36]

The collapse, in towns and cities across Canada, of further work on memorial projects fundamentally reflected the devastating health disaster of the Spanish flu epidemic, labour unrest throughout Canada, and immediate problems of veteran re-establishment, all of which soon captured prominent coverage in both the Liberal-Unionist *Lethbridge Daily Herald* and the Conservative *Lethbridge Telegram*. The collapse of a successful commemoration project may have been inevitable, but the roots of family memories and local connections to the war experience and the search for attaching some permanent meaning to it remained.

Within four years, the Alexander Galt branch of the IODE had begun accepting donations for a war memorial monument, and a series of contributions were quietly received with a sizable balance accruing within five years. In 1927, a year in which cenotaph unveilings were beginning to peak elsewhere in Canada, the fund needed only a further $1,500 to reach its budgeted $10,250. At that point, negotiations were already underway to commission a Montreal-based sculptor, Coeur de Leon MacCarthy, who would become famous for Canadian war monuments. Crucial permission from the Canadian Pacific Railway to erect the cenotaph at the centre of Galt Gardens, on land still held by the railway, was also obtained by the IODE's cenotaph committee. The requisite balance finally came in October 1930 with a loan approved by the municipal council, which had expressed concern over delays in fundraising though MacCarthy was already at work. Disappointment was felt that it could not be unveiled on Armistice Day that year; securing an appropriate bronze wreath delayed that until the summer of 1931.[37] By then, southern Alberta was in the grips of the Great Depression, and annual droughts would soon accelerate a prolonged period of rural out-migration. Nonetheless, the cenotaph in Galt Gardens, which was moved in 2000 to the front of city hall, served the same general purpose cenotaphs did across Canada on November 11—to honour the sacrifice of Canada's fallen soldiers.

Of most recent significance is the Lethbridge Cenotaph Project. Under the aegis of the project, local historian Brett Clifton wishes to connect the names of some 400 soldiers identified on the city cenotaph to newly compiled biographical sketches that will be made available in digital format through the University of Lethbridge library. In each of the three key areas, recruitment and send-offs, voluntary fundraising, and commemoration, a local community-based historical study of Lethbridge helps to shed light on the vital, complex, and often contradictory connections between locale, nation, and empire that continues today as the city, the province of Alberta, and the country mark the centenary of the outbreak of the war in August 1914.

Notes

1   On early development and the National Policy in the Prairie West, see Andrew den Otter, *Civilizing the West: The Galts and the Development of Western Canada* (Edmonton: University of Alberta Press, 1982).

2   Dan Todman, "The First World War in Contemporary British Culture," in *Untold War: New Perspectives in First World War Studies*, edited by Heather Jones, Jennifer O'Brien, and Christopher Schmidt-Supprian (Leiden: Brill, 2008), 424.

3   *Lethbridge Daily Herald*, 27 October 1915, 1. For discussion of Colonel Sam Hughes' strong endorsement of locally based drives for recruitment, including support for newly formed "community regiments," see Ron Haycock, *Sam Hughes: The Public Career of a Controversial Canadian* (Waterloo and Ottawa: Wilfrid Laurier University Press and the Canadian War Museum, 1986), 213.

4   *Lethbridge Daily Herald*, 27 October 1915, 1.

5   Ibid., 5 August 1914, 1 and 6.

6   Ibid.

7   Ibid.

8   Ibid., 3 August 1914, 7.

9   Ibid., 19 August 1914, 4.

10 Ibid.

11 Ibid.

12 Ibid., 15 May 1916, 1 and 7, and *Lethbridge Telegram*, 18 May 1916, 5.

13 See Robert Rutherdale, *Hometown Horizons: Local Responses to Canada's Great War* (Vancouver: UBC Press, 2004), 94–95.

14 Phillip H. Morris, *The Canadian Patriotic Fund: A Record of Its Activities from 1914 to 1919* (n.p., 1920), 15.

15 *Lethbridge Daily Herald*, 15 October 1914, 1.

16 Ibid., 30 November 1914, 1.

17 Ibid., 2 December 1914, 1.

18 Duff Crerar, "1916 and the Great War," in *Alberta Formed, Alberta Transformed*, edited by Michael Payne, Donald Wetherell, and Catherine Cavanaugh (Edmonton: University of Alberta Press, 2006), 400.

19 Ibid.

20 Jonathan Vance, *Death So Noble: Memory, Meaning, and the First World War* (Vancouver: UBC Press, 1997), 219.

21 As Bodnar expresses it, "public memory is a body of belief and ideas about the past that help a public or society understand its past, present, and by implication, its future . . . The major focus of this communicative and cognitive process is not the past, however, but serious matters in the present such as the nature of power and the question of loyalty to both official and vernacular cultures." See John Bodnar, *Remaking America: Public Memory, Commemoration, and Patriotism in the Twentieth Century* (Princeton, NJ: Princeton University Press, 1992), 15.

22 *Lethbridge Daily Herald*, 21 November 1918, 8.

23 Ibid.

24 Ibid., 23 November 1918, 14.

25 Higinbotham's public service in Lethbridge, much of it as a civilian volunteer for war-related causes, was indeed significant. He served as a school board trustee in 1896 and 1897, the earliest period for the local public school system, and later from 1912 to 1915. See Sir Alexander Galt Archives, Souvenir Booklet: Lethbridge Public Schools (Lethbridge: 1915), P19851045017. *Lethbridge Daily Herald*, 22 November 1918, 10, and 23 November 1918, 14.

26 Ibid., 25 November 1918, 7

27 Ibid., 27 November 1918, 7

28 Ibid., 29 November 1918, 14.

29 Ibid., 21 November 1918, 8.

30 Ibid.

31 Ibid., 22 November 1918, 10.

32 Ibid., 30 November 1918, 14.

33 Ibid., 19 December 1918, 10.

34 Ibid., 27 November 1918, 7.

35 Ibid., 21 November 1918, 4.

36 Ibid., 31 December 1918, 4.

37 See Alex Johnston, "Canada's Wars and the Cenotaph in Galt Gardens, Lethbridge, Alberta," copy of occasional paper published by the Lethbridge Historical Society and deposited in the Sir Alexander Galt Archives.

Works Cited

PRIMARY SOURCES

Lethbridge Daily Herald
Lethbridge Telegram

Sir Alexander Galt Archives

SECONDARY SOURCES

Binnema, Theodore. "Old Swan, Big Man, and Siksika Bands, 1784–1815." *Canadian Historical Review* 77 (1996): 1–32.

Bodnar, John. *Remaking America: Public Memory, Commemoration, and Patriotism in the Twentieth Century*. Princeton, NJ: Princeton University Press, 1992.

Crerar, Duff. "1916 and the Great War." In *Alberta Formed, Alberta Transformed*, edited by Michael Payne, Donald Wetherell, and Catherine Cavanaugh. Edmonton: University of Alberta Press, 2006.

Den Otter, Andrew. *Civilizing the West: The Galts and the Development of Western Canada*. Edmonton: University of Alberta Press, 1982.

Durflinger, Serge. *Fighting from Home: The Second World War in Verdun, Quebec*. Vancouver: UBC Press, 2006.

Haycock, Ron. *Sam Hughes: The Public Career of a Controversial Canadian*. Waterloo and Ottawa: Wilfrid Laurier University Press and the Canadian War Museum, 1986.

High, Steven, ed. *Occupied St. John's: A Social History of a City at War, 1939–1945*. Montreal and Kingston: McGill-Queen's University Press, 2010.

Johnston, Alex. "Canada's Wars and the Cenotaph in Galt Gardens, Lethbridge, Alberta." Occasional Paper published by the Lethbridge Historical Society, Sir Alexander Galt Archives.

Kenny, Trevor. "Uncovering the Lessons of War." UNews, University of Lethbridge, 21 December 2010. URL: http://www.uleth.ca/unews/article/uncovering-lessons-war, retrieved 4 November 2013.

Miller, Ian H.M. *Our Glory and Our Grief: Torontonians and the Great War*. Toronto: University of Toronto Press, 2002.

Morris, Phillip H. *The Canadian Patriotic Fund: A Record of Its Activities from 1914 to 1919*. N.p., 1920.

Pitsula, James. *For All We Have and Are: Regina and the Experience of the Great War*. Winnipeg: University of Manitoba Press, 2008.

Rutherdale, Robert. *Hometown Horizons: Local Responses to Canada's Great War*. Vancouver: UBC Press, 2004.

Thompson, John Herd. *The Harvests of War: The Prairie West, 1914–1918*. Toronto: McClelland and Stewart, 1978.

Todman, Dan. "The First World War in Contemporary British Culture." In *Untold War: New Perspectives in First World War Studies*, edited by Heather Jones, Jennifer O'Brien, and Christopher Schmidt-Supprian. Leiden, Netherlands: Brill, 2008.

Vance, Jonathan. *Death So Noble: Memory, Meaning, and the First World War*. Vancouver: UBC Press, 1997.

Red Deer and the First World War

MICHAEL DAWE

War! It was a tragic upheaval that had not touched central Alberta for more than a decade since the end of the Boer (South African) War. Experiences from that war had not prepared the community for the monumental changes—social, economic, and political—that would follow the outbreak of the great global conflict in summer 1914. Some had foreseen the inevitability of global war, as the various imperial powers competed for territory and influence; however, most central Albertans were oblivious to the gathering storm clouds. In fact, on 30 September 1913 a local steering committee was struck to plan for the upcoming centenaries commemorating the end of the Napoleonic Wars and the War of 1812.[1]

The military was marginally prepared. In 1907, the first local militia unit, the Red Deer Troop of the 15th Light Horse Regiment, was formed.[2] The move was greeted with considerable enthusiasm in the community. The troop soon grew enough that the Red Deer Independent Squadron of mounted rifles was organized, again, as a detachment of the 15th Light Horse.[3] These occurrences in Red Deer were typical of other communities across the country—at the time Canada had only local militia regiments and a tiny, regular force.

The Independent Squadron was soon split in two with one troop centred in Red Deer and the second located at nearby Pine Lake. A third troop was later organized at Alix, east of Red Deer. By 1913, the local militia had grown to the extent that it had to be reorganized. A new regiment, the 35th Central Alberta Horse, was established. Red Deer was named the regimental headquarters, and armouries were constructed on the city square.[4]

The new building was a grand one: tapestry brick gave the structure a rich appearance, and the usual concrete blocks were replaced with sandstone. A large brick fireplace was constructed in the assembly room/officers' mess on the second floor of the east end of the building. Two medieval-style battlement towers were added to that section of the building.[5] The armouries were finished at the beginning of 1914 and the timing was fortuitous. Word that war had been declared reached Red Deer on the evening of 4 August 1914.[6] The armouries immediately became a centre of frenzied activity as the community mobilized "For King and Country."

While the military superficially appeared prepared, the reality was quite different. At the time, Canada's permanent force was fewer than 4,000.

Part of Parade. July 1st

Men of the 15th Light Horse in the Dominion [Canada] Day parade in Red Deer before the outbreak of the First World War in the summer of 1914. Red Deer Archives, P5390.

The training that militia regiments received varied greatly. The local militia was entirely composed of mounted rifle units, which fit with the cowboy image often associated with this part of Alberta. The experiences of the Boer War also reinforced the bias of military authorities toward mounted rifle units. Their rapid mobility had worked well in a war in which the British and Canadian forces were fighting Boer farmers, who were highly skilled in commando tactics (the word was derived from the Afrikaans' word *kommando*).

However, cavalry and mounted rifle units were becoming anachronistic, much like the medieval battlement towers on Red Deer's new armouries. Masses of soldiers on horses were poorly suited to a war in which the armies were dug into highly fortified defensive trenches. The use of cavalry and mounted rifles was also disastrous when pitted against such modern weaponry as machine guns. These facts were soon made very clear on the Western Front.

The lack of proper planning and preparation became evident when the men of the 35th Central Alberta Horse (CAH) were called up to serve in the 1st Contingent of the Canadian Expeditionary Force (CEF). The call-up was expected, and the unit had been conducting drills every evening instead of the usual weekly sessions. However, on the morning of 21 August 1914 word reached Red Deer that the 35th was to depart by train for Valcartier, Quebec, within the hour. The men were out on a march. Messengers had to be sent off in all directions to locate them.

A tremendous rush to get back to the armouries followed. After a frenzy of packing and tending to last-minute details, the unit began its march to the train station. The local newspapers described the procession as a "picturesque sight." Some of the men were in old uniforms, while others were dressed in overalls. Several were carrying grips, parcels, and other personal items. The chaos was increased by family members and girlfriends freely mingling with the men as they marched.

A very large crowd gathered at the station to see the young men off. Many tears were shed during the emotional farewells. Several tried to hand over last-minute gifts and keepsakes. The Red Deer

Citizens' Band, which had also been quickly assembled, played a number of patriotic songs and choruses.[7] One recruit, an Austrian, arrived at the CPR station to find that the train had left without him. Several people did what they could to make sure that he was quickly on his way to catch up.[8]

Shortly after the departure of the 1st Contingent, Red Deer was designated as the main recruiting station for central Alberta. The armouries were soon swamped with eager young men wanting to enlist. Many were worried they might miss the "big show," as it was anticipated that the war would end by Christmas. Most of the recruitment during the fall of 1914 was for the 31st Battalion, which was a Calgary regiment and part of the 2nd Canadian Contingent. This was the first mobilization of men from Red Deer for an infantry unit, rather than a mounted rifle troop. Again, the lack of preparedness of the military in Alberta quickly became evident. The recruits were given billets in the swine building at the

Red Deer's new armouries, regimental headquarters for the 35th Central Alberta Horse, January 1914. Red Deer Archives, P389.

Calgary Exhibition grounds. An officer wrote home to Red Deer to assure people that these were the best accommodations in the camp.[9]

While the military scrambled to mobilize, Red Deer began to rally to support the men overseas and their families at home. A local Patriotic Fund committee was formed to raise funds for the wives, children, and other dependents of those on active service. Another new charitable organization was the Red Deer local of the Red Cross. It too focused on providing aid to those on active service and their families. However, for a while, consideration was also given to helping the poor in the community.[10]

Generosity also extended to those living in the war zones overseas; thus, food, clothing, and other essentials were collected for the Belgian Relief Fund, including a carload of wheat.[11] A local real estate firm donated 45 cases of canned milk from the Laurentia Milk Company, which had recently been forced to shut down operations due to spoilage of its product.

Sacrifices for the war effort took many forms. Public bodies such as Red Deer City Council implemented a program of strict financial restraint, anticipating demands on the public purse required by the war. Several employees, including the public works foreman, the sanitary inspector, and the parks superintendent, were laid off. The remaining staff were asked to take pay cuts of between 20 percent and 40 percent. The salary reductions for the Public School District's teachers and maintenance workers were not as severe, at 5 percent.[12]

As the year drew to a close, news of the terrible battles being waged in Belgium and northern France began to fill local newspapers. The Gaetz Cornett Drug and Bookstore had a special telegraph wire installed, and posted the latest war bulletins in its windows. The Lyric Theatre became the first

Major H.L. Gaetz with his wife Grace and sons Ronald and Harold, Red Deer, 1915. Major Gaetz was killed in the Battle of Courcelette during the latter part of the Somme offensive, September 1916. Red Deer Archives, P2442.

establishment in Alberta to show movies of the war. These films accentuated the positives of the Allied situation overseas and were intensely patriotic. They also provided a visual glimpse of what it was like overseas.[13]

In December 1914, the military announced the creation of a new regiment, the 12th Canadian Mounted Rifles, as part of the 2nd Contingent. A full squadron ("C" Squadron) was to be recruited and trained at Red Deer.[14] Temporary billets were provided at the armouries. Meals were furnished at the Commercial and Olympia restaurants. However, the armouries proved to be too small to house a full squadron of men. In addition, the restaurants were nearly bankrupted, since the contracts they signed with the military seriously underestimated the quantities of food that the young men would consume.[15]

The military decided to follow the example used in Calgary and turn the Red Deer fairgrounds into a training camp. The livestock buildings were converted into barracks, and the horticultural building into a dining hall.[16] Because of the general concern over sanitation, the medical health officer arranged to have all the men inoculated for typhoid fever.[17]

In the meantime, the 1st Canadian Division went into action in late April 1915 as part of the Second Battle of Ypres. During the Battle of St. Julien, on April 22 to 24, the Canadians withstood the first use of poison gas as a weapon. The casualty rate was horrendous—approximately one out of every three men

was killed or wounded. Nevertheless, the Canadians held the line and won high honours for their bravery under extreme battle conditions. For several years after the war, the anniversary of the Battle of St. Julien was a special day of remembrance in Canada.[18]

In the following weeks, Red Deer newspapers began to fill with the reports of all of the young local men who had been killed or wounded. The *Red Deer News* of 5 May 1915 had an article titled "Canadian Casualties In Fight North of Ypres Will Be Over 5,000."[19] The horrors of war were beginning to hit home on a large scale. This was demonstrated on 23 May 1915 with the send-off given to the 12th Canadian Mounted Rifles (CMR). A crowd estimated at 1,500 (Red Deer's census population at the time was 3,000) gathered at the CPR station as the young

Crowd gathered at the Red Deer CPR station for the departure of "C" Squadron of the 12th Canadian Mounted Rifles, May 1915. Red Deer Archives, P2130.

Men of the "C" Squadron training on Ross Street near the Red Deer Armouries. Note the multiple unit outhouse in the background. Red Deer Archives, P346.

men departed. The Red Deer Citizens' Band played a number of farewell tunes. In contrast to the previous send-offs, this time there were no formal speeches or rounds of cheering.[20]

With large numbers of young men departing for service overseas, there was a push for more direct support of the military. There was also a growing public realization of the many deficiencies in the training and equipment of the CEF. Hence, in summer 1915, there was a fundraising drive to buy machine guns for units such as the 12th CMR.[21] The realities of modern trench warfare were beginning to strike home for military and civilians alike.

All the recruiting during the rest of 1915 was for infantry battalions such as the 63rd and 66th. Their training took place in Calgary and Edmonton. Then, in the fall of 1915, military authorities announced the raising of the 89th Battalion. Two companies were to be recruited and trained in Red Deer. The shift away from mounted rifle regiments to infantry was now complete.[22]

The community welcomed the training of a significant portion of the 89th Battalion. However, there were huge challenges in accommodating three times the number of men than had enlisted in "C" Squadron of the 12th CMR. The city had severe financial problems arising from the collapse of the prewar real estate speculation bubble and the pressures of the wartime economy. Red Deer and area had experienced tremendous growth between 1900 and 1913.

The start of construction of the Grand Trunk Pacific line from Calgary to Edmonton, and the building of the Alberta Central and Canadian Northern Western lines westward toward Rocky Mountain House and the Brazeau coalfields, increased the flow of traffic in the area, allowing agriculture and forestry to become the mainstay of central Alberta's economy in the first decade of the twentieth century.

Red Deer's growth, however, was not sustainable. Across Alberta, careless real estate speculation left investors with empty subdivisions that were not selling. Land prices were artificially inflated, creating paper profits rather than real ones. Speculators could no longer afford the property taxes, so much of the land was sold back to the city for back taxes. Red Deer was on the verge of bankruptcy, and the council was heavily in debt due to overspending. By 1914, the debt rose to $440,000 (worth $9.3 million in 2015). Floods, a failing sawmill industry, and an exodus of homesteaders created an economic downturn. The treasury was empty, meaning the city could no longer afford utilities or to pay their employees. In addition, the banks would no longer give the city credit. The population stagnated; in 1911, Red Deer was home to 2,118 people, and would only grow by 210 in the next 10 years.

The costs of expanding and improving the military training camp at the Red Deer fairgrounds had to be covered with borrowed funds. The city had agreed to undertake several thousands of dollars' worth of new construction and renovations. New buildings were erected, and a new water main was installed to help meet the needs of the men for cooking and washing.[23] Local authorities tried to save money wherever possible. The new structures remained bare board, without insulation, allowing for savings of $200 per building. The city commissioner justified the large amount of money spent on the grounds by asserting that the new structures would "come in useful for increased stock requirements at the Fair."[24] The new water main to the fairgrounds was installed after the onset of cold weather and froze several times. A heavy coat of manure was put over the lines to try and prevent freeze-ups.

By early 1916, the number of enlistments, and those who had lost their lives, had grown to the extent that the city decided to create an official roll of honour. The large, framed, three-panel scroll was officially unveiled by Lieutenant Governor R.G. Brett at a special ceremony held in the armouries.[25] Because of the acute awareness that the war was far from over, plenty of space was left for the names of future recruits who would pay "the supreme sacrifice."

That anticipation, tragically, was soon fulfilled. The British and Allied forces continued to suffer horrific losses as the bloody stalemate of the war continued. Many units being sent overseas were used as "reinforcing units," as men were transferred to other battalions to fill gaps in the ranks. Losses became so severe that the military announced plans to mobilize a new battalion, the 187th, in central Alberta. It was an exceptionally challenging goal. There was already a widespread perception that almost all available young men in Alberta's towns and cities had enlisted. The farm labour shortage had become so acute that the men of the 89th Battalion were given a special one-month furlough so that they could help with the spring planting.[26]

Despite the enormous challenges, the results were astonishing. Within 10 days, more than 250 volunteers had enlisted.[27] By the time that the colours of the 187th Battalion were officially presented at a ceremony in Innisfail on 16 June 1916, more than

550 recruits had signed up.[28] However, as had been the case so many times during the war, the results were misleading. The 187th Battalion was dubbed the "Veterans' Battalion" because most of the officers had either seen service during the Boer War or had already been overseas in the current war. Many of the recruits were teenagers, with some being as young as 15 years old, technically too young to enlist. In other words, while the recruitment of the 187th seemed impressive, many in the battalion were old, previously wounded, or too young to serve.

Again, finding accommodations for the new recruits was an enormous challenge. The situation eased a bit when the 89th Battalion departed, and space became available at the fairgrounds. Nevertheless, once again the city had to borrow money for new construction and improvements. Incredibly, the Red Deer Fair Board decided to go ahead with the annual summer exhibition. The fairgrounds became extremely overcrowded. Large numbers of tents had to be pitched to handle all the soldiers, fairgoers, and livestock exhibits. Somehow or other, the organizers and the military managed to squeak through. The fair was deemed a surprising success.

Then, as was likely inevitable because of the overcrowding and less than ideal sanitary facilities, disaster struck. A sergeant became fatally ill with a case of typhoid fever. The medical health officer had the drinking water tested, but the results were inconclusive. However, because the areas around the wells were in poor shape, the medical health officer had grounds and wells disinfected with chloride of lime.[29] City council worried that the test results and the new sanitation measures would not be enough to satisfy the military authorities. Hence, a private detective was hired to do more investigations. He reported to council that the strain of typhoid that

had broken out in the camp was one not usually found in Alberta, and it was his "expert opinion" that an enemy agent had put the germs into the officers' food.[30]

While the military authorities and municipal officials struggled to ensure more adequate training facilities, there were growing problems with those who had returned home from active service. Almost all had been seriously wounded. The Red Deer Memorial Hospital was too small to care for all the men who needed hospitalization. In December 1915, a special committee was set up by the city council, the board of trade, and the Patriotic Fund to find ways to assist the returning men.[31] Special public appeals were made for temporary homes for the convalescing.

In the meantime, the Alberta Ladies College in Red Deer became insolvent. The provincial government agreed to buy the building for $125,000. The original intent was to use it as a home for mentally handicapped children; however, with the escalating problem of men returning home with severe injuries to their minds and bodies, the facility was turned into a mental hospital for "shell-shocked" veterans.[32]

The terrible Battle of the Somme commenced on 1 July 1916 with a staggering loss of life over the succeeding weeks and months. The average casualty rate was nearly 3,000 men per day. By the time winter brought an end to the tragic bloodbath, the total number of British and Allied losses exceeded one million. Incomplete records indicate that 47 young men from Red Deer and district were killed at the Somme and roughly three times that number were wounded. By the end of September 1916, Will Richards, who had enlisted with the 12th CMR, was the only surviving non-commissioned officer in his

Nurses and volunteers of the Red Deer branch of the Red Cross in front of a vehicle donated by the Red Deer IODE (Imperial Order Daughters of the Empire), 1916. Red Deer Archives, P2129.

platoon.[33] The incredible losses made it obvious in central Alberta, and across the nation, that voluntary enlistments were no longer adequate to meet the demands for fresh recruits.

Nevertheless, military authorities decided to try recruiting one more battalion, the 191st, with the Red Deer fairgrounds being used for winter training.[34] Although the city's financial position had become even more severe, more construction and improvements were undertaken, including new officers' quarters. Unfortunately, at the end of December 1916, problems developed with the cesspool between the sergeants' quarters and one of the barracks.[35] A whole company of men had to be evacuated to the

Alexandra Hotel, which had been forced to close after the recent imposition of prohibition.[36] The military authorities decided they had enough with the problems in Red Deer, and the 191st was transferred to Calgary. The lease with the city for the fairgrounds was suddenly terminated.[37]

This was a heavy blow to the community's ego, and the local economy. The 191st was the last major unit to be stationed at Red Deer during the war. Some recruitment continued for battalions such as the 223rd (Scandinavians), the Royal Canadian Navy, and the Royal Flying Corps; however, the limit of voluntary recruitment had finally been reached.

The demands for more recruits did not decline. In April 1917, the Canadian Corps, fighting for the first time with all four divisions, captured the strategic Vimy Ridge in northern France. The battle was Canada's greatest victory of the war. It became an enduring symbol of Canadian skill, spirit, and valour, but it exacted a tragic cost: 12 young men from Red Deer and district were killed on Easter Monday, the first day of the assault, and 16 more during the rest of the battle. The Canadian Corps as a whole suffered 10,300 casualties at Vimy.

Finally, decisive action was taken; Prime Minister Sir Robert Borden announced in May 1917 that compulsory military service would be implemented. Conscription became an enormous political issue. At first, Albertans rallied in support of the new Union Government, composed of Conservatives and pro-conscription Liberals.[38] However, as the battlefield losses kept mounting and election promises as to how conscription would be implemented were changed (i.e., that farmers' sons actively involved in food production would be exempted), traditional political loyalties were shattered.

Kathrine Gibson in a Red Cross uniform, 1916. Red Deer Archives, P5403.

The promise made in the federal election campaign was not, in fact, broken until April 1918 in light of the German Spring Offensive. Hence, Dr. Michael Clark, Red Deer's long-time Liberal MP, was easily re-elected as a Union Government supporter over a traditional Liberal candidate in the federal election of December 1917.[39] However, in a provincial by-election in fall 1918, former city mayor Francis Galbraith, running as a Union candidate, was so badly beaten by his Liberal opponent, J.J. Gaetz, that he lost his deposit.[40]

While conscription for overseas service was being implemented with mediocre results, there were growing demands for conscription of wealth. The federal government implemented two "temporary" revenue measures—a business profits tax and personal income tax.

Ironically, while local farmers generally prospered from the wartime demands for food and horses for the military, increasing demands from the military, Britain, and growing cities across Canada meant that locally produced items such as beef and butter were increasingly hard to get. The Red Deer Horticultural Society began a program of planting gardens on vacant lots to improve the local supply of vegetables. Unfortunately, the improved financial position of the local farm community did not spill over into the realm of public finances. The city saw much of its property tax revenue permanently disappear after the collapse of the prewar real estate speculation bubble. Using debentures and treasury notes to fill the revenue gaps became increasingly difficult, as the federal government sucked up most of the available credit for the war effort.

Traditional charities and community support groups also found it difficult to compete for donations with the wartime charities. Even a wartime group, the Patriotic Fund, found itself in difficulties. While contributions to the local fund were among the highest in the province, more money was paid out than raised. The demands of the war were becoming overwhelming. Finally, the city hit a financial brick wall: its banker cut off all credit. Fortunately, the administration managed to find a new bank willing to handle the municipal accounts, but only with a strict overdraft limit. The Memorial Hospital, too, finally cracked under the strain. The board faced an increasing budgetary deficit. Board meetings were only held sporadically. The board chair finally declared that the management of the hospital had largely become "a joke."[41] As a result, the city was forced to take over the management of the hospital. A three-person commission was appointed to oversee the now-defunct Memorial Hospital Board. The commission raised patient fees to increase revenues; however, it also had to implement salary increases to offset the growing shortage of nurses.[42]

The human costs of the war kept growing. Canadian troops suffered immensely in the muddy, bloody, and largely futile Battle of Passchendaele in November 1917, where Canada's casualty rate was over 20 percent.[43] Twenty young men from Red Deer and area were among those killed, and several dozen more were wounded out of total Canadian casualties of nearly 16,000.

Internationally, things continued to get worse. Russia dissolved into revolution and, as a result, the Germans were able to shift more troops to the Western Front. In March 1918, the Germans launched a major offensive that threatened Paris before petering out. As newspapers began to report dramatic Allied breakthroughs in the Battle of Amiens and the subsequent One Hundred Days Offensive, a new scourge emerged in Canada: the Spanish flu pandemic.

The first cases in Alberta were recorded in early October 1918 when a troop train containing ill soldiers arrived in Calgary. Within days, there were growing numbers of cases across the province. Stringent regulations were imposed by the provincial Department of Health. Strict quarantines were imposed wherever the flu appeared. The wearing of "flu masks" became compulsory.[44] In Red Deer, the first case appeared on 23 October 1918; schools were quickly closed, and public meetings and church services cancelled. A special isolation hospital was set up in the old Royal North-West Mounted Police barracks on Victoria Avenue (43rd Street).[45] The pandemic took a terrible toll: 54 people in Red Deer and the surrounding area died, and many others faced months of convalescence.

The terrible four-year war came to an end on 11 November 1918. Plans were quickly made for a civic celebration, despite the Board of Health's injunctions against any public gatherings. A large crowd of returned veterans, local dignitaries, and ordinary citizens paraded through the streets. A boisterous ceremony of celebration and thanksgiving followed on the city square as reported in the *Advocate* on 15 November 1918.[46]

However, joy over the end of the war was soon dampened by a renewed outbreak of the flu. Other monumental challenges remained. Governments were essentially broke and inflation began to soar. In addition, an increasing number of veterans, many with significant wounds to their bodies and minds, began to return home.

Just as the military and government had been largely unprepared for the start of the war, they were also poorly prepared for the end of it. A labour bureau was established to find jobs for the returning soldiers.[47] However, there was not enough work, and unemployment began mounting. The Soldier Settlement Board was eventually established to provide opportunities in farming. However, the weather turned harsh and unforgiving as a prolonged drought set in, and the winters from 1918 to 1920 were some of the worst on record.

While the community was experiencing hard times, it was also determined to remember the terrible years of war and sacrifice in a symbolic way. The newly formed Great War Veterans' Association held a public meeting on 18 December 1918 to discuss a suitable memorial to those who had served and the 118 local men who had lost their lives.[48] City council declined to become directly involved because of its critical financial position. A plan to present medals to returning veterans was also scrapped for financial reasons. Instead, paper certificates of appreciation and remembrance, with a special seal and the signature of the mayor, were handed out.

The impact of the First World War was enormous. A generation of young men lost their lives or had their health permanently damaged. A wave of inflation wiped out savings. The economy collapsed into a prolonged postwar recession. Veterans faced not only poor health but also high unemployment and poor social support programs. The grand dreams of gallant young men galloping across the battlefield on horseback had been shattered by years spent in muddy, bloody trenches where success in battle was often measured in metres of ground captured. Most importantly, the First World War became the turning point between the heady years of the great settlement boom, with its tremendous prosperity and boundless optimism, and a postwar period plagued by economic hardship and enormous suffering on a personal as well as a community level. A time of peace had finally returned, but it also heralded a time of troubles.

Notes

1 "Red Deer Takes Part in Peace Celebration," *Red Deer News,* 1 October 1913.

2 "15th Light Horse Troop for Red Deer," *Red Deer News,* 8 May 1907.

3 "Squadron At Red Deer," *Red Deer News,* 29 April 1908.

4 "$100,000 Post Office and Armouries For Red Deer," *Red Deer News,* 14 May 1913.

5 "The Armoury," *Red Deer News,* 26 November 1913.

6 "The Declaration of War," *Red Deer Advocate,* 7 August 1914.

7 "Call Came Suddenly," *Red Deer Advocate,* 28 August 1914.

8 "Red Deer Contingent Departs On Short Notice," *Red Deer News,* 26 August 1914.

9 "Our Volunteers in Calgary," *Red Deer News,* 25 November 1914.

10 "Red Deer Red Cross Society," *Red Deer News,* 9 September 1914.

11 "A Carload of Wheat," *Red Deer Advocate,* 22 January 1915.

12 G.H. Dawe, *Schools At The Crossing: A History of the Red Deer Public School District No. 104* (Red Deer, AB: Adviser Graphics, 1992), 36.

13 "Belgian War Picture Shown for the First Time in Alberta at Red Deer," *Red Deer Advocate,* 22 January 1915.

14 "Regiment of Mounted Rifles in Alberta," *Red Deer News,* 30 December 1914.

15 Kerry Wood, *A Lifetime of Service: George Moon* (Red Deer, AB: Red Deer Advocate, 1966), 5–6.

16 "City Council," *Red Deer News,* 14 April 1915.

17 "Local And General," *Red Deer News,* 31 March 1915.

18 "St. Julien Canadian Memorial," Veterans Affairs Canada, URL: www.veterans.gc.ca/eng/memorial/belgium/st.julien, retrieved 7 June 2014.

19 "Canadian Casualties In Fight North of Ypres Will Be over 5,000," *Red Deer News,* 5 May 1915.

20 "Departure Of 12th C.M.R.," *Red Deer News,* 26 May 1915.

21 "A Machine Gun For Red Deer: City Falls Into Line," *Red Deer News,* 21 July 1915.

22 "89th Battalion Recruiting In Red Deer," *Red Deer News,* 17 November 1915.

23 "89th Battalion Quarters: Work Being Rushed At Exhibition Grounds," *Red Deer News,* December 1915.

24 "Military Notes," *Red Deer Advocate,* 21 January 1916.

25 "Lieut-Governor Unveils Roll of Honor," *Red Deer News,* 9 February 1916.

26 "The 89th Battalion," *Red Deer News,* 19 May 1916.

27 "Recruiting For 187 off to a Good Start on Wednesday Last," *Red Deer Advocate,* 28 April 1916.

28 "Presenting 187 Colours," *Red Deer Advocate,* 23 June 1916.

29 "City Fathers Meet," *Red Deer News,* 16 August 1916.

30 "The City Council," *Red Deer Advocate,* 16 March 1917.

31 "Annual Meeting," *Red Deer News,* 1 December 1915.

32 "Government Buys Red Deer Ladies College," *Red Deer News,* 10 May 1916.

33 "Letters From The Front," *Red Deer News,* 6 December 1916.

34 "A Welcome To The 191st," *Red Deer News,* 1 November 1916.

35 "Last Regular Council Meeting Of The Year," *Red Deer News,* 3 January 1917.

36 "Regular Council Meeting," *Red Deer News,* 17 January 1917.

37 "Regular City Council Meeting," *Red Deer News,* 31 January 1917.

38 "Union Government Wins In Red Deer," *Red Deer Advocate,* 21 December 1917.

39 Ibid.

40 "Mr. J.J. Gaetz Elected," *Red Deer Advocate,* 1 November 1918.

41 "Red Deer Memorial Hospital President's Report," *Red Deer News*, 22 March 1916.

42 "Memorial Hospital," *Red Deer News*, 26 June 1918.

43 "The Battle of Passchendaele," Veterans Affairs Canada, URL: www.veterans.gc.ca/eng/remembrance/history/first-world-war/fact_sheets/passchendaele, retrieved 7 June 2014.

44 "Efforts To Combat Flu Epidemic," *Red Deer Advocate*, 1 November 1918.

45 "City Organizing For Influenza," *Red Deer News*, 30 October 1918.

46 "Red Deer Celebrates," *Red Deer Advocate*, 15 November 1918.

47 "Provincial Labour Bureau," *Red Deer Advocate*, 22 November 1918.

48 "Central Alberta Veterans' Memorial," *Red Deer News*, 18 December 1918.

Works Cited

PRIMARY SOURCES

Red Deer Advocate
Red Deer News

SECONDARY SOURCES

Dawe, G.H. *Schools at the Crossing: A History of the Red Deer Public School District No. 104*. Red Deer, AB: Adviser Graphics, 1992.

Dawe, Michael J. *Red Deer: The Memorable City*. Red Deer, AB: City of Red Deer, 2013.

Veterans Affairs Canada. "The Battle of Passchendaele." URL: www.veterans.gc.ca/eng/remembrance/history/first-world-war/fact_sheets/passchendaele, retrieved 7 June 2014.

———. "St. Julien Canadian Memorial." URL: www.veterans.gc.ca/eng/memorial/belgium/st.julien, retrieved 26 March 2014.

Wood, Kerry. *A Lifetime of Service: George Moon*. Red Deer, AB: Red Deer Advocate, 1966.

Threads of Life: The 1917 Waskatenau Signature Quilt

ADRIANA A. DAVIES, SEAN MOIR, AND ANTHONY WORMAN

Introduction

Since the beginning of the twentieth century, Canadian women have produced hundreds of thousands of quilts to provide moral and material support to those affected by war. They have been used to raise money for charities supporting Canada's military efforts abroad, aid civilian populations left destitute by war, and comfort the wounded. McKenzie Porter, author of *To All Men: The Story of the Canadian Red Cross*, acknowledges that "no single article produced by women of the Canadian Red Cross Society is remembered with more gratitude than the quilts."[1]

The Royal Alberta Museum has in its collection a signature quilt (ca. 1917) from Waskatenau, Alberta, made for the purpose of raising money for the local Red Cross auxiliary. Citizens from the area paid a nominal sum to have their names, and those of friends and family members, embroidered on the quilt.[2] The money was used to assemble comfort packages for Canadian soldiers and sailors serving overseas.[3] Fundraising activities of this kind were commonplace across Canada during the war as communities looked to heed the call, "For Humanity's Sake, Help the Red Cross."[4] An article from *Modern Priscilla* (December 1917), a women's magazine, suggests what people should be charged in order to have their names included on a quilt, and what could be purchased with the funds raised. Albeit an American publication, it offers some interesting insights. The article suggests that a signature quilt could fetch upwards of $1,000, depending upon the circumstances of those being asked to contribute. In 1917, one thousand American dollars could purchase one ambulance or 280 pounds of yarn; eighteen nurses' uniforms and associated accoutrements; or 129 beds complete with mattresses and bedding.[5] This was not insignificant as wartime costs of enlisting, training, provisioning, and transporting soldiers and equipment mounted.

All of the names appearing on the Waskatenau quilt were entered into a raffle, and the winner of the draw for the quilt was 23-year-old William Cherrington. At the time, he was a member of the Royal Naval Canadian Volunteer Reserve (1914–1923), assigned to the HMCS *Rainbow*. He was on active service from November 1917 to July 1919, and at sea aboard the *Rainbow* for approximately one year.[6]

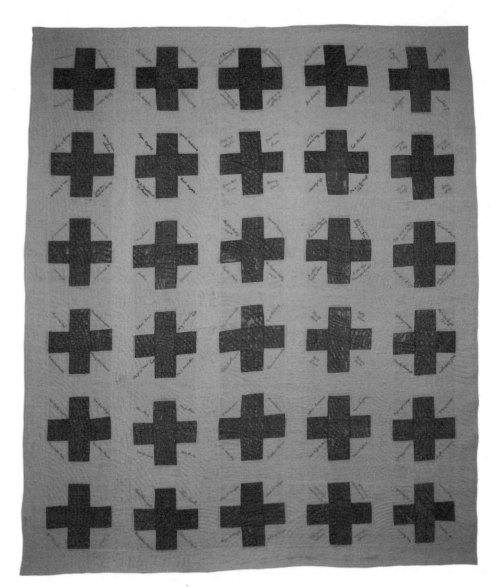

1917 Waskatenau Red Cross signature quilt, post cleaning and stabilization, bearing the names of 300 area residents. Photo courtesy of the Royal Alberta Museum.

The *Rainbow*, one of only two vessels in the Canadian navy at the time, was assigned to patrolling the Pacific coastal waters of North and Central America.[7]

Since William was not in Waskatenau at the time of the draw, his parents kept the quilt and presented it to him and his bride Jeanne (Jones) on their wedding day in 1923. As is evident from the wear, the couple used it regularly, like any other piece of bedding. Their daughter Helen recalls sleeping under the quilt as a child. Subsequently, in 1978, Bill and

(left) The Cherrington family, ca. 1920s. William (Bill), the winner of the raffle, is pictured in the back row, second from left. Photo courtesy of Helen Karvonen; (right) William (Bill) Cherrington, Naval Reserve, ca. 1917. Photo courtesy of Helen Karvonen.

Jeanne gave the quilt to Helen and her husband Alex Karvonen. The Karvonens did not use it, preferring to store it as a keepsake. After discussing the matter with family members, in 1990, they gifted it to the Waskatenau Seniors Association.[8] The association displayed it in a wall-mounted case in the vestibule of their hall. In 2009, concerned by the quilt's deterioration, association members consulted Royal Alberta Museum (RAM) staff. Following several discussions, they decided to donate the quilt to the museum.[9]

By "deconstructing" the quilt, a great deal can be learned about the role of women and communities at war. One might ask, "Why is a military curator collecting quilts; gathering information about quilts; and, for that matter, even interested in quilts?" It is by no means without precedent that military

historians acquire such objects and use them to further understand the wartime home front, past and present. Consider the title of an exhibit mounted by the Wadsworth Atheneum Museum of Art in Hartford, Connecticut (2011–2012), *Colts and Quilts: The Civil War Remembered*. One of the accompanying talks, "Quilts for the Civil War," was described as follows: "Listen to stories from behind the Civil War battle lines told through the period's quilts: stories of patriotism, of challenges in outfitting soldiers, and especially of the enormous efforts of women on the home front to keep soldiers clothed and assured that their presence was missed and their sacrifice honored."[10] Increasingly, museum war-related projects and exhibits examine the impacts, on or upon, and inputs of those left behind. This is what the RAM hopes to achieve by making the Waskatenau quilt the

385

centrepiece of its First World War home front exhibit in the new museum being constructed in downtown Edmonton (opening ca. 2017–2018).

The Community of Waskatenau

Waskatenau, known as Pine Creek before the 1920s, is situated an hour's drive northeast of Edmonton on Highway 28. The name "Waskatenau" is rooted in the name of the Wasatenow Cree people, who inhabited the area prior to the arrival of settlers.[11] Roughly translated, it means "opening in the bank," a reference to the location where the Waskatenau or Pine Creek empties into the North Saskatchewan River.[12] New arrivals were attracted to the region by the land—a combination of natural pastures and wooded areas, the latter providing raw material for building homes, barns, and other structures, as well as fuel for heat and cooking. Shortly after the first settlers arrived in 1904, a small hamlet took shape not unlike thousands of others across western Canada during the pre–First World War immigration boom. Growth was spurred by the announcement of construction of a rail line in 1913; rail service commenced in 1919; and the community of Waskatenau, population 200, was incorporated as a village in 1932.[13]

Role of Women in the War

Traditionally, men went off to war; occasionally women accompanied them—working as nurses or for support agencies—but this was not common. Women were expected to support the decision of husbands, fathers, sons, brothers, and uncles, and endure the aftermath. They suffered the loss of loved ones; dealt with the shattered skeletons and souls of those fortunate enough to return home; and cared for households, farms, businesses, children, and aging parents. Some worked to make ends meet. If they were lucky, what little they earned was supplemented by donations from family and friends, Patriotic Fund payments, and, as time passed, widows' or survivor pensions. Such payments were anything but generous and were only allotted following lengthy, and sometimes contentious, application processes, investigations, and legislative proceedings.[14] Despite these responsibilities, women supported the troops abroad and contributed to the war effort in spiritual and material ways.

As for direct participation, women had but one official role in the military—nursing.[15] This would not change until the establishment of women's divisions in the navy, air force, and army during the Second World War. Women filled numerous roles in support agencies such as the YMCA/YWCA or the Red Cross—from ambulance drivers and vehicle mechanics to cooks, medical aids, and even pen pals. Organizations such as the St. John Working Committee, Patriotic League, United Farm Women of Alberta, Imperial Order Daughters of the Empire (IODE), Junior Red Cross, and Girl Guides enlisted Alberta's women and girls to knit socks, mitts, and other garments and assemble "comfort packages" for soldiers serving in Europe and Britain.[16] The women of Waskatenau organized their own Red Cross auxiliary at the outset of the war. In addition to making the signature quilt, members organized annual picnics, rallies, and raffles to maintain support for the war, and knitted or sewed 1,400 garments for shipment overseas (e.g., mitts, trench caps, mufflers, socks, and sweaters).[17]

About the Quilt

The king-sized "summer quilt," so-called because of its relative light weight and cotton construction, measures 221 by 180 centimetres, and was constructed using fine white and red cotton for the top, cotton batting as filler, and open-weave cotton for the backing. The 30 blocks, each measuring approximately 25 by 26 centimetres, are arranged into five symmetrical columns (vertical) and six rows (horizontal). These blocks are framed by a 9-centimetre-wide border that is folded over the backing and is machine sewn, and they are separated by strips of sashing. The strips between each column run continuously, while those separating the rows coincide with the width of the blocks. All block stitching and meandering stitches (five per inch) were done by hand, and a combination of both hand- and machine-stitching was used to complete various aspects of the quilt construction. The backing is made of two pieces of material, and the hand quilting was done in a clamshell pattern. Lucie Heins, Assistant Curator of Western Canadian History at the RAM and author of the *Alberta Quilt Project*, notes that the irregularity or uneven spacing of the quilting confirms that this was undertaken by several people

Section of the quilt showing the clamshell pattern. Photo courtesy of the Royal Alberta Museum.

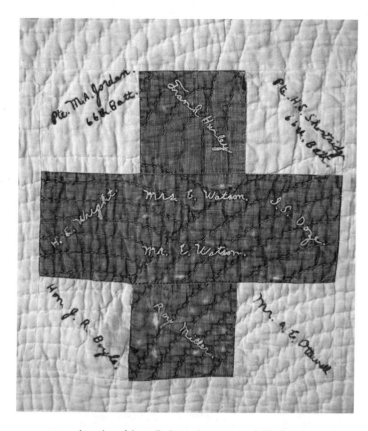

A section of the quilt shows the seven-patch block pattern and varying types of stitches used to embroider the signatures. Photo courtesy of the Royal Alberta Museum.

The red crosses are composed of three patches—one vertically oriented rectangle and two square patches forming the left and right, or horizontal arms, framed by four, white corner patches. This configuration is far less common than the nine-patch pattern typically used to construct quilts of this kind. Aware of it or not, the Waskatenau women used the three-patch "cross" from the "Star and Cross" pattern (#3230), as identified in Barbara Brackman's *Encyclopedia of Pieced Quilt Patterns*. This pattern allowed them to be more frugal with time and the material, as it required less overlap during the piecing process.[19]

One signature, embroidered using red cotton thread, appears on each of the four white corner patches of each block. Black thread was used to

"Star and Cross" pattern as identified in Barbara Brackman's book, *Encyclopedia of Pieced Quilt Patterns*.

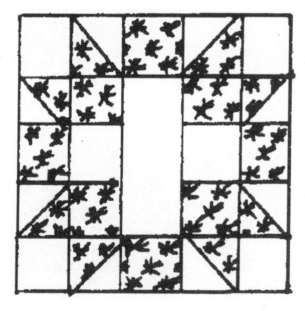

and likely rather quickly so it would be ready for the raffle. Heins suggests that the women likely started in one corner with one of the blocks, piecing it to a segment of horizontal sashing, then repeated this process until the column was complete. These were then pieced to a continuous, vertical strip of sashing. The piecing process would be repeated to assemble each of the five columns and intervening strips of sashing.[18]

embroider the signatures on the red patches; this thread has faded over time and now appears white. At least three different types of stitches—stem, chain, and running—were used to complete the embroidery work. This variation of technique again verifies that construction of the quilt was truly a group effort.[20]

When RAM obtained the quilt in 2009, a conservation plan was developed, and this work was completed in 2011–12. Stabilization work was undertaken to stop further tearing of the quilt top, loss of interior batting, and deterioration of the embroidered signatures. These were all factors caused by use, washing, and exposure to light. Much of the fraying

and tearing was found around the edges of the quilt. The conservation plan called for the application of nylon tulle netting to arrest further tearing of the fabric and loss of the embroidered threads. Nylon tulle netting was selected over other options as it proved to be the least intrusive material with respect to viewing the embroidered signatures.

About the Women Who Made the Quilt

The way in which the women's names were cited on the quilt, or in conjunction with the photo from the 1917 picnic, is revealing of the values of the time.

Women of the Waskatenau Red Cross auxiliary likely in the summer of 1917. Mrs. Bertha Cherrington, William's mother, is fifth from the left in the back row, immediately behind Mrs. Carrie Lunn, sitting front and centre sporting the Red Cross armband. Note the banner in the upper-left corner bearing the Red Cross symbol and regimental numbers of several Canadian Expeditionary Force units. Photo courtesy of Helen Karvonen.

```
      Red Cross picnic, summer 1917, on the
          Bishop farm,   SW 13, 59, 20, W 4
       across from the W. Nicoll place.
Back row, 1 to r:

Mrs. Dale (Josephine) West
  "         ?        Erikson
  "   Sidney (Phoebe) Woodward
  "   Samuel (Lottie) McCartney
  "   George (Bertha ) Cherrington
Miss Lena Ongena      (farm in Charles O. name,bro)
Mrs. Caleb (Annie) New
  "   Chris (Klazina ) Van Manen
  "   Robert (Lizzie ) Brown
  "   James (Jane)       Whale (lived on SW¼,16,59,19,W¼)
  "   John(Malissa) Vance

Front row, 1 to r:

  "   Frank (Elsie) Scott
  "   Robert B. (Mary) Barron
  "   William (Elsie) Carefoot
  "   Francis (Carrie) Lunn
  "   Robert (Mary Ann) New
  "   Edward (Polly) Melbourne
  "   Harvey (Ellen) Lunn

This the group who made the Red Cross Quilt
```

Of the 18 women credited with making the quilt, only two are listed with their own names, and that because they were not married—all others went by the title "Mrs.," followed by the first initial or name of their husbands. In addition, not all of the women who contributed to the project had their names embroidered on the quilt. In some cases, their husbands' names appear instead. Given what we know about the home front attitudes toward certain ethnic groups during the war, and the demographics of the Waskatenau/Pine Creek community in 1917, it is no surprise that almost all of the women involved in the project were of British ancestry. Many were part of the "ruling elite" of the community and were involved in a host of local and regional organizations.[21]

The Serving Military

At the outset of the war, most of the people who lived in the hamlet of Waskatenau were of Anglo-Celtic ancestry.[22] Similarly, a significant percentage of those who resided in the surrounding district were also of British descent. Not surprisingly, they were keen to join the fray in defence of the "Mother Country." Research suggests that 64 men from the community and district signed up for service; seven were killed in action, or died as a result of their participation. This represents an 11 percent fatality rate, equal to the national figures.[23] The quilt bears the names of 36 members of the Canadian and British military—30 are identified as from the Waskatenau

Table 1: Comparative Participation and Casualty Statistics for the Waskatenau Area and Canada[24]

	POPULATION	TOTAL SERVED	SERVED OVERSEAS	KILLED	OTHER CASUALTIES	TOTAL FATALITY %	TOTAL CASUALTY %	OVERSEAS CASUALTY %
Canada	~7,879,000	619,636	424,589	66,655	172,950	11%	38%	56%
Waskatenau Area	–	64[A]	–	7	–	11%	–	–
Waskatenau Quilt Names	–	32	27	5	16	15.5%	66%	78%
10th Battalion[B]	–	–	5,390	1,315	3,266		–	85%
31st Battalion[B]	–	–	4,487	941	2,312		–	72%
49th Battalion[B]	–	–	~4,000	973	2,282		–	81%

A This number is derived from cross-referencing the names on the quilt with those on the Waskatenau and area Honour Roll and using data found in family histories in the local history publication.

B Rows containing information relating to the 10th, 31st, and 49th Battalions are only included to provide a comparison of Waskatenau casualty rates to those of front-line (infantry) fighting battalions. These particular battalions were chosen as the majority of the men whose names appear on the Waskatenau quilt served with these three Alberta-based units at the front.

area, and two of these are readily identified by way of inclusion of their unit names or numbers.

These casualty statistics demonstrate the cost of participation at the community level. Researching the fate of these individuals brings to life the names that appear on the community quilt. In terms of contemporary museum practice, this type of research emphasizes the importance of situating an artifact in a context of meaning within a community.[25] Waskatenau's Red Cross quilt is an archetypal and powerful example of how an artifact can tell many stories. Many more secrets wait to be unlocked by delving into the lives of soldiers, quilters, and settlers alike, and through contacting their descendants. As well, more work needs to be done to determine the uniqueness of this type of quilt in Alberta, if unique at all; to date, only one other example of this kind has been brought to the attention of RAM staff.

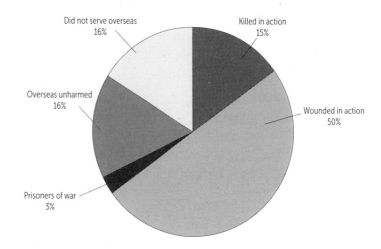

Casualty figures for Albertans whose names appear on the quilt. This information is restricted to those names on the quilt as information relative to all Waskatenau and area participants is not yet known and research is ongoing.

Table 2: Waskatenau Quilt Soldiers and Their Participation Outcomes

NAME	UNIT	SERVED OVERSEAS OR IN CANADA	WOUNDED IN ACTION	RETURNED TO ACTION	MEDICALLY UNFIT	KILLED IN ACTION	RETURNED TO WASKATENAU FOR A MINIMUM OF FIVE YEARS
Pte John Roy Armstrong	151st and 31st Battalions	Overseas	Yes; 3 times (Vimy, Passchendaele, 11 Nov. 1918)	Yes	No	No	Not known
Pte James Barnes	194th and 10th Battalions	Overseas	Yes	Yes	No	No	Yes
Pte Edward Clarence Bibby	202nd and 50th Battalions	Overseas	Yes	Yes	No	No	No – married in the UK and moved to BC.

/continued

NAME	UNIT	SERVED OVERSEAS OR IN CANADA	WOUNDED IN ACTION	RETURNED TO ACTION	MEDICALLY UNFIT	KILLED IN ACTION	RETURNED TO WASKATENAU FOR A MINIMUM OF FIVE YEARS
Pte Walter John Bibby	202nd and 50th Battalions	Overseas	Yes	N/A	N/A	Yes; 23 Aug. 1917 at Lens (Hill 70). Died of wounds.	N/A
Pte Robert Brown	194th and 218th Battalions and Army Medical Corps	Canada (Training Depot)	No	N/A	No	No	Initially moved to New Zealand; returned to Waskatenau in 1922.
William Cherrington	RNCVR; HMCS *Rainbow*	Overseas	No	N/A	No	No	Yes – farmed and ran a business.
Capt John Henry Cherrington	British military	Not known					N/A
Pte Richard Cherrington	British military	Not known					N/A
Pte Frederick Stanley Cockroft	194th and 49th Battalions	Overseas	Yes; 3 times (unknown, unknown, Canal du Nord)	Yes	No	No	Yes – remained in Waskatenau for his entire life.
Pte Milton Cockroft	194th and 49th Battalions	Overseas	Yes	No	Yes	No	Yes – moved away in 1941.
Pte Frank Dodd	Canadian Forestry Company (Southern Alberta)	Overseas	No	No	No	No	Yes – moved to Edmonton in 1963; served in the Veterans Guard of Canada in the Second World War.
Pte J. Frankland	2/7 Cheshires (British regiment) and Army Service Corps	United Kingdom					N/A
Pte Duncan Graham Fraser	151st and 8th Battalions	Overseas	Yes (Vimy)	No	Yes	No	Not known
Pte Clarence Jay Innes	4th Pioneers and 7th Battalion	Overseas	Yes	No	Yes	No	Not known
Pte Marion Albert Jorden (Jordan)	66th and 49th Battalions	Overseas	Yes; and prisoner of war	No	No	No	Yes – moved around Alberta with railway employment.

NAME	UNIT	SERVED OVERSEAS OR IN CANADA	WOUNDED IN ACTION	RETURNED TO ACTION	MEDICALLY UNFIT	KILLED IN ACTION	RETURNED TO WASKATENAU FOR A MINIMUM OF FIVE YEARS
Pte Francis Lunn	194th and 49th Battalions	Overseas	Yes; twice (unknown, Courcelles)	Yes	No	No	Yes
Pte Hugh Charles McDonald	194th and 49th Battalions	Overseas	N/A	N/A	N/A	Yes; 30 Oct. 1917 at Passchendaele	N/A
Pte N. McKellar	Unknown— Possibly British	Not known					Not known
Capt Ernest McNee	RNCVR; HMCS *Niobe* (depot ship), HMS *Niobe*, and HMS *Niobe III* (shore establishment); unknown minesweeper	Canada	No	N/A	No	No	Yes – ran various businesses.
Sgt Leonard Edward Melbourne	19th Alberta Dragoons and 10th Battalion	Overseas; awarded Military Medal	Yes; twice	Yes	No	No	Not known
Pte Alphonse Monserez	194th and 233rd Battalions	No	No	N/A	Yes	No	Yes – farmed.
Pte Edward John Nelson	151st Battalion and 16th Field Ambulance (CSEF)	Overseas (Siberia)	No	N/A	Yes; 1916, re-attested CAMC 1917	No	Not known
Sgt Isaac Nelson	66th and 49th Battalions	Overseas; awarded Military Medal	Yes	No	Yes	No	Not known
Pte William James Nelson	66th and 49th Battalions and 7th Trench Mortar Battery	Overseas	No	N/A	No	No	Not known
Pte John Henry New	151st and 44th Battalions	Overseas	Yes	Yes	No	No	Not known
Pte Young Wheeler New	151st and 44th Battalions	Overseas	Yes	No	Yes (pneumonia)	No	Not known

/continued

NAME	UNIT	SERVED OVERSEAS OR IN CANADA	WOUNDED IN ACTION	RETURNED TO ACTION	MEDICALLY UNFIT	KILLED IN ACTION	RETURNED TO WASKATENAU FOR A MINIMUM OF FIVE YEARS
Sgt Emanuel Pilkington	194th and 10th Battalions	Overseas	Yes (Lens)	No	Yes (gassed)	No	Yes – served as justice of the peace and held other gov't jobs.
Pte Hugh Rogers	202nd and 50th Battalions	Overseas	Yes (Lens)	No	Yes	No	No – lived in Edmonton.
Pte Willard Rogers	202nd and 50th Battalions	Overseas	N/A	N/A	N/A	Yes; 21 Aug. 1917 near Lens (Aloof Trench)	N/A
Pte Carl Roy Sampson	151st Battalion and Canadian Forestry Corps	Overseas (United Kingdom)	No	N/A	No	No	Not known
Pte John Allan Sampson	1st Depot Battalion, Alberta Regiment	Canada (conscripted 23 May 1918)	No	N/A	No	No	Yes
Pte George Sexauer	151st and 44th Battalions	Overseas	Yes (Vimy)	Yes	No	No	Yes
Pte Herbert Stanley Shortridge	66th and 49th Battalions	Overseas	N/A	N/A	N/A	Yes; 9 Oct. 1916 at the Somme (Regina Trench)	N/A
Pte Melvin Blake Stapley	194th and 10th Battalions	Overseas	N/A	N/A	N/A	Yes; 2 Sept. 1918 at the Drocourt-Queant Line	N/A
Pte Edwin Roy Watson	151st and 8th Canadian Railway Troops	Overseas	No	N/A	No	No	Yes – moved to Detroit in 1926.
Pte Frank Woodward	194th Battalion and 2nd Canadian Railway Troops	Overseas	No	N/A	No	No	Never lived in the area – Bowden, AB, resident; relative paid to have name included.

Preserving the Quilt—Cleaning: the first step was to temporarily apply fine netting over compromised areas to facilitate low-suction vacuuming. This was followed by several presoaks, washes, and rinses in a wash table, using deionized water and an additive-free mild detergent. Repeated rinsing was required to ensure that no soap residue remained on the quilt. Drying was done by hand, using quilt pads to blot the surface areas; next, the quilt was rolled onto a clean piece of four-inch ABS plumbing pipe interleaved with towels; lastly, the quilt was laid flat on a drying table, and fans were run for several days to assist the drying process. Photo courtesy of the Royal Alberta Museum.

Initial investigation has resulted in contact with descendants of the Cherrington and Rogers families. Through military service records from Library and Archives Canada, and introductory discussions with family members, a more complete picture of the experiences of the four Rogers brothers, who served Canada during the First and Second World Wars, is now known. Willard, the oldest, was killed in action August 1917 at Aloof Trench (near Lens); Hugh was seriously wounded by an exploding mortar shell in June 1917 and declared medically unfit to return to the front; Elmer received the Military Medal for bravery in the field at the Battle of the Somme and survived the war physically unscathed; and the

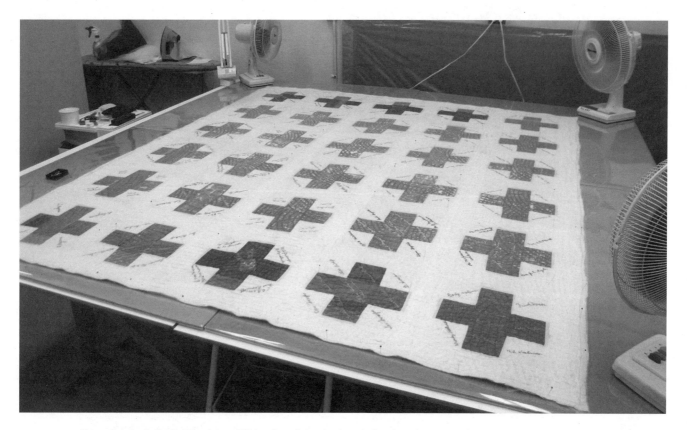

Preserving the Quilt—Stabilization: stabilizing the quilt involved overlaying the red crosses and other damaged areas with nylon tulle netting material to halt further tearing and deterioration of the embroidered signatures. As each cross is slightly different, tracings were made using clear mylar. The mylar cut-outs were marked with numbers and arrows to correspond with the appropriate cross and to ensure that each piece of the tulle material was correctly applied. A curved needle and ultrafine polyester thread were used to affix the netting to the quilt. Photo courtesy of the Royal Alberta Museum.

youngest brother, Ray, served his country during the Second World War and returned to Waskatenau where he raised a family. Time has not permitted a thorough exploration of their family archives, but RAM staff has been told that they possess a letter from Willard, written to his mother days before he was killed. Such circumstances are not unlike those experienced by thousands of Canadian soldiers and their respective families. Exploring and understanding the stories associated with the names on the quilt will provide a detailed understanding of the impact of the war on the community of Waskatenau and, to a lesser extent, on the Alberta home front, in general. For this reason, the quilt will serve as the focal point of the First World War home front story told in the new Royal Alberta Museum.[26]

Mylar tracings of the crosses used to make nylon tulle netting overlays of the exact size. Photo courtesy of the Royal Alberta Museum.

Conclusion

That the Waskatenau quilt has survived is both remarkable and a tribute to the Cherrington family and the members of the Waskatenau Seniors Association. The quilt was well used and well loved; because of this, it is available for current and future generations to discover the stories that it holds. Only one other quilt of this type is known to exist in Alberta; it hails from southern Alberta and remains in private hands. No examples bearing the same pattern can be found among the collections of Canada's national heritage institutions.[30] What began as a curiosity has evolved into a major research project, and the quilt now serves as a portal to a past world. Through continued investigation we will further our understanding of one Alberta community's enduring connection to the First World War.

The work of making quilts for those in need continued. Although signature quilts are not specifically mentioned, members of the Waskatenau chapter of the United Farm Women of Alberta produced quilts in the postwar era to raise funds for the construction of a Great War Veterans Association hall.[31] During the Second World War, Canadian women, including those from Waskatenau, made tens of thousands of patchwork or "crazy block" quilts for distribution to displaced families in Britain and Europe.[32] Today, women such as Lezley Zwaal, founder of Quilts of Valour Canada (QOV Canada), carry on this tradition. The organization began operations in Edmonton in 2006 and now has active participants and chapters across Canada. The society's mission is "to ensure that our injured Canadian Forces members are recognized for their service and commitment to our country . . . through the presentation of quilts to comfort [them] in their time of need." As of April

2013 QOV Canada has made and delivered 3,290 quilts to injured service personnel and veterans.[33]

Notes

1 McKenzie Porter, *To All Men: The Story of the Canadian Red Cross* (Toronto: McClelland and Stewart, 1960), 73.

2 *By River and Train: The History of Waskatenau and Districts*, vol. 1 (Waskatenau, AB: Waskatenau and District Historical Society, 1986), 406.

3 Comfort packages typically included articles of clothing such as mitts, socks, sweaters, and scarves, as well as foodstuffs, tobacco, and writing supplies. Agencies such as the Red Cross, the Imperial Order Daughters of the Empire, United Farm Women of Alberta, and the Alberta Women's Institute, as well as individual families, provided thousands of soldiers with comfort packages to supplement official rations. These also served as tangible links to their loved ones and homes. Information drawn from the following sources: *100 Years of Humanitarian Service: The Canadian Red Cross Society, 1896–1996* (Ottawa: Canadian Red Cross Society, 1996), 14; Donna Fallis, "World War I Knitting," *Alberta Museums Review* (Edmonton: Alberta Museums Association), Fall 1984, 8–10, Canadian Red Cross Society website, URL: http://www.redcross.ca/who-we-are/about-the-canadian-red-cross/historical-highlights/the-first-world-war-1914-1918, retrieved fall/winter 2013–2014.

4 Porter, *To All Men*, 37. Albeit one of many phrases employed by the Red Cross in an effort to encourage and maintain support for the war effort, this slogan was used extensively across the country.

5 "Wartime Activities of Significance to Women: One Thousand Dollars for the Red Cross Can Be Raised on a Memorial Quilt," *Modern Priscilla*, December 1917 (Boston: Priscilla Publishing, 1887–1930), 2. It is important to point out that use of this example is not meant to imply that circumstances are directly transferrable to Canada. Notably, one 1917 American dollar

was equivalent to roughly $1.25 Canadian. The cost of doing business in Canada was higher on account of factors such as import tariffs, higher shipping costs, smaller production capacity, and more modest production runs on account of a smaller market. *Modern Priscilla* (1887–1930) began at Lynn, Massachusetts, as a 16-page Quattro devoted to fancy work, dress patterns, china painting, and needlework in general. Subscription rates were 50 cents a year. In 1894, the publisher relocated to Boston and enlarged the scope of the magazine to cover many other aspects of women's home life. It absorbed *Everyday Housekeeping* in March 1912 and *Home Needlework Magazine* in May 1917. URL: http://www.magazineart.org/main.php/v/womens/modernpriscilla, retrieved 12 November 2013.

6   Karvonen family records (assembled by Helen Karvonen) were accessed at the Karvonen residence in Edmonton, AB, 2012–2013; interview with Helen Karvonen, Karvonen residence, Edmonton, AB, 28 February 2012, by Sean Moir; and Library and Archives Canada, Royal Canadian Navy Ledger Sheets (1910–1941), URL: http://www.collectionscanada.gc.ca/databases/navyledgersheet/001102-130-e.html, retrieved January 2014. Both William and brother Fred served in the Canadian Army during the Second World War; too old for front-line service, William spent several years in Britain training recruits. While overseas he was informed his son George had been killed in action in Belgium on 8 February 1945. His daughter Helen joined the Royal Canadian Air Force (1951–56) and trained and worked as a fighter control officer.

7   Interview with Helen Karvonen; CFB Esquimalt Naval & Military Museum website, URL: http://www.navalandmilitarymuseum.org/resource_pages/ships/rainbow.html, retrieved January 2014.

8   Interview with Helen Karvonen.

9   Royal Alberta Museum accession file H09.35.1 (gifting documents and associated notes pertaining to the acquisition of the quilt).

10   Wadsworth Atheneum Museum of Art, Hartford, CT: URL: http://www.thewadsworth.org/exhibitions/past/, page accessed ca. 2010–13.

11   Saddle Lake Cree Nation website, URL: http://www.saddlelake.ca/noflash/?page_id=223, retrieved January 2014. There are many variations of the spelling of the name *Wasatenow*, which is how it appears on the official website of the Saddle Lake Cree Nation, ca. 2014. This is in contrast to *Washatanow*, the spelling used by government of Canada officials when the Washatanow Reserve, No. 126 was established in 1889.

12   *By River and Train*, vol. 1, 18.

13   Ibid., 118–24.

14   Desmond Morton and Glenn Wright, *Winning the Second Battle: Canadian Veterans and the Return to Civilian Life, 1915–1930* (Toronto: University of Toronto Press, 1987), 155–77 and 202–25, respectively. Recipients of Canadian Patriotic Fund payments were screened to ensure they were doing all possible to manage on the resources available to them; adherence to socially conservative values (e.g., moral virtue) was top-of-mind among fund administrators when reviewing applications. Canadian War Museum website, URL: http://www.warmuseum.ca/cwm/exhibitions/guerre/patriotic-fund-e.aspx, retrieved January 2014.

15   Linda J. Quiney, "'Hardly Feminine Work!': Violet Wilson and the Canadian Volunteer Aid Detachment Nurses of the First World War," in *Framing Our Past: Canadian Women's History in the Twentieth Century*, edited by Sharon Anne Cook, Lorna R. McLean, and Kathryn O'Rourke (Montreal and Kingston: McGill-Queen's University Press, 2001), 289.

16   Fallis, "World War I Knitting," 10.

17   *By River and Train*, vol. 1, 29.

18   Shirley Ellis, "Royal Alberta Museum Conservation: Condition Report," 22 November 2011, RAM; meetings and discussions with Lucie Heins, Assistant Curator, Western Canadian History, RAM, and author of *The Alberta Quilt Project*, Edmonton, Autumn 2011 (in

preparation for Sean Moir's presentation, "Untangling the Threads of the Past: Researching the 1917 Waskatenau Signature Quilt," at the 2012 Canadian Museums Association conference, Gatineau, Quebec, April 26; RAM accession file, H09.35.1 [notes]).

19 Barbara Brackman (compiler), *Encyclopedia of Pieced Quilt Patterns*, 1st ed. (Paducah, KY: American Quilter's Society, 1993), 386–91; Ellis, "Royal Alberta Museum Conservation: Condition Report"; Meetings and discussions with Lucie Heins, Autumn 2011; RAM file, H09.35.1 (notes).

20 Ellis, "Royal Alberta Museum Conservation: Condition Report"; Meetings and discussion with Lucie Heins, Autumn, 2011; *By River and Train*, vol. 1, 406; RAM accession file, H09.35.1 (notes).

21 Summative information derived from reviewing the personal histories of the women credited with making the quilt in the accompanying photograph, and sections relative to community organizations; *By River and Train*, vols. 1 and 2, various pages.

22 For the purpose of this article, the area referred to as "the hamlet and surrounding district of Waskatenau" is a 540-square mile tract of land (12 townships) as indicated in the local history, *By River and Trail*, vol. 1. Specifically, this area is a landscape-oriented rectangle, and incorporates townships 58 through 60, and ranges 18 through 20, as well as township 61, range 19, and township 62, ranges 18 and 19; the majority of this district is located to the north of the North Saskatchewan River. *By River and Train*, vol. 1, 18–19, 30–31, 38, 54–55, 66–67, 80–81, 92–93, and 100–102.

23 *By River and Train*, vol. 1, 374; RAM accession file, H09.35.1 (notes).

24 Museum staff is working to determine the circumstances of four of the individuals whose names appear on the quilt. It is believed they are relatives situated overseas who never lived in the Waskatenau area. Overall statistics for Canada: Government of Canada, Veterans Affairs Canada, "The Aftermath," date modified 20 November 2013, retrieved 10 February 2014, URL: https://www.veterans.gc.ca/eng/remembrance/history/first-world-war/canada/canada19;

Government of Canada, Library and Archives Canada, "Soldiers of the First World War: 1914–1918," date modified 29 January 2014, retrieved 10 February 2014, URL: http://www.bac-lac.gc.ca/eng/discover/military-heritage/first-world-war/first-world-war-1914-1918-cef/Pages/canadian-expeditionary-force.aspx. Regimental Statistics: The Loyal Edmonton Regimental Military Museum, "The Last Few Months," 2010, URL: http://www.lermuseum.org/en/regimental-history/billys-own/the-last-few-months/, retrieved 10 February 2014; Daniel G. Dancocks, *Gallant Canadians: The Story of the Tenth Canadian Infantry Battalion, 1914–1919* (Calgary: The Calgary Highlanders Regimental Funds Foundation, Calgary, 1994), 213; Major Horace C. Singer, *History of the 31st Battalion C.E.F.*, edited by Darrell Knight (Calgary: Detselig, 2006), 431.

25 Beginning in the late 1980s, museologists began to place artifacts in a context of meaning within their community, whether this was a community based on geography, ethnicity, gender, or other types of relationships among groups. They focused on public culture and its political ramifications. The book that came to represent this new type of museum practice was Ivan Karp, Christine Mullen Kreamer, and Steven D. Lavine, eds., *Museums and Communities: The Politics of Public Culture* (Washington, DC: Smithsonian Institution Press, 1992).

26 Data used to prepare the table citing the names of those in the military was derived from the Library and Archives Canada, "Soldiers of the First World War," retrieved December 2013, January/February 2014.

27 Specifically, a 0.3 percent Orvus anionic detergent was used to clean the quilt. An anionic detergent is best described as one that has no additives such as fragrances, and/or optical or colour brighteners. Information extracted from S. Ellis, "RAM Conservation Report, Red Cross Quilt," H09.35.1, Spring 2012, RAM, 1–2.

28 Ellis, "RAM Conservation Report, Red Cross Quilt," H09.35.1, 2.

29 Ibid.

30 E-mail correspondence, Sean Moir to Christina Bates, Curator, History of Canadian Home Life, Costume and Textiles, Canadian Museum of Civilization (now Canadian Museum of History), Gatineau, Quebec, 2 February 2012; Primary quote: "We have nothing like this quilt . . ." Similar responses were received from the Glenbow Museum and The Military Museums (Calgary), the Royal British Columbia Museum (Victoria), The Manitoba Museum (Winnipeg), and the Western Development Museum (Saskatoon), as well as dozens of regional and community museums across Alberta.

31 *By River and Train*, vol. 1, 88.

32 Bridget Long, "Quilt Aid: In Britain's Hour of Need," *Quilter's Newsletter Magazine*, no. 371 (April 2005): 32–34.

33 Quilts of Valour–Canada website, URL: http://www.quiltsofvalour.ca/ (About Us section), retrieved 21 February 2014.

Works Cited

PRIMARY SOURCES

Library and Archives Canada. "Royal Canadian Navy Ledger Sheets (1910–1941)." 2 November 2011. URL: http://www.collectionscanada.gc.ca/databases/navyledgersheet/001102-130-e.html, retrieved 9 June 2014.

Royal Alberta Museum, Edmonton. Accession file H09.35.1, 2009.

SECONDARY SOURCES

Brackman, Barbara, ed. *Encyclopedia of Pieced Quilt Patterns*. 1st ed. Paducah, KY: American Quilter's Society, 1993.

Brunn, Margot. "Royal Alberta Museum Conservation: Condition Report, 22 November 2011." Edmonton: Royal Alberta Museum.

Canadian Museum of Civilization website. "Canada and the First World War: The Canadian Patriotic Fund." URL: http://www.warmuseum.ca/cwm/exhibitions/guerre/patriotic-fund-e.aspx, retrieved 9 June 2014.

Canadian Red Cross Society. *100 Years of Humanitarian Service: The Canadian Red Cross Society, 1896–1996*. Ottawa: Canadian Red Cross Society, 1996.

Canadian Red Cross website. "The First World War: 1914–1918." URL: http://www.redcross.ca/who-we-are/about-the-canadian-red-cross/historical-highlights/the-first-world-war-1914-1918, retrieved 9 June 2014.

CFB Esquimalt Naval & Military Museum website. "HMCS Rainbow." URL: http://www.navalandmilitarymuseum.org/resource_pages/ships/rainbow.html, retrieved 9 June 2014. [Website has been updated and changed since information was retrieved.]

Dancocks, Daniel G. *Gallant Canadians: The Story of the Tenth Canadian Infantry Battalion, 1914–1919*. Calgary: The Calgary Highlanders Regimental Funds Foundation, 1994.

Ellis, Shirley. "RAM Conservation Report." October 2012. Edmonton: Royal Alberta Museum.

——. "Royal Alberta Museum Conservation: Condition Report." 30 October 2012. Edmonton: Royal Alberta Museum.

Fallis, Donna. "World War I Knitting." *Alberta Museums Review* (Fall 1984): 8–10.

Heins, Lucie. "The Alberta Quilt Project." 2011. Royal Alberta Museum website. URL: http://www.royalalbertamuseum.ca/research/culturalStudies/westernCanadianHistory/research.cfm, retrieved 9 June 2014.

——. Personal interviews/discussions. Autumn 2011. Edmonton: Royal Alberta Museum.

Karp, Ivan, Christine Mullen Kreamer, and Steven D. Lavine, eds. *Museums and Communities: The Politics of Public Culture*. Washington and London: Smithsonian Institution Press, 1992.

Karvonen, Helen. "Karvonen family records." Edmonton: Royal Alberta Museum, n.d.

——. Sean Moir interview. 28 February 2012. Edmonton: Royal Alberta Museum.

Library and Archives Canada website. "Soldiers of the
First World War: 1914–1918." URL:
http://www.bac-lac.gc.ca/eng/discover/military-
heritage/first-world-war/first-world-war-1914-
1918-cef/Pages/canadian-expeditionary-force.aspx,
retrieved 9 June 2014.

Long, Bridget. "Quilt Aid: In Britain's Hour of Need."
Quilter's Newsletter Magazine, no. 371 (April 2005):
32–35.

Loyal Edmonton Regiment Military Museum website.
"The Last Few Months." URL:
http://www.lermuseum.org/en/regimental-history/
billys-own/the-last-few-months/, retrieved
9 June 2014.

Magazineart.org website. "Modern Priscilla." URL:
http://www.magazineart.org/main.php/v/womens/
modernpriscilla/, retrieved 9 June 2014.

Modern Priscilla. "Wartime Activities of Significance to
Women: One Thousand Dollars for the Red Cross
Can Be Raised on a Memorial Quilt." December 1917.
Boston: Priscilla Publishing Company, 1887–1930.

Moir, Sean. E-mail correspondence with Christina Bates,
Canadian Museum of Civilization, Gatineau, Quebec.
February 2012.

——. "Untangling the Threads of the Past: Researching the
1917 Waskatenau Signature Quilt." Paper presented
at the Canadian Museums Association conference,
Gatineau, Quebec, 26 April 2012.

Morton, Desmond, and Glenn Wright. *Winning the Second
Battle: Canadian Veterans and the Return to Civilian Life,
1915–1930*. Toronto: University of Toronto Press, 1987.

Palmer, Howard, and Tamara Palmer. *Alberta: A New
History*. Edmonton: Hurtig, 1990.

Porter, McKenzie. *To All Men: The Story of the Canadian Red
Cross*. Toronto: McClelland and Stewart, 1960.

Quilts of Valour–Canada website. "About Us." URL:
http://www.quiltsofvalour.ca/, retrieved 9 June 2014.

Quiney, Linda J. "'Hardly Feminine Work!': Violet Wilson
and the Canadian Volunteer Aid Detachment Nurses
of the First World War." In *Framing Our Past: Canadian
Women's History in the Twentieth Century*, edited by
Sharon Anne Cook, Lorna R. McLean, and Kathryn
O'Rourke, 289–94. Montreal and Kingston: McGill-
Queen's University Press, 2001.

Saddle Lake Cree Nation website. "Amalgamation." URL:
http://www.saddlelake.ca/noflash/?page_id=223,
retrieved 9 June 2014.

Singer, Horace C. *History of the 31st Battalion C.E.F.* Edited
by Darrell Knight. Calgary: Detselig, 2006.

Veterans Affairs Canada. "The Aftermath." URL:
http://www.veterans.gc.ca/eng/remembrance/
history/first-world-war/canada/canada19, retrieved
9 June 2014.

Wadsworth Atheneum Museum of Art website. "Past
Exhibitions." URL: http://www.thewadsworth.org/
exhibitions/past/, retrieved 9 June 2014.

Waskatenau and District Historical Society. *By River and
Trail: The History of Waskatenau and Districts*. 2 vols.
Waskatenau, AB: Waskatenau and District Historical
Society, 1986.

Calgary's Grand Theatre in the Great War

DONALD B. SMITH

Calgary's "Grand Story" began on the evening of Monday, 5 February 1912 with the spectacular opening of what the *Morning Albertan* termed, "Canada's Finest Theatre." Together with the Lougheed Building, also completed that year, the Grand represented Senator Sir James Lougheed's vision for his adopted city. The city would be an economic powerhouse with a rich cultural scene that would bring the world to Calgary. Johnston Forbes-Robertson, one of the greatest stars of the English stage, and his touring London company were booked to open with *The Passing of the Third Floor Back*, a play that had run an incredible 300 performances in London and over 200 in New York.

Under promoter Bill Sherman, the theatre had thrived for a time but eventually not only faced financial problems but also a high-profile racial discrimination suit that tarnished its image and led to calls for a change in leadership. Senator Lougheed sacked Sherman in June 1914.[1] With the flamboyant impresario's departure, the Sherman Grand lost the first half of its two-barrelled name; it simply became "the Grand." Lougheed hired Jeff Lydiatt as the Grand's new theatre manager in late December

1914 and, in February 1915, they welcomed back Forbes-Robertson on his North American farewell tour. The Ontario-educated Lydiatt had strong administrative skills developed working as the private secretary and chief clerk to Alfred Price, superintendent of CPR's western lines. His love of music was developed through involvement with the Yonge Street Methodist Church in Yorkville, where he was involved with the church choir. Lydiatt and his wife Clara moved to Calgary to follow Price, in 1907, when he became general superintendent of the CPR's Alberta division.

The Great War had changed Calgary almost beyond recognition. As part of the British Empire, with no control over its foreign affairs, Canada entered the conflict the instant Britain did. The morning of 4 August 1914 German troops crossed the border into Belgium. Under an 1839 treaty, Britain, France, and Prussia had agreed to protect Belgian neutrality. Immediately upon the invasion of Belgium, Britain issued Germany an ultimatum to withdraw. Twenty minutes after it expired, at 11:00 p.m., August 4, London time, the British Empire entered the war on the side of the Allies—France,

(left) The Lougheed Building and Sherman Grand Theatre, ca. 1912. Glenbow Archives, NA-4385-3; (right) The photo shows a crowd gathered to read the war news on the *Herald*'s bulletin board placed between the Herald and the Lougheed Buildings. Glenbow Archives, NA-5610-35.

Russia, Serbia, and Belgium—against the Central Powers, Germany and Austro-Hungary.

Just after 7:00 p.m. that same evening, news of Britain's declaration of war on Germany reached Calgary. The night staff in the Herald Building hastily updated all the latest bulletins on its news board located in the alleyway between their building and the Lougheed Building/Grand Theatre. Simultaneously the paper sent out its newsboys to distribute pink "extras" throughout the city. As a round, blood-red summer moon rose in the southeastern sky, masses of people, the patriotic and the curious, assembled

along Ninth Avenue between Centre and First Streets. A Scots piper marched up and down in front of the CPR station and the brand new Palliser Hotel, opened just two months earlier. Shouts of "Vive la France!" and "God Save the King!" greeted the impromptu processions of flag-draped motorcars.[2]

Legions of eager volunteers came forward as everyone on the Allied side initially expected the war to be over by Christmas 1914. But the unexpected German thrusts through Belgium into France took the Allies by surprise. Only in October did the Allies check the German advance at Ypres in the tiny corner of western Belgium that remained under their control. The German front lines as the crow flies were now about the same distance from Dover, England, as Calgary was from Banff—approximately a hundred kilometres. Both sides built a series of trenches from the Swiss border to the North Sea. Only two months after Forbes-Robertson's visit, the Canadians entered into their first major battle at Ypres, where they endured the world's first large-scale use of poison gas.

A martial atmosphere dominated in the city in early 1915. Forbes-Robertson visited the city's parade ground where the 31st Battalion marched before him. He later wrote of the experience: "Deeply moved at the honour shown me, I stood erect with bared head as the battalion swung past me in perfect alignment on the hard and slippery snow."[3] Forbes-Robertson felt the war's intensity. He described the German emperor to a Calgary reporter as a "monster," an "incarnation of iniquity."[4]

Lydiatt's office in 1914 was in room 205 on the second floor of the Lougheed Building,[5] which was itself transformed by wartime developments. Dr. Robert O'Callaghan retained his office nearby in room 210, but, in addition to his practice, the McGill-trained surgeon now served as a recruiting officer for the Princess Patricia's Canadian Light Infantry, the military unit named after the Duke of Connaught's daughter.[6] In early 1916, he himself enlisted in the British Royal Army Medical Corps and spent over a year in several hospitals in England and France.[7]

Other military-related activities occurred in the building. As soon as the war broke out, Calgary's naval volunteer headquarters opened an office in the Lougheed's fourth floor.[8] In late October 1915, Senator Lougheed and his business partner Edmund Taylor donated two vacant retail spaces on the building's ground floor for a soldiers' club open to all ranks of enlisted men every evening from 4:30 to 10:30. The four Calgary chapters of the Imperial Order Daughters of the Empire operated the club.[9] The Calgary office of the Patriotic Fund moved into room 300 of the Lougheed in late 1916.[10] The following April the recruiting office for the Army Medical Corps opened in the building as well.[11]

Senator Lougheed, president of the Alberta Boy Scouts Association, provided two rooms rent free for the duration of the war in the Lougheed Building for the association's headquarters.[12] Founded in Britain by Robert Baden-Powell in 1908, the Boy Scout movement reached Calgary in 1910 with the establishment of the St. Stephen's Church Scout troop later designated as "the 1st Alberta Troop." Chief Scout Baden-Powell himself visited Calgary on 21 August 1910.[13] As Robert H. MacDonald has argued in *Sons of the Empire: The Frontier and the Boy Scout Movement, 1890–1918*: "Scouting came to mean King and Country, Duty and Self-Sacrifice."[14] From the outset in Britain, Boy Scouts were thought of as little soldiers with an honorary connection to the military. It trained boys to do their duty.[15] During the Great War, a total of 222 Calgary leaders and Scouts or former Scouts enlisted, of whom 24 died in action.[16]

No information survives on the stand taken on Canada's war involvement by the Lougheed's major fourth-floor tenant, Will Tregillus. Before the outbreak of hostilities he determinedly opposed any involvement for Canada in a European war. But now, preoccupied by his failed brickworks, he made no statement. The German invasion of neutral Belgium, however, did reverse the earlier stance taken by University of Calgary professor Mack Eastman, who just half a year earlier attacked the piling up of arms by the world powers at the expense of the farmers and working class. Horrified by the German invasion of a small neutral country, the history professor now endorsed the war against Germany. "Autocratic government in Germany will yield only to Force," he told a Calgary interviewer in mid-October 1914.[17] Eastman tried to enlist, but the historian failed the stringent physical test.[18] Robert Maclean, Calgary's classics professor, had enlisted successfully immediately after the outbreak of war.[19]

Anxious to help the Allied cause, Eastman devoted long hours that winter to raise money throughout southern Alberta for the Belgian relief fund.[20] During his last months in Calgary, he boarded with George Coutts, Fred Albright's great friend.[21] Albright had taught the university's first economics course, now taken over by Walter Sage, a University of Toronto graduate with further training at Oxford University. Sage, who also taught English and history, was also a great friend of Coutts.[22]

Calgary became an armed camp over the next four years. Nearly 40,000 men enlisted for overseas service.[23] Lydiatt continued the Grand's policy of welcoming soldiers to performances. As guests of the house, he invited the entire 50th Battalion to attend the production of *Baby Mine*.[24] In late February 1915, it was the turn of the 31st Battalion, 1,100 strong, to see the play *The Private Secretary*.[25] The *News-Telegram* on 6 March 1915 congratulated Lydiatt and his counterpart at the Lyric, now called the Pantages Theatre,[26] for doing "all in their power to make life pleasant for the men who will soon be on the firing line." In late April, 900 members of the 50th Battalion returned for the last performance of *My Tango Maid*. The men in khaki joined in singing the chorus lines.[27]

Members of the 50th Battalion parade through Calgary before leaving for Britain, ca. 1914–18. Glenbow Archives, NA-3419-3.

Information survives on one Lougheed apartment resident in the war years: Millicent McElroy, "the lady who played the cornet." She played the send-off for each outgoing train carrying soldiers from the CPR station in Calgary to England and France. Born in England in 1869, she immigrated to Canada with her husband in 1911. George McElroy had been the bandmaster of the Salvation Army Belfast Citadel, and Millicent was a well-known Salvation Army musician in northern England.[28] After the war ended, she returned to the CPR platform and played rousing tunes as the men disembarked.[29] She had moved into the Lougheed apartment with her daughter and family while her daughter's husband was overseas in the war. Her own husband, a painter, was employed with the decoration of the new Vancouver CPR railway station.[30]

Fortunately, correspondence from a Lougheed tenant in the years 1915 to 1916 survives. In 1915, Seabury Pearce, the eldest son of Calgary Planning Commission President William Pearce, moved into offices on the fourth floor, Sixth Avenue side. Unlike his two younger brothers William and Harry, both in the Canadian Army, Seabury could not enlist, even under the more relaxed recruiting standards of the second and third years of the war, as he had lost the sight in his right eye as a young boy.[31] In fact, he wore a glass eye.[32] Although trained as an engineer and a surveyor, Seabury managed his father's company, "Pearce's Limited." Its letterhead read, "Loans negotiated, estates managed."[33] In 1916, both of Seabury's brothers were in Europe. Bill, who had arrived at the front in charge of a machine gun unit during the early spring of 1915, had been badly wounded in May, hit in the back of the neck by a piece of shrapnel.[34] After hospitalization in England, he returned to the trenches. Younger brother Harry

left for England with his Calgary unit in March 1916. Within less than five months, he too was wounded in a bomb accident in France with exploded shrapnel wounds to his head, neck, and both thighs.[35] For two days, the surgeons considered the amputation of his right arm at the elbow, but fortunately, by day three, he began to recover.[36] Once he had recuperated he returned to the front, also in a machine gun battalion like his brother.

Seabury Pearce, the trusted agent of his father, knew the Lougheed Building well, particularly the Cronn's Rathskeller portion. As president of the Calgary Planning Commission in 1913, his dad had chaired executive meetings at Cronn's.[37] Since opening in late 1912, Cronn's Rathskeller had been the spot to dine in the city. Jeff Lydiatt's friends hosted his retirement party from the CPR there. When the Royal Architectural Institute of Canada held its sixth general annual assembly in Calgary in September 1913, the City of Calgary welcomed the delegates at a luncheon at Cronn's.[38] The Rotary Club of Calgary had been planned around one of Cronn's restaurant tables in the winter of 1913–14. William Pearce and the Calgary Planning Committee Executive scheduled their meetings there. But, with the outbreak of war in August 1914, things changed. Now any establishment with a German name became suspect.

As the war continued, anti-German feelings rose. As early as late August 1914, the *Calgary Herald* endorsed the dismissal by the City of Calgary of German and Austrian employees.[39] That same month, Senator Lougheed urged public calm. On August 19, he mentioned to his fellow senators, "at such a time when all the national impulses are stirred it is peculiarly an occasion for dispassionate deliberation."[40] But hysteria mounted as the war, with no end in sight, took more and more victims. One of the first Calgarians to die in active service was Jimmie Leatherby, the Grand's first treasurer. He died of cerebral spinal meningitis in France on 5 March 1915 while serving with the Princess Patricias.[41]

Perhaps more than any other Albertan in the summer of 1915, Senator Lougheed knew the high casualty rate suffered by Canadian troops on the Western front. In July and August 1915, he served as acting minister of the militia.[42] His personal and emotional involvement increased with the enlistment that fall of Clarence, his oldest son,[43] followed by Edgar, his third son.[44] Understandably, the senator lost his footing and alarmingly emphasized the danger posed by Germans within Canada itself. In the Senate on 16 January 1916, he stated that Germany had embarked on "a war for world power, of territorial conquest," Canada being one of its principal objectives. "Germany," he added, "through its system of espionage, has a more thorough knowledge of Canada in the pigeon-holes of its foreign office than would be found in the departments of our own Government."[45]

Long-standing resentment against the enemy surfaced in Calgary in mid-February. Seabury Pearce was a tenant in the Lougheed at the time. His father learned from his son and the newspapers what had occurred. In a note to his daughter Frances, then in Victoria, British Columbia, William Pearce summarized what happened: "The soldiers in garrison, aided to a large extent by civilians, have given vent to their anti-German feelings in wrecking several buildings."[46] They trashed two restaurants on February 10 and a hotel the next night.[47] William was appalled, and added: "It is a deplorable state of affairs, and the saddest part of the whole thing is that public sentiment seems to be largely in support of that class of work, perhaps not to the extent of wrecking buildings, but there is a most insane anti-German and anti-Austrian feeling."[48]

Nor was that all; on the evening of the 11th, a rumour spread that rioters had targeted Cronn's Rathskeller. Twenty-five quickly assembled defenders of the restaurant blocked the doorway, and an armed guard stood across the road in case of trouble.[49] The defenders prevented an attempt to rush it. Long-time Calgarian Leishman McNeill later recorded what Edgar Lougheed told him about the aftermath. Immediately after the mob dispersed, Jimmy Hunter, the Lougheed Building's Scottish-born superintendent, called a truck to cut the wires leading to the large outside sign that read "Cronn's Rathskeller." After the sign was carted away, he turned out all the lights and had the doors locked. The mob did not return. McNeill concludes: "Mr. Lougheed tells me that Mr. and Mrs. Cronn disappeared that night and he never afterwards heard of their whereabouts."[50]

Cronn's Rathskeller suddenly became Cronn's Restaurant,[51] then, by April 1, Cronn's Café.[52] After that it had a new name entirely: the Cabaret Garden.[53] It took its new designation from the bandstand framed in latticework and hung with baskets of flowers.[54] For a new image, the management hired an African-American quartet. In the basement of the Lougheed Building, in February 1917, jazz was first played in Calgary. The Cabaret Garden later changed its name to the Plaza,[55] but it retained its popular African-American jazz bands until 1920.[56]

The Grand Theatre faced a problem with booking shows during the war. The Orpheum Vaudeville Circuit, which came to the Grand three days of every week, stopped its visits to Calgary and all western Canadian cities with the exception of Winnipeg in late 1914. Attendance had fallen after the war's outbreak, but a year later Jeff Lydiatt successfully convinced the Orpheum circuit to return to Calgary.[57] By keeping the Grand full of life, Lydiatt kept it alive, and helped enormously to maintain Calgary's wartime spirits.

The year 1916 proved a terrible one for Calgary, as Canadian casualties in France and Belgium increased. Calgary's 31st Battalion lost more than half its strength, with 130 killed, nearly 300 wounded, and 4 missing in a six-month period. The 50th Battalion, which had also visited the Grand earlier that year, lost 230 men in a fight by the Regina Trench. Of the 260 officers and men who went "over the top" to attack the German lines, only one officer and 30 men returned without a wound.[58]

By the summer of 1916, Calgary's daily newspapers carried long lists of casualties. Amongst the heavy losses that June was Dick Brocklebank, former alderman, killed in action.[59] That September, 25-year-old Ernest Pinkham, the youngest son of the first Anglican bishop of Calgary, W.C. Pinkham, died at the Battle of Courcelette.[60] In some fashion or another, the impact of the mounting casualties was felt in thousands of Calgary homes.

Lydiatt worked very hard throughout the war to lighten the city's spirits. The *News-Telegram* knew him as "the popular manager of the Grand Theatre."[61] The hard-to-please Bob Edwards also praised him. Writing in the *Eye Opener* on 2 December 1916, he tossed this bouquet: "Manager Lydiatt, of the Grand theatre, is to be congratulated on the high quality of theatrical fare he has been feeding his patrons upon of late. There has been quite an epidemic of good things." Bertha Hart, Edwards's secretary in the 1910s,[62] also appreciated what Lydiatt did: "He used to bring in some grand shows."[63]

Through his work for the Rotary Club of Calgary, Lydiatt contributed much in the community. He also generously devoted his time to the Victory Loan campaign.[64] Later in the war, he chaired the publicity committee to raise funds for the YMCA and its overseas work on the war front in Europe.[65] Next, he chaired the Red Shield campaign to collect money for the Salvation Army's war work.[66] On account of all these responsibilities Lydiatt reluctantly resigned in early 1915 as leader of the Wesley Methodist Church choir.

Lydiatt's job was full of minefields. He had to deal with such difficult personalities as Patrick Harcourt-O'Reilly, the Grand's solicitor. In early 1916, the lawyer saved the theatre $3,000 by reducing in court its original assessment of $12,000 to $9,000. But, as a consequence, Harcourt-O'Reilly expected complimentary tickets to all performances. He appeared in full evening dress for big stage shows, without a ticket, and expected to be taken to the best seats. Operating under an extremely tight budget, Lydiatt repeatedly had to explain that there were no free tickets.[67]

Politically, the Grand's manager had to appear totally neutral as the theatre hosted both the Conservative and Liberal political leaders; wisely, Lydiatt identified himself as an independent.[68] In the war years, the leading provincial Conservative R.B. Bennett spoke several times there,[69] but Alberta's Liberal Premier Arthur Sifton also addressed a large gathering at the Grand.[70] In late 1916, Conservative Prime Minister Robert Borden held a massive rally in the theatre,[71] as did Wilfrid Laurier, the former Liberal prime minister turned leader of the opposition, in late 1917.

Finally, in August 1918, the war took a turn for the better with great Allied advances on the Western

Front. But, just as the end of Great War finally seemed imminent, the deadly and highly contagious Spanish flu epidemic struck. Worldwide the virus claimed 20 million lives. In Canada, perhaps 50,000 died, approximately the same number of Canadian service personnel lost in the First World War. From mid-October to mid-November, all churches, schools, and theatres in Calgary remained closed.

The signing of the November 11 armistice in Europe allowed for a slight relaxation of the strict rules against public assemblies. The news reached City Solicitor Clinton Ford when he was arguing a case before the Appeal Court. He and H.P.O. Savary, the opposing counsel, had to wear cotton masks on account of the epidemic. All the members of the court wore them. Nearly half a century later, Ford recalled that during his presentation Savary suddenly stepped out into the corridor. He returned a short time later waving a newspaper. Shouting incoherently through his mask, he interrupted the city solicitor. When Ford read the headline, he understood—"ARMISTICE AGREED ON"—"It meant the war was over. I will never forget the great feeling I had at that moment."[72]

Once news of the armistice reached the mayor, he temporarily relaxed the anti-contagion rules and declared a half-day holiday, even allowing a victory parade. It began that afternoon at the Central Fire Hall on Sixth Avenue, just two blocks from the Lougheed Building, and proceeded around the central part of the city, ending at City Hall at 3:30. The parade ended with the hanging of two effigies of

The Victory Parade in Calgary, 11 November 1918. During the deadly Spanish flu epidemic then underway, face masks were common. Glenbow Archives, NA-431-5.

the Kaiser and the German Crown Prince opposite City Hall, in what today is Olympic Plaza. Five hours later, the effigies were removed from the scaffold and burned. Calgarians crowded the streets in every direction.[73]

The Grand Theatre's Opera Festival in late January marked Jeff Lydiatt's gift to Calgary to celebrate the war's end. The visiting San Carlo Opera Company enjoyed a worldwide reputation.[74] Calgary choir leader Percy Lynn "P.L." Newcombe publicly thanked Lydiatt in an article in the *Albertan*.[75]

The checking of the influenza epidemic, which took 341 Calgarians' lives in late 1918, added to the joy of the five operas.[76] Influenza cases dropped from 938 in December to 13 in January.[77] No one had to wear "flu" masks anymore. With great anticipation, the public came to see and hear *Aida*, *Rigoletto*, *Tales of Hoffmann*, *Il Trovatore*, and *Madame Butterfly*, the San Carlo Opera Company's *pièces de résistance*.

Lydiatt took the Grand through the upheaval of the Great War. An outstanding and imaginative administrator, he selected an effective management team, one which remained in place into the 1920s after he left the theatre. In late 1919, he assumed the vice-presidency of Trans-Canada Theatres Limited, a national theatre circuit, with his office in the Lougheed Building. Senator Lougheed, who was knighted Sir James Lougheed in 1916 in recognition of his Senate and federal cabinet work, had a major financial interest in Trans-Canada. The senator knew well his employee's true worth. When Lydiatt left Trans-Canada in 1923 to manage the Orpheum Theatre in Vancouver, Lougheed wrote: "I could not wish from anyone who has been associated with me in business any greater satisfaction in that association than you have given me."[78]

Notes

The co-editors thank Donald B. Smith for permission to reprint an abridged version of chapter 8: "Jeff Lydiatt: The Grand in the Great War," in *Calgary's Grand Story* (Calgary: University of Calgary Press, 2005), 137–60.

1   "W.R. Sherman Sells Theatrical Interests to a New Company," *Calgary Herald*, 6 June 1914.

2   "War Announcement Gives Rise to Great Outburst of Patriotic Feeling," *Calgary Herald*, 5 August 1914.

3   Sir Johnston Forbes-Robertson, *A Player under Three Reigns* (1925; repr., New York: Benjamin Blom, 1971), 272. See also: "Actor Visits Troops," *Calgary Herald*, 12 February 1915.

4   Sir Johnston Forbes-Robertson quoted in "Forbes-Robertson on Attitude of the United States," *The Albertan*, 9 February 1915.

5   He appears there in the *Henderson's Calgary Directory*, 1914, but not in 1915, when his office as manager would be in the Grand Theatre.

6   "Recruits Needed by Princess Pats," *Calgary News-Telegram*, 22 November 1915; "Another University Company Recruiting. Particulars may be Obtained. Dr. R.B. O'Callaghan, Lougheed Building," *Calgary Herald*, 7 December 1915.

7   "Dr. O'Callaghan Returning after Active Service," *Calgary News-Telegram*, 6 September 1917.

8   "Urgent Appeal Is Being Made for Recruits," *Calgary News-Telegram*, 5 August 1914; "Second Naval Contingent on Way to Coast," *Calgary News-Telegram*, 10 August 1914.

9   "Soldiers Club's Headquarters in the Lougheed Block," *Calgary News-Telegram*, 1 November 1915; "I.O.D.E. Khaki Club to Be Opened Monday," *Calgary News-Telegram*, 25 November 1915.

10 "Patriotic Fund is Forced to Remove," *Calgary Herald*, 27 December 1916.

11 "Physical Standard is Lowered for the Army Medical Corps," *Calgary News-Telegram*, 20 April 1917.

12 "Many Scouts Are Now in the Army," *Calgary Canadian* (*Calgary News-Telegram*), 12 April 1918; Henderson's Calgary directories for 1916–1919.

13 Accounts by various Calgary authors, *Scouting in Calgary: Boy Scout Groups and Activities, 1910–1974* (Calgary: Century Calgary Publications, 1975), 7, 10.

14 Robert H. MacDonald, *Sons of the Empire: The Frontier and the Boy Scout Movement, 1890–1918* (Toronto: University of Toronto Press, 1993), 186.

15 Ibid., 188, 201.

16 Accounts by various Calgary authors, *Scouting in Calgary*, 17.

17 Mack Eastman quoted in "M. Eastman Volunteered Although Anti-Militaries," *Calgary News-Telegram*, 23 October 1914.

18 "Prof. Eastman Debarred," *Calgary News-Telegram*, 31 August 1914.

19 The University of Calgary, Second Annual Calendar, Session 1914/15, 4. See also unidentified clipping, March–April 1962, Former Student Files, Queen's University Archives, Kingston, Ontario.

20 J.H. Woods, Hon. Secretary of the Belgian Relief Committee, dated Calgary, 4 May 1915, box 1, file 3, S. Mack Eastman Papers, University of British Columbia Archives, Vancouver.

21 Eastman to Edward Braithwaite, dated Calgary, 28 December 1914, Braithwaite Papers, Western Archives, Western University.

22 Walter Sage to Leila Gerrens (his aunt), 24 November 1914, box 31, file 29, Walter N. Sage Papers, University of British Columbia Archives.

23 Max and Heather Foran, *Calgary: Canada's Frontier Metropolis* (Calgary: Windsor Publications, 1982), 156.

24 "Col. Mason's Battalion Invited Out," *Calgary News-Telegram*, 15 January 1915.

25 "Grand to Entertain 31st," *Calgary News-Telegram*, 22 February 1915.

26 Jeffrey Goffin, "Lyric Theatre," in *The Oxford Companion to Canadian Theatre*, edited by Eugen Benson and I.W. Connelly (Toronto: Oxford University Press, 1989), 316.

27 "Soldiers Were Pleased," *Calgary News-Telegram*, 30 April 1915.

28 Ada Patton Kelter (granddaughter of Millicent McElroy), interview with the author, Calgary, 13 February 2003.

29 "Lady with the Cornet," *Calgary Herald*, 31 August 1945. Anne White, "Songster and the Preachers: Female Salvationists in Calgary, 1897–1930," in the Canadian Society of Church History, *Historical Papers* (2001), 119–20.

30 Ada Patton Kelter, interview, 13 February 2003.

31 William Pearce to Senator James Lougheed, 17 July 1915, 74-169, file 67.8, William Pearce Papers, University of Alberta Archives, Edmonton (hereafter cited as Pearce Papers).

32 Seabury Pearce to William Pearce, 14 February 1901, 74-169/790, Pearce Papers.

33 Although he appears in the *Henderson's Calgary Directory* for 1915, the first letter to indicate his offices were in the Lougheed Building is dated later—see Seabury Pearce to William Pearce, 9 March 1916, 74-169/792, Pearce Papers.

34 William Pearce to Archbishop of Rupert's Land, Winnipeg, 20 October 1915, 74-169/802, Pearce Papers.

35 William Pearce to Seabury Pearce, 30 August 1916, 74-169/792, Pearce Papers.

36 William Pearce to J.G. Sullivan, 5 January 1917, 74-169/797, Pearce Papers.

37 Minutes of the Executive, Calgary City Planning Commission, Minutes, 1911–1914, box 2, City of Calgary Archives, Calgary.

38 *Souvenir, Sixth Annual Assembly of the Royal Architectural Institute of Canada, Calgary, Alberta, Sept. 15 and 16, 1913*, 5, Glenbow Library, Calgary.

39 "A New Policy Needed," *Calgary Herald*, 28 August 1914.

40 Senate, *Debates*, 19 August 1914, 7.

41 "Dies in France," *Calgary News-Telegram*, 12 March 1915.

42 "Lougheed Quits as Minister of Militia Branch," *Calgary News-Telegram*, 2 September 1915.

43 Clarence Hardisty Lougheed, Attestation Paper, Canadian Over-seas Expeditionary Force, 27 September 1915, Library and Archives Canada, Ottawa.

44 Officers Declaration paper, Canadian Over-seas Expeditionary Force, 24 February 1916. See also his entire military service file housed in Library and Archives Canada.

45 Senate, *Debates*, 18 January 1916.

46 William Pearce to Frances Pearce, 14 February 1916, 74-169/784, Pearce Papers.

47 For a complete summary of the riots see P. Whitney Lackenbauer, "The Military and 'Mob Rule': The CEF Riots in Calgary, February 1916," *Canadian Military History* 10, no. 1 (Winter 2002): 31–42.

48 William Pearce to Frances Pearce, 14 February 1916, 74-169/784, Pearce Papers.

49 "Soldiers Are Armed with Ball Cartridge, and Are Placed on Guard at Threatened Places," *Calgary News-Telegram*, 12 February 1916.

50 Leishman McNeill, *Tales of the Old Town* (Calgary: Calgary Herald, 1966), 63.

51 Engineers Agree with Laws That Protect Public," *Calgary News-Telegram*, 28 March 1916.

52 See advertisement in the *Calgary News-Telegram*, 1 April 1916.

53 "Cabaret Gardens Will Be Established under Grand Theatre. Coloured Entertainers Will Be Brought from Eastern City to Supply Music," *Calgary News-Telegram*, 23 August 1916.

54 Mark Miller, *Such Melodious Racket: The Lost History of Jazz in Canada, 1914–1949* (Toronto: The Mercury Press, 1997), 47. My thanks to Blane Hogue for this reference.

55 "The Plaza Formerly Cabaret Garden," *Calgary Eye Opener*, 3 March 1917.

56 Miller, *Such Melodious Racket*, 47–49. "Colored Musicians No Longer at the Plaza," *The Albertan*, 22 December 1920.

57 "Orpheum Will Be Closed until the War Is Over," *Calgary News-Telegram*, 13 October 1914; "Orpheum Re-Opens in Calgary," *The Albertan*, 14 December 1915.

58 Hugh A. Dempsey, *Calgary: Spirit of the West* (Calgary: Fifth House, 1994), 106–7.

59 "Letters from Front Tell How 'Dick' Brocklebank Met Death," *Calgary News-Telegram*, 20 September 1916.

60 "Capt. Ernest Pinkham Gives His Life for His Country," *Calgary News-Telegram*, 20 September 1916.

61 "Grand Theatre Will Show Musical Motion Pictures; Sets New Standard Here," *Calgary News-Telegram*, 12 February 1916.

62 Bertha Hart Segall, "'Bob' Edwards," *Canadian Cattlemen* (June 1950): 18, 35, 42.

63 Annette Friedman, interview with Bertha Hart Segall, May 1974, transcript, Jewish Historical Society of Southern Alberta Archives.

64 "Publicity Men Are Named for Victory Loan," *Calgary News-Telegram*, 1 November 1917.

65 "Plans Laid for Big Red Triangle Fund Drive Starting Next Week," *Calgary Canadian* (*Calgary News-Telegram*), 4 May 1918.

66 "Red Shield Campaign for the Salvation Army War Work and Children's Home Gets Good Start," *Calgary Canadian* (*Calgary News-Telegram*), 11 September 1918.

67 "Grand Theatre Assessment Is Cut By $3,000," *Calgary News-Telegram*, 24 January 1916. Margaret Lydiatt, interviews, 28 September 2000 and 12 November 2000.

68 "Liberal Government's Leader Tells the Soldiers Why Aliens Will Be Allowed to Vote in Alberta Election," *Calgary News-Telegram*, 17 May 1917.

69 "Sir Robert Borden Speaks in Grand Theatre Dec. 28," *Calgary Herald*, 6 December 1916; "Two Great Calgary Audiences Listen to the Prime Minister," *Calgary Herald*, 29 December 1916.

70 "I Am Out to Win the War, I Have Been from the First and Will Be to the Last," *Calgary News-Telegram*, 13 December 1917.

71 "Principaled by Aberhart, Inspired by Famous Five," *Calgary Herald Neighbours, Zone 1*, 17 August 1995, 4.

72 P.L. Newcombe, "Presentation of 'Madame Butterfly' Is Acclaimed Finest of San Carlo Company," *The Albertan*, 25 January 1919.

73 Janice P. Dickin McGinnis, "A City Faces an Epidemic," *Alberta History*, 24, no. 4 (1976), 1. Forty-three individuals died of the "Spanish flu" in 1919.

74 "Influenza Epidemic Ended in City Twenty Years Ago After Striking Many Down," *Calgary Herald*, 25 November 1938.

75 This information appears in program, *Grand Opera Festival, 23, 24 and 25 January 1919*, 17, Non-Circulating Pamphlet, Local History Room, W.R. Castell Central Library, Calgary.

76 Margaret Lydiatt, interview, 11 February 2001; Grace Lydiatt Shaw, interview, 11 February 2001. Grace Lydiatt Shaw, introduction to *Stratford under Cover: Memories on Tape* (Toronto: NC Press, 1977).

77 For a good summary of the opera, see Mary Ellis Peltz and Robert Lawrence, *The Metropolitan Opera Guide* (New York: Modern Library, 1939), 404–10.

78 James A. Lougheed to R.J. Lydiatt, Calgary, 18 July 1923. A Photostat of the letter is now in the Jeff Lydiatt files in the Calgary Grand Story Fonds, donated by Donald B. Smith to the Glenbow Archives, Calgary.

Works Cited

PRIMARY SOURCES

The Albertan
Calgary Canadian
Calgary Eye Opener
Calgary Herald
Calgary News-Telegram

Ada Patton Kelter, interview with the author, Calgary, 13 February 2003.

Glenbow Library, Calgary. *Souvenir, Sixth Annual Assembly of the Royal Architectural Institute of Canada, Calgary, Alberta, Sept. 15 and 16, 1913*, 5.

Grace Lydiatt Shaw, interview with the author, 11 February 2001.

Jewish Historical Society of Southern Alberta Archives, Calgary. Annette Friedman, interview with Bertha Hart Segal, May 1974, transcript.

Margaret Lydiatt, interviews with the author, 28 September and 12 November 2000; and 11 February 2001.

University of Alberta Archives, Edmonton. William Pearce Fonds, 74–169.

University of British Columbia Archives, Vancouver. Walter N. Sage Papers, box 31, file 29.

SECONDARY SOURCES

Baines, Tom, ed. *Scouting in Calgary: Boy Scout Groups and Activities, 1910–1974: Accounts by Calgary Authors*. Calgary: Century Calgary Publications, 1975.

Dempsey, Hugh A. *Calgary: Spirit of the West*. Calgary: Fifth House, 1994.

Forbes-Robertson, Johnston. *A Player under Three Reigns*. New York: Benjamin Blom, 1971. First published 1925.

Goffin, Jeffrey. "Lyric Theatre." In *The Oxford Companion to Canadian Theatre*, edited by Eugene Benson and I.W. Connelly. Toronto: Oxford University Press, 1989.

Lackenbauer, P. Whitney. "The Military and 'Mob Rule': The CEF Riots in Calgary, February 1916." *Canadian Military History* 10, no. 1 (Winter 2002): 31–42.

MacDonald, Robert H. *Sons of the Empire: The Frontier and the Boy Scout Movement, 1890–1918*. Toronto: University of Toronto Press, 1993.

McNeill, Leishman. *Tales of the Old Town*. Calgary: *Calgary Herald*, 1966.

Miller, Mark. *Such Melodious Racket: The Lost History of Jazz in Canada, 1914–1949*. Toronto: The Mercury Press, 1997.

Segall, Bertha Hart. "'Bob' Edwards." *Canadian Cattlemen* (June 1950): 18–42.

Shaw, Grace Lydiatt. *Stratford under Cover: Memories on Tape*. Toronto: NC Press, 1977.

Smith, Donald B. *Calgary's Grand Story*. Calgary: University of Calgary Press, 2005.

White, Anne. "Songster and the Preachers: Female Salvationists in Calgary, 1897–1930." In Canadian Society of Church History, *Historical Papers* (2001): 119–20.

Student Life on the University of Alberta Campus during the First World War[1]

CHRIS HYLAND AND PAUL STORTZ

From the summer of 1914 to the end of the First World War in November 1918, 484 University of Alberta staff and students served in the Canadian armed forces, and 82 paid the ultimate price for their commitment.[2] One hundred and sixteen students were junior officers, perhaps the most dangerous occupation on the Western Front.[3] These figures represent a huge sacrifice. For such a small university, the University of Alberta can stand proud of its war service with its strong Canadian Officers Training Corps (COTC) program, and its faculty and students serving in all branches of the Canadian Expeditionary Force (CEF), as well as the Khaki University of Canada. This story is not about those who served overseas, however, but about those who stayed behind and experienced the war from campus.

What happens to a university student community when the country goes to war? How are students' lives and cultures affected by the conflict? This essay argues that student life at the University of Alberta became subservient to the needs of a country at war. Student cultures and traditions were modified, or interrupted by the conflict. Demographic patterns on campus changed, creating unique challenges and opportunities for the student body. The loss of senior students led to discipline problems. Further, the return of student veterans was a welcome but troubling addition to the university student community.

The University Campus before the War

Before the outbreak of hostilities in summer 1914, the University of Alberta was a small institution located on the outskirts of the city of Edmonton. Under the university's first president, Dr. Henry Marshal Tory, the university was only six years old when the First World War began. Enrollment in 1908 numbered only 45 students, but quickly expanded to 443 for the 1914–15 school year, 383 of whom were men and 60 women. Freshmen counted 160, sophomores 137, juniors 74, seniors 52, and graduate students 20. Freshmen were 36 percent of the student body, while seniors and graduate students represented 16 percent.[4] The origins of the students reflected the relative youth of the province as only 33 were born in what would become Alberta in 1905. Over 80 percent of the student body was of Canadian or British birth (England, Scotland, and Wales), with 164 from Ontario and 66 from England. Only 13 percent of students were from the United States. About two-thirds of students were born in Canada, while 22 percent hailed from other parts of the British Empire. Despite being born in different parts of Canada and the world, 303 students gave a home address in Alberta, reflecting recent migration to the province.[5] Most students came from Northern Alberta. Historian Rod Macleod, writing about the student body in 1911 in his official history of the university, points out that in reality the University of Alberta was a northern Albertan institution, rather than for the whole province, as Tory and other promoters would claim. He writes: "Of the 196 students registered [in 1911], only ten came from Calgary and fourteen others from rural areas and towns south of Red Deer."[6]

Many students came from remote and rural areas, often knowing no one at the university and none of its traditions.[7] Prior to the First World War, 70 percent of Albertans lived in rural areas.[8] Student home addresses reflected the rural nature of the student body. Outside of Edmonton and Calgary, over 50 different Albertan communities are listed.[9] Further, E.A. Corbett, in *Henry Marshall Tory: A Biography*, writes: "Among the students were some whose social background was extremely limited, as indeed is the case in the freshman year at any university, but there was perhaps less of an idea in this instance of what university life was like than in an Eastern university." Corbett goes on to tell the following anecdote about the recent university senate decision to have students wear academic dress: "One of the students, not knowing how to accommodate himself to the situation, bolted into the President's office and wanted to know if it was necessary to take off his trousers

before putting on the gown."[10] Corbett seems to be politely suggesting that some students were at first quite unfamiliar with the customs and traditions of university life.

Most of the major Christian denominations were represented on campus. In 1914–15, 157 students were Methodist, 135 Presbyterian, 56 Anglican, 33 Baptist, 23 Roman Catholic, and 6 Lutheran.[11] Roman Catholics and Lutherans did not attend the university in large numbers, which is surprising considering the large, vibrant Catholic and Lutheran communities in northern Alberta. With a lack of a definitive reason for the relative absence of these two denominations, it can be speculated that some Albertans perceived the university to be a liberal, Protestant institution, one that was not receptive to other belief systems. The students' average age was 23, ranging from 15 to 43. Most fell between the ages of 19 and 30. The mature, older nature of the student body may have reflected how Albertan students, on average, took longer to graduate from high school than students in other provinces, often due to a lack of high school opportunities in the new province.[12]

A university education was a luxury that few families could readily afford. Tuition and student fees were expensive enough, but adding room and board amounted to approximately $265 per year, or about half a year's salary for a typical blue-collar worker. In theory, the majority of students lived away from home in residence. President Tory and Premier Rutherford held the traditional belief that the residential system gave a sense of unity to the university and added to its traditions.[13] Residences also fit in with the university administration's belief in *in loco parentis*. Students who were on campus were easier to monitor and control. Under watchful eyes, proper behaviour and socio-religious norms could

Athabasca Hall, the first official building of the University of Alberta, Edmonton, 1913. Photograph courtesy of the University of Alberta Archives, AN 69-10-0003.

be enforced. Regulations were developed so that students had to live in residence or at home with their parents. Special dispensation was required from the bursar for students to reside off campus and away from the watchful eyes of their elders.[14] In 1914, the university had two residential halls in operation, Athabasca and Assiniboia, and a third, Pembina, under construction. Athabasca and Assiniboia could accommodate approximately 130 students. Despite the best efforts of university administration, a significant number of students had to find off-campus accommodations.[15]

What was student life like on campus before the war? The answer is somewhat complicated. The typical academic routine of lectures and coursework filled large stretches of the day, as did the corresponding readings and assignments. But the peaceful and serene atmosphere on campus was, at times, punctuated by bursts of high-energy activities and youthful enthusiasm. In 1914, listening to the radio was not an option (CJCA, the city's first radio station, only began broadcasting in 1922) and neither was television. Cinemas were in town, but none on campus. Alcohol was officially banned, reflecting the religious tenor of the time and, from 1916, the law. Students were left largely to their own devices for entertainment, and so they filled their leisure hours with rituals, athletics, clubs, and social events. Initiations were a large part of the school experience. One of the first events in the new school year was the freshman initiation, which, by 1914, had evolved into an elaborate ritual. Sophomores as well as upper classmen dunked, sprayed, or rounded up unsuspecting freshmen in mock trials for undisclosed offences, forcing them to carry ridiculous accruements such as beanies or to wear inappropriate clothes—underwear worn on the outside was a common form of humiliation—while marching about for the wider campus, or even the city, to see.[16] The initiations impressed upon the freshman that respect for older

University of Alberta students, ca. 1911–12. The full names of the students are John Alton, Sandy Caldwell, and Dot Hyssop (the other man in the photograph remains unidentified). Photograph courtesy of the University of Alberta Archives, AN 70-69-27 (Miss Ethel Anderson—Class of 1912).

students was imperative. As many freshmen were unaware of the customs and traditions on campus, these initiations served as an informal indoctrination in which the unofficial rules and regulations were passed on to the next class.[17]

Athletics became a popular diversion, both as a participation sport and spectator activity. The university developed strong athletic traditions in hockey, rugby, and basketball. Boxing, wrestling, tennis, and rifle shooting were also popular.[18] Leisure skating on McKernan Lake, to the south of campus, proved a popular pastime in the winter. Students enjoyed track and field in the summer.[19] Several clubs also offered a welcome relief from the routine of student life. The Literary Society put on programs that included mock parliaments and debates.[20] Performances by the Glee Club and the Dramatic Society were well attended. Both the Young Men's (YMCA) and Young Women's Christian Associations (YWCA) were active on campus. The student newspaper, *The Gateway*, was issued on a monthly and, later, weekly basis. The Philosophical Society organized a series of public lectures.[21] Although no fraternities or sororities were on campus, a women's group formed in 1909—called the Wauneita Club—organized student life for female undergraduates.[22] Throughout the school term, but especially during the winter, the university and students held a number of social events on campus including the freshman reception and the undergraduate ball.

In spring and summer 1914, the mood on campus was relatively positive. Despite a provincial recession, enrollments had been increasing every year. Tory was expanding campus infrastructure and buildings as fast as his budget would allow. Students were developing a sense of group identity, and new traditions were being forged. The years before the

First World War were a time of growth, expansion, and dynamism. But on 4 August 1914, with Britain's declaration of war on Germany, life on campus began to change.

1914–1916

Students at the university greeted Canada's entry into the First World War with general enthusiasm. The vast majority strongly supported the war effort; any dissenting voices kept very quiet. In fall 1914, not much changed on campus. Life continued as it had in 1913; athletic competitions were held as were many club activities and social events. The feeling on campus was that the war would be over in months, if not weeks. It would be a short, decisive war full of mobility and swift movements.[23]

Two exceptions to this trend of normalcy, however, were seen in the fall. The first was large-scale military training on campus. In September, the staff and students who were in Edmonton formed into a small unit for military training under the larger organization, the Home Defence Volunteers of the City of Edmonton. When the university opened in October, the program rapidly expanded, and many students joined. A strictly voluntary, extracurricular program of close-order drill, open-order formations, and lectures was offered three to five times a week.[24] These activities were in addition to the physical training that had always been a requirement for first- and second-year students. The nature of the military training changed when a Canadian Officers Training Corps (COTC) program was authorized for the university in December 1914.[25] The program was considered a regular university course, so students received academic credit for their participation.

With this added stimulus, 192 men enrolled, with an average attendance of 150. Fully half of the male student body was involved with the COTC program. Moreover, accommodations in the Athabasca Hall gym were provided for the COTC men. This was a blow to the social scene on campus, as the area was no longer available at certain times for large gatherings. Another branch of the training was conducted by Heber Moshier, a medical doctor, who began preparing 54 men for entry into the Army Medical Corps.[26]

Yet, involvement in the COTC was not a commitment to serve in the armed forces. A separate, conscious act of "signing up" for military service was required.[27] University students' motivations to enlist reflected a variety of interrelated factors. As military historian Tim Cook writes: "No single reason for Canadians' decision to enlist stands out; what appealed to one man might have no effect on another, but all had a range of allegiances that often intersected and overlapped."[28] For Albertans, patriotism, and loyalty to the British Empire, was one reason.[29] A large majority of students had British origins. A chance for adventure was another reason. The lure of foreign travel may have appealed to the rural and isolated young men from northern Alberta. Many felt that the cause was just, one of freedom and liberty against Prussian despotism and militarism.[30] President Tory was a big proponent of military service and constantly encouraged his students to get involved.[31] Never specifically demanding that students enlist, Tory made his expectations on military service clear in a number of speeches, in which he exhorted students to join up.[32] Both the Methodist and Presbyterian churches supported the war effort. No hints of Christian pacifism existed on campus: the message from the pulpit was for young men to go and fight.[33]

Promising young lieutenants (1916–19). Photograph courtesy of the University of Alberta Archives, AN 73-18-28.

The second noticeable change to campus life in fall 1914 was more subtle and, in some ways, more profound. The war was beginning to capture the attention of students. Debate topics and public lectures shifted their focus to various aspects of the war. Church leaders, school administrators, and professors spoke frequently about the conflict to students. Articles on martial themes appeared in *The Gateway*. The Department of Extension switched from providing information about the latest agricultural techniques to disseminating the latest imperial propaganda. The war was a constant topic of conversation among students.[34]

The year 1915 was a transitional one in the university community's war experience as its grim realities began to set in. In April, the Second Battle of Ypres, in which the Germans used poison gas, cost the 1st Canadian Division 200 officers and almost 6,000 other ranks. Almost one-third of the Canadian force had been wiped out. Following this and other battles on the Western Front, hopes for a quick war died as most recognized that it would be a long and bloody affair. A serious, almost sombre, atmosphere settled over the campus.[35] Friends, peers, and professors left the campus for military service. By November 1915, 130 men from the university were on active service, and three had died. These three deaths had a huge impact on this small community, as evidenced by their long obituaries on the front page of the student newspaper.[36] Reports of university students in combat actions were frequent.[37] War had instilled a deep sense of responsibility in those who remained behind—to be supportive of the war effort and to train hard for military or civilian life.

In spring 1916, the whole campus bore the signs of a community at war. Men in khaki uniforms were everywhere. The COTC drilled frequently. Fundraisers for the war and Red Cross events were a regular occurrence.[38] Twenty-one professors were on active service as were approximately 230 students; 26 members of the university community had died.[39] In fall 1916, 418 students registered—361 men and 57 women—which indicated a slight drop in student enrollment as compared to the 1914–15 school year. What was significant about the 1916 enrollment, however, was the smaller number of students in the upper years: first and second year students totaled 278, while third and fourth year students totalled only 114. This loss of older, mature students would have important consequences in 1917 and 1918.[40] Tory was concerned that the pool of potential university students was drying up: many high school seniors in the province were choosing to serve in the armed forces rather than seek a higher education.[41]

Several other changes to campus life were also evident. The annual freshman initiation was cancelled in 1915. The loss of the ritual was lamented, and students vigorously defended the tradition in the press.[42] The initiation made a return in 1916, but was a shell of its former self, and heavily monitored by university authorities. As well, by the fall, the residential basis of the university was under threat. Not enough students were at the university to fill the residences. Tory was hoping just to fill Athabasca Hall, never mind the other two residences. Assiniboia Hall was rented out to the Presbyterian Ladies College of Red Deer.[43] Pembina Hall was closed for most of 1915 and then used on a limited basis as a military billet and as a residence for a few students.[44]

With two of three residences essentially off limits, the centre of student life was constricted. Participation in athletics declined as well. With all the time and energy spent drilling, a decreasing number of students wanted to play sports.[45] Moreover, the nature of athletic competition changed—instead of travelling to other universities, teams tended to stay closer to campus.[46] One by one, student customs were modified or supplanted by a commitment to the war effort. Student life was being reoriented to serve the needs of a nation at war.

For the most part, students willingly surrendered some of their traditions. Two years into the conflict, strong support for the war was still felt on campus. Students were proud of their peers' service in the armed forces and their sacrifices.[47] Students held onto a strong belief that the war was saving the country and that the sacrifices in men and material were not in vain.[48] The diminishing number of male students on campus and a growing list of casualties, however, began to chip away at the student body's confidence in the war effort.

1917–1918

In fall 1916 and into 1917, the war in Europe took a turn for the worse for the Canadian Corps, and the fighting would have serious consequences in faraway Edmonton. On 15 September 1916, the Corps participated in the battle of Flers-Courcellette, which degenerated into an attritional confrontation that added to a casualty count of just over 24,000 since the outset of the Somme offensive on 1 July 1916. In April 1917, Canadians took part in the Battle of Arras, which included the capture of Vimy Ridge, a notable and important achievement, but at a cost of 3,598 dead and 6,664 wounded. In August 1917, General Sir Arthur Currie orchestrated the capture of Hill 70, but again at huge cost. The Canadian Corps took part in the Third Battle of Ypres, also known as Passchendaele, in fall 1917. After weeks of fighting, the Canadians had suffered another 15,600 casualties.[49] This high casualty rate had significant repercussions in Canada. The pool of volunteers for the armed forces was drying up by late 1916. By spring 1917, the number of new recruits was well below replacement requirements.[50] Moreover, in January 1916, Prime Minister Sir Robert Borden committed Canada to raising a force of 500,000 soldiers. Although conscription was not introduced until the summer of 1917, Canada's huge military commitment and losses had significant ramifications for the University of Alberta.

By 30 June 1917, the composition of the student body had changed significantly: only 305 students were enrolled, down from 443 in 1914. Of the 305 registered, 220 were men and 85 were women. Women, in 1917, made up 28 percent of the student body compared to 13.5 percent in 1914.[51] Only 125 freshmen registered, a drop from 174 in 1916; most worrying for university administration was the loss of upper-class men.[52] In 1917, only 19 seniors registered, down from 54 in 1914.[53] In 1917, the freshman-to-senior ratio was 6.5:1; whereas, in 1914, it was 3:1. These demographic trends reflected the university's strong commitment to the war effort. By June 1917, 329 students had enlisted in the armed forces, and 45 had perished.[54] Many young men were foregoing their university education, opting instead to enlist.

Combined, the course of the war and the changes in demographic patterns altered student life on campus. The diminishing number of male students on campus, and a growing list of casualties, began to erode the student body's confidence in the war effort, and by spring 1917, war weariness blanketed

Interior of the Old Tuck Shop, ca. 1917–19. The Tuck Shop, established in 1917, was a "popular student haunt, where coffee, books, candy, horse race betting, and the odd bottle of whiskey could be found." Photograph courtesy of the University of Alberta Archives, AN 73-18-0030.

the campus. Students were losing interest in the war that had held their attention for three long years. In February 1917, Tory gave a lecture on "Education and the War" on behalf of the Philosophical Society; only four students attended. *The Gateway* was running out of money to distribute the soldiers' newsletter. Students were tired of donating.[55]

Given the recent developments in the war, in late 1916 and 1917, able-bodied male students faced a huge dilemma: they felt an enormous pressure to enlist, but also a need to stay home, in many cases for farming. An editorial from *The Gateway* in December 1916 captured the mood about enlisting.[56] The context was President Tory's address to a recent parade of the COTC. Tory was explicit that the decision to enlist was a matter of personal choice; however, he also clearly expressed his expectations that the University of Alberta would provide two platoons for the spring of 1917 as reinforcements for the 196th Western Universities Battalion.[57] *The Gateway* editorialized that the war was not over yet; students needed to fight for freedom, and they would be lauded for their service. For the other side, an article by the YMCA revealed the tensions that revolved around enlisting and what the author called the "Rural Problem."[58] Too many young men were leaving the farm for either urban war jobs or the war. As a result, the rural way of life and, importantly, agricultural production were threatened. The problem in some areas was so acute that the YMCA recruited both men and women from the city to work on farms. Male students still at the university were under great pressure: one side pulling them to enlist; the other side hoping they would stay and serve the rural community from which many had come.

For some students, the introduction of the Military Services Act in August 1917 resolved their dilemma. All men between the ages of 18 and 60 were to be conscripted for active service. Two exemptions applied to university students: if a person were engaged in work deemed of importance to the national interest—farming, for example—or if a person were in the process of being educated or trained in a field that was in the national interest, such as medicine.[59] Although no exact statistics are available as to how many students were exempted from military service, students who met such stringent exemption criteria and chose to remain in Edmonton were likely in a small minority. Further, it is difficult to ascertain how many University of Alberta students were conscripted. By fall 1917, few students were left on campus to be conscripted. Enlistment rates were very high at the university due to a combination of factors: peer and faculty pressure, patriotism, the call of duty, and pressure to conform to societal expectations. One could speculate that the conscription policy ultimately had relatively little impact at the University of Alberta.[60]

Women students were also involved in the war effort on campus. From 1914 to 1916, traditional gender roles limited women's war work to a few specific areas, mostly in support of the men serving overseas. These activities included knitting, preparing care packages, rolling bandages, fundraising, and volunteering with the Canadian Red Cross or other organizations. These were common experiences for women students and women in general in Alberta. Although no large program was in place to train Volunteer Aid Detachment Nurses or Canadian Army Medical Corps Nurses, as was the case at the University of Toronto or McGill University,[61] some women undergraduates learned to shoot rifles and others took a first aid course with Dr. Moshier.[62] A women's group specific to the University of Alberta

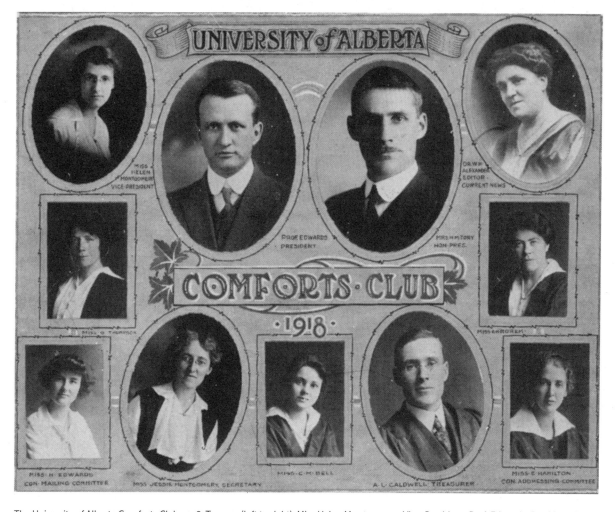

The University of Alberta Comforts Club, 1918. Top row (left to right): Miss Helen Montgomery, Vice-President; Prof. Edwards, President; Dr. W.H. Alexander, Current News; Mrs. H.M. Tory, Hon. Pres.; Miss O. Thompson; Miss C.H. Rorem [?]; Bottom row (left to right): Miss H. Edwards, Cdn Mailing Committee; Miss Jessie Montgomery, Secretary; Miss C.M. Bell; A.L. Caldwell, Treasurer; Miss E. Hamilton, Cdn Addressing Committee. University of Alberta Archives, AN 69-12-76.

was the Soldiers' Comforts Club. Led by Helen Montgomery, it strove to comfort male students on active service.[63] It produced a newsletter that was distributed to the university's soldiers wherever they were stationed. Women's efforts resembled "a productive 'war industry' that generated goods and services that soon became as essential to the war as munitions and soldiers."[64]

From 1917 onward, the nature of the female undergraduate experience changed. With fewer men on campus, especially seniors, women started to fill leadership roles. Katherine McCrimmon was elected president of the Students' Union in 1917. Clara Bell was elected president of the Literary Society in 1918.[65] Moreover, women students were increasingly growing dissatisfied with their gendered roles and the limitations placed on them by society. Outside of the university, women had received the provincial vote in 1916. The Women's Christian Temperance Union succeeded in its drive for prohibition. Women in Alberta were feeling a new sense of empowerment. For women undergraduates, volunteer work failed to satisfy their need to contribute to the war effort. While some women in Alberta joined the Red Cross, and others joined the paid workforce, the lack of opportunities for women students was frustrating. In a revealing article in *The Gateway*, "Women Students and the War," an anonymous member of the Wauneita Society delicately complained:

> Surely, there never was a time before when women had such an opportunity to come forward and show themselves to be of equal value to their country economically and intellectually, as their absent brothers. But the question is, "What can we Wauneitas do"? Are we to stand meekly by with folded hands, "Waiting for the war to cease"? Probably someone will suggest Red Cross work, which must not be neglected, yet are there not some of us who feel we ought to be doing more during a great crisis like this; that we would like to have a share, no matter how small in the making of these great world-wide events? But we cannot all do the heroic and go overseas as Red Cross nurses, or enter munitions factories, and it is for us to "Keep the home fires burning" . . . [We] should spend our every minute in training ourselves for the places which we are to fill in the world. The gallant boys at the front are sacrificing their years of preparation in order that we may have ours. Surely we owe it to them to take this advantage and use it to the utmost, so that in the coming days we may be capable and efficient co-workers in the great business of life.[66]

For many women students, overseas nursing or paid labour options seemed remote and unavailable. Another avenue for channelling women's desire to help their communities and country was encouraging them to study hard and prepare themselves as best as possible for life after university, whether for the workplace or the home. Just as the men conducted military training in order to wage war, women were urged to take maximum advantage of their university experience to prepare for future leadership positions.[67] This thinking was in keeping with the widespread notion at the time that women were agents of social reform and moral uplift.

Without upper-level students to keep social checks on pretentious freshmen, discipline problems arose with younger students. Especially in 1918, the university was faced with an increasingly unruly freshman class. The Board of Governors report elaborated on the reasons for the low level of scholarship and lack of discipline in the male student body. The report cited three factors: first, the student body was more affluent than in past years and had a greater sense of entitlement; second, the older students were away fighting the war and not present to keep the younger students from misbehaving; third, young men were distracted by events concerning the war. Acting president W.A.R. Kerr noted: "I do not mean anything of a real serious nature has occurred, but a careful watch will have to be kept so that we may be sure that a certain irresponsibility which attaches to youth is kept in check and a sense of responsibility is developed."[68]

An instance of the pervasive misbehaviour occurred during 1918, when President Tory was temporarily replaced by Kerr. An editorial in *The Gateway* admonished the student body that its unruliness was a betrayal of trust and disloyal. The students seemed to feel that acting out under the watch of a substitute president was acceptable. A professor had to scold his students "for plain discourtesy" that persisted during his class, and complaints were similarly received "regarding the conduct in the dining room" and "excessive noise in the corridors of the residences."[69] These were serious breaches of student etiquette in 1918.

Postwar Problems

The armistice declared on 11 November 1918 was somewhat anticlimactic because no one was around to celebrate it. The campus had been closed since late October due to the Spanish influenza epidemic, and did not reopen until December 6.[70] The only people on campus were the student and faculty volunteers and others taking care of the sick in Pembina Hall, which had been turned into an isolation hospital.[71] The disruptions associated with the First World War and the influenza pandemic did not end at the university until winter 1919. The student veterans came back from war, preventing a

return to an entirely stable, peaceful campus. Adding a new dynamic to the campus, they were a welcome but troubling aspect of student life. Student veterans were not an unanticipated problem. As early as December 1916, Dr. James C. Miller, university professor and district vocational officer for the Military Hospitals Commission, spoke to business leaders and civic officials about the reabsorption of veterans into civilian life.[72] Writing in late 1917, columnist and former Princess Patricia soldier G.H. Clark foresaw many of the potential problems with returned students: "What exactly will his position be? He will be returning to an environment, associations and responsibilities which are strange to him after a more or less protracted absence."[73] In a subsequent column, he noted that "allowance must be made for the fact that their long absence and the general effect of army life and experiences will make it very difficult for them to settle down for a time."[74]

The veteran presence on campus was first felt in fall 1917 with the return of a few former students. No official welcome was given and no official notice was taken until a banquet in December.[75] Veterans returned in a steady stream throughout 1918, and by November, 57 had resumed their studies.[76] Two distinct cultures clashed: the traditions and customs of campus life conflicted with a culture born in the trenches.

With the support of federal and provincial governments, the university tried to help the veterans transition to civilian life with a number of programs and special curricula. A five-month course in practical agriculture was designed to teach soldiers the basics of farming. In October 1918, the new course was offered every one or two months to accommodate the irregular arrival of veterans. It was organized in cooperation with the Department of Soldiers' Civil Re-establishment, and received financial assistance from both the federal and provincial governments.[77] At the request of the Retail Merchants' Association of Edmonton, the university also provided a short course in retail merchandizing.[78] However, a special summer program was of most importance to those veterans who wanted to resume their undergraduate work. Specifically designed to assist men whose studies were interrupted by enlistment, the provincial Department of Education organized summer courses for high school matriculation and first-year university credits. Starting in May 1919, these courses saved veterans an entire year of academic work and expense.[79]

Despite these programs and all the welcome-back events and speeches, the return of veterans was a considerable disruption to university life, and student veterans had a difficult time readjusting to the university community. A major problem was that veterans did not return all at once but came back at different times of the year. Getting them started in the middle of the term was difficult. Refresher courses were needed, necessitating new curriculum and programs from an already overburdened teaching staff.[80] Veterans had to be reintroduced to the rigours of the classroom, and, in the short term, many struggled. Writing of student veterans and their impact on the university, Tory observed the "disturbance to classes produced by the almost daily return of our men from service overseas . . . [The] constant re-adjustments . . . must react unfavorably on the orderly routine of work."[81]

In fall 1919, freshman initiation reappeared (the one for 1918 had been cancelled because of the influenza outbreak). As student veteran Reginald Lister observed, the sophomores thought they could initiate the veterans but they were badly mistaken.

The veterans would have nothing to do with the initiations, and some bad feelings arose between the two groups.[82] When the veterans refused the initiation, they made a strong, collective statement declaring their uniqueness and separation from the rest of the student body. They were also less willing to accept the university custom of *in loco parentis*. Older, more mature, tired of army discipline, and happy to be alive, veterans wanted to remain a distinct student body. In his report to the Board of Governors, Tory discussed the issue of discipline on campus, admitting: "We had some difficulty at the beginning of the term on account of the demand for social life and the lighter side of college life, and though we admit that some curtailment of such activities in the future will be necessary, we beg to express profound pleasure at the general conduct of the students."[83]

Conclusion

Student life at the University of Alberta was significantly altered by the First World War. The growth of the student body was stunted by the war. Enrollments that had been increasing rapidly previous to the war levelled off in 1916, and then decreased in 1917 and 1918. The student community remained smaller for a longer period of time. The growth of infrastructure and new buildings was limited by a war economy. The atmosphere of campus life changed from one initially of growth and excitement, to one of sombre, grim determination. Leisure time became subservient to the war effort. Instead of carefree playing in athletics or socializing in clubs, students undertook the serious business of training for war, and supporting the war effort financially, materially, and emotionally. Traditions and rituals that had been established prior to the war were absent, or changed during the war. The loss of senior students created a vacuum in leadership and discipline problems with freshmen. During the war, women had a unique, temporary opportunity to rise to prominence on campus. Contravening traditional gender norms, female undergraduates assumed leadership positions. The return of student veterans and their reintegration into the university community proved a difficult transition period full of tension and friction. The war showed, however, the dynamism of academic life and the lived experiences of undergraduate students. The campus was seen to be a place of complex social interaction, not immune to the forces and impact of the society surrounding it and worldwide events. Similar to the off-campus community, the university also contributed to the war effort in important ways, and, in some cases, offered the ultimate sacrifice in brave lives lost.

Notes

1 The authors would like to acknowledge the funding support of the Social Science and Humanities Research Council of Canada. We would also like to thank Jim Franks, Associate University Archivist (University Records), at the University of Alberta Archives for his generous assistance.

2 Rod Macleod, *All True Things: A History of the University of Alberta, 1908–2008* (Edmonton: University of Alberta Press, 2008), 41.

3 University of Alberta Archives (UAA), *Board of Governors Report 1919*, 35.

4 Ibid.

5 Ibid., 4–5.

6 Macleod, *All True Things*, 38–39.

7 Mary Spencer, Kay Dier, and Gordon McIntosh, eds., *Echoes in the Halls: An Unofficial History of the University of Alberta* (Edmonton: University of Alberta Press, 1999), 2.

8 Howard Palmer and Tamara Palmer, *Alberta: A New History* (Edmonton: Hurtig, 1990), 106.

9 UAA, *Board of Governors Report 1915*, 5.

10 E.A. Corbett, *Henry Marshall Tory: A Biography* (Edmonton: University of Alberta Press, 1992), 102.

11 UAA, *Board of Governors Report 1915*, 5.

12 Ibid., *1912*, 7–8.

13 Corbett, *Henry Marshall Tory*, 117.

14 UAA, *Calendar 1915–1916*, 61.

15 Walter H. Johns, *A History of the University of Alberta, 1908–1969* (Edmonton: University of Alberta Press, 1981), 39–40.

16 UAA, "The Initiation," *The Gateway*, 1 October 1912, 36, 38.

17 Student initiation rites were a commonly accepted practice in Canadian universities before the war, and held different and gendered connotations according to ritual and campus. E. Lisa Panayotidis, "Blurring the Boundaries between the Campus and the Community: University Initiations for Women Students in Western Canada, 1920–1950" (paper presented at the annual meeting of the Canadian Historical Association, University of Victoria, British Columbia, 2013).

18 UAA, *The Gateway*, "Sports Column," 1 January 1913, 17; "Editorial," 1 February 1913, 10; "Athletics," 1 April 1914, 48; "Athletics," 1 October 1913, 17.

19 Ellen Schoeck, *I Was There: A Century of Alumni Stories about the University of Alberta, 1906–2006* (Edmonton: University of Alberta Press, 2006), 100.

20 Johns, *History of the University of Alberta*, 45.

21 Ibid., 46.

22 Macleod, *All True Things*, 29.

23 John Herd Thompson, *The Harvests of War: The Prairie West, 1914–1918* (Toronto: McClelland and Stewart, 1978), 23.

24 UAA, "The Military Situation in the University of Alberta since September 1914," *The Gateway*, 1 April 1915, 21–22.

25 See Macleod, *All True Things*, 44–45; Johns, *History of the University of Alberta*, 50, 52–53; and Daniel Thomas

Byers, "The Canadian Officers' Training Corps: Support for Military Training in the Universities of Canada, 1908–1935" (MA thesis, Wilfrid Laurier University, 1993), 77. For a close look at the COTC in an eastern university, see James Leatch, "Academic Militarism: The Canadian Officers' Training Corps at the University of Toronto during the First World War," *Ontario Journal of Higher Education* (1995): 107–24.

26 UAA, "The Military Situation in the University of Alberta since September 1914," *The Gateway*, 1 April 1915, 21–22.

27 Byers, *Canadian Officers' Training Corps*, v.

28 Tim Cook, *At the Sharp End: Canadians Fighting the Great War, 1914–1916* (Toronto: Penguin Group, 2007), 26.

29 Desmond Morton, *When Your Number's Up: The Canadian Soldier in the First World War* (Toronto: Random House of Canada, 1993), 9.

30 Jonathan F. Vance, *Death So Noble: Memory, Meaning, and the First World War* (Vancouver: UBC Press, 1997), 28–29.

31 Tory was particularly sensitive to soldiers' educational needs as is evidenced through his work in establishing the Khaki University, which was designed to provide education for soldiers serving overseas. For a discussion of the Khaki University with its organizational roots at the University of Alberta, see Johns, *History of the University of Alberta*, 61–68; Macleod, *All True Things*, 52–54; and Tim Cook, "From Destruction to Construction: The Khaki University of Canada, 1917–1919," *Journal of Canadian Studies* 37, no. 1 (Spring 2002): 109–43.

32 For just one of many examples see: UAA, "Greetings from President Tory," *The Gateway*, 7 November 1916, 1.

33 Macleod, *All True Things*, 44.

34 UAA, "College and the Job," *The Gateway*, 1 April 1915, 19.

35 UAA, "Editorial," *The Gateway*, 16 December 1915, 4.

36 UAA, "Dead on the Field of Honor," *The Gateway*, 1 November 1915, 1.

37 UAA, "Editorial," *The Gateway*, 9 November 1915, 4.

38 John Macdonald, *The History of the University of Alberta, 1908–1958* (Edmonton: University of Alberta Press, 1958), 20.

39 UAA, *Board of Governors Report 1916*, 4–5.

40 Ibid., 15.

41 Ibid., 8.

42 UAA, "Editorials," *The Gateway*, 16 November 1916, 4; UAA, W.B. Poaps, "On Initiation," *The Gateway*, 23 November 1915, 3.

43 Johns, *History of the University of Alberta*, 56.

44 Schoeck, *I Was There*, 123.

45 "University Sports Held on Saturday," *Edmonton Bulletin*, 30 October 1916, 9.

46 UAA, W. Muir Edwards, "University Athletics," *The Gateway*, 8 November 1917, 1, 10; "Women's Athletics," *The Gateway*, 27 February 1917, 2.

47 UAA, "Editorial," *The Gateway*, 1 February 1916, 4.

48 UAA, "Harold Riddell," *The Gateway*, 22 February 1916, 4.

49 Terry Copp, "The Military Effort, 1914–1918," in *Canada and the First World War: Essays in Honour of Robert Craig Brown*, edited by David Mackenzie (Toronto: University of Toronto Press, 2005), 49–50, 52, 54.

50 J.L. Granatstein, "Conscription in the Great War," in *Canada and the First World War: Essays in Honour of Robert Craig Brown*, edited by David Mackenzie (Toronto: University of Toronto Press, 2005), 64.

51 UAA, *Board of Governors Report 1917*, 11.

52 Ibid., *1916*, 8.

53 Ibid., *1917*, 11.

54 Ibid., 5.

55 UAA, "Editorial," *The Gateway*, 20 February 1917, 4; 27 February 1917, 4.

56 Ibid., 12 December 1916, 4.

57 The 196th (Western Universities) Battalion was created at the request of students and university administrations at the universities of Alberta, British Columbia, Manitoba, and Saskatchewan, who desired to maintain the university identity by fighting

together. They lobbied the minister of militia, who approved the idea, which was initiated in February 1916.

58 UAA, "Enlisting," *The Gateway*, 29 February 1916, 5.

59 Library and Archives Canada, RG 9 III-A-1, Military Service Act, 1917.

60 On 20 April 1918 a federal order-in-council was passed removing some exemptions from the Military Services Act for farmers. This change in policy could have affected a few students. No statistical data are available. However, the issue of farmers' sons being conscripted was not a divisive issue at the University of Alberta, as compared to the protests in Ontario. See W.R. Young, "Conscription, Rural Depopulation, and the Farmers of Ontario, 1917–19," *Canadian Historical Review* 53, no. 3 (1972): 289–320.

61 See, for example: Linda J. Quiney, "'We must not neglect our duty': Enlisting Women Undergraduates for the Red Cross during the Great War," in *Cultures, Communities, and Conflict: Histories of Canadian Universities and War,* edited by Paul Stortz and E. Lisa Panayotidis, 71–94 (Toronto: University of Toronto Press, 2012).

62 UAA, "The Wauneita Society," 1 April 1915, 63; "Ladies," 1 November 1915, 4.

63 Schoeck, *I Was There*, 151.

64 Quiney, "We must not neglect our duty," 72.

65 Johns, *History of the University of Alberta*, 57.

66 UAA, "Women Students and the War," *The Gateway*, 6 February 1917, 6.

67 This desire by women to focus less on war work and more on academic studies was not limited to the University of Alberta, but, for example, was also evident at McGill University. See Quiney, "We must not neglect our duty," 72.

68 UAA, *Board of Governors Report 1918*, 22–23.

69 UAA, "Editorial," *The Gateway*, 10 January 1918, 4; 24 January 1918, 4.

70 "University to Open on Friday December 6th," *Edmonton Bulletin*, 29 November 1918, 3.

71 "Noble Work at Pembina Hall to Save 'Flu' Patients," *Edmonton Bulletin*, 7 November 1918, 4; Macleod, *All True Things*, 57.

72 "Re-absorption in Civil Life of Soldiers," *Edmonton Bulletin*, 11 December 1916, 2.

73 UAA, G.H. Clark, "Problems of the Returned Soldier," *The Gateway*, 29 November 1917, 1, 10.

74 Ibid., 6 December 1917, 1, 10.

75 UAA, "Our Returned Men," *The Gateway*, 1 November 1917, 4.

76 UAA, *Board of Governors Report 1919*, 35.

77 UAA, "Returned Soldiers Agricultural Training," Box 68 9-495 RG3.

78 "University Notes," *Edmonton Bulletin*, 14 April 1919, 3.

79 UAA, *Board of Governors Report 1919*, 28.

80 Ibid., 27.

81 Ibid.

82 Reginald Charles Lister, *My Forty-Five Years on the Campus* (Edmonton: University of Alberta, 1958), 28.

83 UAA, *Board of Governors Report 1920*, 20.

Works Cited

PRIMARY SOURCES

Edmonton Bulletin
The Gateway

Library and Archives Canada (LAC). *196th Battalion (Western Universities)*, RG9 II-B-9; RG24C.
——. Henry Marshall Tory Fonds, MG30 D115.
——. Khaki University, RG9 III-A-2.
——. Military Service Act, 1917, RG9 III-A-1.
University of Alberta Archives (UAA), Edmonton. Henry Marshall Tory Papers.
——. Minutes of the Advisory Committee on Returned Soldier Studies.
——. Report of the Board of Governors 1913–1919.
——. Returned Soldiers Agricultural Training.
——. Senate Meeting Notes 1913–1919.
——. Soldiers' Comforts Club.
——. Student Handbooks 1912–1919.
——. University Calendars 1913–1916, 1918–1919.

SECONDARY SOURCES

Alexander, William Hardy. *The University of Alberta: A Retrospect, 1908–1929*. Edmonton: University of Alberta Press, 1929.

Aytenfisu, Maureen. "The University of Alberta: Objectives, Structure and Role in the Community, 1908–1928." MA thesis, University of Alberta, 1982.

Bilash, Olenka. *Words into Buildings: The University of Alberta 1906–1928*. Ottawa: Society for the Study of Architecture in Canada, 1995.

Bowser, W.E., ed. *The First Fifty Years: A History of the Faculty of Agriculture, 1915–1965*. Edmonton: University of Alberta, Faculty of Agriculture, 1965.

Burke, Sara Z. "Dancing into Education: The First World War and the Roots of Change in Women's Higher Education." In *Cultures, Communities, and Conflict: Histories of Canadian Universities and War*, edited by Paul Stortz and E. Lisa Panayotidis, 95–120. Toronto: University of Toronto Press, 2012.

Byers, Daniel Thomas. "The Canadian Officers' Training Corps: Support for Military Training in the Universities of Canada, 1908–1935." MA thesis, Wilfrid Laurier University, 1993.

Clark, Ralph J. "A History of the Department of Extension at the University of Alberta, 1912–56." PhD diss., University of Alberta, 1985.

Cook, Tim. *At the Sharp End: Canadians Fighting the Great War, 1914–1916*. Toronto: Penguin Group, 2007.

Copp, Terry. "The Military Effort, 1914–1918." In *Canada and the First World War: Essays in Honour of Robert Craig Brown*, edited by David Mackenzie. Toronto: University of Toronto Press, 2005.

Corbett, E.A. *Henry Marshall Tory: A Biography*. Edmonton: University of Alberta Press, 1992.

Currie, Lieutenant General Sir Arthur. "Interim Report on the Operations of the Canadian Corps during the Year 1918." In *Report of the Ministry, Overseas Military Forces of Canada, 1918*. London, UK: Ministry, Overseas Military Forces of Canada, 1919.

Granatstein, J.L. "Conscription in the Great War." In *Canada and the First World War: Essays in Honour of Robert Craig Brown*, edited by David Mackenzie. Toronto: University of Toronto Press, 2005.

Johns, Walter H. *A History of the University of Alberta, 1908–1969*. Edmonton: University of Alberta Press, 1981.

Lister, Reginald Charles. *My Forty-Five Years on the Campus*. Edmonton: University of Alberta, 1958.

Macdonald, John. *The History of the University of Alberta, 1908–1958*. Edmonton: University of Alberta Press, 1958.

Macleod, Rod. *All True Things: A History of the University of Alberta, 1908–2008*. Edmonton: University of Alberta Press, 2008.

McGugan, Angus C. *The First Fifty Years: The University of Alberta Hospital, 1914–1964*. Edmonton: University of Alberta Press, 1964.

Morton, Desmond. *When Your Number's Up: The Canadian Soldier in the First World War*. Toronto: Random House of Canada Ltd., 1993.

Nicholson, Colonel G.W.L. *Canadian Expeditionary Force, 1914–1919: Official History of the Canadian Army in the First World War*. Ottawa: Queen's Printer, 1962.

Palmer, Howard, and Tamara Palmer. *Alberta: A New History*. Edmonton: Hurtig Publishers Ltd., 1990.

Peel, Bruce. *History of the University of Alberta Library, 1909–1979*. Edmonton: University of Alberta, 1979.

Quiney, Linda J. "'We must not neglect our duty': Enlisting Women Undergraduates for the Red Cross during the Great War." In *Cultures, Communities, and Conflict: Histories of Canadian Universities and War*, edited by Paul Stortz and E. Lisa Panayotidis, 71–94. Toronto: University of Toronto Press, 2012.

Reader, W.J. *At Duty's Call: A Study in Obsolete Patriotism*. Manchester, UK: Manchester University Press, 1988.

Schoeck, Ellen. *I Was There: A Century of Alumni Stories about the University of Alberta, 1906–2006*. Edmonton: University of Alberta Press, 2006.

Scott, John William. *The History of the Faculty of Medicine of the University of Alberta, 1913–1963*. Edmonton: University of Alberta, 1963.

Spencer, Mary, Kay Dier, and Gordon McIntosh, eds. *Echoes in the Halls: An Unofficial History of the University of Alberta*. Edmonton: University of Alberta Press, 1999.

Stortz, Paul, and E. Lisa Panayotidis. *Cultures, Communities, and Conflict: Histories of Canadian Universities and War*. Toronto: University of Toronto Press, 2012.

Thompson, John Herd. *The Harvests of War: The Prairie West, 1914–1918*. Toronto: McClelland and Stewart, 1978.

Vance, Jonathan F. *Death So Noble: Memory, Meaning, and the First World War*. Vancouver: UBC Press, 1997.

von Heyking, Amy. *Creating Citizens: History and Identity in Alberta's Schools, 1905 to 1980*. Calgary: University of Calgary Press, 2006.

Wallace, R.C. *The University of Alberta, 1908–1933*. Edmonton: University of Alberta, 1933.

Young, W.R. "Conscription, Rural Depopulation, and the Farmers of Ontario, 1917–19." *Canadian Historical Review* 53, no. 3 (1972): 289–320.

Mobilizing Mount Royal:
Capturing Campus Contributions to the Great War

JARETT HENDERSON

On the eve of the First World War, Mount Royal College was advertised in *Henderson's Directory* as a Calgary institution that provided a "first class college education to young people of both sexes, under the best influences, and a moderate cost."[1] The school's commitment to coeducation was enshrined in the provincial Act that had created the college four years earlier, in December 1910. According to the Act to Incorporate Mount Royal College, Mount Royal was "an institution of learning for the education of youths of both sexes."[2] Less than a year later, students first filled the halls of a red-brick building, popularly known as "The Barn." By the end of the 1911–12 academic year, nearly 200 students had enrolled.[3] For all students at the college, a "first class" education entailed courses in history, geography, religion, and languages, as well as household and domestic science for the girls. Both young men and women played hockey and joined campus clubs. In 1913, and perhaps because they were restricted from enrolling in the college's "public speaking and diction" course, female Mount Royal students took to the streets and marched for women's suffrage. Prior to the outbreak of the war, in 1914, there were nearly equal numbers of male and female students enrolled. Of the 179 students who enrolled at Mount Royal in 1911–12, roughly 25 percent were from locations outside Calgary.

This essay is rooted in archival research done by myself and students in History 1100 (An Introduction to History) at Mount Royal University (MRU). The course aims to teach undergraduate history majors historical methodology through a focus on the history of Mount Royal as an educational institution. Students are required to conduct original research in the university's archives, organize and interpret the data, and make inferences about Mount Royal's knowable history. In the process, many discover that what they want to know cannot be known definitively. Such discoveries—or lack thereof—encourage students to question the nature of the archival material available to them, and the historical consequences that such archival omissions have on the historian's ability to truly *know* the past. Based on a close analysis of materials housed primarily in the MRU Archives, it appears that the Great War shifted attention at the college away from *both* male and female students to what were seen as

(left) The official opening of Mount Royal in 1911. Rev. Dr. Kerby, the college principal, is dressed in his academic regalia on the right. Mount Royal University Archives; (right) These young Mount Royal women marched for suffrage in 1913. Mount Royal University Archives.

the more significant wartime sacrifices of its male "soldier-boy" students. In fact, the lack of available archival materials makes it difficult to capture the campus contributions made by those young female students who attended Mount Royal during the Great War.[4] The masculine nature of the archive—a consequence of contemporaries ascribing a higher value to the wartime contributions made by male students—means that this chapter focuses primarily on the young men whose wartime contributions were considered more worthy of comment, documentation, and preservation.[5]

Students, faculty, and staff at Mount Royal College, like their contemporaries in other parts of Alberta and Canada, experienced the Great War in ways that were simultaneously local and imperial, generational and gendered.[6] Knowledge about the war was cultivated in college classrooms and clubs.

Students in history classes at Mount Royal learned about both Canada and the British Empire, with lessons that reiterated the importance of the war to national and imperial reputations. The student executive of the Mount Royal Literary Society announced, in December 1913, that "the subject of the essay for 1914 shall be: Canada's Duty to the Empire."[7] Two years later, the student-run newspaper, the *Chinook*, reported that Professor Rosborough gave to the members of the Literary Society "a most interesting and instructive map study of the present war."[8] Miss E. Dixon, who arrived in Calgary from Toronto and began teaching at Mount Royal during the war, quickly became the "Honorary President" of the Literary Society. In 1917, the society offered a book prize to the Mount Royal student who composed the best essay on the subject "Why the Allies Must Win." The society also provided the student body with various opportunities to discuss the war, although no record of what they covered remains. According to the *Chinook,* Miss I. Morgan presented a paper on "The Causes of War," and Mr. R. Huff and Miss Orpha King papers on "The Colonies and the War" and "Austria-Hungary, France, and the Kaiser," respectively.[9] That such attention to the war prevailed at Mount Royal is not surprising, nor is the national imperialist sentiment promoted through such events and activities. Yet, as Mary Chaktsiris reminds us, it is important to acknowledge that not *all* students would have shared such sentiments.[10] The 1914 Christmas issue of the *Chinook,* for example, urged students to "hope for a speedy cessation of the awful carnage that has over-clouded Europe."[11] This unnamed contributor to the *Chinook* may have lamented the human costs of war but did not argue that the war itself ought not to be waged.

Mount Royal's first principal, Rev. Dr. George Kerby, makes only occasional references to the war in the archival documentation that remains. Yet, photographs of Kerby published in Mount Royal's *Academic Calendars*, as well as in the *Chinook*, provide snapshots of how he and, by extension, the college mobilized for war. During Kerby's 30-year tenure as principal, official photographs only twice captured him not dressed in the academic regalia of a graduate of Victoria University, the Methodist and liberal arts college in Toronto where he had studied in the late 1880s.[12] On both occasions, this change occurred when Canada was at war.[13] In 1917, just months after Kerby had been appointed Chief Recruitment Officer for Military District No. 13, a photograph of him outfitted in military uniform was published in the *Chinook*. In his dual role as Chief Recruitment Officer and college principal, Kerby oversaw the recruitment of young men in a territory that stretched from the

Alberta foothills to the igneous rock of northwestern Ontario, while remaining a model of duty, loyalty, and citizenship—all important aspects of early twentieth-century manliness and militarism.[14]

Kerby's commitment to the war effort was not lost on the editors of the *Chinook*, who not only published a full-page photo of the principal, but also

Kerby, dressed in military uniform. During the Great War Kerby exchanged his academic regalia for a military uniform. 1917. Mount Royal University Archives.

reported, early in 1917: "During the past few months, since our last issue of the *Chinook* several members from the school have joined the colors, to fight for the right in this great world-wide conflict." Although the paper made no mention of Kerby's recent military appointment, it likely did not have to for the image of Kerby in military uniform greeted anyone who opened that issue of the *Chinook*. It did note the contributions of others at the school. The *Chinook* commended Major Bennett, the Head of the Commercial Department, as well as Oswald McWilliams, Ivan Linton, Max Palmer, and Harry Clarke, for the manly sacrifice that they had so recently made "for the Empire, and the good of the world."[15] Clarke was praised for working as a stenographer in Red Deer, while McWilliams and Linton had enlisted with the 191st and 196th Battalions, respectively. Max Palmer had returned to Toronto, where he was training at the Canadian National Exhibition grounds. These were considered wartime contributions worthy of recording.

The nature of the archival record also makes it impossible to know if Kerby's military appointment influenced male Mount Royal students to enlist. What is knowable, however, is that nearly 20 percent of the male students who enrolled in 1911 also enlisted to fight for Canada during the war. Leonard Gaetz and John Wilder were two students who had completed the double-sided government forms – known as attestation papers – that had to be filled out before one could fight for King and Country. The form asked about John and Leonard's bodies, beliefs, and prior military experience.[16] Everett Boyd Jackson Fallis, who enrolled at Mount Royal in 1914, informed his recruitment officer that he had previously been a lieutenant in the Toronto Cadets.[17] Ewart Cropper, who arrived in September 1914, had served as an officer in the Calgary Cadets

before enlisting later that semester.[18] Other students such as Wesley Steinhaur and Stanley Sweetman had drilled with the Canadian Officers' Training Corps,[19] while John Hawley Ross, who enlisted in Halifax on 23 August 1915, listed that his previous military experience was with the Queen's Own Rifles.[20] At least one Mount Royal student, George Alfred Sales, had worked at the Banff internment camp prior to enlisting on 20 November 1916.[21] Although it remains unclear if Kerby or campus sentiment were important factors in why Fallis, Steinhauer, Sweetman, and Sales decided to enlist, the mandatory drill and Mount Royal Cadet Corps certainly encouraged others to join.

Some young Mount Royal men who enlisted between 1914 and 1918 identified the college's cadet corps as having prepared them for war. Plans had been made to establish a separate, female cadet corps, but the focus on male students during the war meant that this separate corps never materialized. When 20-year-old Albert Edwin Kerslake enlisted on 22 November 1916, he testified that he had one year's experience with "Mt. Royal Cadets." Kerslake was not alone; since 1911, when Mount Royal opened, young men and women were expected to perform drill for at least two half-hours per week.[22] In May 1914 the young men of the cadet corps, which had been created earlier in the semester, were the first cadets in the province of Alberta to be inspected by Major William Outhit. On Friday, 15 May 1914, 40 young men stood along Seventh Avenue and performed their manoeuvres. The commanders, Percy Smith and Alfred Sales (both would later enlist), "took charge of their respective half-companies for rifle exercise and acquitted themselves splendidly, giving their command clearly and sharply without hesitation."[23] Although the *Chinook* reported that the event went off without a hitch, the paper lamented (above) The attestation paper of Mount Royal student, George Alfred Sales. Source: Library Archives Canada; (below) The Mount Royal College Cadet Corps is inspected on Friday, 15 May 1914. Lieutenant Bennett, instructor, is in the foreground and Rev. Dr. Kerby is at the extreme right. Mount Royal University Archives.

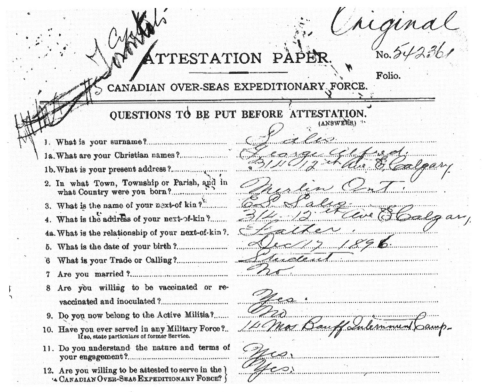

that the young men did not have regulation uniforms. Such uniforms, the editor opined, would remind the young men of the discipline and alertness required by drill, and curtail such "regrettable incidents" as the gum chewing that had occurred among the ranks. He noted further: "It is hoped that the College Board will see their way clear to assist the boys to procure [uniforms] in the near future." Pleased overall with the inspection, the *Chinook* boasted that England had no reason to tremble, as there "are so many cadets from the different organizations who will be ready to do their duty to the British Empire."[24] Of the young men who participated in this first inspection, and whose names can be found

in archival documents, Morley Johnston, Franklin McKay, and Harry Blow all enlisted.

If cadets inspired male students to enlist, the rigid physical culture promoted at the college, and captured in team photographs, vividly reveals that campus contributions to the war were also linked to the physical. In fact, many of those who played on Mount Royal College sports teams would later go to war together. Fortunately, the majority returned to families and friends; some, however, did not. On Monday, 29 May 1916, the *Calgary Daily Herald* reported that Cecil Duke had been "killed in action." The photograph of Duke included with the news of his death had been cropped from the

(left) This image of Cecil Duke was published in the *Calgary Herald* on 29 May 1916. It is cropped from Mount Royal's first boys hockey team photo (1911–12). Peel's Prairie Provinces; (right) The young men on Mount Royal's first lacrosse team. Only five of those pictured did not enlist in the Great War. Mount Royal University Archives.

KILLED IN ACTION

CECIL DUKE
Well known Calgary athlete, whose death at the front is reported.

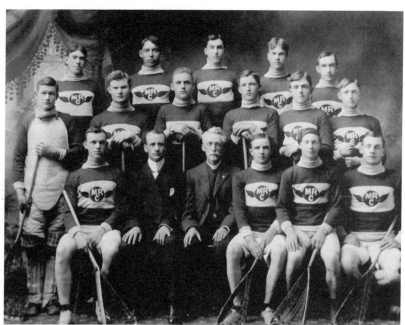

1911–12 Mount Royal boys hockey team picture. The article noted that Duke, a remarkable athlete, was also the "third fatal casualty recorded on the Mount Royal Roll of Honour. Two other students, James Arnell and Hawley Ross [had also been] reported killed in action." The article concluded with thanks to the nearly 40 young men from the college who had, by May 1916, gone forth to "do their bit for the Empire."[25]

A photograph of the 1911–12 lacrosse team originally published in the *Chinook* captures just how many Mount Royal athletes went to war. After August 1914, of the 17 men pictured, 12 became directly involved in Canada's war effort. From just this one team, 10 young men (of whom one was Cecil Duke) enlisted to fight. Of the enlistees, Stanley Sweetman, Jay Gould, and Cecil Duke all resided in Calgary, while Wesley Steinhauer, Charles and Milford Boucher, Fred Riley, Leonard Gaetz, and John Wilder heralded from Morley, Bottrell, Airdrie, Red Deer, and High River, respectively. In addition to the male students captured in this image, the two men in suits, Professor W.G. Bennett, who served as the team coach, and the Reverend Dr. Kerby, the college principal, had each made direct contributions to Canada's war effort. It was Bennett who had, after his successful mustering of the Mount Royal Cadets in 1914, relocated to Red Deer where he took command of the 191st Battalion. This photograph is striking for it illustrates that nearly 70 percent of the young men from this lacrosse team chose to enlist. Cecil Duke was the sole member of the 1911–12 team to be killed in action.

Those Mount Royal students who did not, could not, or chose not to enlist would have been well aware of the costs and consequences of war. When the *Chinook* reported in January 1917 that the list of

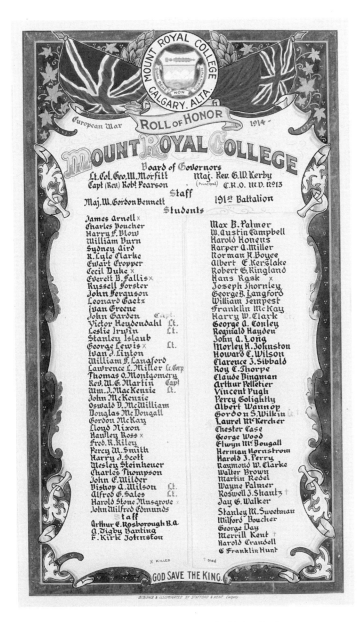

Mount Royal "Roll of Honour" begun in 1914 and added to for the duration of the Great War. Mount Royal University Archives.

names on the honour roll was increasing, over 40 young Mount Royal men had already been mobilized.[26] It is not clear how the passing of conscription later that year affected enrollments at the college, but, by the time the war ended, 79 Mount Royal students, 4 instructors, and 3 members of the college's board of governors had answered the call of war. Their names were recorded on Mount Royal's "Roll of Honour." Of those students honoured, 10 attained a rank higher than private. The same number, according to the crosses and "xs" of red ink on the illuminated version of the honour roll, were killed or died while in service. "To the friends of such," read an article in the *Chinook* that accompanied a reprint of the honour roll, "we extend the sympathy of the student body of Mount Royal."[27]

After November 1918, Kerby once again appeared in college photographs dressed in his academic regalia, an acknowledgment that he and Mount Royal College had begun their transition back to civilian life. It was only once the war had ended that Kerby expressed his opinion on the conflict itself. In the Easter 1919 issue of the *Chinook,* Kerby somberly reflected on the human cost and social consequences of the war, writing:

> Once more it is our privilege to welcome
> the students, new and old, to Mount Royal
> College. We use the word welcome in a deeper
> sense than ever before. The War is over.
> The daily casualty list has ceased. On every
> ship and train are the returning boys. Soon
> all, save those who sleep "In Flanders Field
> where Poppies blow," will be home. Living
> or dead, these brave spirits have blazed out a
> new trail for Canada.[28]

For Kerby, the war provided an opportunity for a *new* Canada; but the "call of a new Canada" could only be met if the same "spirit of sacrifice, courage, and determination" that had been evident among those in uniform was embraced by all "our young people." That new Canada valued education and human endeavour, and offered a "new outlook to life." The ultimate hope of postwar Canada, declared Kerby, "was never so centered in her boys and girls as today."[29]

By locating hope in young women and men, Kerby revealed his belief that war and reconstruction would lead to a new day for Canada. He also reaffirmed for the public—and the archival record—that "youths of both sexes" had a place and a knowable history at Mount Royal College. That the Great War had recalibrated the archives not only makes it difficult for students of history to track the experiences of young Mount Royal women at the college between 1914 and 1919, it also suggests that the wartime contributions of young Mount Royal men, and, by extension, their histories, were considered more worthy of preservation, documentation, and comment. It is certainly possible that young women such as Susie Green, Ada Irwin, and Janet Brown—as female kin in families with male relatives at war—performed citizenship by voting for the first time in the 1917 federal election.[30] It is also likely that young women from Mount Royal, like their counterparts at the University of Alberta and elsewhere, joined voluntary associations such as the Red Cross, the IODE, and the YWCA that provided women across Canada the opportunity to put their lessons in imperial domesticity to the test through patriotic war work.[31] Yet it remains near impossible to know such things for certain because the archives that remain are silent about such matters of history. Such an observation is not meant to dismiss the campus contributions made by boys and young men from Mount Royal during the war, but rather to illustrate the very real ways that the gendered nature of the archive can limit the historian's ability to capture how male *and* female Mount Royal students were mobilized during the Great War.

Notes

My sincere thanks to Jeff Keshen for encouraging me to write this; Pat Roome and Scott Murray for having digitized some of the material I draw on; Alice Swabey for her assistance tracking down provincial legislation; and Carol Shepstone for granting me access to the Mount Royal University Archives. Scott Murray, Mike Wilton, and students in History 1100 read and commented on parts of this chapter for which I am thankful. Thanks also to Cathryn Crocker for taking the pictures of the archival documents used in this chapter.

1   *Henderson's Directory*, 1914, 138, URL: http://peel. library.ualberta.ca/bibliography/2961.9/138.html.

2   *Statutes of the Province of Alberta*, An Act to Incorporate Mount Royal College, 1910, 233, URL: http://www. ourfutureourpast.ca/law/page.aspx?id=2956121.

3   *Academic Calendar, 1912–13*, 46–50, Mount Royal University Archives [hereafter MRUA].

4   For an excellent examination of similar themes at other institutions see: Paul Stortz and E. Lisa Panayotidis, eds., *Cultures, Communities, and Conflict: Histories of Canadian Universities and War* (Toronto: University of Toronto Press, 2012).

5   James M. Pitsula, "'Manly Heroes': The University of Saskatchewan and the First World War," in *Cultures, Communities, and Conflict*, edited by Stortz and Panayotidis, 121–45.

6   See, for example, the essays published in Jarett Henderson and Jeff Keshen, eds. *Canada's Great War,*

7   MRUA, *Chinook*, 1913, 10.

8   Ibid., 1915, 21.

9   Ibid., 1917, 22–23.

10 Mary Chaktsiris, "Not Unless Necessary," in *Canada's Great War, 100 Years On*, edited by Henderson and Keshen.

11 MRUA, *Chinook*, 1914, 7.

12 Michael Owen, "'By Contact and by Contagion': George W. Kerby, 1860–1944," *Vitae Scholasticae* 10, nos. 1 and 2 (1991): 131–57; and Michael Owen, "Rev. Dr. George W. Kerby: Evangelist for the Home and School," *Alberta Journal of Educational Research* (1993): 477–93.

13 Thanks to Cliff Leeson and Michael Macdonald for drawing my attention to this while they were conducting their archival research for HIST 1100.

14 Mark Moss, *Manliness and Militarism: Educating Young Boys in Ontario for War* (Toronto: University of Toronto Press, 2001).

15 MRUA, *Chinook*, 1917, 17.

16 For an excellent analysis of these records, see Tim Cook, "'He was determined to go': Underage Soldiers in the Canadian Expeditionary Force," *Histoire sociale/ Social History* 41, no. 81 (May 2008): 41–74.

17 The originals are available electronically on the Library and Archives Canada [hereafter LAC] website; copies can be found in the MRUA, First World War File. LAC, RG 150, Accession 1992-93/166, Box 2986 – 25.

18 Ibid., Box 2160 – 43.

19 Ibid., Box 9406 – 32; Box 9464 – 16.

20 Ibid., Box 8480 – 41.

21 Ibid., Box 8614 – 36.

22 A.B. McKillop, "Marching as to War: Elements of Ontario Undergraduate Culture, 1880–1914," in *Youth, University, and Canadian Society: Essays in Social History of Higher Education*, edited by Paul Axelrod and John G. Reid (Montreal and Kingston: McGill-Queen's University Press, 1989), 45–93.

23 MRUA, *Chinook*, 1914, 17–18.

100 Years On. Special issue, *Histoire sociale/Social History* 47, no. 94 (June 2014).

24 Ibid.

25 *Calgary Herald*, 29 May 1916.

26 Michael Hayden, "Why Are All Those Names on the Wall? The University of Saskatchewan and World War I," *Saskatchewan History* 58, no. 2 (2006): 4–14.

27 MRUA, *Chinook*, 1919, 19. Today Mount Royal University awards scholarships named in honour of each of these individuals.

28 Ibid., 1919, 5.

29 Ibid.

30 Tarah Brookfield, "Divided by the Ballot Box: The Montreal Council of Women and the 1917 Election," *Canadian Historical Review* 89, no. 4 (2008): 473–501.

31 Linda J. Quiney, "'We Must Not Neglect Our Duty': Enlisting Women Undergraduates for the Red Cross during the Great War," in *Cultures, Communities, and Conflict: Histories of Canadian Universities and War*, edited by Stortz and Panayotidis, 71–94; Sarah Glassford and Amy Shaw, eds., *A Sisterhood of Suffering and Service: Women and Girls of Canada and Newfoundland during the First World War* (Vancouver: UBC Press, 2012); and Adele Perry, "Women, Gender, and Empire," in *Canada and the British Empire*, edited by Phillip Buckner (Oxford: Oxford University Press, 2008), 220–39.

Works Cited

PRIMARY SOURCES

Calgary Herald
Henderson's Directory

Library and Archives Canada. RG 150, Attestation Papers, Accession 1992–93/166.

Mount Royal University Archives, Calgary. *Academic Calendars*, 1911–1919.

——. *The Chinook*, 1911–1919.

——. *Statutes of Alberta*.

SECONDARY SOURCES

Brookfield, Tarah. "Divided by the Ballot Box: The Montreal Council of Women and the 1917 Election." *Canadian Historical Review* 89, no. 4 (2008): 473–501.

Cook, Tim. "'He was determined to go': Underage Soldiers in the Canadian Expeditionary Force." *Histoire sociale/Social History* 41, no. 81 (May 2008): 41–74.

Glassford, Sarah, and Amy Shaw, eds. *A Sisterhood of Suffering and Service: Women and Girls of Canada and Newfoundland during the First World War*. Vancouver: UBC Press, 2012.

Hayden, Michael. "Why Are All Those Names on the Wall? The University of Saskatchewan and World War I." *Saskatchewan History* 58, no. 2 (2006): 4–14.

Henderson, Jarett, and Jeff Keshen, eds. *Canada and the Great War, 100 Years On*. Special issue, *Histoire sociale/Social History* 47, no. 94 (June 2014).

McKillop, A.B. "Marching as to War: Elements of Ontario Undergraduate Culture, 1880–1914." In *Youth, University, and Canadian Society: Essays in Social History of Higher Education*, edited by Paul Axelrod and John G. Reid, 75–93. Montreal and Kingston: McGill-Queen's University Press, 1989.

Moss, Mark. *Manliness and Militarism: Educating Young Boys in Ontario for War*. Toronto: University of Toronto Press, 2001.

Owen, Michael. "'By Contact and by Contagion': George W. Kerby, 1860–1944." *Vitae Scholasticae* 10, nos. 1 and 2 (1991): 131–57.

——. "Rev. Dr. George W. Kerby: Evangelist for the Home and School." *Alberta Journal of Educational Research* (1993): 477–93.

Perry, Adele. "Women, Gender, and Empire." In *Canada and the British Empire*, edited by Phillip Buckner, 220–39. Oxford, UK: Oxford University Press, 2008.

Stortz, Paul, and E. Lisa Panayotidis, eds. *Cultures, Communities, and Conflict: Histories of Canadian Universities and War*. Toronto: University of Toronto Press, 2012.

Under Siege: The CEF Attack on the RNWMP Barracks in Calgary, October 1916

P. WHITNEY LACKENBAUER

Calgary last night was the scene of one of the most serious riots in its history. Several hundred soldiers from Sarcee camp after making a violent demonstration in front of the city police headquarters proceeded to the barracks of the Mounted Police and did considerable damage to the building and its contents. During the melee one soldier . . . was shot and seriously wounded, another soldier was beaten up and a mounted policeman was badly mauled. The central part of the city was kept in a ferment from 8 o'clock to 10 o'clock, and that casualties were not more numerous and damage far greater was in large measure to the forbearance of the police, civic and mounted, and the influence of General Cruikshank and the officers who arrived when the trouble was at its height—almost immediately after the shooting of the soldier.

—*Calgary Daily Herald*, 12 October 1916

It was almost as though there was something in the air in 1916, at the beginning of the third year of the First World War. From Perth, New Brunswick, to Calgary, Alberta, Canadian soldiers took to the streets and battled with local authorities on "various patriotic pretexts."[1] These wartime riots varied in degrees of seriousness, but the sheer number of episodes and men involved bespoke a serious problem. Most of the rioting soldiers were new recruits, yet to embrace the strict discipline and hierarchical control of military life. These were young men willing, if not anxious, to quell the boredom of domestic training and take action. Calgary, in both frequency and severity, was one of the main centres of discontent. Although the military maintained that the various units stationed in Calgary were under control, media and police testimonies indicated that the military officers demonstrated a chronic inability to enforce discipline over their troops, and that non-commissioned officers seemed to lead the mobs. The ensuing destruction was a product of miscommunication and military mismanagement.

Western Canada proved to be the best recruiting ground of the Canadian Expeditionary Force (CEF) in the early years of the war. During the last three months of 1915 alone, 23 battalions raised 21,897

Interior view of the saloon riot at the Riverside Hotel located at Fourth Street SE and Boulevard Avenue, Calgary, AB, 19 February 1916. The riot was supposedly started because the owner was German (*Calgary Daily Herald*, 13 February 1916, 14). Photographer/Illustrator: W.J. Oliver. Glenbow Archives, NA-2365-16.

men. New battalions were formed to handle the enthusiastic throngs of patriotic citizens, and Calgary itself prospered as a result. The city had been made the headquarters of Military District 13 in 1905, and thus served as a centre for concentration under Sir Sam Hughes's mobilization scheme. Veteran militia officer Brigadier E.A. Cruikshank, a man known for his strict discipline and intelligence, oversaw Calgary's burgeoning ranks of aspiring citizen soldiers. The presence of a large military camp teeming with young, thirsty men pleased local business owners, especially hotel owners.[2]

The first rash of riotous activity in Alberta was launched on anti-enemy alien grounds. Canadian society was hypersensitive to perceived "foreign" threats by the winter of 1916, and nativist expression was swirling in the media—and in the highest political arenas. On consecutive evenings in mid-February 1916, hundreds of members of four battalions billeted in Calgary destroyed the two White Lunch restaurants and the Riverside Hotel, on the basis of rumours that had linked the establishments with sympathy for the enemy. Although the military refused to acknowledge its responsibility for the soldier riots, some members of the media and the local police remained unconvinced. Calgary Police Chief Alfred Cuddy was critical of the local military officials, whom he felt had been guilty of inaction in preventing disorder and were thus culpable for the damage to the Riverside if not the White Lunch restaurants. The owners of the establishments were never reimbursed for damages, which the government consistently refused to acknowledge on narrow legal grounds.[3]

Themes that emerged from the courts of inquiry (established by the district military commander to look into the disconcerting behaviour) were the roles of camaraderie and liquor in inspiring participation and relieving inhibitions. The "mob" mentality may have been provoked by anti-alien sentiments, but the participation of individual soldiers was often driven by the more sanguine inducements of comradeship and curiosity. In a show of group solidarity, witnesses withheld individual names (both of fellow soldiers involved in the riots and civilian "friends" who got them liquor) to preserve anonymity. The soldiers stuck together, and it appeared that they could "stonewall" the authorities and get away with just about anything. Furthermore, the city's subsequent decision to fire all civic employees of "enemy alien" descent and offer jobs to returned soldiers seemed to validate the mob action. The recalcitrant

Interior of the Riverside Hotel showing damage, 10 February 1916. Glenbow Archives, NA-3965-11.

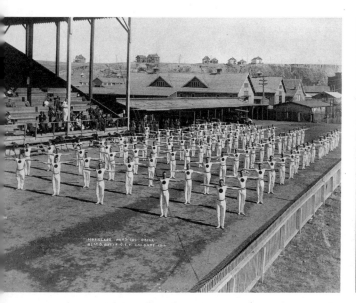 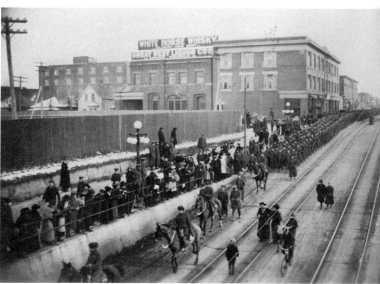

(left) Number 1 physical drill, 82nd Overseas Battalion, Canadian Expeditionary Force, at the Calgary exhibition grounds, 1916. Photographer/Illustrator: W.V. Ring. Glenbow Archives, NA-3171-19; (right) The 56th Battalion, Canadian Expeditionary Force, parading on Second Street and Ninth Avenue SE, before going overseas, Calgary, 1914. Glenbow Archives, NA-988-1

soldiers had indeed succeeded in affecting change in desired directions.[4]

For those citizen-soldiers who were undoubtedly at the crime scenes, drunkenness appeared to have been an acceptable means of denying participation and of evading some responsibility for one's actions. Intoxication was a particularly common defence voiced at the inquiry into the Riverside Hotel incident. For example, Private H.H. Thompson of the 82nd Battalion was caught with a box of cigars that were obviously stolen from the hotel; he claimed that a soldier gave these to him while he was "under the influence of liquor." Private Thomas Howarth of the 56th followed the crowd to the Riverside after having had a half dozen drinks at the Alberta Hotel and was arrested for being drunk and disorderly; like others

who drank before the riot he said he remembered little of the evening's subsequent events.[5]

Of course, drunken disorderliness was an offence, and some soldiers were convicted of crimes committed under the influence. Heavy drinking, however, has always been an element of army culture. If official authorities demanded conformity to the regulations, the informal relations between soldiers stressed quite the opposite. Tim Cook, in an article on the social functions of rum overseas, has demonstrated that the "demon rum" was an important source of morale and courage overseas and played a crucial social function.[6] In the domestic context, alcohol-induced boisterous behaviour, followed by amnesia, was not a defence to get a soldier absolved of all blame for his actions; but drinking was nevertheless a vice to which most soldiers seemed to succumb.

In the summer of 1916, however, provincial liquor laws became much less forgiving, and "completely altered the social fabric of the province."[7] The year before, after an intense crusade, prohibitionists had succeeded in convincing Albertans to outlaw the "devil's brew" in a referendum vote. The Alberta Temperance Act came into force on 1 July 1916. Still, the consumption of alcohol was not eradicated; as James Gray noted, "there were enough loopholes left to enable a determined drunk to drink almost without pause." While historians have been careful to stress that too few police were provided to enforce the temperance regulations, there certainly were arrests.[8] And soldiers stationed in Calgary soon perceived themselves to be an easy and unfair target. In early October 1916, an employee of a downtown cabaret bar allegedly made an uncomplimentary remark to several patrons in khaki, proclaiming that he was there "to serve gentlemen and not soldiers." The report quickly spread, and several hundred soldiers gathered at the bar that night, whooping and shouting "derisively." The chief of police showed up with as many officers as he could assemble, as did the military police. Eventually the proprietor of the bar appeared in the middle of the street, apologized for any wrongdoing, and said he would "do anything" to avoid inciting trouble. The crowd, apparently satisfied, marched off when a "band of the kilties," bagpipes blaring, passed by.[9]

On October 11, the seeds of a more serious disorder were sown. At 11:00 a.m., five men of the 211th Battalion were convicted by the police magistrate of Calgary for offences under the Liquor Act. (Three days earlier, another member of the regiment had been similarly convicted.) The punishment imposed was the minimum allowed by statute: a $50 fine, or 30 days in jail. Accordingly, as the fines could not be paid on a soldier's wages, the city police handed the prisoners over to the Royal North-West Mounted Police (RNWMP). They were to be escorted to the provincial jail at Lethbridge to serve their prison terms.[10] At noon that day, the news of the convictions reached Sarcee Camp and a movement began to take shape, designed to make a demonstration in favour of the detained soldiers and, if necessary, to obtain their release by force.

The 211th Battalion was a unique entity in western Canada. As one of five American Legion battalions raised in Canada, it recruited Americans anxious to join the war effort through a headquarters in Vancouver prior to mobilization at Calgary. Although the original concept had these battalions based on the enlistment of US citizens, this was later expanded to include naturalized Americans and Canadians of American parentage.

Discipline in the American Legion battalions was a problem from the onset, and continuous delays in deployment overseas and high desertion rates frustrated the units and "led to low morale and frequent incidents of alcohol abuse and fist fights." Despite the American Legion brigade leader's policy of temperance, drunkenness was clearly a "chronic problem" in other Legion battalions, and quite possibly in the 211th as well.[11]

Some of these soldiers billeted in the city were convinced that even the minimum punishment levied on the detained soldiers was unacceptable. In their view, the prosecuted soldiers had been unjustly treated and were discriminated against. Had they not enrolled in the United States to fight for the King, and now found themselves in jail according to new laws foreign to their nation?

Sergeant Cohen of the 218th explained that he knew there was going to be trouble the night of October 11 based on

> an idea [the soldiers] were going to get a certain person named Tom Turner and knock his block off . . . because he framed up with his stool pigeons to supply five soldiers with one bottle of whiskey and then went and got them all convicted—the whole five for one bottle of whiskey. [A]nd a week before that I heard that they were going to do this as this same man arrested a soldier of the 211th for drunkenness . . . That started the whole scrap according to what rumours I could pick up around town.[12]

Lance Corporal Webster heard remarks that the soldiers had been arrested "for being drunk on stuff that could be bought at any drug store in the City." Rumours such as these quickly spread through the closed, intimate environment of the military camp at Sarcee. Even if there was no coordinated leadership, a large number of men presumably went into town to prepare for an attempted release of the prisoners, and several buglers took their bugles with them. By 6:15 p.m., Police Chief Cuddy suspected that something was going to happen, and had his day staff all remain for night duty. However, he did not call the RNWMP to warn them of any potential problem until much later.[13]

At about 7:30 p.m., buglers in front of the Canadian Pacific Railway station on Ninth Avenue sounded a "call in" for the local troops. Between two and three hundred soldiers fell into two ranks, and an excited throng proceeded toward city police headquarters. Upon their arrival, they sprawled out on the street in front of the building. They shouted and booed, sang and cheered, interspersing their clamour with threats and demands that the five men sentenced that morning be released. One unidentified soldier addressed the crowd:

> All of you who care anything for justice, join us in getting these men out . . . These men are brave soldiers and good citizens who have committed no crime. They were not even accused of being drunk. The only charge against them was that they smelled of liquor and for that they are treated as criminals and sent down for 30 days. Do you call that justice? These men have volunteered to fight for you: some of them have crossed the border to fight for you people, and is that the way they should be treated?

Another added that "it was a shame that a civilian could be had up for the same thing and only get a $5.00 fine and a soldier getting only $1.10 a day and fighting for his Country, was given $50.00 and costs, when they knew he couldn't pay it so were given 30 days." Several called for city police detective Tom Turner, the man who had arrested the soldiers and was described as a crook and a coward. The mob also questioned: "Why didn't he [Turner] join the colours?"[14] A small force of uniformed police prevented an attack upon the building by opposing the growing mob on the front steps. Chief Cuddy informed the throng of soldiers that the prisoners were not in the police building, but a disbelieving crowd continued to intimidate the authorities. Several projectiles were thrown, and two windows at the police station were broken by a dummy cartridge and a stone.

Sergeant C.C. Campbell of the 211th Battalion, the de facto spokesman for the soldiers, demanded that some of his men go in and verify that the prisoners were indeed not in the building. The chief constable agreed, and two parties of three men proceeded to inspect the cells, where they discovered that the men whom they sought were not there. Sergeant Campbell then stomped upstairs to the chief secretary's office and telephoned the RNWMP barracks. Alleging to speak as a representative of the recruiting office, he inquired as to whether any men from the 211th were being detained in the barracks. As soon as Campbell received an affirmative reply, he returned to the front steps. He stepped up on a wall arch and, leaning against a pillar about fourteen feet above the ground, he proclaimed the prisoners' real location to the crowd of soldiers.[15]

The soldiers were told to "fall in," resumed their "rough formation with bugles blowing," and tramped along Seventh Avenue toward their new destination—the RNWMP barracks. An officer with the garrison military police tried to intervene, but he was shouted down and his pleadings to disperse summarily discarded. The crowd gathered on the lawn around the Fourth Street entrance to the barracks; they now included some two hundred civilians, as well as about three hundred members of the 211th, 218th, and 233rd Battalions.

Several non-commissioned military officers demanded the release of the prisoners, amidst shouts of: "We want justice!" and "Our comrades are inside and we want to get them released!" Inspector Newson informed them that this would be impossible without a higher court order, and promised to telephone a local judge. He did so, but the crowd did not wait for a response.[16] At about 8:45 p.m., some soldiers charged the east door and some succeeded

in forcibly gaining entrance. A few made an inspection of the barracks room, but began to smash things when they realized that the prisoners were not there.

Captain J.L. Main of the 211th, who was valiantly trying to calm the crowd outside the barracks, was then struck over the head with a board and shoved partway through a window. The sound of breaking glass further incited the crowd, and soon, in a general onslaught, the windows on the east side were systematically smashed by the mob. The best efforts of Lieutenant Colonel West-Jones, the officer commanding, the officers of the 211th, and the few police officers and constables to quiet the men failed. They could not stem the rising tide as soldiers flooded into the building, breaking police items in frustration when they could not find the prisoners. The main body of rioters were unable to find the main entrance to the guardroom.[17]

While this attack was being mounted on the east door, a hole was made in the high fence of the prisoners' yard along the west side of the barracks, and a small band of soldiers pushed through it. The "worst agitator of the outfit," Private Julio Pelegrino of 211th, made his way up a fire escape toward the barred window of the guardroom, where four RNWMP men were watching over the prisoners. The two groups began to shout at one another, the RNWMP issuing a warning that they would shoot, and the soldiers retorting, "We can shoot too and we would sooner die here than in the trenches!" As Pelegrino peered over the windowsill, wielding an unknown object in a raised hand and making "a threatening motion" with it, one of the constables on duty, Constable A.N. Eames, fired his service revolver. Fortunately for the soldier, the shot struck only the top of the man's upper arm bone. The bullet split the bone and had to be removed in surgery, rendering the soldier unfit for further service. At the sound of a gunshot and the collapse of Pelegrino, the other soldiers quickly fled the yard. The excited cry that a soldier had been shot led men from the main crowd to rush to the west side of the building and to carry the crumpled Pelegrino out into the street, his gushing wound quickly packed with handkerchiefs. From then on, other than a few stones clinking off the bars of the cell room windows, the well-armed RNWMP contingent reported that everything was quiet.[18]

Shortly after this incident, an RNWMP constable, who was returning to the barracks after having escorted some lady friends from the area, elicited the wrath of an enraged mob. As he approached the building, Constable A. Gammon heard someone shout: "He shot him, get a club and kill him!" About 150 soldiers, under the misapprehension that Gammon had shot Pelegrino, began to yell "mob him! mob him!" Gammon was knocked down, but scrambled to his feet and tried to break away from the mob. At the corner of Third Street West, a soldier managed to trip him to the ground, and the others "piled on top" of him and began pounding his head with sticks. Fortunately, Inspector Newson saw the ominous developments, intervened, and found the constable up against an automobile. His lips were badly cut, and he was "suffering pain internally." Someone in the crowd yelled: "We've got him; we've got rope; lynch him." Fortunately, cooler heads prevailed. Lieutenant Colonel Robinson of the 187th, who assisted the injured man, described the crowd as "murderous at a little distance from the car, but hesitant in its immediate neighbourhood."

The soldiers ceased their attack on Gammon when one of them realized they had the wrong man, but not before he had been "viciously kicked" in the privates. Inspector Newson pulled Gammon into a nearby car and duly protected him until he could be taken away for medical attention.[19] Thankfully, the serious injuries ended there and both casualties, Gammon and Pelegrino, eventually recovered in hospital.

The night's activities, however, were not quite finished. A small group of soldiers broke from the crowd and tried to obtain ammunition from the nearby Martin's Hardware. Six local policemen who had been ordered to stay behind at their headquarters now rushed to action, and attacked the soldiers with batons while they were trying to break down the door of the store. The attempt to secure ammunition was foiled. An RNWMP carbine that had been carried to the scene by a drummer of the 211th was now discarded on the street. Later evidence revealed that twelve carbines and twelve revolvers had been removed from RNWMP barracks. Thankfully, they were never used against the police.[20]

Brigadier General Cruikshank eventually arrived with his staff to address the mob. He assured them "that in the event the men who were incarcerated had any just grievance or had been unfairly treated, [he] would make every effort to see that justice was done to them." After Lance Corporal Webster spoke with Cruikshank he collected a considerable party of men and marched them off. The commanding officer then persuaded the soldiers to withdraw, but the throng of civilians standing around the barracks made the task of dispersing the soldiers much more difficult. Lieutenant Colonel May stated that civilians "failed to see the point that it would help us if they would move off and go home and the majority just stood and leered at us."[21]

By 10:30 p.m. the mob had dispersed, unsuccessful in its attempt to "rescue" the prisoners. A strong military picquet arrived from Sarcee Camp, ensuring that the scene of the action was absolutely quiet by midnight. Although sensationalizing news-papermen reported that saddles, carpets, and other items had been thrown out of the barracks windows and had been burnt, there was, in fact, nothing of the sort in the barracks and the bonfire really consisted of a few wicker chairs that had been left on the tennis court. The principal damage to the barracks was to some of the men's kits "and a few other articles." Damage totalled eight hundred dollars. The RNWMP had taken the precaution of placing all the important documents in a safe and keeping them there until they felt that the danger had passed.[22]

Given the tenuous situation, the RNWMP commanding officer decided to ship the prisoners out of Calgary as quickly as possible. The CPR agreed to stop the southbound train at East Calgary for them at midnight, but the police missed the connection. The prisoners were then rushed by automobile to Midnapore, where they boarded the southbound train to Lethbridge without mishap.

Political and military officials worried about aftershocks. Prime Minister Robert Borden was sufficiently concerned to call for an official inquiry and wrote the following to the Minister of National Defence:

> As this is the second serious disturbance which has taken place in Calgary and as this incident seems graver than anything that has yet occurred insomuch as it was a direct attack upon those responsible for the maintenance of law and order, I must ask that a thorough and rigid inquiry ... be made into the affair and that any who may be found guilty shall receive adequate punishment. Any other course would certainly tend to

bring about a repetition of such disturbances which must be sternly suppressed.[23]

A court of inquiry was established to look into the matter, and lasted seven days. Chaired by Lieutenant Colonel George MacDonald, the proceedings filled 228 typewritten pages and featured testimonies by dozens of soldiers, city police authorities, and RNWMP officers and constables. In addition to the men of the 211th Battalion whose comrades were imprisoned, a number of soldiers from the 218th and 233rd Battalions were identified in the crowd and called to testify.

The court was convinced that the motive behind the agitation, i.e., the "entrapment" of five soldiers by Calgary police, was wholly without foundation. The Calgary police magistrate testified that the action taken in the cases was morally and legally sound, and that he had no option but to impose the penalties that he had. He also satisfied the court that the police actions were taken without discrimination. Detective Tom Turner of the Calgary police force (against whom the soldiers' animosity had been primarily directed) also gave evidence that exonerated him of impropriety. He had intervened in only two of the cases against soldiers, both on the basis of citizen complaints and consequent orders given by his superior officers. Rather than spearheading a supposed campaign against the soldiers, the city police had never assumed the initiative, nor were they interested in the subsequent prosecutions. Stool pigeons were no longer being used by the police; they simply did not have the money to pay them! Furthermore, a provincial officer laid the information in almost every case, and the city police did not accrue any benefits from the fines as the money was payable to the province.[24]

Courts of inquiry are not judicial bodies; they are established pursuant to military regulations at the discretion of the convening officer, "to collect and record information only, or it may be required to give an opinion also on any proposed question, or as to the origin or cause of certain existing facts or circumstances."[25] They resemble a royal commission. Major O.M. Biggar, the assistant judge advocate general and a noted Edmonton lawyer, explained that the evidence provided by the accused could not be used against them, unless they lied—in which case they could be punished for perjury.

Since the military court did not have to conform to civilian legal practices, it featured some interesting dynamics. Those accused of improprieties cross-examined witnesses themselves, and often went on the offensive. When one private was identified as a ringleader, he promptly called the finger-pointing witness a "G—D—liar" and was placed under close arrest. Others played tricks on those testifying to try and demonstrate the limitations of their evidence, but these shenanigans elicited sharp rebukes from the presiding officer. Outside the court at Sarcee Camp, accused soldiers continued to throw insults and threats at RNWMP witnesses. Sergeant Cohen continued to be "the worst of the bunch," passing such remarks as: "You s—of—bi—s we will get you yet, and those in town."[26] It was hardly a congenial environment.

The local media had, of course, followed the developments closely from the onset, and unanimously applauded Cruikshank for his decision to make the court of inquiry public. The various newspapers, however, were divided on other salient matters. The *Calgary Herald* had taken a "wet" position during the battle over prohibition, and was critical of the police and military decisions that contributed to the riots.

It stressed the youth of the soldiers involved in the attack—"about the most meek and mild 'rioters,' as far as their general appearance went, that ever entered a court of enquiry"—and the "harsh penalties" of the temperance laws that "in any other country than this would not be made the cause of a man's permanent disgrace."

Given the American origins of most members of the 211th Battalion, this consideration took on more weight than normal. By contrast, *The Albertan* had been a champion of the "dry" crusade, and blamed the riotous soldiers without reserve or qualification. Brigadier Cruikshank could not have prevented the lamentable events, the paper asserted, and the soldiers had to be tried as civilians since "civil law is superior to military law." If the soldiers were exempted, it would be "a condition of militarism which has caused the whole trouble leading to the present war."[27]

As a result of the investigation, 22 soldiers were handed over to the civil authorities for prosecution. Five men were found not guilty, and in two cases the charges were withdrawn. Two prisoners, Privates Grantly and Sheldon of the 211th, removed the bars from their cell windows in the east guardroom at Sarcee Camp and disappeared. They still had not been rediscovered by mid-November. The remainder were found guilty: seven were fined $25 and costs; four $50 and costs; and one was levied $100 and costs. Private Pelegrino, who had been shot by the RNWMP, was released on suspended sentence due to the wounds he had sustained.[28]

So who was to blame? Characteristically, the "foreigner" became a target of much official criticism. The Mounted Police found it "most humiliating . . . that the ringleaders were all foreigners" with "a big Russian, or German, who could hardly speak

English, leading the attack." Sergeant Major T.H. Irvine and Constable R. Campbell confirmed that the men "that were doing all the bad damage were foreigners who spoke broken English." The media and courts used men like Pelegrino to substantiate such stereotypes.[29] Appeals to public nativist sentiments, however, actually served to deflect responsibility from those who should have borne the brunt of it: the military and the local police. RNWMP officials concluded that their inspectors and non-commissioned officers had acted with "good judgment and a great deal of forbearance" by never indicating where the entrance to the guardroom was located, thus safeguarding the prisoners in custody as well as the office records.

They were much less generous in their assessment of the military and city police. Given the number of soldiers in camp at Calgary and their past history, the military officers arguably should have had a picquet patrolling the town every evening—something the officers themselves had suggested to city council as late as May but not acted upon. The

(left) Detective department, city police, Calgary, AB, 1912. Back row (left to right): C. Cox; J. Burroughs; J. McDonald; D. Ritchie; W. Turner; E.P. Schoeppe. Centre row (left to right): P.D. Rickett; D. Richardson; Chief Alfred Cuddy; A. Yeates; W. Symons. Front row (left to right): D. Milne; Jack Cuddy; J. Hale. Glenbow Archives, NA-2861-17; (right) Alfred Cuddy, police chief, Calgary, AB, ca. 1912–19. He served from 15 March 1912 to 13 July 1919. Glenbow Archives, NA-2861-6.

local RNWMP commanding officer lamented that "there is not a strong arm at the helm in charge of the men at Sarcee Camp as, had there been, all this trouble with the soldiers would certainly have never occurred." The city police, they asserted, also had been negligent in relaying information to Brigadier Cruikshank and the RNWMP, and "this is not . . . the first time that the City Police have acted in this manner towards us." Had they been informed earlier of rumours, they could easily have avoided trouble by moving the prisoners. They were consoled by the fact that Chief Cuddy was "receiving the censure of the majority of the citizens" for his action and inaction![30]

Testimonies before the court of inquiry indicated that the military hierarchy itself was clearly functioning improperly. Non-commissioned officers (NCOs) were supposed to be responsible for instilling and enforcing discipline in the ranks, and were responsible for teaching drill and marching to the recruits. It now seemed apparent that NCOs had led the procession to the police station and RNWMP barracks. Sergeant Campbell testified that he had taken no part in the attack, and had "tried to appeal to them about law and good order" on the way to the barracks "but it was useless." He later helped with picquet duty, but that should not obfuscate the fact that he had spurred the excited crowd to directed action earlier in the evening by announcing the location of the prisoners. Lance Corporal Webster was seen leading a "sort of organized mob" to the barracks in a somewhat more orderly fashion than a mere "rabble" of unguided individuals. Staff Sergeant S.R. Waugh of the RNWMP identified Sergeant Cohen of the 218th Battalion as the "chief agitator" who stood on the steps "yelling and shouting and all around."

The court of inquiry sent all three NCOs to civilian trial for "being particularly blameworthy, both by reason of their rank, and the prominent part which they took" in the riot. Nevertheless, the military stressed that the attack was not premeditated but spontaneous, and therefore they had little control over the actions of the men who happened to be in uniform.[31] However, it was this lack of control that was the most damning indictment against the local officer corps.

An interesting issue, if somewhat tangential to this topic, involves the payment of compensation. In other cases of soldier attacks and "rioting" across the country, military officials strictly denied any legal responsibility for lawless behaviour. "It has always been the policy of the Department not to recognize damages done by the soldiers in riots or otherwise," the deputy minister of defence reported, with "the Department disclaiming all responsibility for such actions on the part of the soldiers and leaving it to the victims to exercise their ordinary legal remedies in recovering damages." Although there was some concern that payment to the RNWMP could represent a dangerous precedent for claims made by the public, the Department of National Defence never seriously considered withholding nearly $800 in compensation from the Mounted Police. The Department of Justice reported that "as the loss is an incident to the war it might very well be repaired out of the war vote, but whatever disposition be made of the matter I do not think it can affect cases like that of the Canadian Club at Waterloo [or White Lunch Restaurants and Riverside Hotel in Calgary] in which a private concern is preferring a claim against the Government." Although this reasoning was never explained, the RNWMP did indeed receive its compensation.[32] If the military's de jure responsibility for the soldiers' recalcitrant behaviour remained questionable, their payment of damages to the RNWMP was a de facto admission of guilt.

Fortunately, the attack on the RNWMP barracks was the last of the so-called "soldier riots" in Calgary during the First World War, and was the only known direct conflict between the RNWMP and soldiers of the CEF. Armed military picquets once again governed Calgary streets after the October 11 attack, quelling any fears of future disturbances. There had been casualties, but no deaths.

The 211th battalion wintered in Calgary before proceeding overseas as a unit. There it suffered the fate of so many CEF battalions in the last few years of the war: once in England in January 1917, it was drafted into the Canadian Railway Troops.[33] Ironically, of course, once overseas these soldiers could indulge in the devil's brew forbidden to them in Alberta. One can imagine members of the former 211th sipping their ration of "demon rum" with comrades in the trenches, conveying the tale of the night they tried to "rescue" their compatriots from the city and mounted police in Calgary.

Acta non verba—"deeds, not words." So read the motto of the American Legion battalions.[34] Predictably, the story of the 211th's brash deeds in Calgary during the autumn of 1916 never made its way into the published histories of the war. When the peace was obtained, it was the unwavering patriotism and discipline of the soldiers and the astuteness of their officers that captured a place in history and in public minds. For Brigadier Cruikshank, who moved on to serve with the army historical section in Ottawa, the attack on the RNWMP barracks in October 1916, like the Calgary riots earlier that year, were a blemish on his own, and the nation's, war record that was best forgotten.

Notes

This article was published in *Alberta History* 49, no. 3 (Summer 2001): 2–12. The co-editors would like to express their thanks to the author and *Alberta History*.

1   Desmond Morton, "'No More Disagreeable or Onerous Duty': Canadians and the Military Aid of the Civil Power, Past, Present, Future," in *Canada's International Security Policy*, edited by David B. Dewitt and David Leyton-Brown (Scarborough, ON: Prentice-Hall, 1995), 135; Department of National Defence, Directorate of History and Heritage, DHH 74/672, E. Pye Papers, folder H, file "Disturbances in Canada 1916."

2   Desmond Morton, *When Your Number's Up* (Toronto: Random House, 1993), 13, 62; Hugh A. Dempsey, *Calgary: Spirit of the West* (Saskatoon: Fifth House, 1994), 107. On Cruikshank, see CGS Report on Calgary Camp (1912), National Archives of Canada (NAC), RG 24, vol. 2507, file HQ5 1308 pt. 1; Inspector General's Report on Camp of Instruction at Calgary (6 July 1911), NAC, RG 24, vol. 357, file HQ 33-24-41; David McConnell, "E. A. Cruikshank: His Life and Work" (MA thesis, University of Toronto, 1965), 50.

3   For an expanded discussion, see P.W. Lackenbauer, "The Military and 'Mob Rule': The CEF Riots in Calgary, February 1916," *Canadian Military History* 10, no. 1 (Winter 2001): 31–42.

4   Lackenbauer and Nikolas Gardner, "Soldiers as Liminaries: The CEF Soldier Riots of 1916 Reassessed" (paper presented at the Canada and War Conference, Ottawa, Ontario, 5 May 2000).

5   1st, 10th, and 42nd witnesses, Proceedings of the Court of Inquiry into the Riverside Hotel, NAC, RG 24, vol. 1255, file HQ 593-1-86, vol. 1.

6   Tim Cook, "'More a medicine than a beverage': 'Demon Rum' and the Canadian Trench Soldier of the First World War," *Canadian Military History* 9, no. 1 (Winter 2000): 6–22. On drinking as an element of army culture, see also Donna Winslow, *The Canadian Airborne in Somalia: A Socio-cultural Inquiry* (Ottawa:

Minister of Public Works and Government Services, 1997).

7   Dempsey, *Calgary*, 107.

8   James Gray, *Booze: The Impact of Whisky on the Prairie West* (Toronto: Macmillan, 1972), 75–78.

9   *The Albertan*, 5 October, 1916, 8.

10 Commissioner, RNWMP, to Comptroller, RNWMP, Ottawa, 25 October 1916, NAC, RG 18, vol. 3274, file 1915-HQ-1184-15-1 (hereafter NAC RNWMP).

11 Clive M. Law, "Colonel Bullock's American Legion of the Canadian Expeditionary Force," *Military Collector and Historian* 51, no. 4 (Winter 1999): 150, 153–55. The 211th had a strength of 747 in July 1916. See RG 24, vol. 359, file HQ 33-24-117, vol. 1. On problems with the American Legion, see also the fine article by Ronald G. Haycock, "The American Legion in the Canadian Expeditionary Force, 1914–1917: A Study in Failure," *Military Affairs* (October 1979): 115–19.

12 Witness Sergeant Cohen, 218th Battalion, Proceedings of a Court of Enquiry re Attack on Calgary Police Headquarters and RNWMP Barracks, 11 October 1916 (hereafter Proceedings of Enquiry), NAC, RG 24, vol. 1257, file HQ 593111108, pt. 1. Cohen admitted that he had personally experienced problems with Turner, who had arrested him on some charges but then "refused to bring them up."

13 Proceedings of Enquiry, Witness L/Cpl Webster; Superintendent F.J. Horrigan, RNWMP report, 16 October 1916, NAC RNWMP.

14 *Calgary Herald*, 12 October 1916, Const. J.E. Kingston, RNWMP report, NAC RNWMP.

15 Insp. C.H. King to OC, RNWMP, Calgary, 12 October 1916, NAC RNWMP; Proceedings of Enquiry, Witness Constable Thomas Ward, City Police.

16 Inspector Newson to OC, RNWMP, Calgary, 13 October 1916, NAC RNWMP.

17 Proceedings of Enquiry, Witness Constable Dan Finlayson, Staff/Sgt S.R. Waugh, RNWMP.

18 Staff Sergeant Waugh, Corporal A.J. Barber, RNWMP report; Proceedings of Enquiry, Witness Corporal A.J. Barber, RNWMP.

19 Supt. Commanding "D" Division to Commissioner, RNWMP, Regina, 16 October 1916; Newson to OC, RNWMP, 13 October 1916, and Gammon, RNWMP report, NAC RNWMP; Proceedings of Enquiry, Witness Gammon. Private Sheldon later testified that Gammon had kicked him in the privates earlier that evening.

20 Proceedings of Enquiry, Witness Constable Dan Finlayson.

21 Proceedings of Enquiry, Witnesses: Brigadier Cruikshank; Lieutenant Colonel May.

22 Comptroller, RNWMP, Ottawa, to Commissioner, RNWMP, Regina, 23 February 1917; Supts Commanding "E" and "D" Divisions to Commissioner, RNWMP, 11 October 1916 and 16 October 1916, NAC RNWMP; Proceedings of Enquiry, Witness. Brigadier Cruikshank; *The Albertan*, 12 October 1916.

23 Borden to Hughes, 13 October 1916, NAC, RG 24, vol. 1257, file HQ 59311/108, pt. 1.

24 Report from Court of Inquiry, 26 October 1916; Proceedings of Enquiry, Witness Detective Tom Turner, NAC, RG 24, vol. 1257, file HQ 593/1/108, pt. 1; *Calgary Herald*, 19 October 1916. The necessity for the shooting of Pelegrino was, however, not established. The constable who had used his revolver was not in Calgary by the time of the inquiry and could not be examined.

25 Major General Sir William D. Otter, *The Guide: A Manual for the Canadian Militia (Infantry)*, 9th ed. (Toronto: Copp Clark, 1914), 150–51.

26 Proceedings of Enquiry, Witnesses: Constable Dan Finlayson; Staff/Sergt Waugh (recalled). Staff/Sergeant Waugh, RNWMP report; letter, Staff/Sergt Waugh to OC RNWMP, Calgary, 13 October 1916; Asst Commissioner to Comptroller, 14 October 1916, NAC RNWMP; handwritten message from phone conversation, Assistant Commissioner and Officer Commanding "E" Division, RNWMP, 13 October 1916, NAC, RG 18, series F-2, vol. 3274, file HQ-1184-K-1; *Calgary Herald*, 14 October 1916. On Biggar, see Chris Madsen, *Another Kind of Justice* (Vancouver: UBC Press, 1999).

27 R.I. McLean, "A 'Most Effectual Remedy': Temperance and Prohibition in Alberta, 1875–1915" (MA thesis,

28 Cruikshank to Secy, Militia Council, 3 November 1916; Captain DAAG for A/Adjutant General, to Military Secy, 16 November 1916, NAC, RG 24, vol. 1257, file HQ 59311/108, pt. 1; *Calgary Herald*, 20 October 1916.

29 Supt Commanding "D" Division to Commissioner, RNWMP, 11 October 1916, NAC RNWMP. On nativism in Alberta during this period, see Howard Palmer, *Patterns of Prejudice* (Toronto: McClelland and Stewart, 1982).

30 Supt Commanding "E" Division to Commissioner, RNWMP, 11 October 1916; Supt Commanding "D" Division to Commissioner, RNWMP, 11 and 16 October 1916, NAC RNWMP; Commissioner, RNWMP to Office Commanding, RNWMP, Calgary, 25 October 1916, NAC, RG 18, series F-2, vol. 3274, file HQ-1184-K-1; letter, GOC MD 13 to Mayor and Councillors, 26 May 1916, City of Calgary Archives, City Clerk Correspondence, box 100, file 720 (miscellaneous military matters, 1916).

31 Report from Court of Inquiry, 26 October 1916; Proceedings of Enquiry, Witness Constable Thomas Ward, City Police; Waugh, RNWMP; Sgt Campbell, 211th; Lt. Col. Robinson; various testimonies, 17 October 1916, all in NAC, RG 24, vol. 1257, file HQ 593/11108, pt. 1. The Camp Sergeant Major testified that Campbell had not helped the authorities and had instead urged the rioters on, while Chief Cuddy testified that Campbell had tried to dissuade the soldiers from doing any damage. It should be clarified that the soldiers at Sarcee Camp did not represent a united front. Other battalions were apparently furious with the 211th for what had happened, and there were rumours that the 211th was going to attack the 187th regiment "for their derogatory utterances" against them. Supt Commanding "E" Division to Commissioner, RNWMP, 11 October 1916, NAC RNWMP.

32 Deputy Minister, DMD, to Deputy Minister of Justice, 2 January 1917, and reply, 8 January 1917, NAC, RG 13, series A-2, vol. 208, file 1917-37.

University of Calgary, 1969) 106–8; *Calgary Herald*, 12, 14, 16 October 1916; *The Albertan*, 14, 17 October 1916.

33 Haycock, "American Legion," 118; Law, "Colonel Bullock's," 155; *The Albertan*, 13 and 16 October 1916.

34 Haycock, "American Legion," 117.

Works Cited

PRIMARY SOURCES

The Albertan
Calgary Herald

City of Calgary Archives. City Clerk Correspondence, box 100, file 720 (miscellaneous military matters, 1916).

Department of National Defence, Directorate of History and Heritage. DHH 74/672, E. Pye Papers, folder H, file "Disturbances in Canada 1916."

Library and Archives Canada. RG 13, series A-2, vol. 208, file 1917-37.

———. RG 18, series F-2, vol. 3274, file HQ-1184-K-1.

———. RG 18, vol. 3274, file 1915-HQ-1184-15-1 (hereafter LAC RNWMP).

———. RG 24, vol. 357, file HQ 33-24-41.

———. RG 24, vol. 359, file HQ 33-24-117, vol. 1.

———. RG 24, vol. 1255, file HQ 593-1-86, vol. 1.

———. RG 24, vol. 1257, file HQ 59311/108, pt. 1.

———. RG 24, vol. 1257, file HQ 593/1/108, pt. 1.

———. RG 24, vol. 1257, file HQ 593/11108, pt. 1.

———. RG 24, vol. 2507, file HQ5 1308, pt. 1.

SECONDARY SOURCES

Cook, Tim. "'More a Medicine Than a Beverage': 'Demon Rum' and the Canadian Trench Soldier of the First World War." *Canadian Military History* 9, no. 1 (Winter 2000): 6–22.

Dempsey, Hugh A. *Calgary: Spirit of the West*. Saskatoon: Fifth House Limited, 1994.

Gray, James. *Booze: The Impact of Whisky on the Prairie West*. Toronto: Macmillan, 1972.

Haycock, Ronald G. "The American Legion in the Canadian Expeditionary Force, 1914–1917: A Study in Failure." *Military Affairs* 43, no. 3 (October 1979): 115–19.

Lackenbauer, P.W. "The Military and 'Mob Rule': The CEF Riots in Calgary, February 1916." *Canadian Military History* 10, no. 1 (Winter 2001): 31–42.

Lackenbauer, P.W., and Nikolas Gardner. "Soldiers as Liminaries: The CEF Soldier Riots of 1916 Reassessed." Paper presented at the Canada and War Conference, Ottawa, Ontario, 5 May 2000.

Law, Clive M. "Colonel Bullock's American Legion of the Canadian Expeditionary Force." *Military Collector and Historian* 51, no. 4 (Winter 1999): 150, 153–55.

McConnell, David. "E.A. Cruikshank: His Life and Work." MA thesis, University of Toronto, 1965.

McLean, R.I. "A 'Most Effectual Remedy': Temperance and Prohibition in Alberta, 1875–1915." MA thesis, University of Calgary, 1969.

Morton, Desmond. "'No More Disagreeable or Onerous Duty': Canadians and the Military Aid of the Civil Power, Past, Present, Future." In *Canada's International Security Policy*, edited by David B. Dewitt and David Leyton-Brown. Scarborough, ON: Prentice-Hall, 1995.

——. *When Your Number's Up: The Canadian Soldier in the First World War*. Toronto: Random House, 1993.

Otter, Major General Sir William D. *The Guide: A Manual for the Canadian Militia (Infantry)*. 9th ed. Toronto: Copp, Clark, 1914.

Winslow, Donna. *The Canadian Airborne in Somalia: A Socio-cultural Inquiry*. Ottawa: Minister of Public Works and Government Services, 1997.

Canada's First National Internment Operations and the Search for Sanctuary in the Ukrainian Labour Farmer Temple Association

KASSANDRA LUCIUK

The Ukrainians who came to Canada were predominantly citizens of the Austro-Hungarian Empire and had formerly resided in the territories of Galicia and Bukovyna. Faced with difficult social, economic, and political conditions and increased efforts by the Canadian government to attract immigrants, approximately 170,000 Ukrainians emigrated between 1891 and 1914.[1] However, the conditions of Ukrainians did not improve, as hoped, in their new home. This was exposed, most notably, between 1914 and 1920, when thousands of Ukrainians and other Europeans were labelled "enemy aliens" and interned across the country.

"A Virtual Canadian Ukraine": Settling the Canadian West

Prior to 1896, Aboriginal peoples inhabited the majority of Canada's prairies. In the 1880s and 1890s, there was an influx of central Canadian and British immigrants. While many settlers remained apathetic toward the arrival of the non-British,

certain populations, such as the ranchers of southern Alberta, began challenging their immigration. This opposition was rooted in ideas of nativism, or an aversion to immigrants and those considered to be different or a threat to the majority. Nativism was beginning to be articulated through the practice of negatively stereotyping groups such as the Mormons, central and eastern Europeans, and the Chinese.[2] Sir John A. Macdonald exemplified the spread of nativism, perhaps most clearly, in an 1890 statement when he spoke out against the influx of immigrants to the United States. He stated that the country would have "its vicissitudes and revolutions" as a result of its immigration policies. He observed, "Look at that mass of foreign ignorance and vice which has flooded [the] country with socialism, atheism, and all other isms." Canada, he asserted, would only seek "northern races" that were "culturally sound" and could conform quickly, and easily, to Anglo-Canadian life.[3]

From 1896 to 1914 there was a dramatic increase in Canadian immigration; between 1901 and 1911 Alberta's population alone grew more than five times, from 73,022 to 374,295.[4] The employment boom that occurred demanded masses of workers, and this instantly ended the vision of a homogenous Canada. The election of Sir Wilfrid Laurier's Liberal government in 1896 and the appointment of Clifford Sifton as minister of the interior reflected the changing nature of Canadian society.[5] Previously blocked from immigrating to Canada, approximately 170,000 Ukrainians arrived between 1892 and 1914, leaving behind quasi-feudal conditions in search of a better life. However, the exploitation and alienation that characterized the experiences of Ukrainians in their homeland followed them to Canada.[6] Sifton's immigration policy was formulated around attracting farmers, regardless of nationality, to Canada. He recognized that due to the limited number of farmers available from Great Britain, and strict emigration laws in Germany, he would have to attract large numbers of immigrants from central and eastern Europe.[7] According to Sifton, "a stalwart peasant in a sheepskin coat born on the soil whose forefathers have been farmers for ten generations" would be ideal for populating the West.[8] In other words, the immigration of Ukrainians could be justified because they were "inured to the cold in their native land and brought up in the hard school of adversity."[9]

Sifton's immigration policies were highly criticized by the Anglo-Canadian population of Alberta. "As for the Galicians," wrote a priest in the *Alberta Tribune*, "they are from the point of civilization, ten times lower than the Indians."[10] Calgary's *Daily Herald* remarked that the Ukrainians "have not the least idea of sanitation. In their personal habits and acts, [they] resemble animals, and even in the streets of Edmonton, when they come to market, men, women, and children, would if unchecked, turn the place into a common sewer." The article continued that, in many cases, the Ukrainians "have been content with building themselves holes in the ground where the family consorts with the animals—all in the common apartment."[11] Banff's *Crag and Canyon* wrote: "The majority of our citizens are of the opinion that the scenic outlook is not vastly improved by the presence of the slouching, bovine-faced foreigners."[12]

The Department of the Interior, and officials from other government departments, upheld these views. Alfred Akerlindh, a government immigration officer, wrote that the Ukrainians were "very filthy in their habits and very dirty about their clothing and their persons." William McCreary, commissioner of immigration, furthered these impertinences by remarking that Ukrainian immigrants were "a low, illiterate, ignorant class."[13] Frank Oliver, an MP who would later become minister of the interior, raised concerns about Ukrainian assimilation, stating that it called for "the intermarriage of your sons and daughters with those who are of an alien race and of alien ideas."[14] Another government official reminded Canadians that physical characteristics are permanent, meaning that while Ukrainians and other European immigrants can be made into Englishmen by transplanting them to Canada, "it is an irrefutable scientific fact that where a higher race breeds with an inferior, the characteristics of the inferior in the long run prevail."[15] The reference to breeding demonstrates that the official was a believer in eugenics, a social philosophy advocating the improvement of human genetic traits through promoting higher reproduction rates of individuals who possessed desirable traits and discouraging the reproduction of so-called "inferior" species. "Selective breeding" had been practised in agriculture for thousands of years and was, in the late nineteenth century, applied to human populations. In short, Anglo-Canadians believed that they were the apex of evolution and human achievement, and furthermore that Canada's greatness was due to its Anglo-Canadian heritage.

Sifton attempted to counter those who opposed his immigration policy when, on 7 July 1899, he raised the issue in Parliament. His defence of the Ukrainians was, once again, rooted in the claim that Canada needed immigrant workers. "If these people were people not accustomed to agricultural life," Sifton stated, "I would unhesitatingly use every power that the Government would place in my hands for the purposes of preventing their going to the North-west." He further noted that "these people are agriculturalists and have been for generations" and, therefore, were "an acquisition to the country. If we are ever going to have the North-west populated, we shall not succeed in doing it by standing on our boundary with a club or putting the microscope on every man who wishes to come into the country." He concluded that the Ukrainians "would be no menace to the future of the country," and, to the contrary, would "assist in the developing of the country and become good citizens."[16]

Canada's "Golden Era" and a New Phase of Immigration Policy

With Frank Oliver's appointment as minister of the interior in April 1905, Canada entered into a new phase of immigration policy. Unlike his predecessor, Oliver was particularly concerned with the ethnic and cultural origins of prospective immigrants and, consequently, moved to make immigration policy more selective. For Oliver, populating the North-West with settlers was the "ultimate result of the efforts being put forward for the building up of a Canadian nationality so that our children may form one of the great civilized nations of the world, and be one of the greatest forces in that civilization." This could never be accomplished, he believed, if the population "should be of such class and character [that] will deteriorate rather than elevate the conditions of our people and our country at large."[17]

Oliver's outlook on immigration was reflected in the legislation he effected. The Immigration Act of 1906 attempted to revise all immigration legislation that preceded it, barring, in the process, a broad spectrum of immigrants.[18] This was followed by the Immigration Act of 1910, which gave the government unlimited power to regulate the volume, ethnicity, and occupational composition of incoming immigrants. "We want to be in such a position," stated Oliver, "to exclude people whom we consider undesirable." Nonetheless, he could not ignore the continued need for immigrants. Canada was entering into a "golden era"—the West was finally being settled, new mineral resources were being discovered, and the building of another transcontinental railway was underway. Large numbers of immigrants, particularly those deemed docile and difficult to unionize, were desired more than ever. As a consequence, Oliver began admitting the largest numbers of Ukrainians to date. They were mostly employed by the railway and mining industries, where they faced deplorable working conditions, poor wages, and high injury and death rates. Furthermore, Ukrainians were generally spurned by the established unions, who saw them as a threat to native wages, and were manipulated by their employers, who used them as scabs to break up strikes.

The Beginnings of the Ukrainian Socialist-Progressive Movement

These conditions undoubtedly increased the hopelessness felt by many Ukrainians who, shunned from all other aspects of Canadian socio-political life, began to participate with increasing enthusiasm in self-regulating trade union activity and socialist-progressive organizations. While socialist ideas accompanied many Ukrainians from their homeland, these politics took on their own, unique form in Canada as many believed that they were being exploited here, just as they had been by the ruling elite in the Austro-Hungarian and Russian empires.[19] Ironically, block settlements implemented by the Anglo-Canadian population at the beginning of the nineteenth century in order to segregate Ukrainians became the ideal breeding ground for the spread of radical ideas.[20] Ukrainians began organizing *chytalni* (reading clubs) and *tovarystva prosvity* (enlightenment societies) that were often radical in nature, counting among their membership followers of the Ukrainian Radical Party (URP) from Western Ukraine, where Marxism had taken root as early as the 1870s.[21] Through these local societies, the socialist-progressive Ukrainians attempted to educate Ukrainian, and other immigrant labourers, on what they regarded as the inherently exploitative capitalist system.[22]

The first considerable effort to organize the socialist-progressive Ukrainians occurred in 1907 with the formation of the Ukrainian Socialist Labour Committee and their *Chervonyi Prapor* (Red Flag) paper. *Chervonyi Prapor,* printed "for that section of the Canadian proletariat which speaks the Ukrainian language," intended to "help this section in awareness, education and organization, and towards a clear understanding of the international idea of socialism," in order to lead "the working masses in the fight against lawlessness, exploitation and slavery."[23] Later that year, the socialist-progressive Ukrainians pledged their support for the Socialist Party of Canada (SPC), an organization dedicated to uniting "workers of all nations and faiths."[24] In addition to their commitment to the SPC, the Ukrainians emphasized the need for the education and mobilization of Ukrainian immigrants. Recognizing the Ukrainians as an asset to the movement due to their "extremely important and strategic position" for reaching foreign-born workers, the SPC established three Ukrainian sections of the party, as well as distributing the Ukrainian language newspaper *Robochyi Narod* (The Working People) throughout western Canada.[25] While organizational strife dominated the early years of the Ukrainian socialist-progressive movement, it was successfully operating by the outbreak of the First World War in 1914, frequently drawing attention to the plight of immigrant labourers while continuing its educational and cultural work on behalf of the Ukrainians it represented.

Canada's First National Internment Operations

The discrimination encountered by Ukrainians continued with the outbreak of the First World War. On 15 August 1914, a proclamation was issued that exposed all citizens of "enemy countries" to threats of arrest and internment. Within a week, the War Measures Act was passed, giving the federal government emergency powers to administer the war without accountability to either Parliament or extant legislation.[26] By October, worsening socio-economic conditions coupled with increased government interest in "enemy aliens" led to an order in council that not only required Ukrainians and other immigrants to apply for permits to cross the border but also implemented mandatory registration according to age, nationality, place of residence, and occupation. All enemy aliens within 20 miles of a registrar's office were required to report within a month of the order in council, and carry special internal travel documents and identification cards. Those considered too dangerous to remain at large were interned.[27]

Some Ukrainians were interned because of increasing economic misfortune since enemy aliens were the first to lose their jobs because of reactions from Anglo-Canadian workers and employers who now preferred "Canadian labour."[28] The soundest justification for internment was a perceived lack of loyalty; any peacetime tolerance of Ukrainians, and others, was immediately overridden during the war.[29] However, close surveillance of the communities in question often revealed that the fear of disloyalty was unwarranted. Colonel Aylesworth Bowen Perry, sixth commissioner of the RCMP (1 August 1900 to 31 March 1923), reported in February 1915 that he had begun discharging many agents hired to infiltrate the immigrant communities because the investigation "has not revealed the slightest trace of any organization or concerted movement amongst the enemy aliens." In his opinion, public fears were groundless, and his agents had yet to find a single case of sabotage or disloyalty. These accounts were furthered by claims of innocence from the Ukrainian community itself. In July 1916, a collection of Ukrainian editors attempted to prove their innocence to the Canadian public. "The Ukrainians ... of Western Canada," they wrote, "have found

themselves heavily handicapped since the outbreak of the war by the fact of their Austrian birth, which has led ... the Dominion Government, as well as Canadian employers of labour, to unjustly class them as ... enemy aliens." They continued noting that Ukrainians "are persecuted, by thousands they are interned, they are dismissed from their employment, and their applications for work are not entertained. And why? For only one reason, that they were so unhappy as to be born into the Austrian bondage."[30]

Despite these defences, between 1914 and 1920, 8,579 enemy aliens, including women and children, were interned.[31] An additional 80,000, mostly Ukrainians, were ordered to report regularly to their local police authorities, and were issued identity papers that they were required to carry at all times.[32] Genuine prisoners of war (POWs), those of German nationality and German-speaking Austrians, were separated from the other internees and placed in "first-class" camps where they were kept in relative comfort. Meanwhile, those described as "Austro-Hungarians," like Ukrainians, were sent to work camps in remote areas of Canada including Castle Mountain, Lethbridge, Cave and Basin near Banff, and Jasper. The internees were not only expected to construct their own camps but were also required to work on land clearing, road building, woodcutting, and railway construction projects.[33]

The daily existence of internees was difficult. General William Otter, who led the internment operations on behalf of the Canadian Army, wrote: "The various complaints made to you by prisoners as to the rough conduct of the guards I fear is not altogether without reason ... and, I am sorry to say, by no means an uncommon occurrence." Samuel C. Reat, the US consul in Calgary, wrote on 11 November

REPORT BY   Major A. E. Hopkins,

Commanding Internment Camp,

Jasper. Alta.

ON WORK DONE BY PRISONERS OF WAR DURING THE WEEK ENDING Feb. 26th. 1916.

Report of Major Hopkins on the work done by prisoners of war in Jasper, AB. Author's personal collection.

Monday, 21st.   125 prisoners cutting posts in the bush.
             20   "   digging water main at Jasper.
Remainderof prisoners hauling water, sawing wood, finishing and clearing in and around Camp generally.

Tuesday,22nd.   125 prisoners cutting posts in the bush.
             20   "   digging water main at Jasper.
Remainder of prisoners building fence gate in Camp, hauling water, sawing wood, finishing and clearing in and around Camp.

Wednesday,23rd. 125 prisoners cutting posts in the bush.
             20   "   digging water main at Jasper.
Remainder of prisoners building fence gate in Camp, hauling water, sawing wood, finishing and clearing in and around Camp generally.

Thursday, 24th.   125 prisoners cutting fence posts in the bush.
             20   "   working on Pipe line at Jasper.
              7   "   hauling Cinders.
Remainder of prisoners hauling water, cutting wood, finishing and clearing in and around Camp generally

Friday, 25th.   100 prisoners cutting fence posts in the bush.
             20   "   workind on pipe line at Jasper.
             25   "   repairing Athabasca River Bridge and cut-
                 ting ice around piers.
Remainder of prisoners hauling water, cutting wood, finishing and clearing in and around Camp generally

Saturday, 26th.   100 prisoners cutting fence posts in the bush.
             15   "   working on Pipe line at Jasper.
             25 n "   repairing Athabasca River Bridge and cut-
                 ting ice around piers.
Remainder of prisoners hauling water, cutting wood, finishing and clearing in and around Camp generally
   "   "   P.M.   Prisoners washing their clothing, etc. and cleaning generally.

Sunday, 27th.   Sunday routine was observed and some prisoners hauling water and bringing in fire wood for general purposes.

A. E. Hopkins

Major.
Commanding Internment Camp

Prisoners of war coming out for roll call in Castle Mountain, AB. Whyte Museum of the Canadian Rockies, W. Buck Collection, V295/LC-51.

1915 that instances of prisoners being placed in dark cells and fed only bread and water "are not only proved but admitted by the authorities. Guards have cuffed prisoners on the slightest provocation and the conduct of some sergeants has been extremely reprehensible." The most reprehensible case, according to Reat, involved a prisoner by the name of Koziol, who was assaulted with a bayonet by a sergeant. "The sergeant made three distinct thrusts," wrote Reat, "but the . . . wounds were very slight. There seems to have been no cause for use of force. Koziol was an exemplary prisoner, according to the record." Watson Kirkconnell, who served as a guard, observed that there were "few on whom the long years

of captivity had not left their mark . . . confinement in a strange land, inactivity and hopeless waiting were in themselves enough to shatter the nerves and undermine the health."[34] Nick Olynyk, interned at Castle Mountain, wrote to his wife that "there are men running away from here everyday because the conditions here are very poor, so that we cannot go on much longer, we are not getting enough to eat. We are hungry as dogs. They are sending us to work, as they don't believe us, and we are very weak."[35]

Word of camp conditions spread through *Robochyi Narod*. "Who built the railroads and cultivated this wasteland where formerly only wind howled?" wrote one Ukrainian internee to the newspaper on 28 August 1915. "We, the victims who today are being tortured ... make our cause known so that all Ukrainians and all the nations of the world might see how the blind, 'civilized' English chauvinists and their Canadian hangers on treat foreigners."[36] Two months later, Banff inmate Dmytro Tkachyk wrote to the newspaper describing how the men were being "mercilessly driven" at bayonet point, and were sometimes chained and fed a diet of bread and water for insubordination. Others spoke openly about their captors, with one prisoner

declaring that he had been "forced to work when he was sick" and on refusing the guard "struck him with his rifle butt and called him a son of a bitch." Another prisoner wrote that he had tried avoiding work, due to the poor state of his clothes and boots, and was driven out of his hiding place by rifle point.[37] Surviving archival records of the internment operations corroborate the stories printed in *Robochyi Narod* and offer insight into the lives of the internees. For example, internee William Cowch wrote to Captain Charles Harvey, the commanding

Internees at Castle Mountain, 1916. Glenbow Archives, NC-54-4336.

officer of his internment camp, appealing for relief from his creditors. Despite being interned and, therefore, unable to keep his affairs in order and earn an income, his landlord was demanding that he pay rent and additional interest. This was expressed in a letter dated 4 August 1916 from the landlord's lawyer, demanding payment of debts, or Cowch's remaining possessions, mostly furniture and trunks, would be sold off. The situation was further complicated upon Cowch's parole when he was freed on work release far away from his home and debt.[38] While the commanding officer kept a record of Cowch's predicament, he did little to assist him in protecting his belongings or securing his permission to travel, while on parole, to settle his debt.

The internment operations also affected those who were not imprisoned. On 22 September 1916, Maria Marchuk appealed to the director of operations for assistance as she and her children were "suffering greatly" and "in great need" because her husband had been interned.[39] Katie Domytryk wrote to her father, who was arrested in Edmonton, that the family had nothing to eat and that "they do not want to give us no wood. It is better with you," she continued, "because we had everything to eat . . . We your small children kiss your hands my dear father. Goodbye my dear father. Come home right away."[40] Others attempted to appeal to the public directly: on 29 February 1917 an assembly of Ukrainian and Austrian women wrote to the *Calgary Daily Herald* proclaiming their innocence and loyalty to Canada. "We, the undersigned . . . wish to bring before the notice of the women of Calgary [that] we came to this country to make Canada our future home . . . We have been discharged from work because we are considered aliens but we are loyal to Canada." The appeal continued, "What are we to do if we cannot

3326

April 10, 1917.

Dear Sir,

The Canadian Pacific Railway Co. have applied for a large number of Prisoners of War to work on their lines.

Enclosed herewith is a list of 133 men who are eligible for release for such employment provided you are not aware of any special reasons for retaining any of them, in which case please give particulars.

I am sending you under separate cover 133 signed release forms and undertakings, to be accounted for, which you may fill out with full particulars when their representative arrives and selects the men.

They are to be paroled to the nearest Police Officer to the point they are required to work, or in the absence of such officer, the nearest Postmaster. Please see that whichever it is is filled in on the forms.

As soon as they are released send here M.F.W.2, also statements of accounts to date of release, Medical History and Conduct Sheets, and signed undertakings.

Yours very truly,

LT. COL.
For Director Internment Operations.

The Commandant,
Internment Camp,
Banff, Alta.

Letter from director of internment operations on CPR request for internee labour. Author's personal collection.

get work? Are we to starve or are we to be driven [to] a life of vice? Will not the women of Calgary speak for us?"[41] While some remained imprisoned, the end of the war saw the release of the majority of internees because the task of caring for them was becoming burdensome. Those who were physically fit, and "non-dangerous," were paroled to work for private companies, the federal and provincial governments, and especially railway companies, who increasingly turned to internment camps to solve their labour shortage problem.[42]

The Creation of the Ukrainian Labour Farmer Temple Association

Hostility toward potentially disloyal aliens continued to the end of, and immediately after, the First World War, allowing nativist sentiments to become even further ingrained in Anglo-Canadian identity. In the eyes of the majority, the image of Ukrainians was transformed from "enemy aliens" to "radicals," and, consequently, they became even more distrusted than their German counterparts.[43] While this had begun much earlier, by February 1919 employers across Canada had announced their willingness to dismiss enemy aliens and offer employment to returning soldiers instead. These concerns were fostered, perhaps most prominently, by the Great War Veterans' Association, who appealed to the Canadian government for mass and forcible repatriation of enemy aliens due to their continued role in labour industries. The government, alarmed by the growing tide of antiwar and pro-Soviet feelings within both Canada and Europe, issued an order in council banning many foreign language newspapers and radical organizations. Among these forbidden organizations

was the Ukrainian Social Democratic Party of Canada (USDP), which was, at the time, representing socialist-progressive Ukrainians and had petitioned the government in regard to their interned membership specifically, and other internees generally.[44]

The threat of forced repatriation was very real, with many internees viewing the deportations associated with the Winnipeg General Strike as precedent. Camp commanders were asked to identify prisoners who were "bitter against Canada and Great Britain," "bitter and troublesome and agitators and insubordinate," "trouble-makers and reported as being Industrial Workers of the World (IWW)," and even those who were "decidedly eccentric." These men were described as being "more or less of a nuisance," "IWW agitators," and "strike fomenters who congregate at secret meetings." As a result, 1,964 enemy aliens were deported, 302 of whom were Ukrainian.[45]

It was under these circumstances that the USDP leadership determined that, in addition to a political organization, a cultural and educational society was needed. Not only would such a society be beneficial in continuing the work of the USDP but it would also help to attract larger numbers of Ukrainians who were uncertain about their safety and future in Canada. Matthew Popovich, a leader of the Ukrainian socialist-progressive movement, recognized just how crucial this would be to maintaining the movement. "For some of us," he stated, "it became obvious that we must take this opportunity to organize a mass cultural-educational association, which would attract those workers who until now have not joined our existing organizations, but have shown great interest in the building of a Ukrainian Labour Temple and have responded generously with their help." He continued that to turn away these workers by diminishing the role of cultural-education work "would be a crime against our movement."[46]

On 14 May 1918, the Ukrainian Labour Farmer Temple Association (ULFTA) was established.[47] The supremacy of both political and cultural identity within the movement is best expressed in the founding constitution of the organization, which pledged "to give moral and material aid to the Ukrainian working people and to the labour cause, in general."[48] The ULFTA's organizers travelled across Canada establishing branches, including in some of the most remote areas of the country. They were most successful in rural Alberta, where many Ukrainian farmers had previously worked in mining and railroad construction and had become familiar with socialist ideas. By the end of 1918, the ULFTA had approximately 1,500 members in Alberta alone.[49]

Conclusion: "An Alternative to the Canadian Way of Life"

Canada's nativist sentiments, immigration policy, wartime xenophobia, and the internment operations undoubtedly took their toll on Canada's Ukrainians. The *Canadian Ruthenian,* in noting the plight of Ukrainians, denounced their harsh treatment at the hands of the Canadian government and public. "The Ukrainians were invited to Canada and promised liberty and a kind of paradise but liberty did not last long," it wrote, and continued: "First they were called 'Galicians' in mockery. Secondly, preachers were sent amongst them, as if they were savages, to preach Protestantism. And thirdly, they were deprived of the right to elect their representatives in Parliament." As a result, the newspaper

ventured that the future of Ukrainians in Canada was uncertain.[50] While some did, in fact, petition the government to allow them to return to their homeland, many more became increasingly uninterested in assimilating into Canadian society and began searching for alternatives.[51]

The ULFTA, which had begun its work as a carrier of radical and socio-economic change prior to the war, was seemingly the solution for many Ukrainians in Alberta. The ULFTA dedicated significant energy to establishing courses for its illiterate membership, Ukrainian children's schools, relief campaigns for victims of the 1921–22 Volga famine, and women's and youth branches of the organization. It eventually established drama clubs, choirs, and reading circles. All the while, the organization remained strongly dedicated to class struggle. "We, the workers," stated an article in *Robochyi Narod,* "regardless of our national origin, each and every one, want a free Ukraine, but the kind of Ukraine in which power belongs only to the workers, the poor peasants and the soldiers. We want socialism in Ukraine."[52]

According to Jim Mochoruk, the ULFTA "stood on the cusp of something quite amazing: the creation of an oasis where they and their families could live their entire lives almost entirely in the context of their own ethnic, radical community yet still reach out to others like themselves in order to bring them within the socialist fold."[53] Therefore, the commitment of adherents to the Ukrainian socialist-progressive movement was due to what it was able to retain, and represent, throughout the years. While the ULFTA and its predecessors were committed to the working-class struggle, they were, first and foremost, outlets of Ukrainian identity. For much of the membership, their ethnicity transcended acknowledgement, and support, of their birthplace and, instead, was a self-identification with their new home of Canada. In other words, it was the membership's experiences in Canada that influenced the ways in which they would think and act. After all, it was within the ULFTA that many of Canada's Ukrainians found a channel for their socio-economic and political needs, and a safe haven from the vehement discrimination and exploitation that greeted them in Canada. The organization had drawn much of its membership from among youth, taught them to read and write, integrated them into its ranks and trained them in various posts and positions. The organization also provided its membership with a social life and haven in what was, at least initially, a strange and alien environment.[54] The ability of the ULFTA to encompass both a political and ethnic identity not only rewarded it with the opportunity to represent the "progressive" version of what it meant to be a Ukrainian in Canada but also profoundly changed the way in which many Ukrainians came to understand their relationship with Canada—and each other.

Notes

1   Stella Hryniuk, "'Sifton's Pets': Who Were They?" in *Canada's Ukrainians: Negotiating an Identity,* edited by Lubomyr Luciuk and Stella Hryniuk (Toronto: University of Toronto Press, 1991), 4.

2   Howard Palmer, *Patterns of Prejudice: A History of Nativism in Alberta* (Toronto: McClelland and Stewart, 1982), 19–21.

3   Notwithstanding, nativism remained minimal throughout the 1880s and 1890s due to limited settlement opportunities. See Donald Avery, "European Immigrant Workers and Labour Protest in Peace and War, 1896–1919," in *The History of Immigration and Racism in Canada: Essential Readings,* edited by Barrington Walker (Toronto: Canadian Scholars' Press, 2008), 125, 126.

4   Statistics Canada, "Population, urban and rural by province (Alberta)," URL: http://www.statcan.gc.ca/tables-tableaux/sum-som/l01/cst01/demo62j-eng.htm, retrieved 13 June 2014.

5   In many ways, Sifton continued to adhere to prevailing notions of Anglo-Canadian superiority in his treatment of other immigrant groups such as the Italian-Americans and the Chinese. In the spring of 1897, Sifton convinced the government to pass the Alien Labour Act to restrict the influx of railway construction workers, mostly Italians, from the United States. He also attempted to increase Chinese capitation taxes and implement the Natal Act, which used educational tests as a means to bar entry to the country. See Avery, "European Immigrant Workers," 125, 126.

6   John Lehr, "Government Perceptions of Ukrainian Immigrants to Western Canada 1896–1902," *Canadian Ethnic Studies* 19, no. 2 (1987): 4, 5.

7   Palmer, *Patterns of Prejudice,* 22, 23.

8   Lubomyr Luciuk, *Searching for Place: Ukrainian Displaced Persons, Canada, and the Migration of Memory* (Toronto: University of Toronto Press, 2000), 13.

9   Lubomyr Luciuk, *Ukrainians in the Making: Their Kingston Story* (Kingston, ON: Limestone Press, 1980), 2.

10 Ibid., 3.

11 "The Affirmation of Witnesses: The Causes and Consequences of Canada's First National Internment Operations, 1914–1920," 7–8 February 2011, http://www.internmentcanada.ca/PDF/Affirmation_of_Witness.pdf, 5.

12 Lubomyr Luciuk, "Truth Takes Its Place alongside Tourism," *The Kingston Whig Standard,* 20 June 2013, 5.

13 Lehr, "Government Perceptions," 4, 5.

14 Bohdan Kordan and Lubomyr Luciuk, *A Delicate and Difficult Question: Documents in the History of Ukrainians in Canada, 1899–1962* (Kingston, ON: Limestone Press, 1986), 20.

15 Luciuk, *Ukrainians in the Making,* 3.

16 Kordan and Luciuk, *Delicate and Difficult Question*, 15, 17.

17 Valerie Knowles, *Strangers at Our Gates: Canadian Immigration and Immigration Policy 1540–2006* (Toronto: Dundurn, 2007), 80–82.

18 This included prostitutes, those with mental disabilities or contagious diseases, and immigrants deemed undesirable.

19 Knowles, *Strangers at Our Gates*, 82–85, 161, 162.

20 Palmer, *Patterns of Prejudice*, 28.

21 Jim Mochoruk, "'Pop&Co' versus Buck and the 'Lenin School Boys': Ukrainian Canadians and the Communist Party of Canada, 1921–1931," in *Re-Imagining Ukrainian Canadians: History, Politics, and Identity,* edited by Rhonda Hinther and Jim Mochoruk (Toronto: University of Toronto Press, 2011), 335; Peter Krawchuk, *Our History: The Ukrainian Labour-Farmer Movement in Canada 1907–1991* (Toronto: Lugus, 1996), xix.

22 They also dedicated considerable energy to organizing unskilled immigrant workers into unions such as the Industrial Workers of the World (IWW), the Western Federation of Miners (WFM), and the United Mine Workers of America (UMWA). See Donald Avery, *Dangerous Foreigners: European Immigrant Workers and Labour Radicalism in Canada, 1896–1932* (Toronto: McClelland and Stewart, 1979), 59.

23 Ibid.

24 Mochoruk, "'Pop&Co' versus Buck," 338.

25 However, even within the SPC, a movement dedicated to internationalism, or international and interethnic working-class solidarity, the Ukrainian membership was often alienated from their English-speaking counterparts and became increasingly aware of the dissension with the party. Troubled by their increasingly marginal role within the party, the Ukrainian language branches called a meeting, bringing together delegates from the Ukrainian socialist-progressive organizations across Canada, to discuss the current situation and strategize for the future. A conference was held on 12 November 1909, with the understanding that the Ukrainian language branches must unite into a cohesive and central organization that could plan and conduct educational work on behalf of the Ukrainian proletariat in Canada. Moreover, it was decided that if the SPC's leadership would not recognize the autonomy of this newly formed centralized organization then it would "work with complete organizational independence, disregarding the official party" as well as make attempts "with others dissatisfied with the present leadership to form a new party, worthy of carrying the name socialist." Ultimately, following continued disagreements with SPC leadership, Ukrainians, along with other language federations, severed ties and, on 20 July 1910, united with the Social Democratic Party of Canada (SDPC) under the designation of the Federation of Ukrainian Social Democrats (FUSD). Unlike the SPC, the SDPC was seemingly interested in cooperation between immigrant and English-speaking party members and even encouraged the unique interests of FUSD. See Krawchuk, *Our History*, 7, 8, and 16.

26 This included media censorship, arrest, detention, deportation, the appropriation and disposal of property, and the elimination of the option of bail.

27 Unemployment rates amongst the Ukrainians were often so high that the internment camps served as shelters for those who were destitute. See Peter Melnycky, "The Internment of Ukrainians in Canada," in *Loyalties in Conflict: Ukrainians in Canada during the Great War,* edited by Frances Swyripa and John Herd Thompson (Edmonton: Canadian Institute of Ukrainian Studies, 1983), 2.

28 Ibid., 3–6.

29 The internment of Ukrainians, and other enemy aliens, was complicated by their problematic status in Canadian law. According to James Farney and Bohdan Kordan, the status of enemy aliens paralleled a deeper conflict between nationalism and imperialism that dominated Canadian public discourse. The idea of citizenship, championed by Laurier's government, had provided a theoretical basis for the incorporation of new immigrants to Canada. This model was created around the idea that immigrants should be understood

as rights-bearing individuals. However, it did not take into account the extenuating circumstances of Canadian sovereignty; mainly, Canada's status as a dominion. Therefore, it could not simply adjust its ideas of citizenship or decide who fully belonged; it had to ensure that these ideas were consistent with imperial statutory law as well. Furthermore, the version of Canada promoted by imperialists implied a direct connection between a relationship with the Crown and legal status. In other words, individuals received protection and benefits from the Crown insofar as their relationship to it was well defined; those with unclear connections to the Crown would only receive limited, if any, rights. In the context of the war, this was exceptionally relevant because immigrants were unable to develop connections to Britain, or prove their loyalty to it, immediately disadvantaging them. See James Farney and Bohdan Kordan, "The Predicament of Belonging: The Status of Enemy Aliens in Canada, 1914," *Journal of Canadian Studies* 39, no. 1 (2005): 75–80.

30 Lubomyr Luciuk, *Without Just Cause: Canada's First National Internment Operations and the Ukrainian Canadians, 1914–1920* (Kingston, ON: Kashtan Press, 2006), 9.

31 According to calculations from General Otter, who led the internment operations on behalf of the Department of Justice, only 3,138 of those interned could have been classified as genuine POWs. The other 5,441, most of whom were Ukrainian, should have been considered civilians.

32 Ibid., 2, 3. While determining the nationality of the internees is difficult since many of the archival materials were destroyed after the Second World War, the records that remain suggest that many of the Austro-Hungarians were, in fact, of Ukrainian origin. Some Poles, Italians, Bulgarians, Croats, Turks, Serbs, Hungarians, Russians, Jews, and Romanians were also interned or categorized as enemy aliens.

33 In November 1915, it was reported that internees were performing labour valued at $1,500,000 a year.

See Lubomyr Luciuk, *In Fear of the Barbed Wire Fence: Canada's First National Internment Operations and the Ukrainian Canadians, 1914–1920* (Kingston, ON: Kashtan Press, 2001), 14.

34 Luciuk, *Without Just Cause*, 7, 8.

35 "The Affirmation of Witnesses," 12

36 "Enemy Aliens, Prisoners of War: Canada's First World War Internment Operations, 1914–1920," Cave and Basin National Historic Site, 20 May 2014.

37 Bill Waiser, *Park Prisoners: The Untold Story of Western Canada's National Parks, 1915–1946* (Saskatoon: Fifth House, 1995), 21.

38 Library and Archives Canada, RG6 H1, vol. 752, CSIS fonds.

39 The request was denied on 6 October 1916, when a staff officer wrote: "I regret to inform you that such is not considered desirable." See Library and Archives Canada, RG18, vol. 1793, CSIS fonds.

40 "The Affirmation of Witnesses," 17.

41 Ibid.

42 By the spring of 1917, nearly all of the internees were released on parole for this reason. The conditions for release included remaining in Canada, reporting frequently to police, and carrying certificates of release as "internal passports" while travelling. See Melnycky, "The Internment of Ukrainians in Canada," 14.

43 Avery, *Dangerous Foreigners*, 76.

44 The USDP specifically protested the classification of Ukrainians as enemy aliens, criticized naturalization restrictions, and called for the establishment of employment bureaus. See Melnycky, "The Internment of Ukrainians in Canada," 13.

45 Ibid., 15–17.

46 Krawchuk, *Our History*, 35.

47 Ibid., 31, 32. When the USDP was banned in September 1918, the Ukrainian Labor Temple Association (ULTA) replaced it as the national organization responsible for promoting socialist and Marxist ideas amongst the Ukrainians. In 1924 it was nationally incorporated as the Ukrainian Labour-Farmer Temple Association (ULFTA), a centralized cultural-

educational labour organization responsible for
the promotion of the communist cause amongst
Ukrainians.

48 Ibid., 34.

49 John Kolasky, *The Shattered Illusion: The History of
Ukrainian Pro-Communist Organizations in Canada*
(Toronto: PMA Books, 1979), 3, 4.

50 Although appeals for mass repatriation were largely
rejected, some deportations did occur following the
Winnipeg General Strike of 1919. This procedure was
not universal for all strikers; while Ukrainians, and
others, were deported, their British counterparts were
processed through the appropriate judicial channels
and did not face the same kinds of punishment. See
Avery, *Dangerous Foreigners*, 76, 77.

51 Ibid., 89. The ULTA eventually became the Ukrainian
Labour-Farmer Temple Association to reflect the
growing numbers of farmers joining the organization.
After the Second World War it became the Association
of United Ukrainian Canadians.

52 Krawchuk, *Our History*, xix.

53 Ibid., 32; Mochoruk, "'Pop&Co' versus Buck."

54 Kolasky, *Shattered Illusion*, 202.

Works Cited

PRIMARY SOURCES

Library and Archives Canada. CSIS fonds, RG6 H1, vol.
752.

——. CSIS fonds, RG18, vol. 1793.

——. CSIS fonds, RG211, vol. 866.

——. *Novyi Shliakh*, NJ.FM.1786, newspaper microfilm
holdings.

——. *Ukrainske Zhyttia*, NJ.FM.1798, newspaper microfilm
holdings.

SECONDARY SOURCES

Angus, Ian. *Canadian Bolsheviks: The Early Years of the
Communist Party of Canada*. Victoria: Trafford, 2004.

Avakumovic, Ivan. *The Communist Party in Canada: A
History*. Toronto: McClelland and Stewart, 1975.

Avery, Donald. *Dangerous Foreigners: European Immigrant
Workers and Labour Radicalism in Canada, 1896–1932*.
Toronto: McClelland and Stewart, 1979.

——. "European Immigrant Workers and Labour Protest
in Peace and War, 1896–1919." In *The History of
Immigration and Racism in Canada: Essential Readings*,
edited by Barrington Walker. Toronto: Canadian
Scholars' Press, 2008.

Carter, David. *Behind Canadian Barbed Wire*. Calgary:
Tumbleweed Press, 1980.

Cave and Basin National Historic Site, Banff, AB. "Enemy
Aliens, Prisoners of War: Canada's First World War
Internment Operations, 1914–1920" exhibit.

Farney, James, and Bohdan Kordan. "The Predicament
of Belonging: The Status of Enemy Aliens in Canada,
1914." *Journal of Canadian Studies* 39, no. 1 (Winter
2005): 74–89.

Hinther, Rhonda. "Raised in the Spirit of the Class
Struggle: Children, Youth, and the Interwar Ukrainian
Left in Canada." *Labour/ Le Travail* 60 (2007): 43–76.

Hinther, Rhonda, and Jim Mochoruk, eds. *Re-Imagining
Ukrainian-Canadians: History, Politics, and Identity*.
Toronto: University of Toronto Press, 2011.

Keshen, Jeffrey. *Propaganda and Censorship during Canada's
Great War*. Edmonton: University of Alberta Press,
1996.

Knowles, Valerie. *Strangers at Our Gates: Canadian
Immigration and Immigration Policy, 1540–2006*.
Toronto: Dundurn, 2007.

Kolasky, John. *Prophets and Proletarians: Documents on the
History of the Rise and Decline of Ukrainian Communism
in Canada*. Edmonton: Canadian Institute of
Ukrainian Studies Press, 1990.

——. *The Shattered Illusion: The History of Ukrainian Pro-
Communist Organizations in Canada*. Toronto: PMA
Books, 1979.

Kordan, Bohdan, and Lubomyr Luciuk, eds. *A Delicate and
Difficult Question: Documents in the History of Ukrainians*

in Canada, 1899–1962. Kingston, ON: Limestone Press, 1986.

Krawchuk, Peter. *Mathew Popovich: His Place in the History of Ukrainian Canadians.* Toronto: Canadian Society for Ukrainian Labour Research, 1987.

——. *Our History: The Ukrainian Labour-Farmer Movement in Canada, 1907–1991.* Toronto: Lugus, 1996.

Lehr, John. "Government Perceptions of Ukrainian Immigrants to Western Canada, 1896–1902." *Canadian Ethnic Studies* 19, no. 2 (1987): 1–12.

——. "People the Prairies with Ukrainians." In *Immigration in Canada: Historical Perspectives*, edited by Gerald Tulchinsky. Toronto: Copp Clark Longman, 1994.

Luciuk, Lubomyr. *In Fear of the Barbed Wire Fence: Canada's First National Internment Operations and the Ukrainian Canadians, 1914–1920.* Kingston, ON: Kashtan Press, 2001.

——. *Searching for Place: Ukrainian Displaced Persons, Canada, and the Migration of Memory.* Toronto: University of Toronto Press, 2000.

——. *Ukrainians in the Making: Their Kingston Story.* Kingston, ON: Limestone Press, 1980.

——. *Without Just Cause: Canada's First National Internment Operations and the Ukrainian Canadians, 1914–1920.* Kingston, ON: Kashtan Press, 2006.

Luciuk, Lubomyr, and Stella Hryniuk, eds. *Canada's Ukrainians: Negotiating an Identity.* Toronto: University of Toronto Press, 1991.

Luciuk, Lubomyr, and Bohdan Kordan, eds. *Anglo-American Perspectives on the Ukrainian Question, 1938–1951.* Kingston, ON: Limestone Press, 1987.

Marunchak, Michael. *The Ukrainian Canadians: A History.* Winnipeg: Ukrainian Academy of Arts and Sciences, 1982.

Momryk, Myron. "The Royal Canadian Mounted Police and the Surveillance of the Ukrainian Community in Canada." *Journal of Ukrainian Studies* 28, no. 2 (2003): 89–112.

Palmer, Howard. *Patterns of Prejudice: A History of Nativism in Alberta.* Toronto: McClelland and Stewart, 1982.

Petryshyn, Jaroslav. *Peasants in the Promised Land: Canada and the Ukrainians, 1891–1914.* Toronto: James Lorimer & Co., 1985.

Piniuta, Harry. *Land of Pain, Land of Promise: First Person Accounts by Ukrainian Pioneers, 1891–1914.* Saskatoon: Western Producer Prairie Books, 1978.

Radforth, Ian. "Ethnic Minorities and Wartime Injustices: Redress Campaigns and Historical Narratives in Late Twentieth-Century Canada." In *Settling and Unsettling Memories: Essays in Canadian Public History*, edited by Nicole Neatby and Peter Hodgins. Toronto: University of Toronto Press, 2012.

Reinisch, Jessica, and Elizabeth White. *The Disentanglement of Populations: Migration, Expulsion, and Displacement in Postwar Europe, 1944–1949.* New York: Palgrave Macmillan, 2011.

Roberts, Barbara. *Whence They Came: Deportation from Canada, 1900–1935.* Ottawa: University of Ottawa Press, 1988.

Sangster, Joan. "Robitnytsia, Ukrainian Communists, and the 'Porcupinism' Debate: Reassessing Ethnicity, Gender, and Class in Early Canadian Communism, 1922–1930." *Labour/ Le Travail* 56 (2005): 51–89.

Swyripa, Frances, and John Thompson, eds. *Loyalties in Conflict: Ukrainians in Canada during the Great War.* Edmonton: Canadian Institute of Ukrainian Studies, 1983.

Timlin, Mabel. "Canada's Immigration Policy, 1896–1910." *The Canadian Journal of Economics and Political Science* 4 (1960).

Waiser, Bill. *Park Prisoners: The Untold Story of Western Canada's National Parks, 1915–1946.* Saskatoon: Fifth House, 1995.

Zembrzycki, Stacey. "'There Were Always Men in Our House': Gender and the Childhood Memories of Working-Class Ukrainians in Depression-Era Canada." *Labour/ Le Travail* 60 (2007): 77–105.

Conscientious Objectors in Alberta in the First World War

AMY J. SHAW

In 1917, Prime Minister Robert Borden returned from a visit to the Western Front and a meeting of the Imperial War Cabinet convinced him that it was necessary for Canada to start conscripting men for compulsory military service. When the war broke out, he had promised there would be no conscription, and he knew that it would be terribly unpopular in certain parts of the country, especially Quebec. But Borden, like many Canadians, felt that it was necessary, and that it was the duty of the government to prosecute the war to its utmost.

The concept of duty was important during the First World War. Participation was framed as a duty to the Empire, to Canada, to more local loyalties such as one's family, and to a sense of appropriate "manliness." However, one's primary duty was, especially for some individuals, not always easy to ascertain. To those for whom military service conflicted with religious or ethical beliefs, conscription brought a difficult dilemma. A letter sent to Borden earlier in the war expressed its signers' conflicted sense of duty:

We are aware that in taking the stand which we have some will consider us to be "shirkers" but this is far from being the case. Some are bound by what seems like a tragic fate to take the lives of our fellow-men whilst they only wish to give their lives for their country—on the other hand some of us are bound to appear the enemies of our country for conscience sake when we wish to serve her with all our powers.[1]

The government, to a certain extent, had a similar dilemma. Conscription was understood as part of its duty to soldiers already overseas. It was also deemed necessary for the home front because the war effort demanded a lot from people within Canada as well. Many of them, it seemed, felt less willing to make the necessary sacrifices—to send off their sons, to conserve food and fuel—if those sacrifices were not broadly distributed. To the minds of many people at home, conscription seemed a necessary, and democratic, equalizer. It would help ensure that there were no slackers.

The federal government had to balance out its competing obligations as well. Beyond the successful prosecution of the war, it was also obliged to respect the promises made to what are called the "historic peace churches" in Canada, namely the Mennonites, Church of the Brethren (also called Tunkers or Dunkards), Hutterites, Doukhobors, and the Society of Friends, or Quakers. Many of these people had immigrated to Canada based on promises that they would not be asked to undertake military service. The Borden administration also had duties to Canada's tradition of liberal democracy. This meant that, like the other democracies fighting in the First World War, conscription legislation included provision for exemption on the grounds of conscientious objection to military service, whether voluntary or conscripted. Conscientious objection is at the core of the individual's relationship to the state because it challenges what is generally seen as the most basic of civic obligations: the duty to defend one's country.

Conscription was not a novelty in Canada, although the First World War was the first large-scale use of it, and the first time Canadians were drafted for overseas service. In spite of the existence of various militia acts since the time of New France, Canadians had had little direct experience with military conscription. The volunteer militia had not been called out since the North-West Rebellion of 1885, and the contingents sent to the South African War had been made up entirely of volunteers paid for, and commanded by, Britain. In many quarters, the tradition of militia service linked to the sense that conscription was "un-British" and demonstrated confidence in the efficacy of the voluntary system. Voluntarism was an important part of many people's sense of Canada's national identity. There was no stronger proponent of voluntarism—and the value of the "citizen soldier"—than Minister of Militia and Defence Sam Hughes.

The Borden administration introduced conscription under the 1917 Military Service Act, drafted by Arthur Meighen, Solicitor General and a future Conservative prime minister of Canada. The act was signed into law on 29 August 1917. It declared that all male British subjects between the ages of 20 and 45 were liable for military service, and grouped them into classes according to age and marital status. When a man's class was called up, he was deemed to be an enlisted soldier subject to military law. The act included various grounds for exemption from conscription, recognizing other duties and abilities that made across-the-board conscription impractical. A man could be exempted from compulsory military service on the grounds of ill health, or by proving that his job was essential to the prosecution of the war or that enlisting would cause serious financial hardship to those dependent upon him. The last grounds for exemption was that a conscript

> conscientiously objects to the undertaking
> of combatant service and is prohibited from
> so doing by the tenets and articles of faith,
> in effect at the date of the passing of this act,
> of any organized religious denomination ex-
> isting and well recognized in Canada, at such
> date, and to which he in good faith belongs.

A series of tribunals was set up across the country. Prominent local citizens judged the claims for exemption, with provision for the claimant, or the military, to appeal the decision to a higher court presided over by Justice Lyman Duff.

The Borden administration did not enforce the act right away. The government had been elected in 1911, which meant that, under normal circumstances, there ought to have been an election in 1916. Because of the war, Britain gave the government special dispensation to continue, and no one seems to have minded much, But introducing something so controversial as conscription under an expired mandate seemed problematic. Borden hoped that the unified front of a coalition government would be the answer. While Wilfrid Laurier, the leader of the opposition, refused to join, based on the negative reaction he knew conscription would give rise to in Quebec, many Liberals did. The election of 1917 was thus between the "Unionists" and the rump of the Liberal party, with a few Labour and independent candidates. Before the election, the government enacted two laws to strengthen its chances at the polls. One was the Military Voters Act, which enfranchised all members of the armed forces, no matter how long they had lived in Canada. The other, the Wartime Elections Act, famously gave the vote to Canadian women who were mothers, wives, sisters, or daughters of servicemen. Less famously, it also disenfranchised some people. Conscientious objectors and naturalized Canadians born in enemy countries, who had settled in Canada after 1902, lost their right to vote. The election campaign of 1917 was negative and bitter, and fought largely around the issue of conscription. The victory of the Unionists seemed to prove Canadians' support of it. However, when conscription was finally enforced, some 93 percent of those drafted claimed exemption.[2]

The clause in the Military Service Act of 1917 providing exemption from military service on conscientious grounds was included specifically for the members of Canada's historic peace churches. The government recognized that it had prior promises to these groups, and hoped that limiting exemption to members of organized churches with clear proscriptions against military service would control the numbers of objectors. The government also hoped to avoid the difficulty of assessing the conscience of individual objectors by putting forward an exemption clause that was a privilege granted members of certain religious denominations, rather than a right accorded all Canadians who might object conscientiously.

Alberta was home to about 1,500 Mennonites living mainly in scattered communities across the south of the province. As well, Doukhobors from British Columbia began settling in Lundbreck and Cowley, east of the Crowsnest Pass, in 1916. Although this recognition simplified matters for them, it did not mean they had an easy time. The churches were not able to present an organized front, and difficulties in the wording of the act, and its various interpretations by tribunals, caused a great deal of anxiety, and led to the imprisonment of several young men. For example, Gordon Weber and Otto Reimer, both from Didsbury, Alberta, were conscripted in spite of being Mennonites, though their status was later recognized. They were imprisoned for their refusal but released before their sentences were up—Weber in August 1918 and Reimer not until December of that year, after the war's end.[3] Insecurity about their position, along with the public antipathy they faced, contributed to the emigration of several Mennonite groups after the war. Conversely, the oppression some Hutterites faced in the wartime United States led groups of them to move to Canada in 1918.[4]

Despite official government recognition, the Mennonites faced public animosity for their stance. A letter to the editor of the *Lethbridge Daily Herald* called "the Mennonite problem" "the biggest thing in Southern Alberta" based on the author's sense that these people "threatened to engulf all the available land in this south country." The land, he thought, should, "in common decency, be saved for the men of the Canadian Army" when they returned. He was also unhappy with their exemption, and noted:

> Just how any conscientious objector can manage to justify his existence at this time puzzles me. The fact that the government, back in 1873, gave these people the freedom of the country, and an undertaking that they would not be called for military service, is no decent excuse for their not being in khaki at this time, for the simple reason that when that undertaking was given our only thought of war was an Indian rising or two, or a small scrap in some out of the way portion of the globe. There was certainly no thought of a world-wide scrap in which the whole efforts of the country would be strained to the utmost.[5]

He believed that these were not the types of citizen Canada wanted, and that "something should be done, and done quickly, to stop the matter going any further, and it is up to the municipalities of the southern half of the province to get busy without any loss of time and petition the government to bar any more of these people coming into Canada."[6]

In the face of this, members of these non-resistant churches emphasized their desire to be obedient to the government. They also, perhaps partly in response to antagonism such as that expressed in the letter to the *Lethbridge Daily Herald*, made efforts to express their thanks for exemption, and join Canadians in the self-sacrificing spirit of the war. A letter discussing a monetary gift to the government expressed this hope and stated:

> We realize that the Government has not assigned us any duty in lieu of military service, and therefore we are not made to share any special part of the burden which our nation is bearing ... while we are sharing in the national burden of trials and fears and labours, it is our purpose, by the grace of God, to undertake voluntarily some share in the sacrifices of our fellow-citizens, and by some means ... express in a more substantial manner our gratitude to the Government for the Christian privileges which we enjoy under the laws of Canada.[7]

Mennonites, however, were not the only ones who felt that their attitudes toward war placed them in the category of conscientious objectors. Members of smaller denominations such as the International Bible Students Association (IBSA; today called Jehovah's Witnesses), Plymouth Brethren, Seventh Day Adventists, and Christadelphians also objected, as did some members of the mainstream Protestant and Catholic Churches. They had a more difficult time.[8]

Advocates of conscription promoted, among other things, its democratizing benefits. One editorial in the *Toronto Globe*, in May 1917, discussed how conscription was a good policy because it "democratize[d] citizenship." The editor wrote:

> The freedom of the individual is bound up with the defence of the nation. The small nations that seek freedom and independence and the untrammeled development of their civil life are forced to adopt a system of universal service. This is the case with Canada. In her search for honour and military strength and freedom she finds it only in compulsory national service.[9]

The broad association of conscription with equality and democracy placed conscientious objectors in a most unfavourable light. The draft promised a parity of sacrifice, and recognition of group goals that many Canadians hoped would continue after the war. Objectors had chosen to differentiate themselves from that picture of unity, and retain allegiance to different, individual goals. It left them open to charges of selfishness, along with the more predictable allegations of cowardice. That the war was often portrayed as a religious crusade also made the option of conscientious objection difficult, both for an individual to take, and for the wider public to understand.

An article in the *Grande Prairie Herald* expressed this suspicion with individual rights in a fairly dramatic way, arguing that the conscientious objectors were actually like the hated Germans in their sense of exceptionality.

It seems . . . that the conscientious objectors are suffering from the same mental malady that afflicts the Germans. In one case the patients consider themselves to be so much finer in sensibility and truer to their ideals than their brothers that they can indulge themselves in these feelings at the expense of these same brothers who are thinking more of the good of others than of themselves. When I think of the stupendous egotism of the Germans, I can't get any farther than the puzzled baffled feeling that I had at the beginning of the war. This same puzzled, baffled feeling comes when I try to get the point of view of the conscientious objectors. How can they be sure that they believe in non-resistance when there are so many brave men between them and danger? How can they be satisfied to be one of the difficulties that these brothers of their have to contend with? How can they keep on worshipping Billikin, the foolish "god of things as they ought to be," while their brothers are serving the "God of things as they are?"[10]

This argument saw the "pacifist" objectors, in a somewhat surprising twist, as like the "militaristic" Germans because of their insistence on making their own judgments about right and wrong. Evidently, being idealistic in a country at war was just as much of a difficulty as cowardice.

Robert Elliott of Calgary was 31 years old and a minister in the Plymouth Brethren Church when he claimed exemption. His case went all the way to the Central Appeal Tribunal, and became the test for whether this denomination would be recognized. Judge Lyman Duff complimented Elliot on presenting the case for the Plymouth Brethren's pacifist stance "with great clearness as well as obvious sincerity," but he refused to grant exemption. Duff explained that he did so based on the fact that Elliott "did not dispute that the taking part in combatant military service would not, according to the corporate views of the Plymouth Brethren, be regarded as a disqualification for membership; wickedness alone, he said, would be a ground of exclusion, and that would not necessarily be regarded as wickedness in all circumstances."[11] The church, then, was not included in the exemption clause because it did not impose harsh enough, or consistent enough, penalties on those who transgressed its pacifist tenets. Adherents of sects with such flexibility made up the largest part of unrecognized conscientious objectors; along with the Plymouth Brethren, these included the IBSA and members of the Pentecostal Assemblies.

Tunker Ernest Swalm was detained with a Plymouth Brother while awaiting trial for his refusal to obey military orders. In his memoirs, he recalled the difficulty caused by this group's reluctance to take on a denominational label, and recalled the questions asked of the Plymouth Brother as follows:

"What church do you belong to?" asked the colonel.
"The Church of Jesus Christ."
"Do you have a creed?"
"Yes, the Bible," replied my friend.
"Where do you originate?"
"At Calvary."
'But where are your headquarters?"
"Heaven."
"Don't get smart, kid," snapped the officer.

While the officer's frustration is understandable, given that he was apparently looking for evidence of organization necessary to exempt the young man, Swalm explained that "the colonel did not know that the Plymouth Brethren boy was answering sincerely in the tradition of his accepted belief."[12] In the Plymouth Brethrens' repudiation of denominational labels, they ran up against the Canadian government's decision to base recognition on denominational, rather than individual beliefs. That it was a sect with strong pacifist principles is evident, but the deliberate lack of structure and organization was a serious handicap in a wartime society impatient with the nuances of radical Christianity.

Another group of Albertans who encountered challenges with their application for exemption

from conscription on conscientious grounds were the Seventh Day Adventists. This denomination had applied for exemption from combatant service, arguing, for example, that "if there is any portion of the Bible which we, as a people, can point to more than another as our creed, it is the law of the ten commandments . . . The fourth of these commandments requires cessation from labour on the seventh day of the week, the sixth prohibits the taking of life, neither of which, in our view, could be observed while doing military duty."[13] The church, like many others that requested exemption, emphasized its members' desire to be good citizens and respect government authority. The appeal court judge granted exemption. However, in the rather makeshift atmosphere surrounding conscription, this did not always filter down to the officials who had to deal directly with conscientious objectors.

This was reflected in the experience of three young Albertans who were drafted into the army training camp at Calgary on 15 April 1918. James Bennett Wagner, at 26 years of age, was the oldest; a year younger was Max Popow, a Russian-born farmer from Lacombe. At 21, Floyd Edwin Jones was the youngest of the group, and another farmer from Strathcona. When they informed the sergeant major of their principles, he first replied that "that [would] be all right" but, later, put the men into military detention when they refused to drill on their Sabbath (Saturday). Wagner recorded that the three men "tried to persuade those in authority to transfer us to the Medical Corps, where we could conscientiously help the sick on the Sabbath; but no, they would not do that, for we were all in good health, and they wanted us as common infantrymen." Wagner spent six weeks in jail in Lethbridge for his refusal, but the military later made the concession, and he was transferred to the Medical Corps. When he got there, he was happy to see Jones, who had been transferred there earlier.

However, this was not the end of their difficulties. If the decisions of the appeal court did not always immediately affect those of the military authorities, conscientious objectors also had to deal with the officers and enlisted men. The three Adventists' refusal to do unnecessary work on their Sabbath annoyed the sergeant major, who complained, "I haven't time to be running after you all the time." Other soldiers expressed their frustrations more violently: "One night [after] Floyd and I had gone to sleep, into the tent came a mob of disguised soldiers. They jumped upon us, beat us, and smeared us with axel grease." A few days later, they were mobbed again, in broad daylight: "When they slipped the canvas bag over my head and carried me out of the tent, I did not resist them, but only offered a silent prayer to the God whom I was serving. Without any injury to me, after smearing my body with tar, they set me free." A few days later, the two men were released from the army.[14]

Conscientious objectors in Alberta faced animosity from many of their compatriots, partly because of their apparent decision to stand aside from the unified front of war service in favour of the more individual duty of allegiance to conscience. The experience of this war, however, shaped that of the next. In the Second World War, the government, working with members of Canada's historic "peace churches," worked out a system of alternative service, whereby those whose conscience forbade them military service could still offer productive service to their country.[15]

Notes

1 David D. Priestman and George Arthur Wigmore to Robert Borden, 5 October 1916, Library and Archives Canada (LAC), Robert Borden Papers, MG26 H1(c), vol. 208, 112599.

2 J.L. Granatstein and J.M. Hitsman, *Broken Promises: A History of Conscription in Canada* (Toronto: Copp, Clark, Pitman, 1985), 85. David Ricardo Williams, *Duff: A Life in the Law* (Vancouver: UBC Press, 1984), 94. There is no record of how many people requested exemption on the grounds of conscientious objection.

3 Amy Shaw, *Crisis of Conscience: Conscientious Objection in Canada during the First World War* (Vancouver, UBC Press, 2008), Appendix: "List of Conscientious Objectors."

4 German-speaking Hutterites from South Dakota established six colonies in southern Alberta in 1918. For further discussion see Rod Janzen, *The Hutterites in North America* (Baltimore, MD: Johns Hopkins University Press, 2010).

5 *Lethbridge Herald*, 7 September 1918.

6 Ibid.

7 S.F. Coffman and Aaron Loucks to Robert Borden, 30 November 1917, Conrad Grebel College, University of Waterloo, Samuel Coffman Papers, XV 11.4.7.

8 William Cassidy, for example, a 29-year-old steam engineer from Barons, Alberta, had, as a Catholic, no support from his church in his conscientious objection. He was sentenced to five years in the Alberta Penitentiary for his refusal to obey orders when conscripted. Shaw, Appendix: "List of Conscientious Objectors."

9 *Toronto Globe*, 21 May 1917, 6.

10 "The Conscientious Objector: Beclouded Viewpoint of Pacifists Is a Puzzle to Others," *Grande Prairie Herald*, 27 December 1917, 3. This article was printed in many Canadian newspapers. Harriet Rashnell, writing for the *New York Outlook*, is cited as its original author.

11 "The Military Service Act, 1917, Report of Cases Decided by the Central Appeal Judge, March 23rd,

1918," Canada *Unpublished Sessional Papers,* 1st sess., 13th Parliament (18 March 1918–24 May 1918), no. 97, 29–30, LAC, RG14, D2, vol. 36.

12 Ernest Swalm, *My Beloved Brethren: Personal Memoirs and Recollections of the Canadian Brethren in Christ Church* (Nappanee, IN: Evangel Press, 1969), 26.

13 General Conference Executive Committee, Statement to the Governor of the State of Michigan, 2 August 1864, quoted in J. Ernest Monteith, *The Lord Is My Shepherd: A History of the Seventh-day Adventist Church in Canada* (Oshawa, ON: Canadian Union Conference of the Seventh-day Adventist Church, 1983), 162.

14 James Wagner to J. Ernest Monteith, n.d., quoted in *The Lord Is My Shepherd*, 163–64. See also service records for #3207837 James Bennett Wagner, LAC, CEFS Records, RG150 accession 92/93, box 9983-21, service record for #3207838 Max Popow, box 7904; and service record for #3207839 Floyd Edwin Jones, box 49933-11. The attacks by the soldiers were precipitated because Wagner and Jones had been deleted from a list of those eligible for a draft to Siberia.

15 These provisions allowed conscientious objectors to serve for four months in "Alternative Service" camps operated by the Department of Mines and Resources. This would later be extended to the duration of the war. The labour was compensated at 50 cents a day, and the government provided maintenance and travelling expenses to and from the camps.

Works Cited

PRIMARY SOURCES

Globe and Mail
Grande Prairie Herald
Lethbridge Herald

Conrad Grebel College, University of Waterloo. Samuel Coffman Papers, XV 11.4.7.
Library and Archives Canada (LAC). Canadian Expeditionary Force Records, RG150 accession 92/93.

———. Government of Canada, "The Military Service Act, 1917, Report of Cases Decided by the Central Appeal Judge, March 23rd, 1918," Canada *Unpublished Sessional Papers,* 1st sess., 13th Parliament (18 March 1918–24 May 1918), no. 97, 29–30, RG14, D2, vol. 36.
———. Robert Borden Papers, MG26 H1.

SECONDARY SOURCES

Granatstein, J.L., and J.M. Hitsman. *Broken Promises: A History of Conscription in Canada.* Toronto: Copp, Clark, Pitman, 1985.
Janzen, Rod. *The Hutterites in North America.* Baltimore, MD: Johns Hopkins University Press, 2010.
Monteith, J. Ernest. *The Lord Is My Shepherd: A History of the Seventh-day Adventist Church in Canada.* Oshawa, ON: Canadian Union Conference of the Seventh-day Adventist Church, 1983.
Shaw, Amy. *Crisis of Conscience: Conscientious Objection in Canada during the First World War.* Vancouver: UBC Press, 2008.
Swalm, Ernest. *My Beloved Brethren: Personal Memoirs and Recollections of the Canadian Brethren in Christ Church.* Nappanee, IN: Evangel Press, 1969.
Williams, David Ricardo. *Duff: A Life in the Law.* Vancouver: UBC Press, 1984.

SECTION FOUR

Aftermath

The men and women who came home from the Front returned to a country and province that had changed dramatically over four years. The war had empowered some; for example, women had been granted the vote on 19 April 1916. They had participated in the 1917 provincial election as voters and also as candidates for the Legislative Assembly of Alberta. Other changes would prove less popular; for example, patriotic fervour spurred Prohibitionists, who believed that returning soldiers should come back to a "dry" homeland that would somehow be thereby rid of all social ills. They were instrumental in the passage of prohibition legislation in 1916.

Returning soldiers suffered from loss of limbs and other unseen symptoms comprising "shell shock," or what is today known as Post-Traumatic Stress Disorder. Measures to help them to adjust were not always adequate. Many returning veterans had to be hospitalized. Medical historian J. Robert Lampard notes that, in the early 1920s, treatment of veterans was centralized in a number of key facilities. In 1922, the federal government built an 84-bed annex at the Strathcona Hospital in Edmonton to house soldiers, and also funded the building of the second wing on the Royal Alexandra Hospital. In Calgary, the Colonel Belcher Hospital opened in 1919 and received the remaining Calgary vets. In 1920, the Keith Sanatorium opened west of Calgary with 185 beds.[1] According to Lampard, by 1921, there were 650 veterans left in Alberta hospitals.[2]

Venereal disease also presented challenges since the rate of infection was so high; an estimated 66,000 Canadian soldiers were infected during the war. An Albertan, Dr. Harold Orr, played an important role in its treatment. A medical officer with the 3rd

Canadian Mounted Rifles in the field hygiene section, Orr developed important disinfection equipment to deal with the scourge of body lice. He undertook postgraduate studies focusing on syphilis and, in 1920, wrote the Venereal Disease Control Act of Alberta, the first in Canada. In 1923, he was appointed director of the provincial Division of Venereal Disease Control.[3]

Having survived the horrors of battle, veterans were among those who succumbed to the so-called Spanish influenza, which returned with them from the front and infected their communities. According to Mark Humphries, in 1918, more than 31,000 Albertans were officially listed as having the ailment; he suggests that the real number was probably at least three times higher. The mortality rate was also extremely high: 3,259 people died in 1918 and an additional 1,049 in the winter of 1918–19. Thus, deaths from influenza in Alberta equalled over two-thirds of deaths on the Front (4,308 compared to 6,140 killed in action).

Section Four: Aftermath explores short- and long-term impacts of the war. Mark Humphries covers the impact of the Spanish influenza pandemic of 1918 and 1919 in Alberta, detailing its devastating results, but also its role in prompting significant public health reforms, such as replacing *pest houses*, where people went to die, with community hospitals. Donald Wetherell links the war to the emergence of modern housing styles emphasizing healthier living conditions, namely through the federal government's 1919 Housing Act. Though inadequately funded, the Act aimed to stimulate the postwar economy and provide better shelter to veterans. Allan Rowe examines the federal Soldier Settlement scheme, a much-trumpetted program providing subsidized loans to veterans to acquire farmland, machinery, and seed. Of the 31,670 veterans who participated in the program, almost one-third (9,883) settled in Alberta, with the federal government directing them to the remote Peace River region. However, this program, like most others for veterans, sparked complaints about underfunding, mismanagement, and uncompromising regulations that produced a high failure rate and a legacy of bitterness.

The final essay in this section, which deals with the centenary of the outbreak of the First World War, offers a more positive message. Communities across Canada have arranged commemorations of the war experience, a principal component of which has been the honouring of local servicemen, an exercise that Rory Cory shows has involved nearly all Alberta museums.

Notes

1 J. Robert Lampard, *Alberta's Medical History: "Young and Lusty, and Full of Life"* (Red Deer: 2008), 293.

2 Ibid., 346–47.

3 Donald R. Wilson and Paul Rentiers, "Evolution of the Venereal Disease Program in the Province of Alberta," in Lampard, *Alberta's Medical History*, 92–96.

War, Public Health, and the 1918 "Spanish" Influenza Pandemic in Alberta

MARK OSBORNE HUMPHRIES

Andrew Robert W. was born along the Ottawa River near Aylwin, Quebec, on 23 June 1893. His Scottish father, John, was then a farmhand struggling to support a family of five children on an income of $150 a year and, as was the case for many Canadian families, emigration to the West promised an escape from poverty.[1] When the Edson Trail opened in 1911, John W. moved to Alberta, clearing a homestead at Bear Lake near Grande Prairie.[2] When war came in 1914, Albertans flocked to the colours to escape a deepening recession, but the conflict seemed very remote from northern Alberta, where the prewar boom continued unabated.[3] At that time, the railway was slowly pushing toward the Peace River country, the town of Grande Prairie was flourishing, and the family's fortunes were on the rise. By 1916 Andrew had set up his own tinsmith operation and was beginning to move into gas engineering.[4] Neither he nor his two younger brothers were eager to join the army. But the Canadian government required more soldiers to fill the ranks of its expeditionary force fighting in Europe; and with volunteerism failing, at the end of 1917 conscription was imposed, requiring all young able-bodied men to serve.[5] In March 1918, 25-year-old Andrew went to the depot office in Grande Prairie for his medical examination, and when he passed he was ordered to report for duty at the end of July in Calgary.[6]

While Albertans like W. may have felt that death and the horror of war were a world away, that fall a new disease—the so-called "Spanish" influenza—appeared in Canada. The flu would kill more people worldwide than the Great War, and nearly as many Canadians as died overseas.[7] When it appeared in Calgary in early October, Andrew W. was training in the foothills of the Rockies. For weeks the epidemic raged and death seemed to be lurking around every corner: more than 4,000 Albertans would eventually die that fall.[8] When the Armistice was announced on November 11 and a masked (to avoid contagion) but joyful population rejoiced in the streets, W. must have thought that he would soon be on his way home, back to Grande Prairie, having escaped the fate of so many Canadians on the Western Front. But demobilization came slowly, as those who were the last to join were also the last sent home. Weeks passed, and then he too began to cough.[9]

On the morning of December 19, W. paraded for duty as usual at Victoria Park Barracks.[10] He looked unwell, so much so that his commanding officer sent him on sick parade. The battalion's doctor, Major H.G. Nyblett, an English-born surgeon from Fort Macleod, Alberta, recorded his temperature at 102° and, an hour later, W. was in Sarcee Camp hospital.[11] On admission, there were no signs of pneumonia; a brief physical examination showed no abnormal heart sounds and his lungs were clear. W. was given Aspirin, a dose of quinine, and Dover's powder (a combination of ipecac and opium) to help him rest—all standard treatments aimed at comforting the patient and reducing symptoms. When he was examined that evening, his cough had worsened, but that was to be expected; nothing seemed amiss and he was left to sleep for the night. The next morning, when Nyblett made his rounds, he discovered that during the night pneumonia had set in. With a stethoscope pressed against W.'s chest—first to one side then the other and back again—the doctor realized that W.'s right lung had almost been completely consolidated; he could hear telltale rales (rattling) beginning in the left. W. was now struggling to breathe. Nyblett pushed a full array of stimulants, including strychnine, brandy, and pituitrin (an extract containing oxytocin and vasopressin) and ordered oxygen to be given as required. But, despite his best efforts, W.'s temperature kept rising past 104° as his breathing became shallow, wet, and laboured. At 9:00 that night he died from acute pneumonia—less than 36 hours after coming down with the sniffles on parade.[12]

The 1918 influenza pandemic killed 35,000 to 50,000 Canadians between September 1918 and April 1919. Many died as quickly and inexplicably as W.[13] Across Canada, public health officials struggled, first to prevent the disease from entering their communities, and then, when it inevitably did, to manage the largest healthcare crisis in modern

history. The 1918 influenza pandemic circled the globe in three successive waves: the first in winter and spring of 1918; the second in the fall just as the war was coming to an end; and the third as troops demobilized in the winter of 1918–19.[14] We do not know where the virus first appeared—it may have been China, the midwestern United States, or even in Europe.[15] Evidence gathered from newspapers, public health reports, and hospital records shows that, during the first wave, many people across the globe became sick—including the King of Spain, who gave the disease its inaccurate but nevertheless enduring moniker. Few, though, actually died. It was in Europe that the virus mutated, emerging late in July with new genetic characteristics that made it a far more deadly disease. The fall wave of flu spread outward from England along the sinews of war: south to Africa on a British ship destined for Sierra Leone; east to Brest and the armies of Europe fighting on the continent; and west to Boston with merchant vessels or empty troop ships arriving to pick up the next drafts of the growing American army. A third wave of flu returned in the spring but was far less deadly.[16]

The second and third waves of flu may have killed as many as 100 million people worldwide.[17] Seasonal cases of influenza tend to incapacitate otherwise healthy victims for a few days, only progressing to pneumonia in those with compromised immune systems, underlying health conditions, or the elderly. The deadly fall wave of so-called "Spanish" flu carved a different pattern: it killed young, healthy adults—like Private Andrew W.—who otherwise appeared to be in the prime of life. Scientists are not sure what made the flu so deadly for young people, or how it could progress from infection to death in a matter of hours. The most likely explanation is that the virus provoked a "cytokine storm," causing

Susie   Jimmie   Alice

Mrs. Herman Hungerbuhler and children, feeding poultry, near Vulcan, Alberta, 1910. Left to right: Susie; Mrs. Hungerbuhler; Jimmie; and Alice. Jimmie, twin to Susie, died in the influenza epidemic in 1918. The Hungerbuhlers were immigrants from Switzerland. Glenbow Archives, NA-2685-49.

the body's immune system to go into overdrive; in this scenario, it was the intensity of the cascading immune response that ultimately may have killed many of the flu's youngest victims.[18]

Albertans were first alerted to Spanish influenza when it arrived in the northeastern United States.[19] On September 18, the *Edmonton Bulletin* reported the deaths of 70 people in Boston from a strange new form of grippe which was said to have shut down the harbour and even all the shoe factories in nearby Brockton.[20] The next day, the paper said that there were more than 3,000 cases of "Spanish influenza" in the army camps of New England and upper New York State.[21] According to Canadian military records, American soldiers from those barracks then carried the disease across the border to a Polish army camp run by the Canadian army at Niagara-on-the-Lake,

Ontario, and to barracks in Montreal and Quebec as they made their way toward waiting troopships bound for Europe. In Sydney, Nova Scotia, sick American soldiers also disembarked from an infected American freighter en route from New Jersey to England and were treated in Canadian hospitals there and in Halifax.[22]

Historians once believed that the flu's primary vector was returning veterans, but with the war effort actually ramping up in Europe and the new threat of German submarines marauding off the Atlantic Seaboard, injured soldiers were not returning home that fall. In fact, the war effort was widening rather than waning. Earlier in the summer, Prime Minister Robert Borden had agreed to create a Canadian military force to go to Vladivostok, Russia, where it would assist forces loyal to the deposed Tsar in their fight against the new Bolshevik government.[23] The mobilization of this newly created Siberian Expeditionary Force (SEF) spread flu across the country.[24] Just as influenza was beginning to cross the border, Canadian troops were assembling in Nova Scotia, New Brunswick, Quebec, and Ontario. Soon they boarded trains destined for Vancouver. When sick soldiers climbed into sealed trains packed to the roof with men, they entered a warm, crowded incubator. Whereas demobilizing veterans would have dispersed flu in a random pattern as they returned home to communities big and small across the country, the speedy and organized mobilization of the SEF ensured that the disease crossed the country in a matter of days, seeding crowded barracks and hospitals in all the major population centres from Halifax to Victoria.[25]

On the morning of September 27, Special Siberian Troop Train 337 took on its first load of passengers at Sussex Camp, New Brunswick.[26] That same morning, the first cases of flu were reported in the camp among soldiers who had brought extra supplies to the over-stretched military hospital at North Sydney. By the time the cars lurched into Montreal, some soldiers were already getting sick and had to be removed to a hospital in the city.[27] The train also took on several new drafts of soldiers from a local barracks already infected with flu.[28] As Special No. 337 rumbled onward across the country, sick soldiers were secretly removed to hospitals in Winnipeg and Regina in the dead of night.[29] At 4:00 a.m. on the morning of October 2, the flu train pulled into downtown Calgary, where one officer and 11 other ranks were removed and sent to the Calgary Isolation Hospital. The assistant director, medical services for Military District No. 13 (Alberta), Lieutenant Colonel Chester Fish McGuffin, wired the director general of medical services, Guy Carleton Jones, asking for "any new suggestions regarding treatment."[30] None were forthcoming.[31]

The mobilization of the SEF was accomplished largely in secret, as the publication of troop train movements had been banned by the Office of the Chief Press Censor in Ottawa.[32] Nevertheless, dire reports from the east continued to stoke fears that the disease would inevitably spread west—even as it was already simmering in the military hospitals of Calgary. On October 3, the *Redcliff Review* noted that Spanish flu was prevalent in many military camps in both eastern Canada and the United States. It warned readers that it was "of a serious type and when not properly taken care of it has, in many cases, proved fatal."[33] When flu arrived, the paper suggested that readers "keep feet and clothing dry; avoid crowds; protect your nose and mouth in the presence of sneezers; gargle your throat three times a day with a mild antiseptic, if only salt and water; don't neglect a cold; keep as much as possible in the sunshine; [and] don't get 'scared.'"[34] But it was difficult to remain calm. Frank Oliver's *Edmonton Bulletin* noted that the flu was killing thousands every day south of the border, and would eventually reach western Canada where it was expected to do the same.[35] He argued, "on the principle that prevention is better than cure this is the time to mobilize the forces to resist the invader. So far as the public are concerned there is a total lack of information as to the cause and nature of the disease, the conditions which favor it, and the precautionary measures which may be employed . . . If there is any way of combating the disease by preventative measures, these should be officially explained and published widely and at once."[36]

Doctors had few weapons at their disposal. The ancient practices of quarantine and isolation might be used to reduce or eliminate person-to-person transmission of the disease by erecting barriers between sick and healthy populations.[37] Restrictions could also be placed on people's movements, behaviours, and socio-economic activities, which might limit transmission of the disease once it reached a city or town. We now know that these non-pharmaceutical interventions could not prevent influenza, but would enable officials to control the epidemic by slowing down the transmission rate, thus reducing strain on public health resources. Across the United States and Canada, non-pharmaceutical interventions were employed with varying degrees of success. Epidemiological studies have shown that cities that were able to implement case reporting procedures, quarantine, and bans on public gatherings before the flu's arrival had lower overall mortality. However, if non-pharmaceutical measures were employed only after the disease was already epidemic, they had little effect on death rates.[38]

Unlike many Canadian provinces that had little in the way of a formal public health infrastructure, Alberta was well situated to organize a robust response to the crisis.[39] In 1918 public health in the province was centrally managed by the Provincial Board of Health, which had been created by the Public Health Act of 1907; the provincial board, in turn, controlled regional health boards across the province.[40] Staffing was limited and, in 1918, the provincial board consisted of a provincial medical officer of health, a sanitary engineer, and a bacteriologist who in turn oversaw the Provincial Laboratory.[41] In the years before the First World War, provincial and local boards focused almost exclusively on improving sanitation in Alberta's growing towns and cities, which amounted to inspecting pit privies and ensuring that "nuisances" were removed, while seeing that the food supply, especially milk, was secure from infection.[42]

While these community problems were not neglected, the province's growing immigrant population was often blamed for "importing" communicable diseases such as smallpox, typhoid, scarlet fever, or diphtheria.[43] "We in the west find that the immigrants coming into that country, not from foreign countries alone, but frequently from the older provinces, arrive in a convalescent stage of disease," read a typical prewar editorial. "They will go among their friends in the west and will say nothing about having been afflicted with disease, and the local authorities have no knowledge of the matter. What is the result? These people go among their friends and among children who attend the schools, and in a short time an epidemic breaks out. The number of deaths from diphtheria and scarlet fever in our western country, due to causes of this kind, is absolutely appalling."[44] Although there was little evidence to support such claims, the association between immigration and disease gave underlying nativist attitudes a scientific veneer, legitimizing fears of outsiders in a province undergoing an unprecedented period of growth and demographic change.[45] The main weapons against disease in Alberta, and Canada more widely, had been a robust immigrant border inspection, strict quarantine procedures, and disinfection when communicable disease was discovered.[46] As one historian has argued, an episodic, reactionary approach to public health and disease management prevailed across the country.[47]

Few public health officials had experience managing outbreaks of influenza, as the last pandemic had been in 1889–90; it had also been much milder.[48] Initially, advice had to be appropriated from British and American sources closer to the epicentre of the outbreak on the east coast.[49] On October 1, Cecil Mahood, medical officer of health for Calgary, told citizens that influenza began rapidly with a "sudden chill, headache, elevation of temperature, pains in various parts of the body, sore throat, herpes on lips, and prostration."[50] In many cases, he warned, it then progressed to pneumonia. Because flu was transmitted by secretions from the nose, mouth, and throat, he recommended that "affected individuals go home and to bed at once, and place themselves under care of a physician." There

Poster issued by the Provincial Board of Health about the influenza epidemic, Alberta, 1918. Glenbow Archives, NA-4548-5.

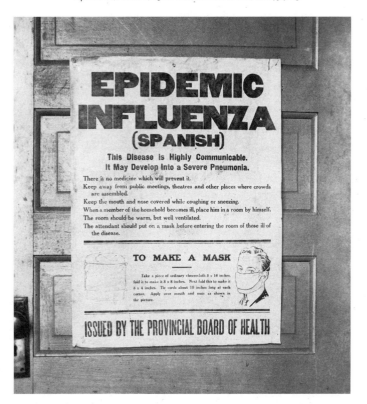

they were to remain, in bed, until the symptoms subsided, lest pneumonia develop.[51] Alberta's health board met to discuss the crisis for the first time on October 4 and issued similar advice.[52] Over the next few days "influenza warnings" were published in local newspapers across the province and posted in public places. Again, Albertans were implored: "Don't Get 'Scared.'"[53]

At first, the official response—that is, the efforts of public health officials—centred exclusively on quarantine and isolation. On October 9, T.H. Whitelaw, the medical officer for health in Edmonton, suggested that the provincial board of health should declare flu a reportable disease, which would give him the power to enforce quarantines against those afflicted with the condition.[54] The next day in Calgary, Mahood announced that he would not wait and would begin to order infected individuals to be isolated and quarantined immediately if discovered.[55] As Janice Dickin points out, although this violated the Alberta Health Act, most physicians and officials in Calgary supported his actions.[56] On October 14, the Alberta health board finally amended its regulations, but decided that flu should be a quarantinable rather than a reportable disease, to minimize panic.[57]

As late as the end of the second week of October—10 days after the first cases of flu arrived in Calgary—public health officials were still discussing flu in the abstract, implying that it had yet to reach the province. Efforts to control the disease likewise focused on prevention through exclusion, rather than on developing the infrastructure necessary to manage an epidemic that was already underway. After a meeting of the provincial board of health on October 13, the minister of health, A.G. MacKay, announced a "sweeping program" designed to prevent flu from reaching the province. Medical inspectors were hired and placed at every road or rail entry point along Alberta's borders, and charged with inspecting travellers on entry into the province. Those whom inspectors determined to be sick were to be placed into isolation or denied entry, while those on through-bound trains were to be quarantined throughout their journey. If flu was detected in a town, that location was to be isolated and cordoned off from the outside world.[58]

Oyen, Alberta, a small town about 150 kilometres north of Medicine Hat near the Saskatchewan border, was the first place to be quarantined. When flu erupted there, the provincial board immediately ordered all theatres, churches, schools, and businesses closed. The town was also placed under a broader quarantine with the board prohibiting the "egress of any person to, or ingress from, Oyen and other nearby places in which influenza exists."[59] On October 17, the entire city of Lethbridge too was placed under quarantine. "Provincial Health Department Takes Unexpected and Drastic Action," read the headline in the *Lethbridge Herald*. "No one may enter or leave the city . . . From the date of the order which was first communicated to the CPR, the movement of passengers was prohibited and doors on trains passing through Lethbridge are locked before coming into Lethbridge and not unlocked until the train is out of the city limits."[60] Guards were also hired by the Royal North-West Mounted Police (RNWMP) to guard the road entrances to the city, blocking all vehicular and carriage traffic into or out of the city.[61] Pincher Creek, Fort Macleod, and Taber were similarly quarantined in the south, as was Legal, north of Edmonton.[62]

The Alberta Board of Health was the only public health authority in Canada to quarantine entire municipalities. Yet this drastic step soon proved impossible to enforce or maintain. For example, at Lethbridge, coal miners returning from the night shift found themselves unable to get home and unable to return to work. Farmers, ranchers, and businessmen who had been in the city overnight when quarantine was imposed were similarly unable to leave despite the pressing needs of the harvest, their livestock, and their families.[63] The provincial board soon reversed course. Within 48 hours of being imposed, the quarantines were lifted, and, in their place, officials were dispatched to inspect incoming and outgoing passengers for flu. But while the citizens of Lethbridge complained about being quarantined, some towns actually imposed their own forms of isolation. The town of Irma, roughly 30 kilometres west of Wainwright, instituted its own quarantine on October 25 "to take steps to prevent the induction [*sic*] of the disease into the community from outside points by stopping travellers both by train and car from alighting here and in restricting the mixing of people in the community as far as possible without stopping business."[64]

Bans on public gatherings and institutional closures were some of the most commonly implemented non-pharmaceutical interventions across Canada. On October 10, for example, the newspapers reported that all schools, churches, and theatres had been ordered closed in New Brunswick.[65] Winnipeg banned all public gatherings two days later, while Toronto outlawed meetings until the middle of November.[66] However, public health officials, worried about restricting commerce or still convinced that flu was primarily confined to the eastern parts of the country, remained reluctant to do so in Alberta long after officials in both British Columbia and Saskatchewan had taken similar steps. "There

Victory parade, Calgary, Alberta, 11 November 1918. The image shows the masks worn during influenza epidemic. The hill in background is thought to be North Hill. Glenbow Archives, NC-20-2.

is no need of closing the theatres in Calgary because of the Spanish Influenza epidemic which is raging in eastern Canada so long as ... precautions are taken," Mahood told the newspapers in mid-October. As Oral Cloakney, the manager of the Allen theatre, reported, this meant washing the premises with carbolic acid every night as one might have cleaned a contemporary operating room. "Some of our patrons complain of the carbolic odor, but we are not going to take any chances," he said. "There is not a home in the city of Calgary where one may feel as immune as in Calgary theatres." Mahood agreed, assuring Calgarians that the city's "theatres are probably the healthiest place in the city as a result—far healthier than the average business house."[67] Both Edmonton and Calgary waited until October 18—more than two weeks after the first cases arrived in the city—to

order theatres, dance halls, public libraries, and poolrooms to close.[68]

Public closures caused significant disruption to not only commerce and patterns of social interaction but also to the spiritual lives of Alberta's terrified communities. In Irma, Pastor C.G. Hockin acknowledged that the severity of the flu outbreak necessitated closing the churches, which placed responsibility for religious observance on the family. "The first teachers of life and truth in every family are the parents and in a time of pestilence they are given more responsibility than commonly falls to their lot in the modern civilization," he told his flock via the local paper. "This includes a deeper religious interest. We would like to suggest that the family become the worship unit during the time of our danger. Make the family altar to be the place where all are found at the hour when public worship would be called and let us hear God's Word in our homes and with boldness make our requests unto the Almighty."[69] Families were not only left to worship together but also to bury their dead. In isolated communities across the province, family units dissolved in the face of disease and further suffered because of the absence of normal, rural community supports for the survivors. In the district of Athabasca, it was reported that "a lad of fifteen is seen digging behind the house, he is asked what he is doing, his answer is that he is burying the dead, asked who was dead, his answer is, father, mother, brother and sister."[70]

By the time churches were shut, quarantine had clearly failed to stem the tide of flu's advance. Once it failed, the Alberta Board of Health sought to control the further spread of the disease by ordering all citizens to wear masks over their mouths and noses when they left their homes, providing instructions on how each might manufacture his or her own version from readily available supplies.[71] "These masks are made of cheese cloth," reported the *Redcliff Review*, "sixteen by eight inches, which are twice doubled alternatively until they are finally eight by four inches in size, and are then tied over the nose and mouth with cord."[72] Many refused to wear them. As Janice Dickin has noted, some complained to the newspapers that they were grotesque, depressing, and even dangerous.[73] Besides being unpopular, the regulation was difficult to enforce. During the first

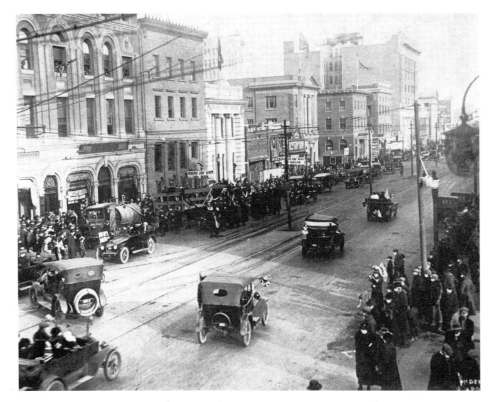

The Armistice Day Parade, on 11 November 1918, took place on Jasper Avenue in Edmonton in spite of the flu epidemic but some people wore masks. McDermid Studio. City of Edmonton Archives, EA-10-655.

few days when the order was in effect, 30 sum-
monses were issued to Edmonton men who refused
to comply.[74] When pressed to explain their actions,
some claimed that they could not smoke while wearing a mask, while others said that they had no money
to buy the necessary materials; one man told a judge
"that if the city wanted him to wear one it would have
to buy him one."[75] Even some physicians refused
to partake in the precautions. The *Bulletin* reported

"How to make [an] influenza mask." 21 October 1918. Provincial
Archives of Alberta, A13187.

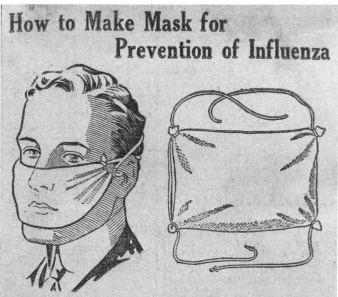

How to Make Mask for Prevention of Influenza

Instructions as to the making and use of masks have been sent out
by the provincial board of health. These are to be used when taking care
of influenza patients, and beginning on Thursday morning on all trains
and street cars in the province. Here is the method of making the mask,
published in The Bulletin some days ago and here repeated by request.
To Make a Mask—Take a piece of ordinary cheesecloth, 8x16 inches.
Next fold this to make it 8x4 inches. Tie cord about 10 inches long at
each corner. Apply over mouth and nose as shown in the picture.
To be worn in the sick room when taking care of the patient and on
street cars and railway trains.
Keep the nose and mouth covered while coughing or sneezing.
A mask should not be worn more than two hours.

that "one doctor who was going about maskless [*sic*]
told the [medical] officer [of health] that he did
not need any and drove on."[76] When A.G. MacKay
visited Calgary, he too complained to Mahood that
only about 20 percent of the population seemed to
be wearing their masks as required.[77] But Mahood
himself refused to enforce the provincial regulation
because he felt that it was a "fruitless endeavour,"
insisting that his efforts were better focused on
implementing other forms of protective measures.[78]
Even when "offenders" were arrested and brought
before the local court, it was frequently pointed out
that those present to hear the cases—including the
judges—were not actually wearing the masks themselves as proscribed by the province. Most offenders
ultimately escaped with a warning.[79]

For many physicians, quarantines and masks
seemed to be relics from another era of less scientific medicine. Ever since Louis Pasteur demonstrated the effectiveness of his artificial rabies
vaccine in 1885, medical researchers had looked to
the laboratory to inoculate the vulnerable against
illness.[80] After all, in the absence of the "magic
bullet" antibiotics would later provide, few diseases
could actually be cured; prevention was thus the best
medicine.[81] In 1918, many doctors hoped to develop
a vaccine that would reduce morbidity and mortality from flu, as had been done against smallpox,
rabies, and a host of other diseases. We now know
that influenza is a viral infection, but in 1918 most
medical professionals believed that it was caused
by Pfeiffer's bacillus—based largely on erroneous
research conducted in German laboratories during
the previous pandemic of 1889–90.[82] This presented
the possibility that a serum could be developed using
a weakened form of the bacteria to confer at least a
degree of immunity on healthy people.[83]

During the fall of 1918, vaccines were prepared across North America containing a potpourri of dead bacteria—and probably live copies of the virus—drawn from the noses and throats of flu sufferers.[84] In Manitoba and Ontario, thousands of doses of vaccine were issued.[85] In Alberta, too, Dr. Heber Jamieson, the provincial bacteriologist and head of the Provincial Laboratory in Edmonton, developed his own version of an American vaccine first prepared in New York.[86] However, the first 1,000 doses were not ready until November 1, when the epidemic was already reaching its height. Even so, it would have had little effect—and may actually have been harmful—because it was designed to inoculate against a bacterial rather than a viral infection. Even at the time, many physicians were skeptical about the usefulness of vaccines against flu. "Since we are uncertain of the primary cause of influenza," read a dispatch from the Royal College of Physicians in London, and printed in the *Edmonton Bulletin* on 12 December 1918, "no form of inoculation can be guaranteed to protect against the disease itself. From what we know as to the lack of enduring protection after an attack, it might in any case be assumed that no vaccine could protect for more than a short period."[87]

The development and distribution of dubious vaccines spoke to the provincial health board's growing sense of desperation. By the middle of the third week of October, it was becoming clear that far more people were getting sick than official case reports suggested; the authorities had lost control of the situation. Rumours swirled that there was a severe epidemic at Drumheller, where two-thirds of the population were said to be sick; death notices began to fill the pages of local papers. Yet officially published numbers suggested that the epidemic

was still limited in scope. The public seemed to be losing confidence. The provincial board suspected that compliance with the suggested procedures was low because the reporting of influenza cases was still voluntary. On October 25, the flu was thus made a reportable disease. This required all physicians across the province to give the patient's name, sex, age, and address for any case of influenza, or pneumonia, as well as report on any deaths.[88] Case reports immediately began to pour in from across towns and cities.

By the end of October, Albertans were dying by the hundreds. Some of the most tragic cases were those of conscripted soldiers, who died alone and far from home. Thirty-three-year-old Private Joseph M. of Nanaimo, British Columbia, was drafted in June 1918 and sent to Calgary for training. He was admitted to the Edmonton isolation hospital on 23 October 1918 suffering from a cough, pain in the chest, headache, constipation, and low fever. The next day, his temperature had risen to 104° and his symptoms worsened. By the 27th, his doctor reported evidence of broncho-pneumonia, and the next day his fever was 105°. M. died on the night of October 30 and was buried far from his family in Mount Pleasant Cemetery. Caregivers could usually anticipate death in cases of Spanish flu by the appearance of a peculiar heliotrope cyanosis, a brief dip and then spike in temperature, and the quickening of pulse and respiration. Unfortunately, there was almost nothing that could be done to save victims when the disease progressed to broncho-pneumonia.[89]

As public health officials came to grasp the enormity of the crisis, the official response shifted from prevention to treatment. At first, flu victims had been encouraged to remain at home in bed. But such directives were most easily followed by those from the middle and upper classes, who could afford a private doctor or nurse, not to mention the luxury of taking a voluntary hiatus from work, as well as extra fuel for the fire. For the working class, living in crowded conditions in the slums of Edmonton or Calgary, medical assistance was usually unaffordable, and isolation and privacy not possible. Failure to attend work, too, carried a significant risk of dismissal and increased financial hardship. Farming families would also have had a difficult time following the health board's advice. The onset of the epidemic coincided with the final weeks of the harvest. Even if the wheat crop was in, household chores still had to be performed and members of farm families who became ill could no more confine themselves to bed rest than could wage workers in the cities. Prescriptions for bed rest and isolation were, thus, ideal remedies that were unrealistic for all but a few Albertans.[90]

Soon, though, it became clear that travellers, soldiers, and the poor had few options but to seek care in the province's hospitals.[91] By the 25th, the wards in Edmonton and Calgary were crowded with victims. Public health officials looked to commandeer public buildings to create makeshift flu wards. In Edmonton, Whitelaw took over the University of Alberta's Pembina Hall as a flu hospital, providing beds for 150 patients.[92] Halls and schools across the province were similarly appropriated, usually staffed with volunteers who ran soup kitchens and changed bedding for those unable to care for themselves.[93]

As public health efforts shifted from prevention to treatment, the role of physicians faded into the background. Although members of the medical profession volunteered their expertise, there was little they could do to treat flu.[94] While physicians might prescribe stimulants or sedatives, these had little effect. The most useful treatments consisted

of bed rest and nursing care. In this respect, both professional female nurses and volunteers now took the lead role in managing the crisis at the level of home and community. Nurses had, in fact, been preparing to minister to the needs of the community long before public health officials abandoned quarantine efforts. On October 15, the Graduate Nurses Association held the first of several emergency meetings to "devise ways and means of coping with the malady if necessary and to do the best that could be done under the circumstance."[95] Lists of trained nurses were prepared should the need arise to call on their services.

Nurses had played an important but often overlooked role in the provision of care even in normal times.[96] Usually confined to hospitals or private residences, there were relatively few professionally trained nurses in Alberta—many had also chosen to go overseas by 1918. Despite early preparations, by October 19 the city of Edmonton was already in the midst of a nursing shortage, forcing Whitelaw to close the city's only isolation hospital to new admissions.[97] The next day, provincial bacteriologist Heber Jamieson told the *Bulletin* that the "scarcity of nursing talent was becoming a serious embarrassment," in part because many wealthy families were employing their own private nurses "to the exclusion of those who had not" the means to pay. "It was not fair," he said, and announced plans to require employers to allow private nurses to service the entire community rather than individual families.[98]

On October 25, Whitelaw announced that the city would be divided into districts to better facilitate management of care.[99] Each district would be placed under the supervision of a graduate nurse appointed by the province. These professionally trained sisters would be responsible for managing cases within

Nurses at the Isolation Hospital, Lloydminster, Alberta and Saskatchewan. Nurses and teachers acting as volunteer nurses pictured during influenza epidemic, 1918. Glenbow Archives, NA-1422-7.

their ward, visiting families in need and arranging assistance as necessary. Each graduate nurse would work out of a school commandeered for the purpose where volunteers and Volunteer Aid Detachment (VAD) nurses would be trained to provide home care for the sick.[100] The decision to organize care by district around the nucleus provided by professional nurses rather than physicians also called on these professional women to take on the traditionally male tasks of hospital organization and administration. Not only were nurses asked to go into the homes of the sick but also to manage care, reporting directly to the provincial board of health, bypassing local medical professionals.[101]

As Linda Quiney argues, VAD service provided women with a "unique opportunity for an active part in the war effort, not available to women through any other form of voluntary patriotic work."[102] Voluntary service during the pandemic was also extremely

dangerous. In Edmonton, Christina Frederickson was one of the first nurses of many to die in the pandemic. As the *Edmonton Bulletin* reported, Ms. Frederickson had "volunteered when the soldiers of the Siberian forces were taken from a troop train some days since suffering from the influenza and placed in the isolation hospital to assist in nursing them, and she had been steadily at work with little respite up to the time that she herself became infected with the disease."[103] It may have been hazardous work, but that did not tend to discourage volunteers. As one nurse said, "It is dangerous—undoubtedly. So is overseas service; yet that did not hinder enlisting to any large extent. It would be better to have the 'flu [*sic*] than to carry through life the uneasy feeling that by your indifference you allowed some other woman to die."[104]

While graduate nurses such as Frederickson organized and managed treatment networks across the province, female volunteers—many of them teenagers and young adults—were responsible for administering to the sick on a daily basis.[105] In 1918, providing basic necessities such as food, heat, and water required a significant amount of effort, often beyond the ability of the stricken. Water had to be pumped, sometimes from an outdoor well a good distance from the house. Fresh food had to be bought and prepared. Sick families across the province were thus in desperate need of assistance. "Volunteers are wanted to give a hand in certain homes," implored the *Edmonton Bulletin*. They "are needed to look after babies and children in homes where there is sickness—an opportunity for girls. The furnaces and stoves have to be looked after—ashes taken out, coal and wood to be got in. Play the game, boys. There's work for everybody."[106] The situation was most acute in the rural parts of the province where there were neither graduate nurses nor doctors to organize care. MacKay told rural Albertans that they "must realize that they cannot depend upon receiving trained nurses; that the local men and women must organize and under the instruction and direction of the local doctors they must give what assistance they can."[107]

As Esyllt Jones found in her study of Winnipeg's response to the pandemic, the flu was truly a community disease that could only be contained through a cooperative effort.[108] Unlike previous outbreaks of illness that were blamed on outsiders and immigrants, the 1918 flu proved the ineffectiveness of prophylactic interventions aimed at specific ethnic minorities and, instead, emphasized the importance of community cooperation.[109] In part, this shift in attitude can be attributed to the work of middle-class female volunteers, who came into contact with the sufferings and daily hardships of the working class for the first time in a meaningful way during the pandemic. Care instructions necessitated a close and sustained period of contact between the sick and their nurses. Caregivers were instructed that fresh air and bed rest were the most important elements of care, while nourishing food and water were to be given at regular intervals. Bed rest was to be so complete that patients were not even to leave their beds to go to the bathroom but were instead to use bedpans that had to be emptied. Patients might be given an antiseptic mouthwash every few hours, and their bedclothes had to be changed and washed, but few other interventions were possible. As Jones has argued, this routine, which might last a week or more, created an unheard-of level of intimacy between members of different social worlds.[110]

In Alberta, as elsewhere, it was the poorest members of society who suffered most during the epidemic. When Edmonton volunteers went door to door, they found families living in squalid conditions in the city's slums. One family of six was said to have been living in a 10 × 12–foot shack with only one window and a door.[111] Throughout the crisis, the family had to sleep in the same bed where the mother and her infant child died.[112] One VAD nurse reported that she had only discovered another fatal victim of flu when two small girls approached her in the street to say that they needed help because they could not wake up their mother.[113] In response to this heart-wrenching story, one Albertan wrote to the *Bulletin*: "Surely our health organization is not in such a wretched state that fatal cases have to be reported in this sad manner. If so, it is an everlasting disgrace to our city authorities and board of health . . . surely there are enough Christian-spirited people left outside of our overworked nurses and volunteers who would be glad to learn what aid they could rather give than leave the sick to die unattended. If there are not such we had better lock our church doors and stop playing at Christianity, and continue to live and die as the heathen."[114]

As with the working class in Alberta's slums, Aboriginal groups suffered a disproportionately higher level of mortality from flu, both in the province and across the country.[115] A Department of Indian Affairs report compiled in 1919 puts the death toll among Aboriginal peoples living on reserves in Canada at 3,694 out of a total population of about 106,000, suggesting an influenza mortality rate of 34.85 per thousand—more than five times the national average for non-Aboriginal Canadians.[116] In Alberta the mortality rate for flu among Aboriginal groups was much higher than the national average, at 53.8 per 1,000 (see table below). The squalid living conditions on many reserves—where Aboriginal people had been forced into inadequate housing provided by the Department of Indian Affairs, where many suffered from malnutrition, and where tuberculosis and other diseases were already in wide circulation—made victims more susceptible.[117] In the Treaty 8 territory of northern Alberta, RNWMP inspectors feared the worst when reports of flu began to trickle in to the north. K.F. Anderson of the Peace River Detachment wrote to R. Field, the commanding officer of N Division, requesting permission to take medicines to "fight the Spanish Influenza" to the people living in the vicinity of Great Slave Lake, as he feared that "if it should get amongst the Natives, most of whom are suffering from pulmonary disease . . . it will commit wide and general destruction."[118] When flu came, 11 percent of the Aboriginal population in Treaty 8 territory alone succumbed to the disease.[119]

On 1 December 1918, a University of Alberta Public Health student named Frank Fish filed a report with RNWMP headquarters in Edmonton accusing the Department of Indian Affairs of neglecting the health of the people on the Hobbema agency. Fish had gone there after hearing that many of the Cree people in the agency were suffering from both influenza and smallpox. "I might say that the housing conditions on the Reserve are not of the best," he wrote in an affidavit filed with the RNWMP. "In fact in many cases I found as many as eight or nine adults living in a one roomed shack which in all cases were absolutely devoid of ventilation . . . I found in many cases, that the families were without food and had gone to relatives or friends in the hope of getting nourishment. In many cases, also, I was asked to inform the [Indian] Agent of the condition of the people with regard to the lack of food."[120] A subsequent RNWMP investigation revealed that the Indian agent had been placing families infected with smallpox in quarantine and then refusing to feed them, forcing the victims to secretly visit friends and family at night to obtain something to eat. "There is no question," read Staff Sergeant Fyffe's report, "that the Official[s] on the Reserve at the present time have no idea whatever as to the number of Indians suffering from smallpox, and apparently very little has been done by them to find out, if the indian [sic] dose [sic] not report it themselves, and as far as I could learn the Indians hide the fact that they have smallpox, as the [sic] say they would be quarantine and would get no food."[121] Over the next few months, the situation improved little, although food and medicine were eventually brought in by the RNWMP. At Hobbema, the combination of smallpox and flu drove the death rate from flu alone above 120 per 1,000, meaning that it killed roughly 12 percent of the population of Hobbema.[122]

Whereas previous epidemics had devastated Aboriginal groups but had little effect on the

Mortality rate from influenza by reserve for the period October 1918 to February 1919

INDIAN AFFAIRS AGENCY	POPULATION (31 MARCH 1918)	DEATHS FROM FLU (1918–19)	MORTALITY RATE (PER K)
Blackfoot	710	25	35.21
Blood	1,112	29	26.08
Edmonton	727	49	67.40
Fort Simpson and Fort Smith	2,544	8*	3.14
Hobbema	831	100	120.34
Peigan	414	10	24.15
Saddle Lake	883	40	45.30
Sarcee	182	7	38.46
Stoney	669	55	82.21
Treaty 8	1,941	216	111.28
TOTAL	10,013	539	53.83
Alberta	495,351	4,308	8.70
Canada	8,100,000	50,000	6.17

* This figure only represents deaths recorded as due to influenza

Source: Population statistics are based on annual treaty payment figures from *Dominion of Canada, Annual Report of the Department of Indian Affairs for the Year Ended March 31 1918* (Ottawa: Department of Indian Affairs, 1919), 111–12; "Influenza Epidemic," 28 May 1919, RG 29, vol. 2970, file 851-4-D96, Part 1, LAC.

European settler population, the 1918 influenza pandemic struck across ethnic boundaries—even though Aboriginal groups still suffered disproportionately due to the legacies of Canada's colonial policies. The 1918 flu was a community disease that necessitated collective action. When the second wave of flu finally crested in late November and rolled back through December, more than 31,000 Albertans had officially been listed as sick—although the real number was probably at least three times as high. A total of 3,259 people died of the disease in 1918. That winter, there were a further 7,185 cases and 1,049 deaths.[123]

To summarize, the official response in Alberta to the Spanish flu epidemic was both paradoxical and lurching. The initial prophylactic measures taken by public health authorities to guard against flu followed established patterns of quarantine and isolation, reflecting a stubborn belief that despite the appearance of a few military cases at the beginning of the month of October, flu could be halted so long as outsiders were prevented from bringing the disease into the province. Strong but unenforceable measures such as municipal quarantine were precipitously proposed and adopted while more realistic and pragmatic steps like school closures were avoided until well after the disease was already in wide circulation.

In part, this approach reflected the lingering dominance of the old quarantine practices that had been used to guard Canadians from disease since the age of cholera. When Albertans looked for a scapegoat to blame, though, this time it was not immigrants or outsiders but public health officials who had made false promises of safety. "Flu is a communicable and therefore quarantinable disease," argued Frank Oliver on the editorial page of the *Edmonton Bulletin*. "The Dominion government have sole authority to enforce quarantine. They did not establish quarantine. They took no notice of the fact that there was an epidemic spreading over the world."[124] In another editorial, Oliver elaborated. "When the menace appeared," he wrote,

> had the Dominion authorities through the war railway board, taken charge of all arrivals at ocean ports and entry ports along the boundary, and subjected them to the inconvenience of two or three days in quarantine, there is every reason to suppose that the disease could not have got past the borders; certainly it could not have attained the proportions of a nation-wide epidemic . . . Certainly there is no excuse for the Government having made no attempt whatever to keep it out. Is human life of no account in Canada?[125]

But the ultimate lesson of the pandemic was that quarantine alone was not sufficient protection and that, so long as the seeds of disease found fertile soil among the poor and colonized, epidemics would be unstoppable. As prophylaxis failed and the attention of public health authorities turned to managing treatment efforts, the entire community was, for the first time, called upon to take responsibility for protecting public health by assisting the less fortunate. It was during the pandemic that Albertans, and Canadians in general, began to see health as a community rather than an individual concern. Flu's lasting legacy was the recognition of this central tenet of modern public health policy: health can only be protected through the cooperation and with the consent of all members of the community.

Notes

This paper is based on a combination of new research as well as research published in Mark Osborne Humphries, *The Last Plague: Spanish Influenza and the Politics of Public Health in Canada* (Toronto: University of Toronto Press, 2013).

1   1901 Census of Canada, RG 31, Reel T-6549, District 200, Sub district C, Division 1, Family 7, 1, Library and Archives Canada (LAC). According to Eric Sager's research, this would place John W. in the lowest 20 percent of wage earners. Eric Sager, "The National Sample of the 1901 Census of Canada: A New Source for the Study of the Working Class," unpublished paper presented at the Social Science History Conference, 16–19 March 1998, web.uvic.ca/hrd/cfp/publications/Eric%20W.%20Sager.pdf, retrieved 2 October 2013; Gerald Friesen, *The Canadian Prairies: A History* (Toronto: University of Toronto Press, 1987), 250–55.

2   Particulars of a Recruit Drafted Under Military Service Act, 1917, Personnel File Andrew Robert W., RG 150, Accession 1992–93, vol. 10433, file 57, LAC.

3   On perceptions of war in the West, see John Herd Thompson, *The Harvests of War: The Prairie West, 1914–1918* (Toronto: McClelland and Stewart, 1978). On enlistment in the province, see C. A. Sharpe, "Enlistment in the Canadian Expeditionary Force,

1914–1918: A Regional Analysis," *Journal of Canadian Studies* 18, no. 3 (1983): 15–29, esp. 20–22.

4   1916 Census of Manitoba, Saskatchewan, and Alberta, RG 31, Reel T-21951, Alberta, Edmonton West, 25, 15, Family 212, Line 2, LAC.

5   J.L. Granatstein and J.M. Hitsman, *Broken Promises: A History of Conscription in Canada* (Oxford, UK: Oxford University Press, 1977), 75–77. For an examination of farmer's responses in Ontario, see W.R. Young, "Conscription, Rural De-Population, and the Farmers of Ontario, 1917–19," *Canadian Historical Review* 53, no. 3 (September 1972): 289–320.

6   Service Card, Personnel File Andrew Robert W., RG 150, Accession 1992–93, vol. 10433, file 57, LAC.

7   Peter Wiliton, "Spanish Flu Outdid WWI in Number of Lives Claimed," *Canadian Medical Association Journal* 148, no. 11 (1993): 2036–40.

8   There were approximately 3,300 excess deaths in the province in 1918–19. Mark Osborne Humphries, *The Last Plague: Spanish Influenza and the Politics of Public Health in Canada* (Toronto: University of Toronto Press, 2013), 106.

9   Records of a Court of Inquiry, Statements of Evidence, Personnel File Andrew Robert W., RG 150, Accession 1992-93, vol. 10433, file 57, LAC.

10   Report re Death of # [redacted], RG 150, Accession 1992-93, vol. 10433, file 57, LAC.

11   Personnel File of Major H.G. Nyblett, RG 150, Accession 1992–93/166, box 7390, file 40, LAC; Records of a Court of Inquiry, Statements of Evidence, Personnel File Andrew Robert W., RG 150, Accession 1992–93, vol. 10433, file 57, LAC.

12   Records of a Court of Inquiry, Statements of Evidence, Personnel File Andrew Robert W., RG 150, Accession 1992-93, vol. 10433, file 57, LAC.

13   For an overview of the historiography, see Guy Beiner, "Out in the Cold and Back: New-Found Interest in the Great Flu," *Cultural and Social History* 3, no. 4 (2006): 496–505; and Howard Phillips, "The Re-Appearing Shadow of 1918: Trends in the Historiography of the 1918–19 Influenza Pandemic," *Canadian Bulletin*

of Medical History 21, no. 1 (2004): 121–34. For a general introduction to the pandemic in Canada, see Humphries, *The Last Plague*; as well as Janice P. Dickin McGinnis, "The Impact of Epidemic Influenza: Canada, 1918–1919," in *Medicine in Canadian Society: Historical Perspectives*, edited by S.E.D. Shortt (Montreal and Kingston: McGill-Queen's University Press, 1981), 471–83; Janice P. Dickin McGinnis, "The Impact of Epidemic Influenza, 1918–19," *Historical Papers* (1977): 120–41. Although somewhat dated, Eileen Pettigrew's *Silent Enemy: Canada and the Deadly Flu of 1918* (Regina: Western Producer Prairie Books, 1983) is still useful, especially for firsthand accounts of the crisis.

14   Humphries, *The Last Plague*, 3–4.

15   Mark Osborne Humphries, "Paths of Infection: The First World War and the Origins of the 1918 Influenza Pandemic," *War in History* 21, no. 2 (2014): 55–81.

16   Alfred Crosby, *America's Forgotten Pandemic: The Influenza of 1918* (New York: Cambridge University Press, 1989), 37–39.

17   Niall P.A.S. Johnson and Juergen Mueller, "Updating Accounts: Global Mortality of the 1918–1920 'Spanish' Influenza Pandemic," *Bulletin of the History of Medicine* 76 (2002): 105–15.

18   Michael T. Osterholm, "Preparing for the Next Pandemic," *The New England Journal of Medicine* 352, no. 18 (5 May 2005): 1839–42; for a broader introduction to cytokine storms, see Jennifer R. Tisoncik et al., "Into the Eye of the Cytokine Storm," *Microbiology and Molecular Biology Reviews* 77, no. 3 (September 2013), http://mmbr.asm.org/content/76/1/16.full.

19   The most complete regional study is Esyllt Jones, *Influenza, 1918: Disease, Death, and Struggle in Winnipeg* (Toronto: University of Toronto Press, 2007). See also Ann Herring, ed., *Anatomy of a Pandemic: The 1918 Influenza in Hamilton* (Hamilton: Allegra Press, 2006); Niall P.A.S. Johnson, "Pandemic Influenza: An Analysis of the Spread of Influenza in Kitchener, October 1918" (MA thesis, Wilfrid Laurier University, 1993); Maureen K. Lux, "'The Bitter Flats': The 1918

Influenza Epidemic in Saskatchewan," *Saskatchewan History* (Spring 1997): 3–13; Maureen K. Lux, "The Impact of the Spanish Influenza Pandemic in Saskatchewan, 1918–1919" (MA thesis, University of Saskatchewan, 1989); Denise Rioux, "La grippe espagnole à Sherbrooke et dans les Cantons de l'Est" (Sherbrooke, QC: Études supérieures en histoire, Université de Sherbrooke, 1993); D. Ann Herring, "'There Were Young People and Old People and Babies Dying Every Week': The 1918–1919 Influenza Pandemic at Norway House," *Ethnohistory* 41, no. 1 (1994): 73–105.

20 "Influenza Takes Heavy Toll in New England," *Edmonton Bulletin*, 18 September 1918, 2.

21 "Epidemic in Three US Army Camps," *Edmonton Bulletin*, 19 September 1918, 6.

22 Mark Osborne Humphries, "The Horror at Home: The Canadian Military and the 'Great' Influenza Pandemic of 1918," *Journal of the Canadian Historical Association* 16 (2005): 241–47.

23 On the SEF, see Benjamin Isitt, *From Victoria to Vladivostok: Canada's Siberian Expedition, 1917–19* (Vancouver: UBC Press, 2010).

24 See Dickin McGinnis, "The Impact of Epidemic Influenza, 1918–19," 120–41; Janice P. Dickin McGinnis, "A City Faces an Epidemic," *Alberta History* 24, no. 4 (1976): 1–11; a more recent example is David Bright, "1919: A Year of Extraordinary Difficulty," in *Alberta Formed, Alberta Transformed*, edited by Donald Wetherell, Catherine Cavanaugh, and Michael Payne (Edmonton: University of Alberta Press, 2005), 420–22.

25 Humphries, "The Horror at Home," 248–53.

26 War Diary (WD), Assistant Director, Medical Services (ADMS), Military District (MD) 7, 28 September 1918, RG 9, vol. 5063, file 978, Part I, LAC.

27 District Records Officer (DRO), MD 4 to DRO MD 7, 7 November 1918 and Memorandum DRO, MD 7 to ADMS MD 7, 27 November 1918, RG 24, vol. 4574, file 3-9-47, vol. 1, LAC.

28 WD, ADMS, MD 4, 29 September 1918, RG 9, vol. 5061, file 976, Part I, LAC.

29 Humphries, "The Horror at Home," 253–54.

30 ADMS MD 13 to Director General, Medical Services (DGMS), 2 October 1918, RG 24, vol. 1992, file HQ-762-11-15, LAC.

31 Janice P. Dickin McGinnis paints a similar picture, although she suggests that these soldiers were returning veterans because they were reported as such in the local papers. See Dickin McGinnis, "A City Faces an Epidemic," 1.

32 RG 6, Reel C-5863, file NSC 1029-6-24, LAC. On wartime censorship in general, see Jeff Keshen, *Propaganda and Censorship during Canada's Great War* (Edmonton: University of Athabasca Press, 1996), especially chapters 3 to 6.

33 "Precautions," *Redcliff Review*, 3 October 1918, 2.

34 Ibid. Identical notices, likely derived from American wire services, were printed in the *Chinook Advance* on the same day.

35 "Time to Take Precautions," *Edmonton Bulletin*, 3 October 1918, 7.

36 Ibid.

37 Heather MacDougall, "Toronto's Health Department in Action: Influenza in 1918 and SARS in 2003," *Journal of the History of Medicine and Allied Sciences* 62, no. 1 (2007): 89.

38 Howard Markel et al., "Non-Pharmaceutical Interventions Implemented by US Cities during the 1918–1919 Influenza Pandemic," *Journal of the American Medical Association* 298 (2007): 644–54; S. Zhang, P. Yan, B. Winchester, and J. Wang, "Transmissibility of the 1918 Pandemic Influenza in Montreal and Winnipeg of Canada," *Influenza and Other Respiratory Viruses* 4, no. 1 (January 2010): 27–31; Lisa Sattenspiel and D. Ann Herring, "Simulating the Effect of Quarantine on the Spread of the 1918–19 Flu in Central Canada," *Bulletin of Mathematical Biology* 65, no. 1 (2006): 1–26.

39 Humphries, *The Last Plague*, 109–11.

40 Adelaide Schartner, *Health Units of Alberta* (Edmonton: Health Unit Association of Alberta/Co-Op Press, 1982), 22–24.

41 Ibid., 22.

42 Ibid., 22–23.

43 Ibid., 23–24.

44 "Dominion Board of Health," *Edmonton Bulletin*, 24 February 1908, 4. For examples, see "Immigrants from US Spread Smallpox," *Edmonton Capital*, 5 August 1910, 1; "Smallpox on the Increase," *Taber Free Press*, 28 May 1908, 4; "Immigrants Should Not Stay in Cities," *Edmonton Bulletin*, 4 April 1914, 6.

45 Alan M. Kraut, *Silent Travelers: Germs, Genes, and the "Immigrant Menace"* (Baltimore, MD: Johns Hopkins University Press, 1994), 5–7.

46 "Dominion Board of Health," *Edmonton Bulletin*, 24 February 1908, 4. On the development of quarantine, see Humphries, *The Last Plague*.

47 Jane E. Jenkins, "Baptism of Fire: New Brunswick's Public Health Movement and the 1918 Influenza Epidemic," *Canadian Bulletin of Medical History* 24, no. 2 (2007): 322–26.

48 On the earlier pandemic, see F.B. Smith, "The Russian Influenza in the United Kingdom, 1889–1894," *Social History of Medicine* 8, no. 1 (1995): 55–73; and Mark Honigsbaum, "The Great Dread: Cultural and Psychological Impacts and Responses to the 'Russian' Influenza in the United Kingdom, 1889–1893," *Social History of Medicine* 23, no. 2 (2010): 299–319. A brief overview of the Canadian experience is provided in Humphries, *The Last Plague*, 58–67.

49 A similar struggle took place in British Columbia, Saskatchewan, Manitoba, and Ontario. See Margaret W. Andrews, "Epidemic and Public Health: Influenza in Vancouver, 1918–1919," *BC Studies* 34 (Summer 1977): 30; Lux, "The Bitter Flats," 9; Jones, *Influenza, 1918*, 43; Province of Ontario, *The Report of the Provincial Board of Health, 1918* (Toronto: Government of Ontario, 1919).

50 "Fifteen Spanish Influenza Cases Come to Calgary," *Calgary Herald*, 2 October 1918, 10; for the verbatim text of Mahood's release, see "Spanish 'Flu Has Reached the Province," *Edmonton Bulletin*, 4 October 1918, 12.

51 "Spanish 'Flu Has Reached the Province," 12.

52 "Health Board Meets to Combat Disease," *Edmonton Bulletin*, 5 October 1918, 3. For the full verbatim text, see "Information on Spanish Influenza," *Claresholm Review-Advertiser*, 11 October 1918, 1.

53 For example, see "Influenza Warning," *Bow Island Review*, 11 October 1918, 1.

54 "Wants Influenza to be Declared Reportable Now," *Edmonton Bulletin*, 9 October 1918, 3.

55 "Health Act Does Not Quarantine Influenza Cases," *Calgary Herald*, 10 October 1918, 9.

56 Janice Dickin, "Pale Horse/Pale History? Revisiting Calgary's Experience of the Spanish Influenza, 1918–19," in *Harm's Way: Disasters in Western Canada*, edited by Anthony Rasporich and Max Foran (Calgary: University of Calgary Press, 2004), 47.

57 "Spanish Influenza Subject to Modified Quarantine," *Edmonton Bulletin*, 14 October 1918, 3.

58 "Sweeping Program of Train Inspection Adopted for Keeping 'Flu Epidemic from Province," *Edmonton Bulletin*, 16 October 1918, 1.

59 "Spanish Flu Visits Oyen," *Oyen News*, 16 October 1918, 1.

60 "Lethbridge Is Now Under Quarantine," *Lethbridge Daily Herald*, 18 October 1918, 1.

61 Ibid.

62 Ibid.

63 "Will Lift 'Flu Ban on City This Afternoon," *Lethbridge Daily Herald*, 19 October 1918, 1, 4.

64 "Steps Taken to Protect Town Against 'Flu," *Irma Times*, 25 October 1918, 1.

65 "New Brunswick Schools, Churches, Theatres Closed," *Edmonton Bulletin*, 10 October 1918, 1.

66 "Suspend Public Gatherings in Winnipeg," *Edmonton Bulletin*, 12 October 1918, 1; "Toronto Conventions Banned for Month," *Edmonton Bulletin*, 12 October 1918, 11.

67 "Dr. Mahood Says No Need to Close Theatres," *Claresholm Review-Advertiser*, 18 October 1918, 8.

68 "City Theatres, Dance Halls, Libraries and Public Rooms Closed," *Calgary Herald*, 18 October 1918, 1.

69 "Church Notice," *Irma Times*, 25 October 1918, 8.

70 "Found Boy Digging Graves," *Edmonton Bulletin*, 14 November 1918, 3.

71 "One More Day Before Masks Obligatory," *Edmonton Bulletin*, 24 October 1918, 1.

72 "Must Wear Mask Now When Travelling," *Redcliff Review*, 24 October 1918, 1.

73 Dickin McGinnis, "A City Faces an Epidemic," 4–6.

74 "No Abatement of Influenza," *Edmonton Bulletin*, 28 October 1918, 1.

75 Ibid.

76 Ibid.

77 Dickin McGinnis, "A City Faces an Epidemic," 4–6.

78 Ibid.

79 Ibid.; see also "Prosecutions Will Be Commenced in City Today for Violations of Order for Wearing of Masks," *Edmonton Bulletin*, 9 November 1918, 1.

80 On the development of the new medicine by the laboratory in Canada, see Christopher Rutty, "Personality, Politics, and Canadian Public Health: The Origins of the Connaught Medical Research Laboratories, University of Toronto, 1888–1917," in *Essays in Honour of Michael Bliss: Figuring the Social,* edited by E.A. Heaman, Alison Li, and Shelley McKellar (Toronto: University of Toronto Press, 2008), 278–79.

81 William Osler, *The Treatment of Disease: The Address in Medicine Before the Ontario Medical Association, Toronto, June 3, 1909* (London, UK: Oxford University Press, 1909), 5–7.

82 Alfred Crosby, *Epidemic and Peace 1918: America's Deadliest Influenza Epidemic* (Westport, CT: Greenwood, 1976), 264–72. For a discussion of how Canadian physicians interpreted his discovery, see "Le bacilli de la grippe," *L'union médicale du Canada* 21, no. 3 (March 1892): 158–59.

83 Pettigrew, *Silent Enemy*, 20–21.

84 Carol R. Byerly, *Fever of War: The Influenza Epidemic in the US Army during World War I* (New York: NYU Press, 2005), 163–64.

85 F.T. Cadham, "The Use of a Vaccine in the Recent Epidemic of Influenza," *Canadian Medical Association Journal* 9, no. 6 (1919): 519; Jones, *Influenza, 1918*, 43;

Pettigrew, *Silent Enemy*, 19–20; John W.S. McCullough, "The Control of Influenza in Ontario," *Canadian Medical Association Journal* 8, no. 12 (1918): 1085.

86 "Peak Not Yet Reached Says Hon. A.G. MacKay," *Edmonton Bulletin*, 1 November 1918, 1.

87 "Influenza and After; Advice from College of Physicians," *Edmonton Bulletin*, 12 December 1918, 3. For a similar reaction in Canada, see J.J. Heagerty, "Influenza and Vaccination," *Canadian Medical Association Journal* 9, no. 3 (1919): 226–27.

88 "Health Authorities Look for Rapid Spread of Disease and Urge More Precautions," *Edmonton Bulletin*, 25 October 1918, 3.

89 Medical Case Sheet, Joseph M., RG 150, Accession 1992–93/166, vol. 6163, file 22, LAC; Commonwealth War Graves Commission Burial Record, http://www.cwgc.org/find-war-dead/casualty/2765430/MILBURN,%20JOSEPH, retrieved 3 October 2013.

90 Jones, *Influenza, 1918*, 139. On the effects of flu on farm families, see Joan Champ, *The Impact of the Spanish Influenza Epidemic on Saskatchewan Farm Families, 1918–1919* (Saskatoon: Saskatchewan Western Development Museum, 2003), http://wdm.ca/skteacherguide/WDMResearch/1918SpanishFlu.pdf. For a description of the problems of rural care in Alberta, see "Nineteen Dead at Drumheller," *Edmonton Bulletin*, 28 October 1918, 3.

91 Dickin McGinnis, "A City Faces an Epidemic," 6.

92 "Pembina Hall Secured for 'Flu Hospital," *Edmonton Bulletin*, 25 October 1918, 1.

93 "How Influenza is Fought at Queen Alexandra School," *Edmonton Bulletin*, 18 November 1918, 3.

94 "Pembina Hall Secured for 'Flu Hospital," *Edmonton Bulletin*, 25 October 1918, 1.

95 "Graduate Nurses Make Plans for Coping with Spanish 'Flu," *Edmonton Bulletin*, 16 October 1918, 4.

96 On the role of professional nurses in Canadian hospitals and private homes, see Kathryn McPherson, *Bedside Matters: The Transformation of Canadian*

Nursing, 1900–1990 (Oxford, UK: Oxford University Press, 1996).

97 "Forty-One Cases of Spanish Influenza in City at Present," *Edmonton Bulletin*, 19 October 1918, 3.

98 "Over 100 Cases of Spanish Influenza Reported by the City Authorities Since Friday Last," *Edmonton Bulletin*, 21 October 1918, 1.

99 "City Divided into Districts," *Edmonton Bulletin*, 28 October 1918, 1.

100 "District Nursing System to Care for 'Flu Cases," *Edmonton Bulletin*, 26 October 1918, 1.

101 "How Influenza is Fought at Queen Alexandra School."

102 Linda J. Quiney, "'Filling the Gaps': Canadian Voluntary Nurses, the 1917 Halifax Explosion, and the Influenza Epidemic of 1918," *Canadian Bulletin of Medical History* 19, no. 2 (2002): 367.

103 "Brave Nursing Sister Dies at her Post from Influenza After Caring for Soldiers," *Edmonton Bulletin*, 29 October 1918, 1.

104 Anon. Volunteer Nurse, "What the 'Flu is Doing to Us,'" *Edmonton Bulletin*, 2 November 1918, 4.

105 See advertisement "Urgent Call for Assistance in fight Against Epidemic," *Edmonton Bulletin*, 29 October 1918, 3.

106 "City Divided into Districts," 4.

107 "Hon. A.G. MacKay Tells of Fight Against Flu," *Edmonton Bulletin*, 29 October 1918, 3.

108 Esyllt Jones, "'Co-operation in All Human Endeavour': Quarantine and Immigrant Disease Vectors in the 1918–1919 Influenza Pandemic in Winnipeg," *Canadian Bulletin of Medical History* 22, no. 1 (2005): 57–82.

109 Ibid., 77–78.

110 Esyllt Jones, "Contact across a Diseased Boundary: Urban Space and Social Interaction during Winnipeg's Influenza Epidemic 1918–1919," *Journal of the Canadian Historical Association* 13 (2002): 119–39; for care guidelines see Provincial Health Department, "Epidemic Influenza: Instructions Regarding Care of Sick Persons," as printed in the *Drumheller Review*, 8 November 1918. For a similar case study of

Montreal, see Magda Fahrni, "'Elles sont partout . . .': les femmes et la ville en temps d'épidémie, Montréal, 1918–1920," *Revue d'histoire de l'Amérique française* 58, no. 1 (2004): 68–71.

111 A.W. Coone, "Living Conditions in Parts of This City," *Edmonton Bulletin*, 26 November 1918, 7.

112 Ibid.

113 Letter to the Editor, "The Epidemic," *Edmonton Bulletin*, 16 November 1918, 7.

114 Ibid.

115 See Mary-Ellen Kelm, "British Columbia First Nations and the Influenza Pandemic of 1918–1919," *BC Studies* 122 (1999): 23–47; and Maureen Lux, "Prairie Indians and the 1918 Influenza Epidemic," *Native Studies Review* 8, no. 1 (1992): 23–33.

116 "Influenza Epidemic," 28 May 1919, file 851-4-D96 Part 1, vol. 2970, RG 29, LAC. Accuracy is always an issue when dealing with statistics compiled by Indian Affairs, but the numbers are confirmed by independent research. Ann Herring calculated that 188 people died at Norway House during the pandemic. The Indian Affairs statistics list 190 deaths, including two which were recorded after the period examined by Herring. See Herring, "There Were Young People and Old People and Babies Dying Every Week."

117 Maureen Lux, *Medicine That Walks: Disease, Medicine, and Canadian Plains Native People, 1880–1940* (Toronto: University of Toronto Press, 2001), 189ff.

118 K.F. Anderson to R. Field, 20 December 1918, RG 18, vol. 1003, file "Spanish Influenza, 1919," LAC.

119 Population statistics are based on annual treaty payment figures from Dominion of Canada, Annual Report of the Department of Indian Affairs for the Year Ended March 31 1918 (Ottawa: Department of Indian Affairs, 1919), 111–12; "Influenza Epidemic," 28 May 1919, RG 29, vol. 2970, file 851-4-D96, Part 1, LAC.

120 Affidavit by Frank C. Fisg, 1 December 1918, RG 18, vol. 1928, file RCMP 1918, no. 160, LAC.

121 Staff Sergeant Fyffe to Commanding Officer, G Division, 2 December 1918, RG 18, vol. 1928, file RCMP 1918, no. 160, LAC.

122 "Influenza Epidemic," 28 May 1919, RG 29, vol. 2970, file 851-4-D96, Part 1, LAC.

123 Dickin McGinnis, "A City Faces an Epidemic," 11, notes 4 and 5.

124 "Union Government and the Flu," *Edmonton Bulletin*, 25 October 1918, 7.

125 "Why the Epidemic?," *Edmonton Bulletin*, 17 October 1918, 7.

Works Cited

Andrews, Margaret W. "Epidemic and Public Health: Influenza in Vancouver, 1918–1919." *BC Studies* 34 (Summer 1977): 21–44.

Beiner, Guy. "Out in the Cold and Back: New-Found Interest in the Great Flu." *Cultural and Social History* 3, no. 4 (2006): 496–505.

Bright, David. "1919: A Year of Extraordinary Difficulty." In *Alberta Formed, Alberta Transformed*, edited by Donald Wetherell, Catherine Cavanaugh, and Michael Payne. Edmonton: University of Alberta Press, 2005.

Byerly, Carol R. *Fever of War: The Influenza Epidemic in the US Army during World War I*. New York: NYU Press, 2005.

Crosby, Alfred. *America's Forgotten Pandemic: The Influenza of 1918*. New York: Cambridge University Press, 1989.

———. *Epidemic and Peace 1918: America's Deadliest Influenza Epidemic*. Westport, CT: Greenwood Press, 1976.

Dickin, Janice. "Pale Horse/Pale History? Revisiting Calgary's Experience of the Spanish Influenza, 1918–19." In *Harm's Way: Disasters in Western Canada*, edited by Anthony Rasporich and Max Foran. Calgary: University of Calgary Press, 2004.

Dickin McGinnis, Janice P. "A City Faces an Epidemic." *Alberta History* 24, no. 4 (1976): 1–11.

———. "The Impact of Epidemic Influenza, 1918–19." *Historical Papers* (1977): 120–41.

———. "The Impact of Epidemic Influenza: Canada, 1918–1919." In *Medicine in Canadian Society: Historical Perspectives*, edited by S.E.D. Short. Montreal and Kingston: McGill-Queen's University Press, 1981.

Fahrni, Magda. "'Elles sont partout . . .': les femmes et la ville en temps d'épidémie, Montréal, 1918–1920." *Revue d'histoire de l'Amérique française* 58, no. 1 (2004): 67–85.

Friesen, Gerald. *The Canadian Prairies: A History*. Toronto: University of Toronto Press, 1987.

Granatstein, J.L., and J.M. Hitsman. *Broken Promises: A History of Conscription in Canada*. Oxford, UK: Oxford University Press, 1977.

Herring, Ann, ed. *Anatomy of a Pandemic: The 1918 Influenza in Hamilton*. Hamilton, ON: Allegra Press, 2006.

Herring, D. Ann. "'There Were Young People and Old People and Babies Dying Every Week': The 1918–1919 Influenza Pandemic at Norway House." *Ethnohistory* 41, no. 1 (1994): 73–105.

Honigsbaum, Mark. "The Great Dread: Cultural and Psychological Impacts and Responses to the 'Russian' Influenza in the United Kingdom, 1889–1893." *Social History of Medicine* 23, no. 2 (2010): 299–319.

Humphries, Mark Osborne. "The Horror at Home: The Canadian Military and the 'Great' Influenza Pandemic of 1918." *Journal of the Canadian Historical Association* 16 (2005): 231–65.

———. *The Last Plague: Spanish Influenza and the Politics of Public Health in Canada*. Toronto: University of Toronto Press, 2013.

———. "Paths of Infection: The First World War and the Origins of the 1918 Influenza Pandemic." *War in History* 21, no. 1 (2014): 55–81.

Isitt, Benjamin. *From Victoria to Vladivostok: Canada's Siberian Expedition, 1917–19*. Vancouver: UBC Press, 2010.

Jenkins, Jane E. "Baptism of Fire: New Brunswick's Public Health Movement and the 1918 Influenza Epidemic." *Canadian Bulletin of Medical History* 24, no. 2 (2007): 317–42.

Johnson, Niall P.A.S. "Pandemic Influenza: An Analysis of the Spread of Influenza in Kitchener, October 1918." MA thesis, Wilfrid Laurier University, 1993.

Johnson, Niall P.A.S., and Juergen Mueller. "Updating Accounts: Global Mortality of the 1918–1920 'Spanish' Influenza Pandemic." *Bulletin of the History of Medicine* 76 (2002): 105–15.

Jones, Esyllt. "Contact across a Diseased Boundary: Urban Space and Social Interaction during Winnipeg's Influenza Epidemic 1918–1919." *Journal of the Canadian Historical Association* 13 (2002): 119–39.

——. *Influenza, 1918: Disease, Death, and Struggle in Winnipeg.* Toronto: University of Toronto Press, 2007.

Kraut, Alan M. *Silent Travelers: Germs, Genes, and the "Immigrant Menace."* Baltimore, MD: Johns Hopkins University Press, 1994.

Lux, Maureen K. "'The Bitter Flats': The 1918 Influenza Epidemic in Saskatchewan." *Saskatchewan History* (Spring 1997): 3–13.

——. "The Impact of the Spanish Influenza Pandemic in Saskatchewan, 1918–1919." MA thesis, University of Saskatchewan, 1989.

——. *Medicine That Walks: Disease, Medicine, and Canadian Plains Native People, 1880–1940.* Toronto: University of Toronto Press, 2001.

——. "Prairie Indians and the 1918 Influenza Epidemic." *Native Studies Review* 8, no. 1 (1992): 23–33.

MacDougall, Heather. "Toronto's Health Department in Action: Influenza in 1918 and SARS in 2003." *Journal of the History of Medicine and Allied Sciences* 62, no. 1 (2007): 56–89.

Markel, Howard, et al. "Non-Pharmaceutical Interventions Implemented by US Cities during the 1918–1919 Influenza Pandemic." *Journal of the American Medical Association* 298 (2007): 644–54.

McPherson, Kathryn. *Bedside Matters: The Transformation of Canadian Nursing, 1900–1990.* Oxford, UK: Oxford University Press, 1996.

Osler, William. *The Treatment of Disease: The Address in Medicine Before the Ontario Medical Association, Toronto, June 3, 1909.* London, UK: Oxford University Press, 1909.

Osterholm, Michael T. "Preparing for the Next Pandemic." *The New England Journal of Medicine* 352, no. 18 (5 May 2005): 1839–42.

Pettigrew, Eileen. *Silent Enemy: Canada and the Deadly Flu of 1918.* Regina: Western Producer Prairie Books, 1983.

Phillips, Howard. "The Re-Appearing Shadow of 1918: Trends in the Historiography of the 1918–19 Influenza Pandemic." *Canadian Bulletin of Medical History* 21, no. 1 (2004): 121–34.

Quiney, Linda J. "'Filling the Gaps': Canadian Voluntary Nurses, the 1917 Halifax Explosion, and the Influenza Epidemic of 1918." *Canadian Bulletin of Medical History* 19, no. 2 (2002): 351–74.

Rioux, Denise. "La grippe espagnole à Sherbrooke et dans les Cantons de l'Est." Sherbrooke, QC: Études supérieures en histoire, Université de Sherbrooke, 1993.

Rutty, Christopher. "Personality, Politics, and Canadian Public Health: The Origins of the Connaught Medical Research Laboratories, University of Toronto, 1888–1917." In *Essays in Honour of Michael Bliss: Figuring the Social*, edited by E.A. Heaman, Alison Li, and Shelley McKellar. Toronto: University of Toronto Press, 2008.

Sattenspiel, Lisa, and D. Ann Herring. "Simulating the Effect of Quarantine on the Spread of the 1918–19 Flu in Central Canada." *Bulletin of Mathematical Biology* 65, no. 1 (2006): 1–26.

Schartner, Adelaide. *Health Units of Alberta.* Edmonton: Health Unit Association of Alberta/Co-Op Press, 1982.

Smith, F.B. "The Russian Influenza in the United Kingdom, 1889–1894." *Social History of Medicine* 8, no. 1 (1995): 55–73.

Thompson, John Herd. *The Harvests of War: The Prairie West, 1914–1918.* Toronto: McClelland and Stewart, 1978.

Tisoncik, Jennifer R., et al. "Into the Eye of the Cytokine Storm." *Microbiology and Molecular Biology Reviews* 77, no. 3 (September 2013). URL: http://mmbr.asm.org/content/76/1/16.full.

Wiliton, Peter. "Spanish Flu Outdid WWI in Number of Lives Claimed." *Canadian Medical Association Journal* 148, no. 11 (1993): 2036–40.

Zhang, S., P. Yan, B. Winchester, and J. Wang. "Transmissibility of the 1918 Pandemic Influenza in Montreal and Winnipeg of Canada." *Influenza and Other Respiratory Viruses* 4, no. 1 (January 2010): 27–31.

Applying Modernity: Local Government and the 1919 Federal Housing Scheme in Alberta

DONALD G. WETHERELL

The outbreak of war in 1914 was accompanied in Alberta by calls to defend the nation and the empire and protect home and family life. These calls were broad and emotive. "Home" was a familiar term, but one laden with varied notions about social continuity, tradition, gender, personal comfort, safety, and belonging. The "house," as the physical space that sheltered the home, was of more than passing importance in the expression of these values. And by 1914 the ideal house could be defined by citing objective criteria that had recently coalesced into a definition of the "modern house." These criteria drew upon relatively new scientific knowledge about health and the cause of disease and theories about how physical space affected social relationships. This knowledge also guided how houses should best be arranged on lots, and how neighbourhoods should be laid out to create social efficiency, healthful surroundings, and, if it could be had, a beautiful environment in which to live and raise families. When the federal government created a housing scheme for postwar reconstruction in 1919, it drew directly on these understandings about modernity and domestic architecture.

"Modernity" was not a style in domestic architecture but rather a loose set of concepts that posited a healthier, more rational future through science, rational design, and technology. By the outbreak of the First World War, advances in scientific knowledge postulating that germs were a major cause of contagious disease had been broadly accepted. It was also understood that germs could be killed or, at least, their impact mitigated by cleanliness, sunlight, openness, and fresh air.[1] The application of this knowledge in house design necessitated the replacement of nineteenth-century closed-in rooms—which were dark, had poor air circulation, and were hard to keep clean—with open plans in which rooms connected one into the other and had plenty of windows that could open. The public was cautioned that every room had to have at least one window. Logically, living areas in basements were, thus, considered to be unhealthy and depressing. Sanitary standards were further enhanced by smooth walls that would shed dust and hard floor surfaces that were easy to clean. This justified the replacement of lath-and-plaster walls covered with wallpaper with ones finished with smooth plaster or panelling, or with various wall-board products. While employing such design principles could help prevent disease, it supported broader social values as well. Open plans were conducive to family life because they brought people together, while openness, light, and fresh air also contributed to sound mental and spiritual health and a positive outlook.[2] For urban houses, the relationship of the house to its community was equally significant. Connection to municipal sewer systems was essential for public sanitation, but houses also needed to be placed within lots (rather than completely fill them) to ensure that sunlight and fresh air could easily reach into the buildings. Sound land-use principles also demanded the prohibition of incompatible land use near housing, and the provision of public open spaces where community life could be focused. As the Canadian town planner Thomas Adams advised in 1916: "The first necessity of good housing is to control all land development by town planning."[3]

Although the elements that defined the modern house were broadly accepted by the time of the outbreak of the war as those needed for decent standards of housing, they were not codified by the state or public agencies. Moreover, only the urban middle class and a few wealthier farmers could afford to implement them; and, at the start of the war, many people lived in crowded, small, poorly constructed houses without adequate sanitation or heating. Mortgages were difficult to obtain; wages were low and job security was rare; while on farms, capital was invested in production rather than housing. All of these problems were intensified in Alberta because of its recent settlement. As A.E. Grauer noted in 1939 in his survey of the history of housing in Canada: "The housing difficulties of low income

groups common to all countries have been complicated by conditions peculiar to a young country—rapid growth, inflated real estate values, speculative activity, and influx of poor immigrants and lack of planning."[4] Nor did the state see itself as having a role in helping people gain access to better housing through mortgages or other programs.

Alberta thus entered the war with ideals about what contributed to good housing that exceeded what most people could afford. The province's economy was also fragile. It had recently experienced a five-year period of increasingly frantic growth and land speculation, but this boom had collapsed suddenly in 1912–13. The most telling consequence in Alberta was a rapid drop in the price of land, which had reached extremely high levels because of speculation driven by the optimism and greed of the previous half decade. Although there was a brief revival of activity in Calgary in 1914 after the discovery of oil at Turner Valley, speculative fever was over for a time.[5]

This collapse left many towns and cities with substantial amounts of vacant land that had been surveyed and serviced by local governments with sewage, electrical, and transportation infrastructure in preparation for what was believed would be imminent private development. When the economy collapsed, the prospects for rapid development of this, as well as other subdivided but unserviced land, disappeared, and much of it was soon being forfeited for nonpayment of taxes. The impact of the collapse of land values on local governments was exacerbated because some cities in the province had earlier adopted a single-tax system in which only land, not improvements, was taxed. In 1912 the provincial government had imposed this system across Alberta. As a method of funding local government, the single tax had many problems, but the most obvious one was that tax revenue fell as land values evaporated. In some places, generous tax incentives that had been offered to attract industry also now weighed heavily on local governments. Although war-related industrial production was minimal on the prairies, unemployment was low because of the enlistment of employable men and a boom in agricultural and resource industries. However, most of the resulting gains disappeared in wartime inflation and, in terms of industrialization, the war probably had a negative impact on the prairies.[6]

For local governments, problems became worse because of falling tax revenues, forfeiture of land for nonpayment of taxes, and slow economic growth. As a result, homeowners, who could ill afford it, were forced to pay higher and higher property taxes. In an attempt to gain control of its finances, Edmonton, for example, brought in a civic income tax from 1918 until 1920; but it was too late. The city and its ratepayers struggled for the next 25 years to overcome the difficulties resulting from the short-sighted policies of the boom years and the added problems of the 1930s.[7]

The war slowed house construction dramatically, and the near collapse of the house-building industry in Alberta ensured that very little new housing was constructed in the province between 1914 and 1918. This meant that there would be even more serious housing shortages at the end of the war than there had been at its beginning. Thus, providing housing was widely recognized as a priority for postwar adjustment and, as Thomas Adams of the Commission of Conservation observed in 1918: "If there is a shortage now, what will be the conditions when several thousand men return from Europe?"[8] Adams's question pointed to the dual housing problem faced at the time of postwar adjustment: taking care of returned soldiers and meeting the already-pressing housing needs of the civilian population.

To grapple with current and impending housing shortages, and the likelihood of social unrest because of it, the federal government developed two separate policies to deal with rural and urban housing. Rural and urban housing needs were different and required different approaches, especially since rural programs further aimed to promote land settlement to create economic stimulus at the war's end. In 1917, the federal government passed the Soldier Settlement Act, which enabled soldiers to obtain loans on a 20-year term to homestead, to purchase land for farming, or to build a farm house. In Alberta, most of this settlement took place in the Peace River country and in the areas north and east of Edmonton. By the end of 1920, almost 20,000 soldier settlers had taken up land in Canada, 5,785 of them in Alberta.[9]

As part of this land settlement program, the federal Soldier Settlement Board also issued architectural drawings for outbuildings and for four different types of modest houses that could be built easily and quickly by soldier settlers. The plans were developed with prairie conditions in mind and included double floors, storm windows, "liberal use of building paper," and an exterior wall finish of asphalt and "flint coated ready roofing"—all of which would "make a wind tight job." The interior was finished with wall board. The houses ranged from a two-room, gable-roof shack of about 22 square metres to a small, six-room, two-storey house with a simple gable roof. All were designed so that they could be easily enlarged in the future. Soldier settlers could buy building materials at reduced prices, and complete packages of the materials required could be purchased from Eaton's and many lumber yards.[10]

To meet the needs of urban people, a postwar adjustment housing scheme was introduced in 1919. It, too, aimed to create employment and stimulate the economy by meeting the obvious demand from low-income urban people for affordable housing. The scheme also reflected tentative stirrings to recognize housing as a social-reform issue. A belief that the war had been caused by materialism, greed, and a lack of cooperation gave new vitality to demands that town planning schemes, public sanitation services, and other civic improvements relevant to housing quality had to be approached systematically, and as part of the state's responsibility for housing.[11] Under this scheme, the federal government lent $25 million at 5 percent interest to the provinces, distributed according to population. The provinces, in turn, lent this to municipalities where jurisdiction in the housing field lay. Loans were made to prospective owners at 5 percent, instead of the current rate of 8 percent, amortized over 20 years. The plan aimed to provide housing in industrial areas for people with incomes of less than $3,000 per year, which constituted the vast majority. Local governments were required to provide land at cost, by expropriation if necessary, in order to eliminate speculation. The land was expected to represent only about 10 percent of the total cost of the house exclusive of local improvements. As well, each province was required to develop a housing plan according to which the houses would be built, ideally as part of a single, serviced site close to amenities and employment. The federal government drew up recommendations for design and construction, which, while not mandatory, were considered the "minimum standards

for health and comfort, and not as ideals that are difficult to attain." Under the scheme the building cost could not exceed $3,500 for a seven-room, wood-frame house.[12]

Reflecting ideas about open plans; the connection between light, sanitation, ventilation, and human health; and the relationship between urban planning and the quality of housing, the houses built under this 1919 scheme were to be of "modern character." This meant that each house had to be part of a general urban plan. The house was to face onto a street, or a large courtyard, and be accessible to playgrounds, parks, and other public services. To ensure light and ventilation, the house could not occupy more than 50 percent of the lot. Houses were expected to have proper sewage disposal systems and ample plumbed-in clean water. The bathroom was to be located on the second floor of a two-storey house, and each room, including the bathroom, was to have a window placed so that it would provide light and good cross-ventilation. Basements were not to be used as living space. Ventilation and access to fresh air were further promoted by setting minimum sizes for rooms; furthermore, all ceilings on the second floor were to be at least 2.4 metres high, and were to cover no less than two-thirds of the floor area.[13]

These standards were promoted not only by the federal government but also, with some slight modifications, by the Ontario Housing Committee, whose recommendations received wide coverage in Alberta newspapers and in Canadian building journals. Clearly, what had been the ideals of modern design before the war were now seen as baseline standards that could be applied across the country. Importantly, these standards drew upon scientific knowledge about health and disease. They also asserted basic standards for comfort and family life, and social amenities. This was one of the most important consequences of the scheme and, as was observed in 1919, "by this legislation, Canada has lifted the study of the homes of her people from a local . . . interest to a national status."[14] Surprisingly, there were few objections to the entry of the state into a field that had so far been wholly in the hands of private enterprise. The importance of the scheme as a model and the need for affordable housing for workers outweighed its challenge to "the virtues of free competition."[15]

The federal housing scheme was introduced in Alberta against the background of troubled local governments, housing shortages, rising costs, and high urban unemployment. Between 1918 and 1920, Edmonton took possession of 70,000 building lots in the city, almost all for tax arrears; by 1919, Calgary owned two-thirds of the land within its boundaries for the same reason. Despite this land glut, there was a housing shortage that pushed up costs. In 1919 rent in Edmonton and Calgary was up 25 percent over the past 12 months, and even as high as 50 percent over the previous year. Most of these increases were due to a shortage of capital for housing and to the cost of materials and labour that by 1920 had risen by between 70 and 80 percent since 1914. Thus, a house that had cost between $4,000 and $6,000 in 1914 now cost between $6,500 and $9,500. The only saving grace was that land was cheap. Lots that had cost $2,000 in 1912 could be had after the war for $500. Inflation had caused the increase in labour costs; calls for cheaper labour were unrealistic in light of wartime hyper-inflation.[16] At the same time, unemployment was high. In 1919 carpenters in Edmonton lobbied the city and the provincial government to initiate building projects to create employment. As the *Calgary Herald* editorialized, most of those who "went to the front were connected

. . . with building and construction work," and given the need for housing and employment, house construction would solve a number of postwar social problems.[17]

In these conditions, it was not surprising that the provincial government was at first enthusiastic about the federal government's housing scheme. Premier Charles Stewart estimated that Alberta would be eligible for about $1.6 million in loans, or enough to build 530 houses at $3,000 each. This new construction would promote urban renewal and prevent the development of "slum conditions" in downtown Edmonton and Calgary. Further, it would help to improve housing in mining communities such as Drumheller, where housing was extremely poor. Critics of the plan observed that payments on a $3,000 house, even at 5 percent, would be about $33 per month including upkeep and taxes, which was more than the "average workingman" could afford. The provincial government also began to reconsider its support. The provincial treasurer argued that a program that encouraged renovation and repair of houses in industrial areas, rather than one directed at new-house construction, would be more beneficial. The province also contended that the federal government should give it the money as a grant, not as a loan. As well, the provincial government was concerned about how it would enforce the minimum construction and urban planning standards required by the scheme, since both of these matters lay in the jurisdiction of local government. Most importantly, it worried that bankrupt municipalities would never repay the loans extended to them by the province. Thus, despite numerous calls for Alberta's involvement in the program, the premier informed a delegation of mayors in 1920 that it had decided not to participate, and, "as to borrowing money from the

Dominion government on municipal securities, he was inclined to think that every municipality in the province was already pretty well up to, or past, its borrowing powers."[18]

Local governments were not eager to participate in the program. Calgary was concerned that the scheme would add to its civic debt, and refused to assume responsibility for loan repayments by issuing debentures. Nor could Alberta cities agree on a uniform set of goals for the program. Edmonton, for example, argued that the money should be made available for renovating, repairing, and moving houses onto serviced lots, while Medicine Hat wanted to make loans to anyone, including landlords, to build what and how they wanted. Moreover, urban governments refused to provide land from their rapidly growing holdings, and all wanted to charge borrowers full administrative and land costs. In practical terms, this would put the houses built under the scheme even further out of reach of the intended market. Of course, had local governments participated in the program, their land holdings would have been reduced, needed houses would have been built on vacant serviced land, and some revenue would have been generated for the cities. However, no urban government took this view, which, along with the provincial government's justifiable reluctance to take any risk in the circumstances, scuttled the program in Alberta.

By 1921, when it was repealed, every province except Alberta had passed housing legislation under the program, and all except Alberta and Saskatchewan had received advances under the program. Despite charges by the provincial opposition that Alberta's failure to participate in the scheme lay solely with a "faint-hearted" provincial government, the program had a number of drawbacks. Indeed, it was not particularly successful anywhere in the country except in Winnipeg. One basic problem was its reliance on local governments, which were too poor and inefficient, and too narrowly fixated on local concerns to make the program work as a provincial one. Because it made no provision for assisting rural home owners, provinces with large rural populations, such as Alberta and Saskatchewan, were also disadvantaged. In addition, Alberta's major urban problems were not slums, as they were in some other parts of Canada, but a large number of small, poor-quality, prewar houses scattered throughout urban areas. In this light, the province's concern for renovation and not new construction was understandable. Moreover, Alberta's urban housing problems were the legacy of prewar land speculation and over-expansion, and the 1919 housing scheme did nothing to solve these problems and, in certain respects, promised to bring further difficulties by over-extending already-burdened civic governments.[19]

By this measure, the 1919 postwar housing scheme was a failure. In Alberta, no houses were built under it, despite the evident need for new housing. Some scholars have contended that its failure helped "to discredit the idea of government assisted home construction" for over a decade.[20] Certainly, critics claimed that government involvement in the housing sector was unrealistic, but what the disappointing results actually proved, in this respect, was that local government could not be relied upon for such programs in the housing field, and that provincial and federal governments would, of necessity, have to lead such programs in the future. And, for certain, the 1919 scheme did not change the nature of the Canadian housing market and its contradictions. As historian John Saywell argues, although the state increasingly accepted responsibility for the safety and sanitation of housing, and thereby increased the costs of "legally adequate housing," it simultaneously refused to control land costs or interfere with market-driven incomes. As Saywell concludes, the consequences were recurring housing crises in Canada.[21]

Yet in other ways, the 1919 scheme had an inadvertent legacy. For the first time, systematic national standards had been devised as a national baseline to measure adequacy of housing. This drew upon the prewar idealization of the modern house. While the standards that emerged in 1919 would evolve, their outline would shape Canadian housing policy for the next half century. Indeed, in 1934 the National Construction Council, a lobby group and clearing house for the Canadian construction industry, drew up minimum standards of housing under two broad categories: health and amenities. Substandard houses were defined as those dangerous to the occupants' health or "incompatible with decency," while amenities set out those things necessary to "provide satisfactory environmental conditions which Canadian customs and standards demand."[22] These standards owed a strong debt to the measures of housing quality that had been devised in the 1919 housing scheme in its attempt to grapple with the legacy of the war.

Notes

This paper, while written by Donald G. Wetherell, relies heavily on Donald G. Wetherell and Irene R.A. Kmet, *Homes in Alberta. Building Trends and Design* (Edmonton: University of Alberta Press, 1991), but reworks the content in some respects. The co-editors of this book would like to thank Wetherell and Kmet and the University of Alberta Press for permission to use this material.

1   For examples of such concepts in popular thinking, see *Calgary Herald*, 23 October 1911, and *Farm and Ranch Review*, 20 October 1909.

2   Donald G. Wetherell and Irene R.A. Kmet, *Homes in Alberta: Building Trends and Design* (Edmonton: University of Alberta Press, 1991), 45–53, 87–93.

3   Thomas Adams, "Planning for Civic Betterment in Town and Country," *American City* 15 (1916): 50.

4   A.E. Grauer, *Housing: A Study Prepared for the Royal Commission on Dominion-Provincial Relations* (Ottawa, 1939), 33.

5   Doug Owram, *The Economic Development of Western Canada: An Historical Overview* (Ottawa: Economic Council of Canada, Paper No. 219, 1982), 14–15.

6   John Herd Thompson, *The Harvests of War: The Prairie West, 1914–1918* (Toronto: McClelland and Stewart, 1978), 45. On the single tax, see Donald G. Wetherell and Irene R.A. Kmet, *Town Life: Main Street and the Evolution of Small Town Alberta, 1880–1947* (Edmonton: University of Alberta Press, 1995), 47–48.

7   Wetherell and Kmet, *Homes in Alberta*, 99–100.

8   Ibid.,153.

9   John McDonald, "Soldier Settlement and Depression Settlement in the Forest Fringe of Saskatchewan," *Prairie Forum* 6 (1981): 37–40.

10   *Eaton's Farm Buildings and Equipment* (1919) (a copy of this soldier land settlement scheme catalogue can be found in Provincial Archives of Alberta, 66); *Farm and Ranch Review*, 21 April 1919.

11   Wetherell and Kmet, *Homes in Alberta*, 106–7.

12   Ibid., 154.

13   Provincial Archives of Saskatchewan, Regina, "Report of the Committee of the Privy Council, February 20, 1919," PC 374, 192.4/298.

14   *Social Welfare*, 1 June 1919.

15   *Conservation of Life*, January 1919, 1.

16   Wetherell and Kmet, *Homes in Alberta*, 155–56.

17   *Calgary Herald*, 24 May 1919.

18   Wetherell and Kmet, *Homes in Alberta*, 156.

19   Ibid., 157.

20   John Bacher, "Canadian Housing 'Policy' in Perspec-
     tive," *Urban History Review* 15 (1986): 5.

21   John Saywell, *Housing Canadians: Essays on Residential
     Construction in Canada* (Ottawa: Economic Council of
     Canada, Paper No. 24, 1975), 4.

22   Wetherell and Kmet, *Homes in Alberta*, 106–7.

Works Cited

PRIMARY SOURCES

Calgary Herald
Farm and Ranch Review

Provincial Archives of Alberta, Edmonton. *Eaton's Farm
     Buildings and Equipment*, 1919.
Provincial Archives of Saskatchewan, Regina. Report of
     the Committee of the Privy Council, 20 February 1919
     (P.C. 374), 192.4/298.

SECONDARY SOURCES

Adams, Thomas. "Planning for Civic Betterment in Town
     and Country." *American City* 15 (1916): 50.
Bacher, John. "Canadian Housing 'Policy' in Perspective."
     Urban History Review 15 (1986): 5.
Conservation of Life, January 1919, 1.
Grauer, A.E. *Housing: A Study Prepared for the Royal
     Commission on Dominion-Provincial Relations*. Ottawa,
     1939.
McDonald, John. "Soldier Settlement and Depression
     Settlement in the Forest Fringe of Saskatchewan."
     Prairie Forum 6 (1981): 37–40.
Owram, Doug. *The Economic Development of Western
     Canada: An Historical Overview*. Ottawa: Economic
     Council of Canada, Paper No. 219, 1982, 14–15.
Saywell, John. *Housing Canadians: Essays on Residential
     Construction in Canada*. Ottawa: Economic Council of
     Canada, Paper No. 24, 1975, 4.
Social Welfare, 1 June 1919.

Thompson, John Herd. *The Harvests of War: The Prairie West,
     1914–1918*. Toronto: McClelland and Stewart, 1978.
Wetherell, Donald G., and Irene R.A. Kmet. *Homes
     in Alberta: Building Trends and Design*. Edmonton:
     University of Alberta Press, 1991.
——. *Town Life: Main Street and the Evolution of Small Town
     Alberta, 1880–1947*. Edmonton: University of Alberta
     Press, 1995.

Soldier Settlement in Alberta, 1917–1931

ALLAN ROWE

"Alberta is far in advance of the other provinces in respect to the number of soldiers settled on the land" boasted the *Farm and Ranch Review* in June 1920. The Calgary-based publication noted with satisfaction that 4,428 soldiers had taken land in Alberta under the federal government's postwar soldier settlement plan, with thousands more eligible to participate in the coming years. The article quoted Red Deer M P Michael Clark, who explicitly linked "Alberta's lead in recruiting" during the war and its lead "in soldier settlement on the land in peace." "Compared with the results from the whole Dominion," concluded the *Review*, "this is a most satisfactory position for Alberta."[1]

The program that drew such praise from the *Review* was governed by the Soldier Settlement Act. Passed in 1917, and amended in 1919, the act offered assistance to veterans who wanted to take up agriculture after the Great War. Successful applicants were eligible for land grants and financial aid. While soldier settlement was a national program, the trend of especially high participation in Alberta, noted by the *Review* in 1920, continued for the rest of the decade. No province attracted more participants than Alberta: of the 31,670 veterans who took advantage of the program, almost one-third (9,883) settled in Alberta.[2]

The optimistic tone of the *Review*, however, obscured a more sober reality. While the program certainly helped many ex-servicemen transition back to civilian life, soldier settlement was far from an unmitigated success. From the outset, the scheme was plagued by significant problems, including economic depression and excessive bureaucracy. Perhaps most significant, however, was the government's unrealistic expectation that soldier settlement would help return Canada to an idealized notion of rural, agrarian ideals—in the face of growing industrialization, class conflict, and regional discontent—by bolstering loyal, steady citizenship. These hopes were compromised by their unrealistic scope, as well as by contradictory anxieties about the suitability of ex-servicemen (and their wives) for such crucial, nation-building responsibilities. The result was a program that could never live up to the high expectations placed on it.

The scheme, launched in 1917, was rooted in a long tradition of soldier settlement in Canadian

DENIED ACCESS TO THE LAND WHICH HE BLED TO DEFEND

This political cartoon from the *Grain Grower's Guide,* 6 March 1918, shows how obstacles were put in the way of potential soldier settlers.

history. Both the French and British colonial regimes had offered soldiers incentives to settle in North America prior to 1867, while the Dominion government had granted land to Canadian soldiers after the North West Rebellion (1885) and the South African War (1899–1902).[3] The scope of the Soldier Settlement Act (1917), however, eclipsed these earlier military-colonization experiments. The legislation offered veterans 160-acre "soldier grants" of

Dominion land and loans of up to $2,500 for stock or equipment. The program was administered by the Soldier Settlement Board, which reserved all "undisposed" federal land within 25 kilometres of railway lines in the Prairie West for soldier settlement.[4] The goal of the plan, according to Minister of the Interior W.J. Roche, was "to assist the returned soldier and increase agricultural production."[5] The unspoken objective, however, was to fill unclaimed Dominion land—soldier settlement would help complete prairie agricultural settlement by directing veterans to regions where significant homestead land was still available.

One such region, prominent in the government's early vision of soldier settlement, was Alberta's Peace River District. Shortly after the act was passed, Ottawa dispatched survey teams to the region to subdivide land specifically for returning veterans. Critics were sceptical—Liberal MP William Pugsley scornfully predicted "not one man in a thousand would be attracted by an invitation to settle on land in the Peace River Country."[6] The surveyors disagreed, reporting that "a considerable number of quarter sections" were suitable for cultivation.[7] By early 1919, 800 veterans had taken up homesteads in Peace River, and surveyors were having trouble keeping pace with demand.[8]

Despite this promising start, the government's determination to direct settlement to unclaimed Dominion land was widely criticized. In January 1918, both Alberta Premier Charles Stewart and the Alberta branch of the Great War Veterans Association (GWVA) urged Ottawa to make more land available for soldier settlement.[9] In March 1918, the *Grain Grower's Guide* condemned the scheme for granting isolated land to veterans while leaving the best available prairie land in the hands of speculators.[10]

The GWVA kept up the pressure through the summer of 1918, calling on Ottawa to expropriate land from enemy aliens and speculators, and to open up "idle" Indian reserve land for soldier settlement.[11] Pressure on the government mounted and, in September 1918, the head of the Returned Soldier Commission conceded privately that Ottawa would be "forced to take some action" and expand the program because "returned men will not take up land 500 miles north of Edmonton."[12]

In 1919 the government amended the act and greatly expanded the soldier settlement program. The number of staff was increased to provide better oversight and assistance for soldier settlers, while the money available to borrow was tripled to $7,500. The board was authorized to acquire Indian reserve land and, through the 1920s, 35,000 hectares were opened for soldier settlement, including 2,700 hectares from the Bobtail Reserve near Hobbema and more than 8,000 acres from the Saddle Lake Reserve near St. Paul de Métis.[13] The board was also authorized to acquire forest reserves, school lands, and privately owned lands, opening up significant new opportunities for soldier settlement.

In Alberta, the board acquired 7,300 hectares of land west of Drumheller from the Pope Grazing Lease, and an additional 4,500 hectares of Hudson's Bay Company land east of Rowley.[14] Most crucially, applicants could use loans to purchase privately owned land and improved farms.[15] Ottawa did not abandon the hope that soldier settlement would fill unclaimed homestead land—56 townships were surveyed in northern Alberta explicitly for soldier settlement after 1919.[16] However, the amendments removed the narrow focus on Dominion land and offered veterans greater choice on where to settle. The impact was dramatic and immediate. While only

2,000 men had participated in the program prior to these amendments, the board was receiving 600 applications per week by August 1919.[17] A substantial majority of veterans (77 percent) who participated in the program after the amendments chose to buy private land rather than accept free homesteads.[18]

The expansion of the program reflected the government's confidence that soldier settlement could serve as a pillar of Canada's postwar transition. Canadians were justifiably proud of the country's contributions to the Allied victory, but that sense of national achievement masked serious social, political, and economic fissures—class conflict, Anglo-French tension, resurgent nativism, and regional discontent—that threatened Canada's orderly adjustment to peacetime. The capacity of soldier settlement to counter this threat was articulated in June 1919 by then Interior Minister Arthur Meighen:

> We believe that we cannot better fortify this country against the waves of unrest and discontent that now assail us . . . than by making the greatest possible proportion of the soldiers of our country settlers upon our land. Of course, every class of citizen is necessary to constitute the national life, but the class of citizen that counts most in the determination of the stability of a country against such forces is undoubtedly the basic class—the agricultural class. That class is the mainstay of the nation.[19]

This speech, delivered a week after the Winnipeg General Strike, fit within in a deeply conservative vision of Canada that idealized the moral superiority of rural life.[20] In Meighen's view, soldier settlement would facilitate Canada's smooth transition to peacetime by returning the country to its agrarian roots. And, while the program was national in scope, the emphasis on social renewal through agricultural settlement clearly pointed to the Prairie West, which had long been viewed in utopian terms by those seeking to foster social and moral improvement.[21]

Alberta remained at the forefront of soldier settlement as the program grew over the next five years.

By the end of 1924, 24,148 veterans had received loans, with just over 7,000 settling in Alberta.[22] In addition, at least 2,400 veterans had settled in Alberta on soldier land grants without financial assistance.[23] Overall, soldier settlers had occupied 8.5 million hectares of land in Alberta from 1917 to 1924, representing 36 percent of the Dominion total.[24] Embedded within these statistics are thousands

Returned soldier's home, implements and some of his stock assisted by the Soldier Settlement Board. Tp 74-3-6, Peace River district. Alberta, 1920. Canada. Dept of Mines and Technical Surveys/Library and Archives Canada, PA-018311.

of individual and family narratives of success and failure, happiness and hardship, and the transition from military to civilian life. One example promoted by the board as representative of Alberta's veterans was Adolphus Lamoureux, who had lived there since moving to Fort Saskatchewan as a child in 1883.[25] A carpenter by trade, Lamoureux enlisted in the 151st Battalion (Canadian Expeditionary Force) in January 1916. In 1918, he received a medical discharge and returned to Alberta, claiming a soldier grant and accepting a $2,500 loan from the board for stock and equipment. Despite early difficulties, Lamoureux was running a profitable farm near Mallaig in east-central Alberta by the end of 1920.[26]

The board characterized Lamoureux's success story as "fairly typical" of soldier settlers in Alberta. Statistical evidence provides some support for the claim that the province's soldier settlers made good progress through 1921. In 1920–21, for example, 72.6 percent of Alberta's soldier settlers who had received loans were able to make their repayments, roughly in line with the national average of 77 percent.[27] By the end of 1921, however, Alberta and the rest of the prairie region were on the verge of an agricultural crisis. The price of wheat fell from a peak of $2.31 a bushel (1919) to a mere $0.77 (1922), while periodic drought took a significant toll on the wheat crop.[28] Though this was a hardship common to all farmers, soldier settlers were especially vulnerable, given that most had only been on their farms for one or two years before the downturn hit. By 1923 soldier settlers in Alberta were facing serious problems. In the 1922–23 collection year, only 49.6 percent of Alberta's indebted soldier settlers made repayments on their loans, and only 29 percent of the total money due was collected—statistics that placed Alberta last

in Canada.[29] Alberta veterans and politicians took the lead in calling for financial relief for soldier settlers. The Alberta GWVA lobbied the government to ease loan repayments and revalue veterans' land, while E.J. Garland, MP for Bow River, called for similar measures in parliament.[30]

Despite such pressure, the federal government proved reluctant to seriously consider significant reforms. Rather than acknowledge the impact of the agricultural crisis, the government insisted through the mid-1920s that the "personal factor was a major reason for failure"—that those who had failed to meet their repayment obligations were likely morally deficient.[31] This claim was extraordinary and illustrated a fundamental contradiction within the soldier settlement program. On one hand, the government celebrated veterans as "the backbone . . . of the nation" and "the best of its manhood"—the ideal candidates to stabilize Canada and return the country to its agrarian roots.[32] At the same time, the government was clearly anxious about the possibility that veterans would return home disabled or robbed of their personal initiative, accustomed to taking orders rather than making their own decisions.[33] This concern was embedded within the settlement board's own preliminary screening process, designed to disqualify anyone who was "indifferent," "thriftless," "careless," or otherwise represented a "moral risk"; only applicants who exhibited "self-reliance," "initiative, competence and resourcefulness" would be accepted—qualities that one would expect the "best of Canada's manhood" to have in abundance.[34]

This essential contradiction manifested itself in the government's suspicion that difficulties encountered by settlers were of their own making rather than the result of larger economic forces. The example of Henry Weed, farm inspector for the Monitor sub-district in southern Alberta, illustrates how this suspicion could turn the board's bureaucracy into an intrusive system of micromanagement. The farm inspector system was originally put in place in 1919 to provide support to soldier settlers but, as J.M. Powell notes, it could evolve into an "extremely intricate, if somewhat paternalistic" process of oversight and control.[35] In early 1921, Weed sent out a remarkable letter detailing his instructions and expectations for the upcoming year. The inspector noted that he wanted more soldier settlers to have "a definite goal, a plan for the future, a well thought out system in laying out the farm."[36] He instructed farmers to "take a complete inventory, in duplicate" of their equipment to prove they were ready for the upcoming year. In perhaps the most paternalistic part of the letter, Weed wrote: "I plan to take a picture of every settler's place this summer and send some to Ottawa. I took a few this summer and Ottawa is well pleased with my settlers' houses; try and have your place as neat and attractive, and a good clean garden, as it is a pleasure to feel that my settlers show up as well as any."[37]

While the farm inspector system undoubtedly rendered important service to many veterans, Weed's letter illustrates how it could also result in extreme (and unwelcome) levels of supervision. When asked to provide a character reference for Weed, local businessman George Lucas praised the inspector for taking "an almost fatherly interest in the settlers," though he conceded that some settlers complained Weed was too "busy with their business."[38]

This paternalism also extended into the domestic sphere through the Home Service Branch. The branch was established across Canada as part of the expansion of the soldier settlement program,

and included offices in Edmonton (opened in August 1919) and Calgary (January 1920).[39] It was led by Jean Muldrew, who had spent several years in Alberta as principal of Red Deer Ladies' College before serving as the director of household economy with the Canada Food Board during the war.[40] The mandate of the branch was to assist wives of soldier settlers (particularly newly arrived brides) through publications, home visits, and short courses in home economics. Through the end of 1921, the branch in Alberta made more than 1,500 home visits and held short courses in Edmonton, Calgary, Red Deer, Lethbridge, Grande Prairie, and Peace River.[41] It also connected wives to other women's organizations, including the United Farm Women of Alberta and the Women's Institute, which helped ease transition to rural life. Perhaps most significantly, the home visits revealed the "lack of maternal care in rural and isolated areas." Responding to this problem, the branch served as an important health resource, providing information on pre- and post-natal care and arranging for nurse visits to remote homesteads.[42]

Despite these valuable contributions, the branch was ultimately guided by the same approach that manifested itself in the farm inspector system— namely, that those involved in soldier settlement could not be trusted with the responsibilities assigned to them. The board conceded that good wives could be a "great help" to a farm, but also warned that wives could be a "serious handicap" if they were "discontented, not interested in farm life, or unthrifty and indolent." It bluntly warned that it was "impossible to estimate the financial injury" a wife could do to a farm if her "mental attitude and her physical condition" undercut her spouse's efforts and "rendered him incapable of repaying" his loan.

Women were thus viewed at once as an asset and a potential threat to the success of soldier settlement; like the farmers, they required careful oversight.[43]

The federal government finally agreed, in 1927, to revalue downward soldier settlement land, thus providing some economic relief to veterans by lowering debt. By that time, however, the agricultural economy had recovered and Alberta's soldier settlers were on a stronger footing. In 1927–28 indebted soldier settlers in the Edmonton District managed to pay back 72 percent of the money they owed, ranking the district first in Canada for repayments; veterans in the Calgary District paid back 66 percent, which was slightly above the national average of 63 percent.[44] The recovery, however, was short-lived, as the Great Depression dealt a massive blow to the province's remaining soldier settlers. The vast majority of Alberta's veterans were unable to make their loan payments after 1930 and, by the end of 1931, only 3,371 (34 percent) of the province's original soldier settlers remained on the land.[45] In 1931 the Soldier Settlement Board was dissolved and the government's experiment in postwar colonization was over.

In the end, judging the success or failure of soldier settlement in Alberta is a highly subjective exercise. The program certainly failed to achieve the lofty goals set by the federal government. Soldier settlement was not a catalyst for rural revitalization, as Alberta (and the rest of Canada) continued to urbanize throughout the interwar years. The program did not contribute meaningfully to national unity—indeed, given the extent to which the farmers' movement (and particularly the United Farmers of Alberta) championed the veterans' cause against Ottawa, the program was likely an additional irritant in the federal government's relationship with the province. Statistically, the program certainly appears to have been a failure, with two-thirds of Alberta's soldier settlers giving up on farming by 1931.

A different perspective, however, is offered by John Black and Charles Hyson in a 1944 article published in the *Quarterly Journal of Economics*. The authors quote a letter from Charles Murchison, director of Canadian soldier settlement, who argued that it was misguided to measure the success of soldier settlement strictly on the basis of "cold figures of an orthodox balance sheet." Rather, Murchison contended that the program had allowed veterans "to get their war experiences out of their systems" before moving on with their lives. He suggested that many soldier settlers had never intended to farm permanently but rather had used the program as a springboard to other ventures where they were "soundly integrated" back into the Canadian mainstream.[46] Murchison may have been rationalizing the program's lack of success, but his analysis raised a very important point: judging soldier settlement on the basis of how many men successfully farmed through the early 1930s assumes that they all shared the same ambition to take up farming as a permanent vocation. The program may not have achieved all that the government hoped, but as Murchison suggests, it may have helped thousands of veterans successfully transition to civilian life, including those who had already quit farming by 1931.

Notes

1   "Alberta Leads in Soldier Settlement," *Farm and Ranch Review* 16, no. 12 (21 June 1920): 35.

2   J.M. Powell, *Soldier Settlement in Canada, 1915–1930* (Clayton, AU: Monash University, Department of Geography, 1979), 27.

3   Desmond Morton and Glenn Wright, *Winning the Second Battle: Canadian Veterans and the Return to Civilian Life, 1915–1930* (Toronto: University of Toronto Press, 1987), 10.

4   Soldier Settlement Board (hereafter SSB), *First Report of the Soldier Settlement Board of Canada*, 31 March 1921, 25.

5   Kent Fedorowich, *Unfit for Heroes: Reconstruction and Soldier Settlement in the Empire between the Wars* (Manchester, UK: Manchester University Press, 1995), 63.

6   Ibid., 64.

7   Canada, *Sessional Paper* No. 25a, Report of the Topographical Survey Board, 1920, 19. See also Judy Larmour, *Laying Down the Lines: A History of Land Surveying in Alberta* (Calgary: Brindle and Glass, 2005), 177–78.

8   Canada, Report of the Topographical Survey Board, 1920, 19.

9   Fedorowich, *Unfit for Heroes*, 107.

10 *Grain Growers' Guide*, 6 March 1918; Sarah Carter, "An Infamous Proposal: Prairie Indians and Soldier Settlement after World War I," *Manitoba History* 37 (1999): 14.

11 Fedorowich, *Unfit for Heroes*, 74; Morton and Wright, *Winning the Second Battle*, 103–4.

12 Glenbow Museum and Archives, Garnet Ellis Fond, M 363: letter from Ellis to his mother, 6 September 1918. Ellis was recruited to be part of the scheme as a land surveyor in 1918, and later served as a farm inspector in northern Alberta.

13 Carter, "An Infamous Proposal," 9; SSB, *Fourth Report of the Soldier Settlement Board of Canada*, 31 December 1925, 8; SSB, *Sixth Report of the Soldier Settlement Board of Canada*, 31 December 1927, 7.

14 SSB, *Fourth Report of the Soldier Settlement Board of Canada*, 8–9.

15 Fedorowich, *Unfit for Heroes*, 77.

16 Larmour, *Laying Down the Lines*, 180.

17 Morton and Wright, *Winning the Second Battle*, 145.

18 Fedorowich, *Unfit for Heroes*, 80.

19 As quoted in Powell, *Soldier Settlement in Canada*, 10.

20 The idea that postwar soldier settlement would act as a bulwark against the forces of class conflict and urban disorder was very popular in Australia as well. See Ken Fry, "Soldier Settlement and the Australian Agrarian Myth after the First World War," *Labour History* 48 (May 1985): 29–43.

21 R. Douglas Francis and Chris Kitzan, "Introduction," in *The Prairie West as Promised Land*, edited by R. Douglas Francis and Chris Kitzan (Calgary: University of Calgary Press, 2007), x–xii.

22 SSB, *Third Report of the Soldier Settlement Board of Canada*, 31 December 1924, 13.

23 As noted by Powell (*Soldier Settlement in Canada*, 27–28), there are significant variances in the year-to-year tallies of this group in the board's annual reports. Whether this reflected problems with recordkeeping or (as Powell suggests) a deliberate effort by the board to skew numbers to improve the statistical measurement of the program's success is unclear.

24 SSB, *Third Report of the Soldier Settlement Board of Canada*, 15.

25 SSB, *First Report of the Soldier Settlement Board of Canada*, 161–62.

26 Biographical information on Adolphus Lamoureux taken from SSB, *First Report of the Soldier Settlement Board of Canada*, 161–62; Mallaig History Committee, *Precious Memories = mémoires précieuses: Mallaig – Therian, 1906–1992* (Mallaig, AB: Mallaig History Committee, 1993), 565–66; and Lamoureux's attestation papers, available on the Library and Archives Canada website, *Soldiers of the First World War – CEF*, URL: http://www.collectionscanada.gc.ca/databases/cef/index-e.html, retrieved 15 November 2013.

27 SSB, *Second Report of the Solder Settlement Board of Canada*, 31 March 1923, 28. The collection year in western Canada, when indebted soldier settlers were expected to make repayments on their loans, ran from early October to early August.

28 Howard Palmer and Tamara Palmer, *Alberta: A New History* (Edmonton: Hurtig, 1990), 198.

29 SSB, *Second Report of the Soldier Settlement Board of Canada*, 30.

30 Morton and Wright, *Winning the Second Battle*, 152;
    Fedorowich, *Unfit for Heroes*, 103.

31 Fedorowich, *Unfit for Heroes*, 99.

32 Canada, *House of Commons Debates*, 1919, 3863; SSB,
    First Report of the Soldier Settlement Board, 8.

33 Desmond Morton, "The Canadian Veterans' Heritage
    from the Great War," in *The Veterans Charter and Post-
    World War II Canada*, edited by Peter Neary and J.L.
    Granatstein (Montreal and Kingston: McGill-Queen's
    University Press, 1998), 21.

34 SSB, *First Report of the Soldier Settlement Board*, 8–9.

35 Powell, *Soldier Settlement in Canada*, 8–9.

36 Provincial Archives of Alberta, W.J. Blair Fonds, PR
    1507, ACC.1984.407/206. The letter is undated; how-
    ever, it offered New Year's greetings, and the chrono-
    logical order of the file suggests that it was sent out in
    January 1921. Unless otherwise stated, all of the quotes
    are taken from this letter.

37 Ibid.

38 Ibid., letter from George Lucas to W.J. Blair,
    12 May 1921.

39 *Edmonton Bulletin*, 13 July 1920; SSB, *First Report of the
    Soldier Settlement Board of Canada*, 123.

40 David C. Jones, "From Babies to Buttonholes:
    Women's Work at Agricultural Fairs," *Alberta History*
    29, no. 4 (Autumn 1981): 28.

41 *Red Deer News*, 19 January 1921; SSB, *First Report of the
    Soldier Settlement Board of Canada*, 119, 124.

42 Diane Dodd, "Helen MacMurchy: Popular Midwifery
    and Maternity Services for Canadian Pioneer Women,"
    in *Caring and Curing: Historical Perspectives on Women
    and Healing in Canada*, edited by Diane Dodd and
    Deborah Gorham (Ottawa: University of Ottawa Press,
    1994), 143; SSB, *First Report of the Soldier Settlement
    Board of Canada*, 41, 119, 123.

43 SSB, *First Report of the Soldier Settlement Board of
    Canada*, 38.

44 SSB, *Ninth Report of the Soldier Settlement Board of
    Canada*, 31 December 1931, 16.

45 Ibid., 15.

46 Murchison's letter quoted in John D. Black and
    Charles D. Hyson, "Postwar Soldier Settlement," *The

Quarterly Journal of Economics 59, no. 1 (November
1944): 7.

Works Cited

PRIMARY SOURCES

Edmonton Bulletin
Farm and Ranch Review
Grain Growers' Guide
Red Deer News

Glenbow Museum and Archives, Calgary. Garnet Ellis
    Fonds.
House of Commons, *Debates*, 1919.
House of Commons, Sessional Paper 25a, *Report of the
    Topographical Survey Board*, 1920–21.
Provincial Archives of Alberta, Edmonton. W.J. Blair
    Fonds.
Soldier Settlement Board, *Annual Reports*, 1921–31.

SECONDARY SOURCES

Black, John D., and Charles D. Hyson. "Postwar Soldier
    Settlement." *The Quarterly Journal of Economics* 59,
    no. 1 (November 1944): 1–35.
Carter, Sarah. "'An Infamous Proposal': Prairie Indian
    Reserve Land and Soldier Settlement after World War
    I." *Manitoba History* 37 (November 1999): 9–23.
Dodd, Diane. "Helen MacMurchy: Popular Midwifery and
    Maternity Services for Canadian Pioneer Women." In
    *Caring and Curing: Historical Perspectives on Women and
    Healing in Canada*, edited by Diane Dodd and Deborah
    Gorham, 135–62. Ottawa: University of Ottawa Press,
    1994.
Fedorowich, Kent. *Unfit for Heroes: Reconstruction and
    Soldier Settlement in the Empire between the Wars.*
    Manchester, UK: Manchester University Press, 1995.
Francis, R. Douglas, and Chris Kitzan, eds. "Introduction."
    In *The Prairie West as Promised Land*, ix–xxiv. Calgary:
    University of Calgary Press, 2007.

Fry, Ken. "Soldier Settlement and the Australian Agrarian Myth after the First World War." *Labour History* 48 (May 1985): 29–43.

Jones, David C. "From Babies to Buttonholes: Women's Work at Agricultural Fairs." *Alberta History* 29, no. 4 (Autumn 1981): 26–32.

Larmour, Judy. *Laying Down the Lines: A History of Land Surveying in Alberta*. Calgary: Brindle and Glass, 2005.

Mallaig History Committee. *Precious Memories = mémoires précieuses: Mallaig – Therian, 1906–1992*. Mallaig, AB: Mallaig History Committee, 1996.

Morton, Desmond. "The Canadian Veterans' Heritage from the Great War." In *The Veterans Charter and Post-World War II Canada*, edited by Peter Neary and J.L. Granatstein, 15–31. Montreal and Kingston: McGill-Queen's University Press, 1998.

Morton, Desmond, and Glenn Wright. *Winning the Second Battle: Canadian Veterans and the Return to Civilian Life, 1915–1930*. Toronto: University of Toronto Press, 1987.

Palmer, Howard, and Tamara Palmer. *Alberta: A New History*. Edmonton: Hurtig Publishers, 1990.

Powell, J.M. *Soldier Settlement in Canada, 1915–1930*. Clayton, AU: Monash University, Department of Geography, 1979.

First World War Centennial Commemoration in Alberta Museums

RORY CORY

For the centennial of the First World War, museums across Canada are rallying to commemorate this important and formative event in our nation's history. What is often lacking in commemorative efforts is the material culture—the physical history. Viewing historical objects is the primary way in which many people connect with history, and to reach this audience, museums must be key players in providing this means of commemoration. To fulfill this public trust obligation, The Military Museums in Calgary are coordinating a consortium of western Canadian museums that are presenting exhibits on the conflict, on display from 2014 through to 2018. This cooperative effort has allowed joint advertising, but also coordination of access to resources such as artifacts. The following article provides a summary of exhibits across Alberta that are part of this initiative.

Among the most significant commemorative events in the province was the exhibit developed and hosted by The Military Museums in Calgary (28 July to 15 December 2014). The *Wild Rose Overseas: Albertans in the Great War* exhibit comprised 2,000 square feet and was one of the largest temporary heritage-based exhibits mounted in the museum's Founders' Gallery. The planning began in 2006 when it was slotted into the exhibit schedule. The original intention was to embrace a national perspective. However, in the course of identifying artifacts and thematic areas, it quickly became apparent that a more focused approach was necessary to fit within the available space. Therefore, the geographic scope was modified to centre on Alberta. Similarly, the thematic focus was narrowed to only military themes, again partly because of space constraints and also in keeping with the museum's mandate.

The core organizational structure of the exhibit was focused on the Canadian Expeditionary Force (CEF) and the infantry battalions. This provided the best way to present balanced coverage of military service from across the province, since the battalions were raised on municipal or regional lines. Artifacts associated with these battalions were also the easiest to identify. However, supporting units such as the artillery and medical services also needed to be discussed to give the most complete picture of Alberta's military commitment. Since The Military Museums is a tri-service (navy, army, and air force) organization, it was necessary to represent all three.

A total of 27 battalions were raised in Alberta, with an additional eight battalions partially raised in or otherwise associated with the province. Since there were too many battalions to have individual themes shaped around each one, groupings were required and, ultimately, the focus came to be on units that had perpetuated their memory after the war. To provide context for the overseas experience and what Albertans did during the fighting, it was also necessary to discuss key battles and the role played in them by units from Alberta and some of their individual members. Other themes were explored to give a full picture of military service during the war, including training, prisoner-of-war experiences, weaponry, German militaria, demobilization, and remembrance.

Once themes had been identified, it was necessary to select representative items that would engage the public. Regimental badges, medals, and uniforms were known to have less appeal than items that connected with personal stories. A broad spectrum of different artifact types was also needed for maximum visual interest and impact, as well as to give better representation of First World War material culture in general. With the stories of the battalions as the core organizational principle of the exhibit, it was also important that the artifact either be clearly associated with a battalion or have interesting provenance connecting it with one.

Artifacts for the exhibit came primarily from the collections of The Military Museums. Since planning began long before the exhibit was mounted, exhibit organizers were also able to draw on new donations. Some additional artifacts not in the museum's collections needed to be acquired, and an intensive search for them began in 2013. The organizers next looked to the province's senior museums: the

Glenbow Museum in Calgary and the Royal Alberta Museum (RAM) in Edmonton. Items from regional museums were obtained to cover gaps; for example, from the Galt Museum and Archives in Lethbridge and the Esplanade Arts and Heritage Centre in Medicine Hat. Searches for artifacts went hand-in-hand with investigations of archival holdings. For several years, temporary displays at The Military Museums had relied, in large measure, on archival materials as display objects. For example, certificates have great visual appeal and convey much information; letters have much stronger emotional impact when presented as originals. Museum collections and archival holdings are too often held completely separately when, in many cases, an original donation came in with components for both that together tell a complete story.

Initially there were gaps, as some of the battalions had few artifacts associated with them, beyond badges. However, as more donations came in from the public and more research was done, all themes and units had good representation of material culture items. These ranged from swagger sticks to pistols, trench art to commemorative medallions, flags, and more. Rare items included a message canister used by carrier pigeons and a jewelled Turkish officer's sword captured by one of the few Albertans to serve in Palestine during the war. All had very good provenance connecting them to a specific Alberta individual or battalion, and there was very little reliance on badges in the end. Many items had compelling stories associated with them, for example a book that had been damaged by shrapnel while being carried by an individual killed by the same shrapnel. Many represented noteworthy individuals such as Frederick Augustus Bagley, one of the oldest to enlist, having come out West with the North-West

(left) Pigeon message canister. This particular canister was used by a signaller from the 187th Battalion from Alberta to send messages across the battlefield when the wires on field telephones were cut. Collection of the Army Museum of Alberta. Photo: Julie Vincent Photography; (right) Next of Kin Medallion issued for Thomas Ralph Shearer (pictured here), one of three brothers who enlisted at Medicine Hat. Two were killed, including Thomas Ralph, and one came home wounded. Next of Kin Medallions were minted by the British government and given to the families of all soldiers from the Empire who were killed. Thomas Ralph served in the Royal Naval Air Service and was killed in an airplane accident. Collection of the Naval Museum of Alberta. Photo: Julie Vincent Photography.

Mounted Police 40 years earlier; the three Shearer brothers who enlisted at Medicine Hat but only one of whom survived the war; and Harold McGill and Emma Griffis, whose love letters were presented along with their uniforms. Well-known Albertans—such as Wop May (who was the last Allied pilot chased by Baron Manfred von Richthofen, "the Red Baron," on the day the Baron was shot down in 1918), Harold Riley (a former MLA and one of the founders of the Old Timers' Association), and Sam Steele (who had fought in the 1885 North West Rebellion and the Boer War)—were also featured.

Some of the more interesting and unusual objects were not associated with battalions but rather with the more general themes. These included a wheelbarrow issued to a returning soldier as part of the Soldier Settlement Act, which sought to direct veterans into farming; and the table created by a disabled soldier while convalescing as part of a work-reintegration project. While mundane, these items conveyed important information about the theme of demobilization. In the end, many more objects were identified than could be used in the exhibit, and these were culled based on such criteria as lack of provenance, limited availability for loan, and the high cost of borrowing them. While provision had been made to acquire highly desirable objects from national institutions such as the Canadian War Museum, in the end this proved unnecessary.

Photographs were needed to illustrate the text panels, and a wealth of them were available from various archives, in particular the Glenbow and Library and Archives Canada. Since both institutions post their holdings online, their photos were the easiest to access. As with the artifacts, a variety of visually interesting subjects was desired, rather than just posed group company or battalion photos. Representations of training, frontline service, or other "action" photos were preferred and generally obtained.

With respect to museum interpretation, use of the "first-person voice" for impact and audience engagement was preferred. This has been a practice in Founders' Gallery exhibits since 2009. The Military Museums, for example, have enriched exhibits pertaining to the Second World War by conducting oral history interviews with veterans, portions of which were then played, with both video and audio components, at listening and projection stations. Because such oral history research could not be conducted

Wheelbarrow issued to a veteran of Alberta's 31st Battalion after the First World War to help integrate him into agricultural production as part of the Soldier Settlement Act. Collection of the Army Museum of Alberta. Photo: Julie Vincent Photography.

for *Wild Rose Overseas*, taped interviews were sought. Some were found in the museum's own collections and others were obtained from the Glenbow Archives. This allowed the exhibit to include the "first person" voice as well. An unexpected benefit of the need to use these materials was that the museum was able to pay for the digitization of these analog materials that would otherwise have continued to degrade and eventually have been lost.

A number of regional museums in the province have military content as part of their permanent exhibit galleries. These include the Esplanade Arts and Heritage Centre in Medicine Hat, the Crowsnest Museum in Coleman, the Fort Museum in Fort Macleod, the Musée Héritage Museum in St. Albert, the Claresholm and District Museum in Claresholm, the Galt Museum and Archives in Lethbridge, the Museum of the Highwood in High River, and Lougheed House in Calgary.

For their First World War centenaries, several museums chose to highlight specific units associated with their communities. The Esplanade focused on the 175th Battalion, 3rd Canadian Mounted Rifles, and 13th Canadian Mounted Rifles, which were specifically raised in and associated with Medicine Hat. As with *Wild Rose Overseas*, the Esplanade borrowed materials from a variety of collections across the province including the Glenbow, the RAM, and The Military Museums. In this sense, the centennial represented a real convergence and opportunity for collaboration among Alberta museums. The exhibit (titled *Medicine Hat's War 1914–1918*) ran from August to November 2014. Similarly, the Crowsnest Museum chose to highlight the role of the 192nd Battalion, the only one raised in the Crowsnest Pass. The exhibit is timed to coincide with the centennial of the formation of the 192nd Battalion in 1916, rather than

the more general centennial of the start of the war. The Fort Museum also concentrated on the sole unit raised locally, the 191st Battalion. However, similar to the Esplanade exhibit, it also sought to feature individuals from the Fort Macleod area who joined other units such as the 13th Canadian Mounted Rifles. There was also coverage of First Nations' soldiers, in particular the Mountain Horse brothers

Steel helmet, 31st Battalion Canadian Expeditionary Force. This helmet was painted as a commemorative souvenir with the battle honours for all the battles that the 31st Battalion out of Calgary fought in. Collection of the Army Museum of Alberta. Photo: Julie Vincent Photography.

War Deed—Story Robe created by Mike Mountain Horse, from the Kainai (Blood) First Nation in southwest Alberta, with the assistance of Ambrose Two Chiefs, to commemorate his overseas service with Alberta's 50th Battalion. Collection of the Esplanade Arts and Heritage Centre.

from the Blood (Kainai) Reserve. Albert Mountain Horse enlisted soon after the beginning of the war and served in the Canadian Army Service Corps, but died of pneumonia a little over a year later. His brother, Mike Mountain Horse, enlisted in the 191st Battalion but fought in the 50th Battalion. He created a wonderful "story" robe as a pictographic record of his overseas exploits, which is held in the Esplanade collections. The Fort Museum's display ran from May to October 2014.

Other museums chose to tell the story of noted individuals, rather than specific units. The Musée Héritage Museum had a unique topic—that of Francophone participation from the area. The exhibit focused on experiences of local men who had been born in Belgium or France and left Alberta to serve with those armies, as well as other Francophones from the area who enlisted in the CEF. Titled *Joining Up! Our Men and Women in the First World War*, the exhibit ran from June to November 2014 and filled half of the temporary gallery at the museum. A separate exhibit titled *Brigadier-General Raymond Brutinel and the Motor Machine Gun Brigades* focused on one of the most notable soldiers from the area and ran from September to November 2014. Brutinel

established the Motor Machine Gun Brigade during the war with his own money. A third exhibit, *The Home Front: Life in St. Albert during the First World War*, was also shown from June to August.

The Claresholm and District Museum also told stories of local individuals, but with the unique perspective of comparing and contrasting the experiences of 18–21-year-olds serving in the war to the experiences of that age group today, and different attitudes toward patriotism. The Claresholm exhibit extends from May 2014 to December 2018, one of the few to run through the centennial of all the war years.

For the Galt Museum and Archives' exhibit *Lethbridge's Experiences in the First World War—1914/1915*, the focus was on the life of Lethbridge's most

Summary panel for the Musée Héritage Museum exhibit *Joining Up! Our Men and Women in the First World War*. The exhibit, in part, focused on experiences of local men who had been born in Belgium or France and left Alberta to serve with those armies, as well as other Francophones from the area who enlisted in the CEF. Courtesy of the Musée Héritage Museum.

The Home Front
Life in St Albert during the First World War
June 17 – August 31

What was St Albert like at the outbreak of the war and how did its citizens react to the conflict? Roughly ten percent of the population of this small, primarily Francophone town went to serve in Europe. Those at home were left to keep the town running, raise money and supplies for the war effort and harvest crops to send overseas for the troops. They rallied to support not only the war effort but also each other in this time of stress and great loss. Through photos, news clippings and artifacts, this exhibit looks at what life was like in St Albert leading up to, during and immediately following the First World War.

Image Credits (top to bottom)
Musée Héritage Museum, St Albert Historical Society fonds, 2003.01.1764,
Musée Héritage Museum, St Albert Historical Society fonds, Pp86.2610

Exhibit Sponsors

Your Logo Here   Your Logo Here

8

Brigadier-General Raymond Brutinel
and the Motor Machine Gun Brigades
September 9 – November 16

This exhibit is the remarkable story of a remarkable man. After serving on one of the last sailing ships, the young Brutinel joined the French Military. In 1904 he moved his family to Alberta. His contributions to the fledgling province include serving as editor for *Le Courrier de l'Ouest*, Alberta's first French language newspaper, surveying routes and resources for the Grand Trunk Railway, playing a central role in the development of the Coal Branch and building the interurban Railway between Edmonton and St Albert. When the First World War began he served in the Canadian Forces, creating the Motor Machine Gun Brigade which he tirelessly championed as a new tactical force in modern warfare. His brigade played a vital role in many crucial battles. During the Second World War he continued the fight, working with the French resistance, to yet again free his homeland.

Exhibit Sponsors

Your Logo Here   Your Logo Here

Image Credits (top to bottom)
Musée Héritage Museum, St Albert Historical Society fonds, 2003.01.795
Brutinel archive
Brutinel archive

9

Two commemorative exhibits at the Musée Héritage Museum, St. Albert, showcased home front history and artifacts and highlighted a local settler and entrepreneur, Raymond Brutinel, who established the Motor Machine Gun Brigades. Courtesy of the Musée Héritage Museum.

well-known soldier: General J.S. Stewart. In addition, the exhibit explored the initial response and mobilization efforts, Lethbridge's militia history, the spread of patriotism, the rise of xenophobia, and recruitment. It ran from May to August 2014.

The Museum of the Highwood also had a small exhibit in 2014 on local individuals who served, including the poignant story of its local championship polo team whose members enlisted together but none of whom returned. This museum's contribution to the centennial deserves special mention, in light of the devastation of 80 percent of its collections as a result of the June 2013 flood in southern Alberta.

The exhibit set up at Lougheed House in Calgary from October 2014 to January 2015 offered an interesting mix focusing on specific units and local individuals. Highlights included photos and artifacts from the Lougheed House collection exploring the roles that Clarence and Edgar Lougheed played in the war, as well as objects provided by The Military Museums showing connections between the Lougheed family and several regiments that fought in the war, namely Princess Patricia's Canadian Light Infantry and Lord Strathcona's Horse. Senator Sir James and Lady Isabella Lougheed's work during and after the war, including helping to establish what is now Veteran's Affairs, was also explored. The display comprised almost 1,000 square feet. Also, the City of Calgary Corporate Archives mounted a largely photo-based exhibit in City Hall on the theme of "Calgary in the First World War," which ran from March to September 2014.

Finally, it is rare to see new war memorials created in any municipality, but the town of Blackfalds built one to recognize the 22 men who served from the community in the First World War, as well as those who fought in the Second World War and other conflicts. The complete poem "In Flanders Fields" was sandblasted into the circumference of the circular memorial, which also features glass mosaic work representing poppies and other motifs. It was unveiled and dedicated in a ceremony on 23 May 2014. A companion publication told the story of each of the 77 individuals represented on the memorial. In a parallel initiative, the community of St. Albert found that three soldiers killed during the First World War had not been included on its pre-existing cenotaph, and worked to get their names added.

These efforts are just some of the highlights of First World War commemorations around the province. Museums, as keepers of the communities' artifacts and documents, have an important role to play in such activities. They collect, study, and interpret material relating to their communities and are "treasure-houses of memory." This is why, whenever any significant community event is commemorated, they are the "go-to" places for setting up remembrance projects. All Alberta communities were touched by the war, and the fact that museum-based centennial commemorations were so widespread is a testament to the conflict's broad impact and profound legacy to this day.

The community of Blackfalds constructed a war memorial in commemoration of the centenary of the First World War. Lieutenant Colonel (Ret'd) Moffat, a Korean War veteran, lays a wreath at the dedication ceremony on 23 May 2014.

APPENDIX

Alberta Formations Raised in the First World War

The following is based on information from John Blue, "Alberta in the Great War," *Alberta Past and Present: Historical and Biographical*, Vol. 1 (Chicago: Pioneer Historical Publishing Co., 1924), chapter XXIII.

FORMATION	DATE AUTHORIZED	LOCATION FOR RECRUITMENT	LEFT CANADA	ARRIVED OVERSEAS	ORGANIZATION OVERSEAS
CAVALRY					
19th Alberta Dragoons	6 August 1914	Edmonton	15 October 1914	Arrived in England, 12 February 1915	Absorbed as "A" Squadron in the Canadian Corps Cavalry Regiment. Changed to Canadian Light Horse.
3rd Regiment, Canadian Mounted Rifles	5 November 1914	Edmonton, Calgary, and Medicine Hat	12 June 1915	Arrived in England, 21 September 1915	Absorbed by 1st and 2nd Battalion, Canadian Mounted Rifles. Perpetuated as 1st Regiment, Alberta Mounted Rifles.
12th Regiment, Canadian Mounted Rifles	1 December 1914	Calgary and Red Deer	9 October 1915	Information unavailable	Absorbed into Canadian Cavalry Depot. Perpetuated in the active militia as the 15th Canadian Light Horse.
13th Regiment, Canadian Mounted Rifles	1 December 1914	Pincher Creek, Cardston, and Macleod	26 June 1916	Information unavailable	Absorbed into various units. Perpetuated in the active militia as 2nd Regiment, Alberta Mounted Rifles.

FORMATION	DATE AUTHORIZED	LOCATION FOR RECRUITMENT	LEFT CANADA	ARRIVED OVERSEAS	ORGANIZATION OVERSEAS
INFANTRY					
9th Battalion	7 August 1914	Edmonton	3 October 1914	Information unavailable	Reorganized as a reserve battalion and sent to reinforce the 1st, 2nd, 3rd and 4th battalions in France. Perpetuated in the active militia as 2nd Battalion, Edmonton Regiment.
31st Battalion	11 November 1914	Throughout Alberta	17 May 1915	Arrived in France, 18 September 1915	Perpetuated in the active militia as 1st and 2nd Battalions, Alberta Regiment.
49th Battalion	4 January 1915	Edmonton	4 June 1915	Arrived in France, 9 September 1915	Perpetuated as the 1st Battalion, Edmonton Regiment.
50th Battalion	15 December 1914	Calgary	27 October 1915	Arrived in France, 11 August 1916	Perpetuated as the 2nd Battalion, Calgary Regiment.
51st Battalion	4 January 1914	England	18 April 1916	Information unavailable	Became a Garrison Duty Battalion. Perpetuated as the 3rd Reserve Battalion, Edmonton Regiment.
56th Battalion	24 January 1915	Calgary	1 April 1916	Information unavailable	Absorbed by the 9th Reserve Battalion. Perpetuated as the 3rd Reserve Battalion, Calgary Regiment.
63rd Battalion	28 June 1915	Edmonton, Calgary, and Medicine Hat	23 April 1916	Information unavailable	Absorbed by the 9th Reserve Battalion. Perpetuated as the 4th Reserve Battalion, Edmonton Regiment.
66th Battalion	21 June 1915	Edmonton	1 May 1916	Information unavailable	Absorbed by the 9th Reserve Battalion. Perpetuated in the active militia as the 5th Reserve Battalion, Edmonton Regiment.
82nd Battalion	1 September 1915	Calgary	20 May 1916	Information unavailable	Absorbed by the 9th Reserve Battalion in England. Perpetuated as the 4th Reserve Battalion, Calgary Regiment.

FORMATION	DATE AUTHORIZED	LOCATION FOR RECRUITMENT	LEFT CANADA	ARRIVED OVERSEAS	ORGANIZATION OVERSEAS
89th Battalion	1 November 1915	Calgary	6 June 1916	Information unavailable	Absorbed in the 9th Reserve Battalion and 97th Battalion. Not perpetuated in the active militia.
113th Battalion	17 November 1915	Lethbridge	18 October 1916	Information unavailable	Perpetuated as the 3rd Reserve Battalion, Alberta Regiment.
137th Battalion	11 November 1915	Calgary	24 August 1916	Information unavailable	Absorbed by the 21st Reserve Battalion. Perpetuated as the 5th Reserve Battalion, Calgary Regiment.
138th Battalion	22 November 1915	Edmonton	24 August 1916	Information unavailable	Absorbed by the 128th Battalion. Not perpetuated.
151st Battalion	26 November 1915	Federal electoral ridings of Battle River, Victoria, Strathcona, and Red Deer	19 April 1916	Information unavailable	Absorbed by the 7th and 9th Reserve Battalions. Perpetuated as the 4th Reserve Battalion, Alberta Regiment.
187th Battalion	20 January 1916	Red Deer district	20 December 1916	Information unavailable	Absorbed by the 9th Reserve Battalion. Perpetuated as the 6th Reserve Battalion, Alberta Regiment.
191st Battalion	21 January 1916	Macleod and district	Information unavailable	Information unavailable	Re-organized in Canada as a draft giving depot battalion. Not perpetuated.
192nd Battalion	25 January 1916	Blairmore and district	3 November 1916	Information unavailable	Absorbed by the 9th Reserve Battalion. Not perpetuated.
194th Battalion	28 January 1916	Edmonton and district	14 November 1916	Information unavailable	Absorbed by the 9th Reserve Battalion. Not perpetuated.
202nd Battalion	4 February 1916	Edmonton and district	24 November 1916	Information unavailable	Absorbed by the 9th Reserve Battalion. Not perpetuated.
218th Battalion	25 February 1916	Edmonton	17 February 1917	Information unavailable	Amalgamated with the 211th Battalion and organized as the 8th Battalion, Canadian Railway Troops. Not perpetuated.

CONTRIBUTORS

David Borys, PhD, is a historian who specializes in civil-military relations and the reconstruction and rehabilitation of war-torn states. He is currently a sessional instructor at both Simon Fraser University and the University of British Columbia.

Juliette Champagne, PhD, is an Alberta-based heritage consultant and author specializing in western Canadian history from contact to settlement. Her book *De la Bretagne aux plaines de l'Ouest canadien, lettres d'un défricheur franco-albertain, Alexandre Mahé (1880–1968)* focuses on French-Canadian community building in northeastern Alberta.

Brett Clifton, BA, works at the Lethbridge Collegiate Institute and, in 2011, received the Historical Society of Alberta's award for the best student essay for his "From Bridges to the Ridge," focusing on the experience of Lethbridge at Vimy Ridge.

Catherine C. Cole, MA (History), MA (Museum Studies), is an arts and heritage consultant. Her exhibitions and publications deal with western Canadian labour, and social and industrial history. Her book *GWG: Piece by Piece* is an illustrated history of Edmonton's Great Western Garment Company.

Rory Cory, MA, is the Senior Curator at the Military Museums in Calgary.

Duff Crerar, PhD, is an instructor at Grand Prairie Regional College specializing in Canadian military, social, and religious history. His publications include *Padres in No Man`s Land: Canadians Chaplains and the Great War.*

Adriana A. Davies, CM, PhD, is a heritage consultant, author, editor, and creator of the *Alberta Online Encyclopedia* (www.albertasource.ca). Her book *From Realism to Abstraction: The Art of J.B. Taylor* was published in 2014.

Michael Dawe, BA, is a western Canadian history specialist and Red Deer historian. His centennial history of Red Deer, *Red Deer: The Memorable City*, was published in 2013.

L. James Dempsey, PhD, is an associate professor in Native Studies at the University of Alberta and the author of *Warriors of the King: Prairie Indians in World War I*.

Antonella Fanella, MA, is an archivist at the Calgary Police Interpretive Centre and a specialist in immigration history, in particular the Italian community, which is featured in her book *Heart and Soul: Calgary's Italian Community*.

Alvin Finkel, PhD, is a professor of history at Athabasca University and a specialist in labour history. His books include *Social Policy and Practice in Canada: A History*.

Ryan Flavelle is a PhD candidate in the Department of History at Western University. An officer with the Canadian Armed Forces, he is the author of *The Patrol: Seven Days in the Life of a Canadian Soldier in Afghanistan*.

David Joseph Gallant is a PhD candidate in the Department of History at the University of Calgary.

Stephen Greenhalgh, MA, MLIS, is a freelance heritage researcher and writer.

Jarett Henderson, PhD, is an Assistant Professor of History in the Department of Humanities at Mount Royal University with research interests in colonialism and social and political reform as well as archives and historical methodologies.

Mark Osborne Humphries, PhD, is Dunkley Chair in War and the Canadian Experience in the Department of History and Director of the Laurier Centre for Military Strategic and Disarmament Studies (LCMSDS) at Wilfrid Laurier University. He has published widely on the medical history of the First World War, including *The Last Plague: Spanish Influenza and the Politics of Public Health in Canada*.

Chris Hyland is a PhD candidate in the Department of History at the University of Calgary.

Kathryn Ivany, MA, is the City Archivist and Supervisor, Heritage and Specialty Facilities at the City of Edmonton, and a western Canadian historian.

Allan Kerr, P Eng, P Geol, is President of the Canadian Militaria Preservation Society and Museum in Edmonton and a collector of militaria.

Jeff Keshen, PhD, is Dean of Arts at Mount Royal University whose books include *Saints, Sinners and Soldiers: Canada's Second World War* and *Propaganda and Censorship during Canada's Great War*.

Norman Knowles, PhD, is a professor of history at St. Mary's University and has recently published *Narrating a Nation: Canadian History Pre- and Post-Confederation*, a two-volume textbook.

P. Whitney Lackenbauer, PhD, is an associate professor and Chair of the Department of History at St. Jerome's College, University of Waterloo, and a specialist in modern Canadian military, diplomatic, and political history.

J. Robert Lampard, MD, MSc, MBA, is the former director of the Michener Centre, Red Deer, and author of *Alberta's Medical History: "Young and Lusty, and Full of Life."*

Michale Lang, MA, is a heritage consultant, author, and former Executive Director of the Whyte Museum of the Canadian Rockies. She recently published *An Adventurous Woman Abroad: The Selected Lantern Slides of Mary T.S. Schaffer*.

Kassandra Luciuk is a PhD candidate in the Department of History at the University of Toronto. She is currently researching the Ukrainian Canadian socialist-progressive movement in the 1930s.

Rod Macleod, PhD, is professor emeritus of history at the University of Alberta. An expert on western Canadian history, his books include *All True Things: A History of the University of Alberta*.

John Matthews, Major (retd.), BA, is a graduate of the Royal Military College Kingston, and served with the Royal 22nd Regiment and the Loyal Edmonton Regiment, retiring in 1995 after 36 years of service. He is a volunteer history researcher at the Loyal Edmonton Regiment Military Museum.

Peter McKenzie-Brown is a freelance journalist and author specializing in energy resources. Together with Gordon Jaremko and David Finch, he authored *The Great Oil Age: The Petroleum Industry in Canada*.

Sean Moir, MA, MLS, is Collections Manager and former Curator of Military and Political History at the Royal Alberta Museum.

Patricia Myers, MA, works for the Royal Alberta Museum as a historian involved in the development of the new facility and is an established author specializing in western Canadian history. She is the author of *Sky Riders: An Illustrated History of Aviation in Alberta, 1906–1945*.

Allan Rowe, PhD, works in the Historic Places Stewardship Program, Alberta Culture, and is a specialist in Canadian ethnic and immigration history.

Robert Rutherdale, PhD, is an associate professor of history at Algoma University whose works include *Hometown Horizons: Local Responses to Canada's Great War*.

Amy J. Shaw, PhD, is an associate professor of history at the University of Lethbridge and the author of *Crisis of Conscience: Conscientious Objection in Canada During the First World War*.

Donald B. Smith, PhD, is a retired professor of history from the University of Calgary specializing in western Canadian history. His recent publications include *Honore Jaxon: Prairie Visionary* and *Calgary's Grand Story: The Making of a Prairie Metropolis from the Viewpoint of Two Heritage Buildings*.

Paul Stortz, PhD, is an associate professor of history at the University of Calgary and is a specialist in the history of education and higher education. With E. Lisa Panayotidis, he has edited *Cultures, Communities, and Conflict: Histories of Canadian Universities and War* and *Historical Identities: The Professoriate in Canada*.

Doug Styles, BA, CD, is a retired City of Edmonton Fire Department Dispatcher and has been an avid collector and researcher of Canadian and Commonwealth military medals for over 50 years. He has also spent 22 years with the Cadet Instructors Cadre of the Canadian Armed Forces Reserve Force.

Ken Tingley, MA, was the first Historian Laureate of the City of Edmonton (2010–12) and has authored many books on western Canadian history including *Ride of the Century: The Story of the Edmonton Transit System* and *My Heart's in the Highlands: The Building of a Historic Edmonton Community*.

Aritha van Herk, MA, is a professor in the Department of English, University of Calgary, and teaches creative writing, Canadian literature, and contemporary narrative. She is an established author, and her historical writings include *Mavericks: An Incorrigible History of Alberta*.

Donald G. Wetherell, PhD, is professor emeritus in the Heritage Resources Management Program at Athabasca University, whose books include *Alberta Formed, Alberta Transformed* (co-edited with Michael Payne and Catherine Cavanaugh).

Anthony Worman, BA, Diploma of Applied Museum Studies, MLIS, is the Acting Curator, Military and Political History at the Royal Alberta Museum.

INDEX